KU-615-426

THE CHANGING CONSTITUTION

University of Liverpool
Withdrawn from stock

THE CHANGING CONSTITUTION

Ninth Edition

EDITED BY

JEFFREY JOWELL
COLM O'CINNEIDE

OXFORD
UNIVERSITY PRESS

OXFORD
UNIVERSITY PRESS

Great Clarendon Street, Oxford, OX2 6DP,
United Kingdom

Oxford University Press is a department of the University of Oxford.
It furthers the University's objective of excellence in research, scholarship,
and education by publishing worldwide. Oxford is a registered trade mark of
Oxford University Press in the UK and in certain other countries

© Oxford University Press 2019

The moral rights of the authors have been asserted

Sixth Edition 2007
Seventh Edition 2011
Eighth Edition 2015

Impression: 1

All rights reserved. No part of this publication may be reproduced, stored in
a retrieval system, or transmitted, in any form or by any means, without the
prior permission in writing of Oxford University Press, or as expressly permitted
by law, by licence or under terms agreed with the appropriate reprographics
rights organization. Enquiries concerning reproduction outside the scope of the
above should be sent to the Rights Department, Oxford University Press, at the
address above

You must not circulate this work in any other form
and you must impose this same condition on any acquirer

Public sector information reproduced under Open Government Licence v3.0
(http://www.nationalarchives.gov.uk/doc/open-government-licence/open-government-licence.htm)

Published in the United States of America by Oxford University Press
198 Madison Avenue, New York, NY 10016, United States of America

British Library Cataloguing in Publication Data
Data available

Library of Congress Control Number: 2019934175

ISBN 978-0-19-880636-3

Printed in Great Britain by
Bell & Bain Ltd., Glasgow

Links to third party websites are provided by Oxford in good faith and
for information only. Oxford disclaims any responsibility for the materials
contained in any third party website referenced in this work.

PREFACE TO THE NINTH EDITION

The title of this work, chosen for the first edition in 1985, one hundred years after the publication of Dicey's seminal *The Law and the Constitution*, reflected the editors' belief that the UK's uncodified constitution would continue to alter incrementally in response to unforeseen situations, while retaining its essential stability. As the eight previous editions of this book have come and gone, this assumption held good—despite certain persisting areas of contestation, such as whether the UK was a majoritarian or rights-based democracy, the legitimacy of an unelected second chamber, and the extent to which the British constitutional system should move in the direction of a federal system in respect of the devolution of powers to Scotland, Wales and Northern Ireland.

However, as we publish this ninth edition, writing this Preface in early 2019, the stability of the UK's unwritten constitutional arrangements has been profoundly tested by the decision in the referendum in June 2016 to exit the European Union. Dicey's assurance that our constitution consists of three fixed pillars—namely parliamentary sovereignty, the rule of law, and conventions of the constitution—has proved less durable than might have been imagined prior to that date. Brexit has starkly highlighted that the inevitable opacity of an unwritten constitution can lead to confusion and instability.

For a start, whichever direction Brexit takes, it has thrown into relief the question as to whether we are a popular or representative democracy. The 2013 Referendum Act makes no mention of whether the result of the Brexit referendum was to be binding on Parliament. However, despite its putative 'advisory' status, the referendum is widely viewed as binding the hands of Parliament. Indeed, at the time we write this, claims are being made that it would be 'undemocratic' for the members of Parliament in any way to question the 'will of the people' by delaying or diluting a 'hard Brexit' or calling for a second referendum—despite the comparative narrowness of the referendum result (52% to 48%), the fact that no specific exit route from the EU was on the ballot paper, and the well-established constitutional position that Parliament is the ultimate law-making authority.

In some ways, these views are understandable. A referendum does confer a kind of special, constitutional status on the policy favoured by its result. Because the choice of policy was legitimated through a universal vote on a single issue, there is force in the argument that it should be shielded from change by a majority of members of Parliament, at least for a considerable period of time. Fidelity to the referendum result must be contrasted with the normal procedures of representative democracy, where periodic elections are held under manifestos covering many issues and where, because ultimately the electors are asked to endorse a particular candidate, fluidity and even U-turns are permitted in accord with the consciences of members of Parliament.

However, the institutional nature of a referendum has limits. Just as courts of law are designed to decide 'yes-no' or 'either-or' questions, such as whether a defendant is guilty or not guilty, or liable or not liable, referendums are similarly suited to decide binary questions, such as whether women should have the vote, or the death penalty be abolished. Matters of the complexity of Brexit raise polycentric issues both of fact and opinion. Such issues do not lend themselves well to a mere yes–no answer. Given this, it is not surprising that the Brexit referendum has served to destabilize the functioning of the UK's constitutional system, built as it has been hitherto around the concept of representative democracy. Demands that Parliament maintain fidelity to the referendum result gloss over the reality that the result left multiple key issues unresolved—and claims that MPs advocating particular ways of resolving such issues are betraying the 'will of the people' disregard how representative democracies are supposed to function. Insofar as leaving the EU involves a constitutional change (as the *Miller*[1] case inferred) it is worth noting that countries with codified constitutions sometimes impose 'super-majority' requirements before substantive amendments can be made to national constitutional orders.

Other areas of constitutional uncertainty have also been exposed by Brexit. For example, the *Miller* case raised the issue of whether formal notice of withdrawal from the EU could be issued by the Prime Minister without prior enabling legislation having been passed by Parliament. The Prime Minister asserted that it was clearly for her to trigger Brexit, as withdrawal from the EU treaties was a matter of international law, which is an area still within the 'prerogative power' of the executive. This view was challenged in the courts by a concerned citizen, Gina Miller, who contended that the Prime Minister lacked this authority, as triggering EU exit would inevitably alter the body of domestic law laid down since we joined the EU in 1973. The matter reached the Supreme Court which, by a majority, agreed with Ms Miller that the constitutional ramifications of EU exit were such that only the elected representatives of the people could trigger that step. It still is perhaps a little surprising that our executive, normally so ready to invoke the sovereignty of Parliament for its benefit in other constitutional contexts, chose to press its insistence on appropriating such a significant decision for itself. It is equally surprising that Parliament, having been conferred the power by the courts, handed it straight back to the Prime Minister to trigger Brexit, in exchange for an ambiguous promise to be consulted on the final deal by means of a 'meaningful vote'. Subsequently, Parliament has attempted to reassert its authority over the nature and shape of Brexit, culminating at the time of writing in a vote by a majority of the House of Commons to reject Mrs May's negotiated deal with the EU. It remains to be seen how this dynamic will play out. But the *Miller* case and the events that have followed show the existence of real uncertainty as to the relationship between the executive and legislature within the UK's constitutional framework (as explored further in the chapters by Craig, Elliott, Norton, and Poole in this edition).

---

[1] *R (Miller) v Secretary of State for Exiting the EU* [2017] UKSC 5.

Outside the courtroom too, the *Miller* case raised uncertainties when sections of the press condemned the judges who found in favour of Ms Miller as 'enemies of the people', and doubted their independence. The Lord Chancellor at the time was hesitant to come to their defence, despite her statutory duty to defend the rule of law. The scope of the rule of law has again been a source of controversy in relation to the provisions of the EU Withdrawal Act 2018, which confers extensive powers upon the executive to alter law by way of subordinate legislation without much in the way of substantive scrutiny by Parliament. Disagreement obviously exists as to what respect for this principle, Dicey's second constitutional pillar, requires—which the Brexit process has served to highlight (as discussed further by Elliott, Jowell, and Le Sueur in this edition).

Finally, the third pillar of Dicey's constitutional edifice, constitutional conventions, was also in issue in *Miller*. The Scottish Government and litigants from Northern Ireland argued that Brexit could not be triggered without the consent of devolved authorities (in relation to those areas falling within their competencies) by virtue of the 'Sewel' constitutional convention, which provides that the Westminster Parliament would not normally legislate with regard to devolved matters without the consent of the devolved legislatures. There was much law to the effect that conventions are not in themselves binding legal obligations—but in the case of Scotland, and now in Wales, the Sewell Convention has recently been set out in statutory form. However, in *Miller*, the Supreme Court nevertheless held that the Sewel Convention was not intended to operate as a binding rule, despite having been incorporated in statute. Therefore, the Supreme Court concluded that it should not adjudicate on the issue of whether the triggering of Article 50 would breach the convention, commenting that the courts would not act as 'parents or guardians of constitutional conventions, but only as observers' (para. 146). This issue raises a host of interesting constitutional questions, but it also highlights the existence of deep uncertainty about the status of conventions within the UK's constitutional structure: they remain essential to its functioning, but their status is ambiguous.

In general, it is fair to say that Brexit has provided a stress test for the UK constitution which has been found wanting. The ambiguity inherent in an unwritten constitution, regarded for so long as a positive feature, has become a problem. Serious tension has been exposed between the assumed constitutional roles of different branches of the state, and there is no written constitutional text to act as a decisive point of reference in settling these issues. We have therefore, for the first time, included a chapter by Jeff King on whether we now need in some way to codify our constitution. It seems to us that this chapter, a revised version of his *Current Legal Problems* paper on the same topic, has now at least appeared on the political agenda—and King's chapter asks questions not only about whether to codify the constitution but the procedures by which it may legitimately be achieved.

Not every aspect of the constitution's development since the last edition has been as dramatic as the Brexit-related disputes just discussed. In other areas, the incremental evolution of the constitutional framework has proceeded along similar lines. In certain areas, such as local government, there has been little change. In other areas, change has been more dramatic, with Brexit often acting as a catalyst. This is particularly the case in relation to devolution, separation of powers, respect for fundamental rights, and the relationship between UK law and supranational legal frameworks.

The uneven way in which constitutional evolution has unfolded over the last few years has prompted us to make substantial changes to this edition of *The Changing Constitution*. Excellent chapters prepared by authors for previous editions of this book—including Ian Leigh on local government, John McEldowney on the control of public finances, Tony Prosser on regulation, Dawn Oliver on integrity in elected office, and Rick Rawlings on the 2010–15 coalition government—have lost none of their relevance or quality. However, readers interested in these topics are directed towards the previous (8th) edition of this book.

For this edition, we have considerably expanded the coverage of devolution issues—with separate chapters for the first time devoted to Northern Ireland, Scotland and Wales, written by Brice Dickson, Aileen McHarg, and Rick Rawlings respectively. We have also focused the third part of the book on emerging new debates and trends within the evolution of the UK constitution. We are delighted to feature a wholly new chapter by Alison Young on the relationship between Parliament, the executive and the judiciary. Patrick Birkinshaw, who in the previous edition wrote on freedom of information, has broadened his chapter to include the related issues of privacy and surveillance. John McEldowney has a new chapter on federalism, and Jeff King on a written constitution (as previously mentioned). We are also pleased that the book incorporates a new and timely chapter on the executive by Tom Poole, as well as revised and updated chapters on the other key structural and institutional features of the changing constitution by Mark Elliott, Paul Craig, David Feldman, Andrew Le Sueur and Lord Norton of Louth. As editors, we have contributed revised versions of our own chapters, on the rule of law and human rights. As ever, we are most grateful to our team of contributors for the outstanding quality of their chapters, as well as their prompt responses to dilatory editorial requests. We believe their work provides an exceptional insight into the dynamics of the UK's constitution, which is arguably changing at a faster rate than ever.

Finally, we would like to acknowledge that this is the first edition of this work which is without the contribution as editor of Dawn Oliver, who has been greatly missed. Our thanks too to the supportive team at OUP: Carol Barber, Emily Cunningham, Nicholas Bromley, Joe Matthews and Jonathon Price. Each provided competent and patient support at different stages of the production process, for which we are deeply grateful.

Jeffrey Jowell
Colm O'Cinneide
January 2019

CONTENTS

PART III NEW DIRECTIONS?

TABLE OF CASES

TABLE OF EUROPEAN CASES

NUMERICAL

TABLE OF PRIMARY LEGISLATION

TABLE OF SECONDARY LEGISLATION

TABLE OF EUROPEAN LEGISLATION

TABLE OF INTERNATIONAL TREATIES
AND CONVENTIONS

LIST OF CONTRIBUTORS

Sir Jeffrey Jowell, QC Practising barrister at Blackstone Chambers, former Director of the Bingham Centre for the Rule of Law and Emeritus Professor of Public Law, University College London

Colm O'Cinneide Professor of Constitutional and Human Rights Law, University College London

Patrick Birkinshaw Emeritus Professor of Public Law and Director of the Institute of European Public Law, University of Hull

Paul Craig, QC, FBA Professor of English Law, St John's College, Oxford

Brice Dickson Emeritus Professor of International and Comparative Law, Queen's University Belfast

Mark Elliott Professor of Public Law, University of Cambridge

David Feldman, QC, FBA Emeritus Rouse Ball Professor of English Law at the University of Cambridge, and Emeritus Fellow of Downing College, Cambridge

Jeff King Professor of Law, University College London

Andrew Le Sueur Professor of Constitutional Justice, University of Essex

John McEldowney Professor of Law, University of Warwick

Aileen McHarg Professor of Public Law, University of Strathclyde

Lord Norton of Louth Professor of Government and Director of the Centre for Legislative Studies, University of Hull

Thomas Poole Professor of Law, London School of Economics

Richard Rawlings Professor of Public Law, University College London

Alison L. Young Sir David Williams Professor of Public Law, University of Cambridge, Fellow of Robinson College

PART I

THE CONSTITUTIONAL FRAMEWORK

1

THE RULE OF LAW

Jeffrey Jowell

SUMMARY

Dicey believed that discretionary power offended the Rule of Law as it would inevitably lead to arbitrary decisions. His critics pointed out that, in the modern state, discretion is necessary to carry out a variety of welfare and regulatory tasks. The Rule of Law contains four central features which cohere and overlap: legality, certainty, equality, and access to justice and rights. These are not only formal values but also substantive. The Rule of Law is a principle of institutional morality inherent in any constitutional democracy. In a country without a written constitution, it constrains the way power is exercised. It is enforced and elaborated through judicial review but also serves as a critical focus for public debate. Although the Rule of Law is not the only requirement of a constitutional democracy, it is of great practical significance in promoting fair decisions, restraining the abuse of power, encouraging investment, and in furthering empowerment and respect for equal human dignity.

INTRODUCTION

In 1885, Professor Albert Venn Dicey wrote that the two principles of our unwritten constitution were the sovereignty of Parliament and the Rule of Law.[1] Although he regarded parliamentary sovereignty as the primary principle—one that could override the Rule of Law—he recognized that, ideally, Parliament and all public officials should

---

[1] A. V. Dicey, *The Law of the Constitution* (1885) referred to here in its 10th edn., edited by E. C. S. Wade (reprinted 1960). For an account of Dicey's conception, see the articles on 'Dicey and the Constitution' in [1985] *Public Law* 583–724; I. Harden and N. Lewis, *The Noble Lie* (1986) Ch. 2; P. Craig, *Public Law and Democracy in the United Kingdom and the United States of America* (1990) Ch. 2; M. Loughlin, *Public Law and Political Theory* (1992); T. R. S. Allan, *Constitutional Justice: A Liberal Theory of the Rule of Law* (2001); A. Hutchinson and P. Monahan (eds.) *The Rule of Law: Ideal or Ideology?* (1987). See also, Lord Bingham of Cornhill, 'Dicey Revisited' [2002] *PL* 39. See also D. Dyzenhaus, *The Constitution of Law* (2006). For a critical view of the Rule of Law see R. Ekins (ed.), *Modern Challenges to the Rule of Law* (2011).

respect the Rule of Law as a quality that distinguished a democratic from a despotic constitution.

What is meant by the Rule of Law and what is its value? Is it any more than a statement that individuals or officials should obey the law as it is? Or does it simply require positive legal authority for the acts of all public officials? Is it a guide to the justice of public decision-making—a framework that constrains the abuse of power? Or is it an assertion that law itself contains inherent moral qualities? Is its proper place not in the realm of constitutional legality but in the rhetoric of liberal–democratic values? Is it, as a distinguished legal historian has written, an 'unqualified human good'[2] or, as alleged by another, a device that 'enables the shrewd, the calculating, and the wealthy to manipulate its form to their own advantage'?[3] Is it 'an impossible ideal'?[4]

These days the Rule of Law is accepted as never before as one of the fundamental principles of our uncodified democratic constitution. It is frequently invoked by the courts as a standard by which to judge whether power has been abused. It is engaged as a yardstick by which to assess the validity of government proposals. One of the most senior and distinguished British judges on his retirement wrote a book extolling the virtues of the Rule of Law and elaborating its content.[5] It has even received statutory recognition in the Constitutional Reform Act 2005,[6] the first section of which states that that Act does not adversely affect 'the existing constitutional principle of the rule of law'. Most significantly, some of our judges have suggested that Dicey's hierarchy of principle, with the Rule of Law playing second-fiddle to the sovereignty of Parliament, might be changing, and that 'the rule of law enforced by the courts is the ultimate controlling factor on which our constitution is based'.[7]

DICEY'S RULE OF LAW: ITS CRITICS AND SUPPORTERS

In analyzing what we mean by the Rule of Law it is probably best, even today, to start with Dicey's interpretation of the Rule of Law, because of the immense authority he has exercised for so long over the perception of our uncodified constitutional arrangements.[8]

For Dicey, the Rule of Law distinguished the British (or 'English', as he preferred to call it) from all other constitutions. He described how foreign observers of English

---

[2] E. P. Thompson, *Whigs and Hunters: The Origin of the Black Act* (1975) 266.

[3] M. Horwitz, book review (1977) 86 Yale LJ 561, 566.

[4] M. Loughlin, *Foundations of Public Law* (2010) 337.   [5] Lord Bingham, *The Rule of Law* (2010).

[6] The Act seeks to further the principle of the separation of powers and independence of the judiciary. In particular, it removes the power of appointment of judges from the Lord Chancellor and places it in the hands of an independent Judicial Appointments Commission. It also precludes the Lord Chancellor from any judicial role and establishes a Supreme Court outside the House of Lords.

[7] Lord Hope, *obiter*, in *Jackson v Her Majesty's Attorney General* [2005] UKHL 56 at [107].

[8] The conception of the Rule of Law has an older provenance than Dicey but was rarely mentioned as such before his account. For an account of its origins in the ancient world, see M. Loughlin, *Swords and Scales* (2000), Ch. 5; B. Tamanaha, *On the Rule of Law: History, Politics and Theory* (2004), Ch. 1.

manners (Voltaire and de Tocqueville in particular) were struck when they visited England by the fact that here was a country distinguished above all by the fact of being under the Rule of Law:

> When Voltaire came to England [from France in the eighteenth century]—and Voltaire represented the feeling of his age—his predominant sentiment clearly was that he had passed out of the realm of despotism to a land where the laws might be harsh, but where men were ruled by law and not by caprice.[9]

That passage encapsulates Dicey's approach to the Rule of Law. By allowing for 'harsh' laws to coexist with the Rule of Law it is clear that he does not equate the Rule of Law with the notion of 'good' law. Nor does he contend that in order to qualify as 'law' a particular rule has to be fair, or reasonable, or just. So what did he mean by the Rule of Law?

According to Dicey, the Rule of Law has at least three meanings. The first is that individuals ought not to be subjected to the power of officials wielding wide discretionary powers. He wrote that no one 'is punishable or can be lawfully made to suffer in body or goods except for a distinct breach of law established before the ordinary courts of the land'. Fundamental to the Rule of Law, therefore, is the notion that all power needs to be authorized. But he took that notion further by contrasting the Rule of Law with a 'system of government based on the exercise by persons in authority of wide, arbitrary or discretionary powers of constraint'.[10] Here Dicey contends that to confer wide discretion upon officials is equivalent to granting them scope to exercise arbitrary powers, to which no one should be forced to submit. He writes that 'wherever there is discretion there is room for arbitrariness'[11] and therefore excludes discretionary powers from what he later calls 'regular law'.

Dicey's second meaning engages a notion of equality—what he calls the 'equal subjection'—of all classes to one law administered by the ordinary courts. He contrasts here what he saw as special exemptions for officials in continental countries, such as France, where he considered that the French *droit administratif* operated a separate form of justice that treated ordinary citizens differently from the way it treated its public officials. 'With us', he wrote, 'every official, from the Prime Minister down to a constable or a collector of taxes, is under the same responsibility for every act done without legal justification as any other citizen.'[12]

Thirdly, Dicey saw the Rule of Law as expressing the fact that there was in England no separate written constitutional code, and that constitutional law is 'the result of the judicial decisions determining the rights of private persons in particular cases brought before the courts'.[13] Like Bentham before him, he was against a basic document setting out a catalogue of human rights and saw our law and liberties as arising from decisions in the courts—the common law.

One of the first attacks on Dicey's meanings of the Rule of Law came in 1928 when William Robson wrote his celebrated book *Justice and Administrative Law*, in which

---

[9] Dicey, *Law of the Constitution*, n. 1 above, 189.   [10] Ibid., p. 188.
[11] Ibid.   [12] Ibid., p. 193.   [13] Ibid., p. 195.

he roundly criticized Dicey for his misinterpretation of both the English and French systems on the question of whether officials were treated differently from others. He pointed out that there were, in England 'colossal distinctions'[14] between the rights and duties of private individuals and those of the administrative organs of government, even in Dicey's time. Public authorities possessed special rights and special exemptions and immunities, to the extent that the citizen was deprived of a remedy against the state 'in many cases where he most requires it'.[15] Robson also convincingly showed how Dicey had misinterpreted French law, where the *droit administratif* was not intended to exempt public officials from the rigour of private law, but to allow experts in public administration to work out the extent of official liability. Robson also noted the extent of Dicey's misrepresentation that disputes between officials and private individuals in Britain were dealt with by the ordinary courts. He pointed to the growth of special tribunals and inquiries that had grown up to decide these disputes outside the courts, and was in no doubt that a 'vast body of administrative law' existed in England.[16]

The attack on Dicey continued a few years later with Professor W. Ivor Jennings's *The Law and the Constitution*, which appeared in 1933. Repeating many of Robson's criticisms of Dicey's second and third meanings of the Rule of Law, Jennings also delivered a withering, and almost fatal, attack upon Dicey's first meaning—his claim that wide discretionary power had no place under the Rule of Law. It should be remembered here that Dicey was a trenchant critic of notions of 'collectivism'. An unreconstructed Whig, he had, throughout his life, believed in a *laissez-faire* economic system and had resisted the increasing regulatory role of the state.[17] He was supported by other constitutional theorists of his time,[18] and had an ally in the 1920s in Lord Hewart, who expressed similar views in his book *The New Despotism*.[19] Robson and Jennings were committed to the expansion of the state's role in providing welfare and other social services. Robson, George Bernard Shaw, Leonard Woolf, John Maynard Keynes, Harold Laski, and others worked together in the 1930s to promote these ideas.[20]

Jennings felt that the Rule of Law implicitly promoted Dicey's political views. He equated Dicey's opposition to state regulation with that of the 'manufacturers who formed the backbone of the Whig Party', who:

> wanted nothing which interfered with profits, even if profits involved child labour, wholesale factory accidents, the pollution of rivers, of the air, and of the water supply, jerry-built houses, low wages, and other incidents of nineteenth-century industrialism.[21]

---

[14] W. A. Robson, *Justice and Administrative Law* (1928; 2nd edn., 1947) 343.   [15] Ibid., p. 345.

[16] Ibid. Robson approved of, and wished to develop, administrative law, but through a separate system outside of the 'ordinary courts'. See his 'Justice and Administrative Law reconsidered' (1979) *Current Legal Problems* 107. For an excellent critique and historic corrective of Dicey, see H. W. Arthurs, 'Rethinking Administrative Law: A Slightly Dicey Business' (1979) 17 *Osgoode Hall LJ*, Part I; and *Without the Law* (1985).

[17] See R. A. Cosgrove, *The Rule of Law: Albert Venn Dicey, Victorian Jurist* (1980), and the review by D. Sugarman (1983) *MLR* 102.

[18] Such as Maine and Bryce.   [19] Published in 1929.

[20] See e.g. Keynes's lecture published by Leonard and Virginia Woolf at The Hogarth Press in 1926, entitled *The End of Laissez-Faire*. See Victoria Glendinning, *Leonard Woolf* (2006).

[21] Sir W. Ivor Jennings, *The Law and the Constitution* (1933) 309–10.

Jennings then turned his attention directly to Dicey, who:

> was more concerned with constitutional relations between Great Britain and Ireland than with relations between poverty and disease on the one hand, and the new industrial system on the other.[22]

Jennings concluded that if the Rule of Law:

> means that the state exercises only the functions of carrying out external relations and maintaining order, it is not true. If it means that the state ought to exercise these functions only, it is a rule of policy for Whigs (if there are any left).[23]

There were not too many Whigs or unreconstructed Diceyists left by the 1930s, when further legitimacy for the growth of official power was provided by the Donoughmore Committee, inquiring in 1933 into the question whether the growth of subordinate legislation (promulgated at the discretion of the executive) violated the Rule of Law.[24] Donoughmore found that it was inevitable, in an increasingly complex society, that Parliament should delegate powers to ministers to act in the public interest. The Second World War then provided further compelling reasons to centralize power, an opportunity built upon by the Labour Government of 1945. As Robson wrote in the second edition of his book in 1947, increasingly Parliament had given powers to resolve disputes between the citizen and the state not to the courts—to Dicey's 'ordinary law'—but to specialized organs of adjudication such as administrative tribunals and inquiries. This was not 'due to a fit of absentmindedness' but because these bodies would be speedier and cheaper, and would possess greater technical knowledge and have 'fewer prejudices against government' than the courts.[25] Here he may have been echoing the words of Aneurin Bevan, Minister of Health in the 1945 Labour Government and architect of the National Health Service, who caused a stir in the House of Commons by establishing tribunals in the Health Service, divorced from 'ordinary courts', because he greatly feared 'judicial sabotage' of socialist legislation.[26]

Despite this onslaught on Dicey's version of the Rule of Law, its epitaph refused to be written. In 1938, the American jurist Felix Frankfurter (later a Supreme Court Justice) wrote that:

> the persistence of the misdirection that Dicey has given to the development of administrative law strikingly proves the elder Huxley's observation that many a theory survives long after its brains are knocked out.[27]

Two particularly strong supporters wrote in favour of the Rule of Law in the 1940s. F. A. Hayek's *The Road to Serfdom* in 1943 graphically described that road as being

---

[22] Ibid., p. 311.   [23] Ibid.

[24] Report of the Committee on Ministers' Powers (1932) Cmd 4060.

[25] Robson, *Justice and Administrative Law* 347.

[26] *Hansard*, HC col. 1983 (23 July 1946). See modern criticisms of the Rule of Law in R. Ekins (ed.), n. 1 above.

[27] F. Frankfurter, Foreword to 'Discussion of Current Developments in Administrative Law' (1938) 47 *Yale LJ* 515, 517. The reference to administrative law is in response to Dicey's view that there should be no separate system of law in relation to the exercise of power by public officials.

paved with governmental regulation and unconstrained discretionary power. C. K. Allen, with less ideological fervour, pleaded for the legal control of executive action, which he felt fully accorded with the Rule of Law.[28] Not much heed was paid to these pleas until the late 1950s when the Franks Committee[29] revived interest in Diceyan notions by proposing judicial protections over the multiplying tribunals and inquiries of the growing state. It was in the 1960s, however, that disparate groups once again started arguing in favour of legal values. Some of these groups were themselves committed to a strong governmental role in providing social welfare, but objected to the manner in which public services were carried out. Recipients of discretionary state benefit, known as 'supplementary benefit', for example, objected to the fact that benefits were administered by officials in accordance with a secret code (known as the 'A Code') and asked instead for publication of a set of welfare 'rights'.[30] They also objected to the wide discretion allowed their case-workers to determine the level of their benefits. The heirs of Jennings and his followers, such as Professor Richard Titmuss, opposed this challenge to the free exercise of official discretion and objected strongly to a 'pathology of legalism' developing in this area.[31]

Another plea for the Rule of Law came at about the same time from individuals who were being displaced from their homes by programmes of urban redevelopment. While not asking for a catalogue of 'rights', their claim was for participation in decisions by which they were affected.[32] Their plea did not primarily concern the substance of the law. Just as the welfare recipients were not simply arguing for higher benefits, but for pre-determined rules and fair procedures to determine the benefits, citizens' groups directed their demands for the Rule of Law less at the content of the decisions ultimately taken than at the procedures by which they were reached. They were by no means adopting the undiluted Diceyan view that all discretionary power is bad. Nevertheless, they asked not to be condemned (in those cases, evicted from their communities) unheard.

In recent years, the Rule of Law has constantly been employed as a yardstick by which to challenge the reduction of legal aid, the opportunity to challenge government decisions by way of judicial review, secret trials, detention without trial, the unconstrained powers of tax or immigration officials, the power of the Executive to alter statutes passed by Parliament, and other issues mentioned below.

---

[28] See C. K. Allen, *Law and Orders* (1945). See also F. A. Hayek, *The Constitution of Liberty* (1960), and *Law, Legislation and Liberty* (2 vols., 1976).

[29] Report of the Committee on Administrative Tribunals and Inquiries (1957) Cmnd 218.

[30] See e.g. T. Lynes, *Welfare Rights* (1969); and in the USA: C. Reich, 'The New Property' (1964) 73 *Yale CJ* 733.

[31] R. Titmuss, 'Law and Discretion' (1971) 42 *Polit Q* 113. See Jeffrey Jowell, 'The Legal Control of Administrative Discretion', *Public Law*, Autumn 1973. Republished in the International Library of Essays in Law and Legal Theory, Administrative Law ed. D. J. Galligan, pp. 241–84.

[32] N. A. Roberts, *The Reform of Planning Law* (1976); Patrick McAuslan, *The Ideologies of Planning Law* (1980) esp. Chs. 1 and 2.

WHAT DOES THE RULE OF LAW REQUIRE?

Dicey's Rule of Law has been criticized, as we have seen, for the fact that it tendentiously seeks to promote an individualistic political theory and because of its inaccurate descriptions of the then-existing systems of governance—both in France and England. Yet it remains a compelling idea, although an 'essentially contested concept'[33] and therefore variously interpreted.[34] Some see the Rule of Law as embodying formal qualities in law (such as clarity, prospectivity, stability, openness, and access to an impartial judiciary).[35] Others criticize that view, called by Ronald Dworkin the 'rule-book conception' of the Rule of Law, and prefer the 'rights conception', under which legal rules contain inherent moral content.[36] Dworkin's view must be seen in the context of his and others' opposition to the view of the positivist thinkers who contend that even extremely harsh and unjust laws, such as the discriminatory laws of Nazi Germany, must be regarded as law, despite their moral repugnance.[37] Dicey and Dworkin are aiming at different targets. Dworkin is seeking a general theory of law, focusing more on the nature of 'law' under the concept of the Rule of Law,[38] whereas Dicey seeks a principle of how power should be deployed under a system of government under law. Nevertheless, Dworkin raises the question as to whether the Rule of Law is a merely formal or procedural concept—the 'thin' version of the Rule of Law, or whether it embodies certain fundamental rights (the 'thick' version of the Rule of Law).[39]

In a book on the Rule of Law which has received much attention, the British judge,[40] Tom Bingham, defines the Rule of Law as follows:

> all persons and authorities within the state, whether public or private, should be bound by and entitled to the benefit of laws publicly made, taking effect (generally) in the future and publicly administered in the courts.[41]

---

[33] J. Waldron, 'Is the Rule of Law an Essentially Contested Concept (in Florida)?' (2002) *Law and Philosophy* 137.

[34] See P. Craig, 'Formal and Substantive Conceptions of the Rule of Law: An Analytical Framework' [1997] *Public Law* 467; N. Barber, 'Must Legalistic Conceptions of the Rule of Law Have a Social Dimension?' (2004) *Ratio Juris* 474.

[35] J. Raz, 'The Rule of Law and its Virtue' (1977) 93 *LQR* 195, and *The Authority of Law* (1979). Compare Lon Fuller's requirements of 'legality': generality, clarity, public promulgation, stability, consistency, fidelity to purpose, and prohibition of the impossible. L. Fuller, *The Morality of Law* (1964) 153. See also R. Summers, 'The Principles of the Rule of Law' (1999) *Notre Dame LR* 1691.

[36] R. Dworkin, *A Matter of Principle* (1985) Ch. 1, p. 11ff.

[37] See generally, H. L. A. Hart, *The Concept of Law* (1961).

[38] See J. Waldron, 'The Concept and the Rule of Law', (2008) *Georgia L. Rev.* 3.

[39] See J. Waldron, 'The Rule of Law and the Importance of Procedure' (2010) New York University Public Law and Legal Theory Working Papers 234.

[40] Former Lord Chief Justice, Master of the Rolls and Law Lord.

[41] Tom Bingham, *The Rule of Law* (2010) 8. Compare the definition of the former Secretary General of the United Nations, Kofi Annan that the rule of law is a 'Principle of governance in which all persons, institutions and entities, public and private, including the State itself, are accountable to laws that are publicly promulgated, equally enforced and independently adjudicated, and which are consistent with international human rights norms and standards. It requires, as well, measures to ensure adherence to the principles of supremacy of law, equality before the law, accountability to law, fairness in the application of law, separation of powers, participation in decision-making, legal certainty, avoidance of arbitrariness and procedural and legal transparency'. *The Rule of Law and Transitional Justice in Conflict and Post Conflict Societies*, Report of the Secretary General, Doc.S/2004/616 23 August 2004, para. 6.

This definition may at first reading sound rather too economical, but it encapsulates a number of features of a state grounded in the Rule of Law. It also seems at first sight to fall into the procedural, or thin version of the Rule of Law, but Bingham expands that definition with eight features, or 'ingredients' of the Rule of Law, including that the law must give protection to human rights.[42]

One of the key problems in explaining the Rule of Law is that it consists of four really rather distinct and separate aspects which are contained within the Bingham definition and his eight ingredients, but not specifically articulated. [I exclude for these purposes the international aspects of the rule of law.][43] It is the lack of appreciation of the fact that the sum of the Rule of Law requires attention to all four parts, which are somewhat distinct, but nevertheless cohere and indeed overlap, that accounts for some of the lack of understanding of the Rule of Law's really rather clear intent and significance.

Legality

At its most fundamental, the Rule of Law requires everyone to comply with the law. Legality is distinct from anarchy, on the one hand, and tyranny on the other. Legality contains two features. First, the law must be followed (Bingham's requirement that all persons must be 'bound by the law'). This requirement of the Rule of Law is often asserted by those who call for 'law and order' in the face of lax enforcement of the law. It speaks both to the public (who are expected to obey the law) and to law-enforcement officials (who are expected reasonably to implement the law).

Secondly, in so far as legality addresses the actions of public officials, it requires that they act within the powers that have been conferred upon them. Whereas, under our system, individuals are free to do as they please unless the law forbids them from doing so (by designating certain behaviour a crime or tort) decisions and acts of public officials need to be legally authorized. The modern view, as we shall shortly discuss, is that the conferment of discretionary power on public officials by the law is not wholly inimical to the notion of legality, but that discretion must be exercised within the scope of legality—in accordance with the purpose and objects of the power conferred on the decision-maker, and not in a way that is capricious or arbitrary.

Certainty

For Dicey, the essence of the Rule of Law was that law should be certain and predictable. His later followers, Hewart and Hayek, extolled the virtue of defined rules to govern the exercise of public power.

There is of course great virtue in the notion of law which is prospective and not retrospectively applied. Fair warning of change in rules is an important requirement of the Rule of Law. However, we have seen that Dicey was less concerned that laws were

---

[42] Bingham's eight features are: Accessibility of the Law; Law not Discretion; Equality before the Law; The Exercise of Power; Human Rights; Dispute Resolution; A Fair Trial; and the Rule of Law in the International Order.

[43] See Feldman's chapter in this book (Ch. 5) on the extent to which international law forms part of our domestic law.

'harsh' than that they be known. Certainty, rather than substantive fairness, was the key value. Maitland wrote that 'Known general laws, however bad, interfere less with freedom than decisions based on no previously known rule.'[44] Hayek said:

> [I]t does not matter whether we all drive on the left or the right-hand side of the roads so long as we all do the same. The important thing is that the rule enables us to predict other people's behaviour correctly, and this requires that it should apply in all cases—even if in a particular instance we feel it to be unjust.[45]

The need for legal certainty was another reason why Dicey mistrusted official discretion.

Rules permit fair warning. They allow affected persons to know what they are required to do—or not do—in advance of any sanction for breach of the rule. Certainty in that sense has an instrumental value in that it allows decisions to be planned in advance and people to know clearly where they stand. However, the value of legal certainty is also grounded in *substantive fairness*. It is unfair to penalize someone for an action that was lawful when it was carried out and it is unfair to punish someone for the breach of a law which they were not able to discover. And, as we shall see, when a person is encouraged by the decision-maker to believe that a particular course of action will take place, certainty will dictate that his 'legitimate expectation' shall not be disappointed.

The notion of legal certainty does of course not mean that the law cannot be changed. But change should be carried out in a way that is transparent so that any amendments, repeals, or new laws should be accessible.

Equality

We have seen that Dicey considered that the Rule of Law required all officials, from the Prime Minister down to a constable or a collector of taxes, to be subject to the same responsibility for every act done without legal justification as any other citizen.[46] Dicey is here claiming formal equality for the Rule of Law, by which he meant that no person is exempt from the enforcement of the law; rich and poor, revenue official and individual taxpayer, powerful and marginalized are all within equal reach of the law's implementation.

This type of equality, although sometimes derided,[47] is important. It is inherent in the very notion of law, and in the integrity of law's application, that like cases be treated alike. And it forbids vices such as corruption, which allow the benefits of law to be sold to the highest bidder. As was said as long ago as 1215 in Chapter 40 of the Magna Carta, 'We will sell to no man, we will not deny or defer to any man either Justice or Right.'[48]

---

[44] *Collected Papers*, vol. i (1911) 81. Maitland equated arbitrary power with power that was 'uncertain' or 'incalculable': ibid., p. 80.

[45] Hayek, *The Road to Serfdom* (1943) 60.   [46] See Dicey, above, n. 1, p. 193.

[47] See the recent case, *R. (Gallaher Group Ltd. v Competition and Markets Authority* [2018] UKSC 25, where Lord Carnwath, at paras. 24–25 held that equal treatment was not a 'distinct principle of administrative law' but a feature of irrational behaviour.

[48] This remains on the statute book in Chapter 29 of the version issued by Edward I in 1297.

An interesting question is whether this notion of equality within the Rule of Law refers not to the content of the law but to its *enforcement* and *application* alone. So long as laws are applied equally, that is, consistently without irrational bias or distinction, then formal equality is complied with. Formal equality does not however prohibit *unequal laws*. It forbids, say, racially biased enforcement of the law, but does not forbid racially discriminatory laws from being enacted. For Dicey, the Rule of Law embraced only formal equality. This is because for him the role of equality in the Rule of Law was instrumental; to buttress the central value of legal certainty. It was not espoused as a virtue for its own sake. We have seen how Dicey's supporters freely acknowledged that it is more important that the law be certain than it be not 'harsh', 'bad', or 'unjust'.[49] Discriminatory or arbitrary enforcement of the law would violate legal certainty, but laws themselves that discriminated against certain groups or classes, but were uniformly enforced within the groups or class, would not violate legal certainty, or therefore the Rule of Law.

There are two opposing views as to whether substantive equality qualifies as a feature of the Rule of Law.[50] Those who believe that discriminatory laws are not 'law' would of course not permit them to qualify as fulfilling the Rule of Law.[51] On the other hand, as Lord Hoffmann has said, equality is in itself 'one of the building blocks of democracy'.[52] And Lady Hale has said that 'democracy values everyone equally, even if the majority does not'.[53] It is therefore not necessary to subsume substantive equality within the Rule of Law in order to demonstrate that discriminatory laws violate one of the fundamental requirements of democratic constitutionalism.[54]

Nevertheless, it is surely wrong to say that South Africa, in the days of apartheid, where laws discriminated against the majority, fulfilled the requirements of the Rule of Law simply because the discriminatory laws were enforced equally against blacks and whites. Or that detention without trial in many parts of the world today fulfills the Rule of Law's requirements simply because everyone is equally liable to be detained without distinction of class, wealth, race or gender. That concept amounts to rule by law rather than Rule of Law.

Access to Justice and Rights

The fourth feature of the Rule of Law requires access to courts or equivalent institutions. Chapter 39 of the Magna Carta provided that no person should be condemned 'except by lawful judgment of his peers or by the law of the land'. The requirement of 'due process' or 'natural justice' (these days called 'procedural propriety' or 'procedural

---

[49] See Maitland, above, n. 44, and Hayek, above, n. 45.

[50] Raz, above, n. 35, thinks not. Bingham, above, n. 5, thinks it does.   [51] See Dworkin, above, n. 36.

[52] *Matadeen v Pointu and Minister of Education and Science* [1999] AC 98 (PC).

[53] *Chester v Secretary of State for Justice* [2013] UKSC 63 at [88] See also *Ghaidan v Godin Mendoza* [2004] 2 AC 557 (same sex partner entitled to same inheritance rights as different sex partner): '[Unequal treatment] is the reverse of rational behaviour ... Power must not be exercised arbitrarily' (*per* Lady Hale).

[54] I have expanded on this point in 'Is Equality a Constitutional Principle?' (1994) 47 *Current Legal Problems* (Part 2) 1. See also R. Singh, 'Equality: The Neglected Virtue' [2004] *EHRLR* 141. For a view that equality (both formal and substantive) is part of the Rule of Law, see Allan, above, n. 1, and *Gallaher*, n. 47 above.

fairness') furthers Bingham's requirement that people should be entitled to the 'benefit' of laws, and to ensure this by being able to challenge its wrong application (or non-implementation). In order to do this, the claimant will need access to the courts or equivalent institutions. Access to justice is therefore a further key element of the Rule of Law. It is a feature very different in kind from the notions of certainty and equality but brings life to the Rule of Law by permitting its practical application.

Whatever degree of legality, certainty, or equality there may be, if a person is not able to challenge the government to assert his rights, including human rights, the Rule of Law cannot be said to obtain. In fact it could be said that perhaps the most important feature of a Rule of Law state is that it provides a person the opportunity to challenge a decision of the government of the day with a reasonable prospect of success in an appropriate case.

Access to justice, however, requires more than a system of courts to which an individual may apply. Once the claimant reaches the court, a further aspect of Rule of Law is engaged, namely the requirement that the decision-maker be unbiased, that is, both independent (in the sense of free of external pressure) and impartial (not apparently interested in the outcome of the case in favour of any one of the participants). Even if perfect impartiality on the part of the adjudicator is an unattainable goal (because we all have unconscious predilections and biases), the system should not give the appearance of bias. Justice must both be done and seen to be done. And the independence must extend not only to the judges but also to the legal profession, who must be able to provide advocacy services without fear or favour.

And once the person reaches a court, there must be a fair trial, with the opportunity to submit arguments and challenge facts. Viewed in that light, access to justice is not a merely formal virtue. Its substantive dimension emerges when we consider that it endorses the notion that every person is entitled to be treated with due regard to the proper merits of their cause. Failure to provide that treatment diminishes a person's sense of individual worth and impairs their dignity.[55] The right to due process goes further than forbidding actual punishment without a trial. It extends to a concern that individuals should not have decisions made about their vital interests without an opportunity to influence the outcome of those decisions. And it requires restrictions on rights, liberties, and interests to be properly *justified*. The culture of justification, rather than the culture of authority,[56] is another mark of the difference between democracy and despotism. Due process therefore provides 'formal and institutional expression to the influence of reasoned argument in human affairs'.[57] Overt reference to irrational

---

[55] For a full account of the variety of justifications of procedural protections, see D. J. Galligan, *Due Process and Fair Procedures* (1996), and see G. Richardson, 'The Legal Regulation of Process', in G. Richardson and H. Genn (eds.), *Administrative Law and Government Actions* (1994). The aspect of natural justice that requires the decision-maker to be unbiased also incorporates an aspect of the principle of separation of powers into the Rule of Law.

[56] E. Mureinik, 'A Bridge to Where? Introducing the Bill of Rights' (1994) 10 *SAJHR* 31.

[57] L. Fuller, 'Collective Bargaining and the Arbitrator' (1963) *Wisconsin L. Rev* 1, 3. See also Rawls's view of natural justice as an element of the Rule of Law, in his *A Theory of Justice* (1972) 241–2.

or particularistic factors (such as the defendant's race) will therefore be difficult to sustain. Because procedural fairness promotes full and fair consideration of the issues and evidence, as Lord Steyn has said, it plays 'an instrumental role in promoting just decisions'.[58]

Although Dicey favoured adjudication through the regular courts of law, adjudicative mechanisms of different kinds provide procedural checks on discretion in order to comply with the Rule of Law. Some are provided through appeals—for example, in planning, from local to central government by means of written representations or a public inquiry; or in immigration and asylum matters, from an adjudicator to an appeal tribunal.

Some decisions decide not only rights between the individual and a public organization, but also questions of policy, such as whether a new railway line or motorway should be built over a stretch of land. In those situations, the decision may be structured by means of an inquiry or tribunal hearing, or may simply be made by an official within a government department. There has been a demand for public participation in those decisions. Even though those seeking participation may have mere interests (rather than a vested property right) in the decision's outcome, they ask for the right to participate in the process of making that decision. Neighbours want to be consulted about an application for planning permission on a local site, and people want to be consulted about the closure of hospitals, local railway lines or coal pits.[59] If the Rule of Law is concerned to protect individuals from being deprived of their rights without an opportunity to defend themselves, the concern is only narrowly stretched to protect group interests from being overridden without the opportunity to express views on the matter to be decided.[60] For example, a challenge to a government review which reversed the 'high policy' against nuclear power was struck down by the Administrative Court on the ground that the review was so deficient in content and form that its process was 'manifestly unfair'.[61]

THE RULE OF LAW AS AN IDEAL

The Rule of Law contains, as we have seen, the values of legality, certainty, equality and access to justice. These features in themselves promote both formal and substantive goals. However, they are not unqualified; they constitute an ideal which may permit of some exceptions.

In relation to legality, not all law can be enforced. Sometimes the prosecuting agency will lack the resources to prosecute the law. This happened when the police withdrew full enforcement of the law against unlawful protesters against the shipping of live

---

[58] *Raji v General Medical Council* [2003] UKPC 24.

[59] *R. v British Coal Corpn and Secretary of State for Trade and Industry ex parte Vardy and others* [1993] ICR 720 (CA).

[60] For an account of 'the ideology of public participation', see Patrick McAuslan, *The Ideologies of Planning Law* (1980); J. Habermas, *Towards a Rational Society* (1971).

[61] *R. (Greenpeace Ltd.) v Secretary of State for Trade and Industry* [2007] EWHC 311 (Admin).

animals across the channel. The House of Lords accepted that the action was justified because it was stretching the chief constable's resources to the detriment of policing elsewhere in the county.[62] Full enforcement may also distort the purpose of the rule and require, for example, the prosecution of a doctor who narrowly exceeded the speed limit on a deserted street late at night while rushing to the scene of an accident. That prosecution makes no sense in furthering the goal of preventing unsafe driving.

In December 2006 the Director of the Serious Fraud Office (the Director) decided to abandon an investigation into allegations of bribery and corruption by BAE Systems Ltd (BAE), in relation to contracts for Al-Yamamah military aircraft with the Kingdom of Saudi Arabia. Threats had been made by Saudi officials that if the investigation were to continue the Saudi government would cancel a proposed order for Eurofighter Typhoon aircraft and withdraw security and intelligence co-operation with the UK.

Despite internal political pressure to drop the investigation, and just at the point when the trail of investigation was extended to Swiss bank accounts, the Director was persuaded to drop the case on the advice particularly of the British Ambassador to Saudi Arabia that national security ('British lives on British streets') would be endangered if the threat were carried out. The Director's decision was challenged through judicial review and the Divisional Court held that the Director had not paid sufficient regard to the danger to the Rule of Law in submitting to the threat.[63] However, the House of Lords disagreed and held that the Director's decision was lawful and that courts should be 'very slow to interfere' in prosecutorial decisions outside of 'exceptional cases'.[64] This was because, first, respect should be accorded to the independence of the prosecutor. Secondly, it was said that prosecutorial decisions are not susceptible to judicial review because it is within neither the constitutional function nor the practical competence of the courts to assess matters concerning the public interest, especially when national security is in issue, as it was in this case.

It seems unfortunate in this case that the House of Lords considered itself powerless to prevent the caving in to threats to our system of justice, and thus to the Rule of Law. Had the threats in this case been made by a British citizen, he would be liable at least to prosecution for perverting the course of justice.

In relation to legal certainty, the benefits of rules—their objective, even-handed features—may be opposed to other administrative benefits, especially those of individual treatment, and responsiveness. The virtue of rules to the administrator (routine treatment and efficiency) and to the general public (predictability and the opportunity to plan) may be a defect to the claimant with a special case (such as the brilliant applicant for a university place who failed to obtain the required grades because of a family upset or illness just before the examination). Officials themselves may consider that a task

---

[62] R. v Chief Constable of Sussex ex parte International Traders' Ferry Ltd. [1999] 2 AC 418. But see also R. v Coventry City Council ex parte Phoenix Aviation [1995] 3 All ER 37, where it was held that substantial non-enforcement of the law was in breach of the Rule of Law.

[63] R. (on the application of Corner House) v Director of the Serious Fraud Office [2007] EWHC 311 (Admin).

[64] [2008] UKHL 6.

requires flexibility, or genuinely want to help a particular client, but feel unable to do so. Hence the classic bureaucratic response: 'I'd like to help you—but this is the rule.'

Our administrative law itself recognizes the limits of rule-governed conduct through the principle against the 'fettering' of discretion. Where an official has wide discretion—for example, to provide grants to industry or to students or to regulate safety standards for taxi drivers—a rule will often be introduced both to assist in the articulation of the standard and its even-handed application, and also to announce the standard to affected persons. The safety rules, for example, may require seat belts, and regular vehicle maintenance inspections. A policy of promoting safe driving could be legalized by a rule specifying speeds of no more than 20 miles per hour on certain streets. The courts do not object to the use of a rule in itself, but they do sometimes object to its rigid application without giving a person with something new or special to say about his case the opportunity to put his argument to the decision-maker. The principle against the 'fettering of discretion' acknowledges how the rigid application of rules can militate against good and fair public administration.[65]

This balance of rule and discretion can be found etched into particular areas of public administration. In town planning, for example, permission is needed for the development of land. By what criteria is that permission granted or refused? Some countries have adopted a system of zoning, by which the local map clearly marks out what can be done in each area. A would-be developer knows from the colour-coding whether he can build a factory or change a shop to an office on a given site. In Britain this approach, whereby the zoning map in effect creates a series of rules about what can be done on the land, is greatly softened. Officials will take into account the formal plan for the area, but account may also be taken of 'other material considerations'.[66] So rule and discretion are mixed together, in an attempt to gain the benefits of each. Thus, an applicant for a craft centre in an area zoned as residential on the plan may nevertheless be granted permission because the centre fits in with the area, does not adversely affect its amenity, and generates local employment. These 'other material considerations' provide the flexibility to mitigate the rigours of a rule-bound plan.

Access to justice may also be subject to limitations. Litigation will not be within the reach of everyone's pocket, and legal aid depends upon national resources. Nor is adjudication an appropriate way to resolve all disputes. In the nineteenth century, writers such as Bentham[67] and his disciple Chadwick voiced strong opposition to the judicialization of administration. They agreed that to introduce such procedures would lead to mindless disputes upon 'such simple questions as to whether a cask of biscuits was good or bad'.[68] Due process may impede speed and despatch. Could we really allow a hearing as to whether firefighters should douse a burning house with water? Or a

---

[65] See D. Galligan, 'The Nature and Function of Policies within Discretionary Power' (1976) *Public Law* 332 and *Discretionary Powers* (1986); C. Hilson, 'Judicial Review, Politics and the Fettering of Discretion' [2002] *Public Law* 111. See Woolf, Jowell, et al., *de Smith's Judicial Review* (8th ed. 2018), Chapter 9.

[66] Town and Country Planning Act 1990, s. 54A.

[67] L. J. Hume, *Bentham and Bureaucracy* (1981) 82.

[68] H. Parris, *Constitutional Bureaucracy* (1969) 82.

pavement hearing before a police officer is able to tow away an illegally parked car? Should there be an appeal from a university lecturer's examination grade? Or from a decision to reject admission to a university? Sometimes parties who have to live with each other after the dispute prefer techniques of mediation which can negotiate an acceptable solution.[69] These forms of resolving disputes differ from adjudication where the final decision is taken by the independent 'judge' and is imposed rather than agreed.

THE PRACTICAL IMPLEMENTATION OF THE RULE OF LAW

The Rule of Law is a principle of institutional morality. As such it guides all forms both of law enforcement and of law making. In particular, it suggests that legality, legal certainty, equality, and access to justice are fundamental requirements of democratic constitutionalism. Nor, as we have seen, are all its virtues simply formal. It promotes accountability, but also fairness and respect for human dignity.

In a country like the UK that does not have a codified constitution, the Rule of Law serves as a principle that constrains governmental power. We return now to Dicey's contention that the Rule of Law stands together with parliamentary sovereignty as a constitutional principle. Although many of Dicey's notions may have delayed the development in this country of a coherent public law, his genius was to recognize that our constitution does contain implied principles. The principle of parliamentary sovereignty, together with what he called conventions, *enables* powers to be exercised by government and specifies how it is to be exercised. The Rule of Law however *disables* government from abusing its power.

In countries with written constitutions, the text itself provides the enabling features (such as who may vote and the composition of the executive and legislature). It also normally provides the disabling features through a Bill of Rights that constrains government, even elected Parliaments, from interfering with certain fundamental rights and freedoms (such as freedom of expression and association) which are considered necessary and integral to democracy.[70] In Britain, the Rule of Law, as an unwritten principle performs a similar disabling function, in the area where its values apply.

How does the Rule of Law operate in practice in the UK? Let us first note that our courts have not yet, outside directly effective European Union Law, felt themselves able to disapply primary legislation that offends the Rule of Law. However, since 1998 the Human Rights Act has incorporated into domestic law most of the provisions of the European Convention on Human Rights (ECHR), some of which contain values that inhere in the Rule of Law (such as the prohibition against retroactive laws, the prohibition of torture, the right to liberty and the requirement of a fair trial). All decisions by public officials, including the courts, must now conform with Convention rights.

---

[69] See V. Aubert, 'Competition and Dissensus: Two Types of Conflict and Conflict Resolution' (1963) *J Conflict Res* 26.

[70] Although in some cases the state has a positive obligation to secure or enforce certain rights.

Parliament's statutes may be reviewed by the courts for compatibility with Convention rights, but the courts may not, under the Act, strike down statutes that offend the ECHR; it may only declare them incompatible with Convention rights.[71]

However, the absence of judicial authority to disapply primary legislation that is contrary to the Rule of Law does not mean that the Rule of Law has no influence on the content of legislation. As a constitutional principle, the Rule of Law serves as a basis for the evaluation of all laws and provides a critical focus for public debate. There have been a number of occasions in recent years where proposals to evade the Rule of Law (for example, by prohibiting judicial review of decisions about asylum or immigration) have been abandoned in the face of strong opposition on the ground that the proposals offended the Rule of Law's moral strictures.[72]

Even before the Human Rights Act 1998 came into force, the courts would seek to reconcile the principles of parliamentary sovereignty and the Rule of Law where possible. For example, in the case of *Pierson*,[73] it was held that, despite the fact that the Home Secretary had very broad discretionary power to set a prisoner's tariff (the minimum sentence prior to parole), the decision to increase the tariff retrospectively—contrary to an earlier indication that the lesser sentence would be imposed—offended the Rule of Law in its substantive sense. Lord Steyn in that case said:

> Parliament does not legislate in a vacuum. Parliament legislates for a European liberal democracy based upon the traditions of the common law . . . and . . . unless there is the clearest provision to the contrary, Parliament must be presumed not to legislate contrary to the Rule of Law.[74]

This presumption in favour of the Rule of Law (and other fundamental constitutional principles, such as freedom of expression) was referred to as the 'principle of legality', described by Lord Hoffmann in a later case as follows:

> Parliamentary sovereignty means that Parliament can, if it chooses, legislate contrary to fundamental principles of human rights . . . But the principle of legality means that Parliament must squarely confront what it is doing and accept the political cost. Fundamental rights cannot be overridden by general or ambiguous words. This is because there is too great a risk that the full implications of their unqualified meaning may have passed unnoticed in the democratic process. In the absence of express language or necessary implication to the contrary, the courts therefore presume that even the most general words were intended to be subject to the basic rights of the individual. In this way the courts of the United Kingdom, though acknowledging the sovereignty of Parliament, apply principles of constitutionality little different from those which exist in countries where the power of the legislature is expressly limited by a constitutional document.[75]

---

[71] See, further, O'Cinneide's Chapter 3 below.

[72] See the account by R. Rawlings, 'Review: Revenge and Retreat' [2005] *MLR* 378; A. le Sueur, 'Three Strikes and You're Out? The UK Government's Strategy to Oust Judicial Review from Immigration and Asylum' [2004] *Public Law 225*; and Joint Committee on Human Rights, *The Implications for Access to Justice of the Government's Proposals to Reform Judicial Review* (2013–14, HL 174, HC 868).

[73] *R. v Secretary of State for the Home Department ex parte Pierson* [1998] AC 539.   [74] Ibid. p. 575.

[75] *R. v Secretary of State for the Home Department ex parte Simms* [2003] 2 AC 115, 131.

JUDICIAL REVIEW OF THE EXERCISE OF PUBLIC POWER

The practical implementation of the Rule of Law has taken place primarily through judicial review of the actions of public officials. During the first half of the twentieth century, a time of reaction to Dicey's Rule of Law, the courts rarely interfered with the exercise of discretionary powers.[76] From that time on, however, they began to require that power be exercised in accordance with three 'grounds' of judicial review, each of them resting in large part on the Rule of Law.

The first ground, 'legality', requires officials to act within the scope of their lawful powers. The courts ensure that the official decisions do not stray beyond the 'four corners' of a statute by failing to take into account 'relevant' considerations (that is, considerations that the law requires), or by taking into account 'irrelevant' considerations (that is, considerations outside the object and purpose that Parliament intended the statute to pursue).[77] This exercise is, as we have discussed, a clear instance of the implementation of the Rule of Law, whereby the courts act as guardians of Parliament's intent and purpose. The definition of the purpose of a given statute is no mere mechanical exercise, and is often complicated by the fact that the statute confers very wide discretionary powers on the decision-maker, for example to act 'as he sees fit'. For example, where a statute conferred broad powers upon a local authority to sell its own dwellings to their inhabitants, and where some local councillors decided to sell those dwellings for the cynical purpose of securing electoral advantage for their party, the courts had to grapple with the question whether the councillors were entitled, as elected politicians, to assist their party to win the next election. The House of Lords held that statutory powers are conferred on trust, and not absolutely, and that the motive of the councillors—party gain—was extraneous to the purpose for which the powers were conferred.[78]

Although there are a number of administrative tasks that cannot be pre-determined by any rule, the courts have reconciled Dicey's fear of any discretion with a view that no discretion is wholly unfettered. As was said in a leading case on the issue of 'legality', even if a discretion were expressly defined as 'unfettered':

> The use of that adjective . . . can do nothing to unfetter the control which the judiciary have over the executive, namely that in exercising their powers the latter must act lawfully and that is a matter to be determined by looking at the Act and its scope and object in conferring a discretion upon the Minister rather than by the use of adjectives.[79]

The second ground of review, that of 'procedural propriety', requires decision-makers to be unbiased and to grant a fair hearing to claimants before depriving them of a right or significant interest (such as an interest in livelihood or reputation). We have seen that the right of due process—the right not to be condemned unheard—is a central

---

[76] For an account of this history, see J. Jowell, 'Administrative Law', and R. Stevens, 'Government and the Judiciary' in V. Bogdanor (ed.), *The British Constitution in the Twentieth Century* (2003).

[77] E.g. *Padfield v Minister of Agriculture, Fisheries and Food* [1968] AC 997.

[78] *Magill v Porter* [2001] UKHL 67.

[79] *Per* Lord Upjohn in *Padfield v Minister of Agriculture, Fisheries and Food* [1968] AC 997.

value of the Rule of Law, which the courts presume Parliament will respect. The courts have affirmed the principle of procedural fairness, even where the statute conferring the power to decide was silent on the matter. In the nineteenth century the courts were not slow to allow the 'justice of the common law' to supplement the legislature's omission, looking back to the Garden of Eden as an example of a fair hearing being granted before Adam and Eve were deported from their green and pleasant land.[80] In the first half of the twentieth century the courts were more reluctant to grant hearings, restricting them to matters where rights were in issue (rather than privileges). The case of *Ridge v Baldwin*[81] then extended the hearing to the protections of more important interests, such as reputation or livelihood.

This kind of procedural protection, whether established by statute or the common law, is a concrete expression of the Rule of Law. Its content is variable, depending on the issue. However, as was said:

> The Rule of Law rightly requires that certain decisions, of which the paradigm examples are findings of breaches of the criminal law and adjudication as to private rights, should be entrusted to the judicial branch of government.[82]

The courts have extended the requirement of a fair hearing even where the claimant does not possess a threatened criminal or private right or even an important interest. A hearing will be required where a 'legitimate expectation' has been induced by the decision-maker.[83] In such a case the claimant has, expressly or impliedly, been promised either a hearing or the continuation of a benefit. The courts will not sanction the disappointment of such an expectation unless the claimant is permitted to make representations on the matter. In some cases the courts have even protected the substance of the expectation. The notion of the legitimate expectation is itself rooted in that aspect of the Rule of Law which requires legal certainty.

The third ground of judicial review, 'irrationality' or 'unreasonableness', also applies aspects of the Rule of Law. Suppose the police enforce laws against dangerous driving only against bearded drivers, or drivers of a particular race. Suppose an education authority chose to dismiss all teachers with red hair. Suppose a prison officer refused to permit a prisoner to communicate with his lawyer. Suppose a minister raised the minimum sentence of a prisoner, having earlier told him that the sentence would be set at a lower level. Would these decisions offend the Rule of Law? If so, the Rule of Law becomes a substantive doctrine and not merely formal or procedural. Our courts, through judicial review, tread warily in this area, interfering only if the decision was beyond the range of reasonable responses.[84] However, where the Rule of Law or other constitutional principles or fundamental rights are in issue, the courts scrutinize the

---

[80] *Cooper v Wandsworth Board of Works* (1863) 14 CB (NS) 180.   [81] [1964] AC 40.

[82] *Alconbury Developments Ltd. v Secretary of State for the Environment, Transport and the Regions* [2001] UKHL 23 at [42], *per* Lord Hoffmann. See also *Runa Begum v Tower Hamlets LBC* [2003] UKHL 5 at [4].

[83] Endorsed in the House of Lords in *Council of Civil Service Unions v Minister of the Civil Service* [1985] AC 374.

[84] *Associated Provincial Picture Houses v Wednesbury Corporation* [1948] 1 KB 223.

decision with greater care[85] and also adopt the 'principle of legality' that we have seen above,[86] which presumes that Parliament intends the Rule of Law to prevail.

In practice, many of the decisions held unreasonable are so held because they offend the values of the Rule of Law discussed above. The concept of 'unreasonableness', or 'irrationality', in itself imputes the arbitrariness that Dicey considered was the antithesis of the Rule of Law. Decisions based upon an insufficient evidentiary basis,[87] or which are inconsistent,[88] fall foul of the Rule of Law's values. Where byelaws are not sufficiently clear they have been held unlawful for 'uncertainty'.[89] Dicey's abhorrence of arbitrary decisions is also endorsed when a decision is struck down because it is simply unreasonably harsh or oppressive.[90]

The practical implementation of the Rule of Law over the years makes it clear that its substantive aims underlie and endorse the striking down of a number of decisions, albeit often without mentioning its name. A local authority which withdrew the licence of a rugby club whose members had visited South Africa during the apartheid regime was held to offend the Rule of Law on the ground that there should be no punishment where there was no law (since sporting contacts with South Africa were not then prohibited).[91] A minister's rules allowing a prison governor to prevent a prisoner corresponding with his lawyer, even when no litigation was contemplated, was held to violate the prisoner's 'constitutional right' of access to justice.[92] The inability of the remaining white farmers in Zimbabwe to challenge the proposed taking of their land, following a constitutional amendment, was held to violate the Rule of Law as a foundational principle of the Southern African Development Community (SADC).[93] And an order seeking to freeze the assets of known terrorists such as Usama Bin-Laden on a consolidated list was held by the Supreme Court to violate the Rule of Law because the person whose name is on the list had no right to challenge the listing before a court.[94]

The legitimate expectation, which began by grounding a procedural right to a fair hearing,[95] has since been extended to a substantive doctrine, grounding a right not merely to a fair hearing but to the promised benefit itself. For example, a local authority that promised the claimants a 'home for life' in an institution for the chronically ill, was not permitted to disappoint the resultant legitimate expectation.[96]

---

[85] Under the Human Rights Act 1998, applying the ECHR, the courts will adopt even stricter scrutiny under the test of 'proportionality'. See Chapter 3 below.

[86] See n. 75 above.

[87] *E v Secretary of State for the Home Department* [2004] EWCA Civ 49.

[88] See R. Clayton, 'Legitimate Expectations, Policy and the Principle of Consistency' [2003] *CLJ* 93. See *R. (Rashid) v Secretary of State for the Home Department* [2005] EWCA Civ 744.

[89] *Percy v Hall* [1997] QB 924. And see *R. (L) v Secretary of State for the Home Department* [2003] EWCA Civ 25 ('Legal certainty is an aspect of the rule of law' at [25]).

[90] See de Smith's *Judicial Review*, above, n. 65, Chapter 11.

[91] *Wheeler v Leicester City Council* [1985] AC 1054 (HL)

[92] *R. v Secretary of State for the Home Department ex parte Leech (No. 2)* [1994] QB 198.

[93] *Campbell et al. v The Republic of Zimbabwe* [2007] SADC (T) Case no. 2.

[94] *Her Majesty's Treasury v Ahmed and others* [2010] UKSC 2.   [95] See above, n. 75.

[96] *R. v North and East Devon Health Authority ex parte Coughlan* [2001] QB 213.

The remarkable elasticity of the Rule of Law, and the richness of its underlying values, was demonstrated in a case that concerned the legal effect of a decision that had not been communicated to the person affected. The relevant legislation permitted asylum seekers' rights to income support to be terminated once their application for asylum had been refused by a 'determination' of the Home Secretary. The refusal in this case was recorded only in an internal file note in the Home Office and communicated to the Benefits Agency, which promptly denied the appellant future income support. The determination was not, however, communicated to the appellant.[97]

The appellant in this case could not easily invoke the normal requirements of the Rule of Law in her favour. The decision did not take effect retrospectively; ignorance of the law does not normally excuse its application. Nevertheless, the House of Lords, by a majority, held that the decision violated 'the constitutional principle requiring the Rule of Law to be observed'.[98] Lord Steyn, with whom the majority of their Lordships concurred, based his argument both upon legal certainty ('surprise is the enemy of justice') and upon accountability: the individual must be informed of the outcome of her case so that 'she can decide what to do' and 'be in a position to challenge the decision in the courts' (this being an aspect of the principle of the right of access to justice).[99] The House of Lords had no truck with the notion that the Home Secretary's determination had formally and strictly been made. This was 'legalism and conceptualism run riot', which is reminiscent of the state described by Kafka 'where the rights of an individual are overridden by hole in the corner decisions or knocks on the doors in the early hours'.[100]

We have seen that access to justice is a key ingredient of the Rule of Law. In a recent case, Lord Reed, for a unanimous Supreme Court, gave this aspect of the Rule of Law practical effect. Holding that fees imposed by the Lord Chancellor in respect of proceedings in employment tribunals and the Employment Appeal Tribunal were so high as to pose a real risk of deterring employees from challenging decisions in those tribunals, he said that 'the constitutional right of access to the courts is inherent in the rule of law'.[101] Without such access, he said, 'laws are liable to become a dead letter'.[102] Access to justice as a value of the Rule of Law (and considered a 'higher order' right) was previously held to have been violated by the Lord Chancellor's imposition of substantial court fees which an impecunious litigant was unable to afford.[103]

The Rule of Law does, therefore, possess substantive content.[104] Its promotion of the core institutional values of legality, certainty, equality, and access to justice do not

---

[97] R. (on the application of Anufrijeva) v Secretary of State for the Home Department [2003] 3 WLR 252.

[98] Ibid., at [28], per Lord Steyn.   [99] Ibid., at [26] and [31], per Lord Steyn.

[100] Ibid., at [32] and [28], per Lord Steyn. See also FP (Iran) v Secretary of State for the Home Department, where Arden LJ invoked the Rule of Law to safeguard access to a tribunal—a right which 'cannot be taken away before it has been communicated to the person entitled to it', at [61].

[101] R. (UNISON) v Lord Chancellor [2017] UKSC 51 at para.66.   [102] Id., at para. 68.

[103] R. v Lord Chancellor ex parte Witham [1997] 1 WLR 104.

[104] This passage was cited with approval by Lord Steyn in R. v Secretary of State for the Home Department ex parte Pierson [1998] AC 539 (HL).

merely, as Jennings would have it, further the aims of free trade and the market economy. They certainly do encourage investment as they signal a society based on stability and fairness. However, they also enhance accountability and promote respect for the dignity of the individual.[105] As Tom Bingham said, rejecting Raz' view of the 'thin' concept of the Rule of Law, in which Raz holds that slavery is compatible with the Rule of Law:

> A state which savagely represses or persecutes sections of its people cannot in my view be regarded as observing the rule of law, even if the transport of the persecuted minority to the concentration camp or the compulsory exposure of female children on the mountainside is the subject of detailed laws duly enacted and scrupulously observed.[106]

THE RULE OF LAW AND PARLIAMENTARY SOVEREIGNTY

What about the Rule of Law's status in relation to the sovereignty of Parliament? In the UK the principle of parliamentary sovereignty has always been able to override the Rule of Law; not on the authority of any written constitution, but on the authority of commentators such as Dicey and repeated assertions by the courts over time. In the absence of any formal constitutional source, is it theoretically open to the Rule of Law to replace the sovereignty of Parliament as our primary constitutional principle? This issue was raised in a most unlikely case involving a challenge to the Hunting Act 2004, which banned the hunting of most wild mammals by dogs.[107] The central issue in the case was the validity of the Parliament Acts 1911 and 1949, which were invoked to ensure the passage of the Bill without the approval of the House of Lords. The Parliament Acts were upheld, as was the Hunting Act 2004, but three significant *obiter dicta* questioned the relation of parliamentary sovereignty to the Rule of Law as had never been done before. Lord Steyn said that:

> in exceptional circumstances involving an attempt to abolish judicial review or the authority of the courts, [the courts] may have to consider whether this is a constitutional fundamental which even a complaisant House of Commons cannot abolish.

Lady Hale said:

> The Courts will treat with particular suspicion (and might even reject) any attempt to subvert the rule of law by removing governmental action affecting the rights of the individual from all judicial powers.

And Lord Hope, even more forthrightly, said that 'it is no longer right to say that [Parliament's] freedom to legislate admits of no qualification' and that 'the rule of

---

[105] See Rawls, *A Theory of Justice* 235–43, and cf. Joseph Raz's view of the Rule of Law as a negative value in 'The Rule of Law and its Virtue' (1977) *LQR* 195–211. See also J. Raz, *Ethics in the Public Domain* (1994) Ch. 16. See P. Joseph, 'The Rule of Law: Foundational Norm' in R. Ekins (ed.), *Modern Challenges to the Rule of Law* (2011), p.47, and other chapters there on this issue.

[106] T. Bingham, above note 5, at 67.

[107] *Jackson v Her Majesty's Attorney General* [2005] UKHL 56.

law enforced by the courts is the controlling principle upon which our constitution is based'.[108]

It may take some time, provocative legislation, and considerable judicial courage for the courts to assert the primacy of the Rule of Law over parliamentary sovereignty, but it is no longer self-evident that a legislature in a modern democracy should be able with impunity to violate the strictures of the Rule of Law.[109] However, the courts get quite close to this position when they review what are called 'ouster clauses', namely, provisions in a statute that seek to protect a tribunal or other body from review by a court. In the case of *Anisminic Ltd v Foreign Compensation Commission*,[110] the statute sought to prevent any 'decision or determination' of the Foreign Compensation Commission from appeal or review in any court of law. The House of Lords held that the decision which the Commission took was outside its 'jurisdiction' (which was defined as any error of law or lack of natural justice). The decision was therefore a 'nullity', or only a 'purported decision' and therefore the role of the courts to review the decision was not ousted. This approach has been followed more recently by invoking the Rule of Law more specifically. In *R. (Cart) v Upper Tribunal*[111] Laws LJ said the 'The court's ingrained reluctance to countenance the statutory exclusion of judicial review has its genesis in the fact that judicial review is a principal engine of the rule of law'.[112] He went on to say that since Parliament cannot interpret its own statutes (for to do so would be to judge in its own cause), and nor can decision-makers judge on the extent of the legality of their own exercise of power (for to do so would be for them to 'write their own laws'), in order for public bodies to be kept within the confines of their own powers which have been prescribed by statute 'the need for an authoritative judicial source of ultimate review cannot be denied.' This, said Laws LJ, is not a denial of parliamentary sovereignty, but 'an affirmation of it'.[113]

At the end of his chapter seeking to reconcile parliamentary sovereignty with the Rule of Law, in a passage which makes a very similar point, Dicey said:

> The fact that the most arbitrary powers of the English executive must always be exercised under Act of Parliament places the government, even when armed with the widest authority, under the supervision, so to speak, of the Courts. Powers, however extraordinary, which are conferred or sanctioned by statute, are never really unlimited, for they are confined by the words of the Act itself, and, what is more, by the interpretation put upon the statute by the judges. Parliament is supreme legislator, but from the moment Parliament has uttered its will as lawgiver, that will becomes subject to the interpretation put upon it by the judges of the land, and the judges, who are influenced by the feelings of magistrates

---

[108] *Jackson v Attorney General* [2005] UKHL 56 at [104]–[107], Lord Hope repeated this view in *AXA General Insurance Ltd and others v Lord Advocate and others* [2011] UKSC 46 at [51].

[109] See J. Jowell, 'Parliamentary Sovereignty under the New Constitutional Hypothesis' [2006] *PL* 562.

[110] [1969] 2 AC 147.

[111] [2010] EWCA Civ 859.

[112] Ibid., para. 34. And see further this case in the Supreme Court, *R(Cart) v Upper Tribunal* [2011] UKSC 28.

[113] Ibid., para. 38. For a different approach, in a case which at the time of writing is on appeal to the Supreme Court, see *R. (Privacy International) v Investigatory Powers Tribunal* [2017] EWCA Civ 1868.

no less than by the general spirit of the common law, are disposed to construe statutory exceptions to common law principles in a mode which would not commend itself either to a body of officials, or to the Houses of Parliament, if the Houses were called upon to interpret their own enactments ... By every path we come round to the same conclusion, that Parliamentary sovereignty has favoured the rule of law, and that the supremacy of the law of the land both calls forth the exertion of Parliamentary sovereignty, and leads to its being exercised in a spirit of legality.[114]

IS THE RULE OF LAW A UNIVERSAL CONCEPT?

The former Attorney General of India, Soli Sorabjee has said:

> It needs to be emphasised that there is nothing western or eastern or northern or southern about the underlying principle of the rule of law. It has a global reach and dimension. The rule of law symbolizes the quest ... to combine that degree of liberty without which the law is tyranny with that degree of law without which liberty becomes licence. In the words of the great Justice Vivien Bose of [the Indian] Supreme Court, the rule of law 'is the heritage of all mankind because its underlying rationale is belief in . . . the human dignity of all individuals anywhere in the world'.[115]

In 2011 the Council of Europe's Venice Commission (the Commission for Democracy Through Law—formed in 1990 to assist the countries of the former Soviet Union with constitutional advice) agreed on a document on the Rule of Law which accepted Tom Bingham's definition and eight ingredients.[116] This was remarkable in a body representing 47 countries with very different traditions, from common law to codified systems and from the German 'Rechsstaat' to the French 'Etat de droit' and onwards. That approach and definition has recently been adopted by a consultation paper on the Rule of Law issued by the Commission of the European Union,[117] and followed up by the Venice Commission with a practical Rule of Law Checklist.[118]

It must of course be acknowledged that there may be different ways of achieving the Rule of Law in countries with very different traditions, history and institutions. That does not, however, lead to the conclusion that the Rule of Law is an entirely relative and shifting concept and therefore may be readily excused by the standard of national convenience. As we have seen, the Rule of Law has a core meaning and a profound purpose in a world where the value of human dignity is too often compromised by oppression and a desire to rule not by law but by ideology—by raw power and by extreme dogma.

---

[114] Emphasis added: A.V. Dicey, *Introduction to the Study of the Law of the Constitution*, 8th Edition, p. 273. In contrast, Dicey noted that the French *droit administratif* had the right to 'fix their own power', and thus to act outside of the supervision of ordinary courts. Ibid., p. 224–5.

[115] 'The Rule of Law: A Moral Imperative for the Civilised World' [2014] Supreme Court Cases 59, at 61.

[116] European Commission for Democracy Through Law (Venice Commission), *Report on the Rule of Law* CDL-AD (2011).

[117] EU Commission, *Communication from the Commission to the European Parliament and the Council, a new EU Framework to Strengthen the Rule of Law* COM 2014 158 final/2.

[118] European Commission for Democracy Through Law (Venice Commission) *Rule of Law Checklist CDL-AD (2016) 007.*

It is surely condescending to say that the Rule of Law is for some parts of the world only. Turn the four features of the Rule of Law on their heads and, as each of its core elements fall to the ground, the unmistakable features of tyranny come ominously into view: laws which are uncertain and retrospective; corruption and favoritism in the implementation of law; no access to courts; unfair trials before judges who routinely decide in favour of the government of the day or other powerful elites. Can we really say that any of those are suitable for any country? Or that the features of the Rule of Law are strictly the preserve of any country or group of countries?

One must also add the instrumental benefits of the Rule of Law. Legal certainty and equal application of the law are central ingredients to accountability and the possibility of legal challenge. These features are normally regarded as necessary to foreign direct investment which in turn provides the engine of economic growth. Investment will shirk countries which do not honour contracts or property rights, or which tax retrospectively, or discriminate, or intimidate selected firms or individuals without any hope of recourse.[119]

But the Rule of Law is not only for the investor or the entrepreneur. It is an instrument of empowerment. We have seen that the ability to challenge public decisions is a key feature of the Rule of Law. An example from South Africa illustrates this starkly: Rule of Law was incorporated as a founding principle of the post-apartheid South African constitution and South Africa was the first constitution in the world to establish a constitutional right to just administrative action—the right to challenge public officials for breach of legal, fair or unreasonable acts.[120] It was the utilization of this provision that permitted access to be provided to retroviral drugs to HIV-ridden women and children in South Africa—a decision that has probably done more for the well-being of women and children in Africa than any other.[121] Without the Rule of Law power and resources tend to fall into—or remain in—the hands of the powerful to the exclusion of the poor and the marginalized.

CONCLUSION

The virtues of the Rule of Law are not only formal and procedural. Its scope is broad,[122] although not broad enough to serve as a principle upholding a number of other requirements of a democracy. Some of the features of the Rule of Law overlap those incorporated in the rights set out in the ECHR—the right to a fair trial, for example, or to liberty, or against retrospective laws, yet other Convention rights go beyond the Rule of Law (such as the right to privacy or sexual freedom).

---

[119] See the critical discussion about law and development in D. Marshall (ed) *The International Rule of Law Movement* (2014). The defence of the Rule of Law in that work is put by J. Goldston, 'New Rules for the Rule of Law', at p. 1.

[120] Section 33 of the Constitution of South Africa, 1994.

[121] See *Minister of Health v Treatment Action Campaign* (TAC) 2002 (5) SA 721 (CC).

[122] See e.g. Lord Steyn in *R. v Home Secretary ex parte Venables* [1988] AC 407, 526, who stated that it would be 'an abdication of the Rule of Law' for the Home Secretary, in sentencing the children, to have regard to views expressed in a campaign by a popular newspaper.

Yet in other respects, the Rule of Law goes further than Convention rights. The case of the asylum seeker whose welfare benefits were removed without her knowledge is a case in point.[123] Or where the Immigration Rules were held unlawful because they were changed by the minister after having been laid before Parliament.[124] Sedley LJ held that the practice abandoned a 'constitutional principle which for four centuries has stood as a pillar of the separation of powers in what is today a democracy under the rule of law'. He held that rules which differed from those approved by Parliament violated 'the certainty which rules must have if they are to function as law'. In a case where the release date of a prisoner was not accurately calculated by the Home Office (due to a morass of legislation and further amending legislation) the Supreme Court held that 'it is simply unacceptable in a society governed by the rule of law for it to be well nigh impossible to discern from statutory provisions what a sentence means in practice'.[125]

Dicey's Rule of Law has indeed been damaged over the years by those who attacked it for failing to recognize that official discretion is necessary to perform the welfare and regulatory functions of modern government. Writing about American law from 1780 to 1860, Morton Horwitz describes the growth of legal power to bring about economic redistribution in favour of powerful groups who carefully disguised under a neutral façade the class bias inherent in the law.[126] Robert Unger distinguishes the Rule of Law, which exists in societies governed by formal rules and procedures, from one in which communal bonds and shared values leave no need for this formal legality.[127] Writing in 2010, Martin Loughlin still considers the Rule of Law's limitations to be evident:

> not least because, founded on eighteenth-century political convictions concerning limited government, it has little bearing on the contemporary world. Like rule by law, the doctrine of the rule of law presents itself as an impossible ideal.[128]

And we have seen above, other similar contemporary attacks on the Rule of Law have been made, in domestic and international contexts. [129]

In his book *Whigs and Hunters*[130] on the origins of the Black Act of 1723, which led to a 'flood-tide of eighteenth-century retributive justice',[131] E. P. Thompson, the Marxist historian, concludes that 'the Rule of Law itself, the imposing of effective inhibitions upon power and the defence of the citizen from power's all-intrusive claims, seems to me to be an unqualified human good'.[132] In a critical review, Horwitz disagreed:

> I do not see how a man of the left can describe the Rule of Law as an 'unqualified human good'! It undoubtedly restrains power, but it also prevents power's benevolent exercise. It creates formal equality—a not inconsiderable virtue—but it *promotes* substantive

---

[123] See n. 97.

[124] R. (Pankina) v Secretary of State for the Home Department [2010] EWCA Civ 719. See also Her Majesty's Treasury v Ahmed and others [2010] UKSC 2, discussed above, n. 94.

[125] R. (Noone) v The Governor of HMP Drake Hall [2010] UKSC 30.

[126] M. Horwitz, The Transformation of American Law 1780–1860 (1977).

[127] R. Unger, Law in Modern Society (1976).

[128] Martin Loughlin, Foundations of Public Law (2010) 337.

[129] See e.g. the recent books by Ekins (n. 1 above) and Marshall (n. 119 above).

[130] E. P. Thompson, n. 2 above (1975).   [131] Ibid., p. 23.   [132] Ibid., p. 266.

inequality by creating a consciousness that radically separates law from politics, means from ends, processes from outcomes. By promoting procedural justice it enables the shrewd, the calculating, the wealthy to manipulate its forms to their own advantage. And it ratifies and legitimates an adversarial, competitive, and atomistic conception of human relations.[133]

Horwitz's view of the Rule of Law is misleading. Law can, of course, be oppressive, but we must be careful about equating the Rule of Law with the substance of particular rules or with the substantive quality of the legal system. To claim that the enforcement of unjust laws demonstrates that the Rule of Law is an instrument of oppression is as misleading as the claim (often made in totalitarian countries) that the world described in Kafka's *The Trial*, with its maze of legal procedures, consistently yet heartlessly enforced, portrays an ideal Rule of Law state. Legality must be distinguished from legalism; rule *by* law is different from the Rule of Law.[134]

Surely Thompson is right that the Rule of Law does impose 'effective inhibitions upon power' and the defence of the citizen from power's 'all-intrusive claims'. The Rule of Law guides all forms both of law enforcement and of law making. Its values are fundamental requirements of democratic constitutionalism which rise, time and again, to defeat the designs of the executive and other officials who step outside their conferred powers or who act unreasonably or unfairly. It is a principle that requires feasible limits on official power so as to constrain abuses on the part of even the most well-intentioned officials or governments.

FURTHER READING

ALLAN, T. R. S., *Constitutional Justice: A Liberal Theory of the Rule of Law* (2001).

BINGHAM, T., *The Rule of Law* (2010).

CRAIG, P., 'Formal and Substantive Conceptions of the Rule of Law: An Analytical Framework' [1997] *Public Law* 447.

DWORKIN, R., 'Political Judges and the Rule of Law', in his *A Matter of Principle* (1985) Ch. 1.

European Commission for Democracy through Law (The Venice Commission) *Report on the Rule of Law* (CDL_AD (2011)003-e-March 2011). And *Rule of Law Checklist* CDL–AD (2016) 007.

RAZ, J., 'The Rule of Law and its Virtue' (1977) 93 *LQR* 195.

---

[133] Horwitz, above, n. 3. Like Horwitz, Unger (above, n. 127) sees general rules as crystallizing and legitimizing the power of the ruling class, yet giving a false appearance of neutrality.

[134] This has been the Chinese government's understanding of the Rule of Law. See further, B. Tamanaha, *On the Rule of Law: History, Politics, Theory* (2004) 92.

2

PARLIAMENTARY SOVEREIGNTY IN A CHANGING CONSTITUTIONAL LANDSCAPE

*Mark Elliott**

SUMMARY

Parliamentary sovereignty is often presented as the central principle of the United Kingdom's constitution. In this sense, it might be thought to be a constant: a fixed point onto which we can lock, even when the constitution is otherwise in a state of flux. That the constitution presently is—and has for some time been—in a state of flux is hard to dispute. Over the last half-century or so, a number of highly significant developments have occurred, including the UK's joining—and now leaving—the European Union; the enactment of the Human Rights Act 1998; the devolution of legislative and administrative authority to new institutions in Belfast, Cardiff and Edinburgh; and the increasing prominence accorded by the courts to the common law as a repository of fundamental constitutional rights and values. Each of these developments raises important issues about the doctrine of parliamentary sovereignty. The question might be thought of in terms of the doctrine's capacity to withstand, or accommodate, developments that may, at least at first glance, appear to be in tension with it. Such an analysis seems to follow naturally if we are wedded to an orthodox, and perhaps simplistic, account of parliamentary sovereignty, according to which the concept is understood in unyielding and absolutist terms: as something that is brittle, and which must either stand or fall in the face of changing circumstances. Viewed from a different angle, however, the developments of recent years and decades might be perceived as an opportunity to think about parliamentary sovereignty in a different, and arguably more useful, way—

* Professor of Public Law, University of Cambridge; Fellow, St Catharine's College, Cambridge.

by considering how the implications of this still-central concept are being shaped by the changing nature of the constitutional landscape within which it sits. That is the task with which this chapter is concerned.

INTRODUCTION

The claim lying at the core of the doctrine of parliamentary sovereignty is—on the face of it—as simple as it is extravagant. In the well-known words of Dicey, it means that the United Kingdom Parliament has 'the right to make or unmake any law whatever' and that 'no person or body is recognized by the law of England as having a right to override or set aside the legislation of Parliament'.[1] Well over a hundred years since Dicey wrote in those terms, the UK constitution has changed significantly—and, in some respects, almost beyond recognition. While the Union remains—albeit in a geographically diminished form following the departure, contrary to Dicey's strongly held views, of what became the Republic of Ireland—the UK has been transformed through the development of a multi-layered constitution. As a result of devolution on the one hand and the UK's membership of pan-European institutions on the other, constitutional actors and theorists alike have had to come to terms with a notion of parliamentary sovereignty that subsists in a constitutional setting that is radically different from that which Dicey contemplated. It would be mistaken and simplistic to assert that parliamentary sovereignty has been caught and killed by a pincer movement effected by new tiers of sub- and supra-national governance. At the same time, however, it would be naïve to suggest that those phenomena sit entirely comfortably with an unreconstructed Diceyan version of the sovereignty doctrine.

This chapter situates parliamentary sovereignty in its wider constitutional setting by examining it from three perspectives, each of which reflects an aspect of the UK's changing constitutional landscape. First, the consequences for parliamentary sovereignty of devolution are considered. Second, attention is given to the implications of the UK's being a party to the European Convention on Human Rights ('ECHR') and to constitutional lessons that emerge from the UK's spell as a member of the European Union ('EU'). Third, the viability of the sovereignty doctrine viewed from the perspective of its *own* constitutional plane—namely, the plane of domestic constitutional law—is addressed. In particular, the role of the common law, and the nature of its interaction with statute law, are considered.

From each of these vantage points, the notion of sovereignty is explored and tested by reference to two key questions:

1. **The legal hierarchy question** The first question asks whether, at any of the three constitutional levels with which this chapter is concerned, we encounter a

---

[1] A. V. Dicey, *The Law of the Constitution* (10th edn., 1959, edited by E. C. S. Wade) 40–1.

competitor institution in the form of law or a law-maker that may viably claim to be the legal superior, or at least equal, of the Westminster Parliament or of its legislative outputs.

2. **The constitutional benchmark question** The second question asks whether there exist benchmarks against which the constitutionality of legislation enacted by the Westminster Parliament may plausibly be tested.

The two questions are related but distinct. They amount to the examination of Parliament's legislative authority through two different lenses that are concerned respectively with purely legal and broader constitutional criteria. The first question has an all-or-nothing quality to it. Which institution—whose law—prevails in the event of conflict? The second question is different in nature. It is concerned not with crisp questions of hierarchical priority, but with the existence of constitutional norms that may amount to standards by reference to which the constitutionality of legislation may be evaluated. The use of these two different lenses implies that the legal validity of legislation and its constitutionality may be distinguishable phenomena. The nature and plausibility of that claim will be examined during the course of the chapter.

DEVOLUTION

In a lecture she gave in 2012, Lady Hale said: 'The United Kingdom has . . . become a federal state with a Constitution regulating the relationships between the federal centre and the component parts.'[2] This is a striking claim about how, in constitutional terms, we ought to characterize devolution.[3] It is certainly the case that the UK system today *resembles* a federal one to a greater extent than ever before. However, for all that it might appear to have some of the trappings of a federal state, the UK constitution clearly deviates from that paradigm. The asymmetric nature of the system—such that different geographical parts of the UK have different amounts of devolved authority from one another—is an obvious example of such deviation.[4] Any attempt to argue that the UK has become 'a federal state' is further complicated by the fact that England has no devolved legislature or administration (albeit that this position is now somewhat ameliorated by an 'English votes for English laws' procedure in the House of Commons).[5] It is true that what might be considered to be forms of devolution exist in respect of London and now also in respect of certain so-called city regions in England, under the Cities and Local Government Devolution Act 2016. However, none of these arrangements is closely comparable to those that pertain in Northern Ireland, Scotland

---

[2] Lady Hale, 'The Supreme Court in the UK Constitution' (Legal Wales Lecture, 12 October 2012), available at http://www.supremecourt.uk/docs/speech-121012.pdf.

[3] For a more detailed discussion of devolution, see Chapters 9–11.

[4] See, e.g., R. Brazier, 'The Constitution of the United Kingdom' [1999] *CLJ* 96.

[5] See further, House of Commons Library, *English Votes for English Laws* (2017), available at https://researchbriefings.parliament.uk/ResearchBriefing/Summary/CBP-7339.

or Wales. Moreover, such arrangements concern only particular *parts* of England. It therefore remains the case that England, as a territorial unit within the UK, lacks devolution in the sense in which it exists within the UK's other three constituent territories.

Lady Hale's claim concerning federalization carries a further implication that is particularly pertinent to our inquiry. If she is right—if the UK is indeed a federal system—then the UK Parliament must no longer be sovereign. Parliamentary sovereignty is flatly incompatible with any conventional understanding of the federal model, since one of its cardinal features is the existence of a constitutionally entrenched balance of power between governing institutions at the national and sub-national levels. This means that no single institution at either level can have the capacity unilaterally to alter the balance of power. If the position were otherwise, the balance of power would not be constitutionally guaranteed, and the system would not be a federal one in any meaningful sense. Yet one of the hallmarks of devolution is that the national legislature, far from *transferring* legislative competence, merely *shares* such competence with devolved institutions. A further hallmark of devolution is that such sharing of authority occurs only for as long as the national legislature so provides, and on whatever terms it sets out. Against this background, it is necessary to ask whether the UK adheres to these essential characteristics of a devolved system of government. If it does, then Lady Hale's claim about the federal nature of the modern UK becomes hard to sustain.

Until recently, the case against Lady Hale's analysis was arguably clear. The UK legislation providing for devolution explicitly repudiated any suggestion that giving powers to the devolved institutions entails a loss of power by the UK Parliament. For instance, s. 28 of the Scotland Act 1998, which is the root of the Scottish Parliament's legal authority to legislate, was (and remains) caveated in the following terms: 'This section does not affect the power of the Parliament of the United Kingdom to make laws for Scotland.'[6] The Government of Wales Act 2006 and the Northern Ireland Act 1998 are similarly caveated.[7] On the face of it, provisions such as these slam the door in the face of any argument that devolution amounts to a form of creeping federalization that would call into question the on-going sovereignty of the UK Parliament. Nor, again until recently, did the devolution legislation contain any indication that it gave rise to legally permanent arrangements. As a matter of law, the UK Parliament, having enacted the devolution statutes, was free to amend them (including by taking powers away from the devolved institutions) or even repeal them (thereby abolishing the devolved institutions).

None of this seems consistent with Lady's Hale's argument about the UK's having become 'a federal state', or with the notion that devolution is a challenge to the sovereignty of the UK Parliament. However, for two reasons, we must exercise caution rather than jumping to these conclusions. First, we need to consider whether recent legislative changes make the legal picture today more complex than that which is sketched above. Second, even if a purely legal analysis seems inconsistent with Lady Hale's

---

[6] Scotland Act 1998, s. 28(7).
[7] Government of Wales Act 2006, s. 107(5); Northern Ireland Act 1998, s. 5(6).

federalization thesis, and with the related idea that devolution challenges the sovereignty of the UK Parliament, the issue also falls to be considered through a broader, political lens—the application of which yields a picture that differs sharply from that which is generated when an exclusively legal perspective is adopted.

RECENT LEGISLATIVE CHANGES

In a referendum held in 2014, the Scottish people determined that Scotland should not become independent but should instead remain in the UK. However, as the debate that preceded the referendum developed, a clear expectation emerged that if Scotland were to remain in the UK, it would do so on revised terms that would entail strengthening and extending its devolution settlement. The upshot was the Scotland Act 2016 which, for present purposes, made two key amendments to the Scotland Act 1998 (which remains the principal legislation governing Scottish devolution arrangements). The Wales Act 2017 subsequently made equivalent changes to the Government of Wales Act 2006, the principal Welsh devolution statute.[8] The first of the relevant amendments relates to the 'permanence' of the devolved institutions; the second concerns the authority of the UK Parliament to legislate on devolved matters.

On the former point, the Scottish and Welsh devolution legislation now provides that the devolved legislatures and governments 'are a permanent part of the United Kingdom's constitutional arrangements'.[9] However, the legislation goes on to say that the purpose of the sections in which the 'permanence' provisions are found is 'to signify the commitment of the Parliament and Government of the United Kingdom' to the Scottish and Welsh devolved institutions.[10] The legislation further provides that '[in] view of that commitment it is declared that' the devolved institutions 'are not to be abolished except on the basis of a decision of the people of' Scotland or Wales 'voting in a referendum'.[11] Does this mean that the UK Parliament has limited its own power to abolish the devolved institutions in Scotland and Wales? And, if so, does that mean that the UK Parliament—because its powers are now restricted—is no longer sovereign?

It would be rash to suggest that either of these questions can straightforwardly be answered affirmatively. While there are some *dicta* in the *Jackson* case in support of the view that the UK Parliament can limit its own authority by imposing preconditions on the enactment of future legislation, it is far from settled that Parliament is capable of restricting its power in that way.[12] Nor are the 'permanence' provisions *themselves* explicitly entrenched, meaning that there is nothing on the face of the legislation preventing their repeal in the usual way. More generally, the provisions are framed in a way that does not unambiguously evidence an intention on the part of the UK Parliament to impose legally binding restrictions on its own authority. For instance, the glossing of

---

[8] However, no comparable provision is currently made in respect of Northern Ireland.
[9] Scotland Act 1998, s. 63A(1); Government of Wales Act 2006, s. A1(1).
[10] Scotland Act 1998, s. 63A(2); Government of Wales Act 2006, s. A1(2).
[11] Scotland Act 1998, s. 63A(3); Government of Wales Act 2006, s. A1(3).
[12] R. (Jackson) v Attorney-General [2005] UKHL 56, [2006] 1 AC 262.

the permanence provisions with the statement that their purpose is merely to 'signify a commitment' to the devolved institutions suggests that their purposes do *not* extend to disabling the Parliament from abolishing those institutions. Meanwhile, the referendum 'condition' is not in fact stipulated as a condition: it is only 'declared' that the devolved institutions are not to be abolished absent a public vote. This language is unusual in a statute. After all, when Parliament legislates, it normally just says what the law is; it does not 'declare' that something is or is not to happen. This casts doubt on whether Parliament intended to limit its own legal power.

The second of the recent key amendments to the devolution legislation concerns the UK Parliament's capacity to legislate on matters that are devolved to the Scottish Parliament and the Welsh Assembly. Shortly after the inception of devolution, a constitutional convention, known as the Sewel convention, emerged in this context. It provides that the UK Parliament will not normally legislate in relation to devolved matters without the consent of the relevant devolved legislature.[13] The convention is now also understood to cover UK legislation that affects the extent of the devolved institutions' powers.[14] The convention has been adhered to almost without exception. Nevertheless, in the wake of the Scottish independence referendum, it was decided that the Sewel convention should be 'put on a statutory footing'.[15] This has now occurred in respect of both Scotland and Wales. As noted above, the devolution statutes stipulate that investing the devolved legislatures with law-making power 'does not affect the power of the Parliament of the United Kingdom to make laws' for the relevant devolved territory.[16] However, the Scottish and Welsh legislation has now been amended. The stipulation remains about Westminster's powers being undiminished, but is now glossed in the following terms: 'But it is recognised that the Parliament of the United Kingdom will not normally legislate with regard to devolved matters without the consent of the [relevant devolved legislature].'[17]

Do these new provisions legally limit the UK Parliament's capacity to enact law on relevant matters without the devolved legislatures' consent? That question was addressed by the Supreme Court in *Miller*.[18] In that case it was held that the process for leaving the EU under Article 50 of the Treaty on European Union could be triggered by the Government only if was authorized to do so by an Act of Parliament. It was recognized that the effect of such legislation would be to enable the UK Government to initiate a process that would (other things being equal) result in the UK's exit from

---

[13] The convention is recorded in the Memorandum of Understanding and Supplementary Agreements entered into by the UK and devolved administrations (available at https://www.gov.uk/government/publications/devolution-memorandum-of-understanding-and-supplementary-agreement).

[14] Department for Constitutional Affairs, *Devolution Guidance Note 10: Post-devolution Primary Legislation affecting Scotland* (2005) (available at http://www.gov.scot/Resource/Doc/37349/0066833.pdf).

[15] The Smith Commission, *Report of the Smith Commission for further devolution of powers to the Scottish Parliament* (2014) (available at https://webarchive.nationalarchives.gov.uk/20151202171017/http://www.smith-commission.scot/), p. 13.

[16] Scotland Act 1998, s. 28(7); Government of Wales Act 2006, s. 107(5); Northern Ireland Act 1998, s. 5(6).

[17] Scotland Act 1998, s. 28(8); Government of Wales Act 2006, s. 107(6).

[18] *R. (Miller) v Secretary of State for Exiting the European Union* [2017] UKSC 5, [2018] AC 61. On *Miller*, see further Chapter 4 (Craig).

the EU, the natural consequence of which would be to remove EU law-related limits on the devolved bodies' powers. That would affect the scope of devolved competence and would thus trigger the Sewel convention. In those circumstances, would it be unlawful for the UK Parliament to legislate without such consent, because the convention was now on a 'statutory footing'? The Court held that it would not. The UK Parliament had not been 'seeking to convert the Sewel Convention into a rule which can be interpreted, let alone enforced, by the courts'.[19] Rather, it had been 'declaring that [the convention] is a permanent feature of the relevant devolution settlement'[20] and 'entrench[ing] it *as a convention*'.[21] And since the Sewel convention remained just that—a convention—the Court declined to rule on whether it applied in these circumstances. Answering questions about the 'operation or scope' of conventions belonged 'in the political world'.[22]

The Supreme Court recently returned to these issues when it considered a challenge to legislation enacted by the Scottish Parliament in anticipation of the UK's withdrawal from the EU.[23] The Scottish Parliament had passed legislation that, among other things, purported to authorize the Scottish Ministers to veto secondary legislation made by UK Ministers under the authority of Acts of the UK Parliament. The Scottish Parliament, said the Court, was attempting to make 'the effect of laws made by the UK Parliament conditional on the consent of the Scottish Ministers', which would 'limit the power of the UK Parliament to make laws for Scotland, since Parliament cannot meaningfully be said to "make laws" if the laws which it makes are of no effect'.[24] This, said the Court, would be 'inconsistent with the continued recognition, by section 28(7) of the Scotland Act, of [the UK Parliament's] unqualified legislative power'.[25] And since the Scottish Parliament has no authority to modify section 28(7),[26] legislation enacted by it purporting to do so was invalid. In the course of reaching these conclusions, the Court said that section 28(7) 'makes it clear that . . . the UK Parliament remains sovereign' and that 'its legislative power in relation to Scotland is undiminished'.[27] The Court even said that the UK's territorial constitutional arrangements remained rooted in a system of devolution not federalism because, 'in contrast to a federal model, a devolved system preserves the powers of the central legislature of the state in relation to all matters, whether devolved or reserved'.[28]

---

[19] *R. (Miller) v Secretary of State for Exiting the European Union* [2017] UKSC 5, [2018] AC 61, [148].
[20] Ibid., [148].   [21] Ibid., [149].   [22] Ibid., [146].
[23] *The European Union (Legal Continuity) (Scotland) Bill—A Reference by the Attorney General and the Advocate General for Scotland (Scotland)* [2018] UKSC 64. On this case, see further Chapter 10 (McHarg).
[24] Ibid., [52].   [25] Ibid., [52], emphasis added.
[26] This follows from s. 29(2)(c) of and schedule 4 to the Scotland Act 1998, according to which section 28(7), like most of the Scotland Act 1998, is a 'protected provision' that the Scottish Parliament lacks the authority to modify.
[27] *The European Union (Legal Continuity) (Scotland) Bill—A Reference by the Attorney General and the Advocate General for Scotland (Scotland)* [2018] UKSC 64, [41].
[28] Ibid., [41].

A BROADER PERSPECTIVE

So far, we have seen that devolution, as originally conceived, was hard to square with Lady Hale's picture of a federalized constitution[29]—and that, correspondingly, devolution, as originally understood, was fully legally compatible with UK Parliament's remaining sovereign. We have seen too that while the picture is arguably complicated by recent legislative changes, it is far from clear that those changes have fundamentally altered the legal position. As such, devolution's legal framework is not self-evidently incompatible with parliamentary sovereignty.

However, to end our analysis there would be remiss—for reasons that will become clear if we return to the two questions set out at the beginning of this chapter. The first of those questions—the legal hierarchy question—requires us to ask whether the devolved legislatures are the legal superiors of the UK Parliament. Can they, for instance, enact legislation that is capable of prevailing over UK legislation? In fact, in certain circumstances, they can. For instance, the Northern Ireland Act 1998 says that 'an Act of the [Northern Ireland] Assembly may modify any provision made by or under an Act of [the UK] Parliament in so far as it is part of the law of Northern Ireland'.[30] Similarly, the Scottish Parliament and the Welsh Assembly can modify, repeal or replace UK legislation insofar as it affects matters upon which they are competent to legislate.

It does not, however, follow that the devolved legislatures, or their legislation, enjoy hierarchical superiority over the UK Parliament, or its legislation, in a presently relevant sense. The devolved legislatures can enact legislation modifying or otherwise asserting priority over UK legislation only because the UK Parliament has, in the first place, authorized the devolved legislatures to do so. It has done that by including in the devolution legislation so-called Henry VIII powers.[31] Any authority the devolved legislatures have to deviate from UK legislation is therefore nothing more than a reflection of the authority of the UK Parliament itself as the author of those legislatures' powers.

The answer to our legal hierarchy question is thus clear: the devolved institutions and the laws they enact are not, in any relevant sense, superior to the UK Parliament or the legislation it enacts. What, then, of our second question? This—our 'constitutional benchmark' question—requires us to ask whether the devolution schemes amount or give rise to benchmarks by reference to which the *constitutionality* of UK legislation might be assessed—and, therefore, found to be wanting. It might appear that our conclusion in relation to the legal hierarchy question makes it unnecessary to ask the constitutional benchmark question. If the devolution schemes have not generated institutions that represent a hierarchical challenge to the UK Parliament, does it not follow that Parliament's capacity to do as it pleases—to make or unmake any

---

[29] Interestingly, Lady Hale was herself a party to the unanimous judgment of the Supreme Court in the *Continuity Bill* case.

[30] Northern Ireland Act 1998, s. 5(6).

[31] 'Henry VIII' powers enable constitutional actors other than the UK Parliament to amend or repeal provisions contained in an Act of Parliament. For discussion of their constitutional implications, see N. Barber and A. Young, 'The Rise of Prospective Henry VIII Clauses and their Implications for Sovereignty' [2003] *Public Law* 112.

law—remains undiminished? And if the UK Parliament can do no legal wrong, can it act unconstitutionally?

Perhaps counterintuitively—because we sometimes think of legality and constitutionality as interchangeable concepts—the answer to that question is arguably 'yes'. As a matter of strict *law*, the UK Parliament's powers may be undiminished by devolution. But if we adopt a *constitutional* perspective, it becomes clear that the devolution schemes both acknowledge and conjure into life a constitutional principle that requires respect for the autonomy of the devolved institutions. It is this principle that animates the Sewel convention, and which thus casts doubt on the constitutional propriety—but not the legality—of UK legislation that impinges upon devolved matters but to which the relevant devolved legislature has not consented.

The principle of devolved autonomy is closely related to a further fundamental principle—namely, democracy. It is engaged by both the democratic background to the implementation of the devolution schemes—including, most significantly, the referendums that preceded their introduction—and the democratic nature of the institutional arrangements to which they give effect. It may seem odd to postulate democracy as a constitutional principle capable of casting doubt upon UK legislation, given that such legislation necessarily enjoys (some form of) a democratic mandate. However, the introduction of devolution suggests that democratic concerns are not exhausted by ensuring adherence to legislation enacted by the UK Parliament. Devolution creates other sites of democratic law-making authority within the polity: as a result, the democratic credentials—and so the constitutional propriety—of UK legislation that cuts across the constitutional remit of devolved legislatures is placed in doubt.

This does not, however, mean that it is politically *impossible* for the UK Parliament to legislate in breach of devolution-related norms, as recent events might be thought to illustrate. The European Union (Withdrawal) Act 2018[32] deals, among other things, with the question of who should exercise powers that were held by the EU but which would be repatriated by Brexit. When the UK Parliament was enacting this legislation, the Scottish and Welsh Governments took the view that the Scottish and Welsh devolved institutions should be the recipients of repatriated powers concerning matters falling within their devolved competences. However, the UK Government was concerned that this could result in differences in the laws applicable in the UK's four constituent territories and that this, in turn, could prejudice the operation of the UK's own internal market in goods and services. As such, the legislation was originally drafted such that powers held by the EU would initially flow back to UK institutions, which would then have discretion to release such powers to devolved institutions. These arrangements were to some extent adjusted in the devolved institutions' favour during the passage of the legislation through the UK Parliament, but the Scottish Parliament remained dissatisfied and withheld legislative consent. The legislation was nevertheless enacted by the UK Parliament.

---

[32] See generally M. Elliott and S. Tierney, 'Political Pragmatism and Constitutional Principle: The European Union (Withdrawal) Act 2018' [2019] *PL* 37.

Whether this amounted to a *breach* of the Sewel convention is debatable. Certainly, the UK Parliament legislated in a way that impacted on devolved competence without securing the Scottish Parliament's consent. But as Lord Sewel himself commented, consent is only 'normally' required, while the Withdrawal Act was passed in anything but 'normal' circumstances. He thus argued that 'the size and the scale' of the legal and constitutional changes involved in Brexit put the withdrawal legislation 'in a class of its own', and that in such circumstances there must be the possibility of the UK Parliament acting unilaterally, without devolved consent.[33] There is, of course, room for disagreement on this point; it can be argued—depending on what we take the 'normally' caveat to mean—that the convention applied and was breached. But even if we adopt such a view, it does not signify that the convention is worthless. Rather, it reminds us that the convention is not a legal limit on the UK Parliament's power, meaning that, if it is prepared to pay the political price, it can legislate in breach of the convention.

Can we go further than this? Does the Sewel convention—and, more broadly, the principle of devolved autonomy that underpins it—amount to anything *more* than something which informs the political ease or difficulty with which the (still) sovereign UK Parliament can legislate, even if it clearly amounts to something *less* than a hard legal restraint on its powers? Arguably it does. The reason why it is politically difficult (but not necessarily impossible) for the UK Parliament to ride roughshod over the devolved institutions is rooted in deeper constitutional principles. That such principles are not enshrined in a written constitution does not detract from the appropriateness of regarding them as constitutional—indeed, as constitutionally fundamental—in character. Understood thus, the devolution schemes may not effect a *legal* division of authority between the UK legislature and its devolved counterparts, but this is not incompatible with the view that the devolution schemes effect a *constitutional* division of authority. As a result, it is entirely plausible to imagine UK legislation that might be lawful (because it cannot be otherwise) but unconstitutional (because it breaches fundamental principles such as those that are institutionalized by the Sewel convention). In this way, the devolved competences set out in the devolution legislation can properly be regarded as benchmarks by reference to which the constitutionality—as distinct from the legal validity—of UK legislation may be assessed.

The conclusion that particular legislation is, or would be, suspect in constitutional (as distinct from legal) terms sounds in the political realm, in that it contributes to—indeed, generates—the political difficulty that attempts to legislate in breach of fundamental constitutional values. This is apparent, for example, from the work of the House of Lords Constitution Committee which (among other things) examines Bills that are before Parliament from a constitutional perspective, drawing the attention of the House to any aspects of Bills that are constitutionally suspect. It is possible to infer from

---

[33] BBC News website, 'Emergency debate on Brexit powers held in Commons' (18 June 2018), available at https://www.bbc.co.uk/news/uk-scotland-scotland-politics-44522940.

the Committee's many reports a suite of constitutional values that serve as benchmarks against which Bills fall to be assessed.[34] However, it would be mistaken to suppose that the incapacity of those values to deprive Parliament of the authority to legislate contrary to them necessarily renders them legally irrelevant. The relationship between the legal, political, and constitutional realms is too porous to permit any such conclusion: the implications of fundamental constitutional values resonate throughout the constitutional system—in both its legal and political guises. As a result, although constitutional values such as devolved autonomy and democracy may not enjoy a legal status that ultimately circumscribes the UK Parliament's legislative authority, they may nevertheless find legal expression in other, more modest, ways, including as norms which influence the interpretation of legislation. In this way, fundamental constitutional values can and do both shape the *meaning* of statute law and serve to determine its *constitutionality*, even if, according to the orthodox theory of parliamentary sovereignty, they are ultimately incapable of determining primary legislation's *validity*. Devolution thus serves as a case study in the importance of contextualizing the notion of sovereignty. Accepted on its own terms, the doctrine concedes unfettered legal authority to the UK Parliament: but that concession does not imply an absence of constitutional standards that may operate both as benchmarks of constitutionality and as powerful interpretative constructs.[35]

THE EUROPEAN UNION AND BREXIT

Over the last several decades, the UK has been associated with two distinct European legal orders—the EU and the ECHR—that have placed in sharp relief questions about the sovereignty of Parliament. The transnational nature of the institutional arrangements from which EU and European human rights law flow instinctively prompts us to think of those arrangements as somehow sitting 'above' the merely 'domestic' constitution. In one sense, this reaction is misplaced; the international law character of the EU and the ECHR does not render them legally *superior* to, but *different* from, domestic law. International law does not, from a domestic-legal perspective, enjoy automatic priority over national law. Rather, the nature and extent (if any) of the domestic-legal status of any given international law measure is a function of domestic law itself. The picture changes, however, when the relationship between international law regimes and domestic law is considered from a different vantage point. From an international law perspective, the ECHR and EU law are, or have been, legally binding upon the UK as a State. In this sense, *national* sovereignty is compromised by participation in arrangements that are binding upon the UK in international law. What, however, about *parliamentary* sovereignty? Is this also curtailed?

---

[34] J. Simson Caird, R. Hazell, and D. Oliver, *The Constitutional Standards of the House of Lords Constitution Committee* (2014).

[35] The role of judicial interpretation in upholding fundamental constitutional values is developed below, in the section entitled 'Common Law'.

SQUARING THE CIRCLE: PARLIAMENTARY SOVEREIGNTY AND THE EU SUPREMACY PRINCIPLE

These questions are explored with respect to the ECHR later in this chapter. For now, our inquiry focuses on the EU. It might be thought that Brexit makes such inquiry unnecessary.[36] However, for two reasons, that is not so. First, the position that applied during the UK's EU membership, and how we make sense in constitutional terms of that position, can tell us a good deal about the nature of parliamentary sovereignty— much of which may be relevant, or at least illuminating, in other circumstances. Second, depending upon the terms on which the UK leaves the EU, EU law (at least to some extent) may remain pertinent in the UK for some time to come.

In considering how we should make sense of the implications for parliamentary sovereignty of EU membership, we will address the two key questions that informed our discussion of devolution above. The first of those questions, it will be recalled, concerns the matters of hierarchical priority. According to the doctrine of the supremacy of EU law, directly-effective EU law takes priority over any incompatible provisions of national law.[37] At the time of writing, it is envisaged that this principle will remain applicable during a transitional period and that it will continue to apply thereafter to parts of the Withdrawal Agreement and to EU law referred to in that Agreement.

The EU supremacy principle goes further than merely asserting the binding force upon Member States of their international obligations under the EU Treaties. Rather, the Court of Justice of the European Union ('CJEU') has held that the EU law 'constitutes a new legal order . . . the subjects of which comprise not only Member States but also their nationals'.[38] As a result, EU law is a body of law which regards itself as binding not only upon Member States as States in the international law sense, but as binding also upon governing institutions *within* Member States. Thus it is considered, as a matter of EU law, to be *unlawful* for a national legislature to enact law that breaches EU law. As a result, it is possible, in certain circumstances, for financial liability to be incurred as a result of such legally wrongful action.[39]

Does this mean that during the UK's membership of the EU—and potentially after withdrawal, if (some) EU law remains applicable in the UK under a withdrawal agreement—Parliament has not been and may not be sovereign? The answer to that question must depend on the perspective from which the matter is viewed. From an EU perspective, the doctrine of parliamentary sovereignty must yield in the face of the overriding force of EU law. However, the position may be different viewed from a domestic law perspective. Admittedly, there are writers—most notably Sir William Wade[40]—who argue that the sovereignty of Parliament was not merely suspended but *terminated* by EU membership. Wade pointed in this regard to the seminal decision of

---

[36] On Brexit generally, see Chapter 4 (Craig).   [37] Case 6/64 *Costa v Enel* [1964] CMLR 425, 455.

[38] Case 26/62, *Van Gend en Loos* [1963] ECR 1, 12.

[39] See, e.g., Cases C-6/90 and 9/90, *Francovich v Italy* [1991] ECR I-5357.

[40] H. W. R. Wade, 'Sovereignty: Revolution or Evolution?' (1996) 112 *LQR* 568.

the House of Lords in *Factortame (No. 2)*,[41] in which EU law was accorded priority over an incompatible Act of Parliament. The UK legislation in question—which conflicted with a right conferred by what is now Article 49 of the Treaty on the Functioning of the European Union—was thus 'disapplied': the operation of relevant parts of the Act was suspended and the Government ordered not to enforce them. This, argued Wade, evidenced a fundamental shift of judicial fidelity from Westminster to the EU through the adoption of a new 'rule of recognition'—that is, the fundamental rule by which other legal rules are identified—which enthroned EU law as the supreme form of law applicable in the UK. Wade's view also implies that if, as a result of Brexit, a time comes when the EU supremacy principle no longer applies to the UK, any resulting restoration of parliamentary sovereignty (as it would be understood on this view) will have to be accounted for in terms of a further judicial 'revolution'. However, this explanation does not accord with the way in which UK courts themselves have rationalized domestic accommodation of the EU primacy doctrine. Indeed, *Miller* rejects the idea that EU membership entailed any shift in the 'rule of recognition' and roundly endorses the notion that Parliament remained sovereign throughout the UK's membership of the EU. The doctrine of parliamentary sovereignty, says the majority in *Miller*, is 'fundamental to the United Kingdom's constitutional arrangements', meaning that EU law has only been able to 'enjoy a status in domestic law which that principle allows'.[42]

But how can this be? If Parliament remained sovereign throughout the UK's membership of the EU, how could EU law have had priority over domestic law, including Acts of Parliament? To the extent that UK courts have supplied a serviceable answer to that question, it lies in the notion that the European Communities Act 1972 ('ECA') is a 'constitutional statute'. This idea was first articulated by Laws LJ in *Thoburn*,[43] developed and endorsed by the Supreme Court in *HS2 Action Alliance*,[44] and relied upon by the same Court in *Miller*. On this approach, the priority that EU law has enjoyed over UK law is attributable to the facts that (i) the ECA provides for this and (ii) the ECA has a special constitutional status which means that it is not susceptible to implied repeal. This means that when, as in *Factortame*, a court is confronted with an Act of Parliament that is (implicitly) inconsistent with EU law, the court will give effect to EU law—because that it what the ECA requires, and because the ECA cannot be impliedly overridden. On this view, Parliament has remained sovereign throughout the period of the UK's EU membership, and has thus remained capable of overriding EU law, albeit that, if it had wished to do so, it would have needed to use express (or otherwise specific) language so as to countermand the effect ascribed to EU law by the ECA. The majority judgment in *Miller* is compatible with this view. It states that 'EU law cannot be implicitly displaced by the mere enactment of legislation which is inconsistent with it',[45] and

---

[41] *R. v Secretary of State for Transport ex parte Factortame Ltd (No. 2)* [1991] 1 AC 603.

[42] *R. (Miller) v Secretary of State for Exiting the European Union* [2017] UKSC 5, [2018] AC 61, [67].

[43] *Thoburn v Sunderland City Council* [2002] EWHC 195 (Admin), [2003] QB 151.

[44] *R. (HS2 Action Alliance Ltd) v Secretary of State for Transport* [2014] UKSC 3, [2014] 1 WLR 324.

[45] *R. (Miller) v Secretary of State for Exiting the European Union* [2017] UKSC 5, [2018] AC 61, [66].

the majority relates its view on this point to the fact that the ECA 'has a constitutional character, as discussed by Laws LJ in *Thoburn*'.[46]

On this approach, EU law has never been a direct challenge to the sovereignty of Parliament, because any primacy it has enjoyed has in the first place been attributable to an Act of Parliament. In this way, counterintuitive though it may at first seem, it has been possible—at least when the matter is analysed in domestic constitutional terms—to square the circle within which EU law has overridden the enactments of a sovereign Parliament. It follows that leaving the EU will not 'restore' the sovereignty of Parliament, because the sovereignty of Parliament was never in the first place lost. This, in turn, informs our analysis of the constitutional position that will apply if (as is envisaged at the time of writing) EU law retains overriding force during a transitional period, and if, after that period ends, relevant parts of the Withdrawal Agreement—which will also have overriding effect—come into effect. None of this will prolong the impairment of parliamentary sovereignty, because—understood as a matter of *domestic constitutional law*—parliamentary sovereignty was never *in the first place* impaired.

THE RULE OF LAW AND RESPECT FOR INTERNATIONAL LAW

Bearing in mind that the case in favour of Brexit was framed, in no small part, in terms of 'taking back control' of the law that applies in the UK, the foregoing analysis may seem surprising—for it implies, apparently counterfactually, that control was never in the first place surrendered. How can we reconcile the fact that (at least on the above analysis) Parliament has remained sovereign while the UK has been an EU Member State with the reality that the UK has *not* been at liberty to enact laws that conflict with EU law? To address this issue, it is necessary to consider the implications of EU membership by reference to the second of our key two questions, concerning the existence of constitutional benchmarks that might make it constitutionally improper for the UK Parliament to do something, even if, on a strictly legal analysis, it has the necessary legal authority.

The practical opportunity that Parliament has had to flex its muscles by asserting its sovereignty in the face of EU law has been heavily circumscribed throughout the period of the UK's EU membership. For instance, had the UK regularly sought to depart from EU laws with which it disagreed by enacting explicitly inconsistent domestic legislation, it would have faced, at the very least, significant political and diplomatic consequences. After all, such derogation would have resulted in a breach by the UK of obligations binding upon it in international law[47]—a consequence that would inevitably have framed political responses to derogation, both internally and externally. However, this leaves open the question whether, from a *domestic* (as distinct from international) perspective, it would have been constitutionally improper

---

[46] Ibid., [67].   [47] See Chapter 5.

for the UK Parliament to legislate in breach of EU law. The answer to that question is 'yes'. The notion of government according to law is a fundamental aspect of the rule of law.[48] It reflects both the Diceyan notion of equality before the law[49]—such that those who wield official authority should not for that reason be exempt from the general obligation that binds everybody else to obey the law—and the need for those who are entrusted with state power to be subject to particular obligations to exercise that power fairly, reasonably and for the public good. The requirement of government according to law extends not only to national but also to international law. As Lord Bingham put it:

> . . . although international law comprises a distinct and recognizable body of law with its own rules and institutions, it is a body of law complementary to the national laws of individual states, and in no way antagonistic to them; it is not a thing apart; it rests on similar principles and pursues similar ends; and observance of the rule of law is quite as important on the international plane as on the national, perhaps even more so . . . The rule of the jungle is no more tolerable in a big jungle.[50]

Lord Bingham thus argues that the rule of law requires 'compliance by the state with its obligations in international as in national law'.[51] For the purpose of the present argument, the effect of this fundamental constitutional principle is to render suspect, as a matter of domestic constitutionalism, any derogation by the UK from its international law obligations. Looked at in this way, the UK's commitments in international law whilst an EU Member State have operated as benchmarks against which the constitutionality of domestic legislation has fallen to be evaluated, even if—in the final analysis, for reasons considered above—the UK Parliament has never lacked the legal capacity to override EU law should it wish to do so.

As the UK leaves the EU, such considerations will remain pertinent for as long as the UK retains obligations to the EU that bear upon the content of domestic law. Thus, even if, during a transitional period, the UK were free as a matter of domestic law to legislate incompatibly with EU law, doing so would involve a repudiation of the rule-of-law requirement to honour commitments that bind in international law. The same point applies to those aspects of the Withdrawal Agreement, and to those provisions of EU law to which it refers, that would bind the UK—including as to the content of national law—once a transitional period had ended. For this reason, the lessons that EU membership have taught us about the nature of parliamentary sovereignty will remain pertinent even after the UK has formally left the EU. In particular, the experience of EU membership has shown us that the question of what parliamentary sovereignty means in practice is acutely sensitive to the perspective—legal or political, domestic or international—from which the question is asked.

---

[48] See generally Lord Bingham, *The Rule of Law* (2010). [49] Above, n. 1, Ch. IV.
[50] Above, n. 48, pp. 110–12.   [51] Ibid., p. 110.

EUROPEAN CONVENTION ON HUMAN RIGHTS

Many of the points made above in relation to EU law apply—with some adaptation—to the ECHR.[52] States that are parties to the Convention have agreed to 'secure to everyone within their jurisdiction the rights and freedoms defined in Section I of [the] Convention'[53] and to 'abide by the final judgment of the [European] Court [of Human Rights] in any case to which they are parties'.[54] The ECHR thus forms a body of international law that is binding upon the UK as a State. In some respects, then, being a party to the ECHR entails legal implications that are similar to those which flowed from EU membership. There are, however, important differences between the ECHR and EU legal regimes.

Thanks to the principle of direct effect, many provisions of EU law are automatically applicable and judicially enforceable within Member States: that is, they take effect without any need for national implementing measures.[55] In contrast, the rights set out in the ECHR do not have direct effect. It is for this reason that, until the Human Rights Act 1998 ('HRA') entered into force, the Convention rights were not straightforwardly enforceable in UK courts.[56] Moreover, to the extent that the ECHR asserts any kind of primacy over domestic law, including over Acts of the UK Parliament that are incompatible with Convention rights, the form of primacy in play is only that which is associated with international law generally. In other words, as a matter of international law, the UK as a State acts unlawfully if a State organ, including the UK Parliament, acts in breach of the ECHR by, for example, enacting legislation that is incompatible with it. However, the ECHR, as a body of law, does not specifically assert primacy over domestic law in the way that EU law does. While, therefore, legislative (or other) infractions of the Convention trigger the UK's international law liability, the Convention regime lays no claim to the invalidation of incompatible domestic legislation. As a result, any argument that the Convention regime represents a competitor institution that places the legal sovereignty of the Westminster Parliament in question would be difficult to sustain. Thus, looked at from the perspective of our legal hierarchy question, ECHR membership does not seem to pose any challenge to parliamentary sovereignty.

What, though, of our second question? It is concerned not with whether the ECHR qualifies Parliament's sovereign capacity lawfully to legislate as it chooses, but with the broader question of whether the ECHR may be characterized as a constitutional benchmark by reference to which UK legislation may fall to be measured. That the Convention can be so characterized is an argument that can be sustained relatively straightforwardly. The Convention is a body of international law by which the UK has agreed to be bound. As a result, domestic legislation that breaches Convention rights is dubious in domestic constitutional terms because it repudiates that aspect of the rule

---

[52] See also Chapters 3 and 5.   [53] ECHR, Art. 1.   [54] ECHR, Art. 46(1).

[55] See, e.g., Case 26/62, *Van Gend en Loos* [1963] ECR 1.

[56] This does not, however, mean that Convention rights were irrelevant in domestic legal proceedings. On the pre-HRA position, see M. Hunt, *Using Human Rights Law in English Courts* (1997).

of law that demands adherence to international obligations. It follows that there are good grounds for doubting the constitutionality—as distinct from the legality—of UK legislation that breaches Convention rights.

Further such grounds are supplied by the fact that some Convention rights mirror or at least intersect with values that are also recognized through the doctrine of common-law constitutional rights.[57] The nature of such rights—and the broader notion that the common-law constitution acknowledges certain values to enjoy a fundamental status—is addressed in the next part of this chapter. For the time being it suffices to say that the breach of at least some Convention rights will imply a breach of a parallel common law constitutional right. The constitutional dubiousness of ECHR-incompatible legislation is thus attributable both to its repudiation of the rule-of-law requirement to abide by international obligations and (at least sometimes) to the simultaneous infraction of common-law constitutional rights.

The HRA allows certain courts to issue a declaration of incompatibility: that is, a declaration that a provision in an Act of Parliament is incompatible with the ECHR.[58] This remedy clearly illustrates the way in which legislative action by the UK Parliament can be simultaneously lawful but unconstitutional. The HRA makes it very clear that the issue of a declaration of incompatibility leaves intact the legislative provision concerned: a declaration 'does not affect the validity, continuing operation or enforcement of the provision in respect of which it is given'.[59] Declarations of incompatibility thus explicitly acknowledge that Convention rights, from a domestic law perspective, do not narrow Parliament's legislative authority. At the same time, however, issuing a declaration of incompatibility sends a clear and powerful signal that the UK is acting in breach of its international law obligations—and, therefore, inconsistently with the domestic rule-of-law obligation to adhere to commitments that bind the UK as a State in international law. In this way, declarations of incompatibility bring into play on the national stage breaches by the UK of international law. This serves to problematize such infractions in domestic terms and ensures that they are understood as something other—and more—than a failure to adhere to exotic norms that lack purchase in the domestic constitutional sphere.

A second aspect of the way in which Convention rights are domesticated via the HRA deserves mention too. As well as authorizing courts to declare that legislation is incompatible with Convention rights, the Act requires courts to interpret legislation compatibly with such rights when possible.[60] This underlines the fact that while the Convention rights lack decisive legal bite at the domestic level, in that they do not operate to circumscribe Parliament's sovereign capacity to legislate, they are far from being without domestic legal impact. To the contrary, the Convention rights operate as a powerful influence upon the judicial-interpretive process, often finding legal expression through successful attempts to read domestic legislation compatibly. In this way, the Convention rights, as international law constructs that also operate as benchmarks

---

[57] See, e.g., R. (Osborn) v Parole Board [2013] UKSC 61, [2013] 3 WLR 1020.   [58] HRA, s. 4.
[59] Ibid., s. 4(6)(a).   [60] Ibid., s. 3(1).

of domestic constitutionality, enjoy substantial domestic-legal impact, albeit that they stop short of curtailing the legal authority of the UK Parliament. This is of a piece with the view, advanced in the section on devolution above, that while constitutional values may not ultimately diminish Parliament's sovereign freedom to legislate, this does not rob them of all legal significance.

COMMON LAW

On one analysis, sub- and supra-national strata within the multi-layered constitution might be thought to stand in tension with—even if they do not amount to an outright challenge to—the sovereignty of Parliament. However, the discussion so far in this chapter has shown that any such tension in fact has its foundations in the domestic constitutional order—the national stratum, as it were. This is so because UK legislation that cuts across the authority of devolved legislatures or that is inconsistent with international obligations engages domestic values, including democracy, devolved autonomy and the rule of law,[61] that find expression in what is often referred to as the common law constitution. The idea of a common law constitution is reflective of the fact that, in the absence of a sovereign constitutional text, many aspects of the constitution are attributable to judicial development of the common law. On one view, for instance, it is in the common law that we find the numerous principles applied by courts when assessing the lawfulness of exercises of executive power;[62] and, as we shall see, it is in the common law that we find constitutional values that shape the interpretation of legislation. It follows that our analysis of the contemporary nature of parliamentary sovereignty must address not only the further extremities of the multi-layered constitution, but also its common law core. This is important both for its own sake—the common law constitution forms the overarching context within which the doctrine of parliamentary sovereignty falls to be understood—and because, for the reason just given, it informs our understanding of the implications for sovereignty of multi-layered constitutionalism.

The analysis in this section will proceed by reference to our two key questions. As far as the first question—the legal hierarchy question—is concerned, the answer may seem obvious. An inevitable implication of any orthodox account of parliamentary sovereignty is that the common law is hierarchically inferior to statute law: Acts of Parliament supersede the common law to the extent of any inconsistency. This suggests that there can be no question of the common law amounting to a competitor institution that places in doubt Parliament's superior claim to legal authority. However, this invites the question of whether the orthodox account accurately captures the relationship between common law and statute law—whether, in particular, the common law should inevitably be regarded as something that gives way in the face of incompatible

---

[61] See discussion in Chapter 1.
[62] For discussion, see C. F. Forsyth (ed.), *Judicial Review and the Constitution* (2000).

legislation. That matter will be addressed, but it is desirable to return to it only once the second of our two key questions has been considered.

COMMON LAW PRINCIPLES AS CONSTITUTIONAL BENCHMARKS

That question asks whether the legal regime in question—here, the common law—can be regarded as a benchmark by reference to which the constitutionality of Acts of Parliament may be measured, as distinct from a constraint that circumscribes the legal capacity of the UK Parliament to legislate as it wishes. The answer to that question is affirmative in the sense that the common law can readily be characterized as (among other things) a repository of constitutional values. That those values are legal in nature is clear from the fact that they receive substantial protection through the mechanism of statutory construction. As Lord Steyn put it in *Pierson*:

> Parliament does not legislate in a vacuum. Parliament legislates for a European liberal democracy founded on the principles and traditions of the common law. And the courts may approach legislation on this initial assumption. But this assumption only has prima facie force. It can be displaced by a clear and specific provision to the contrary.[63]

Understood thus, the 'principles and traditions of the common law'—a category that must overlap considerably with, if it is not merely a synonym for, the rule of law—form a crucial part of the backdrop against which legislation is interpreted. What those principles are is a question whose detailed exploration lies beyond the scope of this chapter, but which is considered in depth elsewhere in this volume.[64] Our focus, rather, must be on the legal and constitutional implications of such principles.

In many contexts, common-law constitutional principles operate so as to deny authority to constitutional actors, such as Ministers of the Crown, executive agencies, local authorities and even devolved legislatures.[65] They do so through the application of the principle of legality, according to which legislation conferring legal authority upon such constitutional actors falls to be interpreted in the way described above by Lord Steyn. Unless the legislation provides in crystal-clear terms to the contrary, the effect of the principle of legality is to yield an interpretation of the statute that withholds from the constitutional actor any authority to act incompatibly with common-law constitutional principles. This, in turn, renders unlawful any such action that cuts across those principles.

A good illustration of this phenomenon is the *UNISON* case, in which the executive government enacted secondary legislation requiring people who wanted to bring claims in Employment Tribunals to pay fees.[66] It was held that such secondary legislation engaged the 'constitutional right of access to the courts' which 'is inherent in

---

[63] *R. v Secretary of State for the Home Department, ex parte Pierson* [1998] AC 539, 587.

[64] See Chapter 1 [Jowell—rule of law].

[65] On the position in relation to devolved legislatures, see *AXA General Insurance Ltd v HM Advocate* [2011] UKSC 46, [2012] 1 AC 868.

[66] *R. (UNISON) v Lord Chancellor* [2017] UKSC 51, [2017] 3 WLR 409.

the rule of law'.[67] This was evidenced by the fact that following the imposition of the fees there had been 'a dramatic and persistent fall in the number of claims',[68] owing to the fact that some potential claimants could not afford to initiate proceedings without 'sacrific[ing] ordinary and reasonable expenditure'.[69] In these circumstances, the question for the court was 'whether the impediment or hindrance [to the enjoyment of the constitutional right] in question had been clearly authorized by primary legislation'.[70] The Court held that it had not, and that the secondary legislation imposing fees was therefore unlawful and invalid: in making the secondary legislation, the Lord Chancellor had violated a common law constitutional right, but Parliament had not provided the legal authority to do so.

The *UNISON* case demonstrates that common law constitutional rights and principles can fundamentally influence the way in which Acts of Parliament are interpreted. But if Parliament really is sovereign, then that is as far as they can go: they cannot serve as outright restrictions upon Parliament's legislative power. As interpretive constructs, their legal effects can be highly significant, as in *UNISON*, but their effects are necessarily limited. This suggests, for instance, that circumstances may arise in which an Act of Parliament is so clearly incompatible with a common law right of principle that there is no option but to interpret it in a way that yields a breach of the relevant constitutional standard. In such a scenario, the infringed common law right or principle would continue to serve as a benchmark by reference to which the *constitutional propriety* of the legislation could be assessed, but the hierarchical inferiority of the common law in the face of an Act of the sovereign Parliament would prevent the common law right or principle from determining the *legal validity* of the legislation. Such an outcome would be consistent with our earlier analysis, in which we observed that, in a constitutional system that acknowledges the existence of a sovereign legislature, circumstances may arise in which legislation is regarded as lawful yet unconstitutional.

COMMON LAW PRINCIPLES AS CONSTRAINTS UPON PARLIAMENT?

The issue remains, however, of whether the role of common law constitutional rights and principles is as constrained as our analysis so far assumes. And this takes us back to the first of our key questions. Are common law constitutional rights and values really inferior to Acts of Parliament? Or do they compete with and place in doubt Parliament's sovereign law-making capacity? This goes to the distinction reflected by the two key questions with which we have been concerned in this chapter. Are common law rights benchmarks that influence our assessment of legislation's constitutionality and which, at most, are capable of shaping the interpretation of legislation? Or do they sit above Acts of Parliament in the legal hierarchy, such that they constrain Parliament's legal authority to legislate?

---

[67] Ibid., [66] (Lord Reed).   [68] Ibid., [39] (Lord Reed).   [69] Ibid., [94] (Lord Reed).
[70] Ibid., [79] (Lord Reed).

For some writers, like Allan, any attempt to limit the legal pertinence of common law rights (or other constructs derived from the rule of law) by reference to such a distinction is doomed to failure. He does not doubt that common law principles can and should shape the interpretation of legislation, but he contends that they can and should go further by, where appropriate, determining its validity. He argues, for instance, that an Act authorizing 'draconian restrictions on personal liberty may be capable of salvage, for example, by implying (or imposing) appropriately rigorous requirements of due process or procedural fairness'.[71] For Allan, however, this possibility is without prejudice to the further possibility that a court unable interpretively to finesse unconstitutionality away would be fully entitled to refuse to enforce the legal provision in question on the ground that an unconstitutional law is not a valid law.[72] Thus, although '[t]here is almost always scope, in practice, for reasonable accommodation between statutory purpose and legal principle', Allan argues that 'even when the scope for accommodation diminishes, or entirely disappears, the court must adhere resolutely to the rule of law'.[73]

This view is self-evidently in tension with the Diceyan conception of parliamentary sovereignty outlined at the start of this chapter. The latter reflects an ultimately positivist view, according to which the validity of an Act of Parliament is decisively determined by virtue of its having been enacted by Parliament, validity being an entirely separate matter from the merits—including the constitutional merits—of the law in question. Such a view is consistent with the idea, noted in this chapter, that questions of legality and of constitutionality are distinguishable and may have different answers. Allan, however, criticizes this perspective, arguing that 'legality [must be] annexed to legitimacy',[74] and that, as a result, it is 'impossible to reconcile . . . the rule of law with the unlimited sovereignty of Parliament'.[75]

Others dispute Allan's view.[76] Oliver, for instance, writes that the notion of parliamentary sovereignty is sustained by 'a pragmatic recognition by politicians and the courts that the functioning of the British system imposes responsibility for the Constitution and the rule of law on every organ of state rather than placing that responsibility solely or primarily in the hands of a Supreme or Constitutional Court'.[77] On this view, the rule of law operates as a constraining force, but is not one that *judges* are ultimately equipped to *impose* upon other constitutional branches. Goldsworthy also argues that, properly understood, the rule of law does not require legal-judicial

---

[71] T. R. S. Allan, *The Sovereignty of Law: Freedom, Constitution and Common Law* (2013) 142.

[72] Ibid., pp. 142–3.

[73] T. R. S. Allan, 'Parliament's Will and the Justice of the Common Law: The Human Rights Act in Constitutional Perspective' (2006) 59 *Current Legal Problems* 27, 50.

[74] Above, n. 71, p. 142.

[75] T. R. S. Allan, *Law Liberty Justice: The Legal Foundations of British Constitutionalism* (1994) 16.

[76] See, e.g., Bingham, above n. 48, Ch. 12.

[77] D. Oliver, 'Parliament and the Courts: A Pragmatic (or Principled) Defence of the Sovereignty of Parliament' in A. Horne and G. Drewry (eds.), *Parliament and the Law* (2018) 294.

restriction of legislative authority[78] and goes on to point out that there is a 'mountain of evidence' demonstrating that parliamentary sovereignty is the 'current orthodoxy'.[79]

There is certainly a great number of *dicta* evidencing judicial recognition of parliamentary sovereignty; and there are no examples, outwith the EU context, of UK courts explicitly declining to apply Acts of Parliament on the ground that they are incompatible with the rule of law. However, we should be careful before allowing ourselves to be convinced by Goldsworthy's 'mountain of evidence'. It is possible to argue—although the argument is not without difficulty—that although courts *profess* fidelity to parliamentary sovereignty, they do not invariably *exhibit* such fidelity. The *Anisminic* case is considered by some to be an example of this phenomenon.[80] Faced with an ouster clause directing that determinations made by the defendant decision-maker 'shall not be called in question in any court of law',[81] the Appellate Committee of the House of Lords held that this did not in fact prevent courts from striking down determinations lying outside the decision-maker's jurisdiction.

One way of looking at what is going on in cases like *Anisminic* is to consider the matter straightforwardly in terms of statutory construction. Taken literally and in isolation, the ouster clause might appear to preclude judicial review. But because a fundamental constitutional principle—namely, the rule of law, which requires government according to law and access to courts for the resolution of legal disputes—is implicated, the court may, if it considers it constitutionally appropriate and linguistically feasible, interpret the ouster clause narrowly, so as to preserve the operational effectiveness of the relevant rule of law value to the extent that that is linguistically possible. Thus, the approach in play is, on this view, an interpretive one. Take, for instance, the *Privacy International* case, in which an ouster clause protecting decisions of the Investigatory Powers Tribunal was in issue. When the case was before the Court of Appeal,[82] Sales LJ took the view that it 'turn[ed] on a short point of statutory construction',[83] and concluded that, properly interpreted, Parliament had *not* intended to preclude judicial review of the Tribunal. In contrast, when the case was before the Divisional Court, Leggatt J tended towards the opposite conclusion,[84] saying that 'statutes are interpreted on the understanding that Parliament does not intend to insulate a court or tribunal from it'[85] and that he was thus 'extremely reluctant to attribute to Parliament an intention to achieve a result which would be so clearly inconsistent with the rule of law'.[86]

---

[78] J. Goldsworthy, *Parliamentary Sovereignty: Contemporary Debates* (2010), Ch. 3.   [79] Ibid., p. 97.

[80] *Anisminic Ltd v Foreign Compensation Commission* [1969] 2 AC 147.

[81] Foreign Compensation Act 1950, s. 4(4).

[82] *R. (Privacy International) v Investigatory Powers Tribunal* [2017] EWCA Civ 1868, [2018] 1 WLR 2572. At the time of writing, the judgment of the Supreme Court in this case is awaited.

[83] Ibid., [24].

[84] Although he did not formally dissent from the view of Sir Brian Leveson P, who considered the ouster clause to be effective in precluding judicial review.

[85] *R. (Privacy International) v Investigatory Powers Tribunal* [2017] EWHC 114 (Admin), [2017] 3 All ER 1127, [50].

[86] Ibid., [59].

In this disagreement between Leggatt J and Sales LJ, we find competing understandings of the relative pull of the constitutional forces—namely, fidelity to parliamentary
intention and enforcement of the rule of law—that are in play. The disagreement thus
plays out in the interpretive sphere, the dispute being as to the lengths to which it is
legitimate for the court to go in reading the ouster clause otherwise than in a way that
gives effect to its natural or literal meaning.

However, another way of looking at cases like *Anisminic* and *Privacy International* is
by reference not to the question of whether Parliament has made its intention to oust
judicial review sufficiently clear, but by asking whether, in the first place, Parliament
is capable of effecting such an ouster. And even commentators who generally take an
orthodox line in relation to matters concerning parliamentary sovereignty have argued
that *Anisminic* is hard to reconcile with it. Wade and Forsyth, for example, state that
Anisminic evidences a judicial conviction that 'administrative agencies . . . must *at all
costs* be prevented from being sole judges of the validity of their own acts',[87] since otherwise 'the rule of law would be at an end'.[88] The judges, say Wade and Forsyth, were
thus forced 'to rebel against Parliament'.[89]

There are, however, two difficulties with this analysis. First, the House of Lords insisted that it was merely construing the statute in *Anisminic*—and, the radical interpretive surgery performed upon the ouster clause notwithstanding, this characterization
of the decision enjoys at least some credence. Lord Wilberforce, for instance, pointed
out that Parliament had conferred only limited authority upon the decision-maker,
and that such limits would be meaningless if there were no way of enforcing them.[90]
On this view, the propriety of some form of judicial control of an agency is implicit in
the fact that Parliament has in the first place sought to limit the agency's authority. A
second problem with Wade and Forsyth's argument is that it is built upon the assertion
that the *Anisminic* judgment rendered the ouster clause 'totally ineffective'.[91] Developments in administrative law doctrine since *Anisminic* mean that Wade and Forsyth's
point is true *now*, but it is not an accurate description of the effect of the case upon the
ouster clause *at the time the case was decided*.[92] This sits uncomfortably with the assertion that judges exhibited disobedience to the statute by denying the ouster clause any
effect whatever.

If, therefore, *Anisminic* was the best that critics of parliamentary sovereignty could
offer in response to Goldsworthy's 'mountain of evidence' in its favour, the empirical
case against sovereignty would look rather weak. However, that case has arguably received a shot in the arm in recent years thanks to several *dicta* by senior judges openly
questioning the idea of parliamentary sovereignty. The *Jackson* case is perhaps the

---

[87] H. W. R. Wade and C. F. Forsyth, *Administrative Law* (11th edn., 2014) 614 (emphasis added).
[88] Ibid., p. 614, quoting Denning LJ in *R. v Medical Appeal Tribunal ex parte Gilmore* [1957] 1 QB 574, 586.
[89] Above, n. 87, p. 614.   [90] Above, n. 87, p. 208.   [91] Above, n. 87, p. 614.
[92] At that time, certain matters—non-jurisdictional errors—that would otherwise have been reviewable,
were immunized by the ouster clause as interpreted by the House of Lords. The category of errors that are
non-jurisdictional but reviewable has fallen away since *Anisminic*; it is this that means that, from a modern
perspective, an ouster clause subjected to an *Anisminic*-style interpretation would be 'totally ineffective'.

leading example. It concerned a challenge to the validity of the Hunting Act 2004.[93] It had been enacted without the House of Lords' consent using the special procedure laid down in the Parliament Act 1911.[94] The particular procedure used was one that derived from amendments made to the Parliament Act 1911 by the Parliament Act 1949, which amendments, the claimants contended, had been invalidly made. This, argued the claimants, called into question the validity of the procedure under which the Hunting Act had been enacted, hence placing in doubt the validity of that Act itself. No part of this argument—which was rejected by the House of Lords—turned upon the suggestion that Parliament's authority to legislate may be limited by rule-of-law values. Nevertheless, in the course of reaching their decision, three of the Law Lords considered (*obiter*) whether sovereignty might be limited by such values.

They did so against the backdrop of a bruising constitutional confrontation a year or so earlier. The executive had promoted a Bill containing an ouster clause that went considerably further than that which was at stake in *Anisminic*, and which would probably have defied the sort of interpretative solution adopted in that case. Doubtless with that firmly in mind, Lord Steyn said in *Jackson* that the 'pure and absolute' notion of sovereignty was 'out of place in the modern United Kingdom', albeit that it is 'still the *general* principle of our constitution'.[95] He went on to say that the Supreme Court ought at least to consider refusing to apply legislation at odds with a 'constitutional fundamental'.[96] Lord Hope[97] and Lady Hale[98] expressed comparable sentiments. Lord Hope subsequently returned to this theme in the *AXA* case, saying that 'whether the principle of the sovereignty of the United Kingdom Parliament is absolute or may be subject to limitation in exceptional circumstances is still under discussion'.[99] In *Cart*, meanwhile, Lord Phillips said that the proposition that Parliament could not exclude judicial review was 'controversial'—thereby declining to reject the proposition as constitutionally heterodox—but said that it would '[h]opefully remain academic'.[100]

These comments contrast sharply with earlier judicial statements of orthodoxy, such as Lord Reid's rejoinder in *Pickin* that the suggestion that courts may disregard 'a provision in an Act of Parliament on any ground must seem strange and startling to anyone with any knowledge of the history and law of our constitution'.[101] Do *dicta* such as those found in *Jackson*,[102] *AXA*[103] and *Cart*[104] therefore signify a profound shift in judicial attitudes? Faced with legislation that might be characterized as unconstitutional—for example, legislation purporting to abolish all judicial review,[105] suspend or abolish general elections,[106] or preclude courts from determining the

---

[93] *R. (Jackson) v Attorney-General* [2005] UKHL 56, [2006] 1 AC 262.

[94] The effect of the Parliament Act 1911 is that, in certain circumstances, Bills can become Acts of Parliament without being passed by the House of Lords.

[95] Above, n. 93, para. 102 (original emphasis).   [96] Ibid., para. 102.   [97] Ibid., para. 104.

[98] Ibid., para. 159.   [99] Above, n. 65, para. 50.

[100] *R. (Cart) v Upper Tribunal* [2011] UKSC 28, [2012] 1 AC 663, para. 73.

[101] *British Railways Board v Pickin* [1974] AC 765, 782.   [102] Above, n. 93.

[103] Above, n. 65.   [104] Above, n. 100.

[105] Lord Woolf, '*Droit Public*—English style' [1995] PL 57, 67–69.

[106] J. Jowell, 'Parliamentary Sovereignty Under the New Constitutional Hypothesis' [2006] PL 562, 573.

meaning of legislation[107]—would a court really adopt the nuclear option and decline to recognize it as a valid law? And, if a court were to take such a step, would *it* be acting in an unconstitutional—or, as Wade put it, revolutionary[108]—way? Such conundrums place in sharp relief the relationship between the two key questions with which we have been concerned in this chapter, ultimately reducing to the issue of whether there exist constitutional principles that enjoy a hierarchical status that limits the authority of Parliament as a matter of law. It is to this matter that we must now turn by way of conclusion.

CONCLUSIONS

THE LEGAL AND THE CONSTITUTIONAL

Lord Hope's aspiration, mentioned above, that the question of whether Parliament is truly sovereign will 'remain academic' is telling.[109] The aspiration reflects the fact that if the question ever arose in a concrete form, it would imply the eruption of an unprecedented constitutional crisis. From the courts' perspective, precipitating such a crisis by declining to uphold a provision in an Act of Parliament would be profoundly unappealing, not least because it cannot be taken for granted that such an adventure would end well for the courts. Oliver argues that it is entirely possible that courts would lose the confrontation with Parliament and the executive that would inevitably ensue. If they did, 'untold damage' would be done to the courts' constitutional position and '[the] rule of law itself would . . . [be] weakened'.[110] At the same time, there is also reluctance on the political branches' part to test such deep and unknown constitutional waters; it is hardly in politicians' interests to risk a bruising encounter with the courts whose outcome cannot be known with certainty. Indeed, political capitulation in relation to the ouster clause that was the elephant in the room in *Jackson* is evidence of precisely this phenomenon.[111] When the Bill containing the ouster clause was published, judges dropped strong hints that the consequences might be severe if Parliament and the government pressed on.[112] Against that background, politicians stepped back from the constitutional brink and the clause was withdrawn.

This suggests that we should be cautious about ascribing too much weight either to Goldsworthy's 'mountain of evidence' in favour of untrammelled legislative authority or to contrary judicial *dicta* found in cases like *Jackson* and *AXA*. The reality of the UK's constitutional framework is that 'what if' questions about the periphery, if any, of Parliament's legislative capacity and about how courts would react were Parliament to transgress any such periphery defy abstract resolution. We cannot know for certain how a direct confrontation between Parliament and the courts would play out because,

---

[107] R. *(Cart) v Upper Tribunal* [2009] EWHC 3052 (Admin), [2010] PTSR 824, paras 36–38, *per* Laws LJ.
[108] Above, n. 40 and H. W. R. Wade, 'The Basis of Legal Sovereignty' [1955] *CLJ* 172.
[109] Above, n. 65, para. 50.   [110] Above, n. 77, p. 306.   [111] Above, n. 93.
[112] See, e.g., Lord Woolf, 'The Rule of Law and a Change in the Constitution' [2004] *CLJ* 317, 329.

in the absence of a written constitution, we have no roadmap that provides for such exceptional circumstances. As a result, while it is perfectly possible to make cogent normative arguments about whether or not courts *should* enforce legislation considered to be constitutionally excessive, it is impossible to predict with certainty what *would* happen in such circumstances.

This does not, however, mean that no predictions whatever can be ventured. Understood by reference to our two key questions, the issue at hand is whether there is some point at which the dubiousness of legislation viewed through a *constitutional* lens is so great as to undermine its validity when the matter is examined through a *legal* lens. At what point, if any, does legislation become so profoundly offensive to fundamental *constitutional* values as to render it *unlawful*? While we cannot be confident about whether—and, if so, where—such a point arises, we can be more confident in our assessment if the matter is conceived of not as a binary question but as one of degree. The *more important* the value and the *greater the extent* of its disturbance by the legislation in question, the *less certain* we can be that a court would straightforwardly enforce the legislation.

We can envisage, therefore, a continuum that tracks the relationship between the legality and constitutionality of legislation. At one end, the images yielded by the legal and constitutional lenses clearly diverge: even if a given statutory provision impinges upon, and is therefore to a degree suspect from the vantage point of, a given constitutional value, this raises no serious prospect of the provision's being deprived of legality. This may be because the constitutional value in question is insufficiently fundamental to call the legality of inconsistent legislation into question, or because the legislation concerned does not represent an attack upon the essence (as distinct from a more peripheral aspect) of the value. However, as we move along the continuum, the images yielded by the legal and constitutional lenses may begin to converge. This reflects the fact that as the constitutional offensiveness of the legislation increases—because the value it engages is peculiarly fundamental and/or the statutory provision cuts across the very core of the value—the purchase of the positivist claim that the legislation should be treated as law merely because it was enacted by Parliament is likely to be regarded as having less purchase. As such, a point may arise at which the images yielded by the constitutional and legal lenses precisely align, signifying that the constitutional offensiveness of a statutory provision might jeopardize its recognition by courts as a valid law. However, even if, as we move along the continuum, we can predict with greater confidence that a court which refused to uphold legislation would be judged to have acted constitutionally, it remains impossible to say for certain whether, and if so where on the continuum, such a point arises. This is because at what point (if any) it becomes constitutionally legitimate for judges to refuse to enforce legislation is a matter that would become apparent only *after* the event, in the light of reactions to it.

This highlights a key difference between the UK's constitution and systems based upon a written text. The latter are predicated upon the possibility of unconstitutional behaviour by constitutional actors: they both define what amounts to unconstitutional legislative action and stipulate its legal consequences. Thus they supply an *ex ante* framework that determines in advance how unconstitutional behaviour should be managed. The UK's constitution provides no such framework. It supplies neither a decisive statement of the periphery of what is constitutionally legitimate nor a road-map for determining what should happen in the event of the transgression of any such boundary. It follows that whether a point arises at which constitutional offensiveness collapses into illegality is a question that could be answered in the UK only on an *ex post* basis. Any judicial refusal to uphold legislation could be no more than the open-ing salvo in a debate about whether the legislation was so constitutionally dubious as to have caused Parliament to exceed a legal limit upon its authority and (the flip-side of the same coin) justified the courts' refusal to acknowledge its legality. The conclu-sion of that debate might be that the judges were right; if so, the outcome would be the recognition of a circumstance in which considerations of legality and constitutionality converge so as to constrain Parliament's legislative competence. However, the conclu-sion might equally well be that the court itself had overreached by refusing to uphold duly enacted legislation; such a conclusion would not decisively establish that there is *no* point at which the legality-constitutionality distinction dissolves, but would cer-tainly establish that the legislation in question did not lie at such a point. The essential matter, then, is that fundamental questions of this nature can be decisively resolved only with the benefit of hindsight. In the absence of explicitly stipulated *ex ante* consti-tutional ground-rules, the existence and content of such rules would fall to be inferred from the aftermath of a constitutional crisis in which judges and politicians sought to test the limits of one another's authority.

Conceding that matters of this nature must, in the absence of a clarifying con-stitutional crisis, remain shrouded in uncertainty is perhaps unsatisfying, in that it may appear to be an obstacle to understanding the form that the inner workings of the constitution takes. Yet such uncertainty, far from obscuring some deeper but unknown constitutional truth, itself represents a fundamental aspect of the UK con-stitution's workings. Indeed, uncertainty might be said to be essential to the effec-tive functioning of the system, thanks to the capacity of such uncertainty to place in doubt which institution—Parliament or court—has the final word in relation to fundamental constitutional values, thereby giving rise to a constructive form of in-stitutional tension-cum-comity. This argument will be briefly elaborated by way of conclusion.

THE VALUE OF UNCERTAINTY

Traditional Diceyan analysis of the UK constitution holds that Parliament's legal au-thority is circumscribed by nothing more than whatever restraint is invited by demo-cratic politics. The notion of 'constitutional'—as distinct from 'political'—restraints upon Parliament's authority might therefore appear inapt within this tradition: such restraints as exist are, on this view, transient artefacts of political expediency rather than embedded features of the constitutional system. The better view, it has been argued in this chapter, is that Parliament's legislative freedom is restrained—even if it is not unambiguously restricted—by values that are genuinely constitutional in nature. That is to say, the values—or at least some of the values—that operate as restraining influences reflect deep-rooted commitments to fundamental principles, including the rule of law, the separation of powers and the autonomy of devolved institutions.

For the most part, at least, such values find expression other than as hard constraints upon Parliament's legislative authority. As we have seen, they constitute, among other things, principles of interpretation that shape the meaning ascribed by the courts to legislation, and they serve to disincentivize the enactment of legislation that is insensitive to them. However, for the reasons explored in this chapter, the possibility cannot be discounted that fundamental constitutional values may have an irreducible core whose infraction would test the courts' commitment to the notion of parliamentary sovereignty. Nor can the possibility be discounted that a court would be judged, in the aftermath of the inevitable constitutional crisis, to have acted properly if it were to uphold the very essence of a truly fundamental constitutional value in the face of a legislative attack upon it. The existence of these possibilities—we can put it no higher than that—serves to underpin the notion that Parliament's legislative authority may subsist within a constitutional order that supplies more than merely political restraint. And while, absent hard-to-conceive-of legislative excess, it is impossible to determine whether basic constitutional values may ultimately form hard legal constraints, the possibility of their taking such effect *in extremis* places the operation of such values in more prosaic circumstances in a different light. At the very least, it serves as a reminder that the depth of their constitutional fundamentality is uncertain, and that they should not readily be dismissed as nothing more than 'political' constructs that are wholly fragile in the face of a bare parliamentary majority.

What this boils down to is that the absence of textual or otherwise clearly articulated constitutional ground-rules should not necessarily be taken to imply that none exists. Nor should it be taken for granted that the *ex ante* unavailability of such ground-rules necessarily precludes the possibility of their *ex post* emergence in the course of a constitutional crisis. This is not to suggest that the opposite propositions should blithely be assumed to be correct. The point, rather, is that uncertainty about the legal status of fundamental constitutional values yields a form of necessary institutional tension between the courts and Parliament. Each is understandably loath to test the limits of the other's authority, and, as a result, each generally observes a self-denying ordinance that avoids the infraction of such constitutional ground-rules as might exist. If courts were to contemplate the rejection of unconstitutional legislation or Parliament its enactment, each would stare into a constitutional abyss. What lies at the bottom of that abyss is unknown, since the depth—if any—of the constitutional bedrock that must be reached before the possibility arises of unconstitutionality transmogrifying into illegality is uncertain. Crucially, however, the existence of that abyss and its uncertain content exert a significant, if generally unarticulated, effect upon our constitutional life. They provide, at the very least, a strong disincentive to legislative—and judicial—excess, and invest constitutional values with a status that transcends the merely 'political'.

So, is Parliament sovereign? For the reasons explored in this chapter, no definitive answer can be given to that question. However, intellectually frustrating though that might be, it is in fact relatively unimportant. What is more important is that to view the authority of Parliament through an exclusively legal lens inevitably yields an incomplete and misleading constitutional picture. The reality of the contemporary UK constitution is that Parliament's legislative authority falls to be exercised within a normatively rich constitutional order and in the light of the restraining influences of multi-layered and common-law constitutionalism. The possibility that the constitutional values associated with those influences may possess irreducible cores that sit in tension with the notion of absolute legislative authority can neither be taken for granted nor rejected out of hand. It is to be expected, and hoped, that these matters will remain 'academic', as Lord Hope put it, and thus shrouded in mystery—for the absence of any definitive resolution of such questions is evidence of the mutual respect which (for the most part) the courts and Parliament exhibit in relation to one another, and without which the UK's unwritten constitution could not function. It is a constitution that is predicated not upon prescribing the consequences that would ensue were the worst to happen, but upon the premise that the worst will not happen in the first place. That system is built upon and presupposes a form of institutional respect that would already have disintegrated if we were ever to find ourselves in a position to resolve decisively the fundamental questions of constitutional authority examined in this chapter. It follows that Parliament might or might not be sovereign, but that this is largely beside the point—for the constitutional system demands and expects that Parliament will desist from exercising the full width of the extravagant powers which it would possess if it were sovereign.

FURTHER READING

T. R. S. ALLAN, *The Sovereignty of Law: Freedom, Constitution and Common Law* (2013)

M. ELLIOTT, J. WILLIAMS, and A.L. YOUNG, *The UK Constitution after Miller: Brexit and Beyond* (2018)

J. GOLDSWORTHY, *Parliamentary Sovereignty: Contemporary Debates* (2010)

D. OLIVER, 'Parliament and the Courts: A Pragmatic (or Principled) Defence of the Sovereignty of Parliament' in A. Horne and G. Drewry (eds.), *Parliament and the Law* (2018)

SIR JOHN LAWS, 'Law and Democracy' [1995] *Public Law* 72

3

HUMAN RIGHTS AND THE UK CONSTITUTION

*Colm O'Cinneide**

SUMMARY

UK law relating to civil liberties and human rights has undergone radical transformation over the last few decades, in part because of the influence exerted by the European Convention on Human Rights ('the ECHR') on British law. The Human Rights Act 1998 ('the HRA'), which incorporates the civil and political rights protected by the ECHR in national law, now plays a key role in the UK's constitutional system. It complements legislative mechanisms for protecting individual rights—such as the Equality Act 2010—and imposes significant constraints on the exercise of public power. However, the current state of UK human rights law is controversial. The HRA is regularly subject to political attack, while leading politicians bemoan the influence exerted by the ECHR over UK law but no consensus yet exists as to how human rights should best be protected within the framework of the British constitution. It remains to be seen whether Brexit will change the dynamics of this debate.

INTRODUCTION

Democratic states like the UK are now expected to respect a range of fundamental human rights, in particular core civil and political rights, such as freedom from torture, the right to fair trial and the right to freedom from discrimination. It is generally recognized that the functioning of any genuine democracy must be based on respect for these rights, without which individuals cannot participate freely or effectively in the political process, enjoy meaningful autonomy, or be accorded genuine equality of status in line with basic rule of law principles.[1]

---

* Professor of Constitutional and Human Rights Law, UCL.

[1] See T. Bingham, *The Rule of Law* (Penguin: 2010); also J. Habermas, 'Constitutional Democracy: A Paradoxical Union of Contradictory Principles?' (2001) 29 *Pol. Theory* 766–9.

Human rights are nevertheless contested concepts, which are capable of being in-terpreted and understood in different ways. Deep disagreement often exists as to what exactly constitutes a breach of a fundamental right. Furthermore, different views also exist as to what role should be played by different institutions in protecting rights, in particular when it comes to the question whether courts should be given wide author-ity to protect individual rights and overturn decisions of public authorities that they deem to violate such rights. Disagreement also exists as to what rights should be rec-ognized in law: arguments are increasingly made that UK law should protect not just core civil and political rights, but also socio-economic rights, the rights of children and other fundamental rights that have been recognized to exist in international human rights law.[2]

In the UK constitutional system, it is generally assumed that the political branches of government should play the leading role in resolving disputes about the scope and substance of individual rights. However, the courts have become increasingly involved in adjudicating human rights issues over the last few decades: the protection of indi-vidual rights is now usually viewed as forming part of the 'mission statement' of the judicial branch of government, and human rights cases now form a considerable ele-ment of the case-load of the UK's superior courts.[3]

This trend is not just confined to Britain: it has become a feature of constitutional systems across the democratic world.[4] In many states, such as the USA, Germany, and South Africa, courts have been given wide-ranging constitutional powers to overturn decisions of elected legislatures if they are deemed to violate basic rights. However, the UK has not followed this approach. Instead, over the few decades, it has devel-oped its own particular system of legal rights protection—which bears a close family resemblance to similar systems adopted in Canada, New Zealand and other 'West-minster' systems which share a common adherence to parliamentary sovereignty as a core constitutional principle. This gives judges the authority to overturn acts of public bodies which violate core civil and political rights, while ensuring that the ultimate law-making authority remains in the hands of the Westminster Parliament. This makes it easier for public authorities to be held legally accountable for interference with fun-damental rights, and it provides individuals and groups who lack political power with a forum to challenge unjust laws—while ensuring that the elected politicians in Parlia-ment retain the final say as to the substance of UK law in this regard.[5]

The Human Rights Act 1998 ('the HRA') is central to this system of rights protec-tion, although the common law and other statutes such as the Equality Act 2010 also

---

[2] For a comprehensive overview of the international human rights treaty regime, see P. Alston and R. Good-man, *International Human Rights* (Oxford: OUP, 2012).

[3] B. Dickson, *Human Rights and the UK Supreme Court* (Oxford: OUP, 2013).

[4] B. Ackerman, 'The Rise of World Constitutionalism' (1997) 83 *Virginia Law Review* 771.

[5] David Feldman has described existing UK human rights law as contributing to the establishment of a culture of 'politico-legal justification', whereby governments can be required to justify the impact their actions have on the individual rights and liberties of persons subject to their jurisdiction: D. Feldman, ' "Which In Your Case You Have Not Got": Constitutionalism at Home and Abroad' (2011) *Current Legal Problems* 117–149.

feature, albeit in supporting roles. The HRA incorporates the civil and political rights protected by the ECHR in national law and makes them enforceable by British courts, but does not give the courts any authority to set aside Westminster legislation—thereby ensuring Parliament's 'final say'. At the level of international law, the ECHR provides an additional safety-net. Individuals who have been unsuccessful in obtaining a remedy for alleged rights violations in national law can bring a case to the European Court of Human Rights (the 'ECtHR') in Strasbourg and seek a finding that the UK has breached its obligations under the Convention—which is binding on the UK as a matter of international law, even if it does not create binding obligations as a matter of domestic law.

However, this system of legal rights protection is controversial. The argument is frequently made that UK human rights law as currently constituted places unjustified limits on the freedom of action of the political branches of the state and accords too great a role to the European Court of Human Rights in shaping its substance. Having said that, considerable support exists for the current status quo—with supporters arguing that it provides effective protection for rights without disturbing the core foundations of the UK constitutional order. This debate is further complicated by the cautious development of more extended forms of human rights protection by the devolved legislatures, as well as by the provisions of the Belfast Agreement which commit the UK to maintain respect for ECHR rights within Northern Ireland. In addition, the HRA/ECHR is not the only game in town: recent developments in the uncertain area of common law rights have complicated the picture, as has the Brexit process.

This chapter begins with a historical overview of the evolution of UK law as it relates to the protection of civil liberties and human rights more generally: this is essential, if the context to current debates about the HRA/ECHR is to be properly understood. It then proceeds to map out the UK's obligations under international human rights law in general, and the ECHR more specifically, so as to highlight this key dimension to the development of contemporary human rights law. The scope of common law rights will then be analysed, followed by the structure of the HRA and key elements of the case-law relating to its requirements. The chapter then concludes with an overview of the debate about the future of the HRA and the UK's relationship with the ECHR, which also takes account of the uncertain impact of Brexit in this area and the complicating factors thrown up by developments in the devolved regions.

PART ONE: OVERVIEW—THE HISTORICAL DEVELOPMENT OF UK LAW RELATING TO CIVIL LIBERTIES AND HUMAN RIGHTS

A respect for civil liberties, i.e. for personal freedoms which allow individuals to participate in public life,[6] is often assumed to be a defining characteristic of the British constitution. Views differ as to the extent to which this assumption has corresponded

---

[6] C. Gearty, *Civil Liberties* (Oxford University Press, 2007), p. 1.

to reality in the past, or the extent to which it holds true today. However, the normative expectation that the various organs of state *should* respect civil liberties has become embedded within British constitutional culture as a result of an extended process of political struggle and legal evolution. More recently, this has been supplemented by a wider commitment to respecting a broader range of human rights standards, which define what positive respect for individual dignity should entail.[7] This embrace of human rights has had significant consequences for the UK constitutional system: to understand how and why it happened, and the tensions this has generated, a brief historical overview is in order.

MAGNA CARTA, DICEY AND ALL THAT: THE LONG EVOLUTION OF THE BRITISH TRADITION OF CIVIL LIBERTIES

The legal origin of the British civil liberties tradition is usually traced back to the issuing of the Magna Carta in 1215, which affirmed that limits existed to the arbitrary power of the sovereign monarch.[8] Sometimes anachronistically described as the foundational text for modern understandings of liberty and rights, in reality Magna Carta is best viewed as an assertion of baronial prerogatives.[9] Nevertheless, it acquired considerable symbolic status over time, as the document came to embody the idea that the exercise of sovereign power should respect established liberties.

Royal disregard of this concept of bounded sovereign power lent fuel to the parliamentary revolt against the Crown in the early seventeenth century. This culminated in the 'Glorious Revolution' of 1688 and the passing of the Bill of Rights 1689, which affirmed parliamentary control over taxation, limited the power of the Crown, and presented personal liberty and representative governance as marching hand in hand.[10]

The symbolic legacy of Magna Carta also exerted a significant influence over the development of the common law. In the early seventeenth century, jurists such as Edward Coke argued that the common law imposed limits on monarchical power, invoking the liberties set out in Magna Carta in support of their reasoning.[11] Subsequently, in cases

---

[7] Plenty of ink has been spilled in attempts to draw a clear distinction between civil liberties and human rights, usually to little effect. I use the term 'civil liberties' here to refer to the historic freedoms that subjects of the British Crown enjoyed (in theory at least) by virtue of the self-restraint of the Crown and later Parliament in making law. I use 'human rights' to refer to the positive entitlements (e.g. the right to fair trial, or to non-discrimination) that individuals are supposed to enjoy by virtue of their inherent human dignity, as recognized by various international human rights instruments. There is considerable overlap between the two terms, with 'human rights' having a wider scope.

[8] The history of human rights law in Scotland differs in several important respects from that of England: see A. Boyle, 'Introduction', in A. Boyle (ed.) *Human Rights and Scots Law* (Oxford: Hart, 2002) 1–8, 1.

[9] See in general, J. C. Holt, *Magna Carta*, 2nd ed. (Cambridge University Press, 1992).

[10] As Anthony Lester has put it, '[t]he alliance of Parliament and the common lawyers ensured that the supremacy of the law would mean the supremacy of Parliament: more realistically, it came to mean, between elections, the supremacy of the government in Parliament': A. Lester, 'Human Rights and the British Constitution', in D. Oliver and J. Jowell (eds.) *The Changing Constitution*, 7th ed., p. 72.

[11] See e.g. *Bonham's Case* (1610) 8 Coke's Reports 114.

such as *Entick v Carrington*,[12] the common law courts set out the basic ingredients of the principle of legality—namely that the exercise of executive power must be expressly authorized by law, and that public authorities must in particular have a clear legal basis for any action they undertake which infringes upon individual freedom.[13] The corollary of this principle also emerged—the presumption of liberty, whereby individuals were free to do anything not clearly prohibited by law. This in turn gave rise to the canon of statutory interpretation that the scope of criminal law and police powers should be given a restrictive interpretation in the interests of protecting individual liberty.[14]

A bias in favour of personal liberty was thus gradually incorporated into the DNA of the common law. By the late eighteenth century, it was established that infringements of personal freedom had to be clearly authorized by statute or common law. This did not in itself prevent the enactment of oppressive laws.[15] However, as the century proceeded, popular mobilization in support of political radicals such as John Wilkes and Brass Crosby played a key role in enlarging the scope of civil liberty.[16]

After the repression that accompanied the Napoleonic Wars and the birth pangs of the Industrial Revolution, the UK political system underwent a process of gradual democratization over the course of the nineteenth and early twentieth centuries. Initially a vehicle for oligarchic control, Parliament gradually became the principal locus for the exercise of democratic rights thanks to the expansion of the franchise in the nineteenth and early twentieth centuries. Furthermore, expectations were established that Parliament should exercise its sovereign law-making powers in a manner that respected both the rule of law and basic liberties such as freedom of religion, freedom of speech and freedom of association.[17]

Writing near the end of the nineteenth century, Dicey argued that respect for the rule of law and civil liberties had become deeply engrained in British political culture and the common law. He compared this state of affairs favourably with the protection afforded to fundamental rights by written constitutions in countries such as France and the United States. In his view, such constitutional bills of rights set out abstract guarantees which often failed to give rise to substantive, enforceable legal entitlements—or alternatively gave judges excessive leeway to determine their content at the expense of the elected legislature.[18]

---

[12] (1765) 19 St.Tr. 1029.   [13] See further Chapter 1 of this volume.

[14] For a recent example of the application of this presumption, see *R. v Zafar* [2008] EWCA Crim 184.

[15] See E.P. Thompson, *Whigs and Hunters: The Origins of the Black Act* (London: Allen Lane, 1975).

[16] For a general overview of the development of 'political liberty' during this time period, see L. Ward, *The Politics of Liberty in England and Revolutionary America* (Cambridge University Press, 2004).

[17] As the former Attorney-General, Dominic Grieve QC, commented: 'how well [these] liberties were in practice maintained through the centuries . . . is very questionable . . . But they are part of an entirely distinctive national narrative [which] has been so powerful that it has acted as an almost mythic restraint on successive British governments trying to curb freedoms'. See D. Grieve, 'Why Human Rights Should Matter to Conservatives', UCL Judicial Institute, 3 December 2014, available at http://www.ucl.ac.uk/constitution-unit/constitution-unit-news/031214a (last accessed 15 December 2018).

[18] A. V. Dicey, *Introduction to the Study of the Law of the Constitution* (London: Macmillan, 1st ed., 1885; 10th ed., 1959), in particular at 144.

Dicey's views were regarded as constitutional orthodoxy for many decades.[19] However, as the twentieth century progressed, his complacent assumption that 'the securities for personal freedom are in England as complete as the laws can make them'[20] gradually began to be called into question, as gaps opened up between constitutional image and reality.

THE SLOW DEFLATION OF DICEYAN COMPLACENCY

As Anthony Lester commented in a previous edition of this book, 'the prevailing British constitutional ideology . . . treated British subjects as "subjects of the Crown" without the benefit of fundamental constitutional rights'.[21] The liberties of the subject were 'residual and negative in their nature':[22] the individual was free to do anything that the law had not forbidden, but enjoyed no positive legal rights as such. Respect for civil liberties in the UK was thus dependent on Parliament and other public authorities choosing to exercise their powers in a way that avoided excessive interference with individual freedom.

Such a protective approach was often adopted, with the legislature acting with restraint when enacting laws which impacted civil liberties. Furthermore, as the twentieth century went on, Parliament periodically enacted legislation which substantively extended the legal protection afforded to minorities and other disadvantaged groups, such as the Sex Offenders Act 1967 (which partially decriminalized homosexuality) and the race relations, equal pay and sex discrimination legislation of the 1960s and 1970s. Furthermore, parliamentary legislation relating to health care, social security, and trade unions gradually established a comprehensive floor of positive protection for social rights—thus providing a comprehensive legal foundation for the post-war welfare state.

However, at times, the legislative record was more mixed—especially in areas such as national security and immigration control, where repressive measures were periodically enacted to the particular detriment of marginalized social groups.[23] Furthermore, the dominance generally exerted by the executive over Parliament, coupled with the post-war expansion of the discretionary powers enjoyed by the organs of the new administrative state, generated concerns that the exercise of public power was subject to insufficient accountability controls.[24]

---

[19] For a penetrating analysis of how Dicey regarded the rule of law as a distinctively English contribution to civilization, which helped to provide a liberal justification for Empire—as well as his ambivalent recognition that the maintenance of imperial rule would at times require arbitrary measures departing from the rule of law—see D. Lino, 'The Rule of Law and the Rule of Empire: A.V. Dicey in Imperial Context' (2018) 81(5) *Modern L. Rev.* 739–64.

[20] Dicey, *Introduction to the Study of the Law of the Constitution*, 220.

[21] Lester, 'Human Rights and the British Constitution', 7th ed., 71.   [22] Ibid.

[23] For example, the Commonwealth Immigrants Act 1968 appeased anti-immigrant sentiment by denying entry to the UK to a large number of British Overseas Passport holders, having been enacted after a rushed three day parliamentary debate. A. Lester, 'Thirty Years On: The East African Case Revisited' [2002] *Public Law* 52–72.

[24] For contrasting right- and left-wing views on the impact of the new administrative state on individual liberty, see Lord Hewart, *The New Despotism* (London: Ernest Benn, 1929); R.H.S. Crossman, *Socialism and the New Despotism* (London: Fabian Tracts, No. 298, 1956); Lord Hailsham, *The Dilemma of Democracy: Diagnosis and Prescription* (London: Collins, 1978).

This created pressure for civil liberties to be accorded greater positive protection in law, which grew as British society liberalized and become more multicultural from the late 1950s on. Political campaigning against race and sex discrimination in the 1960s, coupled with growing resistance against traditional morality-based controls on free speech and personal conduct, lent momentum to calls for more extensive legal protection against the abusive exercise of state power. It also fuelled enthusiasm for the new language of 'human rights', which offered a broader, more positive framing of the obligations of the state to individuals than was available under the older, more circumscribed notion of civil liberties.[25]

Similar consequences flowed from the brutal and divisive Northern Ireland conflict, which began in 1969 after an outbreak of inter-communal violence triggered by sectarian attacks on the civil rights movement that had started to campaign against the widespread discrimination experienced by the Catholic/Nationalist minority. During the ensuing twenty-eight years of the 'Troubles', the use by the state of coercive interrogation methods, internment, and a range of special anti-terrorism powers proved to be highly controversial, while allegations of the existence of 'shoot to kill' policies and state collusion with paramilitary groups persisted for much of the conflict.[26]

In mainland Britain, the use of police stop and search powers to target ethnic minorities also triggered calls for greater rights protection, especially following the race riots that took place in the early 1980s in Brixton, Toxteth and elsewhere. The use of police powers during the coal miners' strike of 1984–5 also proved to be divisive, as did enactment of measures such as the infamous prohibition on 'promoting homosexuality' in schools introduced by section 28 of the Local Government Act 1988.[27]

These controversies eroded trust in the capacity of Parliament and public authorities more generally to protect rights in a way that kept pace with evolving concepts of social justice. In turn, this undermined Diceyan orthodoxy about how best to protect civil liberty within the framework of the UK constitutional order, and encouraged a search for new ways to strike a workable balance between facilitating the exercise of public power and orientating its exercise towards rights-respecting outcomes.

THE EMBRACE OF HUMAN RIGHTS LAW

The political momentum in favour of reform was also influenced by the development of international and European human rights law since 1945. Beginning with the ECHR in 1951, the UK ratified a variety of UN and Council of Europe treaty instruments designed to set out universally applicable human rights standards. In the Cold War era,

---

[25] For an interesting historical perspective on this shift, see C. Moores, 'From Civil Liberties to Human Rights? British Civil Liberties Activism and Universal Human Rights' (2012) 21(2) *Contemporary European History*, 169–92.

[26] See C. Campbell and I. Connolly, 'Making War on Terror? Global Lessons from Northern Ireland' (2006) 69 *Modern Law Review* 935–957, 945–955.

[27] In general, see K. Ewing and C. Gearty, *Freedom under Thatcher: Civil Liberties in Modern Britain* (Oxford: Clarendon, 1990).

compliance with these standards came to be seen as a key marker of respect for basic democratic principles. As a consequence, the civil and political rights set out in the ECHR and the interpretation given to these rights by the European Court of Human Rights in Strasbourg become an important reference point for all European legal systems. From the early 1970s on, judgments of the Strasburg Court began to expose the existence of human rights 'blind spots' in UK law.[28]

This contributed to the growing disenchantment with the Diceyan constitutional orthodoxy, and encouraged a new focus on expanding the protection afforded by domestic UK law to human rights. So too did the development of various modes of constitutional rights review in many European jurisdictions after 1945, and the impact of the civil rights jurisprudence of the US Supreme Court during the 'Warren Court' period of the 1950s and 1960s. The development of EU law also had an effect, as the provisions of rights-protective European legislation such as the Equal Treatment and Pregnant Workers Directives were applied by national courts and the ECJ to read down or suspend conflicting UK laws.[29]

Taken together, all of these factors generated new expectations that British courts should play a more active role in protecting individual rights. In line with Diceyan orthodoxy, the role of the courts in this regard was originally confined to (i) ensuring that public authorities had a legal basis for exercising their powers and (ii) applying the presumption of liberty when interpreting legislation or developing the common law. They had no wider power to review the conduct of public authorities for compliance with fundamental rights. Over time, the situation began to change. With the development of modern administrative law, courts began to subject the use of discretionary and prerogative powers to closer scrutiny—and to recognize the existence of 'common law rights', as discussed further below.[30] However, the scope of the judicial role in this regard remained uncertain, as did the substance of the rights protected.

This state of affairs came under increasing criticism from civil society organizations campaigning in the field of law reform, such as Justice, Charter 88 and the National Council for Civil Liberties (subsequently renamed Liberty), and prompted calls for a new British Bill of Rights.[31] Developments in Commonwealth countries who shared the UK's constitutional commitment to parliamentary sovereignty added impetus to the pressure for change. In 1982, the Canadian Charter of Rights and Freedoms gave the Canadian courts the authority to strike down both acts of the executive and legislative enactments, subject to a 'notwithstanding' clause which gave the federal and provincial legislatures the power to override a Charter judgment for a five-year renewable time period. In 1990, New Zealand introduced a Bill of Rights, which gave

---

[28] See Lester, 'Human Rights and the British Constitution', 7th ed., 75–6.

[29] See e.g. Case 152/84 *Marshall v Southampton and South-West Hampshire Area Health Authority* (Teaching) [1986] ECR 723.

[30] See further Chapter 1 of this volume.

[31] See e.g. Lord Scarman, *English Law—The New Dimension*, The Hamlyn Lectures Twenty Sixth Series (London: Stevens & Sons, 1974); R. Dworkin, *A Bill of Rights for Britain* (London: Chatto & Windus, 1990).

its courts a more limited power to review acts of the executive for compatibility with core civil and political rights. Both these enactments preserved the 'final say' of Parliament over all law relating to human rights, while simultaneously giving courts a strong rights protective function. In so doing, they established a template that could be applied in the UK, where the constitutional centrality of parliamentary sovereignty ruled out a US-style approach of giving the courts the 'final say' on contested issues of fundamental rights.

By 1997, when the Labour Party returned to power after eighteen years of being in opposition, the political climate was thus ripe for reform—which cleared the way for Parliament to enact the HRA in 1998.[32] As discussed further below, this incorporated most of the ECHR rights into UK law and empowered the courts to overturn acts by public authorities which violated these rights, while preserving parliamentary sovereignty: courts were given the power to issue declarations of incompatibility to the effect that legislation was in their view incompatible with ECHR rights, but such declarations are not legally binding. The HRA thus preserved the existing ground rules of the UK constitutional system, while giving courts new powers to protect individual rights.

Significantly, the new devolution legislation introduced at the same time also required the devolved legislatures in Northern Ireland, Scotland and Wales to comply with Convention rights.[33] The devolved legislatures were also to have the authority to take measures to give further effect to the UK's international human rights obligations when acting within the scope of their powers, including but not confined to those that arise under the ECHR.[34] In addition, the 1998 Belfast Agreement, which brought the Northern Ireland conflict to an end, provided that compliance with the ECHR was an essential 'safeguard' of the peace process.[35] It also affirmed that ECHR rights should be incorporated into, and made enforceable by, Northern Irish law.[36] The Agreement also made provision for the establishment of a Human Rights Commission—which would play a leading role in considering whether a new Bill of Rights should be introduced containing supplemental rights to those contained in the ECHR 'to reflect the particular circumstances of Northern Ireland'.[37]

ECHR compliance—and respect for human rights more generally—was thus built into the devolved system of governance from the beginning. This reflected the wide political support that existed in 1998 for ECHR incorporation, and more generally for the embrace of human rights law represented by enactment of the HRA. In this

---

[32] For further analysis of the shift away from Diceyan orthodoxy, see F. Klug, *Values for a Godless Age: The Story of the UK's New Bill of Rights* (London: Penguin, 2000).

[33] S. 6(2)(c) and s. 24(1)(a) of the Northern Ireland Act 1998; s. 29(2)(d) and s. 57(2) of the Scotland Act 1998; s. 81(1) and s. 94(6)(c) of the Government of Wales Act 2006.

[34] Para. 3(c) of Sched. 2 of the Northern Ireland Act 1998; para. 7(2) of Sched. 5 of the Scotland Act 1998; and in general Sched. 5 of the Government of Wales Act 2006.

[35] Belfast/Good Friday Agreement, *Strand One: Democratic Institutions in Northern Ireland*, para. 5(b).

[36] Ibid, *Rights, Safeguards and Equality of Opportunity*, para. 2.

[37] Ibid, *Rights, Safeguards and Equality of Opportunity*, para. 4.

particular context, Diceyan orthodoxy had been decisively displaced. But, as subsequent events showed, this did not mean that a settled consensus had been established about how rights should be protected through law.

WHERE THINGS STAND NOW

The HRA came into force in 2000. In the two decades since, it has become an integral part of UK public law—and has come to play an important role in shaping various aspects of private law as well. Many commentators view it as a healthy addition to the UK constitutional system.[38] In their view, the interaction of the ECHR and HRA ensures a decent level of legal protection for core civil and political rights, adds an important normative dimension to UK law, and enhances public accountability by creating a new legal avenue for challenging government wrongdoing. As such, it helps to provide a counter-balance to the executive domination of Parliament and the majoritarian orientation of party politics—while not intruding too far into the political sphere.

However, the HRA also has its critics.[39] It has been accused of giving courts too much power to determine important matters of social policy, and of limiting the proper scope of democratic decision-making. It has also been accused of tying UK human rights law too closely to the case-law of the European Court of Human Rights—which, in the eyes of its critics, lacks legitimacy because it is a supranational court.[40] Calls have also been made for judges to use their powers under the HRA with great restraint. Support has also been expressed for a new 'British Bill of Rights', which would replace the HRA and introduce new 'home-grown' British rights standards into UK law.[41]

One such proposal was included in the 2015 election manifesto of the Conservative Party, which won the 2015 general election. However, such calls for reform or repeal of the HRA—or for the UK to leave the ECHR, as proposed by Theresa May MP when she was Home Secretary[42]—have attracted resistance. Considerable legal and political support exists for the current status quo: as Prime Minister, Theresa May MP acknowledged in 2017 that there was neither majority support in the House of Commons or a clear consensus in the Conservative Party for repeal of the HRA and/or ECHR repudiation.[43] At the time of writing, Brexit also appears to have drained momentum from the campaign to repeal the HRA: indeed, as discussed in the Conclusion to this

---

[38] See e.g. A. Kavanagh, *Constitutional Review under the Human Rights Act* (Cambridge University Press, 2009).

[39] See e.g. M. Pinto-Duschinsky, *Bring Rights Back Home: Making Human Rights Compatible with Parliamentary Democracy in the UK* (London: Policy Exchange, 2011).

[40] N. Malcolm, *Human Rights and Political Wrongs* (Judicial Power Project, 2017).

[41] Conservative Party, *Protecting Human Rights in the UK*, October 2014, available at https://www.conservatives.com/~/media/Files/Downloadable%20Files/HUMAN_RIGHTS.pdf (last accessed 1 December 2014).

[42] T. May MP, 'Speech on Brexit', 25 April 2016, available at http://www.conservativehome.com/parliament/2016/04/theresa-mays-speech-on-brexit-full-text.html (last accessed 29 May 2016).

[43] *Independent*, 'Conservative Manifesto: Theresa May announces UK will remain part of European Convention of Human Rights', 18 May 2017, available at https://www.independent.co.uk/news/uk/politics/conservative-manifesto-uk-echr-european-convention-human-rights-leave-eu-next-parliament-election-a774236.html (last accessed 16 December 2018).

chapter, one potential side-effect of the Brexit process may be to reinforce the status of the ECHR as a key guarantor of rights protection.

As a consequence, the HRA and the link it establishes between UK law and the ECHR remains, for now, an important, if contested, element of the UK's constitutional system. However, it is not the only aspect of UK law that plays an important role in protecting rights. The controversy surrounding the HRA/ECHR has obscured the significant role played by other legal instruments in orientating the exercise of public power in rights-friendly directions.

The UK's obligations under international human rights law have very limited domestic effect, but are nevertheless beginning to exert more influence on the development of law and policy than they did in the past—especially in the devolved regions. Common law rights have acquired new prominence in recent years, as evidenced by the UK Supreme Court's ground-breaking 2017 judgment in *R. (Unison) v Lord Chancellor*.[44] Domestic legislation such as the Equality Act 2010 still plays an important role in vindicating rights. So too do various aspect of EU law, although its impact in this regard will largely fall away post-Brexit. The role of political mechanisms such as the Joint Committee on Human Rights is also worth a mention in this regard, as are the activities of public bodies such as the Equality and Human Rights Commission.

As a result, before examining the provisions of the HRA in detail, and the ongoing debate about its future, it is necessary to outline the wider framework of human rights protection that has gradually taken shape within UK public law—with particular reference to (i) international and (ii) domestic (non-HRA) standards. Discussion of EU law will be left until the final part of the chapter, given the possible ramifications of Brexit for the future of UK human rights law more generally.

PART TWO: THE RELATIONSHIP BETWEEN THE UK LEGAL SYSTEM AND INTERNATIONAL HUMAN RIGHTS LAW

The international human rights movement emerged in the wake of the horrors of the Second World War. It drew inspiration from natural law and Enlightenment philosophy—including the ideas of British thinkers such as Locke, Paine and Mill—and (as noted above) sought to define the fundamental rights that all individuals should enjoy by virtue of their inherent dignity as human beings.[45] It has inspired the drafting of a range of international and regional human rights treaty mechanisms, which have played an important role in giving a degree of substance to abstract human rights ideals. Two sets of instruments are of particular significance for the UK, namely the UN and Council of Europe human rights treaty frameworks—with the ECHR being of especial significance.

---

[44] [2017] UKSC 51.   [45] See Klug, *Values for a Godless Age*.

THE UN SYSTEM OF RIGHTS PROTECTION

The UN General Assembly in December 1948 adopted the Universal Declaration of Human Rights (UDHR), which set out a range of core human rights principles—which included both civil and political rights such as freedom of speech, and also socio-economic rights such as the right to work. Subsequently, two legally binding treaty instruments were concluded within the UN framework: the International Covenants on Civil and Political Rights and Economic, Social and Cultural Rights were opened for signature in 1966. States such as the UK that signed and ratified these instruments entered into a binding commitment under international law to respect and give effect to the rights set out in their text.

The provisions of the two Covenants have subsequently been supplemented and reinforced by a number of other UN human rights conventions. The UK has signed and ratified the most prominent of these treaty instruments—namely, the Convention on the Elimination of Racial Discrimination (CERD), the Convention on the Elimination of Discrimination against Women (CEDAW), the Convention against Torture (CAT), the Convention on the Rights of the Child (CRC) and the Convention on the Rights of Persons with Disabilities (CPRD).

The UK's compliance with these UN human rights treaty instruments is regularly reviewed by the expert monitoring committees established within the framework of each of these treaty instruments, through a national reporting procedure. It has also ratified the Optional Protocols to two of these instruments, namely CEDAW and the CPRD—which makes it possible for individuals to bring complaints to the relevant expert committees for both treaties alleging a violation of their rights. However, thus far, successive UK governments have been unwilling to sign up to the individual complaint mechanisms that exist for the other treaties—while the CEDAW and CPRD Optional Protocol mechanisms have been little-used.[46] More generally, the UK's compliance with international human rights norms is also monitored through its active involvement in the Universal Periodic Review (UPR) process conducted by the UN Human Rights Council.

But, despite the UK's respectable level of engagement with these UN frameworks, they historically have had little impact within UK domestic law. The UK is a dualist legal system, which means that international treaty commitments have no binding legal force unless their provisions have been incorporated into domestic law.[47] None of the major UN human rights treaties have been incorporated: courts sometimes refer to their provisions in interpreting statute law or developing the common law, but they do not create any enforceable legal obligations in their own right.[48] At the political level, the UK's obligations under the UN human rights treaty regime are periodically taken into account by parliamentary committees, in particular the Joint Committee on Human Rights. They are also occasionally invoked by campaigning civil society

---

[46] At the time of writing, three individual communications have been transmitted under the Optional Protocol to the CEDAW, and one under the Optional Protocol to the CPRD. None have been declared to be admissible by the relevant expert committees.

[47] See in general, D. Feldman, 'The Internationalization of Public Law and its Impact on the UK', Ch. 5 of this volume.

[48] *R. v Secretary of State for the Home Department, ex parte Brind* [1991] 1 AC 696 (HL).

organizations. However, by and large, they remain marginal to the functioning of the UK's constitutional system.

Having said that, there are recent indications that UN human rights standards may be acquiring more salience within British law and policy debates—notwithstanding their lack of binding force within national law, and their very abstract character.

The requirements of Article 3(1) of the CRC, which provides that '[i]n all actions concerning children . . . the best interests of the child shall be a primary consideration,' have increasingly been taken into account by UK courts in interpreting legislation and applying ECHR rights via the HRA.[49] Judicial references have also been made to other instruments, such as ICESCR, the CPT, and the CPRD, again by way of interpreting statutory provisions and ECHR rights.[50]

The use of UN instruments in this way as an interpretative tool is usually confined to situations where the relevant provisions of domestic legislation are ambiguous, or clearly associated with the specific treaty instrument in question.[51] Furthermore, in *R. (SG) v Secretary of State for Work and Pensions*,[52] the majority of the Supreme Court affirmed the orthodox position that the requirements of the CRC did not generate binding legal obligations as a matter of UK law, as distinct from serving as an interpretative tool in particular contexts. However, three out of the five judges who heard the case were willing to make a finding that the UK had breached its obligations under the CRC as a matter of international law—even if Lord Carnwath took the view that any remedy for such an infringement could only be sought through the political process. Also, Lord Kerr in the minority went so far as to argue that international human rights treaties should be regarded as having a special status within UK law, and be regarded as capable of giving rise to enforceable obligations.[53] This is a highly heterodox position, as the law currently stands. But, in general, recent case-law trends suggest that UK judges may be more willing to take international human rights instruments into account than hitherto—albeit only as interpretative tools to be applied in certain specific circumstances.

At the political level, there are also signs that UN human rights standards may be having more of an impact. Reports criticizing the UK's compliance with ICESCR obligations, issued in 2014 and 2018 by the UN Special Rapporteurs on Housing and Poverty respectively, attracted plenty of media publicity—as well as a strong political backlash.[54] More tangibly, the devolved legislatures in Scotland and Wales have taken steps

---

[49] See e.g. *ZH (Tanzania) v Secretary of State for the Home Department* [2011] UKSC 4; *H (H) v Deputy Prosecutor of the Italian Republic, Genoa (Official Solicitor intervening); H (P) v Same (Same intervening); F-K v Polish Judicial Authority* [2012] UKSC 25, in particular [15], [98], and [155]; *In the matter of an application by Siobhan McLaughlin for Judicial Review (Northern Ireland)*[2018] UKSC 48, [40].

[50] Ibid., [40] (ICESCR); *P v Cheshire West and Chester Council* [2014] UKSC 19, [36] (CPRD); *A v Home Secretary (No 2)* [2005] UKHL 71, [35]–[40].

[51] Ibid., [27].   [52] [2015] UKSC 16.   [53] Ibid., [247]–[257].

[54] See UN Human Rights Council, *Report of Raquel Rolnik, the UN Special Rapporteur on Adequate Housing as a Component of the Right to an Adequate Standard of Living: Mission to the United Kingdom of Great Britain and Northern Ireland*, 30 December 2013, A/HRC/25/54/Add.2Report; UN Office of the High Commissioner for Human Rights (OHCHR), *Statement on Visit to the United Kingdom, by Professor Philip Alston, United Nations Special Rapporteur on Extreme Poverty and Human Rights*, London, 16 November 2018, available at https://www.ohchr.org/Documents/Issues/Poverty/EOM_GB_16Nov2018.pdf (last accessed 16 December 2018).

to incorporate UN standards into domestic law. For example, s. 1 of the Social Security (Scotland) Act 2018 affirms that social security is a 'human right', while the Scottish Commission on Social Security established to monitor the functioning of the devolved social security system is required to have regard to 'any relevant international human rights instruments', including in particular ICESCR.[55] The Welsh Assembly passed the Rights of Children and Young Persons (Wales) Measure 2011, which placed a duty on all Welsh Ministers to have due regard to the substantive rights set out in the CRC in performing their public functions. These measures have limited impact. However, they suggest that the UN human rights instruments may be becoming more than paper guarantees in the UK context.

THE ECHR AND THE COUNCIL OF EUROPE SYSTEM OF RIGHTS PROTECTION

The UK has also ratified a number of human rights treaty instruments, drawn up within the regional framework of the Council of Europe.[56] These include the European Social Charter, the Framework Convention for the Protection of National Minorities and the Istanbul Convention on Preventing and Combating Violence against Women and Domestic Violence. These tend to have limited impact on UK law. The same is not true, however, for the crown jewel in the Council of Europe human rights system—namely the ECHR.

The ECHR was drawn up in 1950 with a view to creating a binding code of human rights protection for the liberal democratic states of Western Europe, covering core civil and political rights such as the right to life, freedom of expression, and the right to a fair trial. The Convention made provision for the establishment of what was at the time a unique judicial body: the European Court of Human Rights, made up of judges from each of the contracting states, which was given the authority to hear individual complaints that a state had breached the provisions of the Convention.[57] All state parties to the Convention—which now include all 47 member states of the Council of Europe—are now required to comply with its judgments by virtue of Article 46 ECHR. The Committee of Ministers of the Council of Europe assume responsibility for monitoring how states are giving effect to their obligations in this regard.

The extensive case-law of the European Court of Human Rights is regularly cited and applied by national courts, and has exerted a considerable influence over how rights are protected across Europe. States are subject to strong diplomatic pressure to respect the authority of the Court, and in general feel compelled to demonstrate their commitment to the rule of law and European democratic values by complying with its judgments.

[55] See ss. 21–22 and Sched. 1 of the Act.

[56] The Council of Europe was established in 1949 to promote respect for rights, democracy, and the rule of law across the continent. It should be distinguished from the European Union (EU): all EU states are members of the Council of Europe, but so too are non-EU states such as Norway, Switzerland, Serbia, Russia and Turkey.

[57] The Court can hear complaints brought by one state against another alleging a breach of Convention rights, and also complaints brought by individuals who satisfy certain restrictive admissibility criteria.

The UK is no exception.[58] The UK was the first country to ratify the Convention in 1951, albeit not without reservations on the part of the then Attlee government who were concerned that it might open up the exercise of executive power to external judicial review.[59] Subsequently, the Wilson government in December 1965 decided to accept the right of individual petition to the Court.[60] This decision made it possible for individuals to seek redress in Strasbourg for alleged violations of their human rights, and did open up the UK legal system to external scrutiny.

The majority of cases that have been brought against the UK since it accepted the Court's jurisdiction have been dismissed.[61] However, there have been almost 300 judgments of the ECtHR which have found the UK to have been in breach of the Convention. Some of these decisions have been politically controversial.[62] Others much less so.[63] Unlike EU law, there is no requirement under the ECHR to ensure that judgments of the Strasbourg Court are given direct effect in national law: as a result, national authorities are not required to comply with decisions of the ECtHR as a matter of *domestic* law. Successive UK governments have nevertheless chosen to comply with their *international* law obligations under the Convention by giving effect to the Court's judgments, even those they publicly criticized.

As a consequence, the Court's jurisprudence has played an important role in enhancing protection for human rights in the UK, for example in the areas of freedom of expression,[64] privacy,[65] freedom from discrimination,[66] freedom from inhuman and degrading treatment,[67] and the right to fair trial.[68]

A major fracture opened up between the ECHR system of rights protection and the UK over the Strasbourg Court's controversial 2005 decision in *Hirst v UK (No. 2)*[69] that the blanket legislative ban on prisoners voting in elections was disproportionate. Successive UK governments refused to implement this judgment by amending this blanket ban,

---

[58] E. Bates, *The Evolution of the European Convention on Human Rights* (Oxford: OUP, 2010); G. Marston, 'The United Kingdom's Part in the Preparation of the ECHR, 1950' (1993) 42(4) *ICLQ* 796–826.

[59] See A.W.B. Simpson, *Human Rights and the End of Empire* (Oxford: OUP, 2001); A. Lester, 'Fundamental Rights: The United Kingdom Isolated?' [1984] *Public Law* 46; A. Lester, 'UK Acceptance of the Strasbourg Jurisdiction: What Went on in Whitehall in 1965?' [1998] *Public Law* 237.

[60] With effect from November 1998, Protocol No. 11 (ratified by all the contracting states, including the UK) amended the Convention to require that all state parties accept the compulsory jurisdiction of the Court.

[61] From 1966 to 2010, approximately 14,460 individual applications to the Court related to the UK, of which the vast majority were declared inadmissible. During this time period, only 1.3% of cases brought against the UK resulted in a finding of a violation. See A. Donald, J. Gordon and P. Leach, *The UK and the European Court of Human Rights*, Equality and Human Rights Commission Research Report No. 83 (London: EHRC, 2012), 30–43.

[62] See e.g. the criticisms expressed of the judgment of *McCann v UK* (1995) 21 EHRR 97 by Jacques Arnold MP, reported at *HC Deb.*, 6th March 1996, vol. 273, cc. 308–16.

[63] See Donald et al., *The UK and the European Court of Human Rights*, 44–86.

[64] See e.g. *Tolstoy v UK* (1995) 20 EHRR 442 (excessive damages in libel actions).

[65] See e.g. *Malone v United Kingdom* (1984) (No.282), 4 EHRR 330 (privacy of telephone communications); *S and Marper v UK* (2009) 48 EHRR 50 (DNA evidence).

[66] *Dudgeon v UK* (1981) 4 EHRR 149 (the criminalization of same-sex acts in Northern Ireland).

[67] *Price v UK* (2002) 34 EHRR 1285 (treatment of a disabled person in prison).

[68] *Golder v UK* (1975) 1 EHRR 524 (access to justice).   [69] (2006) 42 EHRR 41.

citing strong opposition in Parliament as a justification for inaction—despite how this stance threatened to put the UK in breach of its international law obligations under the Convention.[70] Finally, in 2018, administrative measures were taken to ensure that two categories of prisoners previously effectively precluded from voting—those on temporary licence and home detention curfew—were now able to vote. The Committee of Ministers of the Council of Europe chose to interpret this as ensuring compliance with the original *Hirst* judgment, a decision based on a dubiously narrow reading of that judgment.[71]

This saga could be viewed as illustrating the weakness of the Convention system of rights protection: the UK was able to deny compliance, and ultimately to water down the impact of the Court's original judgment. However, it also shows the degree to which European governments feel compelled to maintain conformity with the Convention's requirements. Even in the case of a politically charged issue like prisoner voting, where there was substantial cross-party opposition to changing the law, the UK government felt that establishing formal compliance with its requirements was desirable.

As discussed in the final section of this chapter, this pressure to conform to Strasbourg rulings is controversial. Critics claim that the European Court of Human Rights lacks the 'constitutional legitimacy' to impose its interpretation of the abstract rights set out in the text of the Convention on national parliaments and courts, and also attack what they see as expansionist tendencies within the jurisprudence of the Court. However, defenders of the Court respond by arguing that its 'living tree' jurisprudence has proved to be invaluable in giving substance to the guarantees of abstract rights set out in the Convention, and that the Court's authority can be justified on the basis of the democracy- and rights-enhancing role it plays both within the UK and across the wider continent.[72] Whichever view one adopts of the Court's authority, it is clear that the ECHR plays an important role within the current functioning of the UK constitutional system, which has influenced the development of common law rights, as discussed in the next section, while also being amplified by the provisions of the HRA.

PART THREE: DOMESTIC LEGAL PROTECTION— LEGISLATION, ADMINISTRATIVE LAW AND COMMON LAW RIGHTS

At the level of UK domestic law, legislation bears much of the day-to-day burden in securing basic rights and liberties. Statutes such as the Police and Criminal Evidence Act 1986 (PACE), the Freedom of Information Act 2000 and the Equality Act 2010

---

[70] See the conclusions of the Parliamentary Joint Committee on the Draft Voting Eligibility (Prisoners) Bill, *Report: Draft Voting Eligibility (Prisoners) Bill*, 16 December 2013, available at http://www.publications. parliament.uk/pa/jt201314/jtselect/jtdraftvoting/103/10302.htm (last accessed 1 December 2014).

[71] Committee of Ministers, Resolution CM/ResDH(2018)467, 1331st Session (Human Rights) of the Ministers' Deputies, 6 December 2018.

[72] For an analysis of this debate, see E. Bates, 'British Sovereignty and the European Court of Human Rights' (2012) 128 *LQR* 382–411.

shape the relationship between public authorities and individual citizens, as well as the rights and obligations that private individuals owe each other. For example, the fundamental right to non-discrimination, a staple of international human rights treaties, is effectively secured by the provisions of the Equality Act: the ECHR and HRA tend to play a residual role in this context.[73]

As discussed in Part One of this chapter, the application of administrative law controls by the courts, and the application of the presumption of liberty in interpreting statutes, has also been important in protecting rights. Their impact has largely been indirect: the requirement for public authorities to conform to the principle of legality, respect the dictates of natural justice, and have a rational basis for their actions helps to prevent abuse of power, even if the legal tests in question are not directly focused on rights *per se*.

However, a form of common law rights review has started to take shape in recent decades, which complements the operation of these administrative law controls. Beginning in the early 1990s, the English courts began to identify the existence of certain fundamental constitutional rights which were recognized by the common law, including the right to freedom of expression, the right of access to the courts and lawyers, and the right to equal treatment without discrimination. In so doing, they also started to apply a more intense standard of review where public authorities interfered with these rights in the course of exercising their discretionary powers: the standard, light-touch *Wednesbury* 'rationality' standard gave way to a more pressing 'reasonableness' review.[74] Furthermore, the courts also began to interpret legislation as subject to a presumption that Parliament did not intend to permit public authorities to violate these common law rights, unless the statutory text contained express or clearly implied provisions to that effect.[75]

In the leading case of *Simms*,[76] Lord Hoffmann made it clear that this jurisprudence was based around a substantive understanding of the rule of law:

[T]he principle of legality means that Parliament must squarely confront what it is doing and accept the political cost. Fundamental rights cannot be overridden by general or ambiguous words. This is because there is too great a risk that the full implications of their unqualified meaning may have passed unnoticed in the democratic process. In the absence of express language or necessary implication to the contrary, the courts therefore presume that even the most general words were intended to be subject to the basic rights of the individual.[77]

The development of these common law rights appears to have been heavily influenced by the growing influence exercised by the ECHR over UK law. In declaring the

---

[73] See C. McCrudden, 'Equality and Non-discrimination', in D. Feldman (ed.) *English Public Law* (2nd ed.) (Oxford University Press, 2009), 499–572.

[74] See e.g. *R. v Ministry of Defence, Ex parte Smith* [1996] QB 517; [1996] 1 All ER 257; *R. v Lord Saville of Newdigate, Ex parte A* [1999] 4 All ER 860.

[75] See e.g. *Raymond v Honey* [1983] 1 AC 1; *Secretary of State for the Home Department, Ex p Leech* [1994] QB 198; *R. v Secretary of State for Social Security, Ex parte JCWI* [1996] 4 All ER 385.

[76] *R. v Home Secretary, Ex parte Simms* [2000] 2 AC 115.   [77] [2000] 2 AC 115, 131.

existence of these common law rights, the courts began to cite the case-law of the Strasbourg Court in support of their common law reasoning, thereby emphasizing the shared values that underpinned them both.[78] Thus, in *Attorney-General v Guardian Newspapers Ltd. (No. 2)*, Lord Goff of Chieveley expressed the view that there was in principle no difference between English law on freedom of speech and the provisions of Article 10 of the Convention,[79] while the Strasbourg jurisprudence was regularly cited in many of the cases that followed.[80]

Despite the subsequent enactment of the HRA, this common law rights jurisprudence remains an important element of the British framework of legal rights protection.[81] It can play a particularly significant role in the context of freedom of expression and access to justice, where the case-law is most developed.[82] In *Osborn v Parole Board*,[83] the Supreme Court overturned a refusal by the Parole Board to grant prisoners an oral hearing in respect for their application for release or transfer to open conditions: the Court ruled that the common law duty of procedural fairness, an aspect of the right of access to justice, required that such a hearing be provided in the circumstances at issue. In delivering the judgment of the Court, Lord Reed stated that the enactment of the HRA did not 'supersede the protection of human rights under the common law or statute' and emphasized in particular 'the importance of the continuing development of the common law' in this context.[84]

More recently, in its judgment in *R. (UNISON) v Lord Chancellor*,[85] the Supreme Court struck down the system of tribunal fees that had been imposed by the 2010–2015 Coalition government on the basis that it created a real risk that persons would be effectively prevented from having access to justice—which would in turn infringe the constitutional right of access to the courts. This right of access was described by Lord Reed as 'inherent in the rule of law',[86] and the enabling statutory provisions which gave ministers the power to regulate access to tribunals were interpreted as precluding the use of this power to impose a disproportionately restrictive fee regime in the absence of express parliamentary approval for such a step. Described by Bogg as a 'decision of high constitutional importance',[87] the *UNISON* judgment represents a powerful judicial endorsement of the concept and fundamental character of common law rights.

However, the scope of protection afforded by these common law rights remains unclear. Some judges have adopted a 'common law constitutionalist' perspective, and

---

[78] Lester, 'Human Rights and the British Constitution', 7th ed., 76.   [79] [1990] 1 AC 109, at 283–4.

[80] See e.g. the comments of Lord Keith of Kinkel in *Derbyshire County Council v Times Newspapers Ltd.* [1993] AC 534, at 550H- 551A; Lord Cooke in *R. (Daly) v Secretary of State for the Home Department* [2001] UKHL 26, [30]; Lord President Hope in *T, a Petitioner* 1997 SLT 724.

[81] For detailed analysis, see M. Elliott, 'Beyond the European Convention: Human Rights and the Common Law' (2015) 68 *Current Legal Problems* 85–117.

[82] See e.g. *R. (West) v Parole Board* [2005] UKHL 1; *A v BBC* [2014] UKSC 25; *R. (on the application of Laporte) v Chief Constable of Gloucestershire* [2006] UKHL 55.

[83] *Osborn v The Parole Board* [2013] UKSC 61.   [84] Ibid, [54]–[63].

[85] [2017] UKSC 51.   [86] Ibid, [66].

[87] A. Bogg, 'The Common Law Constitution at Work: *R. (on the application of UNISON) v Lord Chancellor*' (2018) 81(3) *Modern L. Rev.* 509–38.

suggested that the courts might even have the authority to refuse to give effect to parliamentary legislation which nullified the right of access to the courts or otherwise failed to respect 'constitutional fundamentals'.[88] Others have expressed grave reservations about 'judicial law-making' and argued that courts engaged in the protection of common law rights should be very slow to convert 'political questions' into justiciable legal issues.[89]

There also exists no fixed list of common law rights: the case-law defining their scope and content is still at an early stage of development.[90] In *Watkins v Home Office*, Lord Rodger expressed doubts about whether it was possible to identify with precision what constituted a 'constitutional right' within the framework of the common law, in the absence of a written constitution.[91] The scope and substance of common law rights is also often lacking in clear definition, and it is unclear what standard of review should be applied by the courts in assessing whether public authorities are justified in interfering with their enjoyment.[92] Judgments such as *UNISON* have established that common law rights constitute an integral part of the UK's constitutional order: but their efficacy as instruments of rights protection remains uncertain.

PART FOUR: THE HUMAN RIGHTS ACT 1998—PURPOSE AND DESIGN

In contrast to the situation under the common law, the ECHR sets out a clearly defined list of rights which contracting parties have agreed to respect, which is more comprehensive than the narrow scope of protection afforded under the common law.[93] The case-law of the Strasbourg Court is also much more developed than the common law rights jurisprudence of the English courts, due in part to the sheer volume of cases received by the ECtHR. Also, in applying the proportionality test to determine whether state interference with 'qualified rights' such as freedom of expression and freedom of association complied with the Convention, the Strasbourg Court uses a more structured mode of review than the 'reasonableness' or 'anxious scrutiny' standard usually applied by the British courts in similar situations.[94]

---

[88] See e.g. Lord Steyn's comments in *Jackson v Attorney General* [2005] UKHL 56, [102].

[89] See e.g. J. Sumption, 'Judicial and Political Decision-Making: The Uncertain Boundary' (2011) 16(4) *Judicial Review* 301–15.

[90] For example, it is not clear whether there exists a common law right to non-discrimination: see *Association of British Civilian Internees (Far Eastern Region) v Secretary of State for Defence* [2003] EWCA Civ 473, especially paras. 85–6.

[91] [2006] UKHL 17, [58]–[64].

[92] See e.g. the different views expressed by different members of the Supreme Court in *Kennedy v Charity Commissioners* [2014] UKSC 20 as to the scope of the common law principle of access to justice and the standard of review to be applied in cases where it was engaged.

[93] In particular, the common law has not recognized the existence of a right to privacy, in contrast to Article 8 ECHR: see *Wainwright v Home Office* [2003] UKHL 53.

[94] Compare the different standards of review applied by the Court of Appeal in *R. v Ministry of Defence, Ex parte Smith* [1996] QB 517; [1996] 1 All ER 257 to that applied by the European Court of Human Rights in *Smith and Grady v UK* (2000) 29 EHRR 493.

As a consequence, even as the common law rights jurisprudence emerged in the 1990s, litigants continued to trek to Strasbourg looking for redress. This was a slow process, as they had to exhaust domestic remedies first. Furthermore, the Convention had not been incorporated into national law—meaning that a disparity persisted between the UK's international law obligations and the limited and uncertain protection afforded to human rights in national law.

As political momentum in favour of reform built in the 1990s (as discussed in Part One of this chapter), this gap between ECHR and national law standards became viewed as a problem in need of a solution. In 1997, the new Labour Government published a White Paper, *Rights Brought Home*, which made the case for incorporation on the basis that it would make it easier for individuals to 'argue for their rights in the British courts' without incurring the delay and cost of a trip to Strasbourg.[95] The White Paper also argued that incorporation would ensure that 'rights will be brought much more fully into the jurisprudence of the courts throughout the United Kingdom, and their interpretation will thus be far more subtly and powerfully woven into our law'. The White Paper's proposals were subsequently translated into law in the form of the Human Rights Act 1998 (HRA) and associated provisions in the devolution statutes of the same year.

The HRA incorporates the key rights set out in the ECHR into UK law: these 'Convention rights', as defined in Schedule 1 of the Act, are made legally enforceable before the UK courts. The Act thus introduces for the first time a comprehensive form of 'rights review' into the British constitutional system. It has been described as a 'constitutional instrument',[96] and has become an integral element of the UK's unwritten constitution.

THE STRUCTURE OF THE HRA

The Act sets out to strike a delicate constitutional balance: it leaves parliamentary sovereignty intact, while modifying the legal framework that governs how British courts interpret and give effect to primary legislation.[97] The courts are not given the power to set aside parliamentary legislation, unlike the case with directly effective EU law under the European Communities Act 1972 or the national constitutions of many democratic states like the USA, Germany and South Africa. However, the British courts are required to interpret primary and secondary legislation under s. 3 HRA 'as far as possible' so as to maintain conformity with Convention rights. Where that is not possible, specified higher courts are given the power under s. 4 to issue a nonbinding 'declaration of incompatibility', stating that the legislation in question was

---

[95] *Rights Brought Home: The Human Rights Bill*, CM 3782, October 1997.

[96] *R. (HS2 Action Alliance Ltd.) v Secretary of State for Transport* [2014] UKSC 3, [207] *per* Lords Neuberger and Mance.

[97] See in general C. Gearty, *Principles of Human Rights Adjudication* (Oxford: OUP, 2004); T. Hickman, *Public Law after the Human Rights Act* (Oxford: Hart, 2010).

incompatible with the Convention. The grant of such a declaration does not affect the legal validity of the legislation, and Parliament is under no obligation to respond to a declaration of incompatibility. However, this does not prevent a litigant taking a claim to Strasbourg and seeking a determination by the ECtHR that the UK is in breach of the Convention.

Furthermore, the Act was intended to be a 'constitutionally holistic' measure, in the sense that 'each branch of government—the legislative and executive, as well as the judiciary—[was] called upon to use its public powers compatibly with Convention rights'.[98] Section 6(1) HRA thus imposes a duty on all public authorities aside from Parliament[99] to act compatibly with Convention rights (unless required to do otherwise by primary legislation).[100] This in essence creates a new constitutional tort: if a public authority acts or proposes to act in a manner contrary to s. 6(1), the courts are able to grant any victim[101] of this breach of duty such relief or remedy as it considers just and appropriate within the scope of its powers.[102]

Courts fall within this definition of 'public authority' and are therefore subject to the duty to exercise their powers in conformity with Convention rights—including when they develop the common law and construe legislation in the course of deciding cases between private parties.[103] As a consequence, this means that the HRA 'weaves Convention rights into the warp and woof of the common law and statute law',[104] by requiring the courts to ensure that the development of tort law, contract law and other areas of private and public law respects the requirements of the ECHR.

While Convention rights do not bind Parliament, as noted above, the power given to courts under s. 4 HRA to issue declarations of incompatibility is intended to ensure that Parliament engages with issues of potential legislative non-conformity with the Convention rights. Furthermore, s. 10 and Schedule 2 of the Act makes it possible for legislation subject to a declaration of incompatibility to be amended via a fast-track parliamentary procedure. Taken together, these provisions make it possible for Parliament to react quickly to a declaration of incompatibility.

Similarly, the provisions of s. 19 of the Act, which requires the Minister in charge of a Bill before Parliament to make a 'statement of compatibility' before its Second Reading

---

[98] A. Lester, 'Human Rights and the British Constitution', 7th ed., p. 79.

[99] The broad definition of 'public authority' set out in s. 6(3) HRA does not include either of the Houses of Parliament or 'a person exercising functions in connection with proceedings in Parliament'.

[100] See the provisions of s. 6(2) HRA, which link back to the provisions of ss. 3 and 4 of the Act.

[101] S. 7 HRA.

[102] S. 8 of the HRA establishes a discretionary jurisdiction by which English courts can award damages for breaches of incorporated ECHR rights. In applying this provision, the UK courts have elected to mirror the approach of the ECtHR in deciding whether to award damages and setting levels of compensation, rather than adopting an approach based on domestic tort law: see *R. (on the application of Faulkner) v Secretary of State for Justice* [2013] UKSC 23. For critical commentary on this approach, see J. Varuhas, in 'A Tort-Based Approach to Damages under the Human Rights Act 1998' (2009) 72(5) *Modern Law Review* 750–82.

[103] See e.g. *X v Y* (2004) ICR 1634; *Pay v Lancashire Probation Service* [2004] IRLR 129; *Turner v East Midlands Trains Ltd* [2012] EWCA Civ 1470.

[104] Lester, 'Human Rights and the British Constitution', 7th ed., 91.

stating whether or not in her opinion its provisions comply with the Convention, are intended to focus parliamentary attention on any issues of potential incompatibility, as well as encouraging the executive to engage actively with the rights implications of a legislative proposal.

THE FUNCTIONING OF THE HRA

Since coming into force into 2000, the machinery of the Act has by and large functioned according to its purpose.[105] Its provisions have made it easier for individuals to challenge national laws and practice which infringe their rights. Decisions by the UK courts applying Convention rights in line with the HRA framework have, for example, reformed defamation law by extending protection for freedom of speech,[106] enhanced the rights of patients undergoing mental health treatment,[107] granted new rights to unmarried would-be adopters in Northern Ireland,[108] established that persons with caring responsibilities benefit from the protection of the right to non-discrimination set out in Article 14 of the ECHR,[109] and struck down a range of discriminatory measures.[110]

In general, the interaction between courts and Parliament as regulated by the provisions of ss. 3 and 4 HRA has also functioned relatively smoothly, despite the political rhetoric surrounding the Act. Parliament has responded positively to all but one of the declarations of incompatibility issued by British courts under s. 4 HRA by amending the relevant statutory provisions. (The single exception has been the declaration issued in 2007 by the Scottish Registration Appeal Court in *Smith v Scott*[111] following the *Hirst* decision of the Strasbourg Court on the blanket legislative ban on prisoners voting.) The government has sometimes been critical of particular judgments which have resulted in the grant of a declarations of incompatibility, but has nevertheless taken action to remedy the issue of potential non-compliance.[112] Issues of incompatibility have usually been resolved through the enactment of new primary legislation, rather than the use of the special fast-track remedial option—which could be argued to be a good thing, as it enhances democratic transparency.

---

[105] See for a general overview A. Kavanagh, *Constitutional Review under the Human Rights Act* (Cambridge University Press, 2009); T. Hickman, *Public Law after the Human Rights Act* (Oxford: Hart, 2010); S. Gardbaum, 'How Successful and Distinctive is the Human Rights Act? An Expatriate Comparatist's Assessment' (2011) 74 *Modern Law Review* 195–215.

[106] *Jameel v Wall Street Journal* [2006] 4 All ER 1279.

[107] See e.g. *HL v UK* (2005) 40 EHRR 32; *P v Cheshire West and Chester Council* [2014] UKSC 19.

[108] *Re G (Adoption: Unmarried Couple)* [2008] UKHL 38.

[109] *Hurley and others v Secretary of State for Work and Pensions* [2015] EWHC 3382 (Admin).

[110] See e.g. *Mathieson v Secretary of State for Work and Pensions* [2015] UKSC 47; *Steinfeld v SS Education* [2017] EWCA Civ 81; *In the matter of an application by Siobhan McLaughlin for Judicial Review (Northern Ireland)* [2018] UKSC 48.

[111] [2007] CSIH 9.

[112] See also G. Phillipson, 'The Human Rights Act, Dialogue and Constitutional Principles', in R. Masterman and I. Leigh (eds.) *The United Kingdom's Statutory Bill of Rights: Constitutional and Comparative Perspectives* (Oxford: OUP, 2013).

Furthermore, the HRA case-law has helped to inform the work of the Joint Commit-tee on Human Rights and other parliamentary committees. Certain major legislative reforms, including the Mental Health Act 2007, the Coroners and Justice Act 2009 and the Protection of Freedoms Act 2012 were passed partially in response to HRA judgments which identified problems with the justice and fairness of existing law. Suc-cessive governments have engaged with the s. 19 statement of compatibility proce-dure, while the courts have been prepared to give Convention rights 'horizontal effect' through the interpretation of statutes and the development of the common law by, for example, recognizing the existence of a breach of privacy action. [113]

Legal issues have arisen in respect of the definition of public authorities set out in s. 6 HRA, which covers two different categories of public bodies: 'core' and 'hybrid'. Core public bodies are legal entities which are inherently 'public' in character and must act compatibly with Convention rights in discharging all their functions, even those which could be performed by a private body.[114] Hybrid bodies are legal entities 'some of whose functions are of a public nature'.[115] Section 6(5) HRA provides that these bodies are only bound to respect Convention rights when performing these public functions, as distinct from acts of a private nature. The inclusion of both 'core' and 'hybrid' bodies within the definition of public authorities in s. 6 HRA was an attempt to ensure that private bodies providing public services as a result of privatization, contracting-out and the establish-ment of other forms of public/private partnership would be obliged to respect Conven-tion rights when providing these services. However, defining when a legal entity comes within the definition of a public authority for the purposes of s. 6 has proved to be a dif-ficult matter. The public/private line is increasingly blurred and indistinct in practice.[116] Furthermore, the case-law of the UK courts has struggled to provide clear guidance as to when private bodies will be deemed to be performing public functions.[117]

In the case of *Weaver*, the Court of Appeal summarized the factors taken into ac-count by the courts in assessing when a legal entity came within the scope of s. 6, which includes whether a body is publicly funded in carrying out the relevant functions in question, whether it is exercising statutory powers or 'taking the place' of central gov-ernment or local authorities, providing a public service or performing acts of a distinc-tively private character.[118] The Court then proceeded to apply an integrated approach, taking account of all these factors. This judgment promised to bring some degree of

---

[113] *Campbell v MGN* [2004] 2 AC 457; *PJS v News Group Newspapers Ltd* [2016] UKSC 26.

[114] Lord Nicholls in *Parochial Church Council of the Parish of Aston Cantlow and Wilmcote with Billesley, Warwickshire v Wallbank* [2004] 1 AC 546 (hereafter *Aston Cantlow*), [7], listed government departments, lo-cal authorities, the police and armed forces as examples of core public authorities.

[115] *Aston Cantlow*, [35] *per* Lord Hope.

[116] To complicate the situation, if a legal entity is classified as a core public authority, it may be unable to qualify as a 'victim' of a Convention breach according to the case-law of the ECtHR. See Lord Nicholls in *Aston Cantlow* at [8].

[117] See *Poplar Housing and Regeneration Community Association Ltd v Donoghue* [2001] EWCA Civ 595; [2001] 3 WLR 183; *R. (on the application of Heather) v Leonard Cheshire Foundation* [2002] EWCA Civ 366; *YL v Birmingham CC* [2007] UKHL 27; *Aston Cantlow*, above.

[118] *R. (Weaver) v London & Quadrant Housing Trust* [2009] EWCA Civ 587.

clarity to what had been a very uncertain area of case-law. However, as Williams has argued, the 'multi-factorial approach' adopted in *Weaver* has, as applied in subsequent cases, been 'a poor friend to the important legal values of certainty and predictability'.[119]

This aspect of the HRA jurisprudence also continues to attract some criticism on the basis that it has generally adopted a relatively restrictive approach to the definition of public authorities.[120] Section 145 of the Health and Social Care Act 2008 now provides that the provision of nursing care and accommodation in a care home which is paid for by a public authority will qualify as a public function: this reverses the immediate effect of the controversial Supreme Court decision in the *YL* case which had adopted a narrower interpretation of the scope of s. 6 HRA.

PART FIVE: THE CONSTITUTIONAL DIMENSION OF THE HRA—ISSUES AND UNCERTAINTIES

Issues have also arisen as to how the HRA's provisions should be interpreted and applied within the general constitutional framework of UK law. Some of these issues have mainly concerned the relationship between the UK courts and the ECtHR, on the one hand, and the relationship between the courts and Parliament, on the other. Questions have also arisen as to when the courts should defer to decisions of other branches of government when determining whether Convention rights have been breached.

THE MIRROR PRINCIPLE

The first set of issues relates to the relationship between UK courts and the ECtHR in Strasbourg, and in particular the nature of the requirement set out in s. 2 HRA that British courts should 'take into account' Strasbourg jurisprudence. This wording makes it clear that UK courts are not bound to treat ECtHR judgments as binding precedents when interpreting and applying Convention rights. However, in the early case of *Alconbury*, the House of Lords indicated that, while the ECtHR's case law was not binding in a strict sense, the courts should, in the absence of some special circumstances, follow any clear and constant jurisprudence of the Strasbourg Court.[121] In the subsequent case of *Ullah* in 2004, Lord Bingham expanded on this approach:

> the Convention is an international instrument, the correct interpretation of which can be authoritatively expounded only by the Strasbourg court . . . [I]t follows that a national

---

[119] A. Williams, 'Public Authorities and the HRA 1998: Recent Trends' (2017) 22(3) *Judicial Review* 247–262.

[120] See e.g. JCHR, *The Meaning of Public Authority under the HRA*, 9th Report of Session 2006/07, HL Paper 77/HC 410; C. Donnelly, 'Leonard Cheshire Again' [2005] *Public Law* 785; J. Landau, 'Functional Public Authorities after YL' [2007] *Public Law* 630.

[121] R. (*Alconbury Developments Ltd*) v *Secretary of State for the Environment, Transport and the Regions* [2001] UKHL 23, [26], *per* Lord Slynn.

court subject to a duty such as that imposed by section 2 should not without strong reason
dilute or weaken the effect of the Strasbourg case law . . . The duty of national courts is to
keep pace with the Strasbourg jurisprudence as it evolves over time: no more, but certainly
no less.[122]

This 'mirror principle' initially exerted a considerable degree of influence over the development of the HRA case-law.[123] However, it also attracted plenty of academic and
judicial criticism, on the basis that it prevented British judges developing their own
'native' approach to the interpretation of Convention rights.[124] For example, Lord Kerr
argued in 2012 that British judges are under a duty to develop their own interpretation
of Convention rights, rather than acting as a 'modest underworker of Strasbourg'. He
also suggested that this would make it possible for UK courts to develop a meaningful
judicial dialogue with Strasbourg as to how Convention rights should be interpreted
and applied in the context of UK law, which could benefit both national jurisprudence
and the case-law of the ECtHR.[125]

These criticisms of the mirror principle appear to have resonated with the British
courts. Writing in 2013, Masterman identified a number of circumstances where the
courts have shown a willingness to depart from the Strasbourg case-law, of which the
following are the most significant:[126]

(i)   when the application of the mirror principle would compel a conclusion which
       would be 'fundamentally at odds' with the UK's constitutional system of sepa-
       ration of powers or some other fundamental procedural or substantive aspect
       of UK law;[127]

(ii)   when it is 'reasonably foreseeable' that the Strasbourg Court would now come
       to a different conclusion than in the available authorities;[128]

(iii) when the UK courts wish to enter into a 'dialogue' with the European Court
       of Human Rights, on the basis that existing Strasbourg case-law may be de-
       fective or difficult to apply in the context of the UK legal system—as demon-

---

[122]   *R. v Special Adjudicator, ex parte Ullah* [2004] UKHL 26, [20].

[123]   See e.g. *Secretary of State for the Home Department v AF (No 3)* [2009] UKHL 28, where Lord Rodger
commented at [98] as follows: '[e]ven though we are dealing with rights under a United Kingdom statute, in
reality we have no choice. *Argentoratum locutum, iudicium finitum*—Strasbourg has spoken, the case is closed.'
See also e.g. *Ambrose v Harris (Procurator Fiscal, Oban) (Scotland)* [2011] UKSC 43.

[124]   See e.g. Lord Irving, 'A British Interpretation of Convention Rights' [2012] *Public Law* 237. For a contrary view, see P. Sales, 'Strasbourg Jurisprudence and the Human Rights Act: A Response to Lord Irvine'
[2012] *Public Law* 253–267.

[125]   Lord Kerr, 'The UK Supreme Court: The Modest Underworker of Strasbourg?', Clifford Chance Lecture,
25 January 2012, text available at https://www.supremecourt.uk/docs/speech_120125.pdf. See also his dissent in *Ambrose*, at [126]; Lady Hale, '*Argentoratum Locutum*: Is Strasbourg or the Supreme Court Supreme?'
(2012) 12(1) *Human Rights Law Review* 65–78.

[126]   R. Masterman, 'The Mirror Crack'd', *UK Constitutional Law Blog*, 13 February 2013, available at http://
ukconstitutionallaw.org/2013/02/13/roger-masterman-the-mirror-crackd/ (last accessed 1 December 2014).

[127]   *Manchester City Council v Pinnock* [2010] UKSC 45, [48] *per* Lord Neuberger.

[128]   *R. (Quila) v Secretary of State for the Home Department*, at [43] *per* Lord Wilson.

strated in the case of *R. v Horncastle*[129] when the Supreme Court refused to follow a judgment of a Chamber of the ECtHR on the admissibility of hearsay evidence;

(iv) when the Strasbourg Court views an issue as coming within the 'margin of appreciation' left to signatory states, i.e. as involving an issue of rights interpretation that should be left to be resolved by national authorities in the absence of a general pan-European consensus on the relevant values to be taken into account in defining the scope and substance of the right at issue. In such a situation, the UK courts will interpret the relevant Convention rights in a manner that is appropriate in light of the specifics of the UK's constitutional system, as held by the Supreme Court in the cases of *In re G (Adoption: Unmarried Couple)*[130] and *Nicklinson*;[131]

(v) when 'special circumstances' or a 'good reason' otherwise exist for departing from the Strasbourg jurisprudence.[132]

As the width of these exceptions suggest, it is clear that the UK courts now no longer regard themselves as bound by the mirror principle—as effectively confirmed by the Supreme Court in *Commissioner of Police of the Metropolis v DSD*.[133] A clear and consistent line of settled Strasbourg jurisprudence will generally be followed,[134] but even this rule of thumb is not absolute.[135] In response, the Strasbourg Court has shown a willingness to look again at its previous judgments and to engage with alternative interpretations of Convention rights put forward by the UK courts.[136] British courts have also shown some readiness to develop their own interpretation of Convention rights in situations where the Strasbourg jurisprudence is under-developed, especially where a particular conclusion could be said to 'flow naturally' from the existing ECtHR case-law.[137]

This shift away from a rigid application of the mirror principle may reflect a more fundamental change in how the courts view the purpose and function of the HRA. In *Ullah*, Lord Bingham made it clear that he regarded the HRA as an instrument designed to ensure more effective compliance by the UK with its international law

---

[129] [2009] UKSC14.   [130] [2008] UKHL 38.   [131] *R. (Nicklinson) v DPP* [2014] UKSC 38.

[132] *R. (Alconbury Developments Ltd) v Secretary of State for the Environment, Transport and the Regions* [2001] UKHL 23, [26], *per* Lord Slynn.

[133] [2018] UKSC 11.

[134] See e.g. *Manchester City Council v Pinnock* [2010] UKSC 45.

[135] *Poshteh v Royal Borough of Kensington and Chelsea* [2017] UKSC 36.

[136] See e.g. *Al-Khawaja and Tahery v UK*, Application nos. 26766/05 and 22228/06 [GC], Judgment of 15 December 2011 (responding to the judgment in *R. v Horncastle*). See also N. Bratza, 'The Relationship Between the UK Courts and Strasbourg' (2011) *European Human Rights Law Review* 505–12; M. Amos, 'The Dialogue between United Kingdom Courts and the European Court of Human Rights' (2012) *International and Comparative Law Quarterly* 557–84.

[137] As noted by Lord Brown in *Rabone v Pennine Care NHS Foundation* [2012] UKSC 2, [112].

obligations under the ECHR.[138] In contrast, many critics of the mirror principle tend to view the HRA as a functional equivalent of a domestic bill of rights, which was intended to allow the UK judges to develop their own approach to interpreting and applying human rights standards. There are arguments to be made in favour of both approaches. However, at present, judicial and academic opinion appears to be favouring the second approach.

THE RELATIONSHIP BETWEEN SECTIONS 3 AND 4 HRA

The relationship between the interpretation obligation set out in s. 3 HRA and the power conferred on courts to grant a declaration of incompatibility under s. 4 HRA has also generated a degree of controversy. Many judges and academic commentators have discussed the potential of 'democratic dialogue' between the courts, government and Parliament, which would involve the different branches of government interacting in a constructive manner to resolve issues of non-conformity with Convention rights.[139] However, how this dialogue should be structured through the interaction of ss. 3 and 4 of the Act remains a matter of debate.

As discussed above, s. 3 requires the courts to interpret legislation 'as far as possible' so as to comply with Convention rights. This requires the courts to recalibrate their standard approach to interpreting statutes, which is primarily focused on giving effect to the intent or purpose of Parliament, and to give legislation a rights-friendly interpretation where 'possible'. However, s. 3 provides no real guidance as to how far the courts can stretch the meaning of a legislative text so as to achieve a rights-compliant interpretation. An excessively cautious approach in this respect risks unduly narrowing the scope of legal rights protection on offer under the HRA. But if judges go too far in re-writing legislation they risk trespassing on the domain of elected legislators.[140]

Some leading academic commentators have argued that s. 3 should be read as giving judges wide interpretative latitude. For example, Aileen Kavanagh has suggested that it is only if an innovative, rights-compliant interpretation is 'so radical and wide-ranging, so beyond the typical expertise of the judicial body, that it deserves the label of "legislation"'.[141] Others have argued for a more restrained approach to the use of the s. 3

---

[138] See A. L. Young, *Democratic Dialogue and the Constitution* (Oxford: OUP, 2017). Developing a similar line of analysis, Aileen Kavanagh has argued that courts should be viewed as engaged in a 'collaborative' project with the other branches of government in advancing common legal goals: see A. Kavanagh, *Constitutional Review under the Human Rights Act* (Cambridge University Press, 2009).

[139] See e.g. T. Hickman, 'Constitutional Dialogue, Constitutional Theories and the Human Rights Act 1998' [2005] *Public Law* 306; A. Young, *Parliamentary Sovereignty and the Human Rights Act* (Oxford: Hart, 2008).

[140] I. Leigh and R. Masterman, *Making Rights Real: the Human Rights Act in its First Decade* (Oxford: Hart, 2008), Ch. 5.

[141] A. Kavanagh, 'The elusive divide between interpretation and legislation under the Human Rights Act 1998' (2004) 24(2) *OJLS* 259–285, 285. See also A.L. Young, *Parliamentary Sovereignty and the Human Rights Act* (Oxford: Hart, 2009), Chs. 5, 6 and 8.

interpretative power:[142] in their view, Parliament is often better placed than the courts to decide how to respond to potential rights violations.[143]

The courts have, by and large, adopted an expansive interpretative approach under s. 3 HRA. However, they have also recognized that this interpretative power is limited, and that it does not permit a radical re-writing of statutory text.

In the early case of *R. v A (No. 2)*,[144] the House of Lords read words into s. 41 of the Youth Justice and Criminal Evidence Act 1999 so as to make it possible for evidence to be introduced as to the previous sexual history between the defendant and the victim in sexual offence trials where necessary to ensure compliance with the accused's right to a fair trial under Article 6 ECHR. Lord Steyn argued that it may be necessary under s. 3 to 'adopt an interpretation which linguistically may appear strained' and that a declaration of incompatibility was a 'measure of last resort'.[145] In contrast, in the subsequent case of *In re S (Minors)*,[146] Lord Nicholls stated that 'a meaning which departs substantially from a fundamental feature of an Act of Parliament is likely to have crossed the boundary between interpretation and amendment. This is especially so where the departure has important practical repercussions which the court is not equipped to evaluate.' [147]

Subsequently, in the key case of *Ghaidan v Godin-Mendoza*, the House of Lords interpreted the word 'spouse' in the Rent Act 1977 to include unmarried homosexual partners. Lord Steyn emphasized that s. 3 required the courts to adopt a 'broad approach concentrating, amongst other things, in a purposive way on the importance of the fundamental right involved'.[148] Lord Nicholls was a little more restrained in his analysis of the scope of s. 3:

> [T]he mere fact the language under consideration is inconsistent with a Convention-compliant meaning does not of itself make a Convention-compliant interpretation under s. 3 impossible. Section 3 enables language to be interpreted restrictively or expansively . . . [However] the meaning imported by application of section 3 must be compatible with the underlying thrust of the legislation being construed. Words implied must, in the phrase of my noble and learned friend Lord Rodger of Earlsferry, 'go with the grain of the legislation'.[149]

Subsequently, Lord Bingham in *Sheldrake v Director of Public Prosecutions* took the view that s. 3 should not be used to read legislation in a manner which 'would be incompatible with the underlying thrust of the legislation, or would not go with the grain of it, or would call for legislative deliberation, or would change the substance of a provision completely, or would remove its pith and substance, or would violate a cardinal

---

[142] See e.g. P. Sales and R. Ekins, 'Rights-Consistent Interpretation and the Human Rights Act 1998' (2011) 127 *LQR* 217–38.

[143] R. Bellamy, 'Political Constitutionalism and the Human Rights Act' (2011) 9(1) *International Journal of Constitutional Law* 86–111; D. Nicol, 'Law and Politics after the Human Rights Act' [2006] *Public Law* 722.

[144] [2001] UKHL 25.   [145] Ibid., [12]–[13].

[146] *In Re S (Minors) (Care Order: Implementation of Care Plan)* [2002] UKHL 10.   [147] Ibid., [39].

[148] *Ghaidan v Mendoza* [2004] UKHL 30, [41].   [149] Ibid., [32]–[33].

principle of the legislation'.[150] However, as confirmed by the majority of the Supreme Court in *GC v The Commissioner of Police of the Metropolis*[151] if a rights-friendly s. 3 interpretation of legislation was not incompatible with the presumed intention of Parliament in enacting the relevant statute or its text, then only 'exceptionally cogent' factors would justify a refusal to apply such an interpretation.[152]

If legislation cannot be given a rights-compliant interpretation under s. 3, then the courts may grant a declaration of incompatibility under s. 4.[153] In two high-profile cases, *Chester* and *Nicklinson*, the Supreme Court emphasized the discretionary nature of the s. 4 power to grant a declaration of incompatibility. In *Chester*, the Court did not grant a declaration to an individual whose own rights had not been violated, other than by being subject to a law which might violate the rights of others.[154] In *Nicklinson*, the majority of the Court elected not to grant a declaration of incompatibility on the basis that the legal issue in question—assisted suicide—was a particularly difficult, controversial and sensitive issue to which Parliament was giving active consideration: Lady Hale and Lord Kerr dissented strongly on this point.[155]

The potential problem with this line of reasoning is that it opens the way for breaches of Convention rights to be denied any remedy, even a declaration of incompatibility, solely on the basis that the issue in question is politically sensitive or a subject of political debate. This was recognized in *Steinfeld*, where the Supreme Court concluded that the prohibition on opposite-sex couples entering into a civil partnership violated Article 14 ECHR, and proceeded to make a declaration of incompatibility.[156] In delivering the judgment of the Court, Lord Kerr rejected the Court of Appeal's conclusion that it would not be appropriate to grant a declaration, on the basis that the issue of opposite sex partnership rights raised complex policy issues and was under consideration by the government: he considered that there no basis for such 'reticence' in the circumstances of this case.

Another twist to the s. 4 HRA tale was added in the *Northern Ireland Human Commission* case, which involved a judicial review challenge to the part-criminalization of abortion in Northern Ireland.[157] A majority of the Supreme Court concluded that the Northern Irish law contravened Article 8 ECHR on the basis that it prohibited abortion in cases of fatal foetal abnormality and in cases of pregnancy as a result of rape or incest. However, a differently composed majority of the Court also held that the applicant, the Northern Irish Human Rights Commission, lacked standing to bring the claim—and thus concluded that no declaration of incompatibility should be issued, on the basis that such a declaration could only be issued if a properly initiated legal claim

---

[150] [2004] UKHL 43, [28].   [151] [2011] UKSC 21.   [152] Ibid., [56] *per* Lord Phillips.
[153] See e.g. *Bellinger v Bellinger* [2003] 2 AC 467.
[154] *R. (Chester) v Secretary of State for Justice* [2013] UKSC 63.
[155] *R. (Nicklinson) v Ministry of Justice* [2014] UKSC 38.
[156] *R. (Steinfeld and Keiden) v Secretary of State for International Development* [2018] UKSC 32.
[157] *In the Matter of an Application by the Northern Ireland Commission for Judicial Review (Northern Ireland)* [2018] UKSC 27.

was before the court. As with *Chester* and *Nicklinson*, this outcome creates a situation where legislation has effectively been found to be incompatible with ECHR rights but no declaration has been issued—which could be viewed as generating unnecessary ambiguity, and as inviting further litigation.

DEFERENCE, RESPECT AND PROPORTIONALITY

The question of how courts should interact with the executive and legislative branches again arises in relation to the interpretation and application of Convention rights, in particular when courts are called upon to determine whether government interference with 'qualified rights', such as freedom of expression and association, can be objectively justified.[158] Space prevents a detailed analysis of the HRA and ECtHR case-law in this respect. However, in general, interference with a qualified Convention right will only be objectively justified if it is prescribed by law and 'necessary in a democratic society', i.e. if it satisfies the proportionality test set out in general terms by the Strasbourg Court and developed in further detail by the HRA case-law of the UK courts. Lord Neuberger summarized this test in *Nicklinson*:[159]

(a)   is the legislative objective sufficiently important to justify limiting a fundamental right?

(b)   are the measures which have been designed to meet it rationally connected to it?

(c)   are they no more than are necessary to accomplish it? and

(d)   do they strike a fair balance between the rights of the individual and the interests of the community?

In determining whether this test is satisfied, the British courts have emphasized the need to respect the democratic legitimacy of Parliament and the overall structure of the constitutional system of the separation of powers, as well as the expertise of other branches of government.[160] In respecting separation of powers, the courts should give due weight to the determination of the relevant issues adopted by the primary decision-maker.[161] The courts should also respect the institutional limits of their expertise.[162]

However, in the words of Lord Neuberger, 'the court has a duty to decide for itself whether the decision strikes a fair balance between the rights of an individual or individuals and the interests of the community as a whole'.[163] Lord Bingham in his leading judgment in the seminal case of *A v Secretary of State for the Home Department* (the

---

[158]   Interference with 'absolute rights', such as right to life or freedom from torture, cannot be justified under the ECHR system of rights protection: see *Chalal v UK* (1999) 23 EHRR 413.

[159]   *R. (Nicklinson) v Ministry of Justice* [2014] UKSC 38, [80].

[160]   *R. (Animal Defenders International) v Secretary of State for Culture, Media and Sport* [2008] UKHL 15.

[161]   [2014] UKSC 38, [296] *per* Lord Reed.

[162]   See in general the majority opinions in *R. (Carlile) v Secretary of State for the Home Department* [2014] UKSC 60; however, note by way of contrast, Lord Kerr's dissenting judgment in the same case.

[163]   Ibid., [57]. See also *Nicklinson* [2014] UKSC 38, [100].

'Belmarsh' case)[164] affirmed that the HRA had conferred a distinct constitutional role on the courts, including the responsibility of delineating the scope of legal protection afforded to Convention rights:

> It is of course true that the judges in this country are not elected and are not answerable to Parliament. It is also of course true . . . that Parliament, the executive and the courts have different functions. But the function of independent judges charged to interpret and apply the law is universally recognized as a cardinal feature of the modern democratic state, a cornerstone of the rule of law itself . . . The 1998 Act gives the courts a very specific, wholly democratic, mandate. As Professor Jowell has put it 'The courts are charged by Parliament with delineating the boundaries of a rights-based democracy' ('Judicial Deference: Servility, Civility or Institutional Capacity?' [2003] *Public Law* 592, 597)'.[165]

In *Nicklinson*, Lord Neuberger emphasized that factors such as relative institutional competence, the 'familiarity and confidence' of judges with the subject matter of the case, and the extent of the interference with the right in question would play a key role in marking out the areas where the courts would be prepared to subject the decisions of other branches of government to close and exacting scrutiny.[166] In his minority judgment in *Bank Mellat (No. 2)*, Lord Reed similarly emphasized the importance of context, the nature of the right at stake and the context in which the interference occurs.[167]

Some judges have suggested that the courts should adopt a broadly deferential approach in HRA cases towards legislative decisions relating to controversial and contested areas of law and policy.[168] However, the majority of the Supreme Court in cases such as *Nicklinson* and *Carlile* were reluctant to endorse this argument. So too were the majority in the *Northern Irish Human Rights Commission* case, who emphasized the specific rights-protective role that had been allocated to the courts by the HRA.[169] Indeed, Baroness Hale suggested that, when it came to the protection of fundamental rights, 'courts may be thought better qualified' than legislatures in some respects due to their ability to 'weigh the evidence, the legal materials, and the arguments in a dispassionate manner, without the external pressures to which legislatures may be subject'.[170] Notably, however, in the same case, Lord Reed cautioned about the dangers of 'preempting democratic debate' and the need for courts to 'respect the importance of political accountability'.[171] The question of how to strike a workable balance between these competing considerations is inherently difficult—and may be impossible to resolve at the abstract level, as distinct from the concrete context of a specific legal claim.[172]

---

[164] *A v Secretary of State for the Home Department* [2004] UKHL 56.   [165] Ibid, [37]–[42].

[166] [2014] UKSC 38, [106]. See also Lord Mance at [166].

[167] *Bank Mellat v HM Treasury (No 2)* [2013] UKSC 39, [68]–[76].

[168] See in particular the judgment of Lord Sumption in *Nicklinson* [2014] UKSC 38, [232].

[169] [2018] UKSC 27.   [170] Ibid, [38].   [171] Ibid, [344].

[172] For a sample of the voluminous academic commentary on the issue of 'deference', see e.g. T.R.S. Allan, 'Human Rights and Judicial Review: A Critique of "Due Deference"' (2006) 65(3) *Cambridge LJ* 671–95; A. Kavanagh, 'Defending Deference in Public Law and Constitutional Theory' (2010) 126 *Law Quarterly Review* 222–50; T. Hickman, *Public Law after the Human Rights Act* (Oxford: Hart, 2010), 128–72; A. Young, 'Will You, Won't You, Will You Join the Deference Dance?' (2014) 34(2) *OJLS* 375–94.

PART SIX: THE CHANGING CONTEXT—DEMANDS FOR REFORM, BREXIT AND THE CONTESTED STATUS OF UK HUMAN RIGHTS LAW

THE HRA DEBATE

These issues arising under the HRA as to how to reconcile judicial protection of rights with respect for democratic decision-making inevitably arise in the context of human rights law. Instruments such as the HRA, by giving judges the power to overturn public authority decisions which are deemed to violate rights, inevitably impose constraints on the freedom of action of those public authorities. These constraints can be extensive: even though only civil and political rights are protected by the ECHR, their scope still ranges from the protection of private, family and home life (Article 8), to freedom of association (Article 11) and even to the right to property (Article 1 of the First Protocol).

Furthermore, as noted in the introduction to this chapter, rights are abstract concepts: everyone might agree that, for example, free speech is a good thing, but sharp disagreement often exists as to what respect for that particular right entails in practice. Under the HRA, courts have to interpret abstract rights guarantees, albeit while 'taking account' of the well-established jurisprudence of the Strasbourg Court, and then determine whether they have been unjustifiably infringed. This inevitably requires them to engage in a degree of creative interpretation, and to enter policy areas where they may lack obvious expertise.

Given all this, it is not surprising that the HRA has been a source of controversy. Politicians have criticized the way in which the Act has limited their freedom of action, in particular in areas such as migration control and national security.[173] Academics have expressed concern about its potential to place undue limits on political accountability.[174] A media narrative has developed which portrays human rights adjudication as being excessively concerned with the rights of minorities at the expense of the public interest.[175]

The HRA is not alone in generating these issues. Similar concerns can arise in respect of the functioning of administrative law controls, especially when it comes to common law rights. The latter are judicial creations, rather than the product of statute. As such, from a democratic perspective, they could arguably be viewed as potentially more problematic than the HRA. However, common law rights tend to be viewed as arising organically from the UK's native constitutional tradition—whereas the HRA is attacked for the link it establishes between UK law and the 'alien' jurisprudence of the

---

[173] See e.g. BBC News Online, 'Theresa May Under Fire Over Deportation Cat Claim', 4 October 2011, available at http://www.bbc.co.uk/news/uk-politics-15160326 (last accessed 20 June 2012).

[174] See e.g. R. Ekins, 'Human Rights and the Separation of Powers' (2015) 33 *University of Queensland Law Journal* 217.

[175] See in general A. Donald, J. Gordon, and P. Leach, *The UK and the European Court of Human Rights*, Equality and Human Rights Commission Research Report No. 83 (London: EHRC, 2012).

European Court of Human Rights. In the eyes of its critics, as discussed above in Part Three, the Strasbourg Court as a supranational body lacks the legitimacy to set standards which have *de facto* binding force in the UK.[176] For Eurosceptics in particular, it represents another intrusion upon the democratic sovereignty of the UK.

As a consequence, the HRA has been subject to sustained criticism from certain quarters. Some argue that Convention rights should be de-incorporated and that the UK should revert back to relying solely on the common law to protect rights.[177] Others would prefer that Convention rights be removed from UK law and replaced with new 'home-grown' standards set out in a Bill of Rights, and/or that the UK courts be freed from any obligation to take the case-law of the Strasbourg Court into account when deciding human rights cases.[178] For example, the latter proposal was advanced by a policy document published by the Conservative Party in 2014, calling for the HRA to be repealed and replaced by a new British Bill of Rights and Responsibilities.[179] Following this, the Conservative party manifesto in 2015 called for a new Bill of Rights which would make UK courts 'supreme' again: this somewhat Delphic wording was presumably designed to imply some revision of s. 2 HRA to dilute any obligation to 'take into account' the Strasbourg case-law.

However, as mentioned in Part One, these attacks on the HRA have been met with stiff resistance. To start with, reform proposals have been greeted with scepticism, in particular because of how they appear to dilute key human rights principles: for example, the 2014 Conservative Party policy paper suggested that non-nationals should enjoy a lower standard of rights protection.[180] Concern has also been expressed at how a repeal of the HRA and/or attempts to weaken the influence of the Strasbourg Court might harm human rights protection across Europe, at a time when the value of such protection is arguably becoming more apparent with the roll-back of rights protection in countries such as Hungary and Poland.[181]

Furthermore, any attempt to amend or repeal the HRA, and in particular to de-incorporate the Convention rights from UK law, will give rise to serious legal and political complications. Given that almost all existing UK human rights law, including the case-law on common law rights, is heavily influenced by the Strasbourg jurisprudence, any de-incorporation of Convention rights would generate considerable legal

---

[176] Lord Hoffmann, 'The Universality of Human Rights' (2009) 125 *LQR* 416.

[177] Society of Conservative Lawyers, *Response to the Commission on a Bill of Rights Consultation*, written by Lord Faulks, Andrew Warnock and Simon Murray, 21 October 2011.

[178] See e.g. M. Pinto-Duschinsky, *Bring Rights Back Home: Making Human Rights Compatible with Parliamentary Democracy in the UK* (London: Policy Exchange, 2011).

[179] Conservative Party, *Protecting Human Rights in the UK*, October 2014, available at https://www.conservatives.com/~/media/Files/Downloadable%20Files/HUMAN_RIGHTS.pdf (last accessed 1 December 2018).

[180] For commentary, see Mark Elliott's views at http://publiclawforeveryone.com/2014/10/03/my-analysis-of-the-conservative-partys-proposals-for-a-british-bill-of-rights, and Alison Young's analysis at http://ukconstitutionallaw.org/2014/10/07/alison-young-hra-howlers-the-conservative-party-and-reform-of-the-human-rights-act-1998 (last accessed 1 December 2014).

[181] Loose talk of a UK withdrawal may already have caused damage to the status and standing of the Court and the Convention in Eastern Europe: see Donald et al., *The UK and the European Court of Human Rights*, 145–8, 174–7.

uncertainty: the status of any or all of these precedents would be called into question, which might open the door to fresh waves of litigation.[182]

Furthermore, as discussed above, the Northern Ireland Act 1998, the Scotland Act 1998 and the Government of Wales Act 1998 all require the devolved legislatures to comply with Convention rights. As a result, any amendment or repeal of the HRA would either have to leave these requirements intact, creating a seriously complex legal regime containing overlapping and potentially conflicting rights standards, or else would involve a revision of the devolved settlement which could generate a degree of constitutional turmoil.[183] There is also the issue of the Belfast Agreement: again, as outlined in Part One, ECHR compliance is a key 'safeguard' of the Agreement, meaning that any attempt to shake off the influence of Strasbourg risks breaching the provisions of the Agreement.

But objections to proposed changes to the HRA are not just based on prudential considerations. Many commentators have argued that the ECHR and HRA taken together have enhanced the quality of British democratic life, by making public authorities more accountable and opening up avenues for marginalized groups to contest decisions which have a disproportionate effect on them. The ECHR and HRA taken together have also infused rights-based values into the development of UK public and private law, filling a normative gap that had existed previously and helping to promote greater self-critique.

Furthermore, this has been achieved without sacrificing a democratic 'final say': Parliament still retains the authority to modify or disregard any judicial finding regarding rights protection, even if this is hemmed in by political pressures to respect the requirements of the ECHR and the dictates of international human rights law more generally. Indeed, good arguments can be made that the ECHR and HRA taken together help to enrich political debate, by foregrounding rights considerations in a way that opens up space for parliamentary committees such as the Joint Committee on Human Rights and public bodies such as the Equality and Human Rights Commission to influence wider public debates.[184]

In general, it appears as if the social and political dynamics that lead to the HRA becoming law in 1998 are still in play. The HRA, in tandem with common law rights, the influence of the ECHR, and international human rights law more generally is widely viewed as enhancing British democracy. No consensus currently exists as to its status, or to the place of human rights law more generally within the UK constitutional system. But, for now, it remains one of the cornerstones of what Vernon Bogdanor has

---

[182] See in general M. Amos, 'Problems with the Human Rights Act and How to Remedy Them: Is a Bill of Rights the Answer?' (2009) 72 *Modern Law Review* 883–908; H. Fenwick, 'The Human Rights Act or a British Bill of Rights: Creating a Down-Grading Recalibration of Rights Against the Counter-Terror Backdrop?' [2012] *Public Law* 468–90.

[183] C. O'Cinneide, 'Human Rights, Devolution and the Constrained Authority of the Westminster Parliament, *UK Constitutional Law Blog*, http://ukconstitutionallaw.org/2013/03/04/colm-ocinneide-human-rights-devolution-and-the-constrained-authority-of-the-westminster-parliament/ (last accessed 1 December 2018).

[184] D. Feldman, 'Parliamentary Scrutiny of Legislation and Human Rights' [2002] *Public Law* 323–48.

described as the new UK constitutional order, whereby the exercise of political and bureaucratic power is subject to substantive constraints linked to the concept of the rule of law and the desirability of protecting individual rights.[185]

THE IMPACT OF BREXIT

Will Brexit change this situation? (Presuming it goes ahead: this is being written in mid-December 2018, at a time when the political dynamics surrounding Brexit have become highly unstable.)

It will certainly remove one layer of rights protection from UK law. EU primary and secondary legislation has played an important role in securing certain categories of human rights, in particular equality and non-discrimination rights, privacy rights (via data protection law) and the family rights of migrants.[186] The supremacy and direct effect of EU law insulates these standards from interference or dilution by UK public authorities—meaning that, for example, UK law must conform to the requirements of the EU equality directives as well as the equal pay provisions of Article 157 TFEU. However, even though the EU (Withdrawal) Act currently provides that these standards will remain part of UK law after the Brexit process is complete, they will no longer enjoy this insulation from revision or repeal.[187]

Furthermore, at present, all EU law and national implementing measures must conform to (i) the general principles of EU law, which include respect for the fundamental rights protected by the ECHR or common to national constitutional traditions, and to (ii) the wide-ranging requirements of the EU Charter of Fundamental Rights. But the EU Withdrawal Act provides that, after the Brexit process is complete, it will not be possible to ground a claim on the general principles—while the Charter will be the only element of EU law not carried over into UK law.[188]

It remains to be seen what substantive impact this removal of the EU rights protection will have. Much depends on how post-Brexit policies unfold over the next few years, and the nature of the final withdrawal and trade agreements reached with the EU. But it may be the case that the UK commits itself to maintaining certain common standards currently fixed in EU law, especially in areas such as data protection and equality.

Furthermore, it is possible that any final withdrawal and trade agreements with the EU may commit the UK to remaining part of the ECHR system of rights protection. At the time of writing, paragraph 7 of the Political Declaration agreed between the

---

[185] V. Bogdanor, *The New British Constitution* (Oxford: Hart, 2009), especially 53–88.

[186] T. Lock, 'Human Rights Law in the UK after Brexit' (2017) *Public Law*, Vol Nov Supp (Brexit Special Extra Issue 2017), 117–134.

[187] Joint Committee on Human Rights, *The Human Rights Implications of Brexit*, 5th Report of Session 2016–7, HL Paper 88/HC 695, 19 December 2016, available at https://publications.parliament.uk/pa/jt201617/jtselect/jtrights/695/695.pdf.

[188] C. O'Cinneide, 'Brexit and Human Rights', in O. Fitzgerald and E. Lein, *Complexity's Embrace: The International law Implications of Brexit* (CIGI, 2018), 297–307.

UK government and the EU in December 2018 provides that '[t]he future relationship should incorporate the United Kingdom's continued commitment to respect the framework of the ECHR'. This wording is ambiguous. However, its presence in the Political Declaration is a clear sign that the Brexit process may result in the status of the ECHR within UK law, and thus the HRA, being reinforced—not least because a UK guarantee that the ECHR floor of rights will continue to apply in Northern Ireland post-Brexit may be required to assuage Irish concerns in relation to the impact of Brexit on the Belfast Agreement.

This of course would be an ironic side-effect of Brexit—namely a Eurosceptic political project serving ultimately to reinforce the status of the ECHR/HRA. But it remains to be seen how the powerful and disruptive political dynamics unleashed by Brexit will play out in this regard.

CONCLUSION

The manner in which fundamental rights are protected within the UK constitutional framework has changed dramatically over the last few decades. The influence of the ECHR and the HRA, taken together with the development of common law rights and other factors, has transformed British law. The HRA was carefully tailored to provide strong rights protection, while leaving the fundamentals of the UK constitutional system unaltered. It seems to have bedded down well, and laid down deep roots in UK public law. However, the HRA, and the relationship it establishes between UK law and the ECHR, remain politically controversial. In general, the place of human rights within British constitutional culture remains uncertain and contested, even if the HRA has far remained relatively impervious to challengers. Brexit may yet add a new dimension to this situation.

FURTHER READING

E. Bates, *The Evolution of the European Convention on Human Rights* (Oxford: OUP, 2010)

B. Dickson, *Human Rights and the UK Supreme Court* (Oxford: OUP, 2013)

C. Gearty, *Principles of Human Rights Adjudication* (Oxford: OUP, 2004)

T. Hickman, *Public Law after the Human Rights Act* (Oxford: Hart, 2010)

A. Kavanagh, *Constitutional Review under the Human Rights Act* (Cambridge University Press, 2009)

F. Klug, *Values for a Godless Age: The Story of the UK's New Bill of Rights* (London: Penguin, 2000)

R. Masterman and I. Leigh (eds.), *The United Kingdom's Statutory Bill of Rights: Constitutional and Comparative Perspectives* (Oxford: OUP/British Academy, 2013)

A.W.B. Simpson, *Human Rights and the End of Empire* (Oxford: OUP, 2001)

A.L. Young, *Parliamentary Sovereignty and the Human Rights Act* (Oxford: Hart, 2009)

USEFUL WEBSITES

www.coe.int/—Council of Europe
http://www.equalityhumanrights.com/—Equality and Human Rights Commission
http://www.echr.coe.int/—European Court of Human Rights
www.ohchr.org/—Office of the UN High Commissioner for Human Rights
http://publiclawforeveryone.com/—Public Law for Everyone blog
http://ukconstitutionallaw.org/—UK Constitutional Law blog
http://ukhumanrightsblog.com/—UK Human Rights Law blog
http://www.un.org/en/law/—UN Human Rights Law

4

BREXIT AND THE UK CONSTITUTION

*Paul Craig**

SUMMARY

This chapter is, for obvious reasons, not a modification of the chapter from the previous edition. It is a completely new chapter, which considers the effect of Brexit on the UK constitution. There is discussion of the constitutional implications of triggering exit from the EU, and whether this could be done by the executive via the prerogative, or whether this was conditional on prior legislative approval. The discussion thereafter considers the constitutional implications of Brexit in terms of supremacy, rights, executive accountability to the legislature, and devolution. The chapter concludes with a discussion of the paradox of sovereignty in the context of Brexit.

INTRODUCTION

The normal pattern for a new edition of a book is that changes to the chapters therein are incremental, highlighting the developments in law and politics that are relevant to the subject matter that occurred in the intervening years. This chapter is different, as attested by the title, which has altered from 'Britain in the European Union' to that set out above. The UK will, in all likelihood, have exited the EU by the time that this book is published. The precise nature of the relationship between the UK and the EU is, however, unclear at the time of writing. This chapter will focus on the constitutional dimensions of Brexit, of which there are plenty to occupy the assiduous reader.

The discussion begins with the issue of constitutional power, which was manifest in litigation as to whether the executive could trigger notification to exit the EU, or whether it required legislative approval before doing so. The sections thereafter deal

* Professor of English Law, St John's College, Oxford. Part of this chapter previously appeared in the following article: Paul Craig, 'Brexit, A Drama: The Interregnum', *Yearbook of European Law*, 36 (2017), 3–45, https://doi.org/10.1093/yel/yex005.

with the constitutional consequences of Brexit flowing from the European Union (Withdrawal) Act 2018. There are separate sections dealing with the effect of the 2018 Act on supremacy, rights, devolution and executive accountability to the legislature. The chapter concludes with some broader thoughts concerning constitutional politics.

It may, however, be helpful at this juncture to identify the key legal instruments that constitute the Brexit jigsaw, since it will facilitate discussion thereafter. There is a Withdrawal Agreement, which includes a transition agreement, and a Political Declaration that outlines the direction of future trade relations, the idea being that a full trade agreement will be negotiated in the years after Brexit.[1] These must be agreed by the House of Commons pursuant to section 13 of the European Union (Withdrawal) Act 2018. If this proves to be impossible then the UK, in accord with Article 50 Treaty on European Union, leaves the EU two years after giving notification of its intent to withdraw. This is the scenario of the 'no-deal Brexit'. If there is no Withdrawal Agreement, there will be no transitional agreement, and the UK will be out of the EU at the end of March 2019, unless all Member States vote for an extension of time. A future trade agreement will be negotiated between the UK and the EU at some time, but the emphasis will assuredly be on the temporal dimension 'future', connoting in this respect not merely that it will apply in the future, but also that it could take 4–5 years to conclude such an agreement.

There are, or will be, numerous domestic statutes designed to effectuate different aspects of Brexit. The European Union (Withdrawal) Act 2018 is already in force and is designed to bring existing EU law into UK law to prevent regulatory black holes when we leave, the idea being that such law can be amended or repealed thereafter, if we do not wish to retain it. There will be a statute to give effect to the Withdrawal Agreement in UK law, assuming that such an agreement is accepted by Parliament. There will, in addition, be several more discrete pieces of legislation, dealing with aspects of Brexit that affect diverse issues such as migration, data protection, and cross-border civil litigation.

CONSTITUTIONAL POWER: THE TRIGGERING OF ARTICLE 50 TEU

Article 50(1) provides that a Member State may decide to leave the EU in accord with its own constitutional requirements. This is amplified by Article 50(2) TEU, which states, inter alia, that a Member State that decides to withdraw shall notify the European Council of its intentions. The referendum signalled that the UK would leave the EU. However, the modality by which this was to be done gave rise to important constitutional issues, as to whether Article 50 TEU could be triggered by the government acting pursuant to the prerogative, or whether it required prior approval from

---

[1] Agreement on the Withdrawal of the United Kingdom of Great Britain and Northern Ireland from the European Union and the European Atomic Energy Community, 25 November 2018.

Parliament. There is a prerogative concerning the conduct of foreign relations, including the making of treaties. The government believed that it could act pursuant to this power when notifying withdrawal from the EU pursuant to Article 50. Gina Miller, a private citizen, believed that this could only be done after Parliament had given its approval through statute. This difference of view set the scene for litigation that gripped the legal community as the case went through the courts.

The Supreme Court in *Miller*[2] upheld the Divisional Court,[3] and decided that the government could not trigger Article 50 TEU to begin withdrawing from the EU without statutory authorization from Parliament. The case concerned structural constitutional review, in which the Supreme Court demarcated the ambit of legislative and executive power, the latter being exercised through the prerogative.

LIMITS ON PREROGATIVE POWER: THE AMBIGUITIES

There are three dimensions to legal control over the prerogative: the first is as to whether it exists; the second is as to its extent; the third concerns the manner of exercise. *Miller* turned on contestation as to the second of these issues. The word 'extent' in this context captures the limits or constraints placed on an admitted prerogative. It is a matter for the courts to decide. They determine the types of constraint that should, as a matter of principle, be placed on prerogative power.

Thus, the courts have fashioned constraints that the prerogative cannot alter the law of the land or affect rights, and that it cannot be used where it would place statute law in abeyance or frustrate statutory rules. The precise meaning of these constraints can be contestable, so too can their application in a particular case. There are, therefore, always two related, but distinct, issues when we consider the extent of the prerogative. What types of constraint should, as a matter of principle, be placed on prerogative power? How does a constraint apply to the facts of a particular case?

CONSTRAINTS ON PREROGATIVE POWER: ALTERING THE LAW OF THE LAND AND RIGHTS

The first limit to prerogative power is that it cannot alter the law of the land, a proposition derived from the *Case of Proclamations*. It concerned the legality of two proclamations made by the King: one prohibited new buildings in London, the other the making of starch from wheat. The court held that the King cannot by his proclamation change 'any part of the common law, or statute law or customs of the realm'.[4] Nor could the King create any new offence by way of proclamation, for that would be to change the law. It was for the courts to determine the existence and extent of prerogative powers. The principal beneficiary was Parliament, since the case concerned the extent of

---

[2] *R. (on the application of Miller) v Secretary of State for Exiting the European Union* [2017] UKSC 5.
[3] *R. (on the application of Miller) v The Secretary of State for Exiting the European Union* [2016] EWHC 2768 (Admin).
[4] (1611) 12 Co. Rep. 74 at 75.

monarchical regulatory power independent from the legislature. The denial of such power meant that if the King wished to attain these ends he must do so through statute.

The principles embodied in the *Case of Proclamations* were reinforced by the Bill of Rights 1688, which provided that 'the pretended power of suspending of laws or the execution of laws by regall authority without consent of Parlyament is illegall'[5] and that 'the pretended power of dispensing with laws or the execution of laws by regall authoritie as it hath beene assumed and exercised of late is illegall'.[6]

The application of the principle from *Proclamations* in *Miller* raised difficult issues concerning the meaning of 'the law' that could not be changed through the prerogative, and the nature of the rights that could not be affected by use of the prerogative. The Supreme Court's reasoning was as follows.

The majority regarded EU law as a novel source of law within the UK legal order.[7] It, and the rights emanating from it, were therefore part of the law of the land that could not be altered through recourse to the prerogative. The majority acknowledged that the EU rights brought into UK law through the ECA 1972 could vary from time to time, and that this would cease when the UK withdrew from the EU. This did not, however, mean that withdrawal, with the consequential impact on rights, could be done through the prerogative without Parliamentary authorization. There was, said the majority, no indication that Parliament had intended this. There was a vital difference between changes in domestic law resulting from variations in EU law arising from new EU legislation, and changes in domestic law resulting from withdrawal by the United Kingdom from the EU.[8]

The principal dissent was given by Lord Reed, who held that the prerogative over the making and unmaking of treaties was a fundamental part of the UK constitutional order, which could only be curtailed expressly or by necessary implication. The ECA 1972 contained no express limitation on the Crown's prerogative power, nor were there any words through which to infer that this was the necessary implication of the statute.[9] Lord Reed denied that triggering Article 50 TEU would impact on rights. Parliament had, he said, recognized in the ECA 1972, section 2(1), that rights given effect under the ECA could be altered or revoked from time to time without the need for a statute, and he rejected the distinction drawn by the majority between such changes in rights and that resulting from withdrawal from the EU.

CONSTRAINTS ON PREROGATIVE POWER: STATUTE COVERING THE AREA OF THE PREROGATIVE

The second constraint on prerogative power is that it cannot be exercised if statute covers the same area. The seminal case was *Attorney General v De Keyser's Royal Hotel*,[10] which arose out of the Crown's decision, acting under the Defence of the Realm

---

[5] Bill of Rights 1688, 1 Will. and Mar. Sess.2, c. 2, Article 1.
[6] Bill of Rights 1688, 1 Will. and Mar. Sess.2, c. 2, Article 2; Sir Stephen Sedley, 'The Judges' Verdicts', https://www.lrb.co.uk/2017/01/30/stephen-sedley/the-judges-verdicts.
[7] *Miller*, above, n. 2, [65].   [8] Ibid,. [76]–[78], [83].   [9] Ibid,. [160], [177], [194], [197].
[10] *Attorney General v De Keyser's Royal Hotel* [1920] AC 508.

Regulations, to take possession of a hotel to accommodate personnel of the Royal Flying Corps. The Crown contended that the hotel owners had no legal right to compensation. The Defence Act 1842 gave broad powers to the Crown to take possession of land, subject to compensation. The Crown maintained that the taking was, however, justified by the prerogative, which was said to warrant temporary seizure of property in time of emergency, without any legal right to compensation.

Their Lordships were unpersuaded by the argument. Lord Atkinson held that it would be absurd to construe a statute so as to enable the executive to disregard limits contained in it by reliance on the prerogative. Lord Parmoor was equally clear in this respect: when executive power had been directly regulated by statute, the executive could no longer use the prerogative, but had to observe the restrictions which Parliament imposed in favour of the subject.[11]

The decision in *Miller* did not turn on application of the *De Keyser* principle as such, but the Supreme Court nonetheless said some important things about it. The majority accepted the principle from *De Keyser*, and its application in subsequent cases. It held, moreover, that it was highly improbable that Parliament had the intention that ministers could subsequently take the UK out of the EU without the approval of the constitutionally senior partner, which was Parliament.[12] If that had been the intent it was, in accord with the principle of legality, incumbent on Parliament to have made this clear, and thus pay the political cost of the choice. There was, said the majority, no evidence that the ECA 1972 was intended to clothe the executive with that far-reaching choice.[13]

Lord Reed also accepted the principle in *De Keyser*, but did not believe that it was applicable to this case. It was central to *De Keyser* that Parliament had regulated the area in relation to which the executive sought to exercise the prerogative. This was not so here. The 1972 Act did not regulate withdrawal from the EU. It merely recognized the existence of Article 50 TEU, but said nothing as to who should take the decision to invoke Article 50.[14]

LIMITS ON PREROGATIVE POWER: VALUES AND THE RESOLUTION OF AMBIGUITIES

The preceding analysis is but a bare summation of the contending views of the majority and the dissent in *Miller*. The contrasting arguments were considerably more complex. Resolution of these intricate arguments is equally difficult and cannot be undertaken here. I believe that the majority in *Miller* was correct, and my views in this regard can be found elsewhere.[15] It is, nonetheless, important to identify the background values that inform doctrinal precepts made by the courts.

---

[11] Ibid. 575.   [12] *Miller*, above, n. 2, [85]–[90].   [13] Ibid., [87]–[88].   [14] Ibid., [233].
[15] Paul Craig, '*Miller*, Structural Constitutional Review and the Limits of Prerogative Power' [2018] PL 48. See also, the articles in the Special Issue of *Public Law* devoted to the *Miller* decision, and Jeffrey Jowell, (2017–18) *Supreme Court Review*.

The value that underlies the twin constraints on prerogative power in *Proclamations* and *De Keyser* is the sovereignty of Parliament. It is Parliament that is the legitimate legislator within the UK and the limits protect that authority from being undermined. If the executive could change the law of its own volition, it could thereby bypass legislation without the need for amendment and repeal, hence the principle in *Proclamations*. If the executive could use the prerogative where Parliament had already addressed the issue in a statute it could then avoid the legislation crafted by Parliament, hence the principle in *De Keyser*, and its extension to cases where the prerogative would frustrate the legislation. *Proclamations* protects Parliamentary sovereignty directly, by preventing recourse to the prerogative where it would change the law; *De Keyser* protects sovereignty indirectly, by precluding use of the prerogative where the formal law is left intact, but the executive seeks to circumvent it by use of the prerogative.

The value underlying recognition of a prerogative power to manage international relations, including the making and unmaking of treaties was identified by William Blackstone.[16]

> This is wisely placed in a single hand by the British constitution, for the sake of unanimity, strength, and despatch. Were it placed in many hands, it would be subject to many wills, if disunited and drawing different ways, create weakness in a government; and to unite those several wills, and reduce them to one, is a work of more time and delay than the exigencies of state will afford.

For Lord Reed, 'the value of unanimity, strength and dispatch in the conduct of foreign affairs are as evident in the 21st century as they were in the 18th',[17] and Timothy Endicott voiced strong views to the same effect.[18] It can be readily acknowledged that unanimity, strength and dispatch are important values in the conduct of international relations. We accept that the executive has the primary responsibility for negotiation of treaties, which cannot be done in a collective.

The argument is, nonetheless, difficult when applied to the issue in *Miller*, which was whether Parliament should have to give statutory approval before the triggering of Article 50 TEU. It is not self-evident that unanimity, strength or dispatch should be regarded as the principal values in this determination; it is not self-evident that the executive has advantages in making this decision over Parliament; and it is not self-evident that the executive values would be placed in jeopardy by requiring a vote in Parliament, nor that the executive is united on these issues. Consider these issues in turn.

The decision to trigger Article 50 and leave the EU ranks among the most significant peace time treaty determinations ever made by the UK. It is an issue on which the country was fiercely divided, notwithstanding the referendum. The UK constitutional tradition is one of parliamentary as opposed to popular sovereignty, which is why

---

[16] Sir W. Blackstone, *Commentaries on the Laws of England* (1765–1769), Book I, Chapter 7, 'Of the King's Prerogative'.

[17] *Miller*, above, n. 2, [160].

[18] T. Endicott, 'This Ancient, Secretive Royal Prerogative', U.K. Const. L. Blog, 11 Nov 2016, https://ukconstitutionallaw.org/.

the referendum was not legally binding, although it was clearly important in political terms. The values that matter here are those that are fundamental to a parliamentary democracy, viz that major decisions are not made without approval by Parliament.

It is not self-evident that the executive would have any advantages over Parliament when making this determination. The executive may claim epistemic advantages and experience in relation to some aspects of foreign policy. The reality is that such advantages were not relevant to the current determination, or to analogous decisions of this nature. MPs knew the issues concerning EU membership as well as the executive.

Nor is it self-evident that requiring a vote in Parliament placed the executive's strategy for triggering Article 50 TEU in jeopardy. To the contrary, the date chosen by the executive, the end of March, had no especial magic; it was not jeopardized by the parliamentary vote, which was accomplished in a matter of weeks; and if the government had not contested the issue in litigation parliamentary approval would have been secured earlier. Indeed, as matters concerning Brexit have progressed further, the divisions within the executive as to the best way to pursue Brexit have become ever more apparent, as attested to by the many ministerial resignations that have occurred since the referendum.

Consideration of the values underlying constraints on prerogative power and the values that underpin a particular prerogative can therefore assist us in resolving the issues that arise in a case such as *Miller*. They serve to explain why for many people the intuitive answer was that the decision to leave the EU should not rest with the executive acting alone but should rather be dependent on statutory approval by Parliament. Respect for parliamentary sovereignty underpinned the constraints on prerogative power as expressed in *Proclamations* and *De Keyser*, while the rationale for according the executive prerogative power over treaty making had scant, if any, relevance to the issue in *Miller*.

It is equally important to ensure that the constitutional principles that inform decisions in one area cohere with those in another. This was relevant here for the following reason. In *HS2* the Supreme Court affirmed that there was a category of constitutional statutes, which included the European Communities Act 1972.[19] It will not readily be accepted that a constitutional statute can be impliedly repealed. While this possibility cannot be ruled out entirely, it is generally accepted that the burden of justification should be set very high, such that in the absence of express repeal the inference would have to be irresistible.[20] The normative justification is that a statute of such importance should not be repealed or amended other than through specific decision by the sovereign Parliament.

The reasoning in *Miller* is a natural corollary of that in *HS2*. A statute worthy of the denomination constitutional should not be rendered devoid of effect through recourse to the prerogative. Thus, while the triggering of Article 50 TEU would not in

---

[19] R. *(on the application of HS2 Action Alliance Ltd) v Secretary of State for Transport* [2014] UKSC 3, [207]; *H v Lord Advocate* [2012] UKSC 24.

[20] *Thoburn v Sunderland City Council* [2003] QB 151, [63].

itself repeal the ECA 1972, withdrawal would deprive it of substance, since we would no longer be party to the EU. The majority in *Miller* believed that this consequence should not ensue without parliamentary authorization, or to put the same point in a different way, recourse to the prerogative could only be countenanced if the executive could show specific authority for this course of action, thereby ensuring, in accord with the principle of legality, that Parliament had thought through the consequences of its action.

The requirement that triggering exit via prerogative power was dependent on proof of specific statutory authorization coheres with the reasoning in *HS2* and is sound in terms of normative principle. The 1972 ECA not only provided the vehicle for EU law becoming part of UK law, but also brought about a new constitutional order involving the supremacy of EU law. If statutes of such importance should not generally be susceptible to implied repeal, in order thereby to safeguard the sovereign Parliament, then it follows that they should not be capable of being deprived of effect by the executive, without specific authorization from the sovereign Parliament. The range of statutes, over and beyond constitutional statutes, that should be treated in this manner remains to be seen. This argument is reinforced by the point made earlier to the effect that the triggering of Article 50 does not involve the values commonly associated with prerogative power in relation to treaty making, and that by contrast it is the very kind of determination that should be made by Parliament.

CONSTITUTIONAL CONSEQUENCE: SUBSEQUENT PARLIAMENTARY APPROVAL

The *Miller* decision demanded statutory approval before notification of withdrawal could be given under Article 50 TEU. It was then for Parliament to impose whatsoever controls or conditions it thought fit. The political reality was that Parliament was largely quiescent in this respect. Immediately after the *Miller* judgment, the PM introduced the European Union (Notification of Withdrawal) Bill 2017, which had undoubtedly been drafted earlier. The House of Commons duly passed the Bill by a large majority. There were attempts to impose substantive and procedural constraints on how the government conducted the negotiations, but they were not successful, and the Bill secured its majority without amendment. There was stronger opposition in the House of Lords, but there was never any likelihood that it would block the legislation.

This begs the question as to why Parliament was quiescent in this respect, to which the answer is eclectic. Some MPs might genuinely have felt that the issue should, for reasons of principle, be left to the executive; others, particularly, hard Brexiteers, were committed functionally to the prerogative, since they were concerned in the aftermath of the referendum at attempts to undo their victory on the floor of the House. The principal explanation as to why most MPs did not, at that stage, seek to impose statutory conditions concerning conduct of the negotiations, or a requirement of statutory approval of the withdrawal agreement, was political. They were fearful of backlash from their constituents who had voted to leave, who would be angered if they felt that their victory was in danger of being undermined by demands for such a statute. The issue did, however, arise again in relation to the European Union (Withdrawal) Act 2018. It is to the constitutional implications of this Act that we now turn.

CONSTITUTIONAL CONSEQUENCE: SUPREMACY, AND THE EU (WITHDRAWAL) ACT 2018 ('EUWA')

THE EUWA: RATIONALE

Brexit will generate numerous pieces of legislation, as the UK seeks to navigate the legal terrain towards a post-Brexit world. The European Union (Withdrawal) Act 2018 is, however, a cornerstone of this legal map. The Act is long and complex, and cannot be examined in detail here.[21] The present focus will be on the principal constitutional dimensions of the legislation. It is, however, important to be clear at the outset as to the rationale for the European Union (Withdrawal) Act 2018, henceforth EUWA.[22]

The UK has been a member of the EU since 1972, and many areas of life are regulated by EU law. Directives have already been transposed into UK law. There is, however, much EU law, such as regulations, that is directly applicable, taking effect in domestic law when enacted by the EU, without the need for further national legislation. The European Communities Act 1972, section 2(1), furnished the legal foundation for direct applicability and direct effect within the UK constitutional order. The regulatory architecture in any area is typically an admixture of Treaty provisions, directives, regulations and decisions. It is, moreover, composed of EU legislative acts, in conjunction with delegated and implementing acts.[23]

It is not, in reality, possible simply to dispense with this material in a post-Brexit world, since this would lead to chaos. The existing EU rules regulate matters from product safety to the creditworthiness of banks, from securities markets to intellectual property and from the environment to consumer protection. There cannot be a legal void in these areas, and pre-existing UK law will often not exist. Moreover, the UK helped to fashion much of this EU law.

This is the rationale for the EUWA. The foundational premise is that the entirety of EU law is converted into UK law. Parliament can then decide, in two stages, which measures to retain, amend or repeal. Stage one is to ensure that the EU rules retained as domestic law are fit for legal purpose when we leave the EU, since there may be provisions that do not make sense in a post-Brexit world, such as reporting obligations to the Commission, which must be altered by exit day. Stage two is the period post-Brexit, when Parliament can decide at greater leisure whether it wishes to retain these rules.

---

[21] For detailed analysis, see, P. Craig, 'Constitutional Principle, the Rule of Law and Political Reality: The European Union (Withdrawal) Act 2018' (2019) MLR 319.

[22] Legislating for the United Kingdom's Withdrawal from the European Union, Cm 9446 (2017), [1.13].

[23] Arts 289–291 TFEU.

To this end, section 1 EUWA repeals the European Communities Act 1972, which was the legal vehicle through which EU law became part of UK law. Sections 2–4 EUWA then deal with different types of EU law, preserving, or converting it, into UK law. Section 2 EUWA provides for the saving of EU-derived domestic legislation, which is principally EU directives that were implemented in UK law pursuant to section 2(2) of the ECA 1972; section 3 EUWA is concerned with the incorporation of direct EU legislation, which primarily covers EU measures, regulations and decisions that were directly applicable in the UK legal order without the need for separate national implementing legislation; and section 4 EUWA preserves directly effective EU rights.

THE EUWA: SUPREMACY OF EU LAW

The European Court of Justice asserted the supremacy of EU law over national law from the inception of the European Economic Community, the predecessor of the current EU Treaty arrangements, such that if there is a conflict between the two EU law prevails. National courts have not unconditionally accepted the ECJ's supremacy doctrine, and have suggested a range of possible limits.[24] It is, nonetheless, the case that all Member States accept that if there is a clash between EU law and national law in an area where the EU undoubtedly has competence, and there are no issues relating to, for example, fundamental rights or national constitutional law, then EU law will be accorded priority.

It was felt that when the UK joined the EU, our tradition of parliamentary sovereignty, whereby the latest statute has priority over earlier law, would pose problems in this regard. The UK courts, nonetheless, accommodated the precepts of traditional parliamentary sovereignty and the demands of EU membership. They accepted that EU law would take precedence in the event of a clash with national law,[25] but also made clear that the decision concerning supremacy resided with the UK courts as a matter of national constitutional law.[26] The Supreme Court held, moreover, that the supremacy of EU law would not necessarily pertain if there was a clash between EU law and a UK constitutional statute. What would have happened if Parliament had expressly stated an intent to depart from a particular provision of EU law was, moreover, never tested.

The EUWA provisions dealing with supremacy are set out in sections 5(1)–(3). These sections do not have any sacrosanct status. The principle of parliamentary sovereignty means that a later Parliament could, if it so wished, repeal or amend these provisions.

> (1) The principle of the supremacy of EU law does not apply to any enactment or rule of law passed or made on or after exit day.

---

[24] P. Craig and G. de Búrca, *EU Law: Text, Cases and Materials* (Oxford University Press, 6th ed., 2015), Ch. 9.

[25] *R. v Secretary of State for Transport ex parte Factortame Ltd (No. 2)* [1991] 1 AC 603; *R. v Secretary of State for Employment, ex p. Equal Opportunities Commission* [1995] 1 AC 1.

[26] *Thoburn v Sunderland City Council* [2003] QB 151; *R. (HS2 Action Alliance Ltd) v Secretary of State for Transport* [2014] UKSC 3.

(2) Accordingly, the principle of the supremacy of EU law continues to apply on or after exit day so far as relevant to the interpretation, disapplication or quashing of any enactment or rule of law passed or made before exit day.

(3) Subsection (1) does not prevent the principle of the supremacy of EU law from applying to a modification made on or after exit day of any enactment or rule of law passed or made before exit day if the application of the principle is consistent with the intention of the modification.

Section 5(1) embodies the logic of Brexit, by providing that the supremacy of EU law does not apply to any enactment or rule of law made on or after the UK leaves the EU. It will, moreover, require modification in the light of the Withdrawal Agreement. Article 4(1) invests its provisions, and the provisions of EU law made applicable by the agreement, with the same legal effects as they would have in the EU and the Member States. Direct effect and the supremacy of EU law therefore continue to apply post-exit day during the transitional period, which is presently scheduled to run until 31 December 2020.

Section 5(1) is qualified by section 5(2), which provides for the continuance of the supremacy principle 'so far as relevant to the interpretation, disapplication or quashing of any enactment or rule of law passed or made before exit day'. It means that if there is a conflict between pre-exit domestic legislation and EU law retained under sections 2–4 EUWA, the latter takes precedence; it also means that pre-exit domestic law should be interpreted, as far as possible, in accordance with EU law. Section 5(1) is further qualified by section 5(3), which allows the supremacy principle to continue to operate in relation to modification made after exit to laws enacted prior thereto, provided that this is consistent with the intention underlying the modification.

The House of Lords Constitution Committee was very critical of these provisions for three reasons. The first was uncertainty as to the scope of application of section 5(2). Thus, while the government's intention was that this would apply to law retained via sections 3 and 4, and would not apply to EU law that had already been incorporated into domestic law via section 2, this was not clear from the wording of section 5(2).[27] The HLCC's second critique was that the government's avowed intent was that the supremacy principle preserved in section 5(2) would be applicable in relation to any enactment or rule of law passed or made before exit day, including thereby common law rules as well as statutes. This was, said the HLCC, problematic because the common law emerges and develops. It was therefore difficult to regard it as having been 'made' on a particular date.[28] The HLCC's third critique was more far-reaching. It stated that 'maintaining the "supremacy principle" following exit amounts to a fundamental flaw at the heart of the Bill,'[29] since 'following exit, there will be no "EU law" within the domestic legal system',[30] it will have been converted into UK law via sections 2–4 EUWA.

---

[27] House of Lords, Select Committee on the Constitution, European Union (Withdrawal) Bill (HL 69, 2018) [81]–[83].
[28] Ibid. [86]–[87].   [29] Ibid. [89].   [30] Ibid. [88].

There is undoubtedly force in this critique, but there must, however, be some way of dealing with the issue should it arise.[31] The issue could, however, have been addressed without resort to the language of the supremacy of EU law. Thus, a replacement for clause 5(2) could have read as follows: if, on or after exit day, there is any inconsistency between measures that have been made part of UK law through sections 2, 3 or 4, and a UK enactment or rule of law in force before exit day, priority shall be accorded to the former over the latter.

CONSTITUTIONAL CONSEQUENCE: RIGHTS AND THE EU (WITHDRAWAL) ACT 2018

RIGHTS AND EU LAW: PRE-BREXIT

Brexit also has implications for the protection of rights. A condition precedent to consideration of this issue is to have some understanding of the way in which the EU impacted on rights while the UK was in the EU. It is important in this respect to distinguish between two ways in which this occurred.

Direct Effect

Direct effect is a cornerstone of EU law. It connotes the idea that individuals can bring actions in national courts in order to vindicate rights secured to them by the Treaty, or regulations, directives, or decisions made thereunder.[32] The general test is that a Treaty article will have direct effect provided that it is intended to confer rights on individuals and that it is sufficiently clear, precise, and unconditional.

Direct effect also attaches to rules made pursuant to the Treaty. There are various types of such rules. Regulations are defined in TFEU, Art. 288 as having general application. They are binding in their entirety and directly applicable in all member states. The ECJ had no reluctance in concluding that regulations were capable of having direct effect, provided that they were sufficiently certain and precise, which was normally the case.[33]

There has been more difficulty over directives. These are, according to TFEU, Art 288, binding as to the result to be achieved while leaving the choice of form and methods to the states to which they are addressed. Moreover, while regulations are binding on all states, directives are only binding on the specific states to which they are addressed. Directives have proved to be a particularly useful device for legislating in

---

[31] The Constitution Committee's solution was to invest all EU direct retained law with the status of primary legislation, but this would have been problematic, P. Craig, 'The Withdrawal Bill, Status and Supremacy', U.K. Const. L. Blog (19 February 2018), https://ukconstitutionallaw.org/2018/02/19/paul-craig-the-withdrawal-bill-status-and-supremacy/.

[32] Case 26/62, *Van Gend en Loos v Nederlandse Administratie der Belastingen* [1963] ECR 1; Case 2/74, *Reyners v Belgian State* [1974] ECR 631; Case 43/75, *Defrenne v Sabena* [1976] ECR 455.

[33] Case 93/71, *Leonosio v Italian Ministry of Agriculture and Forestry* [1973] CMLR 343; Case 50/76, *Amsterdam Bulb v Produktschap voor Siergewassen* [1977] ECR 137.

an enlarged European Union. They enabled the EU to specify the ends to be attained, often in great detail, while leaving a choice of form and methods of implementation to the individual member states. The ECJ held that directives are capable of having direct effect,[34] but that this only operated against the state, known as vertical direct effect, and not against an individual, known as horizontal direct effect.[35] The correctness of this distinction, and the rationale for this limitation of direct effect, are by no means self-evident.[36] The existence of this limitation has, moreover, generated a very complex case law, since the ECJ has created exceptions and qualifications to the idea that directives do not have horizontal direct effect.[37]

Direct effect had two important constitutional implications. First, it enabled individuals to derive rights that are enforceable in their own national courts from an international treaty and legislation made thereunder. The general position in public international law is that individuals do not derive such rights, even where they are the beneficiaries of the rules laid down in an international treaty.[38] There are instances where individuals have been held to have such rights, but they are exceptional and there has been nothing on the scale of the direct effect doctrine as developed by the ECJ. This meant that law derived from sources other than Parliament and the common law would, as recognized by the Supreme Court in *Miller*,[39] avail individuals before their own national courts in a way which had not been so on this scale hitherto.

The second reason why direct effect was of constitutional significance resided in the connection between this concept and the supremacy of EU law. Direct effect allowed the supremacy doctrine to be applied at national level, and thereby made it far more potent than it would otherwise have been. It enabled the supremacy of EU law to be enforced by individuals through their own national courts. The national courts become EU courts in their own right, being able to pass judgment on national primary legislation in the context of an action brought by an individual. Where the ECJ had already considered a legal issue, national courts were encouraged to apply the ruling in analogous cases without the need for further recourse to the ECJ, unless they sought clarification of the earlier ruling.[40] This is exemplified by the *Equal Opportunities*

---

[34] Case 41/74, *Van Duyn v Home Office* [1974] ECR 1337, para. 12.

[35] Case 152/84, *Marshall v Southampton & South West Hampshire Area Health Authority (Teaching)* [1986] ECR 723; Case C-91/92, *Faccini Dori v Recreb Srl* [1994] ECR I-3325.

[36] W. van Gerven, 'The Horizontal Direct Effect of Directive Provisions Revisited: The Reality of Catchwords', in T. Heukels and D. Curtin (eds.), *Institutional Dynamics of European Integration, Liber Amicorum for Henry Schermers* (1994); P. Craig, 'The Legal Effect of Directives: Policy, Rules and Exceptions' (2009) 34 ELR 349.

[37] Craig and de Búrca, above, n. 24, Chap. 7.

[38] I. Brownlie, *Principles of Public International Law* (8th edn., James Crawford, 2012), Chaps. 4, 16. And see Chapter 5 (Feldman).

[39] *Miller*, above, n. 2, [65].

[40] Cases 28–30/62, *Da Costa en Schaake NV, Jacob Meijer NV and Hoechst-Holland NV v Nederlandse Belastingadministratie* [1963] ECR 31; Case 283/81, *Srl CILFIT and Lanificio di Gavardo SpA v Ministry of Health* [1982] ECR 3415, [14].

Commission case,[41] where not only did the House of Lords make a declaration that provisions of a UK statute were incompatible with EU law, but it did so without making a reference to the ECJ, having satisfied itself that the existing ECJ precedents meant that the national statute was indirectly discriminatory.

Fundamental Rights

In the UK, most rights-based claims are brought under the Human Rights Act 1998 (HRA 1998).[42] While the UK remained in the EU, it was however open to claimants to use rights-based arguments derived from EU law. The European Union promulgated a Charter of Fundamental Rights in 2000, but the ECJ developed a fundamental rights' jurisprudence prior to this.

The original EEC Treaty contained no list of traditional fundamental rights. The catalyst for the creation of such rights was the threat of revolt by some national courts. Individuals who were dissatisfied with an EC regulation argued before their national court that it was inconsistent with rights in their national constitutions. The ECJ denied that EC norms could be challenged in this manner. However, in order to stem any national rebellion, it also declared that fundamental rights were part of the general principles of EC law, and that the compatibility of an EC norm with such rights would be tested by the ECJ.[43] Fundamental rights, as recognized in the ECJ's case law, were conceptualized as one type of general principle of law.

It became clear that national laws could also be challenged for compliance with fundamental rights, where the national action fell within the scope of EU law.[44] The supremacy doctrine applied with the consequence that national norms, including primary legislation, which were inconsistent with EC law could be declared inapplicable in the instant case. This is by way of contrast with the Human Rights Act 1998 where the courts are limited, in cases involving primary legislation, to making a declaration of incompatibility under section 4.

The Charter of Fundamental Rights of the European Union was promulgated in 2000.[45] It includes economic and social rights, as well as traditional civil and political rights. The Charter is legally binding and has the same legal value as the TEU and the TFEU.[46] The Member States are bound by the Charter only when they are implementing EU law,[47] which has been interpreted by the CJEU to mean that they are bound whenever they act within the scope of EU law.[48]

---

[41] *R. v Secretary of State for Employment ex parte Equal Opportunities Commission* [1995] 1 AC 1.

[42] See Chapter 3 above.

[43] Case 11/70, *Internationale Handelsgesellschaft v Einfuhr- und Vorratstelle für Getreide und Futtermittel* [1970] ECR 1125, 1134.

[44] Case 222/84, *Johnston v Chief Constable of the Royal Ulster Constabulary* [1986] ECR 1651; Case 5/88, *Wachauf v Germany* [1989] ECR 2609; Case 63/83, *R. v Kent Kirk* [1984] ECR 2689; Case C-260/89, *Elliniki Radiophonia Tileorassi AE v Dimotki Etairia Pliroforissis and Sotirios Kouvelas* [1991] ECR I-2925; Case C-159/90, *Society for the Protection of Unborn Children Ireland Ltd v Grogan* [1991] ECR I-4685.

[45] Charter of Fundamental Rights of the European Union [2000] OJ C364/1.

[46] TEU, Art. 6(1).   [47] Charter, Art. 51(1).

[48] Case C-617/10, *Åklagaren v Hans Åkerberg Fransson*, EU:C:2013:105.

RIGHTS DERIVED FROM EU LAW: POST-BREXIT

Direct Effect

It might be thought that since direct effect is a concept of EU law, it will, therefore, no longer be applicable in the UK in a post-Brexit world. There is some force in this, but the legal reality is that the concept of direct effect will continue to be applicable in a post-Brexit world as a matter of UK law. This is so for two related reasons.

First, section 3(1) EUWA stipulates that 'direct EU legislation, so far as operative immediately before exit day, forms part of domestic law on and after exit day.' Direct EU legislation is defined to include EU regulations and decisions that took effect in the UK legal order prior to Brexit via the ECA 1972.[49] Many such regulations and decisions had direct effect, provided that the particular article thereof was sufficiently certain, precise and unconditional. The consequence was that they were enforceable by individuals before a national court, and this superseded any rule as to whether an individual would, as a matter of domestic law, derive enforceable rights from an enactment. The logic of retaining such regulations and decisions via section 3 EUWA, and bringing the EU acquis into national law, is that measures retained by section 3 should continue to have direct effect in accord with the criteria in EU law,[50] subject to anything to the contrary in the EUWA,[51] and subject to later UK enactment to the contrary.

Secondly, section 4(1) EUWA preserves in UK law directly effective rights derived from EU law, which had taken effect within the UK legal order via section 2(1) ECA. This preserves, inter alia, directly effective rights derived from Treaty articles. It is then open to the UK Parliament to amend, repeal or retain such rights in accord with the process in the EUWA. Many such directly effective rights, such as those pertaining to free movement of workers or services, will be repealed, since they make no sense in a post-Brexit world. This does not alter the fact that, until such repeal or amendment occurs, the directly effective rights function as part of the UK legal order.

Fundamental Rights

The position in relation to fundamental rights derived from EU law in a post-Brexit world is more complex and uncertain.

First, the Charter of Fundamental Rights is not part of domestic law on or after exit day.[52] The official explanation for not retaining the Charter was that it did not create new rights, but merely affirmed existing EU rights and principles, and therefore by converting the EU acquis into UK law, those underlying rights and principles would be converted into UK law, as provided for in the EUWA. There is, however, a marked difference between retention of particular rights singularly, in a disaggregated manner, as compared to their inclusion in a separate rights-based document. It is, moreover,

---

[49] EUWA 2018, s. 3(2).

[50] This is, moreover, supported by s. 4(2)(a), the wording of which assumes that rights can attach to law retained via section 3.

[51] See, e.g., EUWA Sched. 1, para. 4, excluding the *Francovich* damages action post-exit day.

[52] EUWA, s. 5(4).

uncertain whether all Charter rights and principles will be retained through a combination of sections 4 and 6 EUWA.[53]

Secondly, section 5(5) EUWA states that the exclusion of the Charter does not, however, affect 'the retention in domestic law on or after exit day in accordance with this Act of any fundamental rights or principles which exist irrespective of the Charter'.[54] The key phrase, 'exist irrespective of the Charter', is open to various interpretations.[55] Fundamental rights existed prior to the Charter, and, as noted above, they were conceptualized as general principles of law. Their status in this respect was not altered by the enactment of the Charter, which was, in any event, said to be merely declaratory of existing rights, and not constitutive of new rights.[56] On this view all Charter rights and principles could be regarded, in the language of section 5(5) EUWA, as 'existing irrespective of the Charter', since the Charter was declaratory of existing law. The Explanatory Notes attached to the EUWA incline to this view.[57] If this is the legal effect of section 5(4)–(5) EUWA then it calls into question the legislative strategy, which was to exclude the Charter from the front door, while including all rights and principles therein via the back door.

Thirdly, general principles of EU law can be part of domestic law after exit day, provided that they were thus recognized by the CJEU before exit day.[58] There is, however, no right of action in domestic law, on or after exit day, based on a failure to comply with general principles of EU law;[59] and no court, tribunal or other public authority may, on or after exit day disapply or quash any enactment or other rule of law, or quash any conduct or otherwise decide that it is unlawful, because it is incompatible with any general principle of EU law.[60] It would seem, therefore, that general principles of law can only operate as interpretive guides to legislators, administrators and courts.

CONSTITUTIONAL CONSEQUENCE: EXECUTIVE ACCOUNTABILITY AND THE EU (WITHDRAWAL) ACT 2018

DELEGATED LEGISLATION: THE BASIC PROBLEM

A central feature of constitutional law concerns executive accountability to the legislature. This issue can arise in a number of different contexts, and it can be addressed in a number of different ways. Thus, Prime Minister's question time

---

[53] A. Lang, V. Miller and J. Simson Caird, 'EU (Withdrawal) Bill: The Charter, General Principles of EU law, and "Francovich" Damages', House of Commons Briefing Paper, Number 8140, 17 November 2017, 14–15.

[54] EUWA, s. 5(5). References to the Charter in any case law are, so far as necessary for this purpose, to be read as if they were references to any corresponding retained fundamental rights or principles.

[55] Craig, above, n. 21.

[56] Charter of Fundamental Rights of the European Union [2010] OJ C83/02, Preamble [5].

[57] European Union (Withdrawal) Act 2018, Explanatory Notes, [107].

[58] EUWA, Sched. 1, para 2.   [59] EUWA, Sched. 1, para 3(1).   [60] EUWA, Sched. 1, para 3(2).

can, in principle, foster accountability, by rendering the political leader subject to questions from the opposition leader that are not published in advance. Select committees provide for more in-depth scrutiny of government policy, and their reports furnish valuable evidence concerning failures or shortcomings in this respect.

Executive accountability to the legislature is, however, placed under particular strain in relation to the enactment of delegated or secondary legislation. The paradigm in democratic systems is for legislation to be enacted by the legislature. Primary legislation cannot, however, cover all issues. The primary legislation is then complemented by delegated legislation, which fleshes out the principles contained in the enabling statute. This is because the legislature may not be able to foresee all ramifications of the legislation when the initial statute is made. It may well have neither the time, nor the expertise, to address all issues in the original legislation. The measures consequential to the original statute may have to be passed expeditiously, which precludes the use of procedures for primary legislation.

There are endemic problems as to how to legitimate such delegated legislation, which is drafted by the executive. The numbers help to place matters in perspective. There are approximately 2,500 pieces of delegated legislation per year, as compared to roughly 40 primary statutes. The reality is that most such delegated legislation receives scant scrutiny by the legislature. The great majority of such measures are subject to what is known as the negative procedure, whereby they enter into force unless annulled pursuant to a motion in the House of Commons, which hardly ever occurs. A minority of such measures are subject to the affirmative procedure, whereby it is for the government to secure a majority in favour of the measure for it to be enacted, although once again governmental failure is rare.

DELEGATED LEGISLATION AND BREXIT: THE PROBLEM COMPOUNDED

Brexit did not change the nature of the problem of securing effective scrutiny of delegated legislation. It did, however, take it to a whole new level in quantitative terms. The reason is not hard to divine. The EUWA strategy was, as we have seen, to bring the entire corpus of EU law into UK law, and then to proceed in two stages: stage one, was to make the necessary changes so that the law was fit for purpose by exit day; stage two, was then to decide thereafter, at greater leisure, whether to retain, amend or repeal the legislation.

The precise number of EU measures thereby domesticated is in the order of 20–25,000. There was a very short time to complete stage one, meaning that it could only be done through changes made by delegated legislation. The EUWA, therefore, gave ministers sweeping powers to propose delegated legislation, the great majority of which are subject only to the negative procedure. The problem was further compounded by liberal recourse to what are known as 'Henry VIII' clauses, which provide that delegated legislation can alter primary statute. The EUWA contains a number of provisions that give the executive powers to make delegated regulations, the principal provisions of the Act being sections 8, 9, 23, and Schedule 8. Space precludes detailed elaboration of all such complex provisions,[61] and thus the focus will be on section 8 EUWA, which is the principal provision dealing with the remedying of deficiencies in laws arising from withdrawal.

Section 8(1) accords a minister broad powers to deal with deficiencies arising from withdrawal.[62] He or she can, by regulations, make such provision as the 'Minister considers appropriate to prevent, remedy or mitigate' any 'failure of retained EU law to operate effectively', or 'any other deficiency in retained EU law', arising from the withdrawal of the United Kingdom from the EU.[63] This power is reinforced by section 8(5), which contains a Henry VIII clause: regulations made under section 8(1) can make any provision that could be made by an Act of Parliament, subject to the limits set out in section 8(7).[64] The list of possible deficiencies in section 8(2) augments the ministerial discretion accorded by section 8(1).

(2) Deficiencies in retained EU law are where the Minister considers that retained EU law—

    (a) contains anything which has no practical application in relation to the United Kingdom or any part of it or is otherwise redundant or substantially redundant,

    (b) confers functions on, or in relation to, EU entities which no longer have functions in that respect under EU law in relation to the United Kingdom or any part of it,

    (c) makes provision for, or in connection with, reciprocal arrangements between—

        (i) the United Kingdom or any part of it or a public authority in the United Kingdom, and

        (ii) the EU, an EU entity, a member State or a public authority in a member State, which no longer exist or are no longer appropriate,

    (d) makes provision for, or in connection with, other arrangements which—

        (i) involve the EU, an EU entity, a member State or a public authority in a member State, or

        (ii) are otherwise dependent upon the United Kingdom's membership of the EU, and which no longer exist or are no longer appropriate,

    (e) makes provision for, or in connection with, any reciprocal or other arrangements not falling within paragraph (c) or (d) which no longer exist, or are no longer appropriate, as a result of the United Kingdom ceasing to be a party to any of the EU Treaties,

---

[61] For detailed analysis, see Craig, above, n. 21.

[62] There is a sunset clause in EUWA, s. 8(8), which precludes recourse to s. 8(1) two years after exit day.

[63] EUWA, s. 8(1)(a)–(b).

[64] EUWA, s. 8(7) provides that regulations under section 8(1) may not: impose or increase taxation or fees; make retrospective provision; create a relevant criminal offence; establish a public authority; be made to implement the withdrawal agreement; amend, repeal or revoke the Human Rights Act 1998 or any subordinate legislation made under it; or amend or repeal the Scotland Act 1998, the Government of Wales Act 2006 or the Northern Ireland Act 1998, subject to certain limited qualifications.

    (f) does not contain any functions or restrictions which—

        (i) were in an EU directive and in force immediately before exit day (including any power to make EU tertiary legislation), and

        (ii) it is appropriate to retain, or

    (g) contains EU references which are no longer appropriate.

Section 8(3) further provides that there is also a deficiency in retained EU law where the minister considers that there is anything in retained EU law which is similar to the deficiencies listed in section 8(2), or there is a deficiency in retained EU law of a kind described, or provided for, in regulations made by a minister. It is, therefore, open to a minister to create new heads of deficiency in such regulations, subject to the limits set out below, and such regulations partake of the Henry VIII power in section 8(5).

The EUWA imposes certain procedural obligations on the exercise of this ministerial power. Thus, the minister must make a statement to the effect that in the minister's opinion the draft regulation does no more than is appropriate; that there are good reasons for it; and that the provision made by the draft regulation constitutes a reasonable course of action.[65]

The EUWA makes provision for legislative scrutiny of draft regulations made pursuant to section 8(1). The default position is that regulations to address deficiencies from withdrawal made under section 8(1) are subject to the negative resolution procedure; it is for either House of Parliament to vote the measure down in order to prevent it from becoming law.[66] There are, however, conditions that are applicable before this procedure can be invoked.[67] A minister cannot make an instrument subject to that procedure unless 'condition 1' is met, combined with either 'condition 2 or 3'.[68]

Condition 1 is that a minister must make a written statement to the effect that it is the minister's opinion that the instrument should be subject to annulment by resolution of either House of Parliament; and the minister must lay before each House of Parliament a draft of the instrument, combined with a memorandum setting out the statement and the reasons for the minister's opinion.

Condition 2 is that a sifting committee of the House of Commons and a sifting committee of the House of Lords, have within the relevant period, each made a recommendation as to the appropriate procedure for the instrument. Condition 3 is that the relevant period has ended without condition 2 being met.[69]

If either sifting committee recommends that the affirmative resolution procedure should be used, whereby Parliament would have to approve the measure, rather than the negative resolution procedure proposed by the minister, then if the minister wishes to persist with the latter procedure he or she must make a statement explaining why the minister disagrees with the committee before the instrument is made, or failing that must make the statement thereafter.[70]

---

[65] EUWA, Sched. 7.   [66] EUWA Sched. 7L, para 1(3).   [67] Ibid., para. 1(4).
[68] Ibid., paras. 3(2)–(5).   [69] Ibid., paras. 3(10)–(11), the basic period being 10 days.
[70] EUWA Sched 7, paras. 3(6)–(8).

The creation of sifting committees is undoubtedly positive in terms of enhancing legislative accountability.[71] This should not, however, serve to conceal the fact that the balance of power remains firmly with the executive. Thus, even if the sifting committee differs from the ministerial view, and recommends use of the affirmative procedure, the minister can persist with the negative procedure, provided only that he or she furnishes reasons for disagreeing with the committee, and these reasons may be given before or after the instrument is made.

The provisions in EUWA concerning delegated legislation raise concerns as to constitutional principle and the rule of law. The practicalities of leaving the EU were always likely to place strains on the relationship between the legislature and the executive, given the very scale of the task at hand. The need to bring the entire acquis of EU law into UK law, and to do so within a very narrow time frame, has resulted in the grant of very broad delegated power to the executive, and led to apprehension as to the adequacy of legislative oversight. This is exacerbated by the frequent recourse to Henry VIII powers, whereby the executive can alter primary legislation through delegated power. There are, in addition, concerns as to the ability or people to plan their lives cognizant of the legal consequences of their action, which is a core element of the rule of law, whatsoever other elements it might contain. This will not be easy in a post-Brexit world, as individuals try to understand and navigate their way among the plethora of complex legal rules that apply within their area.

CONSTITUTIONAL CONSEQUENCE: BREXIT AND DEVOLUTION

The long-term effect of Brexit on the UK devolution settlement remains to be seen, and is not readily predictable at the time of writing. It is, nonetheless, clear at this juncture that Brexit has had a negative effect on the relationship between the centre and the devolved regions, in particular Scotland and Wales. This is apparent in relation to the negotiations and the EUWA.

BREXIT, NEGOTIATIONS, AND DEVOLUTION

The devolved administrations were very much side-lined in the Brexit negotiation process. The UK entered the EU, and Brexit is destined to take the UK out. The flip side to this conception of indivisibility was that the plan was meant to be beneficial to all parts of the UK, including Scotland, Wales and Northern Ireland, and they were to be accorded a voice in its shaping. Thus, in the Prime Minister's Lancaster House speech she

---

[71] The changes to the Bill owe much to arguments advanced by the House of Lords Constitution Committee, and those who submitted evidence to it, House of Lords, Select Committee on the Constitution, European Union (Withdrawal) Bill (HL 69, 2018).

stated that the 'devolved administrations should be fully engaged in this process';[72] this would occur through the Joint Ministerial Committee on EU Negotiations, 'so ministers from each of the UK's devolved administrations can contribute to the process of planning for our departure from the European Union';[73] and the net result would be a Brexit that works for the whole of the United Kingdom.

There was, however, a gap between this rhetoric and reality. Truth to tell the substantive fault lines between Westminster and the devolved assemblies were significant, and the procedural engagement a good deal less than the reader would divine from the official Westminster documentation, with the consequence that while the devolved bodies exercised voice, its impact at Westminster was muted.[74] The Scots had voted to remain in the EU, and were clear that if Brexit was to occur then it should be a soft version thereof. The Welsh voted to leave, but also favoured a soft version of Brexit. This did not cohere with thinking emerging from Westminster, where the Prime Minister, under pressure from Brexiteers, was inclining to a hard version of Brexit. The tensions surfaced when the Prime Minister gave her Lancaster House speech, in which she opted for a hard Brexit, two days before a Joint Ministerial Committee meeting, without having discussed Scotland's policy document released a month earlier. It prompted an angry response from Michael Russell, the Scottish Minister responsible for JMC discussions, who spoke in terms of Scotland being treated with contempt in the negotiating process.[75] Similar tensions were to surface throughout the negotiations, with the devolved administrations feeling that their views were largely ignored.

BREXIT, THE EUWA AND DEVOLUTION

The devolved administrations also expressed their discontent with the way in which they were treated by the EUWA 2018. The legislation was enacted, it will be recalled, in order to bring EU law into UK law, in order that it could be made fit for purpose by exit day, such that it could then be determined thereafter whether to repeal, amend or retain the relevant provisions. The complexity of the 2018 legislation resulted in part from the fact that it had to deal with EU rules that would, in a post-Brexit world, be the responsibility of Scotland, Wales or Northern Ireland, rather than Westminster. This necessarily entailed the detailed replication of provisions in the EUWA concerning Westminster, as they pertained to the other areas.

---

[72] Prime Minister Theresa May sets out the Plan for Britain, including the 12 priorities that the UK government will use to negotiate Brexit, 17 January 2017, p. 5 (hereafter referred to as the Lancaster House speech), https://www.gov.uk/government/speeches/the-governments-negotiating-objectives-for-exiting-the-eu-pm-speech; The United Kingdom's Exit from and New Partnership with the European Union, Cm 9417 (2017) [3.1].

[73] Ibid., 6.

[74] P. Craig, 'Brexit, A Drama: The Interregnum' [2017] *Yearbook of European Law 3*, 17–20; S. Douglas-Scott, 'Brexit and the Scottish Question', in F. Fabbrini (ed.), *The Law and Politics of Brexit* (Oxford University Press, 2017) Chap. 6.

[75] https://news.gov.scot/news/jmc-meeting-on-brexit.

There was, however, very considerable disquiet in the devolved administrations concerning an issue of principle. The logic of the EUWA was, they contended, that when subject matter currently dealt with by the EU was repatriated, it should fall within the power of the devolved administrations, if power of that kind had been devolved to them. It would then be for the devolved administration to decide what to do with the EU law thus retained. The UK government was unwilling to accept this. Thus, while it repeatedly stated that power over most such matters would be returned to Scotland, Wales and Northern Ireland, it also insisted that Westminster must hold the initial key as to the fate of such provisions. The government feared that there might otherwise be serious impediments to the internal market within the UK, which could only be prevented by uniform rules for the relevant area made by Westminster.[76]

The Scottish and Welsh governments were unconvinced, and were highly critical of the provisions in the European Union (Withdrawal) Bill 2017. A joint press release from the Scottish and Welsh leaders stated that while the Bill lifted from the UK Government and Parliament the requirement to comply with EU law, it did the opposite for the devolved legislatures, since it imposed new restrictions, which made no sense in the context of the UK leaving the EU.[77] The Bill operated asymmetrically, such that the UK Parliament regained the ability to legislate without restriction, whereas in devolved areas the devolved administrations would only be allowed to do so if the UK government granted permission by Order in Council. The devolved administrations recognized that there might be a need for common frameworks in certain areas but contended that these should be agreed between the UK government and the devolved administrations, rather than be imposed by Westminster.[78]

The critique from the devolved administrations had some effect and there were amendments to the Bill before it became an Act. The bottom line is, nonetheless, that Westminster retains control.[79] It is, therefore, not open to the devolved administrations to modify retained EU law, so far as the modification is of a description specified in regulations made by a Minister of the Crown. Before seeking approval from the Westminster Parliament, such draft regulations must have been presented to the relevant devolved administration and there must be a consent decision, or the passage of 40 days without such a decision. It is, however, clear that, for these purposes, a 'consent decision' includes the refusal of consent. Thus, a draft regulation made by a Westminster minister specifying that a devolved administration cannot modify certain types of retained EU law must be presented in draft to the devolved administration, and a consent decision must be secured, before proceeding with the making of such regulations in the UK Parliament, but the requirement to secure a 'consent decision' is met even if the consent is refused. The ministerial power is subject to a two-year sunset clause.

---

[76] The United Kingdom's Exit from and New Partnership with the European Union, above, n. 72, [4.01]–[4.06].

[77] https://news.gov.scot/news/eu-withdrawal-bill.

[78] https://news.gov.scot/news/eu-bill-doesnt-reflect-reality-of-devolution.   [79] EUWA, s. 12.

Scottish disquiet concerning the devolution provisions in the EU (Withdrawal) Bill led the Scottish Parliament to reject the measure. The Sewel Convention provided that the UK government will not legislate for devolved matters in Scotland without the consent of the devolved legislature. This was embodied in the Scotland Act 2016, which amended section 28 of the Scotland Act 1998, by providing that the UK Parliament will not normally legislate with regard to devolved matters without the consent of the Scottish Parliament. The UK Parliament, nonetheless, overrode the will of the Scottish Parliament, and the Bill was duly enacted as legislation. The Scottish government did not regard this with equanimity, Michael Russell stating that 'the UK Government acted in an unprecedented and constitutionally improper way in ignoring the views of the Scottish Parliament on legislative consent for the EU (Withdrawal) Act'.[80] Russell made clear that Scotland would, as a result, not consider proposals for regulations made under the EUWA, and that it would press for clarification or amendment to the Sewel Convention. The fallout from these events continues to unfold, and has clearly had a negative impact on the relationship between the centre and the devolved administrations.

The Supreme Court is, however, reluctant to become embroiled in the interpretation of the Sewel Convention. This is evident from *Miller*, where the Supreme Court held that, while the Sewel Convention was undoubtedly politically important, it was not legally enforceable. Courts of law 'cannot enforce a political convention'.[81] Judges were 'neither the parents nor the guardians of political conventions; they are merely observers'.[82] The fact that the Sewel Convention had been enshrined in legislation by section 2 of the Scotland Act 2016 did not thereby render a political convention legally enforceable.[83]

CONCLUSION: BREXIT AND THE PARADOX SOVEREIGNTY

This chapter has been concerned with Brexit and the UK constitution. There will be no attempt to summarize the preceding discussion. It is, however, worth dwelling, by way of conclusion, on the sovereignty paradox that underpins Brexit. The leave campaign was driven, inter alia, by the desire to repatriate power and restore UK sovereignty. It was embodied in language, oft-repeated by ardent Brexiteers, to the effect that the UK would now be able to govern itself, and make its own decisions freed from the need to comply with constraints imposed by EU law. There is both an external and an internal paradox to this sovereignty discourse.

---

[80] https://beta.gov.scot/publications/strengthening-the-sewel-convention-letter-from-michael-russell-to-david-lidington/.

[81] *Miller*, above, n. 2, [141].   [82] Ibid., [146].

[83] The Supreme Court however side-stepped the argument that notification would necessitate amendment to the legislation relating to Scotland, Northern Ireland and Wales.

The external paradox is that even if UK takes the hardest of hard Brexit strategies, there will, nonetheless, be very significant constraints on the sovereign choices available to the UK Parliament. This flows, in part, from the fact that many trading standards are set at the global level, largely as a result of negotiation between the EU and the USA, and these will continue to apply to the UK in a post-Brexit world. It flows, in part, also from the fact that there will, even in the event of a hard Brexit, be very great pressures on the UK not to diverge from EU trading rules broadly conceived. The reason is not hard to divine. A very great many companies will continue to trade with the EU in a post-Brexit world. When they do so they will have to comply with EU rules, or rules that are strictly equivalent thereto. While it is therefore open to a sovereign UK Parliament to enact rules that are substantively different, it would be economically irrational, since the price of doing so would be to impose a double regulatory burden on UK firms. If, by way of contrast, the UK opts for a soft form of Brexit, then sovereignty will be diminished because the UK will be a rule-taker, not a rule-maker. It will be bound to follow EU rules and have no voice at the table in the making of such provisions.

The internal sovereignty paradox is that while Brexit was advocated, inter alia, because it would reinforce UK sovereignty, the abiding theme behind pretty much all post-referendum Brexiteer strategy has been to deny either Parliament or the people any further say in the events that have unfolded. Consider these in turn.

UK constitutional orthodoxy is that sovereignty resides in Parliament. We have parliamentary, not popular sovereignty. It was the return of powers to Parliament that underpinned the Brexit campaign. Yet at every stage Brexiteers have sought to deny Parliament any say in the decision to leave, and the terms on which this is done. The exclusion of Parliament was manifest in the desire to trigger notification of exit via the prerogative without recourse to Parliament; it was evident in the unwillingness to accept any amendments to the notification of withdrawal legislation when it went through Parliament; it was a key feature of many of the skirmishes concerning the EUWA, including most prominently, debates about the extent to which Parliament should have a say about the terms of the withdrawal agreement with the EU; and it surfaced yet again in the post-EUWA exchanges between the legislature and the executive concerning the way in which the limited powers accorded to Parliament concerning the terms of any such deal might be exercised, with the executive seeking to limit very significantly the impact of any such legislative oversight.[84]

UK popular sovereignty was manifest in the referendum itself. This has been the principal argument deployed by Brexiteers to limit parliamentary sovereignty, with repeated iteration of the idea that the will of the people would thereby be undermined. This is not the place for detailed exegesis concerning the relationship between parliamentary and popular sovereignty. Suffice it to say the following in the present context. Parliamentary sovereignty is the principle that underpins the UK constitution, and this in no way precludes respect for the results of popular sovereign choice expressed

---

[84] https://www.parliament.uk/business/committees/committees-a-z/commons-select/procedure-committee/.

through a referendum. The idea that such respect demands unquestioning quiescence from Parliament as to what should happen thereafter does not withstand examination. The idea that any questioning of the results of the referendum, or what the vote meant, is akin to undermining the popular will is not tenable. This is evident, most ironically, from Brexiteer reaction on the night of the referendum when they thought that they had lost the vote. The immediate reaction of the UKIP leader, Nigel Farage, was that UKIP would live to fight another day. There was no sense in which he regarded what was then thought to be the will of the people, to remain in the EU, as the reason to disband or alter UKIP's campaign. It is, moreover, very doubtful whether prominent Brexiteer MPs would have regarded a vote to remain as meaning the end of their op-position to the EU. Lastly, and most importantly, opposition to a second referendum that is grounded on the idea that the people have spoken, and that this per se precludes the need for any second popular vote, is not sustainable. There may well be issues con-cerning the questions to be asked and the timing of any such event. This does not alter the central underlying fact: when the people voted they had imperfect knowledge as to the terms on which the UK would leave, and scant understanding of the effect that this might have on their jobs, and livelihood. This is evident, at one stage removed, in the parliamentary context, in which rival groups of MPs take different messages from the referendum as to what precisely the people really voted for. It can be readily accepted that the result of the referendum should be treated with constitutional respect. It should not be revisited without good cause. Uncertainty as to what form of Brexit the people voted for became, however, more, rather less evident over time, and this became all the greater as the details of the rival versions of Brexit on offer were more sharply defined.

The internal sovereignty paradox concerning parliamentary and popular sover-eignty embodies a significant measure of political realpolitik. Brexit is sold on the basis that sovereignty will be augmented; parliamentary involvement over the terms thereof is, however, repeatedly curtailed and circumscribed on the basis that it will undermine the will of the people; and popular sovereignty is, in turn, circumscribed by unwill-ingness to give the people any further voice lest they give an answer that does not ac-cord with the Brexiteer vision. The take away message is stark and simple: when you have the answer you want, do not allow the question to be asked again, even though the people have far more detailed knowledge concerning the nature of disengagement than they did before. This strategy is readily understandable in terms of political real-politik. We should, however, see it in those terms, and not allow it to be shrouded in some veneer of respect for sovereignty.

FURTHER READING

ANTHONY, G., *UK Public Law & European Law, The Dynamics of Legal Integration* (2002).

ARMSTRONG, K, *Brexit Time, Leaving the European Union—Why, How and When?* (2017).

BIRKINSHAW, P. and BIONDI, A., (eds.), *Britain Alone! The Implications and Consequences of United Kingdom Exit from the EU* (2016).

CRAIG, P., *The Lisbon Treaty, Law, Politics and Treaty Reform* (2010).

CRAIG, P. and DE BÚRCA, G., *EU Law, Text, Cases and Materials* (6th edn., 2015).

DOUGAN, M. (ed.), *The UK after Brexit, Legal and Policy Challenges* (2017).

ELLIOTT, M., WILLIAMS, J., and YOUNG, A. (eds.), *The UK Constitution after Miller* (2018).

FABBRINI, F., (ed), *The Law & Politics of Brexit* (2017).

SLAUGHTER, A.-M., STONE SWEET, A., and WEILER, J. H. H. (eds.), *The European Court of Justice and National Courts: Doctrine and Jurisprudence* (1998).

USEFUL WEBSITES

European Union: **http://europa.eu**

Department for Exiting the European Union: **https://www.gov.uk/government/organisations/department-for-exiting-the-european-union**

5

THE INTERNATIONALIZATION OF PUBLIC LAW AND ITS IMPACT ON THE UK

*David Feldman**

SUMMARY

Municipal public law (by which is meant the public law of national or sub-national polities, including but not limited to local government) is always influenced by events taking place elsewhere in the world and the activities and norms of other polities. For example, the existence of a state depends at least partly on its recognition by other states, and political theories and legal ideas have always flowed across and between regions of the world even if they provoked opposition rather than adoption or adaptation. Yet despite, or perhaps because of, this, any state has good reasons for controlling the introduction of foreign legal and constitutional norms in to its own legal order. It is important to check that the norms are compatible with one's own national values and interests before allowing them to operate within one's own system. A state which values a commitment to the rule of law, human rights, or democratic accountability is entitled to place national controls over potentially disruptive foreign influences. This chapter considers the nature and legitimacy of those national controls, particularly as they apply in the UK, in the light of general public law standards, bearing in mind that influences operate in both directions, not only between states but also between municipal legal standards and public international law.

* I am grateful to the Rev'd Professor John Bell, His Honour Ian Campbell, Dr Veronika Fikfak, Professor Constance Grewe, Professor Sir Jeffrey Jowell, Professor Didier Maus, Professor Nicolas Maziau, Professor Dawn Oliver, Judge Tudor Pantiru, Professor Cheryl Saunders, Anna-Lena Sjolund, Christian Steiner, and Dr. Rebecca Williams for valuable discussions of the subject-matter of this chapter and helpful comments on drafts. Remaining errors and idiosyncrasies are entirely my responsibility.

INTRODUCTION

'Internationalization of public law' refers to several phenomena. They include the influence of public international law, and (related but distinct) of international institutions such as the UN, on municipal systems of public law; development of general principles of public law and their adoption by municipal systems; adoption of rules of municipal law which require officials, including judges, to apply municipal rules of public law to events outside the state's territory or to apply rules developed outside the state; and acceptance by international lawyers and institutions for their purposes of principles derived from the constitutional and administrative laws of states. This chapter focuses on the first three of those phenomena, but we should note that advocates of the use of public-law principles to regulate international law and institutions recognize that such principles help to legitimate the use or threat of force, which may be important for systems and institutions with no democratic accountability.[1]

In its municipal manifestations, internationalization of public law has an obvious but complex relationship to multilayered governance and the expansion of judicial review, two of the themes of this book. The problems in relation to multilevel governance are that international law does not fit straightforwardly into the hierarchy of legal norms operating within states. Different states assign different levels of authority to international law, and sometimes (as in the UK) to different types, sources, or individual norms of international law. Some international influences, such as judgments of courts in other states, have no legal status, and operate outside any hierarchy of norms. In respect of judicial review, when judges are given jurisdiction to determine issues arising outside the state's territory (for example, by virtue of the need to apply human rights law) they may be required to deal with matters which have never before been within their remit, such as the behaviour of UK armed forces operating overseas. This presents novel problems of both law and judicial competence.

Only extremely isolated states can avoid having limits placed by other states on their domestic and external policies. When states seek each other's cooperation and enter into treaties, they agree to restrict the range of options open to them in exchange for the benefits of pursuing objectives unattainable without coordination. International organizations can help to maintain peace, bolster social or economic stability, and foster free trade and open markets. The UK as we know it is partly a result of an extreme form of such an agreement. In 1706–7, the Treaty of Union between England and Scotland led to the foundation of the United Kingdom of Great Britain. It was an instrument of international law, negotiated between the representatives of two sovereign nations and given effect in national law by a combination of Acts of their respective Parliaments and action taken by the monarch of each state (who happened by coincidence to be the same person).[2]

---

[1] See e.g. Philip Allott, *Eunomia: New Order for a New World* (2001), esp. Chs. 12 and 13, on constitutionalizing international law; Spyridon Flogaitis, 'I principi generali del diritto nella giurisprudenza del Tribunale Amministrativo delle Nazione Unite' in Marco D'Alberti (ed.), *Le Nuove Mete del Diritto Amministrativo* (2010), 93–114, on developing general principles of administrative law in the UN's Administrative Tribunal.

[2] For discussion of the implications of this, see Elizabeth Wicks, 'A New Constitution for a New State? The 1707 Union of England and Scotland' (2001) 117 *LQR* 109–26, and Elizabeth Wicks, *The Evolution of a Constitution: Eight Key Moments in British Constitutional History* (2006), Ch. 2.

Events on the international plane continue in the twenty-first century to help shape the UK's constitution through international human rights and other treaties, and participation in international organizations such as the United Nations, the Council of Europe, NATO, and (at the time of writing, at least) the European Union (EU). For example, the devolution legislation prevents the devolved legislatures and ministries from acting in a manner incompatible with the UK's obligations under the European Convention on Human Rights (ECHR) (so far as they have been made part of municipal law in the UK by the Human Rights Act 1998) or EU law.[3] International law is woven into the fabric of public law.

At the same time, cooperation involves significant costs and responsibilities, as well as benefits, for states. They must take account of internationally agreed objectives and values in their internal decision-making. Sometimes they must subordinate their own interests to those of other states. This may compromise systems of accountability for the exercise of public power which are traditionally based on the political and legal processes operating within states. Traditional criteria for the legitimacy of state action, such as democracy, compliance with rule-of-law standards, or respect for fundamental rights, may be hard to apply when decision-making processes are shaped by international agreements or institutions which do not contain equivalent systems for control and accountability of the exercise of power. This leads some people to argue that a 'democratic deficit' in the European Union leads to a crisis of legitimacy which the process of constitutional reform leading up to the Treaty of Lisbon, leading to increased involvement of the European Parliament in law-making and to some extent constraining the power of the European Commission and Council, only partly addressed—and which has, at least in part, contributed to Brexit.[4]

This has consequences for UK public law. The structures of important state institutions are potentially challenged by such organizations as the Group of States against Corruption (GRECO), operating under the aegis of the Council of Europe,[5] and the

---

[3] Northern Ireland Act 1998, ss. 6, 14(5), and 26; Scotland Act 1998, ss. 29(2), 35(1), and 58; Government of Wales Act 2006, ss. 80–2. The European Union Withdrawal Act 2018, s. 12, if and when it comes fully into force, will maintain the limitation of competence so far as it relates to 'retained EU law'. See Craig, Chapter 4.

[4] See Chapter 4 in this volume.

[5] GRECO, *First Evaluation Report on the United Kingdom* (2001), criticized the UK Parliament's handling of complaints against members, because (e.g.) the Parliamentary Commissioner for Standards, who dealt with the House of Commons, had not been put on a statutory basis, and there was no independent system for dealing with complaints against members of the House of Lords. See A. Doig, 'Sleaze Fatigue: An Inauspicious Year for Democracy' (2002) *Parliamentary Affairs* 389; GRECO RC-I (2003) 8E, *Compliance Report on the United Kingdom*, 7–11 July 2003, paras. 27–31; GRECO RC-I (2003) 8E Addendum, 1 July 2005, paras. 9–13. The position changed in 2009 after it was revealed that some members of both Houses had made highly questionable use of their entitlement to claim reimbursement of expenses. The House of Commons is now subject to the statutory Independent Parliamentary Standards Authority: see Parliamentary Standards Act 2009, as amended by the Constitutional Reform and Governance Act 2010. The House of Lords is still self-regulating, but since 2010 peers and their staff are required to comply with Codes of Conduct: see *Code of Conduct for Members of the House of Lords; Guide to the Code of Conduct; Code of Conduct for Staff of Members of the House of Lords*, 4th edn, HL Paper 3 of 2015–16 (2015) (https://www.parliament.uk/mps-lords-and-offices/standards-and-financial-interests/house-of-lords-commissioner-for-standards-/code-of-conduct-for-the-house-of-lords/). Complaints are investigated by an independent House of Lords Commissioner for Standards (www.parliament.uk/mps-lords-and-offices/standards-and-interests/the-commissioner-for-standards/), who reports to the Lords' Conduct Sub-Committee of the Committee on Privileges and Conduct. Members may appeal to the Committee against a recommendation of the Commissioner or Sub-Committee.

European Charter of Local Self-Government,[6] which the UK ratified with effect from 1 August 1998, and its Additional Protocol on the right to participate in the affairs of a local authority (which the UK signed in 2009 but has not yet ratified). This chapter attempts to draw out three characteristics of the relationship between national systems of public law and international developments. The first is the importance of international influence over the very existence and fundamental structures of states. No state is an island (although some islands are states). Secondly, the channels between national and international planes normally permit influence to be exerted in both directions and are usually subject to filters allowing states to preserve an element of autonomy, although the nature and effectiveness of the filters depends on national traditions and interests. Thirdly, the mechanisms by which states allow foreign influences to affect their systems of public law reflect their constitutional traditions and patterns of social interaction, and their legitimacy depends at least in part on their compatibility with those traditions and patterns.

FOREIGN INFLUENCES ON THE FOUNDATIONS OF PUBLIC LAW

THE EXISTENCE OF A STATE AND ITS CONSTITUTION

An entity or group of entities may seek the status of statehood in a variety of circumstances: for example, following the break-up of an existing state, the attempted secession of part of a state, a merger of existing states, or an exercise of foreign control over a state. In such situations, the reaction of other states is of great consequence when deciding whether the entity has the necessary characteristics of statehood. International lawyers agree that recognition by other states is important, although they disagree about its strictly legal significance. Whether recognition by other states is legally constitutive of the new state in international law (the 'constitutive theory') or is important only as evidence that the new state already has that status in international law (and the balance of opinion currently tends towards the latter, 'declaratory' theory),[7] lack of recognition is at least persuasive evidence that an entity is not a state,[8] and international recognition may be crucial, as when the United Nations agreed to the establishment of the state of Israel in 1948. Sometimes other states or international institutions may intervene in the process of developing or renewing statehood, and control the form and content of the new state's constitution. If the international community uses armed force to end a conflict and secure a state's continued existence, it may impose a new constitution designed to protect the interests of the various parties to the conflict in order to give effect to

---

[6] European Treaty Series No. 122 (1985).

[7] See the discussions in James Crawford, *The Creation of States in International Law* (2nd edn., 2006), Ch. 1, esp. 26–8; James Crawford, *Brownlie's Principles of International Law* (8th edn., 2012), 144–6; Malcolm Shaw, *International Law* (8th edn., 2017), 164.

[8] Shaw, *International Law*, 329–36; Crawford, *Brownlie's Principles*, 146.

the agreement which brings it to a close, as in Bosnia and Herzegovina in 1995,[9] or effectively dictate the terms of a defeated state's constitution as an aspect of the peace settlement, as in Japan and West Germany following the Second World War.[10]

But there are no internationally accepted criteria for recognition. Individual states must decide on what grounds to recognize other entities as states. Most states look for an organized governmental authority exercising effective control over a permanent population and a defined territory, together with an ability to carry on external relations independently of other states and give effect to international obligations.[11] Other relevant factors may include: respect for the UN Charter, human rights, and established international frontiers; a commitment to peaceful resolution of international disputes; and respect for the rights of minorities.[12] None of these factors is necessarily decisive. For example, when the constituent parts of the former Yugoslavia broke up from 1992, the government of one of the republics claiming the status of a new state, Bosnia and Herzegovina, controlled only about half its territory when it was recognized by (among others) the UK. The remainder was under the control of anti-secessionist military groups. The integrity of the new state was secured only when military action by the North Atlantic Treaty Organization (NATO) ended three years of war, and the Dayton–Paris Accord of 1995 imposed a General Framework Agreement for Peace (GFAP) on the warring parties. Among other things, this set in stone an internationally agreed constitution, and put in place continuing international control through an international Peace Implementation Council and a High Representative with extensive powers. It has been argued that this external control makes it hard to accept that Bosnia and Herzegovina is an independent sovereign state.[13]

POLITICAL AND CONSTITUTIONAL IDEAS

It is some time since the UK has faced that level of external intervention in its affairs, but ideas from abroad have shaped its structure for centuries. Medieval feudalism was imported from Western Europe,[14] and overlay the pre-Norman structures to produce a

---

[9] For an illuminating analysis of the kinds and consequences of international intervention in the formation of states and their constitutions, see Nicolas Maziau, 'L'internationalisation du pouvoir constituant' (2002) 3 *Revue Générale de Droit International Public* 549–79.

[10] On Japan, see Ray A. Moore and Donald L. Robinson, *Partners for Democracy: Crafting the New Japanese State under MacArthur* (2002). On West Germany and Italy, see Chris Thornhill, *A Sociology of Constitutions: Constitutions and State Legitimacy in Historical-Sociological Perspective* (2011), 327–41.

[11] See e.g. Montevideo Convention on the Rights and Duties of States 1933, Art. 1; American Law Institute, *Restatement of the Foreign Relations Law of the United States* (3rd edn., 1987), § 201.

[12] See Shaw, *International Law*, 157–63.

[13] For an analysis of efforts to end the war and the Dayton Agreement, see Christine Bell, *Peace Agreements and Human Rights* (2000), esp. pp. 91–117. On whether post-Dayton Bosnia and Herzegovina is a state, see Gerald Knaus and Felix Martin, 'Lessons from Bosnia and Herzegovina: Travails of the European Raj' (2003) 14(3) *Journal of Democracy* 60–74; Crawford, *The Creation of States in International Law*, 398–401; Shaw, *International Law*, 161.

[14] See R. C. van Caenegem, *An Historical Introduction to Western Constitutional Law* (1995), Ch. 4.

system of government which made possible the growing central authority of the monarchy and the standardization of law across the country. Similarly, between the tenth and twelfth centuries, Scotland

> was regulated by a complex patchwork combining a typically western European feudal framework with Celtic custom, which can be traced in many of its details to Irish law tracts of the seventh or eighth centuries. The result was what has been called a 'hybrid kingdom', and one of its marks was the emergence of a composite common law of Scotland by the end of the twelfth century.[15]

Public law and political theory in England and Scotland were essentially modelled on those of Western Europe at that period. In the thirteenth century, the model was extended to Wales by military conquest. As elsewhere in Europe, there was a tension between the gradual centralization of law and bureaucracy and the vigorous desire of the nobility and a developing class of free men for an increased role in decision-making.[16] The tension remained, but the structures of the constitution developed so as to accommodate both central and local authority and recognize the interests of a wider variety of free people than previously within the 'community of the realm',[17] encapsulated in such instruments as Magna Carta (1215) and the Statute of Marlborough (1267), which provided that writs should be issued freely against those who were alleged to have committed breaches of Magna Carta, putting it (or at least those parts of it which were capable of judicial enforcement) on the same footing as a statute.

By the sixteenth century, British public lawyers and administrators travelling to Avignon, Paris, Pavia, and other European universities to study Roman law and Greco-Roman political theory at the fountainhead of the Renaissance brought their learning home.[18] In the seventeenth century, the English state was effectively re-founded three times (in 1649 after the Civil War and the execution of King Charles I, at the end of the Protectorate in 1660, and after the flight of King James II in December 1688). The royalists in the lead-up to the Civil War relied on ideas derived from the law of nations (*ius gentium*) or natural law to bolster their claim to the divine right of kings,[19] and political philosophers, including Thomas Hobbes on the side of absolute monarchy and John Locke for constitutional monarchy, were part of major Western European philosophical traditions.[20]

---

[15] Michael Lynch, *Scotland: A New History* (1992) 53 (footnotes omitted).

[16] van Caenegem, *An Historical Introduction to Western Constitutional Law*, Ch. 5.

[17] See Sir Maurice Powicke, *The Thirteenth Century 1216–1307* (2nd edn., 1962), 131–50, 216–18.

[18] W. Gordon Zeefeld, *Foundations of Tudor Policy* (1969), Chs. I–VI, esp. 20–2, 50–1, 79–80, 129–31; David Ibbetson and Andrew Lewis, 'The Roman Law Tradition' in A. D. E. Lewis and D. J. Ibbetson (eds.), *The Roman Law Tradition* (1994), 1–14.

[19] See e.g. J. W. Gough, *Fundamental Law in English Constitutional History* (1955), 12–174. The parliamentarians looked more to the pre-Norman period of English constitutional history: see Christopher Hill, 'Sir Edward Coke: Myth-Maker' in Christopher Hill, *Intellectual Origins of the English Revolution* (1972), 225–65.

[20] On the Western European roots of the idea of public law as developed in the UK, see Martin Loughlin, *Foundations of Public Law* (2010), Introduction and Pt I; John Allison, *The English Historical Constitution: Continuity, Change and European Effects* (2007).

INTERNATIONALIZATION AND PROTECTION FOR NATIONAL INTERESTS: INFLUENCES, CONTROLS, AND FILTERS

PROTECTION AGAINST INTERNATIONAL LAW: FILTERS AND CHANNELS

As foreign influences can derail national arrangements, national authorities do not usually allow ideas from elsewhere to permeate national institutions unless two conditions are met. First, the state must have something to gain from accepting the ideas, either in terms of rationalizing or guaranteeing its own organization and security (as in the case of Bosnia and Herzegovina in 1995) or because of a promise of reciprocal benefits from other states. Secondly, unless the state faces irresistible armed force or economic pressure it will insist on being able to influence the development and application of the ideas which it agrees to accept. Internationalization is thus a two-way street. Benefits must flow inwards to the nation, and the state must have the benefit of being able to influence or export as well as import ideas.

International law reflects this in that a treaty does not bind a state unless it has accepted the obligations arising under it. Internally, state constitutions usually impose filters to ensure that the state's legislative organs maintain control of the impact on municipal law of international treaties (binding agreements between two or more states), customary international law (those state practices internationally accepted as obligatory by most states),[21] and general principles of law.[22] Constitutions usually adopt a position lying on a continuum between two poles, commonly known as 'monism' and 'dualism'. A 'monist' approach draws no clear division between national and international law, allowing both customary international law and treaties[23] to produce effects in national law without the need for national legislation to give effect to them. In civil law systems, the influence of classical Roman law ensured that *ius gentium*, which by the time of Justinian had come to be seen as founded on human reason assumed to be common to Roman citizens and foreigners alike,[24] encouraged the adoption of constitutions which made at least some international obligations directly part of municipal law, treating national and international law as parts of a single, continuous fabric of law, rather than two entirely separate systems. This makes it easier to allow standards of civilized behaviour which form part of international law, including respect for human rights and prohibitions on genocide, torture, and other crimes against humanity, to take effect within states without the need for legislation, and to some extent to control inconsistent national laws: whatever may be the level in the municipal hierarchy of legal norms at which the relevant rule of international law takes effect (a matter which depends on municipal constitutional law), municipal legal norms which are lower in the hierarchy will give way to the requirements of

---

[21] Shaw, *International Law*, 53–69.   [22] Ibid., 72–81.   [23] Ibid., 96–138.
[24] See Barry Nicholas, *An Introduction to Roman Law* (1962), 54–9; Wolfgang Kunkel, *An Introduction to Roman Legal and Constitutional History*, trans. J. M. Kelly (2nd edn., 1973), 100.

the international norm.[25] Furthermore, if the existence of a state and its legal system depend on that state being recognized as meeting criteria for statehood set by international law (the 'constitutive theory' mentioned earlier), there can logically be no separation between national and international law.[26] Constitutions in civil law countries, and some common law countries like the USA, which rebelled against British control, usually adopt some form of monism.

But there are sound reasons for having filters at national level to control the way in which the obligations affect national law- and policy-making. The principled reason is the desire to uphold constitutional guarantees, including the rule of law, and keep in the hands of the nations the democratic control of and accountability for national law and policy, in order to maintain the legitimacy of politics and public law in the state. The pragmatic reason is that international obligations may be contrary to the national interest and may derail important national objectives. 'Dualism' provides such a filter by treating national and international law as two separate systems. This prevents international law from directly affecting national law. The UK has traditionally adopted a broadly dualist approach in relation to treaties, not treating them as part of municipal law unless municipal legislation provides for them to have that effect.

However, there is no sharp distinction between monist and dualist approaches. The principled and pragmatic considerations mentioned earlier ensure that few monist states are without controls over the incorporation of international law, while in dualist states the separation between municipal and international law has never been total. Monist states typically maintain essential national interests in the face of international pressure by providing that treaty obligations become enforceable through national law without national legislation only under strict conditions: they must be reciprocal obligations, binding on all the states parties to the treaty; and they must be compatible with the national constitution, which remains hierarchically superior to treaties as a matter of national constitutional law. For example, Art. 25 of the *Grundgesetz* (Basic Law) of the Federal Republic of Germany makes the 'general rules of public international law' integral to federal law, creating rights and duties directly for inhabitants of the federal territory and taking precedence over national laws. This is an understandable reaction to the disregard, during the Third Reich, of the norms of public international law. On the other hand, under Art. 59.2 treaties which regulate the political relations of the Federation or relate to matters of federal legislation must have the consent or participation, in the form of a federal statute, of the bodies which are competent to make such federal legislation, and treaties affecting federal administration must have the consent or participation of the competent bodies for federal administration. Even then a treaty, when it takes effect in the legal hierarchy, has the status of a federal statute, subordinate

---

[25] See e.g. Hersh Lauterpacht, 'International Law: The General Part', in Hersh Lauterpacht, *International Law: Collected Papers*, ed. Elihu Lauterpacht, 5 vols. (1970) I, 153 ff; Hans Kelsen, *General Theory of Law and State*, trans. Anders Wedberg (Cambridge, Mass.: Harvard University Press, 1949), Part 1, Ch. XI on the hierarchy of norms and Part 2, Ch. VI on the relationship between international and national law.

[26] Hans Kelsen, above, n. 25, 363–80; Hans Kelsen, *The Pure Theory of Law*, trans. Max Knight (1967), 328–47.

to the Basic Law. It is therefore of no effect in the municipal system if it is incompatible with a provision of the Basic Law, including those protecting state sovereignty, democracy, and fundamental rights.[27]

Furthermore, the constitutional structures of monist states normally allow the legislature to control the exercise of treaty-making power by state institutions authorized by the constitution to exercise that power. For example, the US Constitution provides that treaty obligations, together with the Constitution and federal laws made in pursuance of it, are the supreme law of the land,[28] but the President may make treaties only with the concurrence of two-thirds of the members of the Senate who are present.[29] The legislative arm has a veto—at least in theory—over the USA's treaty obligations, and so over the state of federal law, although executive agreements, such as those recognizing foreign states, do not require Congressional approval, and may allow federal authorities to enforce obligations arising from them despite the Tenth Amendment, which reserves to the states all powers not conferred by the Constitution on federal authorities.[30] In France, the Constitution of the Fifth Republic (1958), Art. 52 provides for the President of the Republic to negotiate and usually also ratify treaties. Under Art. 55, once ratified or approved, they prevail over legislation if the other state party reciprocally gives similar effect to the treaty obligations in its own law. But Art. 53 preserves parliamentary control by providing that certain kinds of treaties may be ratified or approved only under an enactment and take effect only after ratification or enactment.[31] What is more, no cession, exchange, or annexation of territory is valid without the consent of the population of the territory.[32]

THE UK'S PARTIAL DUALISM AND THE FEEDBACK LOOP BETWEEN MUNICIPAL AND INTERNATIONAL LAW

In the UK, too, dualism is only partial. Courts have long accepted that, in contrast to treaties, 'customary international law', the part of international law consisting of standards accepted by states by common consent without the need for multinational

---

[27] *Internationale Handelsgesellschaft mbH v Einfuhr- und Vorratstelle für Getreide und Futtermittel* [1974] 2 CMLR 540 (BvfG); *Re the Application of Wünsche Handelsgesellschaft* [1987] 3 CMLR 225 (BvfG); *Unification Treaty Constitutionality Case* (1991) 94 ILR 42 (BvfG); *Lisbon Treaty Constitutionality Case*, BVerfG, 2 BvE 2/08, 30 June 2009, available at www.bverfg.de/entscheidungen/es20090630_2bve000208.html[I; English translation available at www.bundesverfassungsgericht.de/entscheidungen/es20090630_2bve000208en. html. On which see Jo Erik Khushal Murkens, '"We want Our Constitution Back"—The Revival of National Sovereignty in the German Federal Constitutional Court's Decision on the Lisbon Treaty' [2010] *PL* 530–50.

[28] US Constitution, Art. VI *bis*.

[29] Ibid., Art. II.2 *bis*.

[30] See *United States v Belmont*, 301 US 324 (1937) on the recognition by the USA of the USSR. See also *Breard v Commonwealth* 248 Va 68, 445 SE 2d 670 (1994), cert. denied 513 US 971 (1994).

[31] The types of Treaty are: 'peace treaties, trade treaties, treaties or agreements concerning international organizations, those which commit national resources, those which modify provisions of a legislative character, those concerning personal status, and those involving the cession, exchange, or annexation or territory', Art. 53, trans. in S. E. Finer, Vernon Bogdanor and Bernard Rudden, *Comparing Constitutions* (1995), 229.

[32] For further examples, see Shaw, *International Law*, 126–35.

treaties or resolutions of international organizations, forms part of municipal law automatically, by incorporation, without the need for legislation, if sufficiently clear.[33]
However, this is subject to the operation of certain filters.

First, customary international law is incorporated only so far as it is compatible with
national statutes and binding case law. But, since customary international law responds
to state practice, the influence works in both directions. For example, state immunity—
the principle that a state may not be impleaded before the courts of another state—is
part of customary international law, and as such formed part of English common law
until it was codified in statute by the State Immunity Act 1978. In *Al-Adsani v Government of Kuwait* the Court of Appeal held that torture, too, was contrary to customary
international law, but that the plaintiff, who claimed to have been tortured by Kuwaiti
officials in Kuwait, could not sue the Government of Kuwait in English courts because,
by clear words, the 1978 Act established that the defendant could still rely on state
immunity notwithstanding any violation of customary international law.[34] This is an
example of statute giving one principle of international law—state immunity—priority over another—the prohibition of torture in customary law—and, partly because
state practice is a source of customary international law, international law currently
has the same priority rule. In both municipal and international law, state immunity is
not (yet) subject to any exception even in respect of alleged violation of a peremptory
norm of general international law (sometimes called *jus cogens*), defined in the Vienna
Convention on the Law of Treaties 1969, Art. 53 as 'a norm accepted and recognized
by the international community of States as a whole as a norm from which no derogation is permitted and which can be modified only by a subsequent norm of general
international law having the same character', so that it overrides incompatible rules in
customary international law or treaties. Whilst the rule against torture is *jus cogens*,
state immunity even protects individual torturers against civil liability if they acted as
agents of their state in exercising its public, rather than commercial, activities.[35] The
immunity has been restricted by the Convention against Torture and other Cruel, Inhuman or Degrading Treatment or Punishment 1984 (the CAT) to allow criminal proceedings against state agents, but it has not been limited so as to allow civil proceedings

[33] See Shaw, *International Law*, 106–112; *Trendtex Banking Corporation v Central Bank of Nigeria* [1977]
QB 529 (CA); *J. H. Rayner (Mincing Lane) Ltd v Department of Trade and Industry* [1990] 2 AC 418 (HL);
Campbell McLachlan, *Foreign Relations Law* (Cambridge: Cambridge University Press, 2014), Ch. 3, on the
interaction of municipal and international law.

[34] (1996) 107 ILR 536 (CA). This was held not to violate the right to be free of torture or the right to a fair
hearing under ECHR, Arts. 3 and 6.1: Application no. 35763/97, *Al-Adsani v United Kingdom*, judgment of 21
November 2001, RJD 2001-XI, 34 EHRR 273.

[35] *Jones v Ministry of the Interior of the Kingdom of Saudi Arabia and another (Secretary of State for Con-
stitutional Affairs and others intervening)* [2006] UKHL 26, [2007] 1 AC 270 (HL); *Jones v United Kingdom*,
Application no. 34356/06, judgment of 14 January 2014, 59 EHRR 1, applying *Al-Adsani v United Kingdom*,
and *Germany v Italy*, ICJ Reports 2012, 99, paras. 81–97; *Belhaj and others v Straw and others (United Nations
Special Rapporteur on Torture and others intervening)* [2017] UKSC 3, [2017] AC 964, SC; *Benkharbouche v
Embassy of the Republic of Sudan (secretary of State for Foreign Affairs and others intervening)* [2017] UKSC
62, [2017] ICR 1327, SC, where provisions of the State Immunity Act 1978 were disapplied where their effect
would have been inconsistent with the EU Charter of Fundamental Rights; Shaw, *International Law*, 715–6.

against representatives of foreign states for torture. (Officials of the UK, by contrast, cannot rely on state immunity in UK courts as a defence in actions alleging that they participated in mistreatment of the claimants by officials of other states.)[36]

Secondly, crimes in customary international law do not automatically become crimes justiciable before domestic courts in England and Wales. The common law is no longer capable of generating new crimes, and there are good constitutional reasons for requiring parliamentary authorization for new crimes and extensions to the criminal jurisdiction of domestic courts.[37] The requirement preserves parliamentary sovereignty and the integrity of municipal common law, and protects people against uncontrolled creation of criminal liabilities. The value of filters protecting a state's constitution and law from being changed without national authorization explains the decision in *R. v Jones (Margaret)*[38] that the crime of aggression in international law was not part of English criminal law, so people who used force to try to prevent the UK's preparations for the attack on Iraq in 2003 could not rely on the defence under Criminal Law Act 1967, s. 3 of having used reasonable force to prevent an unlawful act. Nevertheless, it points up the moral argument for a more monistic approach in order to uphold international criminal law.

The interplay of customary international law, international treaty obligations, and UK statute is illustrated by *R. v Bow Street Metropolitan Stipendiary Magistrate and others, ex parte Pinochet Ugarte (No. 3)*.[39] The applicant was a former President of Chile who was alleged to have authorized acts of torture and murder during his period in power, including some against Spanish citizens. A Spanish judge had issued an international arrest warrant seeking his extradition to Spain to face trial. The applicant had been arrested in England while on a visit to receive medical treatment. The question was whether he could be extradited. An exceptional seven-judge appellate committee of the House of Lords decided a number of issues.

(a) They held unanimously that a head of state would normally be entitled to claim immunity from legal process in the UK by virtue of a combination of customary international law and UK statutes dealing with state immunity and diplomatic immunity.[40]

(b) By a majority of four to three,[41] they held that, as noted above, torture (unlike murder) is an international crime against humanity by virtue of customary international law, and a peremptory norm of general international law, or *jus cogens*, overriding incompatible rules in customary international law or treaties.

---

[36] See *Belhaj*, n. 35 above.

[37] Roger O'Keefe, 'Customary International Crimes in English Courts' [2001] *BYIL* 293, 335.

[38] [2006] UKHL 16, [2007] 1 AC 136 (HL).   [39] [2000] 1 AC 147 (HL).

[40] See State Immunity Act 1978, s. 20(1) read together with Diplomatic Privileges Act 1964, Sched. 1, para. 39 (giving effect to the Vienna Convention on Diplomatic Relations).

[41] Lords Browne-Wilkinson, Hope of Craighead, Hutton, and Saville of Newdigate. Lords Millett and Phillips of Worth Matravers dissented on the ground that conspiracy to murder in Spain was also an international crime for which no immunity would be available. Lord Goff dissented on the ground that the statutory immunity applied even in relation to torture.

(c) They held unanimously that the Extradition Act 1989 in the UK prevented extradition for a crime which was not a crime in the UK (as well as in the state which has requested extradition of the suspect) at the time when it was committed (known as the 'double criminality rule').

(d) By a majority of four to three,[42] they held that torture committed outside the UK did not become a criminal offence in the UK until two conditions were met. First, there had to be legislation to make it a criminal offence. This was done by the Criminal Justice Act 1988, which came into force on 29 September 1988. Secondly, all the relevant states (Spain, Chile, and the UK) had to have ratified the Convention against Torture, which required states to recognize and provide in their own law for universal jurisdiction over offences of torture. In other words, every state party to the CAT was then obliged in international law both to accept jurisdiction over such cases in its own courts (wherever the torture was alleged to have been committed) and to recognize that other states' courts had similar jurisdiction. That happened on 8 December 1988.

(e) By a majority of six to one, it was held that after 8 December 1988 torture committed abroad was a criminal offence in the UK and so was an extradition crime.

This makes three constitutional principles clear. First, the UK operates a dualist filter not only in respect of treaties, but even in respect of a peremptory norm of general international law which establishes a crime against humanity. Only a legislature can authorize courts in the UK to impose criminal liability. Secondly, even when legislation is in place, English law[43] may recognize a treaty binding on the states involved in a case as an additional necessary step in establishing that there is international jurisdiction. In other words, English courts do not give effect to treaties as such, but may require a treaty before accepting that there is jurisdiction to extradite someone for an international crime against humanity, even when that crime has been shown to exist under statute and customary international law. Thirdly, so far as UK statutes dealing with state and diplomatic immunity are designed to give effect to international treaties, they will be interpreted in the light of those treaties, which themselves may be subject to a peremptory norm of general international law.

TERRITORIALITY AND INTERNATIONAL LAW

A further constitutional filter is the territorial principle. The scope of UK legislation is generally limited to the territory of the UK, even when giving effect to international obligations, although the legislation will be read in the light of those obligations, which

---

[42] Lords Browne-Wilkinson, Goff, Hope of Craighead, and Saville of Newdigate. Lord Hutton argued that it became an offence in the UK from the 29 September 1988 when Criminal Justice Act 1988, s. 134 came into force. Lords Millett and Phillips of Worth Matravers argued that it had been an international crime under customary international law before that, so there could be no immunity.

[43] This is probably also the position in Northern Ireland. Nothing is said here about the applicability of the *Pinochet Ugarte (No. 3)* decision in Scotland.

may require courts to give limited extraterritorial effect to the legislation. For example, the Human Rights Act 1998 gives domestic effect to rights under ECHR, Art. 1, which requires the high contracting parties to secure the rights to everyone within their jurisdictions. The European Court of Human Rights has interpreted this as imposing obligations towards people in areas outside a state's territory if the state has actual control there or, perhaps, exercises factual or *de jure* authority over the victim of the alleged violation.[44] The House of Lords and the Supreme Court held that it should follow the Strasbourg Court's recognition of extraterritorial effect for the ECHR, but only so far as a clear line of case law in the Strasbourg Court requires. At first, a majority of the Supreme Court regarded the Strasbourg jurisprudence on this matter as extending jurisdiction only to areas directly and effectively controlled by the UK's armed forces.[45] The Grand Chamber of the Strasbourg Court decided, however, that the notion of jurisdiction is more elastic, including cases where a state's agents have effective, extraterritorial control over persons or premises. As a result, civil liability may arise under the Human Rights Act 1998, although there may also be cases which give rise to issues in private, rather than public, international law.[46]

COUNTERVAILING OBLIGATIONS IN INTERNATIONAL LAW

Where international law operates as a source of domestic law, the courts have regard to the whole of public international law when establishing the scope of any right or obligation that is to have effect in domestic law. Elements cannot be examined in isolation. We have already seen one example of this: tort liability for torture is limited by the international as well as national law of state immunity.[47] Other international law rules capable of limiting human rights obligations in international and domestic law include those concerning diplomatic immunity[48] and the capacity of UN Security Council Resolutions made under Chapter VII of the UN Charter, protecting international peace and security, to authorize states to act inconsistently with their international human-rights obligations, if the authorization is sufficiently explicit.[49] Where a UK court has to apply rights in the ECHR, taking effect in municipal law by virtue of the Human Rights Act 1998, to events occurring outside the UK in territory subject to

---

[44] See e.g. *Banković v Belgium*, Application no. 52207/99, judgment of 12 December 2001 (GC); *Ilascu v Moldova and Russia*, Application no. 48787/99, judgment of 8 July 2004 (GC); Marko Milanovic, *Extraterritorial Application of Human Rights Treaties: Law, Principles, Policy* (2011), esp. Chs. 2 and 4.

[45] *R. (Al-Skeini) v Secretary of State for Defence (The Redress Trust and another intervening)* [2007] UKHL 26, [2008] AC 153 (HL); *R. (Smith) v Oxfordshire Assistant Deputy Coroner (Equality and Human Rights Commission intervening)* [2010] UKSC 29, [2010] 3 WLR 223 (SC).

[46] *Al-Skeini v United Kingdom*, Application no. 55721/07, judgment of 7 July 2011, 53 EHRR 589, (GC); *Smith v Ministry of Defence (JUSTICE intervening)* [2013] UKSC 41, [2014] AC 52 (SC); cf. *Al-Jedda v Secretary of State for Defence* [2010] EWCA Civ 758, [2011] QB 773 (CA).

[47] *Jones v Ministry of the Interior of the Kingdom of Saudi Arabia and another (Secretary of State for Constitutional Affairs and others intervening)* [2006] UKHL 26, [2007] 1 AC 270 (HL).

[48] *R. (B.) v Secretary of State for Foreign and Commonwealth Affairs* [2004] EWCA Civ 1344, [2005] QB 643 (CA).

[49] *Al-Jedda v United Kingdom*, Application no. 27120/08, judgment of 7 July 2011, 53 EHRR 789 (GC).

a Chapter VII resolution, Convention rights may have to be adjusted to accommodate the requirements of the resolution.[50]

Thus, dualism operates in the UK, but the division between municipal and public international law should be seen as a semi-permeable membrane, which allows rules to pass through it in different directions for different purposes. The matter is further complicated by two decisions going in different directions. In one, the Strasbourg Court held that acts of a country's armed forces operating abroad under the authority of a UN Security Council resolution made under UN Charter, Chapter VII were attributable to the United Nations rather than the state concerned, which was accordingly not liable for any violation of the ECHR, but the Grand Chamber has since made it clear, following the International Law Commission and the House of Lords, that this depends on the UN Security Council having effective control over (or at the very least ultimate authority for) the conduct of forces.[51] In the other, the European Court of Justice held that the European Union is an autonomous legal order independent of international law, so that its fundamental rights are not affected by developments such as UN Security Council Chapter VII resolutions.[52] This will have effect in the UK in relation to EU norms and acts, including those carried out by UK authorities on behalf of the European Union's organs until the UK leaves the EU and thereafter in respect of 'retained EU law' if and when the European Union (Withdrawal) Act 2018 comes fully into effect.

DUALISM, TREATIES, AND INTERNATIONAL ORGANIZATIONS

The UK's dualist filter has been most fully applied in respect of treaties, the action of international organizations established under treaties, and the activities of the Government relating to external affairs, conducted under the authority of the royal prerogative, more generally. Usually, rights and obligations arising under treaties do not take effect in municipal legal systems with a dualist principle unless legislation has been passed to give effect to them. For example, rights under the ECHR, as a multilateral treaty, could not be directly litigated before courts in the UK until the Human Rights Act 1998 had made them effective in municipal law.[53] This has two effects. First, it prevents the Crown (in reality the government of the day, which normally conducts foreign affairs under the royal prerogative) from exercising its treaty-making prerogative in ways which change the law in the UK without parliamentary

---

[50] *Al-Waheed v Ministry of Defence; Serdar Mahammed v Ministry of Defence (No. 2) (Qasim and others intervening)* [2017] UKSC 2, [2017] AC 821, SC; *R. (Al-Saadoon) v Secretary of State for Defence* [2016] EWCA Civ 811, [2017] QB 1015, CA.

[51] *Behrami v France*, Application no. 71412/01, admissibility decision of 2 May 2007 (GC); *R. (Al-Jedda) v Secretary of State for Defence* [2007] UKHL 23, [2004] 1 AC 185 (HL); *Al-Jedda v United Kingdom*, Application no. 27021, judgment of 7 July 2011 (GC), para. 84.

[52] Joined Cases C-402/05P and C-415/05P, *Kadi v Council of the European Union* [2008] ECR I-6351, [2009] AC 1225 (CJEC). See also *A. v HM Treasury* [2010] UKSC 2, [2010] 2 WLR 378 (SC).

[53] See e.g. *Malone v Metropolitan Police Commissioner (No. 2)* [1979] Ch 344; *R. v Secretary of State for the Home Department, ex parte Brind* [1991] 1 AC 696 (HL); *R. v Ministry of Defence, ex parte Smith* [1996] QB 517 (CA).

approval. However, in the absence of a statutory requirement, there is no need to obtain parliamentary approval before negotiating, signing, or ratifying a treaty,[54] or undertaking other activities relating to external affairs. This can be limited by Act of Parliament. For example, the European Union Act 2011 (to be repealed when the European Union (Withdrawal) Act 2018 comes fully into force) prohibited ministers from ratifying a treaty or taking some other steps increasing the specified competences of the EU without an Act of Parliament or, in certain cases, holding a referendum. The Supreme Court also held, by a majority, that ministers were not allowed to exercise the foreign-affairs prerogative to give notice of intention to withdraw from the EU without that notice being authorized by an Act of Parliament, since, on the (perhaps erroneous but uncontested) assumption that that step would lead inexorably to EU law and rights no longer being available in the UK, it would have been inconsistent with the spirit or intendment of the European Communities Act 1972.[55] It is not yet clear whether, or when, this style of statutory interpretation might lead to other international activities of the Government being regarded as unlawful in the future if not authorized expressly by Act of Parliament.

In other cases, to compensate for the loss of democratic control, dualism prevents the treaty-making prerogative being used to extend the power of the executive and protects the legislative supremacy of Parliament against attrition. It also protects both the government and Parliament against the direct imposition of the will of other states, contrary to the UK's national interests, through international treaties and the resolutions of international organizations. Thus, the UK Parliament can refuse to give effect to treaty obligations in municipal law. It, and the government of the day, can also refuse to accept that a treaty imposes any binding obligation. For example, the previous (Labour) government's view of economic and social rights arising under the International Covenant on Economic, Social and Cultural Rights and the Convention on the Rights of the Child was that the obligations were aspirational rather than immediate, and did not require the state to guarantee an ascertainable level of protection by a particular time.[56] Refusing to recognize or comply with treaty obligations might lead to sanctions for breach of international law if any are available, but it leaves the UK's legislatures ultimately in control of their own legal systems.[57]

[54] See *JH Rayner (Mincing Lane) Ltd v Department of Trade and Industry* [1990] 2 AC 418 (HL), 500, *per* Lord Oliver of Aylmerton. Statutory requirements for parliamentary approval are rare.

[55] *R. (Miller) v Secretary of State for Exiting the European Union* [2017] UKSC 5, [2018] AC 61, SC; Mark Elliott, 'The Supreme Court's Judgment in Miller: In Search of Constitutional Principle' [2017] *CLJ* 257–288. Compare Jeffrey Jowell, 'Brexit Judicialised: Crown v Parliament Again', 2016–17, *Supreme Court Yearbook*, 238, and other articles in that volume. See also Craig's Chapter in this volume, Chapter 4.

[56] For the government's position on the Convention on the Rights of the Child and criticism of it, see Joint Committee on Human Rights, Tenth Report of 2002–3, *The UN Convention on the Rights of the Child*, HL 117/ HC 81 (2003), paras. 21–3.

[57] This fundamental point has been lost in the heated exchanges concerning cases in which the European Court of Human Rights has held that the UK's blanket prohibition on convicted prisoners' voting in elections violates the right to vote under ECHR Protocol 1, Art. 3. See David Feldman, 'Sovereignties in Strasbourg' in Richard Rawlings, Peter Leyland and Alison L. Young (eds.), *Sovereignty and the Law: Domestic, European, and International Perspectives* (2013), Ch. 12, esp. 223–4.

This protection for state autonomy can be attenuated. The European Communities Act 1972 provides (until its repeal by the European Union (Withdrawal) Act 2018 takes effect) for some EU rights and obligations to be enforced directly in courts and tribunals in the UK.[58] This allows ministers to change the law in the UK by agreement in Brussels without parliamentary approval. There are some safeguards for national interests. When the supremacy of EC law was established by the Court of Justice of the European Communities (CJEC), the Council needed to agree unanimously in order to legislate. This has since changed. The range of decisions requiring unanimity has steadily narrowed, most recently in the Treaty of Lisbon, and there is no legal protection for parliamentary sovereignty, although some procedural safeguards have been put in place. These include the 'scrutiny reserve' which usually prevents the UK government from agreeing to measures being adopted in Brussels until they have been scrutinized by the Houses of Parliament, a task performed with distinction by committees in both Houses.[59]

In relation to treaties which do not directly alter municipal law, Parliament's position is weak, despite (or because of) dualism. At present, the two Houses normally have no right to be consulted before the text of a treaty is concluded, much less a veto over its signing or ratification. The government makes treaties and is usually accountable to Parliament only afterwards. There used to be a constitutional convention (the 'Ponsonby rule', dating from 1924) that treaties would not be ratified until they had been laid before both Houses of Parliament for 21 days. This did not apply to treaties which did not require ratification and were merely technical;[60] but the government would 'inform the House of all agreements, commitments and undertakings which may in any way bind the nation to specific action in certain circumstances'.[61] The rule, with certain adjustments to limit its impact on governmental freedom, was put on a statutory footing by the Constitutional Reform and Governance Act 2010, ss. 20–25. However, this gives Parliament no more than a right to receive information about the government's treaty-making activities.

Treaties by which the UK becomes a member of supranational or international organizations whose institutions have law-making powers especially call for filters to protect the municipal legal systems against adverse effects, but also make it more difficult to secure that protection. The value of filters in such a system depends on the power of the state to influence the content of obligations imposed on it by treaty bodies. When the UK became part of the European Economic Community (EEC) in 1973 it was an

---

[58] European Communities Act 1972, s. 2, discussed further later.

[59] See the resolutions of the two Houses at *Hansard*, HC, cols. 778ff. (17 November 1998), and *Hansard*, HL, cols. 1019ff. (6 December 1999); K. M. Newman, 'The Impact of National Parliaments on the Development of Community Law' in F. Capotorti (ed.), *Du Droit International au Droit de l'Integration: Liber Amicorum Pierre Pescatore* (1987), 481–97; T. St. John Bates, 'European Community Legislation before the House of Commons' (1991) 12 *Stat LR* 109–24.

[60] 'Technical' is not a technical term. It is capable of covering treaties establishing procedures for giving effect to already existing substantive obligations, and perhaps treaties concerned with the way states deal with fields in which their jurisdictions overlap, for instance in relation to double-taxation agreements.

[61] *Hansard*, HC (5th series), vol. 171, col. 2001 (1 April 1924).

association of a small group of Western European nations designed to remove national barriers to economic development and to turn the member states into a single market (the 'Common Market') in goods and services. At that stage, national interests were strongly protected by equal state representation on the main law-making body and (as noted earlier) a requirement for unanimity to make law. The veto power of each member state gave reasonable protection for the UK's national interests, making possible the UK's acceptance of the direct effect of some Community legislation and of the doctrine of the supremacy of Community law. Over time, however, the number of member states and the diversity of their interests increased, and the law-making activities of the institution grew in range and complexity. The EEC turned into the European Community and later the European Union, dedicated to harmonizing a growing range of economic and social policies, including the regulation of police and judicial cooperation and other fields of common concern. As qualified majority voting was introduced, the safeguards for vital national interests, which had originally justified relaxing the national filters by accepting the direct effect of EC law, became progressively weaker, and the Treaty of Lisbon in 2007 (which came into force on 1 December 2009) continued that trend. Parliament's attempt in the European Union Act 2011 (now to be repealed by the European Union (Withdrawal) Act 2018 when it takes effect) to restrict the government's power to agree to EU measures was in part a response to it.

Some international organizations never demand unanimity in decision-making. From its establishment in 1946, the United Nations had such a large membership that unanimity was never a practical option. Each member state has a seat in the General Assembly, but that body's recommendations do not bind states in public international law except in relation to the internal governance of the United Nations[62] (although resolutions may be evidence of the emergence of binding rules of customary international law if they reflect state practice). The main power to impose obligations binding states in international law is conferred on the Security Council, which forms the executive group of the United Nations with special responsibility for preserving international peace and security.[63] Decisions of the Council (but not mere recommendations) bind all member states.[64] Only 15 states are members of the Security Council. Five of them, the 'great powers' of the period following the Second World War (China, France, Russia, the UK, and the USA), are permanent members. The other ten members are elected for a period of two years from among the remaining members of the General Assembly, as laid down by UN Charter, Art. 23.2. Security Council Resolutions must be approved by an affirmative vote of at least nine members, but any of the permanent members may veto any proposed resolution, except in relation to procedural matters (such as the agenda for sessions, or the states which should be given the opportunity to address the Council in matters affecting them), where there is no veto.[65] This offers asymmetric protection to national interests. Those of the five permanent members are well protected by their veto. Those of the non-permanent members can be

---

[62] UN Charter, Art. 17.   [63] Ibid., Arts. 23, 24, 25, and 28.
[64] Ibid., Art. 25.   [65] Ibid., Art. 27.

subordinated to the interests of nine concurring members, although they may benefit from overlapping the vital interests of one of the permanent members. States without a seat on the Security Council are even less well protected. As members of the United Nations they can use diplomatic techniques in defence of their interests, but their success will depend significantly on the balance of power and the interests of the 'great powers'.

For historical reasons, the UK is a permanent member of the UN Security Council, so it has a measure of control over the most important decisions. In other international organizations, it has influence rather than control, and the extent of its influence depends on the arguments and pressure it can apply. By contrast, the USA, the Russian Federation (formerly the USSR), and today China, as world superpowers in terms of their military or economic might, can exercise great influence by offers of aid with strings attached, or by explicit or implicit threats of trade sanctions, withdrawal of aid, or in extreme cases invasion. Such influence does not depend on the quality of the superpower's arguments or the morality of its stance. It extends beyond organizations of which the superpowers are members, although even a superpower must sometimes take account of other states' points of view, as the aftermath of the second Gulf War in 2003 has shown.

MECHANISMS FOR INTERNATIONALIZATION, CONSTITUTIONAL STRUCTURES, AND LEGITIMACY

Those international influences to which states are inevitably subject must be channelled into municipal law and made to fit within the state's constitutional law and traditions. How is this done?[66]

INCORPORATION OR DIRECT APPLICATION OF INTERNATIONAL OR SUPRANATIONAL LEGAL RULES

The most direct form of international (or at least supranational) influence arises when rules made by another state or states, or accepted at inter-state level, are automatically incorporated into the municipal legal system, without the need for any prior or subsequent legislative action. In the UK, the most straightforward example of this is the automatic incorporation of rules of customary international law (subject to inconsistent legislation or earlier judicial decisions), as mentioned in the previous section.

Marginally less direct, but more powerful, was the process whereby certain rules of EU law became part of the municipal legal system. The European Communities Act 1972, s 2(1) created what was, in effect, a statutory rule of automatic incorporation of what it called 'enforceable Community rights'. Because of the doctrine of the supremacy of EC law over national law, this form of incorporation had a greater impact than the incorporation of customary international law. Enforceable Community rights

---

[66] David Feldman, 'Modalities of Internationalisation in International Law' (2006) 18 *ERPL* 131.

did not need to be compatible with previous or subsequent parliamentary legislation. Instead, inconsistent parliamentary legislation had to be disapplied to the extent that it was inconsistent with enforceable Community rights.[67]

In addition, s. 2(2) of the Act allowed Her Majesty in Council or designated ministers and departments to give effect to or implement other EC obligations or rights (including those arising under directives which do not have direct effect) in municipal law by way of statutory instruments, a form of subordinate legislation. These were usually subject only to the negative resolution procedure: they took effect unless either House passed a resolution annulling them.[68] Statutory instruments under s. 2(2) could make any provision that could be made by Act of Parliament. They could even amend or repeal Acts of Parliament; and any provision of primary legislation was to be construed and to have effect subject to the provisions of the statutory instrument.[69] A subsequent Act of Parliament could revoke the statutory instrument, as long as that would not be incompatible with enforceable Community rights. Nevertheless, the filters protecting parliamentary control over the implementation of EU law were limited: the negative resolution procedure is hardly a strong form of scrutiny or protection, and the best filter was the pre-adoption scrutiny of EU measures by the House of Commons EU Scrutiny Committee and the House of Lords EU Select Committee and its subcommittees.[70] What is more, in some fields the member states delegated power to the European Commission to negotiate treaties on their behalf with non-member states, including agreements on tariffs and trade and arrangements for extradition. The impact of such agreements on the rights and obligations of member states was uncertain.[71] If the UK withdraws from the EU, most of the body of EU law applicable to the UK beforehand will be transformed into municipal law in the UK by virtue of the European Union (Withdrawal) Act 2018, which will also hand exceptionally extensive power to ministers to make changes to that law by subordinate legislation. It remains to be seen how much control, in practice, the two Houses of Parliament will be able to exert over that subordinate legislation.

Following the establishment of the United Nations in 1946, Parliament conferred power on the government to implement certain decisions of the UN Security Council by way of subordinate legislation, with limited or non-existent parliamentary oversight. When the Security Council, acting to preserve international peace and security under UN Charter, Chapter VII, calls on the government to apply any measures to give effect to any decision of the Council under UN Charter, Art. 41 (that is, decisions not involving the use of armed force), United Nations Act 1946, s. 1(1) allows Her Majesty by Order in Council to make 'such provision as appears to Her to be necessary or expedient for enabling the measures to be effectively applied'. The Order must be laid before Parliament forthwith after it is made, and, if it relates to a matter within

---

[67] See Chapter 4 in this volume.   [68] European Communities Act 1972, Sched. 2, para. 2(2).
[69] Ibid., s. 2(4).   [70] See discussion in Chapter 4 in this volume.
[71] See Vienna Convention on the Law of Treaties between States and International Organisations and between International Organisations 1986; Shaw, *International Law*, 1004–6.

the legislative competence of the Scottish Parliament, before that Parliament as well,[72] but neither Parliament can annul the Order save by means of an Act. Still less do such Orders require the approval of either House. The only control available is through judicial review. An Order can be quashed if it is outside the scope of the power conferred by the Act or is incompatible with a Community right (such as the right to be free of quantitative restrictions on free movement of goods)[73] or a Convention right under the Human Rights Act 1998. But if it acts compatibly with EU law (including, after withdrawal from the EU, any relevant retained EU law so far as not changed by Act or by ministers by subordinate legislation) and Convention rights, the government has a very wide discretion as to the terms of the Order and the Treasury has a very wide discretion as to the manner of its implementation.[74]

The scope of the power is enormous, and Orders can directly affect individuals. For example, after the terrorist attacks on the World Trade Center on 11 September 2001 the UN Security Council passed Resolution 1373 of 28 September 2001, calling on the governments of member states to apply measures to give effect to decisions of the Council to combat terrorist activities. It required steps to be taken to freeze terrorist assets. In the UK, the government implemented this by Orders in Council making it a criminal offence to make funds or financial services available to or for the benefit of people participating in acts of terrorism or to fail to report suspicions that people are intending to use funds for such a purpose, and allowing the Treasury to freeze the funds of such people whom the Treasury has reasonable grounds for suspecting may be holding funds for the purpose of committing, facilitating, or participating in acts of terrorism.[75] These Orders were subject to no parliamentary control or scrutiny either before or after they were made. In reliance on them, the Treasury froze the assets of several dozen people, and announced its action in press releases.[76] The Security Council resolution thus authorized a direct attack by the British government on individuals' property, with very limited safeguards and filters within the jurisdiction for rule-of-law requirements and the democratic process.

However, the Supreme Court reasserted respect for fundamental rights, holding that several of these orders were ultra vires the United Nations Act 1946, s. 1. This was partly because they infringed fundamental rights without a fair hearing and subordinate legislation could not validly do that unless an Act of Parliament had expressly conferred a power to do so, and partly because the orders were drafted more broadly than was justified by the Security Council resolutions. The government introduced an emergency bill to preserve the orders until new legislation was passed to define the

---

[72] European Communities Act 1972, s. 1(4), as amended by the Scotland Act 1998.

[73] See *R. v HM Treasury, ex parte Centro-Com Srl* [1997] QB 863 (CJEC).

[74] See *R. v HM Treasury, ex parte Centro-Com Srl, The Independent*, 3 June 1994 (CA), affirming (in relation to municipal law) [1994] 1 CMLR 109. On the implications of EC law, see the decision of the Court of Justice on the reference from the Court of Appeal: [1997] QB 683 (CJEC).

[75] Terrorism (United Nations Measures) (Channel Islands) Order 2001 (SI 2001/3363); Terrorism (United Nations Measures) (Isle of Man) Order 2001 (SI 2001/3364); Terrorism (United Nations Measures) Order 2001 (SI 2001/3365).

[76] See e.g. Treasury Press Release 110/01, 12 October 2001, which includes a list of names.

asset-freezing power more closely and provide for appeal to or review by courts of Treasury decisions.[77]

Today, a provision in a bill allowing the government to introduce international obligations to municipal law by delegated legislation would be likely to face more intensive parliamentary scrutiny than in 1946. In particular, the House of Lords Select Committee on Delegated Powers and Regulatory Reform, which scrutinizes all provisions in bills before Parliament which confer power to make delegated legislation, would seek to insist on including sufficient safeguards in the bill by way of a requirement for adequate parliamentary scrutiny of proposed subordinate legislation to protect the rule of law and human rights. Where the proposed power could affect human rights or constitutional principles, the Joint Select Committee on Human Rights and the House of Lords Select Committee on the Constitution would provide additional pressure. It is noteworthy that the powers included in the Anti-terrorism, Crime and Security Act 2001 to permit EU initiatives on police and judicial cooperation in criminal matters to be given effect in the UK by way of subordinate legislation included far more safeguards than are found in the United Nations Act 1946.[78] Even then the government agreed that legislation to implement the Framework Decision on the European Arrest Warrant would be introduced by way of a bill (now Extradition Act 2003, Pt 1) rather than by using the power to make subordinate legislation under the 2001 Act.[79]

Similar caution about authorizing subordinate legislation can be seen in the Human Rights Act 1998 and the devolution legislation to making rights under the ECHR ('the Convention rights') effective in municipal law in the UK.[80] The Human Rights Act 1998, s. 1, applied in the devolution legislation,[81] appears to import the rights bodily from international law (the ECHR) to national law. However, the transplant is complicated by two factors. First, the rights in international law bind states, whereas in municipal law they bind public authorities within the state. This necessitated adjustments designed, among other things, to adapt the rights for municipal application and maintain consistency with constitutional principles such as parliamentary sovereignty and parliamentary privilege.[82] Secondly, there is a difference between formulating a right and understanding what it means when applied in practice. Both the scope of the Convention rights and the circumstances (if any) in which it is justifiable to interfere

---

[77] *Ahmed and others v HM Treasury (JUSTICE intervening) (Nos. 1 and 2)* [2010] UKSC 2, [2010] 2 WLR 378 (SC); Terrorist Asset-Freezing (Temporary Provisions) Act 2010; Terrorist Asset-Freezing etc. Act 2010, Pt 1.

[78] See Anti-terrorism, Crime and Security Act 2001, ss. 111 and 112. For further primary legislation on cross-border cooperation, see Crime (International Co-operation) Act 2003. The same point was made by Lord Hope of Craighead DPSC in *Ahmed v HM Treasury* [2010] UKSC 2, [2010] 2 WLR 378 (SC), at [48]–[53], arguing that the government should have used either primary legislation or the procedure under the 2001 Act to give effect to the Security Council resolutions.

[79] See Joint Committee on Human Rights, Second Report, 2001–2, *Anti-terrorism, Crime and Security Bill*, HL 37/HC 372, para. 13.

[80] See Chapters 4 and 9 in this volume.

[81] See Scotland Act 1998, ss. 29(2), 54(2), 100 and 126(1); Northern Ireland Act 1998, ss. 6(2), 24(1) and 98(1); Government of Wales Act 2006, ss. 81, 108A and 158(1).

[82] See e.g. the partial delimitation of the term 'public authority' in the Human Rights Act 1998, s. 6.

with them in international law depend on the extensive case law of the European Commission and the European Court of Human Rights. Parts of it, such as the notion of the 'margin of appreciation', arise from the position of international tribunals vis-à-vis national authorities and cannot be transferred to municipal law. Even if a particular line of case law can be transferred to the municipal sphere, there may be good reasons for limiting its impact. The Human Rights Act 1998, s. 2 therefore provides that courts and tribunals in the UK must take into account the case law of the Strasbourg organs when interpreting the Convention rights, but does not make it binding. Courts in the UK have on occasions declined to follow judgments of the European Court of Human Rights.[83] For example, the House of Lords has held that normal rules of precedent generally require a lower court in England and Wales to follow an earlier decision of a higher domestic court on the application of Convention rights in preference to a later, inconsistent decision of the European Court of Human Rights, unless it is clear that the policy justification for the earlier English decision no longer applies.[84] This introduces a filter into the channel by which the Convention rights enter municipal law: courts and tribunals in the UK are not required to follow decisions of international tribunals if they seem inappropriate to the structure of the domestic legal order or plainly wrong.

The Act also empowers ministers to make statutory instruments for various purposes, providing further channels for bringing municipal law into line with the ECHR. With relatively few preconditions or procedural filters a Secretary of State can make a statutory instrument adding an extra right to the list of Convention rights which became part of municipal law by virtue of s. 1 of the Act. With equally little formal constraint, a Secretary of State can add a reservation to the newly recognized right to the list of reservations in s. 1 of, and Pt 1 of Sched. 3 to, the Act, or add a derogation from a Convention right to those recognized in s. 1 of, and Pt 2 of Sched. 3 to, the Act. Any UK court or tribunal interpreting a Convention right must then read it subject to the reservation or derogation in question. There have been two changes to the derogations recognized in the Act, both in relation to terrorism: the original derogation was repealed, and later a new one was inserted;[85] but the derogation order adding the new derogation was subsequently held to be ultra vires because the measures concerned were not strictly required by the exigencies of the terrorist

---

[83] On the circumstances in which courts in the UK should follow Strasbourg judgments, see e.g. *R. (Alconbury Developments Ltd) v Secretary of State for the Environment, Transport and the Regions* [2001] UKHL 23, [2003] 2 AC 295 (HL), at [26], per Lord Slynn of Hadley; *R. (Ullah) v Special Adjudicator* [2004] UKHL 26, [2004] 2 AC 323, at [20], per Lord Bingham of Cornhill; *R. v Horncastle* [2009] UKSC 14, [2010] 2 WLR 47 (SC); *Manchester City Council v Pinnock* [2010] SC 45, at [48]–[49]; *Rabone v Pennine Care NHS Foundation Trust* [2012] UKSC 2, [2012] 2 AC 72, SC; *R. (Chester) v Secretary of State for Justice* [2013] UKSC 63, [2014] AC 271 at [27] per Lord Mance; *R. (Haney and others) v Secretary of State for Justice* [2014] UKSC 66 at [18]–[40] *R. v McLoughlin, R. v Newell, Attorney General's Reference (No. 69 of 2013)* [2014] EWCA Crim 188, [2014] 1 WLR 3964, CA.

[84] *Kay v Lambeth LBC; Leeds City Council v Price* [2006] UKHL 10, [2006] 2 AC 465 (HL), not overruled on this point in *Manchester City Council v Pinnock*, and reaffirmed in *R. (Haney)* (see n. 83).

[85] Human Rights Act 1998 (Amendment) Order 2001, SI 2001/1216 and Human Rights Act 1998 (Designated Derogation) Order 2001, SI 2001/3641 respectively.

threat and consistent with the UK's other international obligations so as to meet the requirements of Art. 15 of the ECHR, so at present (as of April 2019) there is no designated derogation.[86]

If the Strasbourg Court or a UK court decides that UK legislation is incompatible with a Convention right, the Human Rights Act 1998, s. 10 empowers the appropriate Secretary of State to make a 'remedial order'. This is an Order in Council amending or repealing the incompatible provision, which will usually be in an Act of Parliament. As this is a power to amend or repeal Acts of Parliament by Order in Council (sometimes known as a 'Henry VIII' provision), the House of Lords Select Committee on Delegated Powers and Deregulation,[87] scrutinizing the Human Rights Bill in 1997, recommended that this 'Henry VIII' power should be hedged about with preconditions and procedural requirements to ensure proper parliamentary scrutiny of any proposal to make such an Order. The Bill was accordingly amended, and very strict, time-consuming provisions are now contained in s. 10 of, and Sched. 2 to, the Act. As a result, making a remedial order is a long-drawn-out, complex process, which inhibits the use of remedial orders even though their purpose is to protect and extend, rather than to interfere with, human rights. By contrast, an order to introduce a new derogation from a Convention right into the Human Rights Act was not hedged about with special restrictions, with the result that it is easier to make a statutory instrument under section 15 of the Act to restrict Convention rights by requiring courts in the UK to interpret them in the light of a new derogation than to make one which protects rights amending or repealing previously incompatible legislation.

INFORMAL INFLUENCE OF INTERNATIONAL LEGAL RULES

Even where there is no express legislative authority for allowing international standards and treaties to influence municipal law, both treaties and the judgments of international and foreign tribunals can influence parliamentary and judicial decision-making in the UK. Parliament and government departments are increasingly aware of the UK's obligations as a result of the work of the government's legal advisers and select committees and individual members in Parliament. This is affecting both the content

---

[86] See Human Rights Act 1998 (Amendment) Order 2001 (SI 2001/1216), removing a derogation from ECHR, Art. 5 in relation to detaining terrorist suspects without charge for up to seven days before being brought before a judicial officer; Human Rights Act 1998 (Designated Derogation) Order 2001 (SI 2001/3644), introducing a new derogation from Art. 5 to allow indefinite detention without trial of suspected international terrorists who were not UK nationals if they could not be removed abroad for legal or practical reasons under the Anti-terrorism, Crime and Security Act 2001; Human Rights Act 1998 (Amendment) Order 2004 (SI 2004/1574), replacing Protocol 6 with Protocol 13 in the list of Convention rights; and Human Rights Act 1998 (Amendment) Order 2005 (SI 2005/1071), removing the derogation from Art. 5 after the House of Lords had held it to be invalid in *A v Secretary of State for the Home Department* [2004] UKHL 56, [2005] 2 AC 68 (HL). Lord Scott of Foscote expressed doubt as to the applicability of Art. 15, as it was not one of the provisions made part of the legal systems of the UK by the Human Rights Act 1998, s. 1, but the Home Secretary had conceded its relevance.

[87] The forerunner of the Select Committee on Delegated Powers and Regulatory Reform.

of legislation and the way in which scrutiny of government is conducted.[88] If it cannot yet be said that the influence is pervasive, it is at least significant and growing. The main constraint is the government's unwillingness to accept that economic, social, and cultural rights can impose immediate, binding, and justiciable obligations on the UK,[89] but this may change over time. This use of international standards is fully consistent with parliamentary democracy. When used within Parliament, the standards merely help to inform debate rather than foreclose it. When judges look to international standards as guides to the implementation of legislation, they do so on the assumption that legislation is to be given effect compatibly with the UK's international obligations (in the absence of a clear indication to the contrary). Neither this nor any effect on the common law can limit or extend either the UK's international obligations or the freedom of the Queen in Parliament to legislate inconsistently with those obligations for the purpose of municipal law.[90]

JUDGES AS COMPARATISTS AND INTERNATIONALISTS

The judiciary too is a channel for allowing foreign influences into national public law systems. Judges in many countries round the world have a keen interest in foreign and international public law standards, including—but not limited to—human rights. In many common law jurisdictions they consider and draw illumination from public law judgments of courts elsewhere in the world. Judges do not simply adopt solutions or interpretations which have found favour elsewhere. The differences between constitutional and political structures in different countries make that undesirable: there may be no certainty that the solutions would fit a local context. Instead, they find it helpful to see how courts in different constitutional traditions have conceptualized and analysed the conflicting interests relevant to public law problems. This can help to crystallize issues and suggest approaches without dictating an outcome. Courts in the UK regularly use comparative law as a source of ideas for developing the common law and interpreting human rights.[91] Senior British judges have long been familiar with different constitutional and human rights arrangements through sitting regularly as members of the Judicial Committee of the Privy Council on public law appeals.

Interaction with academics also encourages judges to take an interest in comparative law. Judges regularly participate in academic seminars and conferences concerning

---

[88] See e.g. Lord Lester of Herne Hill, QC, 'Parliamentary Scrutiny of Legislation under the Human Rights Act 1998' [2002] *EHRLRev* 432; David Feldman, 'The Impact of Human Rights on the Legislative Process' (2004) 25 *Stat L Rev.* 91; Janet Hiebert, 'Parliamentary Review of Terrorism Measures' (2005) 58 *MLR* 676; Janet Hiebert, 'Interpreting a Bill of Rights: The Importance of Legislative Rights Review' [2005] *BJPS* 235; Carolyn Evans and Simon Evans, 'Legislative Scrutiny Committees and Parliamentary Conceptions of Human Rights' [2006] *PL* 785.

[89] See above, n. 56.   [90] See Feldman, 'Sovereignties in Strasbourg'.

[91] For a critical analysis of the uses made of comparative law, see Mads Andenas and Duncan Fairgrieve, '"There Is a World Elsewhere"—Lord Bingham and Comparative Law' in Mads Andenas and Duncan Fairgrieve (eds.), *Tom Bingham and the Transformation of the Law: A Liber Amicorum* (2009), 831–66.

international and comparative public law. The Judicial College increasingly involves academics in judicial discussions and seminars. A growing number of senior judges have had previous experience as legal academics.

Senior judges in different jurisdictions communicate extensively with each other, building up personal friendships and professional links through judicial colloquia and email. The internet offers access to a huge archive of legal materials from many jurisdictions.[92] The Law Commission and other bodies entrusted with the task of law reform now routinely undertake comparative research on the areas of law under review. English judges have also become far readier than before to make use of international legal materials in their judgments, including opinions, recommendations and resolutions of experts and international bodies that do not bind states in public international law. This 'soft law' influences outcomes by establishing a normative framework which tends to favour one outcome of the 'hard law' dispute over another. In England and Wales, judges sometimes assume that its appropriateness is self-evident, but may in many cases be able to justify it on the ground that it represents customary international law. Where that is so, it is tenable to argue that treaty obligations should be interpreted in the light of the matrix of international obligations within which they operate, and 'if, and to the extent that, development of the common law is called for, such development should ordinarily be in harmony with the UK's international obligations and not antithetical to them'.[93] This open intellectual atmosphere, influenced by judges' growing familiarity with international and comparative methods through their work with the Human Rights Act 1998, various commercial law conventions, and other sources, is likely to grow stronger. Judges will be keen to compare techniques of constitutional reasoning and hear how courts elsewhere approach such matters as the interpretation of legislation so as to make it compatible with human rights.

This approach offers benefits, but it can be taken too far if, without constitutional authority, one makes comparative legal methods a judicial duty rather than an optional aid. For example, in *Lange v Atkinson and Australian Consolidated Press NZ Ltd*[94] David Lange, a former prime minister of New Zealand, sued for libel in both New Zealand and Australia in respect of a magazine article criticizing his performance as a politician and suggesting that he suffered from selective memory loss. One issue was whether 'political expression' was entitled to either absolute or qualified privilege against liability. The High Court of Australia decided that a common-law qualified privilege applied, as long as the publishers proved that they had acted reasonably.[95] In New Zealand, however, the Court of Appeal held that the publications attracted

---

[92] See A.-M. Slaughter, 'A Global Community of Courts' (2003) 44 *Harvard International Law Journal* 191.

[93] *A v Secretary of State for the Home Department (No. 2)* [2005] UKHL 71, [2006] 2 AC 221 (HL), at [27], *per* Lord Bingham of Cornhill; see also [28]–[29]. See further, e.g., cases on the implications for law in the UK of allegations of torture abroad: *Jones v Ministry of the Interior of the Kingdom of Saudi Arabia (Secretary of State for Constitutional Affairs and others intervening)* [2006] UKHL 26, [2007] 1 AC 270 (HL).

[94] [2000] 1 NZLR 257 (PC).

[95] *Lange v Australian Broadcasting Corporation* (1997) 189 CLR 520 (HC of Australia).

qualified privilege, but, unlike the High Court of Australia, held that at common law in
New Zealand only malice could deprive the publishers of the privilege, so the reasonableness of the publishers' conduct was irrelevant.[96] Mr Lange appealed to the Privy
Council against the New Zealand decision of the Court of Appeal, but, before the Privy
Council delivered its judgment, the House of Lords ruled on the same issue in *Reynolds
v Times Newspapers Ltd*.[97] In its judgment in *Lange*, the Privy Council, whilst noting
differences between the Australian, New Zealand, and English approaches to an issue
which 'calls for a value judgment which depends upon local political and social conditions' with 'a high content of judicial policy', and accepting that 'different solutions may
be reached in different jurisdictions without any faulty reasoning or misconception',
nevertheless sent the case back for a further hearing in New Zealand because the Court
of Appeal had not had the opportunity to consider the Law Lords' decision in *Reynolds*
before making its decision.[98]

This comes close to imposing a duty on top common law courts to have regard to
(though not to follow) each other's leading decisions. Yet the decision does not explain
the legitimate basis for having regard to foreign authorities as guides to developing
one's own public law, let alone justify allowing an appeal in order to force another court
to do so.

On constitutional grounds, the decision is hard to justify. Unstructured picking and
choosing between sources can undermine or evade the filters which, for good constitutional reasons, constrain foreign influences on domestic legal systems. There has
been heated disagreement in the USA about the propriety of taking account of either
international law standards which do not form part of municipal law in the USA or
decisions of courts in other common law countries. American judges are comfort-
able with comparative law techniques, as federal law must take account of dozens of
state legal systems and constitutions, but some have challenged the legitimacy of relying on international developments when taking US constitutional jurisprudence in
a new direction. In *Atkins v Virginia*,[99] the US Supreme Court, in a footnote to the
majority judgment of Stevens J, adverted in passing to the fact that 'within the world
community, the imposition of the death penalty for crimes committed by mentally re-
tarded offenders is overwhelmingly disapproved' as evidence for an evolving standard
of decency making such punishment cruel and unusual, and so contrary to the Eighth
Amendment to the US Constitution.[100] The dissent by Rehnquist CJ (in which Scalia
and Thomas JJ joined) argued that only standards within the USA, evidenced by federal and state legislation and decisions of juries, were relevant when deciding whether

---

[96] *Lange v Atkinson and Australian Consolidated Press NZ Ltd* [1998] 3 NZLR 424 (CA of New Zealand).

[97] [2001] 2 AC 127 (HL). On the meaning of a duty to publish, see now *Jameel (Mohammed) v Wall Street
Journal Europe Sprl* [2006] UKHL 44, [2007] 1 AC 359 (HL).

[98] *Lange v Atkinson and Australian Consolidated Press NZ Ltd* [2000] 1 NZLR 257 (PC). For the further
proceedings in the Court of Appeal of New Zealand, see [2000] 3 NZLR 385.

[99] 536 US 304 (2002).

[100] Ibid., n. 21 of the judgment, referring to the Brief for the European Union as *Amicus Curiae* in *McCarver
v North Carolina*, O.T. 2001, No. 00–1727, 4.

a punishment is cruel and unusual for constitutional purposes. It would be illegitimate to decide US constitutional law by reference to foreign standards.

This does not mean that the dissentients are unaware of developments elsewhere. In *Lawrence v Texas*,[101] the majority of the US Supreme Court held that there was no rational basis for a state law criminalizing homosexual sodomy. Scalia J's dissent (in which Rehnquist CJ and Thomas J joined) referred to a Canadian decision[102] as part of a 'slippery slope' argument, suggesting that judicially striking down laws which discriminate against homosexuals could lead to the judicial imposition on the legislature of homosexual marriage, which would be unacceptable under the US Constitution. Where the national constitution does not authorize courts to draw on foreign decisions, it may (as Rehnquist CJ pointed out in *Atkins v Virginia*) be difficult to justify being guided from elsewhere in interpreting one's own constitution. As aids to articulating issues and becoming aware of possible approaches, not to mention a state's international obligations, comparative and international studies are hard to better, but in the USA, unlike most other jurisdictions, the matter is being approached as one of constitutional principle.[103]

It is rare for a codified constitution either to authorize or prohibit courts from taking account of international legal standards or judgments of foreign or international tribunals when deciding municipal public law cases, but the 1996 Constitution of the Republic of South Africa is an exception. The Constitution is an outward-looking document. The formulation of the Constitution's Bill of Rights was heavily influenced by the examples of Canada, Ireland, India, and Nigeria, but the formulation of the rights and their constitutional status was a response to the particular needs of post-apartheid society. Section 39(1) of the 1996 Constitution provides that a court, tribunal, or forum, when interpreting the Bill of Rights:

a. must promote the values that underlie an open and democratic society based on human dignity, equality and freedom;

b. must consider international law; and

c. may consider foreign law.

As a result, the judgments of the Constitutional Court of South Africa are a valuable repository of learning on international and comparative human rights law, and their constitutional legitimacy is beyond question.

Courts in the UK are not required to be as systematic as those in South Africa in their use of international and foreign law, but UK judges have regularly used

---

[101] 539 US 558 (2003), overruling *Bowers v Hardwick* 478 US 186 (1986).

[102] *Halpern v Toronto*, 2003 WL 34950 (Ontario CA).

[103] See e.g. *Printz v United States*, 521 US 898 (1997); *Foster v Florida*, 537 US 990 (2002); *Roper v Simmons*, 125 S Ct 1183 (2005); Norman Dawson, 'The Relevance of Foreign Legal Materials in US Constitutional Cases: A Conversation between Justice Antonin Scalia and Justice Stephen Breyer' (2005) 3 *Int J Const Law* 519, available at www.wcl.american.edu; Ruth Bader Ginsburg, ' "A Decent Respect to the Opinions of [Human] Kind": The Value of a Comparative Perspective in Constitutional Adjudication' (2005) 64 *CLJ* 575.

both international and comparative law.[104] Treaties can be used to interpret legislation, on the assumption that Parliament does not intend to violate the UK's
international obligations unless an intention to do so appears clearly.[105] Where a
statute is designed to give effect to international obligations, the assumption is that
Parliament intended to achieve that and nothing else.[106] A treaty may give rise to a
legitimate expectation, enforceable in administrative law, that the government will
act in accordance with the UK's international obligations, although this has been
criticized as a 'constitutional solecism' amounting 'to a means of incorporating the
substance of obligations undertaken on the international plane into our domestic
law without the authority of Parliament'.[107] Treaties may provide a guide to the
requirements of public policy,[108] and can guide courts when exercising discretion
in relation to such matters as levels of damages.[109] Where an administrative act or
decision infringes a human right in international law, courts will anxiously scrutinize it, giving more attention than usual to the evidence, though not necessarily applying a higher than usual intensity of review, when deciding whether it is
'unreasonable'.[110]

However, UK courts maintain a certain reserve in the face of treaties. Unless a treaty
has been transformed into municipal law by legislation, like parts of the ECHR, they do
not usually consider that they are under any obligation to take account of them:[111] for
the UK lawyer, the dualism of the constitution means that treaties generally still exist
as part of a different system of law. In cases reported in 11 leading series of law reports
for England and Wales in 2001 and 2002, only two international conventions apart
from the ECHR were considered, in a total of six public law cases: the Convention and
Protocol relating to the Status of Refugees, and the Convention on International Trade

---

[104] Historically, Roman law (including the notion of *ius gentium*) had an influence on parts of the common
law: see Andrew Lewis, '"What Marcellus Says Is Against You": Roman Law and Common Law' in A. D. E.
Lewis and D. J. Ibbetson (eds.), *The Roman Law Tradition* (1994), Ch. 12; Daan Asser, '*Audi et Alteram Partem*:
A Limit to Judicial Activity', ibid., Ch. 13. Courts have also had regard to treaties, although only relatively recently in Scotland: see *T., Petitioner* 1997 SLT 734 (Court of Session (Inner House)), and see this chapter under
heading 'Territoriality and International Law'.

[105] See e.g. *Waddington v Miah* [1974] 1 WLR 683 (HL).

[106] See e.g. *R. (on the application of Mullen) v Secretary of State for the Home Department* [2004] UKHL
14, [2005] 1 AC 1 (HL), where the problem was to decide how the international treaty should be interpreted.

[107] For the origin of the application of the doctrine to human rights treaties, see *Minister for Immigration
and Ethnic Affairs v Teoh* (1995) 183 CLR 273 (HC of Australia); *R. v Secretary of State for the Home Department, ex parte Ahmed and Patel* [1998] INLR 570; *R. v Uxbridge Magistrates' Court, ex parte Adimi* [2001] QB
667 (DC), esp. at 686, *per* Simon Brown LJ. For the criticism, see *Behluli* v. *Secretary of State for the Home Department* [1998] Imm AR 407, 415, *per* Beldam LJ; *R. (European Roma Rights Centre) v Immigration Officer at
Prague Airport (United Nations High Commissioner for Refugees intervening)* [2003] EWCA Civ 666, [2004] QB
211 (CA), at [99] and [101], *per* Laws LJ (the source of the quotation in the text), and see also Simon Brown LJ,
at [51]. On appeal in the *Roma Rights* case, the House of Lords did not consider the issue.

[108] See e.g. *Blathwayt v Baron Cawley* [1976] AC 397 (HL).

[109] See e.g. *John v MGN Ltd* [1997] QB 586 (CA).

[110] See e.g. *Bugdaycay v Secretary of State for the Home Department* [1987] AC 514 (HL), and Ch. 4 in this
volume.

[111] See e.g. *R. v Secretary of State for the Home Department, ex part Brind* [1991] 1 AC 696 (HL).

in Endangered Species of Wild Fauna and Flora.[112] UK courts clearly felt no obligation to delve into a wide range of treaties such as is imposed on the South African judiciary in cases on constitutional rights. In the first seven months of 2010, a broadly similar pattern emerged: apart from the ECHR, the Refugee Convention and its Protocol were considered in three cases, and in one of them the court also considered the Statute of the International Criminal Court.[113] More recently, the UN Convention on the Rights of the Child and the Council of Europe Convention on Action against Trafficking in Human Beings have also been considered.[114] This might be an indication of a growing willingness to regard treaties as providing guidance on interpreting and developing municipal law, but the evidence remains sparse.

Direct application of foreign judgments in public law cases is also limited, though they may have persuasive authority. One must leave aside decisions which have to be considered as a matter of law, such as foreign judgments in certain cases in the Privy Council, decisions of the Court of Justice of the European Communities and the Court of First Instance, and those of the European Court of Human Rights. Studying *The Law Reports 2013 Cumulative Index*[115] reveals that no more than four foreign, public law judgments received, in the opinion of the editors of *The Law Reports*, significant consideration in just two cases in the courts of England and Wales reported in the main series of law reports in 2013. Both the domestic cases arose in private law. One concerned pleas of sovereign and diplomatic immunity in a claim concerning employment rights;[116] the other, direct and indirect discrimination on the ground of sexual orientation.[117] This is a significant drop since 2001, when an equivalent study revealed the very modest total of 13 foreign public law cases (12 decided by the Privy Council) receiving substantial consideration in 17 English public law cases. The decline may result from the increased dominance of the ECHR and EU in our public law, leaving little room for seeking guidance from the courts of Canada, Australia, New Zealand, and elsewhere in the Commonwealth.

That is not to say that foreign decisions have a minimal impact. Many more have been cited to and by courts, and might have influenced their thinking, without being expressly analysed, followed, or distinguished in judgments. Some public law principles have been shaped, at least partly, by foreign influences. The rule against anyone being a judge in his own cause derives from Roman law,[118] as does much else in the

---

[112] *The Consolidated Index 2001–2002 to Leading Law Reports* (2002), 347.

[113] *Law Reports Cumulative Index August 2010* (2010), 144.

[114] See e.g. *R. (SF (St Lucia)) v Secretary of State for the Home Department* [2015] EWHC 2705 (Admin), [2016] 1 WLR 1439, Admin Ct.

[115] Incorporated Council of Law Reporting for England and Wales, *The Law Reports Cumulative Index 2013* (2013), 162–225.

[116] *Wokuri v Kassam* [2012] EWHC 105 (Ch), [2013] Ch 80, Newey J, at [13]–[26], discussing *Tabion v Mufti* (1996) 73 F 3d 535, US CA, 4th Circuit, *Baoanan v Baja* (2009) 627 F Supp 2d 155, US DC Southern District of New York, and *Swarna v Al-Awadi* (2010) 622 F 3d 123, US CA, 2nd Circuit.

[117] *Black v Wilkinson* [2013] EWCA Civ 820, [2013] 1 WLR 2490 (CA), at [22]–[23], *per* Lord Dyson MR, discussing *Rodriguez v Minister of Housing of Government of Gibraltar* [2009] UKPC 52, [2010] UKHRR 144 (PC).

[118] See Asser, 'Audi et Alteram Partem'.

common law. Coercive interim remedies against the Crown entered English law after they came to be available to protect Community rights in EU law.[119] The principle of proportionality has been significant in national law because of its importance in EU and ECHR law, and there has been some support for applying it in preference to *Wednesbury* unreasonableness, even in cases not involving EU law or Convention rights.[120] Whilst it is hard to see what role it could have except as a tool for evaluating a purported justification for interfering with a vested right, it offers another example of the capacity of the common law to develop eclectically and its taste for the exotic.

CONCLUSION

The internationalization of public law in the UK is a process of long standing and is continuing. It has benefits, but there are also risks. These are, first, that a borrowed solution will not be workable in a constitution with the special balance of power and democratic accountability found within the state, and, secondly, that reasoning relying on foreign thinking will not be regarded as a legitimate way of deciding public law cases under the constitution. The latter concern is evident in the Chief Justice's dissenting opinion in the US Supreme Court in *Atkins v Virginia*, mentioned earlier. Where in the UK's constitutional rules are judges authorized to look for emerging standards abroad to guide UK public law? Statutes can authorize or require courts to look abroad, as the European Communities Act 1972 and the Human Rights Act 1998 show. But in the absence of such express provisions, there is a danger to the perceived constitutional legitimacy of judicial decisions if courts resort to foreign guidance without a legal basis in national law.

For these reasons, international influences must be treated with caution in developing the structures of an established state and constitutional arrangements. Filters are needed. If the relationship between national and international legal planes is not defined in a constitutional document (such as South Africa's 1996 Constitution) or statute, a case-by-case approach can lead to distinct oddities. We can conclude with two questions about the UK to illustrate this. First, how well are the fundamental values of representative democracy, executive accountability to Parliament, and parliamentary sovereignty protected against the inappropriate introduction to municipal law (either by the executive or by judges) of obligations derived from international law or EU law, and how will the UK's withdrawal from the EU affect this? Secondly, why did UK judges seem more receptive to foreign judicial developments than to international treaties?

---

[119]   *R. v Secretary of State for Trade and Industry, ex parte Factortame (No. 2)* (Case C-213/89) [1991] 1 AC 603 (CJEC and HL); see now e.g. *R. v Secretary of State for Health, ex parte Imperial Tobacco Ltd* [2002] QB 161 (CA).

[120]   See e.g. *R. (Daly) v Secretary of State for the Home Department* [2001] 2 AC 532, 548–9, *per* Lord Cooke of Thorndon; *R. (Alconbury Developments Ltd) v Secretary of State for the Environment, Transport and the Regions* [2001] UKHL 23, [2003] 2 AC 295, at [51], *per* Lord Slynn of Hadley; *R. (Association of British Civilian Internees: Far East Region) v Secretary of State for Defence* [2002] EWCA Civ 473, [2003] QB 1397, at [34]–[37].

One could argue that treaty obligations binding the UK in international law impose standards which should be respected by all organs of the state, including courts, and that there can be no justification in terms of UK constitutional law for having regard to judgments of foreign courts in jurisdictions which have no current constitutional link to the UK. This distinction is recognized by the Constitution of South Africa: there is a duty to consider treaties, but no duty to consider foreign judgments, in cases on constitutional rights. It will be interesting to see whether the influence of the ECHR and the European Court of Human Rights under the Human Rights Act 1998, ss. 1 and 2, bringing with it other treaties which the European Court of Human Rights uses to interpret the ECHR, will gradually lead UK courts to give greater weight to a range of treaties than they presently feel able to do. It will also be interesting to see whether the political furore surrounding a small number of Strasbourg decisions of which some politicians disapprove, notably concerning whether prisoners should be allowed to vote and whether the UK should be allowed to remove suspected terrorists to countries where they face the prospect of torture and other violations of their rights, will lead to political action to remove the UK from the authority of Strasbourg and other international human rights bodies. It needs to be reiterated, however, that international institutions like the Strasbourg Court exercise authority over the UK because the UK has repeatedly bound itself by treaty to accept their rulings (an exercise of, rather than interference with, national sovereignty), and that has nothing to do with the legislative sovereignty of the Queen in Parliament or the political sovereignty of the UK's electorate, which rely on municipal, particularly constitutional, law and cannot be reduced by international law.[121]

FURTHER READING

ALLISON, JOHN W. F., 'Transplantation and Cross-fertilisation in European Public Law' in Jack Beatson and Takis Tridimas (eds.), *New Directions in European Public Law* (1998), Ch. 12.

BELL, J., 'Mechanisms for Cross-fertilisation of Administrative Law in Europe' in Jack Beatson and Takis Tridimas (eds.), *New Directions in European Public Law* (1998), Ch. 11.

BREWER-CARRÍAS, A. R., 'Constitutional Implications of Regional Economic Integration' in John Bridge (ed.), *Comparative Law Facing the 21st Century* (2001), 675–752, on the way in which integration of markets between states depends on and in turn influences national constitutional structures and rules.

CHIGARA, B., 'Pinochet and the Administration of International Criminal Justice' in Diana Woodhouse (ed.), *The Pinochet Case: A Legal and Constitutional Analysis* (2000), Ch. 7, on the interaction of Treaties, peremptory norms of customary international law, and the criminal law.

DUPRÉ, C., *Importing the Law in Post-Communist Transitions: The Hungarian Constitutional Court and the Right to Human Dignity* (2003), esp. Ch. 2 on the importation by nascent or

---

[121] See Feldman, 'Sovereignties in Strasbourg'.

re-nascent states of constitutional law and constitutional values from other systems; but contrast Dupré's less sanguine view of Hungary's 2011 Fundamental Law and its reaction against European constitutional values: 'Human Dignity: Rhetoric, Protection, and Instrumentalism', in Gábor Attila Tóth (ed.), *Constitution for a Disunited Nation: On Hungary's 2011 Fundamental Law* (Budapest: Central European University Press, 2012), 143–69.

ELLIS, E. (ed.), *The Principle of Proportionality in the Laws of Europe* (1999), for essays on the use of a single public law principle in a variety of legal systems.

European Review of Public Law (2006) 18(1) (Spring) 25–653 contains papers derived from a valuable colloquium of the European Group of Public Law in 2005 on the internationalization of public law, including general surveys and studies of particular European jurisdictions.

FATIMA, S., *Using International Law in Domestic Courts* (2005), for full consideration of the various ways in which municipal legal systems can take account of different kinds of public international law.

FELDMAN, D., 'The Role of Constitutional Principles in Protecting International Peace and Security through International, Supranational and National Legal Institutions' in Claudia Geiringer and Dean R. Knight (eds.), *Seeing the World Whole: Essays in Honour of Sir Kenneth Keith* (2008), 17–47, examines the relationship between UN Security Council resolutions under UN Charter, Chapter VII and national constitutional law. (A slightly earlier version can be found at (2008) 6(1) *New Zealand Journal of Public International Law* 1–33.)

FELDMAN, D., 'Sovereignties in Strasbourg' in Richard Rawlings, Peter Leyland, and Alison L. Young (eds.), *Sovereignty and the Law: Domestic, European, and International Perspectives* (2013), Ch. 12, on the relationship between human rights treaty bodies in international law and legislative and democratic sovereignty in municipal politics and law.

HENKIN, L., PUGH, R. C., SCHACHTER, O., and SMIT, H., *International Law: Cases and Materials* (3rd edn., 1993), Ch. 3, on the relationship between public international law and municipal law.

SMITH, E., 'Give and Take: Cross-fertilisation of Concepts in Constitutional Law' in Jack Beatson and Takis Tridimas (eds.), *New Directions in European Public Law* (1998), Ch. 8.

ZINES, L., *Constitutional Change in the Commonwealth* (1991), Ch. 1, on the development of the constitutional orders of Australia, Canada, and New Zealand towards autonomy from the UK.

USEFUL WEBSITES

Foreign and Commonwealth Office: **www.fco.gov.uk**

The website of the Foreign and Commonwealth Office includes a link to an Official Documents page, which allows further links to useful information, including an explanation of UK treaty practice and procedure, a Treaty Enquiry Service giving access to a searchable database of treaties to which the UK is a party, and the texts of the treaties.

United Nations: **www.un.org**

The United Nations website provides (among much other information and material) the text of the UN Charter, information about the working of the institutions of the United Nations including the General Assembly and the Security Council, the texts of many international treaties, and information about international tribunals.

Venice Commission: **www.venice.coe.int**

This website, maintained by the European Commission for Democracy through Law (the 'Venice Commission') under the auspices of the Council of Europe, offers a wealth of material, including reports, recommendations, and *amicus curiae* opinions, together with summaries of significant decisions of, and links to, constitutional courts and other courts with similar jurisdictions in Europe and elsewhere.

Virtual Institute of the Max Planck Institute for Comparative Public Law and International Law: **www.mpil.de/ww/en/pub/news.cfm**

This website offers both valuable documentation and links to many other useful sources.

World Legal Information Institute: **www.worldlii.org**

The website of the World Legal Information Institute provides links to web-based sources on international and national law throughout the world. It includes decisions of international tribunals as well as constitutional texts and decisions of national courts.

Yale University Law School's Comparative Administrative Law Blog: **http://blogs.law.yale.edu/blogs/compadlaw**

This is an interesting website with information about developments in many jurisdictions.

PART II
THE INSTITUTIONAL CONTEXT

6

PARLIAMENT:

THE BEST OF TIMES,
THE WORST OF TIMES?

Philip Norton

SUMMARY

Parliament fulfils functions that are long-standing, but its relationship to government has changed over time. It has been criticized for weakness in scrutinizing legislation, holding government to account, and voicing the concerns of the people. Despite changes in both Houses in the twentieth century, the criticisms have persisted and in some areas Parliament saw a constriction in its scope for decision-making. The twenty-first century has seen significant steps that have strengthened both Houses in carrying out their functions, the House of Commons in particular acquiring new powers. Members of both Houses have proved willing to challenge government. It remains a policy-influencing legislature, but a stronger one than in the preceding century. While strengthening its position in relation to the executive, it has faced major challenges in its relationship to the public. It has seen a greater openness in contact with citizens but has had to contend with popular dissatisfaction and declining levels of trust.

Parliament has its origins in the thirteenth century. It has developed over the centuries, though its core functions developed within the first two centuries of its existence. Knights and burgesses were summoned in order to approve the King's request for additional taxation. Granting supply, that is, money, was core to its existence. However, Parliament used its power of supply to ensure that petitions were accepted by the King. These were presented by the King's subject for a redress of grievances and Parliament began to make voting supply conditional on petitions being granted. The first known instance of this was early in the fourteenth century.[1] The petitions developed into statutes. These required the approval of the Commons, Lords, and monarch, and were separate from ordinances, which were orders promulgated solely by the monarch. Statutes

---

[1] Albert B. White, *The Making of the English Constitution 449–1485* (1908), 369.

soon came to dominate and in the fifteenth century the task of writing them passed from the King's scribes to Parliament.

There were various clashes between monarch and Parliament, not least in the sixteenth and seventeenth centuries, resulting in a civil war and later the Glorious Revolution of 1688–9, when the King was forbidden by the Bill of Rights 1689 from making law without the consent of Parliament. Parliament was thus central to the law-making process, but nonetheless continued to look to the monarch to come forward with proposals for approval. The onus for determining matters of state remained with the Crown.

From this, various generalizations can be drawn that remain germane to understanding Parliament in the twenty-first century. The key characteristic is that it is a reactive legislature. For most of its history, it has looked to the executive—initially the monarch, but, from the eighteenth century onwards, the King's ministers—to bring forward measures of public policy for it to consider.

Law *making*, in the sense of initiating and drafting measures of public policy, has thus not been the defining function of Parliament. Rather, as with other legislatures, its defining function has been that of assenting to measures of public policy.[2] However, before giving (or withholding) its assent, it has debated those measures. It has also given voice to the grievances of the monarch's subjects. These functions have provided the basis of parliamentary activity over the centuries. They have developed or been refined, but they have remained at the heart of the political system.

Although the functions have largely endured, the nature of the relationship between Parliament and the executive has changed. Leadership by the monarch has given way to leadership by ministers heading a major political party. Achievement of a mass suffrage has facilitated the rise and dominance of political parties. Virtual representation—MPs speaking for others, even if not chosen by them—has given way to a representative democracy, with MPs subject to election by all adult citizens.[3] The nineteenth century saw not only the widening of the franchise, but also the outlawing of electoral malpractices. The twentieth century saw a significant change in the nature of membership of the House of Commons, partly a product of the payment of MPs and also the emergence of a working-class party in the form of the Labour Party.[4]

THE 'DECLINE' OF PARLIAMENT

Parliament has been portrayed as a subordinate and at times ineffectual body. The perception of decline developed towards the end of the nineteenth century and was pervasive throughout the twentieth. In his book, *Modern Democracies* (1921), the statesman

---

[2] Philip Norton, 'General Introduction' in Philip Norton (ed.), *Legislatures* (1990), 1.
[3] See David Judge, *Representation: Theory and Practice in Britain* (1999).
[4] See Michael Rush, *The Role of the Member of Parliament Since 1868: From Gentlemen to Players* (2001).

and scholar, Lord Bryce, titled one of the chapters 'The Decline of Legislatures', ascribing that decline largely to the effects of party and the growth of group influence. The growth and organization of mass-membership political parties were seen as conduits for the transfer of decision-making power from Parliament to the executive. This view was not confined to developments in the United Kingdom, but as part of an international phenomenon.

The perception was arguably overstated. It was not clear that there had been any significant shift—a 'decline'—of power from Parliament to the executive. Rather, the shift had been from monarch to the King's ministers assembled in Cabinet. That was the most significant effect of the growth of the franchise and mass-membership parties. Before the nineteenth century, royal patronage and bribery had usually ensured Parliament acceded to the King's wishes. From the nineteenth century onwards, it was political parties that delivered cohesive voting and ensured the ministry got its measures through.

Perceptions, however, persisted and the two Houses were the subject of criticisms and proposed reforms throughout the twentieth century. Both Houses were chamber-oriented bodies, often sitting for only a part of each year, with members frequently being part-time and with the executive getting its business done without undue difficulty. Professor Ramsay Muir told the Procedure Committee of the House of Commons in 1931 that there was no country in north-western Europe 'in which the control exercised by Parliament over the Government—over legislation, taxation, and administration—is more shadowy or unreal than it is in Britain.'[5] The reputation of Parliament was enhanced during the Second World War, when both Houses continued to meet and to scrutinize the wartime government, but this was the exception and not the rule.[6] The growth of government and the welfare state led to a growth in the volume of legislation. Bills became longer and more complex. Government dominance of Parliament meant that bills passed through all their stages in both Houses with little difficulty. In the Commons, after second reading—when it was agreed in principle by the chamber—a bill was sent usually to a standing committee. These committees were standing in name only, with members appointed anew for each bill and with the committee unable to take evidence and operating as a mini-version of the adversarial chamber. Ministers and whips were appointed to the committees to ensure the legislation got through unscathed. The Lords usually took bills for all their stages in the chamber.

Bills had to be passed within the session, otherwise they fell, and the increase in the volume of legislation put pressure on each House to get through more each session without any notable increase in resources to cope with the expansion.

There was a growth not only in primary legislation, but also in the use of secondary legislation, with more and more order-making powers being vested in ministers through primary legislation. The volume increased decade by decade. Neither House had effective means of scrutinizing the orders when they were promulgated.

---

[5] Cited in Philip Norton, *The Commons in Perspective* (1981), 202.

[6] Philip Norton, 'Winning the War, But Losing the Peace: The British House of Commons during the Second World War'(1998) 4(3) *The Journal of Legislative Studies* 33–51.

The growth of the state also increased the burden on individual MPs, constituents having greater contact than before with public bodies. Constituents contacted their MP in greater numbers than before and expected greater engagement with the constituency. Constituency 'surgeries' developed—MPs holding meetings which constituents could attend to raise problems—and MPs expected to live in their constituencies.[7] Collectively and individually, the burden on MPs increased, but was not matched by a capacity to cope with the demands.

The negative perception of Parliament was encapsulated in the 1964 book by the pseudonymous authors, Hill and Whichelow, *What's Wrong with Parliament?*[8] The view was not confined to observers. 'Well, it's dead', declared one MP in 1963, 'power has now by-passed the House of Commons'.[9] This view, that there was something wrong with Parliament, was an enduring feature of the century.

It endured despite changes within Parliament. The House of Lords underwent major reform, primarily but not exclusively in 1958 and 1999. The Life Peerages Act 1958 introduced the concept of life peerages, enabling individuals to be ennobled solely for their own lifetime. This facilitated bringing into the House people who otherwise would not have accepted peerages. Life peerages helped contribute to a reawakening of the House.[10] The House of Lords Act 1999 removed over 500 hereditary peers from membership, retaining only 92 in the House, of whom 90 were elected by the House or the political groupings in the House. The two Acts transformed the House, which become a much more active, and assertive chamber, engaging in detailed scrutiny of legislation and—like the Commons—becoming a more specialized body through the use of investigative committees.[11]

The House of Commons saw not only improvements in the resources made available to MPs, both individually and collectively,[12] but also in its own structures and procedures. The most significant reform of the latter half of the century was the introduction of departmental select committees in 1979.[13] These provided the House with

---

[7] See Anthony Barker and Michael Rush, *The Member of Parliament and His Information* (1970), Ch. 4, and Philip Norton and David M. Wood, *Back from Westminster* (1993), Ch. 3.

[8] Andrew Hill and Anthony Whichelow, *What's Wrong with Parliament?* (1964). The authors were clerks in the House of Commons. See, for other literature, Philip Norton, *The Commons in Perspective* (1981), 201–4.

[9] Quoted in Ronald Butt, *The Power of Parliament* (1967), 10.

[10] Nicholas Baldwin, 'The House of Lords: Behavioural Changes' in Philip Norton (ed.), *Parliament in the 1980s* (1985), 107–8.

[11] See below and Philip Norton, *Reform of the House of Lords* (2017), 23–27.

[12] A secretarial allowance was introduced in 1968, which developed into an office cost allowance, enabling an MP to hire permanent staff. The research services of the House of Commons Library also expanded, enabling the Library to provide bespoke briefings to MPs on particular topics as well as more generic research reports.

[13] See e.g. Gavin Drewry (ed.), *The New Select Committees* (revised edn., 1989); Derek Hawes, *Power on the Back Benches? The Growth of Select Committee Influence* (1993); Michael Jogerst, *Reform in the House of Commons* (1993); David Natzler and Mark Hutton, 'Select Committees: Scrutiny à la Carte' in Philip Giddings (ed.), *The Future of Parliament: Issues for a New Century* (2005); and Andrew Hindmoor, Philip Larkin and Andrew Kennon, 'Assessing the Influence of Select Committees in the UK: The Education and Skills Committee, 1997–2005' (2009) 15 *The Journal of Legislative Studies* 71–89.

the means for more detailed and consistent scrutiny of government departments. It enabled not only greater specialization by the House, but also by its members. It provided a new agenda-setting capacity—the committees determined their own agenda—and a means of informing the House independent of government. They contributed to destroying the government's near monopoly as a supplier of information to Parliament.

Structural changes were accompanied by changes in behaviour. MPs became more independent in their voting behaviour. The high point of party loyalty was the 1950s. The period from the 1970s onwards saw MPs willing to vote against their own side more often, in greater numbers, and with greater effect than before.[14] This independence resulted on occasion in the government being defeated in the division lobbies. Defeat in the lobbies was a more noticeable feature of the House of Lords. A Tory-dominated hereditary House was not afraid frequently to defeat a Labour government, but the Tory government of Margaret Thatcher regularly suffered defeats at the hands of their lordships.[15] The frequency of defeat was less than under a Labour government, but nonetheless more extensive than that seen in the Commons.

Both Houses not only became better resourced, but also more visible. Each voted to admit the television cameras. (Sound broadcasting had been permitted since the 1970s.) Televising proceedings began in the Lords in 1985 and in the Commons in 1989. People could now watch parliamentarians in action.

However, despite these changes, the perception of Parliament appeared not to improve. Indeed, the televising of proceedings in the Commons may have contributed to the negative perception. The disproportionate coverage accorded prime minister's question time reinforced public perceptions of adversarial politics and what amounted to almost yobbish behaviour by MPs.[16] If the collective behaviour of MPs contributed to a poor public perception, then so too did the behaviour of individual MPs. In the 1990s, media stories of MPs accepting money for tabling parliamentary questions—the 'cash for questions' scandal—enhanced public perceptions that MPs were in politics for their own benefit rather than the public good. In the wake of the scandal, surveys showed that most people questioned thought that MPs were in politics for personal gain. A 1994 MORI poll found that 64 per cent of those questioned thought that 'most' MPs made lots of money by using public office improperly (up from 46 per cent in 1985) and 77 per cent agreed that 'most MPs care more about special interests than they care about people like you'. New rules were introduced, a code of conduct instigated, and a Parliamentary Commissioner for Standards appointed.

In the event, any good work done by the reforms of the 1990s were swept away in 2009 by media revelations of the expenses claimed by MPs.[17] A daily newspaper obtained unredacted files of claims made by members. Some were revealed to have

---

[14] Philip Norton, *Dissension in the House of Commons 1945–74* (1975); Philip Norton, *Conservative Dissidents* (1978); Philip Norton, *Dissension in the House of Commons 1974–1979* (1980); Philip Norton, 'The House of Commons: Behavioural Changes' in Norton (ed.), *Parliament in the 1980s*, 212–47.

[15] Philip Norton, 'Introduction' in Norton (ed.), *Parliament in the 1980s*, 14.

[16] See Hansard Society, *Audit of Political Engagement 11: The 2014 Report* (2014), 62–73.

[17] Robert Winnett and Gordon Rayner, *No Expenses Spared* (2009).

been utilizing expenses—that is, public money—for inappropriate purposes and, in some cases, making claims that were illegal. Four were tried and jailed. Inappropriate claims by peers also became the subject of press scrutiny, leading to two peers being imprisoned. Both Houses also variously used their power of suspension (the Lords having resuscitated the power, not previously employed since the seventeenth century) in respect of members who contravened the rules of conduct.

These events affected Parliament's reputation. Wider constitutional changes also appeared to diminish Parliament's capacity to legislate and to protect the rights of the citizen.[18] Membership of the European Communities (now the European Union) limited its capacity to determine public policy that was to apply throughout the United Kingdom. By virtue of membership, European regulations had binding applicability in the United Kingdom. With devolution, law-making powers in areas other than those reserved to Westminster were vested in the Scottish Parliament, Northern Ireland Assembly, and, later, the National Assembly for Wales. Not only was the power to determine laws devolved, but the capacity to discuss matters affecting the devolved parts of the United Kingdom was limited in both Houses, the Commons adopting what *Erskine May* dubbed a 'self-denying ordinance'.[19] The formal remit of Parliament was thus restricted.

The enactment of the Human Rights Act 1998 was perceived as Parliament passing the capacity to determine the rights of citizens to the courts. Although the senior courts were not empowered to strike down legislative provisions deemed incompatible with articles of the European Convention on Human Rights, they could issue declarations of incompatibility.[20] Though Parliament was not formally obliged to change the law to bring it into line with the judgments of the court, it has done so, mostly expeditiously. It resisted taking action for several years on the issue of prisoner voting rights, after a ruling that a blanket ban on voting was incompatible with Convention rights, but in 2017 the government agreed a modification that proved acceptable to the Council of Europe.[21]

The use of referendums was also seen as a means of limiting Parliament through giving the final say on an issue to the people. Previously unknown to the constitution, referendums were utilized in the 1970s in different parts of the United Kingdom on

---

[18] Philip Norton, *Parliament in British Politics* (2nd edn., 2013), 151–95.

[19] *Erskine May's Treatise on The Law, Privileges, Proceedings and Usage of Parliament* (24th edn., 2011), 190. By standing order, the House provided that questions could not be tabled on matters for which responsibility had been devolved, unless they covered information which the UK government was empowered to seek from a devolved executive or related to legislative proposals, concordats between the UK government and devolved administrations, or matters in which UK ministers had taken an official interest.

[20] Norton, *Parliament in British Politics*, 184–7.

[21] A declaration of incompatibility was made in *Smith v Scott*, 2007 SLT 137. A draft Voting Eligibility (Prisoners) Bill was published in 2013 and considered by a joint committee of both Houses. The committee's report, recommending prisoners serving up to 12 months in prison be entitled to vote, was published in 2014. Joint Committee on the Draft Voting Eligibility (Prisoners) Bill, *Report*, Session 2013–14, HC 103, HL Paper 924. The government agreed changes in 2017 that fell short of the committee's recommendations, covering prisoners released on temporary licence and on remand, as well as those imprisoned for contempt of court or for default in paying fines.

the issue of devolution (and Northern Ireland remaining part of the United Kingdom) and throughout the UK on continued membership of the European Communities. They were again variously utilized after 1997. There were referendums again on devolution and, in the new century, UK-wide referendums on a new electoral system for parliamentary elections[22] and on remaining in or leaving the European Union, and in Scotland on whether it should become an independent nation. Though some argued they complemented representative democracy, others contended that their use undermined the concept of parliamentary democracy.[23] By the beginning of the twenty-first century, one could see the continuing relevance of the question posed by Hill and Whichelow. Powers to determine or modify issues of public policy had passed to the institutions of the EU, to elected legislatures in different parts of the United Kingdom, and to the courts (both EU and UK). The UK constitution had acquired a juridical dimension lacking since the time of the Glorious Revolution.

Constitutional changes were diminishing Parliament's capacity to legislate on behalf of the people. Even where it retained the power to legislate, the perception was of an institution still too responsive to the wishes of the executive, not least under the 'presidential' and lengthy premierships of Margaret Thatcher (1979–1990) and Tony Blair (1997–2007): what the executive wanted, the executive got. There was also the perception that the membership was more geared to its own interests, and the interests of party, than to the interests of the public. MPs individually were generally viewed in a positive light by their constituents, but MPs collectively, as we have seen, were not.[24] In surveys of professions that people would trust to tell the truth, MPs fared poorly.

PARLIAMENT REDIVIVUS?

Against this, there is an argument that Parliament is demonstrating a new assertiveness in its relationship to the executive. Parliament remains at the nexus between government and the people. The distinguished parliamentarian, Enoch Powell, observed that Parliament was the body through which the people, through their representatives, spoke to the government and through which the government spoke to the people.[25] The institution has been strengthened significantly in speaking to the government and it is developing the means for listening to the people, albeit in a difficult and increasingly noisy environment.

Parliament has witnessed significant changes in the twenty-first century. The most notable in terms of the relationship between the House of Commons and the executive

---

[22] The Parliamentary Voting System and Constituencies Act 2011 provided that the decision in the referendum was not to be advisory and in the event of a 'yes' vote the Alternative Vote was to be introduced for elections to the House of Commons.

[23] See Constitution Committee, House of Lords, *Referendums in the United Kingdom,* 12th Report, Session 2009–10, HL Paper 99, and Stephen Tierney, *Constitutional Referendums* (2012).

[24] See Norton, *Parliament in British Politics,* 234–5.

[25] Enoch Powell, 'Parliament and the Question of Reform' (1982) 11(2) *Teaching Politics* 169.

have been in respect of constitutional change (war-making, treaty-making, confidence), structural and procedural change (scrutinizing the executive, debate, legislative scrutiny), and political change (no single-party majority). There have also been significant changes in the work of the House of Lords. There have been some notable developments in the relationship between Parliament and the public, with the institution becoming more open and outward looking, at a time when trust in the legislature and its members has been under strain.

CONSTITUTIONAL CHANGE

When power passed from monarch to ministers, the use of prerogative power passed in effect to the Prime Minister. Prerogative powers were exercised formally by the Crown, but on the advice of the monarch's first minister. Prerogative powers are those powers which traditionally have been exercised by the monarch and have not been displaced by statute. They have encompassed the power to declare war, to ratify treaties, and to determine the dates of general elections within a maximum period stipulated by statute. All three have been affected fundamentally by statute or by parliamentary action.

WAR-MAKING POWERS

One of the most important prerogative powers throughout history has been the war-making power. The Crown can commit armed forces to action abroad. This may encompass a declaration of war, as with the two world wars, or limited military engagement. Parliament has been informed usually of such action and has been able to debate it, but the control, in so far as it existed, was retrospective and with parliamentarians reluctant usually to criticize military engagement when British troops were in action. Some engagement has been highly controversial, as with the invasion of the Suez Canal in 1956, but Parliament has not been in a position to prevent the Prime Minister taking such action as he or she thought necessary. Towards the end of the century, military action had been debated prior to the engagement of troops, most notably in respect of action to retake the Falkland Islands in 1982 and of UK involvement in the Gulf War in 1991. In the latter case, military action had been discussed on a motion for the adjournment. Opponents of action forced it to a vote, losing by 534 votes to 54.[26] As MPs opposed to action had complained on the previous day, it was not a substantive motion—the House was being invited to discuss, but not to endorse, action—and could not be amended.

A major change was proposed during the premiership of Gordon Brown (2007–10). He was keen to transfer a number of prerogative powers to Parliament. These formed part of his *Governance of Britain* agenda[27] and encompassed the war-making power. On 3 July 2007, he told the House of Commons that the government 'will now consult

---

[26] House of Commons Debates (*Hansard*), 15 January 1991, cols. 821–5.
[27] See Ministry of Justice, *The Governance of Britain*, CM 7170, July 2007.

on a resolution to guarantee that on the grave issue of peace and war it is ultimately the House of Commons that will make the decision'.[28] However, as the Government White Paper on *War Powers and Treaties* declared:

> In seeking to give Parliament the final say in decisions to commit UK troops to armed conflict overseas, it is nevertheless essential that we do not undermine the ability of the executive to carry out its proper functions. The responsibility to execute such operations with minimum loss of British lives has to remain with the executive.[29]

The statement encapsulated the conundrum that faced those responsible for finding a form of words giving Parliament the capacity to say yes or no to engagement by British forces abroad, but leaving government with the flexibility deemed necessary to respond quickly to defend British interests and lives. The White Paper canvassed various options, including legislation, but in the event, no agreement was reached and no motion or bill brought before Parliament.

Rather, the practice has developed of the House of Commons being consulted, and if necessary voting, on government proposals to commit forces in action abroad.

The precedents were set in 2002 and 2003 in respect of war in Iraq. The Foreign Secretary, Jack Straw, believed that any decision to go to war should be approved by the House of Commons and, along with the Leader of the House of Commons (and former Foreign Secretary), Robin Cook, he persuaded Prime Minister Tony Blair that he should seek parliamentary approval before committing forces in action in Iraq.[30] The principal debate took place on 18 March 2003 and the motion supporting the government was carried by 412 votes to 149. The vote saw the largest rebellion by Labour MPs in post-war history, the motion being carried with the support of the Opposition. The key point, though, was that, as Tony Blair recorded, 'It was the only military action expressly agreed in advance by the House of Commons.'[31]

This set the basis for any future military engagement, at least where such engagement was contemplated and could be a matter of public debate. In 2013 the presumed use of chemical weapons against its citizens by the Assad regime in Syria generated calls for military action by the UK government. Parliament was recalled on 29 August 2013 to debate the use of force in Syria. A combination of a switch in the Opposition's stance—expected initially to support the use of force—and opposition from a sizeable number of Tory MPs resulted in a government defeat. The House rejected an Opposition amendment, but then proceeded to defeat the government motion supporting action by 285 votes to 272. Prime Minister David Cameron immediately accepted the outcome. 'It is very clear tonight that, while the House has not passed a motion, the British Parliament, reflecting the views of the British people, does not want to see British military action. I get that, and the Government will act accordingly.'[32]

---

[28] House of Commons Debates (*Hansard*), 3 July 2007, col. 816.
[29] Ministry of Justice, *War Powers and Treaties: Limiting Executive Powers*, Consultation Paper CP26/07, CM 7239, October 2007.
[30] Jack Straw, *Last Man Standing* (2012), 375.   [31] Tony Blair, *A Journey* (2010), 428.
[32] House of Commons Debates (*Hansard*), 29 August 2013, cols. 1555–6.

The vote was important not only politically, but also constitutionally. The House of Commons had prevented Her Majesty's Government from engaging in military action. It was the most important defeat of the government on a matter of military involvement since the emergence of party government in the United Kingdom. It also confirmed in the eyes of some commentators that it was now a convention that no government could embark on military action without first getting the endorsement of the House of Commons,[33] though such a status was not endorsed by Downing Street. In 2014, Prime Minister David Cameron indicated he was willing to authorize some military action in Iraq against Islamic State (IS) militants, 'if the UK were judged to be at risk', and seek retrospective, rather than prospective, approval from Parliament.[34] In 2018, Prime Minister Theresa May authorized air strikes in Syria, in conjunction with the USA and France, justifying her action on the grounds that revealing the plans for action 'would have fundamentally undermined the effectiveness of their action and endangered the security of our American and French allies'.[35] She then appeared before the Commons in two emergency debates to defend her action. The action thus exemplified the conundrum identified above. The very fact that the Prime Minister was at the Despatch Box explaining why approval had not been sought from the House in advance of action reflected a major change in expectations.

TREATY-MAKING

Before 2010, treaties were negotiated by government and ratified by the Crown. In practice, most treaties were laid before Parliament under the 'Ponsonby Rule', dating from a statement in 1924 by junior Foreign Affairs minister, Arthur Ponsonby, and followed consistently by government since 1929. Under the rule, treaties were published and laid before Parliament as Command Papers and then 21 sitting days elapsed before ratification took place. Should a request be made to debate a treaty within the 21 days, the government acceded to the request. Both Houses also got to debate legislation that was necessary to give effect in UK law to treaty obligations. Parliament did not ratify the Treaty of Accession to the European Communities, for example, but it was necessary to enact the European Communities Act 1972 in order to give effect to obligations arising under the treaty. The same applied to subsequent European treaties. Such legislation was normally enacted prior to ratification to avoid any possibility of the UK being in breach of its international obligations.

---

[33] James Strong, 'Why Parliament Now Decides on War: Tracing the Growth of the Parliamentary Prerogative through Syria, Libya and Iraq' (2014) 17 (4) *The British Journal of Politics and International Relations* 19–34; Constitution Committee, House of Lords, *Constitutional Arrangements for the Use of Armed Force*, 2nd Report, Session 2013–14, HL 46.

[34] Sam Coates, 'We Can Bomb Jihadists without Asking MPs, Says Cameron', *The Times*, 2 September 2014, 1.

[35] House of Commons Debates (*Hansard*), 17 April 2018, col. 207.

Some parliamentary committees recommended that treaties, especially treaties with significant financial, legal, or territorial implications, should be subject to parliamentary debate and approval.[36] The Brown government responded positively to such proposals and consulted on them as part of the *Governance of Britain* agenda. The result was the displacement of the prerogative by statute through the Constitutional Reform and Governance Act 2010. Part 2 of the Act provides that treaties shall be ratified if within 21 sitting days neither House has resolved that the treaty shall not be ratified. If the House of Commons votes against ratification, and persists in voting against, the treaty is not ratified. Provision was made for exceptional cases, though in such cases ratification was prohibited if either House had already resolved that the treaty should not be ratified. The government also accepted a backbench amendment that a treaty had to be accompanied by an explanatory memorandum explaining the provisions of the treaty and the reasons for seeking ratification.[37] It had become the practice to supply such memoranda, but this put it in on a statutory basis.

The change was formally more definitive than the change to the war-making power. The Constitutional Reform and Governance Act transferred a convention to statute, whereas parliamentary approval for committing forces in action acquired or was close to acquiring the status of a convention. However, the latter was politically more significant. Putting the Ponsonby Rule in statute meant that about 30–35 treaties each year fell within the purview of the law, but few treaties are of major political significance and, under the Ponsonby Rule, a debate could have been triggered and, if both Houses objected, it was unlikely ratification would have taken place. Either House could also have refused to enact the legislation necessary to give effect in UK law to a treaty's provisions. This became especially important in the context of legislation necessary to facilitate the UK's withdrawal from the European Union.

Indeed, two of the constitutional developments that critics saw as limiting the capacity of the House of Commons to affect outcomes—the use of referendums and greater judicial involvement—were to result in a notable elevation of Parliament's role in relation to the UK's withdrawal from the European Union. Following the outcome of the 2016 referendum, the government proposed to use the Crown's prerogative powers to give notification of the UK's withdrawal from the EU under Article 50 of the Treaty on European Union. This was challenged through judicial review and in *R. (Miller) v Secretary of State for Exiting the European Union* [2017] UKSC 5 the Supreme Court held that notification required an Act of Parliament. Prerogative powers, it concluded, may not be used to nullify rights that Parliament has enacted through primary legislation. As a result, the government introduced the European Union (Notification of Withdrawal) Bill to provide authority for it to give notification of the UK's withdrawal under Article 50.

---

[36] See e.g. Public Administration Select Committee, House of Commons, *Taming the Prerogative: Strengthening Ministerial Accountability to Parliament*, Fourth Report, Session 2003–4, HC 422.

[37] The author declares an interest as he was the peer responsible for the amendment.

CONFIDENCE

Her Majesty's Government rests on the confidence of the House of Commons for its continuance in office. Until 2011, it was a convention of the constitution that if a government was defeated on a vote of confidence, the prime minister either tendered the resignation of the government or requested the dissolution of Parliament. The precedent was set in 1841 and was maintained thereafter. Three types of confidence vote existed.[38] One was explicitly worded motions expressing confidence, or lack of it, in the government. A second was on motions designated as confidence votes by the Prime Minister. In the Second Reading debate on the European Communities Bill in February 1972, for example, Prime Minister Edward Heath made clear that confidence attached to the vote. He informed the House that 'if this House will not agree to the Second Reading of the Bill . . . my colleagues and I are unanimous that in these circumstances this Parliament cannot sensibly continue'.[39] The third category comprised issues of such significance that they were regarded as implicit votes of confidence, such as the Queen's Speech and the budget.

The government could suffer defeats on motions that were not matters of confidence and these did not engage the convention.[40] Between 1972 and 1979, the government suffered an exceptional 65 defeats in the division lobbies of the House of Commons,[41] but only the last of these—on 28 March 1979, when the House carried a motion of no confidence—triggered a general election.

As part of the negotiations between the Conservatives and the Liberal Democrats following the 2010 general election, a bill providing for fixed-term Parliaments was conceded by the Conservatives and included in the coalition agreement. A Fixed-term Parliaments Bill was subsequently introduced, although deviating somewhat from the terms of the coalition agreement. The bill provided for an early election if two-thirds of all members voted for it or if the government was defeated on a vote of confidence and if within 14 days of the defeat a new government could not be formed and gain the confidence of the House. The reference to losing a vote of confidence was ambiguous. There was no definition as to what constituted a vote of confidence. The bill was amended during its passage in the House of Lords to provide that the motion 'That this House has no confidence in Her Majesty's Government' had to be carried in order to engage the provision.[42]

The Fixed-term Parliaments Act 2011 took effect upon Royal Assent in September 2011. Its consequences were twofold in relation to the power of the Prime Minister.

---

[38] Philip Norton, 'Government Defeats in the House of Commons: Myth and Reality' [1978] *Public Law* 362–70.

[39] House of Commons: Official Report (*Hansard*), 17 February 1972, col. 752.

[40] Norton, 'Government Defeats in the House of Commons: Myth and Reality', 360–78.

[41] There were six in the 1970–4 Parliament, 17 in the Parliament of Feb.–Oct. 1974, and 42 in the Parliament of 1974–9. On those in the 1974 and 1974–9 Parliaments, see Norton, *Dissension in the House of Commons 1974–1979*, 491–3.

[42] See Philip Norton, 'From Flexible to Semi-fixed: The Fixed-term Parliaments Act 2011' (2014) 1(2) *Journal of International and Comparative Law* 203–20.

The first and intended effect was to deny the Prime Minister the power to determine the date of a general election through requesting the Queen to dissolve Parliament. Instead, the Act effectively transferred a veto power from the Crown to the Opposition. As long as the Opposition has at least one-third of the membership of the House, it can prevent a motion being carried by a two-thirds majority of all MPs: abstention would be sufficient to deny its passage. The veto was not employed in April 2017, when Prime Minister Theresa May sought a motion for an early election. The Opposition supported it and an early election took place under the provisions of the Act. Although it may be politically difficult for an Opposition not to support an early election, it nonetheless holds the power now to do so.

The second largely overlooked consequence has been to remove the power to maximize the government's voting strength by saying that a vote is of confidence, with an election to follow if the vote is lost.[43] A prime minister can still announce a vote is one of confidence, but if the vote were lost it would not engage any provision of the Act. It would be open to the Prime Minister to offer the resignation of the government or to ask the House to vote for an early election. The Prime Minister would need not only the Opposition to support such a motion, but also government backbenchers.

The Fixed-term Parliaments Act 2011 has thus affected substantially the relationship between the government and the House of Commons, though the full effects have yet to be fully realized. The most obvious area of uncertainty is in the unlikely, though not unprecedented, event of a government resigning without a motion of no confidence having been passed.[44]

STRUCTURAL AND PROCEDURAL CHANGE

The House has also witnessed changes in its own structures and procedures that have served to strengthen it in its relationship to the executive.

SCRUTINIZING THE EXECUTIVE

The 2010 Parliament saw notable changes in how the House of Commons scrutinizes the executive. These encompassed both Select Committees and debates on the floor of the House. A number of MPs had been pressing for some time for a further strengthening of the House in its ability to scrutinize the executive. Various reform manifestos had been published, both by bodies outside and inside the House. However, the most notable changes occurred as a result of the expenses scandal of 2009.

---

[43] See Norton, 'From Flexible to Semi-Fixed: The Fixed-term Parliaments Act': 203–20, and Philip Norton, 'The Fixed-term Parliaments Act and Votes of Confidence' (2016) 69 (1) *Parliamentary Affairs* 3–18.

[44] Arthur Balfour tendered his government's resignation in December 1905, the government having run out of steam and hoping to wrong-foot the Liberal opposition. See R. J. Q. Adams, *Balfour: The Last Grandee* (2007), 227; and A. K. Russell, *Liberal Landslide: The General Election of 1906* (1973), 34–5.

The start of the twenty-first century saw some expansion of scrutiny by select committees. Most notably, a Joint Committee on Human Rights was established in 2001 and proved to be an active, and productive, body. It appears to have contributed to a greater rights culture on the part of both Houses.[45] References by MPs and peers to committee reports were notable in the 2005–10 Parliament, in the context of a marked increase of references to human rights in both Houses, but especially in the House of Lords.[46]

However, the most important changes occurred at the start of the 2010 Parliament. The genesis for reform has its roots in the expenses scandal. Prime Minister Gordon Brown described it as 'the biggest parliamentary scandal for two centuries'.[47] It reinforced the public's negative perceptions of politicians, dented MPs' morale and fed the belief that something had to be done to restore public trust.[48] A Select Committee on Reform of the House of Commons was appointed, under Labour MP Tony Wright, and it quickly produced a report entitled *Rebuilding the House*.[49] Among its recommendations were that select committees should be strengthened and that the chairs should be elected by the House, and members by their respective parliamentary parties. It also proposed the creation of a House business committee to allocate business in government time and a backbench business committee to allocate backbench business, until then within the gift of the government.

The recommendations on select committees were approved by the House and then implemented at the beginning of the 2010 Parliament. Some committee chairs were hotly contested, including that of the Treasury Committee.[50] (As in previous Parliaments, parties agreed as to which parties should hold the chairs, divided proportionate to party strength in the House.) Election meant that those wanting to chair committees now needed the support of fellow MPs, indeed MPs on both sides of the House, in order to secure election and not the endorsement of the whips. Previously, the whips had been able in effect to offer the chairs of select committees as rewards for good service or consolation prizes for those who had missed out on ministerial office. Now they had lost a significant patronage tool. Power shifted from the whips to backbench MPs. The same applied to membership of the committees. Those wanting to serve on a particular committee no longer needed to gain the endorsement of their party whips, but their fellow backbenchers. The focus of attention thus shifted paradigmatically. MPs collectively were in control.

---

[45] Philip Norton, 'A Democratic Dialogue? Parliament and Human Rights in the United Kingdom' (2013) 21(2) *Asia Pacific Law Review* 141–66.

[46] Murray Hunt, Hayley Cooper and Paul Yowell, *Parliaments and Human Rights* (2012), 25–6.

[47] Winnett and Rayner, *No Expenses Spared*, 349.

[48] See J. Van Heerde-Hudson (ed.), *The Political Costs of the 2009 British MPs' Expenses Scandal* (2014), and Philip Norton, 'Speaking for Parliament' (2017) 70 (2) *Parliamentary Affairs* 200.

[49] Select Committee on Reform of the House of Commons, Rebuilding the House, *First Report*, Session 2008–9, HC 1117.

[50] The elections were by the Alternative Vote (AV), though in practice all chairs that were elected in contested elections in 2010 triumphed in the first round.

The elections also served to give the committees a higher profile, both in the House and in the media. Those elected to chair committees enjoyed the kudos of election and the concomitant attribute of independence. They were not seen as party appointees. Some committees, and especially their chairs, gained a notable media profile. Some committees undertook high-profile inquiries, summoning major public figures as witnesses. A number of the hearings attracted widespread media coverage, though not all were as successful as the committees may have wished.[51] Media magnate Rupert Murdoch had shaving foam pushed in his face by a member of the public when appearing before the Culture, Media and Sport Committee.

The profile of scrutiny by committee was enhanced by the appointment in 2012 of a Parliamentary Commission on Banking Standards to consider professional standards and culture in the UK banking sector, lessons to be learned about corporate governance, transparency and conflicts of interest, and to make recommendations for legislative action. This was established as a ten-member joint committee, had a substantial support staff, and was empowered to work through panels, which could comprise only one or two members.[52] It proved highly productive, producing reports on banking reform, proprietary trading, and the collapse of HBOS, before publishing its final report, *Changing Banking for Good*, in 2013. Its work formed the basis of regulatory reform and banking legislation. As the government acknowledged in response to the Commission's final report, it 'strongly endorses the principal findings of the report and intends to implement its main recommendations'.[53]

The combined effect of these changes was to develop further, both qualitatively and quantitatively, the scrutiny of government. The committees engaged with government, affected interests, and achieved in some cases notable media coverage and policy changes.

DEBATE

The work of both Houses was not only to subject the actions and proposals of government to scrutiny, but also to raise the concerns of citizens and at times to fulfil an agenda-setting role, raising issues that had never before or not recently been on the political agenda. The established means of debate in both Houses was through debate in the chamber.

However, the most notable reforms took place in the House of Commons. In 1999, the House had approved the creation of a parallel chamber, housed in the Grand Committee Room off Westminster Hall, but styled as sittings in Westminster Hall. Sittings in Westminster Hall can be held while the chamber is in session and any member can

---

[51] See Norton, *Parliament in British Politics*, 277–8.

[52] The commission was chaired by Andrew Tyrie, chair of the Treasury Committee, and it achieved an increased public profile when one of its members, Justin Welby, the Bishop of Durham, became the Archbishop of Canterbury.

[53] *The Government's Response to the Parliamentary Commission on Banking Standards*, Cm 8661, July 2013, 5.

attend. They are employed to debate topics raised by private members—similar to the half-hour adjournment debates at the end of daily sittings (though the first debates are normally of 90 minutes in duration)—as well as select committee reports and petitions. Meetings are held on Tuesdays, Wednesdays, and Thursdays, and may also be held on some Mondays to discuss petitions. The sittings provide notable additional time to that available in the chamber for MPs to raise issues of concern. Though meetings are not usually well attended, they serve a useful purpose in enabling MPs to put matters on the public record and to ensure that there is a ministerial response.

The House in 2010 agreed to the creation of a Backbench Business Committee. The membership of the committee, like other select committees, is elected, though—unlike other committees—the election is sessional. The committee allocates backbench business on 35 days each session, 27 of them on the floor of the House and the rest in Westminster Hall. The committee proceeds by inviting MPs to put forward proposals for debate, taking into account the extent to which a proposal is supported, on a cross-party basis, by other MPs.

Although the government decides on which days the debates take place, removing from government the decision as to topics for debate represents a substantial shift of agenda-setting from government to the House. Some of the debates have been well attended, attracting more attention from backbenchers than the normal run of government business, and influencing public policy. The Committee has scheduled for debate subjects that the government might not have chosen and which may cause some embarrassment to it.

According to the analysis of Mark Stuart, the debates appear to have played a part in getting government to alter policy on a range of issues. These have included compensation for victims of contaminated blood and blood products, government funding of the BBC World Service, the release of documents relating to the Hillsborough Disaster, and the freezing of fuel duty. They may also have played a part in other decisions, including holding a referendum on the UK's membership of the EU and the delay in giving some prisoners the right to vote, and had an indirect effect on the eventual government defeat on Syria in 2013.[54]

The 2015–17 Parliament saw a further change, this time dealing with petitions. In the 2010–15 Parliament, petitions submitted via a government website that attracted 1000,000 or more signatures were referred to the Backbench Business Committee. The Committee could then decide to schedule a debate (and usually did) if there was support from some MPs and could also schedule one even if a petition fell short of the 100,000 signatures. In 2015, the House established a Petitions Committee to consider petitions submitted to the House through a dedicated website (https://petition.parliament.uk/). The committee has the power to refer a petition to the appropriate investigative select committee, decide to pursue the issue itself, or schedule it for debate in Westminster Hall. (As in the previous Parliament, petitions attracting 100,000

---

[54] Backbench Business Committee, House of Commons, *Work of the Committee on the 2010–15 Parliament*, First Special Report, Session 2014–15, HC 1106, para. 22.

signatures or more are usually debated.) In the first year of its existence (July 2015–July 2016) it received more than 23,000 petitions. The activity, as we shall see, constituted an important development in the relationship between the House and the public.

LEGISLATIVE SCRUTINY

Legislative scrutiny by the Commons has been identified by some commentators, and by members, as a weak, if not the weakest, part of parliamentary scrutiny.[55] 'Parliament is at its weakest', declared the Commission to Strengthen Parliament in 2000, 'in scrutinising legislation. It needs new tools.'[56] Time in the Commons for considering bills is limited and has been constrained by the use of guillotine motions, imposing a timetable for the remaining consideration of a bill, and since 1997 by the use of timetable motions, time-tabling bills following Second Reading. Committee stage was seen as unproductive, government supporters being encouraged to be silent and anecdotally reported to use the occasion to get on with correspondence.

There were proposals to scrutinize bills in draft (pre-legislative scrutiny) and for the use of evidence-taking committees. Experiments with special standing committees (SSCs), which were empowered to receive evidence, had been seen as productive.[57] Pre-legislative scrutiny developed after 1997, with various government bills being published in draft and being sent to a select committee, or a joint committee, for pre-legislative scrutiny. The experience was seen as improving the quality of legislation, the government being more willing to listen to proposals for change prior to the formal introduction of the bill. Between 1997 and 2010, 76 bills were published in draft, though not all received pre-legislative scrutiny (either because they were published too late or because the relevant select committee was too busy). The Joint Committee on the Communications Bill in 2002 was indicative of what could be achieved: of 148 recommendations made in its report, 120 were accepted by the government. Though pre-legislative scrutiny creates additional pressure on parliamentary resources and can create major time pressures if a bill is published late in a session, it is recognized as a valuable means of parliamentary scrutiny. There have been recommendations for it to be used routinely, rather than leaving it to the discretion of government.[58] However, the number has shown no underlying increase, though in the long session of 2010–12, the Coalition government published twelve bills in draft.

Another notable reform was achieved in 2006 when the House voted for the introduction of public bill committees, essentially to replace standing committees. Public bill committees are empowered, other than in certain circumstances (for example, when a bill comes from the Lords) to take written and oral evidence, before

---

[55] See especially *Making the Law: The Report of the Hansard Society Commission on the Legislative Process* (1993).

[56] *Strengthening Parliament: The Report of the Commission to Strengthen Parliament* (2000), 22.

[57] See *Making the Law: The Report of the Hansard Society Commission on the Legislative Process*, 75.

[58] Constitution Committee, House of Lords, *Parliament and the Legislative Process*, 14th Report, Session 2003–04, HL Paper 173-I.

considering amendments to the bill. The change represented a notable advance on the old standing committees.[59] Problems remain in that committees remain appointed afresh for each bill, witnesses tend to be selected because of the stance they are expected to take, and the time between taking evidence and reverting to the traditional format of considering amendments is constricted, limiting the opportunity to digest and utilize evidence effectively.[60] The government still manages to gets its bills through, with amendments approved normally being government amendments. The committees, as Louise Thompson has shown, tend to be working harder, though with less obvious material gain. Nonetheless, as she notes, 'A much greater number of amendments are introduced by the government at the report stage in response to bill committees.'[61]

One other proposed change to the legislative process achieved particular visibility following the referendum on Scottish independence in September 2014. As a response to the West Lothian Question, the Conservative Party had previously pursued the possibility of 'English votes for English laws' (EVEL)—that is, measures that were exclusive to England (or England and Wales) being voted on in the House of Commons solely by MPs from English (or English and Welsh) constituencies, either at some or all stages of a bill's passage. The Coalition government established a Commission (the McKay Commission) to examine ways of achieving this. The Commission reported in 2013,[62] but no legislation or changes to Standing Orders were forthcoming in the light of objections from the Liberal Democrats. Prime Minister David Cameron did, though, establish a Cabinet Committee chaired by William Hague MP, Leader of the House, to examine how to proceed. The Committee reported in December 2014, outlining different options. Once returned to power in 2015 with an absolute majority, the Conservative moved to implement EVEL through standing orders of the House of Commons. Rather than providing for a measure to be passed on the basis solely of votes by MPs from English constituencies, the standing orders inserted extra stages in a Bill's passage where provisions certified by the Speaker as affecting only England could be blocked by MPs from English seats. EVEL was thus not so much English Votes for English Laws as an English Veto over English Laws. Various provisions have been certified by the Speaker, but consideration has tended to be cursory, not resulted in any veto being exercised, and, according to a study of the procedure, has not enhanced England's voice in the process.[63]

---

[59] See Norton, *Parliament in British Politics*, 92.

[60] See Jessica Levy, 'Public Bill Committees: An Assessment. Scrutiny Sought; Scrutiny Gained' (2010) 63 *Parliamentary Affairs* 534–44.

[61] Louise Thompson, 'More of the Same or a Period of Change? The Impact of Bill Committees in the Twenty-first Century House of Commons' (2013) 66(3) *Parliamentary Affairs* 477. See also Louise Thompson, *Making British Law* (2015), 92–3.

[62] McKay Commission, *Report of the Commission on the Consequences of Devolution for the House of Commons* (2013).

[63] Daniel Gover and Michael Kenny, *Finding the Good in EVEL: An Evaluation of 'English Votes for English Laws' in the House of Commons* (2016).

POLITICAL CHANGE

Linked to some of the foregoing changes, in some cases facilitating them, but also operating independently of them, has been political change deriving from the absence of a single-party majority. For much of the twentieth century there was a party with an overall majority in the House of Commons, though on occasion in coalition with one or more parties. That majority—for most of the time a notably cohesive major-ity—enabled the executive to get its way. However, the 1970s witnessed a period of minority government (1974, 1976–79) with the Labour Government operating on a hand-to-mouth basis, vulnerable to defeats at the hands of opposition parties combin-ing against it (and some of its own MPs voting with the Opposition).[64] The decade witnessed government defeats on a scale not witnessed since the 1860s.

The twenty-first century witnessed a coalition government, the first to be formed in the era of modern British politics as a result of the electoral arithmetic of a general election. The Conservatives joined with the Liberal Democrats after the 2010 general election to form a minimum-winning coalition.[65] The government thus had to con-tend with the potential not only of intra-party conflict (its own MPs voting against it), but also of inter-party conflict (conflict between the parties to a coalition). MPs in both parties were wary of those in the other party and the challenge to the Prime Minister was to maintain good relations with his own backbenchers and with his co-alition partner, something difficult to achieve where each side pursued conflicting goals. This strengthened the position of backbench MPs. The Parliament witnessed unprecedented levels of backbench dissent and tensions between the two parties,[66] David Cameron initially focusing on maintaining unity between the coalition parties, before switching to keeping his own backbenchers on side.[67] The latter included a com-mitment to an in/out referendum on the UK's membership of the EU.

However, the biggest change in relationships occurred as a result of a confluence of the outcomes of the 2016 referendum on EU membership and the 2017 general elec-tion. As a result of the referendum, the Conservative government was committed to achieving the UK's exit from the EU. The outcome of an early election in 2017 left the Conservatives lacking an overall majority. The party leadership negotiated a pact with the Democratic Unionist Party to sustain the party in power. However, even with the pact, the government had an overall majority of only twelve. It was thus vulnerable to dissent from its own backbenchers. Conservative MPs were badly divided between

---

[64] Philip Norton, 'Parliament', in Anthony Seldon and Kevin Hickson (eds.), *New Labour, Old Labour* (2004), 190–206.

[65] Philip Norton, 'The Politics of Coalition', in Nicholas Allen and John Bartle (eds), *Britain at the Polls 2010* (2011), 242–65.

[66] Philip Norton, 'Coalition Cohesion', in Timothy Heppell and David Seawright (eds), *Cameron and the Conservatives* (2012), 181–93; Philip Cowley, 'The Coalition and Parliament', in Anthony Seldon and Mike Finn (eds.), *The Coalition Effect 2010–2015* (2015), 146–54.

[67] Philip Norton, 'The Coalition and the Conservatives', in Anthony Seldon and Mike Finn (eds.), *The Coalition Effect 2010–2015* (2015), 467–91.

those committed to a clean break in exiting the EU and those who favoured remaining in the EU or at least a 'soft' exit. The result was that the government had to look two ways in ensuring an effective withdrawal: it had to deal with the EU negotiating team to agree terms of exit and the House of Commons to mobilize a majority to support the necessary legislation.

The House achieved significance at two levels, though—as we shall see—the distinction was far more significant in terms of outcomes in the House of Lords. One was at the high political level, that is, achieving the key votes necessary to deliver on the government's policy. The other was in terms of legislative scrutiny, examining the detail, in effect the means rather than the ends, seeing if the provisions could be improved. The focus in the Commons was on the former. In the Lords, it was both, but especially the latter in terms of making a difference to the legislation.

The passage of legislation to facilitate the UK's withdrawal, both the formal exiting and the implementation of an agreement on future relations, created major challenges for the government's business managers. The passage of the European Union (Withdrawal) Bill, making provision for the repeal of the European Communities Act 1972 on 'exit day', while retaining extant EU law in UK law, was fraught. The government achieved its enactment, suffering only one defeat in the Commons, but only after making concessions to backbench critics (and in response to defeats in the House of Lords). The concessions not only included requiring an Act to be passed in order to give effect to a withdrawal agreement before it could be ratified, but also the opportunity for the House to discuss and vote in the event of withdrawal without a settlement (a 'no deal' outcome). The government also agreed to proposals for each House to have a dedicated sifting process for orders made under the Act that were subject to the negative resolution procedure. The House was thus not only exerting political pressure in the specific circumstances of negotiating withdrawal from the EU, but was also achieving more embedded structural changes in respect of legislative scrutiny consequent to withdrawal.

The passage of the European Union (Withdrawal) Bill was symptomatic of the extent to which Parliament was a significant actor in determining the outcomes of public policy. The process of the UK withdrawing from the EU was the most significant constitutional development since the UK joined the then European Communities in 1973 and was even more fraught in terms of achieving parliamentary approval than was the case with the European Communities Act 1972. The House of Commons was now a prominent political actor and not seen simply as a body for formally approving whatever the government negotiated and laid before it.

HOUSE OF LORDS

ACTIVITY

The House of Lords, like the Commons, has continued to utilize existing methods of scrutinizing and debating issues of public policy, as well as becoming a more specialized body, making greater use of investigative select committees.

It too expanded its committee work in the new century, complementing existing committees on the European Union and Science and Technology with others on the Constitution, Economic Affairs, Communications, and International Relations. It has also developed its capacity to scrutinize delegated legislation through two dedicated committees, the Delegated Powers and Regulatory Reform Committee (examining the provisions in Bills for parliamentary approval of secondary legislation) and the Secondary Legislation Scrutiny Committee (examining secondary legislation once laid by government). This focus on delegated legislation is particular to the Lords.

The extent of committee work is reflected through the engagement of members and in output. The EU Committee works through six-committees, with the result that more than 70 peers are engaged on the scrutiny of proposals for EU law. The permanent investigative select committees are complemented by ad hoc committees as well as by domestic committees, such as the Procedure Committee. The committees absorb the attention each year of more than 300 peers. (In the 2016–17 session, 358 peers sat on committees.) The investigative select committees tend to be productive in generating reasoned, evidence-based reports. In the 2016–17 session, the six EU sub-committees alone produced a total of 41 reports.

The House is also notable for its role in legislative scrutiny. This has continued to occupy most of the time of the floor of the House and, increasingly, of grand committee. To facilitate its detailed scrutiny of bills, the House has moved from taking the committee stage of most bills on the floor of the House to sending the less politically contentious bills to grand committee. The grand committee (similar to sittings in Westminster Hall) is a form of parallel chamber. The grand committee can meet while the chamber is in session. Any peer can attend and participate. This enables those peers interested only in particular parts of a bill to attend for discussion of those matters of concern to them. Sittings normally take place in the Moses Room, a dedicated committee room close to the chamber, though occasionally it meets in a normal committee room. No votes are taken in grand committee. As a result, only amendments that are not opposed are made at this stage. Any amendments to which objections are made have to be held over until report stage. The use of grand committee has effectively created more time for the House to devote to scrutinizing legislation.

There have also been advances in post-legislative scrutiny. Post-legislative review of Acts began in 2008, which entailed government departments assessing whether Acts of Parliament, three to five years after enactment, achieved what they were intended to do.[68] The reviews were published and sent to the relevant Departmental Select Committee in the Commons, but the committees had little or no time to consider them. The House of Lords, however, began utilizing ad hoc committees to review Acts in particular areas. Each year since 2012, an ad hoc committee has been appointed to examine either a particular body of legislation or a particular Act. Committees have been appointed to consider adoption law and extradition legislation as well as six specific Acts: the Inquiries Act 2005, the Mental Capacity Act 2005, Equality Act 2010,

---

[68] Norton, *Parliament in British Politics*, 100–1.

Licensing Act 2003, Natural Environment and Rural Communities Act 2006, and the Bribery Act 2010.

These changes complemented developments in the means for debate. Peers can raise issues through Questions for Short Debate (previously known as Unstarred Questions) and balloted debates. In the 2016–17 session, there were a total of 154 debates. Though the Government Whips' Office plays a facilitating role in business, the House, as a self-regulating chamber, retains ultimate responsibility. The timetable is not wholly within the gift of government. Unlike in the Commons, there is formally no distinction between government and private members' time, though in practice most days are normally given over to government business. As in the Commons, the House also has a Question Time. This occupies thirty minutes—half the time of a Commons' Question Time—but provides for more extensive scrutiny than in the Commons. No more than four questions can be taken, meaning each occupies several minutes, facilitating several supplementary questions. Ministers have to be well briefed in order to respond.

The House can claim to be effective in fulfilling its scrutiny function. The ad hoc committees engaged in post-legislative scrutiny have influenced government. Thus, for instance, of the 61 recommendations of the Committee on Adoption Legislation, the government accepted 39 and partially accepted a further nine. The report of the Committee on the Mental Capacity Act found that the Act's Deprivation of Liberty Safeguards (DOLS) scheme was not fit for purpose. Subsequent to this (and a high-profile court judgment), the government asked the Law Commission to produce a report, which it did, recommending replacement of the scheme. In July 2018, the government introduced into the House of Lords the Mental Capacity (Amendment) Bill to provide for a replacement scheme.

The House is also regarded as important in securing amendments to government bills, and more successful than the House of Commons.[69] Each session, anything between a few hundred to a few thousand amendments are secured to government bills. In the 2016–17 session, for example, 2,270 amendments were made. (A record number of 4,761 amendments were achieved in the 1999–2000 session.) The vast majority of amendments that are agreed are introduced by ministers, but as the research of Meg Russell has shown, the genesis of most is to be found at earlier stages, not least amendments moved by members in committee.[70] Nor do amendments encompass the totality of the impact on the content of bills: opposition by peers has led to some clauses and schedules of bills being taken out at committee stage.[71]

The impact of the House in terms of scrutiny, both of government policy and legislation, is most notably illustrated by its examination of the process and legislation for withdrawing from the EU. Both the EU Committee and the Constitution Committee

---

[69] Louise Thompson, *Making British Law* (2015), 92.

[70] Meg Russell, *The Contemporary House of Lords* (2013), 173.

[71] Each clause and schedule has to be approved on a motion that it stand part of the Bill. On occasion, the motion has been negatived. See, for example, the removal of a controversial schedule—Schedule 7—to the Public Bodies Bill in 2010–11: Meg Russell, *The Contemporary House of Lords*, 188–9.

were active in scrutinizing the process for withdrawing from the EU.[72] The Consti-tution Committee produced influential reports on the legislation resulting from the decision.[73] Its report on the European Union (Withdrawal) Bill helped shape debate on the Bill and led to constructive engagement with government. During the Bill's pas-sage in the Lords, the government suffered fifteen defeats on amendments, including on key aspects of the government's withdrawal policy. The government accepted one of the defeats and achieved majorities in the Commons to reject the others (or to ac-cept amendments in lieu); the Lords did not persist in the amendments. It was these high-level defeats, on issues such as remaining in the European Economic Area as a negotiating objective, which attracted media attention. What was less noticed was the detailed debate on improving the Bill's provisions, not least in respect of strengthen-ing parliamentary scrutiny, creating greater legal certainty, and covering the position of the devolved parts of the UK. In the light of the detailed scrutiny, the government brought forward amendments of its own or accepted others tabled by peers. In total, just over 200 amendments were secured during the Bill's passage: 170 of these were at report stage in the House of Lords.

The capacity of the House of Lords to influence legislation has been ascribed to the nature of the membership of the House and to the extent to which the House is prepared to carry amendments against the wishes of the government. The House has been characterized as a House of experience and expertise, members being appointed because of holding senior office in a wide range of sectors (government, the arts, in-dustry, trade unions) or because they are leading experts in their field.[74] The political composition is also significant. The House of Lords Act 1999 removed the Conserva-tive bias of the membership. Since 1999, no party has enjoyed an overall majority in the House. As can be seen from Table 1, the cross-bench peers—those with no party-political affiliation—constitute more than 20 per cent of the membership.

Between 1999 and 2010, it was the Liberal Democrat peers who were the swing vot-ers, given that they were more likely to turn out in force, and to vote more cohesively, than cross-bench peers.[75] After the creation of a Coalition government in 2010, with the Liberal Democrats forming part of the Coalition, the cross-bench peers assumed a new significance as holding the balance of power. They demonstrated a willingness on occasion to turn out in large numbers and, if they divided disproportionately against

[72] See European Union Committee, House of Lords, *The Process of Withdrawing from the European Union*, 11th Report, Session 2–15–16, HL Paper 138; *Scrutinising Brexit: The Role of Parliament*, 1st Report, Session 2016–17, HL Paper 33; *Brexit: Parliamentary Scrutiny*, 4th Report, Session 2016–17, HL Paper 50; Constitution Committee, House of Lords, *European Union (Notification of Withdrawal) Bill*, 8th Report, Session 2016–17, HL Paper 119, *The 'Great Repeal Bill' and Delegated Powers*, 9th Report, Session 2016–17, HL Paper 123, *Euro-pean Union (Withdrawal) Bill*, 9th Report, Session 2017–19, HL Paper 69.

[73] Constitution Committee, House of Lords, *European Union (Withdrawal) Bill*, 9th Report, Session 2017–19, HL Paper 69.

[74] See Meg Russell and Meghan Benton, *Analysis of Existing Data on the Breadth of Expertise and Experience in the House of Lords: Report to the House of Lords Appointments Commission* (2010).

[75] See Meg Russell and Maria Sciara, 'Why Does the Government Get Defeated in the House of Lords? The Lords, the Party System and British Politics' (2007) 2 *British Politics* 571–89.

Table 1 Membership of the House of Lords, 12 August 2018

Conservative	249
Labour	188
Cross-bench	186
Liberal Democrats	98
Bishops	26
Other parties	16
Non-affiliated	29
Lord Speaker	1
TOTAL	793

the government, voting with the Opposition, the government went down to defeat.[76] Since the end of the coalition, the government has been vulnerable to defeat as a consequence of the two main opposition parties voting against it and/or the crossbenchers dividing significantly against the government. In the 2015–17 Parliament, it suffered 98 defeats.

The independence of the House in its voting behaviour is a result of how the different political groupings in the House come together, rather than as a consequence of dissenting behaviour by party members.[77] The defeats, though, are the exception rather than the rule in getting amendments accepted. Most amendments—well in excess of 97 per cent—are accepted by the House and agreed without a division.

The activity of the House has been facilitated by a growth in numbers. Prior to the 1999 Act, the House had over 1,200 members. In the wake of the Act, it had 666. This number grew as creations outnumbered deaths. The Labour Government under Tony Blair was keen to bolster Labour ranks in the House. When the Conservative–Liberal Democrat coalition was formed in 2010, more Conservative and Liberal Democrat peers were created. Tony Blair and David Cameron created a record number of peers. By 2016, the membership reached 800, but fell back a little thereafter. By mid-August 2018, there were 793 members. (The figure excludes members on leave of absence and those not eligible to sit, for example, because of serving on the Supreme Court.) This growth in numbers since 1999 has affected the average daily attendance, which has continued to rise decade by decade, and in each session since 2012–13 has exceeded 480, up from 475 in the long 2010–12 session and 388 in the 2009–10 session. The number attending has put pressure on facilities, including on the chamber. During Question Time in the House, and major debates, there is not enough space in the chamber for all peers wishing to attend. Seats that are below the bar of the House, and

[76] Between May 2010 and the summer of 2014, the government suffered 88 defeats in the House, almost all attributable to how the cross-benchers voted.

[77] Party cohesion in divisions is a feature of the House. See Philip Norton, 'Cohesion without Discipline: Party Voting in the House of Lords' (2003) 9(4) *The Journal of Legislative Studies* 57–72.

previously used for visitors, are now occupied by peers, while others stand by the bar or, at the other end of the chamber, by the throne. Various commentators and peers have made the case for a reduction in numbers,[78] either by having a moratorium on new appointments or by having a cap on the total membership. The House agreed a motion, without a vote, in December 2016, that it was too large and calling for steps to reduce its number. In response, the Lord Speaker, Lord Fowler, established a small committee to examine ways to reduce the size of the House.

REFORM

The functions of the House of Lords are generally accepted as appropriate to an appointed second chamber and well fulfilled. Criticism has, however, regularly been levelled at the composition. Lords' reform has been an enduring feature of political debate for more than a century.[79] The Labour Party when returned to office in 1997 implemented its manifesto pledge to reform the House, resulting in the removal of all bar 92 of the hereditary peers. This was deemed the first stage of its reform process. It appointed a Royal Commission on Reform of the House of Lords (the Wakeham Commission) to make recommendations for the second stage. However, the Commission's recommendations[80]—for a partially elected House—attracted widespread criticism and were not implemented. The government advanced other proposals, initially for a 20 per cent elected element and then 50 per cent, before agreeing, following votes in the Commons in 2007 on various options for reform (in which a majority had voted for an 80 per cent and 100 per cent elected membership), to accept the case for a largely elected House.[81] No legislation, however, was brought forward.

The measures agreed by the Conservatives and Liberal Democrats in 2010 as part of their negotiations to form a coalition included one to create a largely elected second chamber. The government in May 2011, as part of a White Paper on Lords Reform, published a draft House of Lords Reform Bill, providing for 80 per cent of members of the second chamber to be elected. The bill was sent to a joint committee set up for the purposes of pre-legislative scrutiny. It reported in March 2012 and recommended that the proposal be subject to a referendum.[82] Almost half the members of the committee, including a majority of the Conservative members, published an alternative report opposing election.[83] The government introduced the bill three months later. It was expected to have a difficult passage through the Lords, but in the event faced immediate criticism in the Commons. It was opposed by a number of Conservative MPs,

---

[78] See e.g. Meg Russell, supported by Lord Adonis et al., *House Full* (2011).

[79] See Philip Norton, *Reform of the House of Lords* (2017).

[80] Royal Commission on Reform of the House of Lords, *A House for the Future*, Cm 4534, 2000.

[81] Norton, *Reform of the House of Lords*, 27–8.

[82] Joint Committee on the Draft House of Lords Reform Bill, *Draft House of Lords Reform Bill: Report*, Session 2010–12, HL Paper 284-I, HC 1313-I, 92–6.

[83] *House of Lords Reform: An Alternative Way Forward* (2012).

who ran a well-organized campaign against it.[84] In the vote on Second Reading, 91 Conservatives voted against the bill and a further 19 abstained from voting. The Opposition voted in favour, but made clear that it would not support a programme motion to limit debate on the bill. Given that a combination of the Opposition and Conservative rebels was sufficient to defeat the motion, the government decided not to move it. This opened the prospect for endless debate on the bill, similar to that experienced during an earlier attempt in 1968–9 to reform the Lords, when MPs from both sides, led by Enoch Powell on the Tory benches and Michael Foot on the Labour benches, had effectively talked out the bill.[85] On 6 August, Deputy Prime Minister Nick Clegg announced the government would not be proceeding with the bill.

Although the government's House of Lords Reform Bill did not make it to the statute book, two private member's bills did. The first, introduced by Conservative MP Dan Byles, emanated from a cross-party and cross-chamber group (the Campaign for an Effective Second Chamber) formed in 2001 to oppose an elected second chamber, but to support reform of the existing House.[86] The bill was not opposed by government and made it to the statute book.

The House of Lords Reform Act 2014 took effect in August 2014 and enables peers to resign, removes non-attending peers (those who have not attended for a session) from membership, and provides for the expulsion of peers convicted and sentenced to 12 months or more in prison. By mid-2018, more than 80 peers had used its provisions to retire from the House. A further six had ceased to be members as a result of non-attendance.

The other bill that made it to the statute book, also a product of the Campaign for an Effective Second Chamber, was the House of Lords (Expulsion and Suspension) Act, introduced in the Lords by former Lord Speaker, Baroness Hayman, and taken through the Commons by Sir George Young. The Act extends the House's power of suspension and gives it a power—which it had never had before—to expel a member.

Although large-scale reform favoured by successive governments since 1999 has failed to materialize, peers have variously pressed for reform within the House to strengthen it in fulfilling its functions. The 2014 and 2015 Acts were the fruits of this pressure. The Leader of the House and the Lord Speaker have also variously appointed working groups to examine changes to structures and procedures. In 2018, the Liaison Committee of the House began an inquiry into the committee structure. The prospect of the demise of the EU committee, and its six sub-committees, in the wake of the UK exiting the EU created scope for reviewing committee resources and looking more strategically at how the House employed committees. Although major reform of the House was seen as off the political agenda for the foreseeable future, significant changes to the structures and practices of the House were not.

---

[84] See Philip Norton, 'The Coalition and the Conservatives' in Anthony Seldon and Mike Finn (eds.), *The Coalition Effect, 2010–2015* (2015), 481.

[85] Janet Morgan, *The House of Lords and the Labour Government 1964–1970* (1975), 208–22.

[86] The author is convenor of the group.

PARLIAMENT–PUBLIC RELATIONS

There have also been significant developments in the relationship between Parliament and the public. Both Houses have expended considerable resources in seeking both to educate and to engage. They have done so at a time of considerable public distrust of Parliament and its members.

The challenge to Parliament has been a mismatch between what it is doing and how the public sees it. As we have seen, Parliament has seen major developments in strengthening its position in relation to the executive. However, the impact of the institution in affecting public policy or scrutinizing the executive has been marginal relative to how the public views the behaviour of its members.[87] The 'cash for questions' scandal of the 1990s and the expenses scandal of 2009 have reinforced, rather than created, cynical attitudes towards politicians. There are low levels of trust. Although this is not peculiar to Parliament in the UK—it is just above the average in terms of European legislatures[88]—the level of trust is declining and only about one-third of those surveyed 'tend to trust' Parliament.

Parliament has devoted resources both to educating and informing the public about its activities and to engaging with citizens. In terms of educating and informing, Parliament has invested in an Education Centre and developing its educational resources. It has devoted significant resources to developing the parliamentary website (www.parliament.uk). It has widened access to the media. In addition to there being a dedicated BBC Parliament channel, debates are live-streamed on the Internet and all public committee sessions are webcast.

In addition to making proceedings and material more accessible—essentially a one-dimensional educational role—there has also been more effort to be two-dimensional and engage with organized interests and members of the public. Public Bill Committees, as we have seen, can take evidence. Some committees have utilized online consultations. These have covered topics as diverse as family tax credit, electronic democracy, hate crimes in Northern Ireland, and the role of prison officers. Online consultations have also been employed by the Parliamentary Office of Science and Technology (POST) and by some all-party groups. In utilizing such consultation, Parliament was, according to Professor Stephen Coleman, ahead of other parliaments.[89] Some committees also utilize Twitter to invite comments. The use of e-petitions has also facilitated greater input from the public. As we have noted, the 2015 Parliament saw the creation of a dedicated petitions website and Petitions Committee. In the first year of its existence, over 10 million unique email addresses were used to sign petitions.[90]

---

[87] See J. E. Green, 'Analysing Legislative Performance: A Plebeian Perspective' (2013) 20 *Democratization* 418.

[88] See Philip Norton, 'Speaking for Parliament' (2017) 70 (2) *Parliamentary Affairs* 197–8.

[89] Modernisation Committee, House of Commons, *Connecting Parliament with the Public*, First Report, Session 2003–4, HC 368, 20–1.

[90] Houses of Parliament, *Your Petitions: A Year of Action*, Petitions Committee 2 July –15 July 2016: 2.

The work of the House and its committees has been complemented by members individually seeking, or being willing, to engage with members of the public. Demands on MPs by constituents have grown decade by decade. In 2011, MPs newly elected in 2010 estimated that they spent 59 per cent of their time when the House was sitting on constituency business.[91] (This compares with 49 per cent for MPs newly elected in 2005 and surveyed in 2006.) Email correspondence has increased as ordinary mail to MPs has decreased.[92] Apart from utilizing email to correspond with constituents, most MPs have also been proactive through the use of social media, notably Facebook, Twitter, and the use of blogs. By 2009, 92 per cent of MPs used email and 83 per cent had websites.[93] By 2011, over 40 per cent were using Twitter.[94] MPs are far less detached in their contact with people outside the House than ever before.

Parliament has thus reached new levels of openness and engagement. It is, however, an uphill struggle, essentially for three reasons, two external to Parliament and the other intrinsic to it. One of the external factors is popular confusion as to the role of the legislature, with attitudes influenced by wider social and political developments. 'Studies suggest that electoral outcomes, the type of parliamentary system, an individual's demography, and a country's overall economic prosperity can all affect democratic satisfaction, yet these factors reside outside the control of parliamentary officials . . .'[95] There is also the allied problem that people do not make links between the activity of the local MP and the institution in which the MP serves. Even if there is a local satisfaction with the MP, this does not feed into positive perceptions of the House of Commons.[96] Levels of satisfaction are low and declining. The Hansard Society 2017 *Audit of Political Engagement* reported: 'Satisfaction with Parliament over the course of the Audit series has been on a shallow downward trajectory, and this year the situation is largely unchanged. Only three in 10 people (30 per cent) report being at least "fairly satisfied" with the way Parliament works'.[97] Only a minority of respondents, and never more than 40 per cent, thought that Parliament did a good job in carrying out its principal functions.[98]

It is also not clear that signing an e-petition contributes to positive attitudes about Parliament. Most petitions are, in any event, not admissible as they are duplicates or call for action for which neither government nor Parliament are responsible.

The second reason is that Parliament suffers from limited public interest. Citizens are increasingly distracted from politics by other interests, not least through social

---

[91] Hansard Society, *A Year in the Life: From Members of Public to Members of Parliament* (2011), 6.

[92] Norton, *Parliament in British Politics*, 223.

[93] Andy Williamson, *MPs Online: Connecting with Constituents* (2009), 8.

[94] David Harrison, 'OMG! MPs Spend 1,000 Hours a Year on Twitter', *Sunday Telegraph*, 31 July 2011.

[95] Annika Weerasinghe and Graeme Ramshaw, *Fighting Democratic Decline Through Parliamentary Communications: The Case Study of the UK Parliament*, PSA Parliaments Blog (2018). https://parliamentsandlegislatures. wordpress.com/2018/01/31/communications-uk-parliament/#more-2324.

[96] Philip Norton, 'Parliament and Citizens in the United Kingdom' (2012) 18 (3/4) *The Journal of Legislative Studies* 13–14.

[97] Hansard Society, *Audit of Political Engagement 14: The 2017 Report* (2017), 26.

[98] *Audit of Political Engagement 14*, 29.

media, and while they may express views on politics they are not interested in getting involved. There has been the rise of 'e-expressives', people who follow and comment on politics, but who do not engage in politics beyond the Internet.[99] Parliament may devote resources to making information publicly available, but accessing that material is a minority interest.

The intrinsic limitation is the absence of leadership in promoting and defending the interests of the institution.[100] If members of either House are criticized publicly, or either House attacked by the media, there is no institutional leadership able to respond immediately. Parliament comprises two distinct Houses, each made up of several hundred members. There is no one person able to speak for Parliament. Although the two Houses have acquired Speakers more willing than their predecessors to make public statements, each has limited institutional resources for the purpose and neither can speak for the other. The problem is compounded by the lack of collective will on the part of parliamentarians to tackle negative coverage. The most notable impact of the expenses scandal of 2009 was not the impact on public trust in Parliament—it reinforced negative views, but the level of trust, or distrust, soon returned to its pre-scandal level[101]—but rather on the morale of MPs.[102] That, compounded with the political absorption of MPs after 2016 with the issue of the UK's exit from the EU, has meant that MPs individually and collectively have not focused on the challenge of building trust in the institution of which they are members. What response there has been has come more from officials, who have limited capacity to act on behalf of either House (informing rather than engaging), than from parliamentarians.

CONCLUSION

For Parliament, the first two decades of the twenty-first century have proved the best of times and the worst of times.[103] They have proved the best, or at least the better, of times in terms of its relationship to the executive. In facing the government, Parliament is now stronger than at any time since the development of mass-membership, organized political parties in the 1860s. It has a capacity to fulfil its functions to an extent that was previously lacking. That does not mean that it has necessarily achieved an ideal state. It remains, as it has been normally throughout history, a reactive, or policy-influencing legislature, waiting for the executive to bring forward

---

[99] M. Cantijoch, 'Will joke, won't vote: The Internet and Political Engagement', in Philip Cowley and Richard Ford (eds.), *Sex, Lies and the Ballot Box* (2014), 69–72.

[100] Philip Norton, 'Speaking for Parliament' (2017) 70 (2) *Parliamentary Affairs* 201.

[101] N. Allen and S. Birch, 'Tempests and Teacups: Politicians' Reputations in the Wake of the Expenses Scandal', in J. Van Heerde-Hudson (ed.), *The Political Costs of the 2009 British MPs' Expenses Scandal* (2014), 132–52.

[102] Philip Norton, 'Speaking for Parliament', 200.

[103] This was the theme of the author's 2016 Michael Ryle Memorial Lecture: Philip Norton, 'Speaking for Parliament', 200.

measures,[104] but as a policy-influencing legislature it has been strengthened in recent years. The bottle of parliamentary scrutiny is far from full, but it may at least be half-full or better.

There have been calls for reform to fill the bottle further, though these have frequently lacked any overall coherence. There is no agreement on what constitutes the ideal relationship between the legislature and the executive. Calls for 'parliamentary reform' have rarely focused on Parliament as Parliament. Rather, calls for reform of the Commons have focused on structures and procedures, while reform of the Lords has concentrated on composition.[105] Nonetheless, they seek to build on what has been achieved in recent years, namely stronger, more emboldened Houses in scrutinizing the executive and its measures. The government can no longer take Parliament for granted to the extent that was possible for much of the twentieth century.

However, they have proved the worst of times in the relationship between Parliament and the public. Though there has not been a collapse of trust in the legislature, the institution and its members do not command high levels of trust. Members of the public tend to take the view that MPs put party and self before the public interest and that they are not necessarily doing a good job. Scandals affecting MPs and peers reinforce, but are not the cause of, negative perceptions. However good each House is in fulfilling the functions ascribed to it, popular attitudes towards Parliament are shaped more by members' behaviour and by developments external to the institution. For Parliament, the challenge is to raise awareness and engage with the public at a time when members of the public, while having views on political issues, are not inclined to engage directly with politics, nor explore in any detail what either House is doing. Although both Houses recognize the problem, and are devoting resources to education and engagement, there remains the challenge that Parliament is the sum of its parts. Moving quickly as an institution at a time of media criticism is a hurdle not yet overcome.

FURTHER READING

EMMA CREWE, *The House of Commons: An Anthropology of MPs at Work* (2015)

PHILIP NORTON, *Parliament in British Politics* (2nd edn, 2013)

PHILIP NORTON, *Reform of the House of Lords* (2017)

ROBERT ROGERS and Rhodri Walters, *How Parliament Works* (7th edn, 2015)

PETER RIDDELL, *In Defence of Politicians* (2011)

MEG RUSSELL, *The Contemporary House of Lords* (2014)

MEG RUSSELL and Daniel Gover, *Legislation at Westminster* (2017)

---

[104] See Norton, *Parliament in British Politics*, pp. 69–70.
[105] Philip Norton, *Parliament in British Politics*, ch. 14.

USEFUL WEBSITES

Constitution Unit, University College London: **www.ucl.ac.uk/constitution-unit/research/parliament**

Parliament: **www.parliament.uk**

Hansard Society for Parliamentary Government: **www.hansard-society.org.uk**

7

THE EXECUTIVE IN PUBLIC LAW

Thomas Poole*

SUMMARY

This chapter focuses on the executive, the branch of government responsible for initiating and implementing the laws and for acting where necessary to secure the interests of the state. We trace its development out of a medieval model of government structured around the king and his court, to a modern world of offices exercising executive functions, grouped under the legacy term 'the Crown'. The resulting institutions display a complicated pattern of law and custom, and legal concepts and principles relate to them often in convoluted ways. Our analysis focuses on how executive power is normally understood from the legal point of view—deriving from an authorizing statute via rules made within a government department to eventual application by subordinate officials or agents—and traces some of the ways the courts monitor that process. But we also examine the executive's non-statutory or 'prerogative' powers, the two main compartments of which are treated separately, as the general executive powers and the general administrative powers of the Crown respectively.

INTRODUCTION

The executive is the most powerful of state institutions. It exercises the basic powers of state (military, police, fiscal, diplomatic, organizational) and is responsible for many other functions necessary for social well-being such as health and education. It makes the majority of the policies and rules that structure public life, and organizes the most significant part of the public administration. As the institution that governs, it is the

* I would like to thank Mark Aronson, Shukri Bin-Ahmad-Shahizam, Robert Craig, David Kershaw, Martin Loughlin and Adam Tucker for their comments on an earlier draft, and my Administrative Law students for helping me work through the themes discussed in the chapter.

one branch of state capable of action: 'the preserve of the executive is to do. While the role of the legislature is to speak and that of the judiciary is to judge, governments act.'[1] Hamilton unpacked that 'doing' part in *The Federalist* No. 70: 'Energy in the Executive is a leading character in the definition of good government', he wrote, essential not only for 'the steady administration of the laws' but also to protect us from external attack and internal corruption and cooption.[2]

Hamilton's aim was to persuade newly independent Americans, sensitive to the dangers of a strong executive, of the need for a sufficiently powerful federal government. In Britain, where the political structure has grown out of and around the institution of the Crown,[3] the issue has been almost the opposite: how to subject already existing executive power to constitutional constraint. If the British constitution resembles a palimpsest, a text whose amendments have been superimposed on successive earlier texts, then its basic script is of medieval origin. Here, the modern executive emerged out of the governing councils through which the King ruled. That medieval world rested on a distinction between *gubernaculum* and *jurisdictio* (government/administration and law) which entailed that while there were conventional limits on his legal powers, the king enjoyed more or less uncontrolled discretion in respect of his administration.[4]

Modern constitutional additions, including parliamentary sovereignty, the rule of law, and the separation of powers, have done much to alter the relationship between government and law. But the modern executive remains relatively obscure in public law scholarship. It tends only to be glimpsed in legal texts, usually seen 'in some sense, as the reflection of some other organ's concerns and functions.'[5] We continue to be drawn to more formal elements, 'the surface and the showy parts of the constitution',[6] where Parliament and the courts are prominent, working backwards to the still somewhat arcane ecosystem of the central executive. The result is to mask the executive's central position in the constitution in two important ways. It produces a misleading account of Parliament, whose first task is to maintain the government in office: we might say, with a little exaggeration, that its legislative role is generally better described as the institution through which the government legislates.[7] It also skews our sense of public law jurisprudence, the lion's share of which turns on how executive power is exercised.

---

[1] Paul Craig and Adam Tomkins, 'Introduction' in Craig and Tomkins (eds.), *The Executive in Public Law: Power and Accountability in Comparative Perspective* (2006), 1.

[2] *The Federalist Papers* is the generic title of 85 essays written by Alexander Hamilton, James Madison and John Jay that were published in New York newspapers between autumn 1787 and spring 1788.

[3] See e.g. Sir William Wade, 'The Crown—Old Platitudes and New Heresies', *New Law Journal* (18 September 1992).

[4] Charles McIlwain, 'Constitutionalism in the Middle Ages' in McIlwain, *Constitutionalism: Ancient and Modern* (1975), 72.

[5] Terence Daintith and Alan Page, *The Executive in the Constitution: Structure, Autonomy, and Internal Control* (1999), 2.

[6] F.W. Maitland, 'The Shallows and the Silences' in his *Collected Papers, Vol. 1* (1911), 478.

[7] Adam Tomkins, *Public Law* (2003), 95.

The emergence of the central executive out of the councils through which the King ruled shaped an institution that is relatively light on law.[8] This does not mean that law is absent. Executive functions are legal powers. They derive normally from statute, which typically vest powers to perform a statutory purpose in a Secretary of State. Alternatively, executive authority derives from prerogative powers. These are non-statutory powers: residues of kingly power now retained by the Crown, almost all of which are now exercised by government ministers. But these formal distributions of power form only part of the picture. To operate, the executive relies heavily on constitutional conventions, or non-legal rules that nevertheless acquire some sort of binding force. Conventions regulate what executive officers may and may not do, the latter crucial in respect of the Monarch (e.g. in fixing the limits of the prerogative of royal assent). They also in some instances determine the nature of those officers. The Prime Minister and Cabinet, the supreme executive authority made up of the ministerial heads of departments, have been the epicentre of British government since the eighteenth century, but neither was created by law.[9] Despite the tremendous political power these offices wield, their formal legal power is negligible.[10]

The prevalence of conventions in the executive branch is neither all that unusual nor necessarily undesirable. It is, after all, a highly political context that requires operational flexibility. But the executive is also light on law in a second sense. Significant confusion surrounds many of the legal concepts that pattern its operations. Underlying these is the enigma of the Crown. That term tends to connote the executive ('Her Majesty's Government') of which the Monarch is formally the head and the historical source of at least some of its powers. But it has been used variously to refer to the Monarch in her public or, less frequently, private capacity;[11] to the executive branch of government, potentially including the Monarch, Ministers and at least parts of the administration; as a structuring fiction or symbol—an 'hieroglyphic of the laws' in the words of the seventeenth-century judge Edward Coke;[12] even occasionally as a kind of synonym for the kingdom or state as a whole.[13]

This lack of definitional clarity stems almost paradoxically from the constitution's success in deriving new content out of old forms. The centrepiece of that process was the insinuation of a Republic beneath the folds of a Monarchy, in Bagehot's redolent

[8] F.W. Maitland, *The Constitutional History of England* (1908), 387: the executive is not 'a legal organization. Of course I do not mean it as an illegal organisation; rather I should prefer to say it is an extra-legal organisation: the law does not condemn it, but it does not recognise it—knows nothing about it.'

[9] From early in his reign, George I absented himself from cabinet meetings, his place being taken by the senior minister, who eventually came to be known as the Prime Minister.

[10] For that reason, there are no court cases directed at the Cabinet and almost none at the Prime Minister. Rare examples include *R. (Gentle) v Prime Minister* [2008] UKHL 20 (whether public inquiry required into the circumstances surrounding the invasion of Iraq in 2003, including the steps taken to obtain legal advice); *R. (Campaign for Nuclear Disarmament) v Prime Minister* [2002] EWHC 2777 (whether a United Nations Security Council resolution authorized military operations against Iraq).

[11] For the evolution of that distinction see *Hill v Grange* (1556–1557) Plowden 163; *Duchy of Lancaster Case* (1561) Plowden 212; *Calvin's Case* (1608) 7 Co. Rep. 1. See also *M v Home Office* [1994] 1 AC 377.

[12] *Calvin's Case* at 11b.

[13] Janet McLean, *Searching for the State in British Legal Thought* (2012).

phrase.[14] This transformation, set in train by the 1688–9 constitutional settlement,[15] saw a monarchy ('the King') morph into a constitutional monarchy ('the Crown'), whittling royal authority down eventually to a vanishing point.[16] Today, nominally the same source of authority is still invoked, especially in relation to prerogative powers. But no-one questions that those powers are exercised in almost all significant cases by government ministers, whose authority stems ultimately from the electorate.[17]

There are almost as many solutions to the problem of the Crown in constitutional law as there are commentators on it. Some write it off as 'metaphysical nonsense'[18] and would have us start over again.[19] Others prefer to stick quite closely to something like its original meaning (i.e. the Queen and her advisers).[20] In my view, the best way forward is to think of the Crown as part of a series of interconnected offices of state that together comprise the UK Government. 'Office' here indicates a corporate entity defined by rules providing that a fictional person shall be deemed to exist and ascribing certain powers, rights and duties to it. An office continues across generations of incumbents and implies the independence and endurance of the office as an entity in its own right. Her Majesty's Government becomes on this reading 'a complex corporate entity with many parts', including the Crown, but also the Queen, ministers, Secretaries of State, and other figures such as the Attorney General. 'Rules of attribution provide that any valid act by a minister shall count as an act of the Crown. But there need not be a relation of identity between the entities ["minister" and "Crown"], nor perfect symmetry between rules of attribution and liability that operate between them.' [21]

---

[14] Walter Bagehot, *The English Constitution*, 44.

[15] The key enactments are the Bill of Rights 1689, the Coronation Oath Act 1689 (requiring the sovereign to swear to maintain the Protestant religion), the Triennial Act 1694 (requiring the sovereign to summon parliament regularly), the Civil List Act 1697 (making the sovereign dependent on parliament for annual fixed grants), and the Act of Settlement 1701 (providing for the successor to the throne).

[16] 'The metaphysics of limited monarchy do not easily lend themselves to critical discussion. On no element in the Constitution is our knowledge so inexact.' Harold Laski, *Parliamentary Government in England* (1938), 388.

[17] Vernon Bogdanor identifies the Catholic Emancipation Act 1829, enacted despite George IV's strenuous efforts to block it, as 'mark[ing] an important watershed in the evolution of constitutional monarchy, by which the sovereign was ceasing to be an independent power in the realm': *The Monarchy and the Constitution* (1995), 15.

[18] F.W. Maitland, *The Constitutional History of England* (1908), 418. See also Maitland, 'The Crown as Corporation' in David Runciman and Magnus Ryan (eds.), *Maitland: State, Trust and Corporation* (2003), 41: 'The way out of this mess, for mess it is, lies in a perception of the fact, for fact it is, that our sovereign lord is not a "corporation sole", but is the head of a complex and highly organised "corporation aggregate of many"—of very many. I see no great harm in calling this corporation a Crown. But a better word has lately returned to the statute book. That word is Commonwealth.'

[19] *Town Investments Ltd v Department of the Environment* [1978] AC 359, at 381 (Lord Diplock): it would be better, 'instead of speaking of "the Crown", to speak of "the government"—a term appropriate to embrace both collectively and individually all of the ministers of the Crown and parliamentary secretaries under whose direction the administrative work of government is carried on by civil servants in the various government departments'.

[20] H.W.R. Wade, 'The Crown, Ministers and Officials: Legal Status and Liability' in Sunkin and Payne, *The Nature of the Crown*, 24.

[21] J.G. Allen, 'The Office of the Crown' (2018) 77 *Cambridge Law Journal* 298, 298–9.

It follows that we do not need to get too hung up on working out what the Crown actually 'is'. We should instead identify and refine the rules that circumscribe and so define that office, and those of the offices it relates to or abuts.[22] Not only is this a more manageable exercise, it also tracks the journey the constitution has undertaken from seigneurial to lawful modes of government: the former structured around the will of the ruling sovereign; the latter on the reason of law and requiring the active presence of 'an intermediary political class to which the exercise of sovereignty could lawfully and perpetually be exercised and maintained.'[23] The more we hold the idea of government through public offices of state in focus, the clearer the general direction of travel within the law—a movement captured in the move from personal liabilities (and immunities) on public servants sounding mainly in private law to public law liability for acts undertaken in an official capacity.[24]

But even if we see the Crown in these terms, we must still concede the executive's ambivalent status. Its first task may be to put the laws into practice—'executing' in the narrow sense of 'carrying out'—but that does not exhaust its functions. We expect government to take necessary measures to ensure public safety, in response to an emergency or foreign attack naturally, but not only in such extreme cases. This second function calls for a different set of qualities from those needed to fulfil its normal 'executive' or regulatory operations. We might call this second function the executive's custodial role since it relates to an idea of government as *custodes patriae* or protector of the realm.[25] It is the requirements of this second role that explains Hamilton's insistence on energy as the defining quality of a functioning executive.

Hamilton was building out of John Locke's elaboration of liberal constitutional principles within the English model of government. The *Second Treatise of Government* contains what at first seems a surprising account of the executive. Locke identifies legislative power as constitutionally supreme and executive power as constitutionally subordinate. But he also accords the executive (the Prince) very wide powers in practice, both in relation to the legislature (e.g. the power to call and dissolve Parliament) and also more generally to perform actions outside the law for the public good (the prerogative).[26] He introduces, in so doing, a double-facing conception of the executive which combines theoretical weakness with practical strength. Generalising the

[22] In fact, it is much more complicated than this. The UK's former colonies, dominions, territories and other dependencies have various notions of the Crown attached to them, and the Crown is clearly divisible in relation to them. See Anne Twomey, 'Responsible Government and the Divisibility of the Crown' [2008] *Public Law* 742. This issue still crops up in the cases (generally involving Crown Dependencies and Overseas Territories): see e.g. *R. (Quark Fishing Ltd) v Secretary of State for Foreign and Commonwealth Affairs* [2005] UKHL 57.

[23] Daniel Lee, '"Office Is a Thing Borrowed": Jean Bodin on Offices and Seigneurial Government' (2013) 41 *Political Theory* 409, 411.

[24] Culminating in the Crown Proceedings Act 1947. Or, rather, in *M v Home Office* [1994] 1 AC 377 where the House of Lords held that injunctions and contempt of court proceedings could be brought against a government minister acting in her official capacity.

[25] Sir Ivor Jennings made a similar distinction between the 'regulatory' and 'police' functions of the executive: see *The Law and the Constitution* (5th ed., 1959), 193–94.

[26] John Locke, 'Second Treatise on Government' in *Two Treatises of Government* (ed. Peter Laslett, 1960), Chapters 11–14.

point, we might say that the modern executive trades on precisely this ambiguity. The notion of the modern or constitutional executive connotes, Harvey Mansfield argues, 'not weakness but the semblance of weakness, a presumed drawing of its own strength from the strength of another: the retiring disguise, combined with the efficient activity, of the *éminence grise*.'[27]

This ambivalent nature makes a legal study of the executive particularly demanding. We encounter in the executive a world that is institutionally multifaceted, indeed quite Byzantine in its complexity, but which presents more fundamentally a variegated pattern of law, custom and practice where trade-offs between principle and pragmatism are common. The plan to navigate this terrain in what follows is to work out from more straightforward aspects of executive power, focusing on its rule-making activities, to less clearly defined areas of authority, dividing the category of prerogative into two more precise fields of inquiry, namely general executive powers and general administrative powers.

THE CENTRALITY OF RULE-MAKING

We tend to think of the *executive* in the singular.[28] It is true that it must be capable of acting as a unit if it is to perform the tasks expected of it—acting consistently in making and applying policy, or decisively in response to a crisis. But 'the executive' is also something of a placeholder—an umbrella term that shields an extensive array of actors and ways of acting. To manage this complexity, I draw up a standard model that captures the main features of the executive process as the law sees it. The model centres on the power to make rules and to give instructions to officials on how to put those rules into operation. The reason I give such prominence to this model is that it represents what the executive does most of the time—making rules and seeing that they are applied—and how it most often does it—translating statutory powers into action through the departments of state. Focusing on these rule-making functions has the added merit of pushing the executive's non-statutory (prerogative) powers, which tend to receive disproportionate attention from public lawyers, to the periphery of a conception of the constitutional executive.

I first sketch the standard model in a handful of propositions, before elaborating on some of them. My aim is to identify the primary legal matrix through which the workings of executive power are understood, not to cover the full spectrum of ways in which the law engages with executive action. Within the standard model so understood: (a) authority for executive action comes from a parent statute (legislation); (b) the authority takes the form of a power to make rules to structure a

---

[27] Harvey C. Mansfield Jr, *Taming the Prince: The Ambivalence of Modern Executive Power* (1989), 13.

[28] See e.g. *R. (BAPIO Action Ltd) v Secretary of State for the Home Department* [2008] UKHL 27, [33] (Lord Rodger): 'In England the executive power of the Crown is, in practice, exercised by a single body of ministers, making up Her Majesty's Government.'

certain field of operations (delegation); (c) the authority is granted to the Secretary of State (discretion); (d) the grant of authority assumes a capacity on the part of the Secretary of State to issue instructions to officials on how to implement the rules (administration).

We see this structure, or variations on it, time and again in the cases. *Ex p Simms*, a decision of general importance as we shall see, is illustrative of the classic scenario: a descending chain of authorizations, originating in statute and moving from the general (rule) to the particular (application). In a challenge to the lawfulness of a rule or its application, the court's task is to construe those authorizations in order to determine whether the rule or application was in fact authorized or whether it went beyond the powers of (ultra vires) the relevant decision-maker. So, in *ex p Simms*, the Prison Act 1952 empowered the Home Secretary to make rules for the management of prisons and the treatment of prisoners (s. 47(1)). The statute required that power to be exercised by statutory instrument, the most common type of delegated legislation (to which we turn shortly). At issue in the case were provisions regulating oral interviews with journalists made in the exercise of the statutory power (paragraphs 37 and 37A of Prison Service Standing Order 5A) which provided that such visits should not generally be allowed but that, where they were, a written undertaking was required that information obtained would not be used except as permitted by the prison governor. The government argued that these rules authorized the Home Secretary to impose a complete or blanket ban on journalists interviewing prisoners for any purpose. The Law Lords found the Secretary of State's interpretation of the rules too broad, and an unjustified infringement of a prisoner's right to free expression, hence unlawful.[29]

Before looking more closely at the law, one word on history and two on politics are in order. On history, we should note that this way of doing things—via rule-making in central government departments—was not always the main way things were done. It has never been the *only* way of doing things,[30] which partly explains why there is so much variety. Another common way of organizing government functions is to run them through boards, agencies and other non-departmental public bodies (NDPBs). The exact relationship between such bodies and the executive varies from body to body. But generally they act at arm's-length from government, appearing 'under the umbrella of a central department but operating effectively outside the departmental structure',[31] and are an extraordinarily pervasive feature of modern public administration. On politics, we should recall that the authorizing (or parent) statute comes about by means of executive initiative. So in a sense the executive is generally granted more or less the power it asked for. We should also recall that, besides the specific rules governing parliamentary authorization of regulations that we touch on in a moment, the minister

---

[29] *R. v Secretary of State for the Home Department, ex parte Simms* [1999] 2 AC 115.

[30] For a concise historical overview see Martin Loughlin, 'Why the History of English Administrative Law is not Written' in David Dyzenhaus, Grant Huscroft and Murray Hunt (eds.), *A Simple Common Lawyer: Essays in Honour of Michael Taggart* (2009).

[31] Frank Vibert, *The Rise of the Unelected: Democracy and the New Separation of Powers* (2007), 19.

always remains accountable to Parliament for actions taken by their department (and bound by conventions of collective Cabinet responsibility).[32]

DELEGATED LEGISLATION

Let us look more closely at the executive's powers to make rules on the basis of a statutory authorization, known as delegated or subordinate legislation. Lord Neuberger provides a useful summary of that process in the *Public Law Project* case, a successful challenge to the lawfulness of a proposal to introduce a residence test for civil legal aid. 'Subordinate legislation consists of legislation made by members of the Executive (often, as in this case, by Government ministers), almost always pursuant to an authority given by Parliament in primary legislation.' The case concerned a statutory instrument, the standard form of this type of legislation which must be laid in draft before Parliament. It is for the parent Act to decide which of the two available procedures is to be used. As Lord Neuberger observed: 'Some statutory instruments are subject to the negative resolution procedure—i.e. they will become law unless, within a specified period, they are debated and voted down. Other statutory instruments . . . are subject to the affirmative resolution procedure—i.e. they can only become law if they are formally approved by Parliament.'[33]

Lord Neuberger's summary raises the question: why the need for delegated legislation in the first place? While the constitution accords paramountcy to Parliament in its legislative capacity (the 'Crown-in-Parliament'), it also accommodates the need to make more detailed rules under the shadow of the laws passed by Parliament. The need for such a facility has grown enormously with the expansion of state functions.[34] The inter-war Donoughmore Committee on Ministers' Powers was established to examine what had become a controversial issue, responding to the widespread concern about the growth of executive power and the more particular worry that the delegated legislative process was allowing bureaucrats to dominate elected politicians.[35] The following list of rationales for delegated legislation is often reproduced: pressures on parliamentary time, the technicality of the subject matter, dealing with unforeseen contingencies, the need for flexibility, opportunity for experimentation, and the requirement for emergency powers.[36]

By the time that Report was written, delegated legislation was already an established feature of the administrative landscape. The practice was common enough by 1893

---

[32] On which see Philip Norton's contribution to this volume, Chap. 6.

[33] *R. (The Public Law Project) v Lord Chancellor* [2016] UKSC 39, [21]. Some statutes require strengthened procedures: e.g. some delegated legislation under the Legislative and Regulatory Reform Act 2006 is subject to a *super-affirmative* procedure, which involves a 60-day consultation period and enhanced power (in both Houses) for Committees to prevent the passage of instruments.

[34] Edward L. Rubin, 'Law and Legislation in the Administrative State' (1989) 89 *Columbia Law Review* 369.

[35] See especially Lord Hewart, *The New Despotism* (1929). The author was the incumbent Lord Chief Justice.

[36] Committee on Ministers' Powers, Report (Cmd 4060, 1932), 51–2. See D.G.T. Williams, 'The Donoughmore Report in Retrospect' (1982) 60 *Public Administration* 273.

for Parliament to enact the Rules Publication Act,[37] which remained in force until the Statutory Instruments Act 1946 established the procedures Lord Neuberger described. Writing in 1921, barrister Sir Cecil Carr claimed that delegated legislation exceeded parliamentary legislation in bulk: 'the child now dwarfs the parent'. For reasons of efficiency, flexibility and competence, it had become the practice to enact framework or 'skeleton' legislation, the Act itself becoming 'a kind of preliminary announcement for legislation' indicating that Parliament 'has had a legislative idea, has sketched an outline, has laid down a principle—and has left it at that', relying on departmental officials and technical advisers to work it up into a functional legal framework.[38] A more positive reading of delegated legislation's relationship with statute is possible, consistent with Carr's analysis. We might see the existence of delegated legislation as enabling primary legislation to be 'as clear, simple, and short as possible', assisting Parliament in so doing to focus on the essential points, policies and principles.[39]

Today, 3,000 or so statutory instruments reach the statute book each year, outnumbering Acts of Parliament by nearly 100 to one.[40] 'Delegated legislation is not merely a common practice; in some senses it is fair to say that it is the standard form of lawmaking.'[41] The practice of delegated legislation belongs to a world of 'subgovernment' where the action takes place largely within the interstices of government departments. This is a relatively secluded world, with junior ministers and civil servants at its heart and consultation limited to a relatively small number of (mainly repeat) players.[42] There is some institutional capacity for parliamentary oversight of the legal results of this process: the Joint Committee on Statutory Instruments, looking largely for non-merits based or 'technical' defects; the House of Lords Secondary Legislation Scrutiny Committee; and ad hoc delegated legislation committees in the Commons.[43] In practice, though, this scrutiny is almost nugatory. The Commons seems never to vote against delegated legislation; the Lords never votes to annul negative instruments. As Adam Tucker concludes in a recent survey, 'scrutiny is inadequate and fails to meet the demands of constitutional principle. There is not enough scrutiny of the merits of delegated legislation, and proposals are not sufficiently vulnerable to defeat.'[44]

Delegated legislation can be challenged in court on all the ordinary public law grounds: legality, fairness, rationality, and on Human Rights Act grounds. As Lord Neuberger writes in *Public Law Project*, a statutory instrument can be held invalid 'if it has an effect, or is made for a purpose, which is ultra vires, that is, outside the

---

[37]   For a useful outline of the history of delegation see C.K. Allen, *Law and Orders* (3rd ed., 1965), Chapter 2.

[38]   Cecil T. Carr, *Delegated Legislation: Three Lectures* (1921), 2 & 16.

[39]   Robert Baldwin, *Rules and Government* (1995), 63.

[40]   For details see House of Commons Library, *Acts and Statutory Instruments: The Volume of UK Legislation, 1950 to 2016* (21 April 2017).

[41]   Adam Tucker, 'The Parliamentary Scrutiny of Delegated Legislation' in Alexander Horne and Gavin Drewry (eds.), *Parliament and the Law* (2018), 350.

[42]   Edward C. Page, *Governing by Numbers: Delegated Legislation and Everyday Policy-Making* (2001), 5–6 & 89.

[43]   For further analysis see Philip Norton's contribution to this volume, in Chapter 6.

[44]   Tucker, 'Parliamentary Scrutiny of Delegated Legislation', 370.

scope of the statutory power pursuant to which it was purportedly made'.[45] This is a straightforward elaboration of constitutional principle, since in so doing, the court not only applies the rule of law but also, by policing the bounds of an authority delegated to the executive, respects the separation of powers and the constitutional supremacy of Parliament. Similarly, if an item of delegated legislation is being used for purposes other than those envisaged by the parent Act, unfairly or unreasonably, it may be held unlawful.[46]

Constitutional principle is most obviously at stake in cases involving a 'Henry VIII clause', that is, where the parent statute includes an executive power to amend primary legislation.[47] Confronted by such a clause, the courts' 'role in upholding Parliamentary supremacy is particularly striking' and the scrutiny they apply correspondingly high.[48] A limited capacity to fine-tune legislative provisions may in principle be justified on expediency grounds, particularly in fast-paced environments.[49] This trade-off between constitutional propriety and efficiency is replicated in the European Union (Withdrawal) Act 2018, but on a massive scale. As Paul Craig explains in Chapter 4 of this volume, the Act paves the way for the UK's departure from the EU by taking a snapshot of EU law as it exists immediately before Brexit, converting it into domestic law ('retained EU law'), and giving extensive power to the government to amend domestic law (not only retained EU law) to address the 'deficiencies' arising from Brexit. That power extends, subject to certain exceptions, to allowing ministers to do anything that could be done by statute (s.8). The House of Lords Constitution Committee has described these powers as 'breath-taking' in their scope and potency. They 'fundamentally challenge the constitutional balance of powers between Parliament and Government' and could 'represent a significant—and unacceptable—transfer of legal competence'.[50] It is a reasonable assumption that, because of this Act, Henry VIII clauses will become a more keenly contested topic in the years to come.

THE MINISTER AND THE DEPARTMENT

Much administrative activity is routed through agencies operating often at arm's-length from central government.[51] But the law retains its focus on government departments, much of administrative law seemingly calibrated to the review of policy-making in that

---

[45] *Public Law Project*, [23].

[46] *Padfield v Minister of Agriculture, Fisheries and Food* [1968] AC 997 (in relation to a statutory discretion vested in the minister).

[47] The most striking examples are prospective Henry VIII clauses: those which create a power to amend statutes passed even after the empowering statute. On which see N.W. Barber and A.L. Young, 'The rise of prospective Henry VIII clauses and their implications for sovereignty' [2003] *Public Law* 112.

[48] *Public Law Project*, [25].

[49] The Consumer Credit Act 2006, s.68 is the example given in Andrew Le Sueur, Maurice Sunkin and Jo Murkens, *Public Law: Text, Cases and Materials* (2010), 453.

[50] House of Lords Select Committee on the Constitution, 'European Union (Withdrawal) Bill: Interim Report' (7 September 2017).

[51] See e.g. Matthew Flinders, 'MPs and Icebergs: Parliament and Delegated Governance' (2004) 57 *Parliamentary Affairs* 767.

context. This world is one over which Parliament exerts little control. Much that goes on within it does so even beyond the control or knowledge of the minister responsible for it. 'In fact', Page writes, 'much of the everyday life of a minister and his or her top brass in Whitehall has rather little directly to do with the everyday practice of government as revealed in the bulk of the measures that government produces, such as decrees, guidance, direct instructions to public and private bodies, and regulatory decisions.'[52]

The courts accommodate many of the practical realities of departmental life. The law assumes that departmental officials exercise the powers given to ministers, and that it is generally acceptable that they do so. 'Public business could not be carried on if that were not the case.'[53] The *Carltona* principle, as this idea is known, is a carve-out from the general administrative law rule that a person given discretion cannot delegate it to another. Justifying the principle in the more recent case of *Bourgass*, Lord Reed said that it 'is not one of agency as understood in private law. Nor is it strictly one of delegation . . . Rather, the principle is that a decision made on behalf of a minister by one of his officials is constitutionally the decision of the minister himself.'[54]

It may well be that *Carltona* represents, as another senior judge has remarked, 'a cornerstone of the conformity between our system of law and our system of government.'[55] But turning the department into something of a black box as far as the delegation of power is concerned can prevent the development of suitably tailored principles designed to enhance good administration. The five decades after *Carltona* did see the creation of certain exceptions as a matter of principle.[56] But these were almost never applied in practice. *Bourgass*, mentioned a moment ago, may signal a change of mood. The case concerned the procedure followed when a prisoner is kept in solitary confinement. The relevant power authorized the prison governor to order segregation for a maximum of 72 hours. Longer periods required the authorization of the Secretary of State, which meant in practice senior officials from outside the prison. The UKSC decided that the rules were intended to provide a safeguard for the prisoner, a safeguard that was only meaningful if the power is exercised by an official from outside the prison and held that the *Carltona* principle did not therefore allow the governor to exercise the Secretary of State's powers.[57]

We will see in time whether *Bourgass* leads to a more serious involvement in structures of delegation.[58] But the courts are already more active in relation to other

[52] Edward C. Page, *Policy without Politicians: Bureaucratic Influence in Comparative Perspective* (2012), 63–4.

[53] *Carltona Ltd v Commissioners of Works* [1943] 2 All ER 560, 563.

[54] *R. (Bourgass) v Secretary of State for Justice* [2015] UKSC 54, [49].

[55] Sir John Laws, 'Crown Proceedings' in Mark Supperstone and James Goudie (eds.), *Judicial Review* (1992), 258–9.

[56] The most important being *R. v Secretary of State for the Home Department, ex p Oladehinde* [1991] 1 AC 254. See also *Lavender v Minister of Housing* [1970]

[57] *Bourgass*, 88–90.

[58] See also e.g. *R. v Gerard Adams* [2018] NICA 8, especially at [42] where the legal position relating to the *Carltona* principle is outlined in six propositions. At the time of writing, the UKSC had granted permission to hear an appeal from this decision.

elements of departmental practice. Three developments are particularly noteworthy. The first is an increased attention to transparency and honesty in policy-making, including how policy is communicated to the public (the 'duty of candour'). This new focus has sometimes meant that courts have had to get to grips with the less formal or 'soft law' elements of the bureaucratic toolkit.[59] In the *BAPIO Action* case, the Law Lords held unlawful a policy change issued by the Health Secretary in guidance published on the NHS Employers' website, which worsened the employment prospects of foreign medical graduates resident in the UK, negatively impacting their immigration status.[60] In *Lumba*, in the context of non-published changes to immigration detention policy, Lord Dyson said that a transparent statement by the executive on how a broad statutory power will be exercised is a requirement of the rule of law. There is a 'right to know', he said, arising out of the rule of law, what the 'currently existing policy is, so that the individual can make relevant representations in relation to it.'[61]

A second strand of interest is the willingness to take a deeper dive into the fairness of the process by which a policy was made or applied. Courts often emphasize the intrinsic as well as instrumental value of fair process: that is, not just its value in producing better results but also for treating people with respect and dignity. In *Osborn v The Parole Board*—another case involving departmental guidance to officials—Lord Reed noted that 'justice is intuitively understood to require a procedure which pays due respect to persons whose rights are significantly affected by decisions taken in the exercise of administrative or judicial functions.'[62] This position builds on earlier cases such as *Anufrijeva*, where it was held that the lack of notice of the failure of the claimant's asylum application left her in a 'Kafka-esque world' where she was affected by a decision she was not told of, and which she could not challenge.[63] And it in turn provided a platform for the Court of Appeal's judgment in *Lord Chancellor v Detention Action* that a new fast track process for asylum appeals was unlawful on the basis that the scheme as a whole was 'structurally unfair and unjust'.[64]

The third strand, the influence of rights, sounds both in the particular and in the general. In the particular, rights are naturally the point of departure in Human Rights Act cases.[65] A relevant example given our focus on rules and their application is *Huang v Home Secretary*, where the Law Lords clarified the role of immigration appellate

---

[59] See e.g. Richard Rawlings, 'Soft Law Never Dies' in Mark Elliott and David Feldman (eds.), *The Cambridge Companion to Public Law* (2015).

[60] *BAPIO Action*, above.

[61] *Walumba Lumba v Secretary of State for the Home Department* [2011] UKSC 12, 34–5.

[62] *Osborn v The Parole Board* [2013] UKSC 61, [68]. See also *Bourgass*, above, [100] (Lord Reed).

[63] *R. v Secretary of State for the Home Department, ex p Anufrijeva* [2003] UKHL 36.

[64] *The Lord Chancellor v Detention Action* [2015] EWCA Civ 840, [45]. See also *R. (Howard League for Penal Reform) v Lord Chancellor* [2015] EWCA Civ 819.

[65] These cases take place under the shadow of the jurisprudence of the European Court of Human Rights: Human Rights Act 1998, s. 2. See e.g. *Tsfayo v United Kingdom* [2006] ECHR 981 (system of appeals to Housing Benefit Review Boards, manned by elected members of the local authority who fund and make decisions about the allocation of housing benefit, insufficiently independent and thus in breach of Article 6 ECHR).

authorities when deciding appeals on human rights grounds.[66] Rights also perform a similar role in some non-HRA cases. In *UNISON*, the UKSC invoked the constitutional right of access to the courts[67] as the lens through which to assess, and ultimately find wanting, a new fees structure imposed in respect of employment tribunals.[68] But rights have also had an extended influence on jurisprudential development, largely through the infusion of the normative orientation that informs rights-based jurisprudence into the general body of administrative law.[69] This is clear in relation to the major decisions just noted, including *Bourgass*, *BAPIO Action*, *Lumba*, *Osborn* and *Anufrijeva*. It is also evident in another case discussed earlier, *ex p Simms*, best known for articulating the 'principle of legality' which holds that fundamental rights can only be overridden by a clear and unambiguously worded statute.[70]

GENERAL EXECUTIVE POWERS

Our aim has been to identify what the executive looks like from the legal perspective. While acknowledging the kaleidoscopic reality of modern executive processes, we isolated a common core based on the idea of power being delegated to government by Parliament, and the exercise of the discretion afforded by that power being subject to legal limits, grounded in principles of legality, fairness, rationality and rights. We now consider the prerogative, which I defined earlier as the non-statutory powers of the executive, the residue of kingly power retained by the Crown. Prerogative follows a different logic from statutory grants of power because it derives from a different source of authority, namely the Crown. That alternative source explains why, in the exercise of prerogative power, the executive does not require authorization from Parliament.

The prerogative corresponds in practice to a fairly wide-ranging bundle of powers, perquisites and immunities. I will split that bundle into two. The first category could be called the prerogative properly understood, since it contains powers that correspond to the second function of the executive mentioned in the Introduction, its custodial responsibility to defend the realm and protect the state's vital interest. These powers include: the making and ratification of treaties; the conduct of diplomacy; the deployment of the armed forces overseas, including involvement in armed conflict, or the declaration of war; and the use of the armed forces within the UK to maintain the peace in support of the police.[71] I call these powers general executive powers, and argue that while they may be necessary for the realization of the government's

---

[66] *Huang v Secretary of State for the Home Department* [2007] UKHL 11.

[67] *R. v Secretary of State for the Home Department, ex p Leech* [1994] QB 198.

[68] *R. (UNISON) v Lord Chancellor* [2017] UKSC 51, 66–8.

[69] Thomas Poole, 'The Reformation of English Administrative Law' (2009) 68 *Cambridge Law Journal* 142.

[70] *Ex p Simms*, at 131 (Lord Hoffmann). For further analysis on this theme see Jeffrey Jowell's chapter on the rule of law in Chapter 1 of this volume.

[71] House of Commons Public Administration Select Committee, 'Taming the Prerogative: Strengthening Ministerial Accountability to Parliament' (2004), 6–7.

protective function, they nonetheless remain 'constitutionally volatile'.[72] I contrast this set of powers with a second category which are increasingly called general administrative powers and include the power to form contracts, to convey property, and to hire and fire staff. Powers belonging to this second category may share the same historical source in king's prerogative. But in practice they raise different conceptual and practical issues, not least because they correspond to the first function of the executive noted earlier, that of executing the laws.

Writing at an important stage in the long-term process of domesticating the prerogative, Bagehot recognized the gap that often exists between form and reality where prerogative is concerned. He noted how so many supposed prerogatives 'waver between reality and desuetude', and suspected that the whole idea of prerogative might thrive on ambiguity: 'Its mystery is its life'.[73] Moving on 150 years, and the mystery element to prerogative is substantially reduced. The most important developments since Bagehot's time have been political. Constitutional conventions surrounding the power and influence of the Monarch have hardened.[74] A prerogative power is now either unquestionably the province of government ministers (e.g. treaty-making); or else it remains a personal power (e.g. royal assent[75]) but edged round with conventions of such force as to make it all but non-existent as a personal power. More generally, the increased recourse to statute, even in areas that were once prerogative's heartland (e.g. war,[76] public emergency[77]), have narrowed the scope left for prerogative.[78]

Our focus, though, is the law relating to prerogative. All accounts start with an origins story, situating prerogative in the kingly power of the king (as lord and overlord), as understood in the English version of the medieval constitution. They then try to explain prerogative's attenuated existence within the modern constitution based on parliamentary supremacy. Dicey isolated prerogative's *residual* nature, defining it as 'the remaining portion of the Crown's original authority' and as such 'the name for the residue of discretionary power left at any moment in the hands of the Crown, whether

---

[72] Margit Cohn, 'Medieval Chains, Invisible Inks: On Non-Statutory Powers of the Executive' (2005) 25 *Oxford Journal of Legal Studies* 97, 97.

[73] *The English Constitution*, 49 & 50.

[74] The one personal prerogative to survive more or less intact is the right to advise, encourage and warn ministers.

[75] On what might happen were a monarch to exercise this power see Mike Bartlett's brilliant play *King Charles III* (2014).

[76] *Burmah Oil Co. v Lord Advocate* [1965] AC 75: 'it would be impracticable to conduct a modern war by use of prerogative alone . . . The mobilization of the industrial and financial resources of the country could not be done without statutory emergency powers. The prerogative is really a relic of a past age, not lost by disuse, but only available in a case not covered by statute.'

[77] See e.g. Civil Contingency Act 2004.

[78] Another development that has had the effect of reducing recourse to prerogative is the end of empire. From the late seventeenth century onwards, the prerogative was much more heavily used in the colonial and imperial context than in the domestic sphere. The occasional case continues to crop up from this context, notably *R. v Secretary of State for Foreign & Commonwealth Affairs, ex p Bancoult (No. 2)* [2008] UKHL 61, where a majority of the UKHL determined that the imperial prerogative—but definitely not the domestic prerogative—allowed the Crown to remove inhabitants from their native land.

such power be in fact exercised by the King himself or by his Ministers'.[79] This definition is too general for our purposes, since it includes the general administrative as well as executive powers of the Crown. Blackstone defined prerogative in narrower terms, as the more specific ('singular and eccentrical'[80]) bundle of powers relating specifically to sovereign authority, in the exertion of which 'the *king is and ought to be absolute*; that is, so far absolute, that there is no legal authority that can either delay or resist him.'[81]

Courts often find little help in these definitions.[82] This is partly due to their age, the law relating to prerogative changing with our conception of kingship. But they are also rather general, largely retrospective and conflict in important ways. The courts have developed their own set of rules. Though most of the relevant domestic cases go back no further than 1915, these rules reinforce settled constitutional principle.[83] We can discern two distinct phases in the development of the law. The first we might call 'constitutional law review', since it deals with aspects of the relationship between statute and prerogative, protecting the constitutional supremacy of the former from incursion by the latter. The second sounds more in administrative law, since it deals with the review of the exercise of prerogative power, and is a more recent development.

Precursors of the first phase—'constitutional law review'—can be found in the old jurisprudence, stemming especially from the turbulent first half of the seventeenth century.[84] But the position only solidified after 1689. In clipping the prerogative's wings, the Bill of Rights implied the supremacy of Parliament over the Crown and law over prerogative.[85] It became settled that prerogative powers, while not themselves created by the common law, were subject to the determination of the common law courts.[86] By the start of the twentieth century, increased legislation meant that prerogative more often bumped up against statute. Two more concrete principles emerged from the cases. The first, the 'abeyance' principle, established that a prerogative power cannot be used when a statutory power appears to have superseded it.[87] Where there is direct overlap between statute and prerogative, then, the prerogative goes into abeyance—it effectively disappears from the scene and can no longer be used. The second,

---

[79] A.V. Dicey, *The Law of the Constitution* (ed. J.W.F. Allison, 2013), 189.

[80] William Blackstone, *Commentaries on the Laws of England* (1979) I, 239.

[81] Emphasis in original: *Commentaries* I, 243.

[82] As Lord Reid said in *Burmah Oil* (at 99), 'the views of institutional writers and text writers are not always very helpful'.

[83] Lord Reid in *Burmah Oil* (at 99): 'I think we should beware of looking at older authorities through modern spectacles. We ought not to ignore the many changes in Constitutional law and theory which culminated in the Revolution Settlement of 1688–1689 and there is practically no authority between that date and 1915.'

[84] See especially *The Case of Proclamations* (1611) 12 Co. Rep. 74: 'the king hath no prerogative, but that which the law of the land allows him' (Coke CJ).

[85] For historical analysis see Sebastian Payne, 'The Royal Prerogative' in Sunkin and Payne, *The Nature of the Crown*, 95–101.

[86] This was visible even of the imperial prerogative: see e.g. *Campbell v Hall* (1774) 98 Eng. Rep. 1045, which placed clear limits on the king's prerogative to make law for a conquered territory.

[87] *Attorney-General v De Keyser's Royal Hotel Ltd* [1920] AC 508: 'When the power of the Executive . . . has been placed under Parliamentary control, and directly regulated by statute, the Executive no longer derives its authority from the Royal Prerogative of the Crown but from Parliament' (Lord Parmoor).

the 'frustration' principle, established that where a statute and prerogative are inconsistent, but not overlapping, the prerogative cannot be used to frustrate or go against the intention of Parliament as expressed in statute.[88]

The frustration principle was first clearly articulated and applied in the *Fire Brigades Union* case. The Criminal Justice Act 1988 provided for a new criminal injuries compensation scheme. Instead of triggering the powers delegated by the Act, the Home Secretary drew up a different scheme for a tariff-based system in the purported exercise of prerogative powers. The Law Lords held that while the minister is under no legally enforceable duty to bring the provisions of the Act into force, his alternative scheme was unlawful. As Lord Browne-Wilkinson observed: 'It would be most surprising if, at the present day, prerogative powers could be validly exercised by the executive so as to frustrate the will of Parliament as expressed in a statute and, to an extent, to pre-empt the decision of Parliament whether or not to continue with the statutory scheme.'[89]

The second phase of development—'administrative law review'—connects more directly to the rise of judicial review of administrative action since the 1960s. The older position, exemplified by Blackstone's definition quoted above, was that the courts could rule on the existence and extent of a prerogative power but could not inquire into the propriety of its exercise (a proposition fleshed out by the abeyance and frustration principles). That changed with the *GCHQ* case. The case involved a challenge to the use of the prerogative by the Prime Minister, in her capacity as Minister for the Civil Service, to ban workers at signal intelligence headquarters, GCHQ, from belonging to a trade union. The case stands for the proposition that in principle an exercise of prerogative is reviewable on the ordinary public law grounds of legality, fairness and rationality. In Lord Diplock's words, 'I see no reason why simply because a decision-making power is derived from a common law and not a statutory source, it should *for that reason only* be immune from judicial review.'[90]

What was made possible in principle in *GCHQ* is now increasingly plausible in practice. The courts have become more consistent in their defence of the proposition that its powers 'cannot be ousted merely by invoking the word "prerogative".'[91] Indicative in this regard is the Brexit case, *Miller*, where the UKSC upheld a High Court judgment that the government did not have the power under the foreign relations prerogative to give notice to EU institutions of the UK's intention to withdraw from the EU, since to do so would compromise existing statutory rights.[92] It is a little odd that the case has caused such controversy among public lawyers. In doctrinal terms, *Miller* was a fairly straightforward application of the frustration principle—especially as the government conceded in court that the notification power in Article 50 of the Lisbon Treaty was irrevocable and that leaving the EU would necessarily interfere with existing statutory

---

[88] *Laker Airways v Department of Trade* [1977] 1 QB 643.
[89] *R. v Secretary of State for the Home Department, ex p Fire Brigades Union* [1995] 2 AC 513.
[90] Emphasis added: *Council of Civil Service Unions v Minister for the Civil Service* [1985] AC 374, 410.
[91] *R. v Secretary of State for the Home Department, ex p Everett* [1989] QB 811 (per Taylor LJ).
[92] *R. (Miller) v Secretary of State for Exiting the European Union* [2017] UKSC 5.

rights.[93] In terms of constitutional principle, *Miller* was an even more straightforward defence of the idea that it is for Parliament via statute and not the executive through prerogative to effect substantial legal change, especially where (as here) the legal change has constitutional ramifications.[94]

Largely unnoticed in the melee surrounding the Brexit case, the UKSC handed down a trio of Act of State cases in the same month as *Miller*. These cases arose out of the post-2001 counterterrorism climate, focusing specifically on the UK government's complicity in the unlawful detention and rendition, assault, torture and cruel and inhuman treatment for the most part (in these actions) by foreign state officials. In *Belhaj*, the UKSC refused to extend the range of acts recognized by the common law as protecting a foreign state's sovereign acts from legal scrutiny and held that complicity in certain acts, including torture, could receive no protection.[95] *Al-Waheed* concerned the power to detain in foreign conflict situations, authorized by the United Nations Security Council, and identified a core set of rights that must apply and an attendant procedure to make those rights meaningful.[96] *Serdar Mohamed*, concerning extensive periods of detention, subjected the Crown's legal immunity for 'acts of a governmental nature, committed abroad' to a review modelled on ordinary public law principles. The government must show to the court's satisfaction that the act in question was 'so closely connected to' a legitimate foreign policy objective as 'to be necessary in pursuing it'.[97] Collectively, these cases further diminish the worldview that used to sustain the prerogative, understood in something like its original form as a reservoir of imperative or directive authority.

GENERAL ADMINISTRATIVE POWERS

But the Crown's general executive (prerogative) powers do not exhaust its discretionary powers. The executive also has at its disposal a significant number of general administrative powers. Such powers, Adam Perry writes, are 'unglamorous but important. They range from the power to form contracts to the power to circulate written material, and include powers to convey property, hire and fire staff, consult with officials, make ex gratia payments, and create policies.' Unlike the general executive powers, which correspond to the protective role unique to the executive, these administrative

---

[93] Robert Craig, 'A Simple Application of the Frustration Principle: Prerogative, Statute and Miller' [2017] *Public Law* 25.

[94] Thomas Poole, 'Devotion to Legalism: On the Brexit Case' (2017) 80 *Modern Law Review* 696.

[95] *Belhaj and Rahmatullah v Straw* [2017] UKSC 3. The court also rejected the argument that the court could not investigate any acts of a foreign state where the government asserted that to do so would embarrass the UK in its international relations.

[96] *Al-Waheed and Serdar Mohamed v Ministry of Defence* [2017] UKSC 2.

[97] *Rahmatullah (No. 2) and Serdar Mohammed v Ministry of Defence* [2017] UKSC 1, [33] & [37] (per Lady Hale).

powers 'are shared by the Crown with its subjects; none of them derive from custom; and together they account for much of the ordinary business of government.'[98]

We have encountered these general administrative powers already, for instance when discussing the capacity of departmental officials to give instructions to those lower down the chain ('soft law'). Perry's statement indicates that these powers often go unnoticed, assumed to exist in as much as they are thought about at all.[99] Changes in the structure of government, however, especially in the provision of public services, did focus some more attention on them.[100] The growth of the 'contract state' since the 1980s included the restructuring of relations between some public bodies on pseudo-contractual lines (e.g. framework documents between government departments and satellite executive agencies).[101] Not only did changes of this sort entail modifications in the structure of government, they also produced a host of new governance arrangements. These are customarily grouped under the umbrella term 'regulation', connoting here the power outside the central government context to make rules and apply them. Significant examples include: arrangements adopted after privatization for the regulation of the telecommunications, gas and electricity, water and railways sectors; and financial services regulation, where a number of bodies such as the Bank of England, the Financial Conduct Authority and the Panel on Takeovers and Mergers operate largely independent of government.[102]

Awareness of these changes induced some modifications in judicial review doctrine. In a move that paralleled the change of direction from *GCHQ* onwards from a focus on form to one on substance, the courts in *Datafin* signalled a move away from the 'sources' test of distinguishing a public authority on the basis of where it obtained its power, to a 'functions' test that looked more at what the body actually did.[103] This approach could have opened up considerably the range of bodies susceptible to judicial review, but in practice its effect was muted. Courts insisted that judicial review applied only to entities performing a 'governmental' function.[104] And even where private entities fell within that description, the courts tended to review their activities with a light touch. 'Most attempts to push *Datafin* further into the realm of privately sourced power which affects the public generally have failed'.[105]

---

[98] Adam Perry, 'The Crown's Administrative Powers' (2015) *Law Quarterly Review* 652 at 652.

[99] An interesting exception is a House of Lords Constitution Committee report on 'The Pre-emption of Parliament' (1 May 2013), which considers the use of the government's general administrative powers to make preparations, sometimes substantial, in anticipation of Parliament passing a bill.

[100] See e.g. Mark Freedland, 'Government by Contract and Public Law' [1994] *Public Law* 86.

[101] For discussion see Carol Harlow and Richard Rawlings, *Law and Administration* (3rd ed., 2009), Chapter 8.

[102] See e.g. Julia Black, 'Paradoxes and Failures: "New Governance" Techniques and the Financial Crisis' (2012) 75 *Modern Law Review* 1037, and more generally Robert Baldwin, Martin Cave and Martin Lodge, *Understanding Regulation* (2nd ed., 2012).

[103] *R. v Panel on Takeovers and Mergers, ex p Datafin* [1987] 1 All ER 564.

[104] See *R. v Disciplinary Committee of the Jockey Club ex p Aga Khan* [1993] 2 All ER 853 and in the context of the Human Rights Act 1998 *YL v Birmingham City Council* [2007] UKHL 27.

[105] Mark Aronson, 'A Public Lawyer's Response to Privatisation and Outsourcing' in Michael Taggart (ed.), *The Province of Administrative Law* (1997), 46.

More recently, the propensity observed earlier for the courts to dig deeper into the further reaches of government departments has resulted in more direct encounters with general administrative powers. *New London College* concerned the lawfulness of new Guidance issued by the Home Secretary, which set out conditions for the grant of a sponsor licence, essential to universities for enrolling international students. The College argued that since the Guidance contained mandatory requirements for sponsors, it ought to have been laid before Parliament as required by the parent statute, the Immigration Act 1971.[106] The UKSC held that the Guidance did not contain rules calling for compliance by the migrant, but wholly concerned the position of the sponsor. Lord Sumption for the majority said that 'the Crown possesses some general administrative powers to carry on the ordinary business of government which are not exercises of the royal prerogative and do not require statutory authority.'[107] These powers gave the Home Secretary, he said, a basis to adopt non-coercive administrative measures, so long as they do not go against the statute or transgress principles of legality, fairness and rationality. Lord Carnwath was concerned about the breadth of this incidental power identified by the majority. These powers should not be understood as incidental to the governing function in a general sense, he argued, but as 'adjunct of the specific function' identified in the legislation and thus 'reasonably incidental' to the authorizing statute.[108]

The UKSC left the theoretical underpinnings of the Crown's general administrative powers unclear.[109] But it is likely that judges and jurists will acknowledge 'that there are express statutory powers, accompanied by powers necessarily implicit in the statutory scheme, and also a residue of [general administrative] powers which can be used to write contracts, hire staff, issue guidelines and so on.'[110] This approach tracks the reality of executive practice, but is capable of subjecting that practice to public law constraints.[111] This contrasts with recent decisions of the High Court of Australia in cases relating to the executive power to contract and spend. The Court held in *Williams v Commonwealth*, primarily on the basis of federal and parliamentary accountability

---

[106] A similar argument had succeeded in *R. (Alvi) v Secretary of State for the Home Department* [2012] UKSC 33, where it was held that the 'powers of control that are vested in the Secretary of State in the case of all those who require leave to enter or to remain are now entirely the creature of statute', [32] (Lord Hope).

[107] *R. (New London College) v Secretary of State for the Home Department* [2013] UKSC 51, [28].

[108] At 37–8.

[109] Quite rightly, there seems to be little support for the doctrine contained within the 'Ram memorandum' (1945, but published in 2003), sometimes relied on by the government, that the Crown, like a private individual, is permitted to do anything not permitted by statute. For criticism see HL Constitution Committee, 'The Pre-emption of Parliament', Chapter 3; Harry Woolf, Jeffrey Jowell, Catherine Donnelly and Ivan Hare, *De Smith's Judicial Review* (8th edition, 2018), Chapter 5–024 ff.

[110] Paul Daly, 'I contract, therefore I am: the Third Source Powers of Government Entities: Part One' (Administrative Law Matters, 31 July 2013).

[111] Per Lord Sumption in *New London College*, at [29]: 'Without specific statutory authority, [the Secretary of State] cannot adopt measures which are coercive; or which infringe the legal rights of others (including the rights under the Human Rights Convention); or which are irrational or unfair or otherwise conflict with the general constraints on administrative action imposed by public law.' See also e.g. *Porter v Magill* [2002] AC 357 (misuse of statutory powers to dispose of land by local councillor essentially for party political gain).

considerations, that Commonwealth executive power is not coextensive with Commonwealth legislative power and that, in most circumstances, the Commonwealth executive requires statutory authority before it can enter into contracts with private parties and spend public money.[112] While praiseworthy for the attention it gives to government financial powers, the decision puts an enormous volume of Commonwealth programmes and financial commitments in a state of legal limbo.[113]

So has the money unlawfully spent by the Australian government been paid back? No: the government announced that the payments would not be recovered. Things go on much as before, except that under heightened conditions of legal risk more thought is no doubt being given to law-proofing future grants. My point is not to comment on the propriety or otherwise of these actions, but to draw attention to them in order to underscore a general observation about the executive's relationship to law.

CONCLUSION

'The proper constitutional relationship of the executive with the courts is that the courts will respect all acts of the executive within its lawful province, and that the executive will respect all decisions of the courts as to what its lawful province is.'[114] So wrote Nolan LJ in his Court of Appeal judgment in *M v Home Office*, one of the seminal cases on the relationship between law and executive power in modern times. It is hard to think of a better summary of the material covered in this chapter. But, as we have seen many times in the course of our investigation, the precise contours of the executive's 'lawful province' changes over time—*M v Home Office* itself being a case in point. The project of subjecting government to law necessarily takes this evolutionary shape. The executive's regulatory functions change over time, as does its protective role (or at least the context in which it is realized). The modern executive is unquestionably bounded by law; but it is not in a straightforward sense entirely circumscribed by it.

FURTHER READING

VERNON BOGDANOR, *The Monarchy and the Constitution* (1995)

PAUL CRAIG and ADAM TOMKINS (eds), *The Executive and Public Law* (2006)

TERENCE DAINTITH and ALAN PAGE, *The Executive in the Constitution* (1999)

---

[112] *Williams v Commonwealth of Australia* [2012] HCA 23.

[113] See *Williams v Commonwealth of Australia (No.2)* [2014] HCA 23 (provisions of the Financial Framework Legislation Amendment Act which attempted to validate the programme invalidated by *Williams (No. 1)* and other similar Commonwealth spending programmes that were invalid as they extended beyond the scope of Parliament's power under the Constitution).

[114] Per Nolan LJ in *M v Home Office* [1992] QB 270 (CA), 314, adopting a formulation of the relationship between courts and the executive that had been presented in argument by Stephen Sedley QC (as he then was).

SIR IVOR JENNINGS, *Cabinet Government* (3rd ed., 1959)

HARVEY C. MANSFIELD JR., *Taming the Prince: The Ambivalence of Modern Executive Power* (1989)

House of Lords Select Committee for the Constitution, 'The Legislative Process: The Delegation of Powers' (2018)

MAURICE SUNKIN and SEBASTIAN PAYNE (eds.), *The Nature of the Crown* (1999)

Ministry of Justice, 'Review of the Executive Royal Prerogative Powers: Final Report' (2009)

JANET MCLEAN, *Searching for the State in British Legal Thought* (2012)

EDWARD C. PAGE, *Governing by Numbers* (2001)

THOMAS POOLE, *Reason of State: Law, Prerogative and Empire* (2015)

ANNE TWOMEY, *The Veiled Sceptre: Reserve Powers of Heads of State in Westminster Systems* (2018)

8

THE FOUNDATIONS
OF JUSTICE

Andrew Le Sueur*

SUMMARY

There is broad consensus that the constitutional principle of judicial independence is important. In relation to the core judicial functions of hearing cases and writing judgments, the central meaning and application of the principle is fairly straightforward: people holding public office (politicians, parliamentarians, and officials) must refrain from interfering with judicial decision-making in individual cases; and judges should be protected from illegitimate pressure from the news media and other organizations. But hearings and judgments do not 'just happen'; they have to be facilitated by a wide array of institutions and processes (the justice infrastructure), covering matters as diverse as court buildings, litigation procedures, judicial careers, and legal aid. In the absence of a codified constitution, in the United Kingdom the justice infrastructure is set out in Acts of Parliament, delegated legislation and 'soft law' (including the 2003 'Concordat'). The day-to-day running of the justice infrastructure can be understood in terms of who carries out functions related to the administration of justice—the judges, government (in particular, the Lord Chancellor), functions shared between judges and government, and functions given to arm's length bodies. Periodically, the justice infrastructure is reshaped. This is a constitutionally significant activity that may take place in different settings—the political environment, expert environments, and blended environments. The day-to-day running of this infrastructure, along with its periodic reshaping, presents numerous and complex challenges for a legal system intent on respecting judicial independence and facilitating access to justice.

* School of Law, University of Essex.

THE JUSTICE INFRASTRUCTURE

'All rise.' Every day, with words like this, thousands of court and tribunal sittings start across the United Kingdom.[1] In the minutes, hours, or days that follow, judges adjudicate on disputes of fact, decide what the common law is, and interpret and apply legislation to the situations before them. In the higher courts and some tribunals, writing judgments is also part of this core judicial function. Judges, and the courts and tribunals they sit in, are the embodiment of the state's judicial power, authorized to impose criminal sanctions, order compensation and other remedies, and adjudicate on the legality of governmental action. These core functions are constitutionally important activities that give practical implementation to the rule of law. In most countries round the world, there is a strong consensus that judges must be insulated from instructions or influences from government or other illegitimate pressures on the outcome of the particular case. Sometimes this understanding is presented as an aspect of the rule of law; sometimes as a strand of the concept of separation of powers; and sometimes as a free-standing principle of judicial independence.

Court and tribunal hearings and judgment writing do not, however, 'just happen'. Behind every sitting and judgment there is a complex array of institutions and processes that facilitate the delivery of justice by the legal system's 27,000 judges. To facilitate the delivery of justice, courts and tribunals must be created and funded. Jurisdiction (the legal power to decide types of cases) is created, transferred, modified, and sometimes 'ousted' by the legislature. There need to be rules of procedure guiding the steps to be taken in litigation. Entitlement, if any, to legal aid, must also be defined. Rules on rights of audience before courts, which in turn may depend on rules about regulation of the legal profession, are required. The practical work of listing hearings, allocating cases to judges, and ensuring parties, lawyers, witnesses, and documents are where they are needed is vital (and in many legal systems increasingly dependent on information technology).[2] Buildings for courts and court staff need to be provided and managed. Judges must be selected and appointed (perhaps thousands each year),[3] disciplined (occasionally), dismissed (very rarely), and eventually allowed to retire with a pension. This 'justice infrastructure' is the focus of this chapter.

It is easy to see what an adverse impact a weak justice infrastructure could have on the quality of court sittings and judgments in particular cases. Imagine a system in which politicians make dramatic changes to the structure of courts without consultation, lawyers

---

[1] There are separate justice infrastructures in England and Wales (with Wales in recent years acquiring features distinct from the English legal system), in Scotland, and in Northern Ireland; each is a distinct legal system; and, under the devolution settlement, justice is a policy field devolved to governments and legislatures in Scotland and Northern Ireland. This chapter focuses on England and Wales.

[2] In England and Wales, a £375 million investment programme started in 2014, designed to use information technology, online services, and video links to reduce delays and costs—described by Lord Thomas CJ as 'of a scale that has not been undertaken since the reforms of the late 19th century' (Lionel Cohen Lecture, 15 May 2017).

[3] e.g. in 2017–18, 749 individual judicial appointments were made in England and Wales, which involved processing over 5,000 applications.

without adequate professional expertise are appointed as judges, and chronic underfunding delays litigants obtaining judgments and prevents many people from affording access to the courts. Worse, a justice infrastructure could be affected by endemic corruption. As Lord Phillips of Worth Matravers (a former Lord Chief Justice of England and Wales) said, repeating the sentiments of Lord Browne-Wilkinson (a former Senior Law Lord): 'Judicial independence cannot exist on its own—judges must have the loyal staff, buildings and equipment to support the exercise of the independent judicial function.'[4]

The justice infrastructure in England and Wales has in recent years been buffeted by some poorly planned reform attempts and (like almost every other part of the public sector) has been reeling from financial cuts introduced by government in the wake of the 2008 Financial Crisis. The Ministry of Justice (the government department responsible for the courts and judiciary) had a 40 per cent cut in its funding in real terms between 2011 and 2020. Pay freezes, job cuts, and court closures are affecting the morale of judges and court staff.[5] Many judges and practitioners are deeply concerned about recent radical changes to the legal aid system.[6]

This chapter explores the justice infrastructure in England and Wales, which has undergone significant reforms in recent years. It does this by looking at two levels— 'running' and 'shaping'. The first level (running) is the routine operation of the system, where decisions are taken within the framework of the existing infrastructure. This encompasses day-to-day matters (for example, listing of cases for hearing, making individual judicial appointments, granting or refusing legal aid) and annual planning cycles (such as the allocation of resources to HM Courts and Tribunals Service, the organization that runs many aspects of the infrastructure). The second level (shaping) is strategic, concerned with changing the infrastructure, which typically involves the addition or abolition of a major new process or institution or significant new rules. Examples of shaping are the institutional changes introduced by the Constitutional Reform Act 2005 (reforming the office of Lord Chancellor, creating the UK Supreme Court, and a new process for appointing judges in England and Wales).

Both levels of the infrastructure—running and shaping—are of constitutional significance. They generate direct and indirect risks of damaging or enriching judicial independence for the core functions of hearing cases and writing judgments.[7] It may be tempting to think that a neat solution would be to hand over the wholesale running and shaping of the justice infrastructure to the judiciary. But, as we will see, a solution along these lines needs to be rejected as being too difficult to square with other constitutional values, especially accountability and the need to reflect the broad public

---

[4] House of Commons Select Constitutional Affairs Committee, *The Creation of the Ministry of Justice*, 6th Report of 2006–7, HC 466, Ev 27.

[5] See C. Thomas, *2016 Judicial Attitude Survey* (UCL Judicial Institute, 7 February 2017); Owen Bowcott, 'Peers Warn of Low Morale in Judiciary and Call for Greater Diversity', *The Guardian*, 2 November 2017.

[6] See F. Wilmot-Smith, 'Necessity or Ideology?' (2014) 36(21) *London Review of Books* 15.

[7] For a detailed statement of the specific norms grouped under the umbrella term 'judicial independence', see *The Mount Scopus Approved Revised International Standards of Judicial Independence* (2008, as amended) http://www.jwp.org.

interest.[8] Running and shaping of the justice infrastructure also has direct and indirect implications for the constitutional principle of access to justice.

THE BLUEPRINT FOR THE INFRASTRUCTURE

Where do we find the blueprint—the instruction manual—for the justice infrastructure? In countries with codified written constitutions, the constitution is a source. In the United Kingdom, primary and secondary legislation and specific pieces of 'soft law' provide the detailed rules and requirements that keep the system ticking over.

CONSTITUTIONS

In countries with codified constitutions, the major elements of their justice infrastructure are laid down in part of the constitutional code.[9] It should not surprise us to find that the justice infrastructures are different across constitutional, political, and legal cultures. What is normal in one system (for example, selecting judges through highly politicized elections in some states of the USA) is anathema in others (where professional merit is the criterion for appointment). There is, however, broad consensus about some general abstract principles that in the mid-twentieth century came to be included in international human rights treaties. The judicial infrastructure must enable hearings that are 'independent and impartial', in public (unless there is an overriding public interest in closed hearings), and within a reasonable time.[10]

LEGISLATION

As the United Kingdom muddles through without a codified constitution, it is Acts of Parliament that do the work of creating the institutions, rules, procedures, and conferring executive power for the most important elements of the national judicial infrastructure.[11] The Acts are amended quite frequently through the normal parliamentary legislative process in the House of Commons and the House of Lords.

---

[8] On accountability, see further A. Le Sueur, 'Parliamentary Accountability and the Justice System' in N. Bamforth and P. Leyland (eds.), *Accountability in the Contemporary Constitution* (2013).

[9] See e.g. the Australian Constitution, Part III (Judicature); Spanish Constitution, Part VI (Judicial Power); Constitution of Ireland, Arts. 34–7; and so on.

[10] Universal Declaration of Human Rights, Art. 10 ('Everyone is entitled in full equality to a fair and public hearing by an independent and impartial tribunal, in the determination of his rights and obligations and of any criminal charge against him'); European Convention on Human Rights, Art. 6.

[11] These include: the Courts Act 1971 (creating the Crown Court); the Magistrates' Courts Act 1980; the Senior Courts Act 1981 (regulating the High Court and Court of Appeal); the County Courts Act 1984; the Legal Aid Act 1988 (replaced by the Access to Justice Act 1999 and subsequently by the Legal Aid, Sentencing and Punishment of Offenders Act 2012); the Courts Act 2003 (creating HM Courts Service, the agency to administer courts, expanded in 2007 to include tribunals); the Constitutional Reform Act 2005 (reforming the office of Lord Chancellor, setting up the UK Supreme Court, and creating a new judicial appointments system); the Legal Services Act 2007 (regulating the legal profession, in conjunction with the Courts and Legal Services Act 1990); and the Tribunals, Courts and Enforcement Act 2007 (creating the First-tier Tribunal and Upper Tribunal in place of the previous maze of separate tribunals); Criminal Justice and Courts Act 2015 (modifying arrangements for trials, appeals and judicial review).

Beneath these Acts of Parliament lies a conglomeration of delegated legislation. As with delegated legislation on other topics, most of this comes into force with little parliamentary scrutiny or public controversy. It fills in detail. Occasionally, however, changes sought to be made in this way do receive high-profile scrutiny. This can take place in Parliament, such as when the blandly named Civil Legal Aid (Remuneration) (Amendment) (No. 3) Regulations 2014 prompted an outcry, with Lord Pannick leading a 'motion of regret' debate in the House of Lords critical of government proposals to restrict legal aid in judicial review claims.[12] Only one member of the House of Lords—the junior minister representing the government's views—defended the new rules; he assured the House that he 'would take back the observations that were made during the course of the debate' to the Ministry of Justice.[13] Lord Pannick did not press the debate to a vote and the new rules came into force. The legality of delegated legislation may also be adjudicated on in the courts, as in August 2018 when the High Court held that the Criminal Legal Aid (Remuneration) Regulations 2013, which sought to reduce fees for solicitors defending people accused of crimes, was unlawful because the government had used an unfair consultation process and carried out flawed analysis of data in making the new policy.[14]

THE CONCORDAT

Beyond the statute book is a variety of 'soft law' documents, one of which is of special general significance. 'The Concordat' reflects the outcome of an intense period of negotiations in the second half of 2003 between Lord Woolf (the then Lord Chief Justice) and Lord Falconer (the minister in Tony Blair's Labour government responsible for judiciary-related matters).[15] The impetus for the negotiations was the unexpected announcement made by the prime minister's office in June 2003 of several far-reaching changes to the justice infrastructure, including abolition of the ancient office of Lord Chancellor, a new top-level court of the United Kingdom (by creating a UK Supreme Court to replace the Law Lords sitting as the Appellate Committee of the House of Lords), a new judicial appointments system for England and Wales, and disqualification of all senior judges from membership of Parliament. This was dramatic stuff and prompted political opposition in Parliament (primarily from the Conservatives) and criticism from some senior members of the judiciary (though others supported the gist of the proposals).[16] A negotiating team was formed by Lord Woolf to discuss with the government how responsibility for running the infrastructure would be divided between the proposed new Secretary of State (who would, under the Blair plan, have replaced the Lord Chancellor) and the judiciary. In January 2004, after six months

---

[12] BBC, 'Grayling Accused of Not Understanding the Legal System', http://www.bbc.co.uk/democracylive/house-of-lords-27319557.

[13] Hansard, HL, vol. 753, col. 1567 (7 May 2014), Lord Faulks.

[14] R. (The Law Society) v Lord Chancellor [2018] EWHC 2094 (Admin).

[15] Constitutional Reform: The Lord Chancellor's Judiciary-related Functions: Proposals, Since Referred to as 'the Agreement' and also 'the Concordat' http://webarchive.nationalarchives.gov.uk/+/http:/www.dca.gov.uk/consult/lcoffice/judiciary.htm.

[16] For a detailed analysis, see A. Le Sueur, 'From Appellate Committee to Supreme Court: a Narrative' in L. Blom-Cooper, G. Drewry and B. Dickson (eds.), The Judicial House of Lords 1876–2009 (2009).

of behind-closed-doors brokering, the Concordat was published: it was a relatively short document setting out the principles that would govern the transfer of functions in England and Wales and providing details of the application of those principles to the proposed arrangements.[17] Lord Woolf told the House of Lords: 'In agreeing the proposals, the judiciary has regarded as its primary responsibility, not the protection of its own interests but the protection of the independence of the justice system for the benefit of the public.'[18] Major elements of the Concordat were incorporated into the Constitutional Reform Act 2005 (CRA 2005); but one central aspect was not. Following sustained opposition from Conservative MPs and peers (and some others) in Parliament, the office of Lord Chancellor was retained though in a much-altered form: the office-holder was a government minister, but no longer the constitutional head of the judiciary nor necessarily in the House of Lords, nor a professionally qualified lawyer.

After the enactment of the CRA 2005, the question arose as to the continuing status of the Concordat. On one view, the document had done its job: it was a statement of the outcome of a negotiation and, once implemented, could be filed away as a mere footnote to the policy-making process. Some, however, take a different view, seeing the Concordat as either a 'constitutional convention' or a 'living document', which remains a reference point and in future to be developed. In 2005, Lady Justice Arden, giving evidence on behalf of the Judges' Council (the official non-statutory body set up by the judiciary to develop collective policy) to a House of Lords select committee scrutinizing the bill that became the CRA 2005, called for the bill or the bill's explanatory notes to make express reference to the Concordat, arguing 'there is a role for the Concordat even after the bill has been enacted', adding 'not every iota of the Concordat can be reflected in statutory language. There are some matters which have to, as it were, survive within the Concordat and one way in which the Concordat may be relevant in future is when the court is construing what will then be the Constitutional Reform Act, it may be necessary for it to look at the Concordat.'[19] The committee was not convinced, reporting: 'We do not consider it possible, beyond the provisions made by the bill, to accord the Concordat a quasi-statutory status.'[20] Two years later, a different House of Lords committee carrying out an inquiry into the relations between the judiciary, government, and Parliament heard evidence from one academic (Professor Robert Hazell) describing the Concordat as 'a constitutional convention' and the committee went on to describe the Concordat as 'a document of constitutional importance' and called for the Concordat to be amended whenever necessary 'to ensure it remains a living document reflecting current arrangements.'[21] No such formal mechanism for change

---

[17] Hansard, HL, vol. 756, col. 13 (26 January 2004).

[18] Hansard, HL, vol. 756, col. 25 (26 January 2004).

[19] House of Lords Select Committee on the Constitutional Reform Bill, *Report*, Session 2003–4, HL Paper 125-I, para. 75.

[20] House of Lords Select Committee on the Constitutional Reform Bill, *Report*, Session 2003–4 (HL Paper 125–1), para. 85.

[21] House of Lords Constitution Committee, *Relations between the Executive, the Judiciary and Parliament*, 6th Report of 2006–7 (HL Paper 151), para. 14.

has been put in place and no revisions have been made to the Concordat since it was agreed in 2003 and has rarely been referred to in Parliament since 2016.

OTHER SOFT LAW

In addition to the Concordat (whatever its status), there are other documents of key importance in the justice infrastructure. Of general importance is HM Court and Tribunals Service Framework Document, which was laid before the UK Parliament in July 2014.[22] The document describes itself as reflecting 'an agreement reached by the Lord Chancellor, the Lord Chief Justice and the Senior President of Tribunals on a partnership between them in relation to the effective governance, financing and operation of HM Courts & Tribunals Service' (HMCTS), which is an executive agency sponsored by the Ministry of Justice.[23]

RUNNING THE INFRASTRUCTURE

Running the justice infrastructure covers routine decision-making of various kinds: making decisions about individuals (should applicant W be selected for appointment as a judge; should claimant X receive legal aid), about managing workflow (which judges should form the panel of the Court of Appeal hearing case Y next week; should court building Z be closed to save money; are more circuit judges needed in the South West), about supervision of the system (how effectively is the tribunal system operating), and so on. The general characteristic of 'running' is that it takes place within the existing infrastructure.

Who runs the national infrastructure on a day-to-day basis? Who ought to run it? In trying to answer these descriptive and normative questions, it soon becomes clear that there are no straightforward answers for England and Wales. Mapping out the intricacies of the system is a colossal task; although some of this detail is needed, we concentrate on the broad constitutional questions about the allocation of decision-making power. A standard approach is to use the framework of separation-of-powers theory. An elementary and rather eighteenth-century account of this principle is that there are three types of state power, each of which ought to be wielded by different state institutions: executive power (exercised by government, in other words ministers and civil servants), legislative power (the law-making powers of Parliament), and judicial power (exercised by judges).[24] This framework is, however, too broad-brush to provide solutions as to who should run the justice infrastructure. A better approach is to focus

---

[22] HM Court and Tribunals Service Framework Document, Cm 8882.

[23] The main function of HMCTS is to administer the work of magistrates' courts, the County Court, Family Court, Crown Court, High Court, Court of Appeal and most tribunals. It employs approximately 17,000 staff.

[24] For a more sophisticated account, see N. Barber, 'Prelude to the Separation of Powers' [2001] *CLJ* 59; R. Masterman and S. Wheatle, 'Unpacking Separation of Powers: Judicial Independence, Sovereignty and Conceptual Flexibility in the UK Constitution' [2017] *PL* 469; and A. Young (Chapter 12 below).

on the four main models in use in the infrastructure of England and Wales that can be discerned: (i) functions run by judges; (ii) functions run by politicians and their officials; (iii) functions which are shared between judges and politicians; and (iv) functions which have been allocated to arm's length bodies, independent of both judges and politicians.

FUNCTIONS RUN BY JUDGES

The CRA 2005 made the Lord Chief Justice of England and Wales (LCJ) 'head of the judiciary'. Where infrastructure functions are led by the judiciary, in practice it is the LCJ (or his nominee) who makes decisions. The LCJ is assisted by the Judicial Executive Board (consisting of ten senior members of the judiciary and a senior administrator), which meets monthly. In 2017, the LCJ had a staff of 207 officials in the Judicial Office, which supports his work, including 'professional trainers, legal advisers, HR and communication experts, policy makers and administrators'.[25] The Judicial Office, which has an annual budget of £29 million, is funded by the Ministry of Justice but staff are answerable to the LCJ—not to government ministers—for their day-to-day work.

The Concordat lists six aspects of the infrastructure as ones to be primarily carried out by judges: oath taking—judges take oaths of office in the presence of the LCJ (not a government minister); deployment—the LCJ is responsible for the posting and roles of individual judges, within a framework set by the government; nomination of judges to fill posts that provide judicial leadership (such as senior presiding judges, the deputy Chief Justice, the Vice-Presidents of the Court of Appeal) 'should fall to the Lord Chief Justice either with the concurrence of or in consultation with' the government; the LCJ determines which individual judges are appointed to various committees, boards, and similar bodies; the LCJ makes 'practice directions', with the concurrence of the government, providing guidance to judges on relative minor procedural matters; judicial training is led by the LCJ, within the resources provided by the government.

After reforms to the judicial appointments process in 2013, the LCJ now has a final say in approving selections of candidates made by the independent Judicial Appointments Commission (JAC) to judicial posts below the High Court in the hierarchy, with a similar role in relation to tribunal judges carried out by the Senior President of Tribunals.[26] Previously this function was carried out by government (through the Lord Chancellor); but in practice, only in a tiny number of cases did the government reject the recommendation made by the JAC.

Another major component of the infrastructure led by judges is the operation of the UK Supreme Court (which as well as England and Wales, serves as the highest level appeal court for civil cases from Scotland and civil and criminal cases from Northern Ireland). Before the CRA 2005, the top court was the Appellate Committee of the House of Lords, consisting of 12 professional judges (colloquially called the Law Lords) who

---

[25] See http://www.judiciary.uk.
[26] Courts and Crime Act 2013, Sched. 13, amending the CRA 2005.

on appointment to the court were granted peerages enabling them to take part in non-judicial as well as judicial work of the upper house of the UK Parliament. Cases were heard in a committee room in Parliament and judgments (or 'speeches') were delivered in the House of Lords chamber at times when politicians were absent. Some of the Law Lords integrated themselves into the political work of the House of Lords, for example by listening and speaking in debates on legislation in the chamber and chairing non-judicial committees (such as one on scrutiny of EU legislation). Other Law Lords sought to distance themselves from non-judicial work as much as possible, uneasy about the blurring of lines between judicial and political roles. The CRA 2005 ended the role of the Appellate Committee, transferring the Law Lords to a new UK Supreme Court physically and institutionally separated from Parliament (though it was not until October 2009 that the new court was ready to start work).

Three infrastructure questions relating to the UK Supreme Court were considered in detail during the debates in 2004–5. The first was who should make the rules of court? Initially, the government proposed that it should have a controlling influence, with power to disallow rules proposed by the President of the court. Responding to criticisms, the government backed down and agreed that the President should have sole rule-making power, with a duty to consult the legal profession and government. The government's only role is to lay the rules before Parliament for formal approval as delegated legislation.

A second issue was how the administration of the court should be organized. Initially, the bill provided: 'The Minister may appoint such officers and staff as he thinks appropriate for the purpose of discharging his general duty in relation to the Supreme Court.' Critics, including the Law Lords, argued that this would give the government too much influence over the court's day-to-day operations. Under pressure, the government agreed to amend the bill so that the CRA 2005 now provides: 'The President of the Supreme Court may appoint officers and staff of the Court' (s. 49). Until 2013, the government remained responsible for appointing the court's chief executive, after consulting the President of the Court; but the Crime and Courts Act 2013 amended the CRA 2005 so that s. 48 now reads: 'It is for the President of the Court to appoint the chief executive.'

A third issue was funding. During the passage of the bill, the government gave the reassurance that 'the Minister will simply be a conduit for the Supreme Court bid and will not be able to alter it before passing it on to the Treasury'. The CRA provides that the government (i.e. the Lord Chancellor) 'must ensure that the Supreme Court is provided' with 'such other resources as the Lord Chancellor thinks are appropriate for the Court to carry on its business'. This arrangement is difficult to square with the reassurance and has caused misunderstanding and some ill-will between the court and the government in the ensuing years. Giving a public lecture in 2011, Lord Phillips (President of the court) told his audience about government pressure to make dramatic cost reductions, a 'peremptory' letter he had received from the minister, and his conclusion:

> that our present funding arrangements do not satisfactorily guarantee our institutional independence. We are, in reality, dependant each year upon what we can persuade the

Ministry of Justice of England and Wales to give us by way of 'contribution'. This is not a satisfactory situation for the Supreme Court of the United Kingdom. It is already leading a tendency on the part of the Ministry of Justice to try to gain the Supreme Court as an outlying part of its empire.

The following morning, the government responded in the news media. Kenneth Clarke, the Lord Chancellor, was reported as saying 'judicial independence was at the heart of the country's freedom but that Phillips could not be in the "unique position" of telling the government what its budget should be'.[27]

FUNCTIONS RUN BY GOVERNMENT

Most of government's powers to run the justice infrastructure are legally and constitutionally speaking in the hands of the Lord Chancellor. Before the CRA 2005, prime ministers selected senior, experienced lawyers for the role; the Lord Chancellor and senior judges therefore knew each other professionally and moved in the same social circles. On taking up the post, the office-holder became the constitutional head of the judiciary and with that came the right to sit as the presiding judge in the top-level courts (even though, prior to appointment, many Lord Chancellors had little experience of sitting judicially).

The 2003 Blair government's proposal was to abolish the Lord Chancellor and transfer government responsibilities for judiciary and court-related functions to a new post of Secretary of State.[28] Once the announcement had been made, a broad consensus quickly emerged that it was no longer appropriate for a government minister to be the constitutional head of the judiciary or to sit as a judge. But the Conservatives (then in opposition), supported by many cross-bencher peers in the House of Lords, were vehemently opposed to the outright abolition of the office of Lord Chancellor: they wanted the government minister responsible for judiciary-related matters and the courts to retain some of the characteristics of previous Lord Chancellors. The minister should, they argued, continue to be called 'the Lord Chancellor', and should be a professionally qualified lawyer, sit in Parliament in the House of Lords (not in the Commons), and be somebody at the end of their political career (rather than being an ambitious mid-career politician keen to please, and therefore be under the patronage of, the prime

---

[27] H. Mulholland, 'Kenneth Clarke Rejects Claim of Threat to Supreme Court Independence', *The Guardian*, 9 February 2011.

[28] In law, all Secretaries of State hold a single office. Acts of Parliament confer powers and impose duties on 'the Secretary of State' without further elaboration as to which minister will in practice exercise those powers or carry out those duties. The Interpretation Act 1978 provides that a reference to 'Secretary of State' is a reference to 'one of Her Majesty's Principal Secretaries of State for the time being'. The previous practice of creating statutory ministerial posts responsible for particular areas of policy (e.g. the Minister of Transport or the Minister of Agriculture, Fisheries and Food) has fallen into disuse. The Prime Minister has considerable scope for making what are often called 'machinery of government' changes, creating new Secretaries of State and departments, and transferring work between Secretaries of State and departments. These are normally done with little parliamentary scrutiny. Changes are given legal effect by secondary legislation made under the Ministers of the Crown Act 1975.

minister). The protracted political wrangling was brought to an end by the need for the bill to become the CRA 2005 before the general election that year. The outcome in relation to the Lord Chancellor was that the name was retained, but there would be no requirement for the office-holder to be lawyer, or to sit in the House of Lords. The new 'Lord Chancellor' was in most respects a mainstream government minister. There were, however, some special features of the new ministerial office.

Although the CRA 2005 is completely silent on this, the role of Lord Chancellor is in practice combined with that of Secretary of State, so that one person holds two ministerial posts. Between 2005 and 2006, the Secretary of State was called 'Secretary of State for Constitutional Affairs', heading the Department for Constitutional Affairs (DCA). After May 2006, he became 'Secretary of State for Justice', heading a new department— the Ministry of Justice—that combined some of the DCA's responsibilities with areas previously under the remit of the Home Office. In this conjoined-roles ministerial office, the Lord Chancellor is responsible for judiciary and court-related functions (along with a few other areas, such as the Law Commission)[29]—in other words, the justice infrastructure—and the Secretary of State deals with everything else in the Department. Since the CRA 2005 was enacted, the 'everything else' element of the job has grown significantly, to include now the large and inevitably controversial areas of prisons and offender management (moved to the Ministry of Justice from the Home Office).

The distinctive nature of the office of Lord Chancellor—distinguishing it from that of Secretary of State—is achieved by several different means. First, the CRA 2005 and numerous other statutes confer powers and duties on the Lord Chancellor (rather than the Secretary of State). It is difficult to quantify the precise number of these functions: many predate the CRA 2005; between January 2006 and July 2018, Parliament enacted 78 Acts of Parliament referring to the Lord Chancellor, many of which will contain multiple specific statutory powers and duties. Secondly, CRA 2005, s. 20 prevents many powers of the Lord Chancellor (those listed in Sched. 7 to the CRA 2005) from being transferred by the prime minister to other ministers under the general machinery of government provisions of the Ministers of the Crown Act 1975. These Lord Chancellor powers are, in effect, ring-fenced and require primary legislation to allocate them elsewhere (so giving Parliament the final say on whether such changes are made); but the Lord Chancellor also has statutory functions that are not ring-fenced in this way, for example those under the Legal Services Act 2007 (to do with regulation of the legal profession). Thirdly, the CRA 2005, s. 17 makes the oath of office taken by the Lord Chancellor different from that sworn by a Secretary of State: 'I, [name], do swear that in the office of Lord High Chancellor of Great Britain I will respect the rule of law, defend the independence of the judiciary and discharge my duty to ensure the provision of resources for the efficient and effective support of the

---

[29] The Law Commissions Act 1965 set up independent law reform agencies in England and Wales, and in Scotland. The Law Commission of England and Wales carries out research projects and publishes reports and draft Bills containing recommendations designed to 'ensure that the law is as fair, modern, simple and as cost-effective as possible'.

courts for which I am responsible. So help me God.' Fourthly, the CRA 2005, s. 2 sets out factors that the prime minister 'may take into account' in selecting a colleague to be Lord Chancellor: (a) experience as a Minister of the Crown; (b) experience as a member of either House of Parliament; (c) experience as a qualifying practitioner; (d) experience as a teacher of law in a university; (e) other experience that the Prime Minister considers relevant. In reality, these words—described as 'vacuous' during the debate on the bill—provide almost no political or legal constraints on the prime minister's discretion.

This model of conjoined ministerial offices is complex and probably understood by few people outside the Ministry of Justice and the handful of academics specializing in this esoteric area of public law. What do Lord Chancellors think about it? In February 2010, Jack Straw MP (Lord Chancellor in the Labour government 2007–10) told the Constitution Committee:[30]

> I am perfectly comfortable about exercising both roles. They are distinct. Many of your Lordships will remember the great debate that took place following the original proposals in the Constitutional Reform Bill, which led to the continuation of the position of Lord Chancellor. I happen to think that was the right decision, for all sorts of reasons. The distinction in practice—I believe in theory but actually in practice—is a very important one, because on the one hand you have the Justice Secretary functions, which in terms of their operation and how they are moderated by other colleagues in Government are no different from any other secretary of state functions. The functions may differ but how they are operated is no different. On the other hand, the functions of Lord Chancellor are principally related to the judiciary and the maintenance of the independence of the judiciary. On those, in turn, I act independently of other colleagues in Government.

Giving evidence to the same committee in September 2014, Chris Grayling MP (Lord Chancellor in the Coalition government from 2012 and not a lawyer) spoke strongly in favour of the conjoined-ministers model:[31]

> I think now, given the constitutional changes that took place a decade ago, the role of the Lord Chancellor would be massively devalued if the roles were separated. It is not something I had fully understood until I took the job. But now I have truly understood in carrying out the role myself, I think it would be just the opposite. The danger would be that you would end up with the Secretary of State for Justice holding the Cabinet position. The Lord Chancellor's role is not what it used to be.

The risk, Mr Grayling said, was that if the roles were split the Lord Chancellor would become a junior minister outside the Cabinet whereas 'You want the Lord Chancellor, in a role that is not what it used to be, to be at the top table heading a substantial department with weight around the Cabinet table. I think it would be a big mistake to move away from that.'

---

[30] http://www.publications.parliament.uk/pa/ld200910/ldselect/ldconst/80/10022402.htm.

[31] http://data.parliament.uk/writtenevidence/committeeevidence.svc/evidencedocument/constitution-committee/the-office-of-lord-chancellor/oral/14379.html.

The senior judiciary also support the practice of a single person holding both ministerial offices, as Secretary of State for Justice and Lord Chancellor. Speaking to the House of Lords Constitution Committee in April 2018, the Lord Chief Justice said:

> I am confident that the Lord Chancellor has a very clear understanding of the constitutional position of his office and of the differences between being Secretary of State for Justice and being Lord Chancellor. I would like to think that Lord Chancellors might occasionally ask their officials, 'Give me the advice that you would give me as Secretary of State, and now give me the advice that you would give me as Lord Chancellor'. That may be too much to ask, but it is a distinction that I am confident the Lord Chancellor has in mind.[32]

So what parts of the justice infrastructure does the government—through the Lord Chancellor—run? The Courts Act 2003, s. 1 provides: 'The Lord Chancellor is under a duty to ensure that there is an efficient and effective system to support the carrying on of the business of [the courts], and that appropriate services are provided for those courts'. To ensure accountability, the Lord Chancellor must 'prepare and lay before both Houses of Parliament a report as to the way in which he has discharged his general duty in relation to the courts'. A comparable duty in relation to the UK Supreme Court, is created by the CRA 2005: the Lord Chancellor 'must ensure that the Supreme Court is provided' with 'such other resources as the Lord Chancellor thinks are appropriate for the Court to carry on its business'. Appearing before a parliamentary committee in 2010, Lord Judge (the then Lord Chief Justice) provided insight into the behind-the-scenes discussions that go on between the judiciary and the government in setting annual budgets for the courts. He said there were three possibilities:[33]

> the first is that when the figures are examined, I come to the conclusion that the arrangement is a reasonable one that I can sign up to—that is called a concordat agreement. The second is that he offers a figure that I do not think is necessarily going to enable me to fulfil my responsibilities, and I write to him and say, 'Well, that's all you've got. I understand the difficulty you're in. I have reservations about it, but let's do the best we can'. I do not sign the concordat agreement, but we all get on as best we can and see what events turn out. The third would be a disaster and a crisis of great magnitude and is that the Lord Chancellor of the day offers the Lord Chief Justice money that the Lord Chief Justice is completely satisfied is derisory for the purposes of running the administration of justice, in which case the option available to the Lord Chief Justice is to bring the concordat to an end.

Lord Judge envisaged that if the third eventuality were ever to come about, a new concordat would have to be negotiated between the judiciary and the government, with the Lord Chancellor 'very anxious to exercise such power as is left to him in the context of the parliamentary process' by involving relevant House of Commons and House of Lords Committees and making a written statement to Parliament under CRA 2005, s. 5.

[32] Lord Burnett of Maldon, Select Committee on the Constitution, Corrected oral evidence, The Lord Chief Justice, 25 April 2018 (available on www.parliament.uk).

[33] House of Lords Constitution Committee, *Meetings with the Lord Chief Justice and the Lord Chancellor*, 9th Report of Session 2010–11, HL Paper 89, Evidence from 15 December 2010, Q9.

The Concordat also recognized that the government 'is responsible for the pay, pensions and terms and conditions of the judiciary' (para. 21). A key aspect of judicial independence recognized internationally is that judicial salaries should never be reduced (as this would enable government to place pressure on judges); in the United Kingdom this is secured by the Senior Courts Act 1981, s. 12 ('Any salary payable under this section may be increased, but not reduced'). There is no legal impediment to government imposing pay freezes, which is what happened for three years from 2010, followed by a 1 per cent increase. The LJC (Lord Thomas) recently told the Review Body on Senior Salaries (SSRB), an independent body advisory body, that it was 'deeply regrettable' that SSRB recommendations to government on pay increases and a major review of salaries were not being implemented by government and said 'there was a justifiable sense of real grievance among the judiciary'.[34]

Changes to judicial pensions have, similarly, been a source of tension between judges and government. Announcing the new scheme to the House of Commons in 2013, the Lord Chancellor said:[35]

> The Government recognise that although there is a longstanding practice that the total remuneration package offered to the judiciary, including pension provision, should not be reduced for serving judges, this forms part of a broader constitutional principle that an independent judiciary must be safeguarded. However, in the particular context of difficult economic circumstances and changes to pension provision across the public sector, we do not consider that the proposed reforms infringe the broader constitutional principle of judicial independence. Nonetheless we have listened to the concerns of the judges and we have modified our proposals.

Since then, judges dissatisfied with the new arrangements have taken legal action to challenge the legality of the new scheme.[36]

FUNCTIONS SHARED BETWEEN JUDGES AND GOVERNMENT

There are several areas in which judges and the government have shared responsibilities for functions required to run the justice infrastructure. One major area for joint-working is HM Courts and Tribunals Service (an agency of the Ministry of Justice), which 'uniquely operates as a partnership between the Lord Chancellor, the Lord Chief Justice and the Senior President of Tribunals as set out in our Framework Document'.[37]

---

[34] Senior Salaries Review Body, *Thirty-sixth Annual Report* (Report No. 84), Cm 8822, para. 5.6.

[35] Chris Grayling MP, Hansard, HC, vol. 592, col. 7WS, 5 February 2013.

[36] More than 200 younger judges successfully argued in the Employment Tribunal and Employment Appeal Tribunal that part of the scheme unlawfully treated them less favourably than older judges by reason of their age (direct age discrimination); a further appeal in that case has been heard by the Court of Appeal, with judgment expected in early 2019. In separate long-running proceedings, a barrister, who worked for 27 years as a part-time judge and was paid a daily fee, challenged the MOJ's failure to provide pensions for part-time judges. In July 2017, the Supreme Court referred a question to the Court of Justice of the EU for a preliminary ruling (*O'Brien v Ministry of Justice* [2017] UKSC 46).

[37] HM Courts and Tribunals Service, https://www.gov.uk/government/organisations/hm-courts-and-tribunals-service.

Leadership is provided by a ten-person board, which includes non-executive directors, Ministry of Justice officials, and three senior judges. Staff working at 650 different locations provide administrative support to courts and tribunals. The aims and objectives of the agency are set by the government (Lord Chancellor) and the judiciary (the LCJ and the Senior President of Tribunals). The Courts and Tribunals (Judiciary and Functions of Staff) Bill 2019 will enable new ways of working across all courts, with 'authorized staff' being permitted to carry out tasks previously reserved to judges. A 'judicially-led' rules committee will decide in detail what kinds of routine and uncontroversial tasks authorized staff are able to handle (examples could include changing the time a hearing will start and pre-trial case management) but the Bill makes clear that there will be limits on what decision-making may be delegated to staff (such as authorizing a person's committal to prison or arrest and making search orders).

A second area of shared functions are the numerous specific responsibilities where, following the agreement reached in the Concordat, the CRA 2005 and other legislation requires there to be 'concurrence' between the judiciary (the LCJ) and the government (the Lord Chancellor). One such area is the system for considering and determining complaints against the personal conduct of the judiciary. A body known as the Judicial Conduct and Investigations Office (JCIO) 'supports the Lord Chancellor and the Lord Chief Justice in their joint responsibility for judicial discipline'.

A third shared function relates to the constitutional principle of the independence of the judiciary. Section 3 of the Constitutional Reform Act 2005 sets out a statutory 'guarantee of judicial independence', under which the Lord Chancellor 'must have regard to the need . . . to defend that independence'. What this duty requires has been tested in different scenarios that have arisen since 2005. In 2007, the House of Lords Constitution Committee reviewed the operation of the arrangements, looking in particular at what happened with the Home Secretary, and publicly expressed strong criticism of a judge for providing what the Home Secretary thought was a lenient sentence on a man (Sweeney) convicted of sexual assault on a child. A junior minister then repeated the criticisms on a radio programme. In fact, the judge was constrained from giving a harsher sentence by legislation passed by Parliament! The Committee pulled no punches, concluding that 'The Sweeney case was the first big test of whether the new relationship between the Lord Chancellor and the judiciary was working properly, and it is clear that there was a systemic failure'. The Committee found that the Lord Chancellor (Lord Falconer) 'did not fulfil his duty in a satisfactory manner'. But the Committee was also critical of the judiciary, stating that 'The senior judiciary could also have acted more quickly to head off the inflammatory and unfair press coverage which followed the sentencing decision' and recommended that the 'judges should consider making the Judicial Communications Office more active and assertive in its dealings with the media in order to represent the judiciary effectively.[38] A more recent test of

---

[38] House of Lords Constitution Committee, *Relations Between the Executive, the Judiciary and Parliament* (6th Report of Session 2006–07, HL Paper 151) paras 49 and 171. The Judicial Communications Office is now known as the Judicial Press Office, part of the Judicial Office supporting the work of the Lord Chief Justice.

the arrangements arose from newspaper coverage of the *Miller* judgment,[39] in which the High Court ruled that a vote in Parliament was required for the Brexit process to start. On 4 November 2016, the *Daily Mail* front page featured photographs of the three judges, with the headline 'Enemies of the People'. When no statement was forthcoming from the Lord Chancellor (Liz Truss), the Bar Council of England and Wales (the representative body for the barristers' profession) expressed concern; 48 hours after the headlines, and with mounting criticism of the newspaper and the Lord Chancellor, Ms Truss issued a very short written statement saying 'The independence of the judiciary is the foundation upon which our rule of law is built and our judiciary is rightly respected the world over for its independence and impartiality'. Some (including Lord Judge, a former Lord Chief Justice) suggested that this was insufficient to fulfil her legal duty under s. 3 to 'have regard to the need to defend' judicial independence and the Lord Chancellor had therefore acted unlawfully.[40] The episode is evidence of the political reality that Lord Chancellors cannot now be relied on to provide wholehearted defences when judges are attacked.[41]

FUNCTIONS GIVEN TO ARM'S LENGTH INDEPENDENT BODIES

Several aspects of the justice infrastructure have been entrusted to 'arm's length' bodies, independent of both government and the judiciary. These bodies may have an executive function (deciding things) or an advisory function. The degree of independence from government and the judiciary varies according to the body.

A body with a high degree of independence is the Judicial Appointments and Conduct Ombudsman office (a team of eight), the remit of which is to resolve grievances about how complaints about judicial conduct have been handled and complaints about the judicial appointments process. It is 'a Corporation Sole who acts independently of Government, the Ministry of Justice (MoJ) and the Judiciary'.[42] Another specialist ombudsmen service working in the justice infrastructure is the Legal Ombudsman for England and Wales, set up by the Office for Legal Complaints (the Board) under the Legal Services Act 2007, to deal with grievances against legal practitioners.

The Judicial Appointments Commission for England and Wales (JAC), another arm's length body, was set up by the CRA 2005, aiming 'to maintain and strengthen judicial independence by taking responsibility for selecting candidates for judicial office out of the hands of the Lord Chancellor and making the appointments process clearer and more accountable'.[43] The government consulted on three different models for the JAC, examples of which already operated in other legal systems—an appointing commission (where the JAC itself would directly advise the Queen on who to appoint),

---

[39] *R. (Miller) v Secretary of State for Exiting the European Union* [2016] EWHC 2768 (Admin).

[40] H. Agerhold, 'Liz Truss may have broken law in failing to defend Brexit judges, warns former lord chief justice', *The Independent*, 19 November 2019.

[41] For further discussion, see Chapter 1 above.

[42] Judicial Appointments and Conduct Ombudsman, Annual Report 2013–14, 4.

[43] Judicial Appointments Commission, http://www.jac.judiciary.gov.uk.

a recommending commission (with the JAC making recommendations to a minister, who in turn would advise the Queen), and a hybrid model (in which the JAC would give direct advice to the Queen in relation to less senior judicial posts and to ministers for more senior posts).

The final design choice for the JAC was that it should be a hybrid commission. It consists of 15 commissioners, including judges, legal practitioners, and lay people (one of whom is the chair). To ensure the members' independence, none are nominated by the government, but by their own governing bodies. The JAC runs competitions for appointment to tribunals and courts across England and Wales (except for magistrates or for the UK Supreme Court). A variety of modern human resources processes are used, including application forms, written assessments, and selection days at which applicants role-play. The JAC makes recommendations either to the Lord Chief Justice (for positions below the level of the High Court) or the Lord Chancellor (for the High Court and Court of Appeal): in almost all cases the LCJ or Lord Chancellor accept the recommendation though they have a residual power to ask the JAC to reconsider the recommendation or to reject it with reasons.

The routine updating of procedural rules are carried out by the Criminal Procedure Rules Committee, the Civil Procedure Rules Committee, and the Family Procedure Rules Committee established by the Courts Act 2003. These are judge-led expert groups, each described as an 'advisory non-departmental public body, sponsored by the Ministry of Justice'. Their membership categories, defined by statute, are mostly judicial, with legal practitioners and lay members (for example, the Civil Procedure Rules Committee includes 'two persons with experience in and knowledge of the lay advice sector or consumer affairs'). The Rules Committees consult, submit rules to the Lord Chancellor, who 'may allow, disallow or alter rules so made' but 'before altering rules so made the Lord Chancellor must consult the Committee'. The Rules are made law through the statutory instrument procedure in Parliament, which is usually a formality.[44]

Some arm's length bodies were abolished as part of the Coalition government's 'bonfire of the quangos', implemented under the Public Bodies Act 2011, which sought to cut public spending, increase accountability, and 'simplify the quango landscape'. For a body to survive the cull, it needed to be shown that it performed a technical function, or that its activities require political impartiality, or that it needed to act independently to establish facts. One important body that did not survive was the Administrative Justice and Tribunals Commission (AJTC) (an advisory non-departmental public body or NDPB), created by the Tribunals, Courts and Enforcement Act 2007 and abolished in August 2013, with the government moving some of its functions in-house to the Ministry of Justice. The AJTC's purpose was 'to help make administrative justice and tribunals increasingly accessible, fair and effective by: playing a pivotal role in the development of coherent principles and good practice; promoting understanding, learning and continuous improvement; ensuring that the needs of users are central'. There

---

[44] Courts Act 2003, Pt 7, as amended, and other legislation.

was strong opposition to the AJTC's demise in Parliament. The chair of the House of Commons Justice Committee argued 'because the administrative justice and tribunal system deals with disputes between the citizen and the executive, moving the process closer to Ministers has serious disadvantages. It is vital that oversight is seen to be independent'.[45] In the House of Lords, peers debating the motion that 'this House regrets the proposed abolition of the AJTC, which will remove independent oversight of the justice and tribunal system at a time when it is undergoing major change' called for the AJTC to be retained but the government narrowly won the vote.[46] Despite the abolition of the AJTC, there was a continued appetite for independent expert input into thinking about the administrative justice system. The Ministry of Justice set up the Administrative Justice Forum of experts 'to bring an independent perspective to policy and practice' but this too was wound up in 2017. A new body called the Administrative Justice Council, run by JUSTICE (the human rights reform group) and chaired by a senior member of the judiciary with modest funding from the Ministry of Justice, was set up in 2017 and held its first meeting in July 2018.[47]

DISCUSSION

The previous sections have illustrated which bodies run the different parts of the justice infrastructure. Working inductively, it is possible to detect some general principles of constitutional design in the current network of institutions and processes.

First, independent, arm's length bodies are favoured where decisions relate to individuals—such as in relation to handling grievances against judges, the JAC, and lawyers, and in relation to individual decisions on appointments to judicial office. One of the reasons that the Legal Aid, Sentencing and Punishment of Offenders Act 2012 (LASPO) was controversial is because it transferred decision-making about individual legal aid applications from a body that had substantial operational independence from government to a body closely integrated into the Ministry of Justice.[48]

Secondly, the more closely intertwined with the core judicial function (hearing cases and writing judgments) a function is, the more control or influence judges should have in the running of that function. It has been recognized for many years that (as Lord Mackay of Clashfern, a Lord Chancellor in Conservative governments in the 1990s put it) 'in order to preserve their independence the judges must have some control or influence over the administrative penumbra immediately surrounding the judicial process', for example the listing of cases.[49]

---

[45] http://www.parliament.uk/business/committees/committees-a-z/commons-select/justice-committee/news/ajtc-report/.

[46] See further, C. Skelcher, 'Reforming the Oversight of Administrative Justice 2010–2014: Does the UK Need a New Leggatt Report?' [2015] PL 214.

[47] See https://justice.org.uk/ajc/.   [48] Discussed later.

[49] Lord Mackay, lecture 6 March 1991 quoted in Lord Bingham, 'Judicial Independence' (a lecture to the Judicial Studies Board on 5 November 1996) published in T. Bingham, *The Business of Judging: Selected Essays and Speeches, 1985–1999* (2011), 55.

Thirdly, the more a function involves decisions about allocation of scarce public resources to the justice infrastructure, the greater the control or influence of government. As John Bell argues:[50]

> when it comes to managing the judicial service and setting its budgets, then we are not dealing with potential interference with individual cases, but with the setting of priorities between categories of legal activity, and this involves giving a direction to society, which is an inherently political activity. The suggestion that the judiciary should be given untrammelled authority in this area is seriously problematic.

Not everybody agrees with this principle. Sir Francis Purchas (a Court of Appeal judge) made the bold argument in 1994 that:[51]

> Constitutional independence [of the judiciary] will not be achieved if the funding of the administration of justice remains subject to the influences of the political market place. Subject to the ultimate supervision of Parliament, the Judiciary should be allowed to advise what is and what is not a necessary expense to ensure that adequate justice is available to the citizen and to protect him from unwarranted intrusion into his liberty by the executive.

Lord Bingham (who during his long judicial career held office as Master of the Rolls, Lord Chief Justice of England and Wales, and Senior Law Lord) recognized that such a call lacked democratic legitimacy. Even the judges, he acknowledged:[52]

> cannot overlook the existence of other pressing claims on finite national resources. We would all recognize the defence of the realm as a vital national priority, but I suspect that we would shrink from giving the chiefs of staff carte blanche to demand all the resources which they judged necessary for that end. We would all, probably, recognize the provision of good educational opportunities at all levels as a pressing social necessity, but might even so hesitate to give educational institutions all the money which they sought. We would all regard the health of the people as a vital national concern, but could scarcely contemplate the demands of health service professionals being met in full, without rigorous democratic control. I do not myself find these choices, even in theory, offensive; but in any event they must surely, in the real world, be inevitable.

This does not, however, mean that the government's decisions about resource allocation to the justice infrastructure are unconstrained by constitutional principles and rights, as was demonstrated by the Supreme Court's ruling in *R. (UNISON) v Lord Chancellor (Equality and Human Rights Commission and another intervening) (Nos 1 and 2)*.[53] The Lord Chancellor sought to implement a policy, through delegated legislation, that applicants using the Employment Tribunal and Employment Appeal Tribunal had to pay fees. The rationale for the policy was to introduce a 'user pays'

---

[50] 'Sweden's Contribution to Governance of the Judiciary' in M. Andenas and D. Fairgrieve (eds.), *Tom Bingham and the Transformation of the Law* (2009).

[51] F. Purchas, 'What Is Happening to Judicial Independence?' (1994) 144 *New Law Journal* 1306, 1324.

[52] T. Bingham, 'Judicial Independence' in T. Bingham, *The Business of Judging: Selected Essays and Speeches, 1985–1999* (2011), 57.

[53] [2017] UKSC 51; [2017] 3 WLR 409.

approach, so that litigants rather than taxpayers paid for the tribunal service; it was also thought that fees would deter unmeritorious claims and encourage earlier settlement. The Supreme Court held that this was unlawful. Lord Reed stressed the importance of the right of access to the courts and tribunals, which has been recognized in the common law for centuries, in maintaining the rule of law, holding that 'In order for the fees to be lawful, they have to be set at a level that everyone can afford, taking into account the availability of full or partial remission. The evidence now before the court, considered realistically and as a whole, leads to the conclusion that that requirement is not met'.[54]

SHAPING THE INFRASTRUCTURE

The justice infrastructure is always a work in progress: rarely a fortnight goes by without a reform proposal. This flux can be illustrated, for example, by the changing responsibility for legal aid, which was started by the Labour government in 1949 introducing a national system for public funding of civil litigation for people unable to afford legal fees; the United Kingdom was the first country in the world to recognize legal aid as a component of a welfare state. At first, the scheme was administered by committees of local lawyers organized by the Law Society (the solicitors' regulatory body), rather than by government or the courts; the government's role (through the Lord Chancellor) was one of general supervision. In 1989, the Law Society was replaced by the Legal Aid Board (a government agency) as the main administrator. The Legal Aid Board was, in turn, replaced by the Legal Services Commission in 2000 (a non-departmental public body working at arm's length from government). The Legal Aid, Sentencing and Punishment of Offenders Act 2012 remodelled the system again, replacing the Legal Services Commission with the Legal Aid Agency (an executive agency tightly integrated within the Ministry of Justice). The current set-up gives government more direct control than at any time since 1949 (though the newly created post of 'director of legal aid casework', and a large team of caseworkers, is not subject to the direction of the Lord Chancellor in relation to individual legal aid applications).

Shaping the justice infrastructure is a constitutionally significant activity. It facilitates—or restricts—access to justice and may affect the independence of the core judicial function (hearing cases and writing judgments). An important question is therefore who controls and influences the process of change and what methods do they use for developing ideas about change. As with running the system (discussed in the previous section), shaping is not susceptible to analysis based on a pure separation-of-powers theory. Almost all shaping involves government action, input from the judiciary, and scrutiny and law-making by Parliament. What matters is the balance of influence among these institutions and the techniques they and other participants use to develop and discuss ideas for change. A model of what this looks like can be

---

[54] [2017] UKSC 51; [2017] 3 WLR 409, [91].

postulated which emphasizes a spectrum of decision-making environments. Towards one end, the environment is highly politicized ('political environment') and at the opposite end the environment is based on expert knowledge ('expert environment'); in the middle the environment is mixed ('blended environment'). Each environment of change has advantages and disadvantages. The challenge for the constitutional system is to find optimal points at which good-quality decisions are likely to be made; this point may differ according to the area of the infrastructure under review and the types of issues under consideration.

POLITICAL ENVIRONMENT

In this environment, proposals for reforming the justice infrastructure are typically led by government ministers. The House of Commons and House of Lords are the fora in which change is debated. The infrastructure is assumed to be an inherently party-political artefact, in which opposing viewpoints rest on different values and conflicts are capable of being resolved through the cut-and-thrust of the political argumentation. The justice system tends to be seen as a public service to be reformed according to party-political preferences.[55] In the political environment, judges and lawyers have no guaranteed or preferential status at the formative stages of the process; they are merely consultees. Facts about the infrastructure are often asserted as true rather than being demonstrated to be true through use of empirical research. The government may have limited (or no) appreciation that its proposals have constitutional implications. The style of presentation of the changes may be confrontational and populist.

An example of change through the political mode is the events that eventually resulted in the CRA 2005. The package of reforms (on the office of Lord Chancellor, creating a supreme court, radical changes to how judges were appointed, and disqualifying all serving judges from membership of Parliament) was announced inauspiciously in a press briefing by officials at 10 Downing Street during one of Tony Blair's annual Cabinet reshuffles. These complex policies had not been subject to detailed legal or constitutional analysis. The senior judges had not been consulted before the announcement; many heard about the proposals through the news media. The changes were the subject to protracted, sometimes poor-quality, and often highly partisan debates in Parliament over two years. The end result was shaped by behind-the-scenes party political negotiations in Parliament under pressure of time because of the impending 2005 general election. Tony Blair candidly admitted that 'I think we could have in retrospect—this is entirely my responsibility—done it better.'[56] The Conservatives were implacably opposed to the Lord Chancellor ceasing to a lawyer yet in 2012 Conservative Prime Minister David Cameron became the first prime minister to select a non-lawyer for the role (Chris Grayling MP).

[55] See D. Oliver, 'Does Treating the System of Justice as a Public Service Have Implications for the Rule of Law and Judicial Independence?', UK Constitutional Law Association Blog, 19 March 2014, www.ukcla.org.

[56] Tony Blair, Minutes of Evidence, Liaison Committee, 3 February 2004 (HC 310-I, 2003–4).

The government seemed not to learn many lessons from the debacle of the 2003–5 reform saga over the Lord Chancellorship. In 2007, there was a new failure to consult the judiciary about developments to the justice infrastructure that had constitutional ramifications. The government decided to create a Ministry of Justice, combining responsibility for judiciary and court-related matters (dealt with by the Department for Constitutional Affairs) with responsibility for the weighty and always politically emotive area of prisons and offender management (previously in the Home Office). The senior judiciary first learnt of these plans through a report in the Sunday newspapers; they were concerned the justice infrastructure would, as part of a new huge department, become devalued as resources and political energy were diverted to prisons; moreover, they saw risks of conflicts of interests within a department that was simultaneously responsible for prisons and defending judicial independence (when many of the most controversial and politically unpalatable cases involve prisoners and sentencing). A parliamentary committee lamented that:[57]

> The creation of the Ministry of Justice clearly has important implications for the judiciary. The new dispensation created by the Constitutional Reform Act and the Concordat requires the Government to treat the judiciary as partners, not merely as subjects of change. By omitting to consult the judiciary at a sufficiently early stage, by drawing the parameters of the negotiations too tightly and by proceeding with the creation of the new Ministry before important aspects had been resolved, the Government failed to do this. Furthermore, the subsequent request made by the judiciary for a fundamental review of the position in the light of the creation of the Ministry of Justice was in our view a reasonable one to which the Government should have acceded in a spirit of partnership.

Another illustration of change through the political mode are reforms to the judicial review procedure initiated by the Coalition government in 2012. Judicial review is a process for challenging the legality of decisions taken by public bodies in the Administrative Court (part of the High Court); it is a vital way in which the rule of law is protected.[58] Using the opportunity of a speech to the Confederation of British Industry conference in November 2012, the prime minister described judicial review as 'a massive growth industry in Britain today' and said:[59]

> We urgently needed to get a grip on this. So here's what we're going to do. Reduce the time limit when people can bring cases. Charge more for reviews so people think twice about time-wasting. And instead of giving hopeless cases up to four bites of the cherry to appeal a decision, we will halve that to two.

The Lord Chancellor, Chris Grayling, later wrote an opinion piece in the *Daily Mail* in which he warned that judicial review should not be 'a promotional tool for countless Left-wing campaigners' and 'Britain cannot afford to allow a culture of Left-wing-dominated, single-issue activism to hold back our country from investing in

---

[57] House of Lords Constitution Committee, Relations between the Executive, Parliament and the Judiciary, 6th Report of 2006–7, HL Paper 151, para. 67.

[58] See Chapter 1 above.

[59] Available at http://www.gov.uk/government/news/prime-ministers-cbi-speech.

infrastructure and new sources of energy and from bringing down the cost of our wel-fare state'.[60] Specific proposals were published piecemeal in two consultations several months apart; academics and practitioners criticized them as unsupported by empiri-cal evidence (the Joint Committee on Human Rights concurred) and damaging to the rule of law.[61] Several elements of the proposals were enacted in Part 4 of the Criminal Justice and Courts Act 2015, despite strong criticism in parliamentary debates in the House of Lords.[62]

Standing back from these illustrations, what are the advantages and disadvantages of changing the justice infrastructure through a political environment? One advan-tage is that it can provide real impetus to decisive change: if the government decides to do something, it may be done speedily. It is also well suited to dealing with issues of distributive justice and reaching judgments about how, on a national scale, scarce resources are allocated to different areas of government activity. The political environ-ment may also score highly for its democratic credentials: initiatives are typically led by ministers who are accountable to Parliament, where their proposals can be scrutinized.

The political environment has potential disadvantages. Ideas may be formulated by people without detailed knowledge or broad understanding of the implications of their proposals; the range of knowledge and research drawn on may therefore be limited. Of particular concern, is that inadequate regard is had to constitutional principles—notably judicial independence, access to justice, and the rule of law, in developing re-form proposals. Expert views are typically sought only after key preferences have been formed; when experts contribute through a consultation process, this may have little or no influence on a government already determined to carry out its plans. Further-more, proposals are prone to being announced before sufficient research and policy development work has been undertaken. Some forms of communication (for example, political speeches) do not provide good opportunities for points of detail to be refined or complexities to be explored.

EXPERT ENVIRONMENT

A different way of steering change to the justice infrastructure is in an expert envi-ronment. Experts and expertise come in various forms. Research may be commis-sioned or used by the Ministry of Justice, parliamentary select committees, the Law Commission, and other institutions. Academics specializing in the legal system can make expert contributions, carrying out empirical socio-legal research (through the collection and evaluation of data), analytical and normative studies (for example, of

---

[60] Available at http://www.dailymail.co.uk/news/article-2413135/CHRIS-GRAYLING-Judicial-review-promotional-tool-Left-wing-campaigners.html#ixzz3IUbXriTU.

[61] See e.g. V. Bondy and M. Sunkin, 'Judicial Review Reform: Who Is Afraid of Judicial Review? Debunking the Myths of Growth and Abuse', UK Const. L. Blog, 10 January 2013; M. Fordham et al., 'Streamlining Judicial Review in a Manner Consistent with the Rule of Law' (Bingham Centre Report 2014/01), Bingham Centre for the Rule of Law, BIICL, London, February 2014.

[62] Hansard, HL, vol. 756, col. 952, 27 October 2014.

the competing constitutional values in the system), and comparative work. Expertise may also be found in the practical knowledge of people deeply immersed in the justice infrastructure, especially judges and legal practitioners, able to reflect on many years of experience of how the system runs to offer insights into how it could be improved. The style of deliberation in expert mode is generally apolitical and predisposed towards searching for consensus.

An example of an expert environment can be seen in how the Law Commission works. Many of its law reform projects relate to the justice infrastructure. For example, after ten years detailed work and consultation, in 1976 the Law Commission published recommendations that previously disparate High Court procedures be unified into a single 'application for judicial review procedure'. Further recommendations were made in 1994, including on which types of applicant should have standing to use the judicial review procedure. Expert working can also take place within the court system. In 1999–2000, a small committee was commissioned by the Lord Chancellor to address the pressures on judicial review thought likely to result from the Human Rights Act; chaired by Sir Jeffery Bowman (an accountant with expertise in managing change), it consisted of civil servants, court administrators, an academic, and the director of a NGO.[63] More recently, a judge-led committee developed proposals for the 'regionalization' of judicial review, making it available at High Court centres outside London.[64]

On a larger scale, a paradigm example of shaping through an expert environment was the complete overhaul of thinking about civil procedure rules that took place between 1994 and 1999.[65] Although the reform process was initiated by government, the development work was left to Lord Woolf (the Master of the Rolls). In a two-stage inquiry, Lord Woolf worked with a team of five 'assessors' (members of the judiciary and the legal profession), an academic consultant, and a consultant on information technology. Several academics were commissioned to undertake original research. The inquiry team visited four overseas jurisdictions for comparative studies. The procedural reforms were implemented by the Civil Procedure Act 1997 and the Civil Procedure Rules, neither of which caused any significant party-political controversy in Parliament.

Another notable illustration of large-scale change through an expert environment was the comprehensive restructuring of the tribunal system. In 2000, the government appointed Sir Andrew Leggatt (a Court of Appeal judge) 'to review the delivery of justice through tribunals other than ordinary courts of law'; he worked with a retired civil servant to produce a detailed analysis and far-reaching recommendations on the changes that needed to be made. These included reducing

---

[63] See T. Cornford and M. Sunkin, 'The Bowman Report, Access and the Recent Reforms of the Judicial Review Procedure' [2001] *Public Law* 11.

[64] S. Nason and M. Sunkin, 'The Regionalisation of Judicial Review: Constitutional Authority, Access to Justice and Legal Services in Public Law' (2013) 76(2) *MLR* 223.

[65] For a critical account, see J. Sorabji, *English Civil Justice after the Woolf and Jackson Reforms: A Critical Analysis* (2014).

the number of tribunals from over 70 to 2 (the First-tier Tribunal and the Upper Tribunal). The government followed best-practice in publishing a draft bill to implement the recommendations but this had so little political resonance that no parliamentary committee was interested in scrutinizing it. The Tribunals, Courts and Enforcement Act 2007 reached the statute book generating no notable party-political controversy.

Expert-led proposals do not, however, always have a smooth ride to the statute book and may be derailed by political events. The Prisons and Courts Bill was abandoned by the Conservative government in April 2017 as it curtailed its legislative programme ahead of the dissolution of Parliament for the unexpected general election in June. The bill contained provisions designed to implement carefully crafted plans, including a judge-led review of the civil courts,[66] to transform civil and criminal justice through use of technology—described by the Lord Chief Justice as being on 'a scale that has not been undertaken since the reforms of the late 19th century.'[67] More than a year after dropping the Prisons and Courts Bill, the new Conservative government introduced the Courts and Tribunals (Judiciary and Functions of Staff) Bill to Parliament—and promised other legislation to implement the original proposals; but, at the time of writing, in a Parliament preoccupied with Brexit, it remains unclear how much progress will be made.

In some contexts, the power of experts has been criticized and the limits of their role debated. Writing about the dominance of experts (a 'technocracy') in how the European Union develops policy ideas, it has been suggested:[68]

> The technocrat believes that rational analysis and scientific examination of the facts will bring about unanimous consensus on policy solutions. By contrast the technocrat feels uneasy under conditions of political conflict, ideological debates, and controversies on distributive issues of social justice.

So, some questions about the shaping of justice infrastructure cannot satisfactorily be solved by experts and expert knowledge alone. These include, for example, whether it would be beneficial for the UK to withdraw from the European Union and European Convention on Human Rights (points of deep political conflict) or what proportion of GDP should be allocated to fund legal aid (a distributional issue). There are other possible limitations and disadvantages of an expert environment. Expert working may be regarded as undemocratic: ideas may emerge from people who are unelected and unaccountable. Moreover, if there is a disconnection between the priorities of government and those of experts, proposals developed through expert working (for example, by the Law Commission) may lie on the shelf, unimplemented. In some situations, it may be difficult to disentangle expertise from self-interest, an accusation levelled

---

[66] Lord Justice Briggs, *Civil Courts Structure Review: Final Report* (July 2016).

[67] See n. 2 above.

[68] C. Radaelli, 'The Public Policy of the European Union: Whither Politics of Expertise' (1999) 6(5) *Journal of European Public Policy* 757.

at the legal profession when it seeks to influence justice infrastructure reforms. For example, in June 2013 a government minister was reported as saying: ' "Let's not kid ourselves. We are in a wage negotiation," Lord McNally warned lawyers this week at the Bar Council's Legal Aid Question Time event at Westminster. "You have a vested interest in this outcome. To deny that, I think, is absurd".'[69]

BLENDED ENVIRONMENT

The political and expert environments for bringing about reform of the justice infrastructure represent points at the extreme ends of a spectrum of styles of decision-making. Between these points, there are ways of working that blend politicization and expertise.

Blended environments may be located within institutions. The government department responsible for judiciary-related and court matters was, in the past, led by people who were experts in the sense that they had insider-knowledge of law and the legal system. The department was known successively as the 'Lord Chancellor's Department' (1885–2003), 'the Department for Constitutional Affairs' (2003–7), and latterly 'the Ministry of Justice'. A government department is led by a politically neutral civil servant—the permanent secretary—who remains in post even if the political party in government changes after a general election. From the nineteenth century until 1997, it was a requirement that the permanent secretary in the Lord Chancellor's Department was a qualified legal professional. As one commentator wrote in the late nineteenth century:[70]

> It probably owes its statutory existence to a wise reform initiated by Lord Selborne, who made the office of Principal Secretary to the Lord Chancellor a permanent one. The obvious object of this reform was to give some chance of continuity to the legal policy of successive Lord Chancellors, and to create what might be the nucleus of a department of Law and Justice. Any one acquainted with the working of a public office must be aware of the wholesale confusion which would result if the staff was changed with every change of government. The hitherto backward state of all non-contentious law reform in this country has probably been due in no small degree to the absence of any body of permanent officials charged with its supervision.

The end of the lawyer-as-permanent-secretary requirement in 1997 came about in consequence of the growth of the department; legal expertise was no longer regarded as the most important—or even particularly relevant—attribute of the most senior official. Legal advice—and sensitivity to constitutional values closely associated with the legal system—were, it was thought, available from other lawyers within the department. There is a perception that, in recent years, the quality of legal advice and sensitivity in the department has diminished. This view is, however, contested by officials.

---

[69] J. Robins, 'Cuts Will "Destroy" Legal Aid System' (2013) 177(26) *Criminal Law and Justice Weekly*, online at http://www.criminallawandjustice.co.uk/.

[70] M. Chalmers, 'County Courts Consolidation Act 1888' (1898) 5 *LQR* 1.

In evidence to a House of Lords committee in October 2014, Rosemary Davies, Legal Director, Ministry of Justice, said:[71]

> It does slightly worry me that there is a perception that the Lord Chancellor is not getting the quality of legal advice that he used to get and perhaps there is an issue about visibility that we should think about. There are 60 lawyers in the in-house public law advisory team, two legal directors and seven other senior Civil Service lawyers. For example, the lawyer responsible for the team advising on the judiciary and courts is about to retire, but he has been in the department and its predecessors for I think 38 years. Likewise, the lawyer responsible for the judicial review reforms has been in the department for something like 27 years. I am not quite sure where this perception has come from that everybody has gone. Obviously, there are lots of new people and people do move around—and generally that is a good thing—but there is no shortage of continuity.

As discussed above, the professional background of Lord Chancellors has also changed. Another change is the typical duration in office. The last two old-style Lord Chancellors were Lord Mackay (3,475 days) and Lord Irvine (2,233 days). Since then, Lord Chancellors have served shorter terms: Lord Falconer (1,447 days); Jack Straw MP (1,049 days); Kenneth Clarke MP (847 days); Chris Grayling MP (978 days); Michael Gove MP (433 days); Elizabeth Truss MP (333 days); David Lidington MP (212 days).

Since the CRA 2005 it has been possible for the prime minister to appoint somebody with no legal background as the minister responsible for judiciary and court-related matters; this possibility was made real with David Cameron's appointment of Chris Grayling MP to the role in September 2012. A history graduate, Grayling worked as a television producer and management consultant before becoming an MP. As an opposition MP, he developed a reputation for strongly confrontational questioning of the government (described by some journalists as 'an attack dog' style). The reason given by the Labour government in 2005 for abandoning the requirement that Lord Chancellors be lawyers was that the nature of the role had changed and enlarged so that skills at political leadership to 'deliver' policies had become much more important than in the past; such skills were not necessarily best found among politicians with legal backgrounds; and the prime minister should therefore have a broad discretion to select the best person for the job. At the time, Conservatives in Parliament argued that a lawyer (preferably a senior one in the House of Lords, rather than the House of Commons) would always be better equipped to carry out the Lord Chancellor's functions as the link-pin between government and the judiciary, to defend judicial independence within government, and to act as a guardian of the rule of law across government. Ten years later, the (Conservative) Lord Chancellor Chris Grayling MP told a parliamentary committee:

> My view is that it is a positive benefit for the Lord Chancellor not to be a lawyer. The reason I say that is, certainly at this moment in time, when we are having to take and would be taking difficult decisions [about reducing public spending] regardless of the

---

[71] Revised transcript of evidence taken before the Select Committee on the Constitution, Inquiry on the Office of Lord Chancellor, Evidence Session No. 4, Q53, 15 October 2014.

situation, if we had a distinguished member of the House of Lords occupying the traditional role of Lord Chancellor overseeing the courts today, there would still be the same financial pressures that my department and my team are currently facing. I think that not being a lawyer gives you the ability to take a dispassionate view: not from one side of the legal profession or the other, not from the perspective of the Bar, not from the perspective of the solicitors' profession and not from the perspective of the legal executives. As long as you take very seriously the duty to uphold the principles I talked about earlier—uphold the independence of the judiciary, uphold the independence of our courts—I think there are benefits in not having a lawyer. It does not mean a lawyer cannot do the job, but it is really important to say I think there are benefits to having a non-lawyer in the job as well.

Whatever the merits of moving from a requirement for both the permanent secretary and the government minister to be lawyers to a situation where neither is a lawyer, it is clear that the government department responsible for the justice infrastructure has become in important respects a less blended environment than previously.[72]

Blending of political and expert environments can, however, be seen to be thriving elsewhere in the system. In Parliament, the House of Lords Constitution Committee has grown into a significant institution connecting politics, law, and the judiciary. The committee has produced several reports on aspects of the justice infrastructure and holds annual meetings with the Lord Chancellor and LCJ. Since its creation in 2001, the committee (whose membership is broadly reflective of the political composition of the House of Lords as a whole) has included retired judges (Lord Woolf and Lord Judge), a former Lord Chancellor (Lord Irvine), former Attorney Generals, and senior members of the legal profession. Expertise is also brought into its work through a legal adviser (all have been senior academics), specialist advisers appointed to assist with particular inquiries, and experts who contribute written and oral evidence to the committee's inquiries.[73]

Blended working may also take place more informally outside institutions where there is a predisposition by politicians to involve people with expertise at a formative stage of their thinking. An illustration of this is an initiative of the former shadow Lord Chancellor Sadiq Khan MP (now Mayor of London) to invite Sir Geoffrey Bindman (a leading solicitor with expertise in public law) and Karon Monaghan QC (a barrister and author on equality law) to lead a review of how to improve diversity in the judiciary. They were encouraged to consider more radical measures such as positive discrimination and gender quotas; academics contributed to a private seminar on the legality and feasibility of gender quotas.[74]

---

[72] David Gauke MP, appointed Lord Chancellor in January 2018, is a law graduate and practised as a commercial solicitor for several years before being elected to Parliament.

[73] See further A. Le Sueur and J. Simson Caird, 'The House of Lords Select Committee on the Constitution' in A. Horne, G. Drewry and D. Oliver (eds.), *Parliament and the Law* (2013).

[74] See N. Watt, 'Labour Prepared to Introduce Judge Quotas to Achieve Balanced Judiciary', *The Guardian*, 21 April 2004, 4; UCL Constitution Unit, Monitor 58, 7.

DISCUSSION

The illustrations outlined above show how policies to change the justice infrastructure are developed in a variety of different environments. A blended environment which captures the strengths of political and expert methods of working, and minimizes their weakness, is likely to be the best way of reaching considered, evidence-based consensus (so far as possible) on many types of reform question. A predisposition to blended environments can be encouraged if the Lord Chancellor were required to apply three presumptions when contemplating change.

First, the more directly a proposed infrastructure change affects the constitutional principles of judicial independence and access to justice, the stronger the presumption that detailed analysis of the problem and recommendations are developed by an expert body—an ad hoc one (Woolf, Leggett, Bowman), the Law Commission, or (for truly landmark change) a Royal Commission. A decision to develop policy 'in–house' within the Ministry of Justice (such as the recent judicial review reforms) or other part of government (10 Downing Street in relation to decisions that led to the CRA 2005) should be carefully justified. Secondly, there should be a strong presumption that infrastructure change should be based on sound evidence and analysis. Academic and other expert research should be commissioned, evaluated fairly, and used at formative stages of thinking about all significant reform proposals. Thirdly, where reforms require legislative backing to be implemented, the government should publish bills and secondary legislation in draft. This will enable parliamentary and other expert scrutiny of detailed proposals.

CONCLUSIONS

The British constitution provides high levels of judicial independence in relation to the core functions of judges (hearing cases and writing judgments). This chapter has explored the constitutional implications of the 'running' and 'shaping' of the justice infrastructure. It has been argued that both of these activities are constitutionally significant. They create opportunities to enhance, or risk of undermining, the principles of judicial independence, access to the courts, and the rule of law.

FURTHER READING

A. Le Sueur, 'Parliamentary Accountability and the Justice System' in N. Bamforth and P. Leyland (eds.), *Accountability in the Contemporary Constitution* (2013)

A. Le Sueur, 'From Appellate Committee to Supreme Court: A Narrative' in L. Blom-Cooper, G. Drewry and B. Dickson (eds.), *The Judicial House of Lords 1876–2009* (2009)

G. Gee et al., *The Politics of Judicial Independence in the UK's Changing Constitution* (2015)

S. Shetreet and S. Turenne, *Judges on Trial: The Independence and Accountability of the English Judiciary* (2nd edn, 2013)

Lord Thomas of Cwmgiedd, 'The Judiciary within the State—Governance and Cohesion of the Judiciary' (Lionel Cohen Lecture, 15 May 2017)

Lord Thomas of Cwmgiedd, 'The Judiciary within the State—The Relationships between the Branches of the State' (Michael Ryle Memorial Lecture, 15 June 2017)

USEFUL WEBSITES

Ministry of Justice: **https://www.gov.uk/government/organisations/ministry-of-justice**

HM Courts and Tribunals Service: **https://www.gov.uk/government/organisations/hm-courts-and-tribunals-service**

Courts and Tribunals Judiciary: **http://www.judiciary.uk**

Judicial Appointments Commission: **https://www.judicialappointments.gov.uk**

9

DEVOLUTION IN NORTHERN IRELAND

Brice Dickson

SUMMARY

Northern Ireland has had a devolved legislature and government, off and on, since 1921. This chapter first examines the nature of the devolution arrangements in place between 1921 and 1972 and then explains what was done to keep Northern Ireland running during the periods of direct rule from Westminster and Whitehall between 1972 and 1999 and between 2002 and 2007. The third section looks at how devolution operated under the Belfast (Good Friday) Agreement from 1999 to 2002 and from 2007 to 2017. The chapter then considers the reasons for the failure since 2017 to get devolution re-established and concludes by canvassing what the future constitutional arrangements for Northern Ireland might be. Taken in the round, Northern Ireland's experience of devolution during the past 98 years has been very troubled. Brexit, alas, seems unlikely to make it less so in the years ahead.

INTRODUCTION

Northern Ireland was the first part of the United Kingdom to be granted devolution and to date the experience amounts to some 64 years. It comprises the period 1921 to 1972, during which there was a bicameral Parliament and a unionist government in Belfast, and the periods 1999 to 2002 (except for about three months) and 2007 to 2017, during both of which, in line with the Belfast (Good Friday) Agreement of 10 April 1998, there was a unicameral Assembly and a power-sharing Executive in Belfast. From 1972 to 1999, for almost three months in 2000 and during the period 2002 to 2007, there was 'direct rule' from London: the Westminster Parliament made legislation for Northern Ireland (very often in the form of Orders in Council rather than Acts) and the UK government exercised executive powers through its Northern Ireland Office, a department headed by the Secretary of State for Northern Ireland with three or four Ministers of State assisting in the task. For a few months in 2000 and from early 2017 until the present (April 2019) Northern Ireland has functioned without a government. This has been due to the inability of the major political parties represented in the Assembly to reach an agreement on how power should be shared in the Executive, coupled with the reluctance of the UK government to resurrect direct rule because of the offence that would cause to nationalists in Northern Ireland as well as to the Irish government, a co-sponsor of the Belfast Agreement.

This chapter will therefore analyse devolution in Northern Ireland in five sections. First the nature of the devolution arrangements in place between 1921 and 1972 will be sketched. Then there will be an explanation of what was done to keep Northern Ireland running during the periods of direct rule from 1972 to 1999 and from 2002 to 2007. The third section, the longest, will examine the workings of devolution from 1999 to 2002 and from 2007 to 2017. Section four will consider the reasons for the impasse there has been since 2017 and the final section will consider possible futures for Northern Ireland, including that of a re-unified Ireland.

THE 'UNIONIST ERA': 1921 TO 1972

By the Government of Ireland Act 1920, the long-running desire for Irish home rule was finally realized after several failed earlier attempts. The process had been delayed by the First World War, during which some Irish rebels sought to take advantage of Britain's military vulnerability by staging the so-called Easter Rising in 1916. It was quickly suppressed and, after many arrests and trials, fifteen of the rebels were executed. In 1919 more widespread violence broke out, continuing until July 1921 in what later became known as the War of Irish Independence. The price paid for the 1920 Act was that Ireland was partitioned. Southern Ireland, comprising 26 of the island's 32 counties, was to be given its own Parliament and government, while Northern Ireland ('the six counties') was to be given the same. It was imagined that in due course both parts of the island might want to re-unite, so the establishment of a cross-border Council of Ireland was provided for in order to facilitate such a development. But most of the people of Southern Ireland did not think that this form of home rule went far enough to allow them full self-governance.

After the July 1921 truce, negotiations took place over the following few months, leading to an Anglo-Irish Treaty in December which significantly altered the 1920 Act. It changed the name of Southern Ireland to the Irish Free State and granted it the status of an autonomous 'dominion' within the British Commonwealth, a status shared by Australia, Canada, Newfoundland, New Zealand and South Africa. Southern Ireland was given 12 months to ratify the Treaty, which it did on the last day of that period. Northern Ireland, which had come into being on 5 May 1921, was given the right to become a part of the Free State as a dominion or to opt out and remain a fully integrated part of the United Kingdom. The Irish Free State officially came into existence on 6 December 1922, when King George V issued a Proclamation to that effect. A day later the Parliament of Northern Ireland voted not to become a part of the Irish Free State. From then onwards the United Kingdom was no longer the United Kingdom of Great Britain and Ireland but the United Kingdom of Great Britain and Northern Ireland.

The degree of autonomous self-governance conferred on Northern Ireland by the Government of Ireland Act 1920 was not as extensive as that conferred on the Irish Free State by that territory's self-designed Constitution, the legality of which was confirmed in UK law by the Westminster Parliament passing the Irish Free State (Constitution) Act 1922. But Northern Ireland remained the first part of the United Kingdom to be given any kind of devolution at all and in some respects the type of devolution was broadly analogous to that which had been granted to dominions. Its essence was that the Parliament of Northern Ireland was empowered to make laws 'for the peace, order and good government of Northern Ireland',[1] the same phrase that was included in the various Acts conferring dominion status on other jurisdictions in previous years.[2] The exact meaning of the phrase was nowhere specified but its underlying intent seems to have been to allow the dominion in question to exercise any powers it wished to, except those which the devolving Act specifically excluded.[3]

In modern jargon it was a 'reserved powers' model rather than a 'conferred powers' model of devolution, meaning that the devolved legislature could enact laws on any matter apart from those which were specifically 'reserved' to the Westminster Parliament. In Northern Ireland's case the legislation reserved at least 13 matters (called 'excepted matters'). They were: (1) the Crown, (2) the making of peace or war, (3) the armed forces, (4) relations with foreign states, (5) dignities or titles of honour, (6) treason and domicile, (7) trade with any place outside Southern or Northern Ireland, (8) submarine cables, (9) wireless telegraphy, (10) aerial navigation, (11) lighthouses and beacons, (12) coinage, legal tender and negotiable instruments, and (13) intellectual property. An additional set of matters were reserved on a temporary basis, either until appropriate measures could be taken by Northern Ireland's Parliament (e.g. on policing[4]) or by the proposed Council of Ireland (e.g. on the postal service[5]). Northern Ireland's Parliament also had the power to impose taxes, but not customs and excise duties, taxes on profits or income tax (or 'any tax substantially the same in character as any of those duties or taxes').[6]

Notwithstanding these limitations on Stormont's powers[7] it still had a great deal of freedom to mould Northern Ireland society in particular ways. In general it tended to

---

[1] Government of Ireland Act 1920, s 4(1). For discussion of the possibility of creating a federal United Kingdom see McEldowney in Chapter 14 of this book.

[2] See e.g. British North America Act 1867, s 91; Commonwealth of Australia Constitution Act 1900, s 51; Union of South Africa Act 1909, s 59.

[3] For an analysis of how the 'peace, order and good government' clause was applied in practice more broadly, see Hakeem Yusuf, *Colonial and Post-Colonial Constitutionalism in the Commonwealth* (2014). The Statute of Westminster 1931 extended the powers of dominions so that they could make laws on any matter except those which they specifically agreed should remain with the UK Parliament.

[4] Government of Ireland Act 1920, s 9(1).   [5] Ibid., s 9(2)(a).   [6] Ibid., ss 21 and 22.

[7] 'Stormont' is the name of the area in East Belfast where the Parliament of Northern Ireland sat from 1932 onwards after an impressive building was constructed for it there. Prior to that it sat in a building in the Queen's University area of Belfast which was formerly the headquarters of the Presbyterian Church in Ireland.

follow the lead given by legislators at Westminster, with many Acts passed at Stormont simply being mirror images of those passed a year or so earlier at Westminster. But in some areas the Stormont Parliament adopted a more conservative stance. It did not replicate the radical reforms relating to land ownership introduced for England and Wales in the 1920s and it refused to countenance a law permitting divorce until 1939 or any liberalization of the law on abortion and homosexuality, both of which were decriminalized in Great Britain in 1967. The Government of Ireland Act 1920 prescribed that elections in Northern Ireland had to be conducted under a system of proportional representation,[8] but it allowed the regional Parliament to change the voting system after three years.[9] It did so in 1929,[10] having already removed the PR system for local government elections in 1922[11] (though, uniquely, Royal Assent for that reform had been temporarily withheld for a few months, as permitted by section 12 of the 1920 Act).

Stormont also discouraged support for the view that Northern Ireland should leave the United Kingdom and become part of a united Ireland. The population of the six counties was two-thirds Protestant and pro-Britain, in other words 'unionist'. The remaining one-third were Catholic, nearly all of whom would have preferred to be living in a united independent Ireland, hence the designation 'nationalists'; those who were extreme in this position, prepared to support the use of violence in their cause, came to be separately designated as 'republicans'.[12] A series of special laws were passed to clamp down on those who supported the use of force for political ends.[13] While there was some initial justification for these, given the sectarian violence that had blighted Northern Ireland in 1920 and 1921,[14] the Civil Authorities (Special Powers) Acts soon began to be abused.[15] In 1936 the National Council for Civil Liberties, a London-based human rights organization (now called Liberty), issued a hard-hitting report condemning police malpractice, the gerrymandering of constituencies and discrimination in the allocation of jobs and housing.[16] Such injustices continued into the 1960s, when a series of civil rights marches took place, such as from Coalisland to Dungannon in August 1968,[17] within Derry in October of that year,[18] and from Belfast to Derry in

---

[8] Government of Ireland Act 1920, s. 14(3).   [9] Ibid., s 14(5).

[10] House of Commons (Method of Voting and Redistribution of Seats) Act (NI) 1929, for elections to the Parliament of Northern Ireland.

[11] Local Government (Elections and Constitution) Act (NI) 1922, for local government elections.

[12] Later the unionists who were prepared to support the use of violence in their cause were called 'loyalists'.

[13] Civil Authorities (Special Powers) Act 1922. This was initially to last just one year, but it was renewed during each of the subsequent five years; in 1928 it was re-enacted for a further five years and then made permanent.

[14] It has been claimed that 636 people were killed between July 1920 and July 1922: R. Lynch, 'The People's Protectors? The Irish Republican Army and the "Belfast Pogrom", 1920–1922' (2008) 47 *J British Studies* 375, 377, n. 9.

[15] See generally L. Donohue, *Counter-Terrorist Law and Emergency Powers in the United Kingdom 1922–2000* (2001) Chaps. 1 and 2.

[16] NCCL, *Report of a Commission of Inquiry Appointed to Examine the Purpose and Effect of the Civil Authorities (Special Powers) Acts (NI) 1922 and 1933.*

[17] Organised by the Campaign for Social Justice, formed in 1964.

[18] Organised by the Northern Ireland Civil Rights Association, formed in 1967.

January 1969.[19] During the last of these the marchers were attacked with stones and iron bars by a crowd of loyalists at Burntollet Bridge. The Royal Ulster Constabulary (RUC)—the police force—treated the marchers harshly and did little to arrest the attackers, thereby increasing nationalist opposition to the RUC. This civil unrest was in due course exploited by the illegal Irish Republican Army (IRA), which had been formed back in 1919 to fight in the War of Independence. The first fatality of the euphemistically named 'troubles' was Francis McCloskey, who died on 14 July 1969 a day after being hit on the head by a police truncheon during street disturbances in Dungiven.[20]

The British army was brought on to the streets of Northern Ireland in August 1969 in an attempt to assist the police in controlling the disorder. Indefinite detention without trial was introduced in the same year to reduce the likelihood of violence by removing trouble-makers from the streets. Most commentators now agree that this measure actually had the effect of encouraging more people to join the IRA. In 1969 14 people were killed in Troubles-related incidents, but by 1972 the annual figure had risen to 470. The Stormont Parliament did, belatedly, take measures to meet most of the demands of the civil rights marchers. An independent Police Authority was established to reduce the control exercised over the RUC by the Ministry of Home Affairs:[21] changes were made to the electoral laws to ensure that those who owned businesses (who were predominantly unionists) did not have an additional voting right in local elections;[22] the boundaries of local council areas were changed[23] and the powers, duties and processes of the local councils were reformed;[24] an independent body was established to decide on the allocation of social housing;[25] and an Ombudsman was appointed to investigate and remedy, amongst other matters, instances of religious or political discrimination by official bodies.[26] Local judges, too, upheld the rule of law.[27]

Opinions differ over the extent to which the Stormont regime operated in practice as a unionist dictatorship. Going that far would be an exaggeration, since by and large the rule of law prevailed throughout the period 1921 to 1972, but it is undeniable that there was widespread discrimination against Catholics and nationalists, particularly in the public sector.[28] While the Government of Ireland Act 1920 prohibited the Northern Ireland Parliament from making a law restricting the free

[19] Organised by the People's Democracy, a new political organization formed after the Derry march in 1968 which campaigned for a socialist republic covering the whole of Ireland. One of its activists, Bernadette Devlin, was elected to be an MP at Westminster in April 1969, the youngest woman until then to achieve that accolade.

[20] But three Catholics had been killed by 'the Ulster Volunteer Force' in 1966, leading to that group being declared illegal.

[21] Police Act (NI) 1970.   [22] Electoral Law Acts (NI) 1968, 1969 and 1971.

[23] Local Government Boundaries Act (NI) 1972.   [24] Local Government Act (NI) 1972.

[25] Housing Executive Act (NI) 1971.

[26] Parliamentary Commissioner Act (NI) 1969 and Commissioner for Complaints Act (NI) 1969.

[27] In particular in *R. (Hume) v Londonderry Justices* [1972] NI 91 (on which see the text at n 42 below); contrast the House of Lords' decision in *McEldowney v Forde* [1971] AC 633.

[28] See J. Whyte, 'How much discrimination was there under the unionist regime, 1921–68?' in T. Gallagher and J. O'Connell (eds), *Contemporary Irish Studies* (1983).

exercise of any religion or imposing any disadvantage on account of religious belief,[29] it did not prevent local councils from acting in a discriminatory way. In the
private sector, employers on each side of the community often preferred to employ
'their own sort'. It is also the case that to some extent 'the Protestant North' was a
reaction to 'the Catholic South', where the dominance of the Catholic church over
the governance of that part of the island following partition was such that the size of
the Protestant population went into a rapid decline.[30] Lord Craigavon, the first Prime
Minister of Northern Ireland, is notorious for proclaiming in 1934 that 'All I boast of
is that we are a Protestant Parliament and a Protestant State',[31] but he prefaced this by
reminding people that politicians in the South—he was probably referring to Éamon
de Valera—had spoken of wanting the South to be a Catholic state. When Ireland
adopted a new Constitution in 1937 this recognized 'the *special position* of the Holy
Catholic Apostolic and Roman Church as the guardian of the Faith professed by the
great majority of the citizens'.[32] This provision was not removed from the Constitution until 1972.[33]

Under section 51 of the Government of Ireland Act 1920, if an Act of the Northern
Ireland Parliament was suspected of exceeding the powers of that Parliament it could
be referred to the Judicial Committee of the Privy Council (JCPC) for a ruling on that
point. The JCPC was a court which sat in London as a final court of appeal for many
of the UK's dominions and colonies. Such a reference seems to have been made on just
one occasion, in relation to Stormont's imposition of a duty on ratepayers to contribute
to the cost of education services, but on the facts the JCPC found no breach of the Parliament's powers.[34] Otherwise the Northern Ireland Parliament was left to get on with
governing Northern Ireland as it liked: a convention developed whereby Westminster could make laws dealing with matters transferred to Belfast only if the Northern
Ireland Parliament consented to that, and the Speaker of the House of Commons in
Westminster ruled in 1923 that questions relating to transferred matters could not be
asked of any minister at Westminster.[35]

There were several challenges in the courts of Northern Ireland to the legality of
particular legislative provisions on the basis that the Stormont Parliament did not have
the power to enact them, but only three succeeded. The first was *Huntley v McKinley*,[36]

---

[29] S. 5(1).

[30] Protestants formed about 10% of the population in the South in 1921 but by 1991 the figure was 3%: John
Coakley, 'Society and Political Culture' in J. Coakley and M. Gallagher, *Politics in the Republic of Ireland* (4th
edn., 2005) 44.

[31] Hansard, House of Commons of Northern Ireland, 24 April 1934, vol 16, p 1095.

[32] Art 44(2) (emphasis added); Art 44(3) recognized the other denominations existing in Ireland at the
time, including the main Protestant churches, but made no mention of their 'special position'.

[33] Fifth Amendment of the Constitution Act 1972.

[34] *Re Section 3 of the Finance Act (NI) 1934* [1936] AC 352.

[35] HC Debs., vol 163, col 1625 (3 May 1923). See too Brigid Hadfield, *The Constitution of Northern Ireland*
(Belfast, SLS Legal Publications, 1989) 81.

[36] [1923] 2 IR 165.

where the Court of Appeal struck down a sub-section in the Constabulary Act (NI) 1922[37] because it had the effect of banning police officers from voting in Westminster elections: the Government of Ireland Act 1920 prohibited the Parliament of Northern Ireland from altering the law on elections to the Westminster or Northern Ireland Parliaments during the three-year period following the first meeting of the Northern Ireland Parliament in 1921.[38] The second successful challenge was in *Ulster Transport Authority v James Brown & Sons Ltd*,[39] where the Court of Appeal held that a sub-section in the Transport Act (NI) 1948[40] restricting the operations of a certain type of transport business (the moving of furniture) was void as it breached the prohibition in the Government of Ireland Act 1920 on legislation that took away property without compensation.[41] The third and by far the most significant successful challenge was in *R. (Hume) v Londonderry Justices*,[42] where a Divisional Court invalidated regulations allowing soldiers to disperse a crowd because, as noted earlier, in the 1920 Act the power to regulate the armed forces had been specifically excluded from the list of powers devolved to the Stormont Parliament.[43] None of these decisions was appealed to the House of Lords.

THE NATURE OF 'DIRECT RULE': 1972 TO 1999 AND 2002 TO 2007

Whenever it became clear that the Northern Ireland Parliament and Government could not contain the civil unrest that had developed in the late 1960s and early 1970s the UK government decided to first of all suspend (or 'prorogue') and then abolish (or 'dissolve') those institutions. Power was transferred to a Secretary of State, and the UK government, acting through the Privy Council (a body of senior ministers who in theory advise the monarch), was authorized to make laws for Northern Ireland in the form of Orders in Council. These had to be approved by Parliament before they could come into force, but such approval was perfunctory because the time allocated for debate of the Orders was very limited and during those debates the Orders could not be amended—they had to be accepted in full or rejected. These law-making arrangements were set up on a temporary basis in 1972 but, except for a few months in 1974, were renewed at least annually over the course of the next 27 years, during which time no fewer than 508 Orders in Council were issued. UK government Ministers also made secondary legislation, which was published as Statutory Rules (comparable to Statutory Instruments in Great Britain[44]). From January to May 1974, as a result of a deal reached between the political parties of Northern Ireland at Sunningdale in Berkshire in 1973, a Northern Ireland Assembly and

---

[37] S. 1(3). [38] S. 14(5). [39] [1953] NI 79. [40] S. 18(1). [41] S. 5(1). [42] [1972] NI 91.

[43] The Northern Ireland Act 1972 was very swiftly enacted at Westminster to retrospectively legitimize the exercise of all such army powers in Northern Ireland since 1920.

[44] Orders in Council were themselves allocated Statutory Instrument numbers.

power-sharing Executive were established, with the power to make 'Measures', but regrettably they were closed down when the UK government found itself unable to deal with disruption to public services caused by strike action encouraged by extreme loyalist groups.[45]

Apart from reinforcing the notion that Northern Ireland was as much a part of the United Kingdom as any region of Great Britain, the direct rule arrangements divorced the law-making process from the people of Northern Ireland and created a sense that they were being governed remotely. Occasionally laws would be made for Northern Ireland by Acts of the Westminster Parliament on matters that were no longer 'transferred' or on transferred matters which were deemed particularly sensitive. 'Emergency powers' fell into the former category[46] while anti-discrimination laws fell into the latter. Under the Fair Employment (NI) Act 1976, for example, it became unlawful for employers in Northern Ireland to discriminate in the recruitment or promotion of workers on grounds of religious belief or political opinion, a step which was not mirrored elsewhere in the UK (or in Europe) until the early 2000s.[47] A Fair Employment Agency was created to oversee the implementation of the Act. In 1989 the Act was amended to extend protection against *indirect* discrimination and the Agency was replaced with a Commission with stronger enforcement powers. Following further reviews conducted by the Standing Advisory Commission on Human Rights, a statutory body established in Northern Ireland in 1973,[48] the law in this area was further reformed by the Fair Employment and Treatment (NI) Order 1998, which extended protection against religious and political discrimination to consumers of goods and services.

Direct rule by way of Orders in Council was the system of governance which was re-introduced in 2002 after the collapse of the new Northern Ireland institutions described in the next section. Given the dilution of the influence of the UK government in the running of Northern Ireland by the Belfast Agreement 1998, there was increased opposition to this form of direct rule on the part of the nationalist community. It did mean, however, that legislation which would have been very difficult to get enacted in the Northern Ireland Assembly—such as the law which allowed gay people to enter into civil partnerships—was able to be passed at Westminster with the overwhelming consent of UK MPs, even though Ulster Unionist and DUP MPs voted against it, including David Trimble and Peter Robinson.[49]

---

[45] See the account in Don Anderson, *14 May Days* (1994). The 1974 Assembly was created by the Northern Ireland Constitution Act 1973, ss. 17 and 19 of which prohibited it (and most public authorities in Northern Ireland) from discriminating against anyone on religious or political grounds.

[46] See e.g. the Northern Ireland (Emergency Provisions) Acts 1973, 1975, 1978, 1987, 1991, 1996 and 1998.

[47] Pursuant to the EU's Framework Directive on Equal Treatment in Employment and Occupation 2000.

[48] Northern Ireland Constitution Act 1973, s. 20.

[49] House of Commons Debs, vol 425, cols. 250–253, 12 October 2004: Second Reading of the Civil Partnership Bill (approved by 426 votes to 49).

HOW DEVOLUTION OPERATED BETWEEN 1999 AND 2017

The Belfast Agreement of 1998 was a hugely important milestone in the history of Northern Ireland. It was the culmination of political talks which had been initiated in the late 1980s, a few years before the ceasefires announced by the main republican and loyalist paramilitary organizations in 1994.[50] The IRA's ceasefire was breached in 1996, when bombs were exploded at Canary Wharf in London and in Manchester's city centre, but it was reinstated shortly after Labour, led by Tony Blair, won the UK general election in 1997. Unionists and nationalists each won an important victory in the Agreement. The former obtained a repetition of the statutory guarantee that the status of Northern Ireland as a part of the United Kingdom would not change without the consent of a majority of the people living in Northern Ireland,[51] and also a pledge by the Irish Government that Articles 2 and 3 of the Irish Constitution would be reworded to ensure that they reflected more accurately the current political reality that Northern Ireland is a separate jurisdiction from the Republic of Ireland. Nationalists, on the other hand, won the right to share in the governance of Northern Ireland, not only through having one of their representatives as the joint head of the Northern Ireland Executive but also through being guaranteed a number of Ministries in that Executive proportionate to the size of their electoral vote; they also secured the establishment of a North-South Ministerial Council at which matters with an obvious all-Ireland dimension, such as trade, food safety, waterways and coastal fisheries would be discussed.

Political scientists call this kind of power-sharing 'consociationalism', one of its early advocates being the Dutch academic Arend Lijphart. Amongst the leading lights in the field today are Brendan O'Leary and John McGarry, who have written extensively on Northern Ireland's experience of the system.[52] On the whole it has worked relatively well there to date, even if it is currently suspended. A downside of power-sharing— evidenced by the difficulties experienced by other coalition governments around the world—is that the time required to reach agreement on issues, and then to implement those agreements, can be much longer than in societies where a majority government can fulfil its manifesto promises by simply relying on its stronger voting capacity in the legislature. The fragility of power-sharing in Northern Ireland is exacerbated by the fact that it is not a sovereign state: the local parties know that if they do not agree to the sharing of power there is a safety-net available in the shape of the UK government and Parliament, which can at least ensure that money continues to be made available to government departments in Northern Ireland.

---

[50] The Hume–Adams talks, between the leaders of the SDLP and Sinn Féin, began in 1988 and were followed after the 1994 ceasefires by talks amongst 110 representatives elected to a Northern Ireland Forum for Political Dialogue in 1996.

[51] This was already enshrined in the Northern Ireland Constitution Act 1973, s. 1 and Sched. 1.

[52] See e.g. J. McGarry and B. O'Leary, *The Northern Ireland Conflict: Consociational Engagements* (2004).

The reaching of the Belfast Agreement coincided with two other developments in the United Kingdom. One was the commitment to devolve powers to Scotland and Wales, as well as to Northern Ireland, and the other was to ensure that most of the rights guaranteed by the European Convention on Human Rights should be claimable in courts throughout the country rather than only in the European Court of Human Rights in Strasbourg.

As is made clear in other chapters in this book, the devolution arrangements for the three devolved regions differed depending on local circumstances; neither Scotland nor Wales had to bear in mind the need for 'power-sharing' or for other measures designed to ensure that violent conflict would not again erupt. Those circumstances have meant that the rate at which devolution has developed in Northern Ireland has not kept pace with that in Scotland and Wales. In some people's eyes, in fact, the devolution experiment in Northern Ireland has failed. The failure is not a result, thankfully, of the re-emergence of widespread politically-motivated violence.[53] It is rather a product of increased political polarization within the electorate, with voters abandoning 'moderate' political parties on the unionist and nationalist sides and turning instead to more hardline parties, the Democratic Unionist Party and Sinn Féin. Cross-community parties have not been able to make a sizeable dent in the support given to those two big parties, each of which tends to attract voters on the basis of sectarian claims that, respectively, 'the union is safe only if you vote for the DUP' and 'if you want a united Ireland any day soon vote for Sinn Féin'. Some observers might also say that there has been a failure of political leadership in the last decade, not just within those parties but also within the British and Irish governments. Cynical unionists have been heard to claim that Sinn Féin has no desire to make Northern Ireland a success: the more it can be seen to be 'a failed entity' the more likely it is that a united Ireland will be a preferred option for the majority of people living there. Cynical nationalists, on the other hand, would argue that the DUP is not genuine when it says that it wishes to share the governance of Northern Ireland with those who are keen to promote the Irish side of their identity.

Likewise, while the Human Rights Act 1998[54] greatly changed the human rights picture in Northern Ireland, as it did in the rest of the United Kingdom, the Belfast Agreement suggested that additional protection of human rights might be required to deal with the particular circumstances of Northern Ireland and that any such legislation could supplement the Human Rights Act to form a Bill of Rights for Northern Ireland. Sadly, that suggestion has not been realized either. The Northern Ireland Human Rights Commission submitted proposals for a Bill of Rights to the UK government in 2008 but the then government, as well as subsequent ones, have dismissed most of the proposals as unnecessary and unrealistic.

---

[53] Though approximately 150 people have been killed in troubles-related incidents since the Belfast (Good Friday) Agreement 1998 was reached.

[54] It received Royal Assent ten days before the Northern Ireland Act, on 9 November 1998.

THE NORTHERN IRELAND ASSEMBLY

The centerpiece of the new institutional arrangements was a 108-member Assembly, six MLAs being elected for each of 18 constituencies coterminous with those used for the election of MPs to the House of Commons. The Assembly was empowered to make laws on anything that was not an excepted or reserved matter,[55] the essential difference between these being that excepted matters are ones which are unlikely to be transferred to any devolved area of the UK in the foreseeable future and are therefore largely mirrored in the Scotland Act 1998 and the Government of Wales Act 2006 (in both of which, unhelpfully, they are referred to as reserved matters[56]), whereas in Northern Ireland reserved matters are those which may in due course be transferred to Northern Ireland.[57] As already noted, the Government of Ireland Act 1920 conferred wide-ranging powers on the Parliament of Northern Ireland but imposed a number of limitations on them,[58] as well as identifying some 'reserved matters' which in due course would be devolved.[59] The Explanatory Notes for Schedule 5 to the Scotland Act 1998 include an alphabetical list of 117 matters and indicate where each of them can be located within the Schedule, but unfortunately there is nothing similar in the Explanatory Notes for the Northern Ireland Act (or for the relevant Acts for Wales). This sometimes means that identifying whether a particular matter is transferred or not in Northern Ireland can be a time-consuming exercise.

During the period December 1999 to October 2002, the Assembly passed 36 Acts, a relatively high output given that the Scottish Parliament, which is not based on consociationalism, passed only 45 (25 per cent more). From 2007 to 2016 it managed to pass 137 Acts, just 14 short of the tally in Scotland.

To date there have been six elections to the Assembly. Initially the dominant unionist and nationalist parties were the Ulster Unionist Party and the Social Democratic and Labour Party respectively but, as Table 9.1 below demonstrates, since 2003 they have been the Democratic Unionist Party and Sinn Féin, both of which are more extreme in their respective unionism and nationalism, thereby indicating that the voters of Northern Ireland have become more polarized than at the time of the Agreement in 1998. It has to be remembered, too, that representatives of the DUP walked out of the negotiations which culminated in the Agreement and urged their supporters to vote against it in the referendum on the Agreement in May 1998. The DUP did however

[55] See, respectively, Scheds. 2 and 3 to the Northern Ireland Act 1998.

[56] See Sched. 5 to the Scotland Act 1998 and Sched. 7A to the Government of Wales Act 2006, inserted by the Wales Act 2017, s. 3(2).

[57] The Acts governing devolution in Scotland and Wales also contain lists of 'reserved matters'. These are sub-divided into 'general' and 'specific' reservations even though nothing really turns on the differentiation; some of the reservations have exceptions (but this does not turn them into 'excepted matters'); and some of the exceptions have what the Explanatory Notes call 'carve-outs' (i.e. exceptions to the exceptions, making them into reserved matters after all).

[58] S. 4(1).

[59] S. 9(1) reserved 'policing' for at least three years and s 9(2) reserved the postal service (and related matters), the registration of deeds and the Public Record Office of Ireland until Irish union was achieved.

Table 9.1 Party representatives elected to the Northern Ireland Assembly, 1998–2017

	1998	2003	2007	2011	2016	2017
Ulster Unionist Party	28	27	18	16	16	10
Democratic Unionist Party	20	30	36	38	38	28
Social Democratic and Labour Party	24	18	16	14	12	12
Sinn Féin	18	24	28	29	28	27
Alliance Party	6	6	7	8	8	8
Others	12	3	3	3	6	5
Total:	108	108	108	108	108	90[60]

agree to the St Andrews Agreement, which was reached in 2006 by way of a supplement to the Belfast Agreement.

The initial stumbling block to the Assembly and Executive getting off the ground was the reluctance of unionists to share power with Sinn Féin until substantial progress had been made with the commitments given by participants in the talks leading up to the Belfast Agreement 'to the total disarmament of all paramilitary organisations' and 'to use any influence they may have to achieve the decommissioning of all paramilitary weapons'. While the devolved institutions in Scotland and Wales became operational on 1 July 1999 this did not occur in Northern Ireland until 2 December 1999, 17 months after the Assembly had met for the first time. The functioning of the institutions was then interrupted in both 2000[61] and 2001[62] due to ongoing concerns about the lack of decommissioning. During the second interruption, the DUP, through its then deputy leader Peter Robinson, challenged the re-election of David Trimble as First Minister because it had not occurred within the six week time limit set out in the Northern Ireland Act 1998. The case eventually reached the UK's highest court, the Appellate Committee of the House of Lords, but Mr Robinson lost by the narrow majority of three to two: the judges in the majority said, in effect, that the peace process in Northern Ireland was too important to be

---

[60] The number of MLAs was cut from 108 to 90 by the Assembly Members (Reduction of Numbers) Act (NI) 2016. This was in accordance with one of the points accepted in the Stormont House Agreement 2014.

[61] This suspension was triggered on 11 February by then Secretary of State Peter Mandelson, under powers conferred on him by the hastily enacted Northern Ireland Act 2000. The institutions were restored on 30 May.

[62] Two one-day suspensions in August and September resulted from the resignation of David Trimble as First Minister in July.

limited by the restrictive wording of legislation,[63] and Lord Bingham equated the Northern Ireland Act 1998 to a Constitution for Northern Ireland.[64] A more serious breakdown occurred on 14 October 2002, when Secretary of State John Reid suspended the Assembly a week after the police conducted a search of the Sinn Féin offices at Stormont and arrested three Sinn Féin members on suspicion of spying. Charges were laid against them but were later dropped; one of them, Denis Donaldson, who had been the Chief Administrator for Sinn Féin at Stormont, later confessed to being a British agent. He fled into hiding in Donegal but in 2006 persons as yet unknown, presumably former IRA associates, tracked him down and killed him.

The suspension of the Assembly did not prevent new elections to that body going ahead in 2003 but those elected were powerless to pass any laws. In October 2006 the political parties and the British and Irish governments reached a further agreement at St Andrews in Scotland. Again there was something in it for both unionists and nationalists. The former secured the promise of a statutory 'Ministerial Code', a restriction on the ability of MLAs to alter their designation as 'unionist', 'nationalist' or 'other' (Alliance Party MLAs had changed their designations in order to keep the Assembly and Executive up and running in 2001), and an amendment to an Order in Council ensuring that the Assembly could, if it wanted to, legislate for academic selection in secondary schools. For nationalists there was the promise of a statutory duty on the Executive to develop strategies relating to the Irish language, poverty and social exclusion, and a change to the way in which First and Deputy First Ministers are elected so that the right to nominate someone to the post of First Minister rested with the largest party in the Assembly, rather than, as it did before, with the largest party within the largest 'designation' in the Assembly. The latter reform means that even if there are more unionist than nationalist MLAs in the Assembly, if Sinn Féin is the largest single party it is able to claim the post of First Minister. While symbolically such an outcome would not play well with unionists, in practice it should not matter very much because under the Northern Ireland Act the posts of First and Deputy First Minister are joint and equal, so much so that if one resigns the other has to leave office as well.[65]

A significant boost to the restoration of the Executive was the support given at a Sinn Féin Ard Fheis (Party Conference) in January 2007 for the policing arrangements in Northern Ireland—prior to then the party had refused to take up its seats on the Northern Ireland Policing Board, the statutory body empowered to hold the Police Service of Northern Ireland to account. Further elections to

---

[63] *Robinson v Secretary of State for Northern Ireland* [2002] UKHL 32, [2002] NI 390.

[64] 'The 1998 Act does not set out all the constitutional provisions applicable to Northern Ireland, but it is in effect a constitution . . . [T]he provisions should, consistently with the language used, be interpreted generously and purposively, bearing in mind the values which the constitutional provisions are intended to embody.' Ibid., para 11.

[65] Northern Ireland Act 1998, s. 16, as amended. Several other sections require the two Ministers to act jointly. By s. 20(2) they jointly chair the Executive Committee.

the Assembly occurred in March 2007 and after another slight delay devolution was restored on 5 May 2007.[66] Subsequent developments concerning policing are outlined below.[67]

PETITIONS OF CONCERN

The Belfast Agreement focused on power-sharing and for that to happen it was deemed necessary to know who was representing whom so that power could be shared fairly. Hence the Agreement stipulated that Members of each Assembly must 'register a designation of identity—nationalist, unionist or other'.[68] The election of the Assembly's Chair and Deputy Chair was to take place on a cross-community basis,[69] as was the election of the First and Deputy First Minister, the adoption of Standing Orders and the allocation of budgets. Other decisions would require cross-community support if 30 MLAs voted in favour of 'a petition of concern' on the issue.[70] Cross-community support was defined as *either parallel consent*, where there is a majority of unionists, of nationalists and of all MLAs (present and voting in all three cases) in favour of the proposition, *or a weighted majority*, where at least 60 per cent of MLAs present and voting and at least 40 per cent of both the unionists and the nationalists present and voting support the proposition.[71]

All of those clauses in the Agreement were transposed into sections of the Northern Ireland Act 1998[72] or the Assembly's Standing Orders.[73] In addition, Standing Orders require cross-community votes if a Bill is to receive accelerated passage[74] (but even then no Bill is allowed to pass through all its stages in less than ten days[75]), if a vote is to be taken on the report of an Ad Hoc Assembly Committee on Conformity with Equality Requirements,[76] if a motion is put to suspend Standing Orders,[77] or if appointments are being made to the Assembly Commission, the statutory body which ensures that the Assembly has the property, staff and services it requires.[78]

One might have thought that use of the petition of concern procedure would be limited to issues on which the unionist and nationalist parties traditionally disagree,

---

[66] For more details on the running of the Assembly from 1998 to 2007 see its website: http://www.niassembly. gov.uk/about-the-assembly/general-information/history-of-the-assembly. See too the useful timeline on the BBC's website: http://news.bbc.co.uk/1/hi/northern_ireland/2952997.stm. A further excellent source for details of political events in Northern Ireland are the various Standard Notes issued by the House of Commons Library, e.g. SN 4291, *Political Developments in Northern Ireland since February 2007* (27 March 2007).

[67] See 'Policing and Justice' below.   [68] Strand One, para. 6.   [69] Ibid., para. 7.

[70] Ibid., para. 5(d).   [71] Ibid.

[72] Ss. 4(5) (definition of 'cross-community support' and 'designation'); 39(7) (election of Presiding Officer, also called Speaker); 41(2) (Standing Orders); 42 (petitions of concern).

[73] Standing Orders 3(11) (designation); 4, 5(1) and 5A (election of Deputy Speakers and Principal Deputy Speaker, rather than Deputy Chair); 26(1)(b) (voting on allocations of money out of the Consolidated Fund or on tax rises). The current Standing Orders, last updated in October 2016, area available on the Assembly's website.

[74] Standing Order 42(4).   [75] Ibid., 42(5).   [76] Ibid., 35(20) and 60(3).   [77] Ibid., 77.

[78] Ibid., 79(3); Northern Ireland Act 1998, s 40.

such as flags, parades, policing, victims and minority languages, but in fact it has been used in a much wider variety of situations. A report commissioned by the Assembly and Executive Review Committee revealed that by March 2014 (i.e. 14 years and 4 months after the Assembly was first empowered to make legislation, during which time it had been operational for 9 years and 6 months) a petition of concern was successfully raised on 63 occasions.[79] Petitions became commoner as the years went on, so much so that in the four years immediately prior to the report it was resorted to on 43 occasions (68 per cent of the total). However, only 27 of the 63 uses of the procedure were in relation to proposed legislative provisions, spread across just nine Bills.[80] The other uses related to Assembly motions unconnected with proposed legislation. Both types of use—legislative and non-legislative—were at times deployed on 'moral' issues rather than on issues traditionally related to the conflict in Northern Ireland. For example, in 2012 it was deployed by the DUP to defeat a motion calling for same-sex couples to have the right to marry[81] and in 2013 it was used by Sinn Féin, the Alliance Party and the Green Party to block a legislative amendment that would have extended the criminalization of abortion.[82]

The members of the Assembly and Executive Review Committee could not reach a consensus on how to reform the petition of concern procedure. [83] The only point they did agree about was that if the number of MLAs was reduced, as planned, from 108 to 90,[84] the number of votes required to trigger a petition of concern should fall proportionately (presumably to 25). In fact, that change did not occur when the number of MLAs fell to 90 in 2017. This may be a blessing in disguise, since it will make it more difficult than before for any single party to secure the total number of votes required for a petition of concern: today the DUP have 28 seats in the Assembly and Sinn Féin have 27. But it would still be easy for the two main unionist parties or the two main nationalist parties to combine in order to frustrate the wishes of their rivals.

A few days before the Committee published its report, Alex Schwartz of Queen's University Belfast produced his own analysis of the petition of concern procedure.[85] The reform he most favoured was the establishment of a political mechanism to control

[79] Ray McCaffrey, *Additional Information on Petitions of Concern*, Northern Ireland Assembly, Research and Information Service Briefing Paper, 66/13, Table 1.

[80] These were the Victims and Survivors (Disqualification) Bill (later a 2008 Act); the Caravans Bill (later a 2011 Act); the Armed Forces and Veterans Bill (not enacted); the Justice Bill (later a 2011 Act); the Local Government Disqualification Bill (not enacted); two Planning Bills (only one of which, in 2011, became an Act); the Welfare Reform Bill (not enacted); and the Criminal Justice Bill (later a 2013 Act).

[81] Northern Ireland Assembly Official Report, Session 2012–13, 1 October 2012; the motion was defeated by 50 votes to 45.

[82] Northern Ireland Assembly Official Report, Session 2012–13, 12 March 2013; the proposed amendment was supported by 53 votes to 40, but neither definition of cross-community support was satisfied.

[83] *Review of Petitions of Concern*, NIA 166/11–15, 25 March 2014. Although the Report itself is comparatively brief, its Appendices contain a lot of views submitted to the Committee by political parties and others.

[84] This was eventually provided for by the Assembly Members (Reduction of Numbers) Act (NI) 2016.

[85] *Petitions of Concern*, Northern Ireland Assembly, Knowledge Exchange Seminar Series, 20 March 2014.

its use. He suggested that the Presiding Officer (the Assembly's Speaker) should be empowered to reject a proposed petition if it seems to relate to an issue that does not meet pre-agreed criteria. A useful precedent is the provision inserted into the Northern Ireland Act 1998 as a result of the St Andrews Agreement in 2006: if 30 MLAs raise a petition of concern that a decision taken by a Minister relates to 'a matter of public importance', the Presiding Officer must consult with all the parties in the Assembly, rule on whether the decision does in fact relate to such a matter and, if it does, refer it to the Executive Committee for its consideration.[86] The criterion of 'public importance' hardly seems sufficient to control the use of petitions of concern more generally, but the principle of designating as arbiter the Presiding Officer (who of course is meant to be politically neutral) is a sound one.

THE EXECUTIVE COMMITTEE

This is the Committee which comprises all the departmental Ministers and is co-chaired by the First and Deputy First Ministers.[87] It is, in effect, Northern Ireland's cabinet. According to the Belfast Agreement, to which there is a cross-reference in the relevant section of the Northern Ireland Act 1998,[88] the Executive Committee provides a forum for reaching agreement on issues which cut across two or more departments, for prioritizing executive and legislative proposals, and for producing an annual programme for government and a linked budget for approval by the Assembly on a cross-community basis.

Ministries are allocated by using the d'Hondt formula, named after a nineteenth-century Belgian mathematician. It is legislated for in the Northern Ireland Act 1998[89] and is designed to ensure a distribution of ministries proportionate to the seats won by the various parties in the Assembly. The only exception is the highly sensitive post of Minister for Justice, which is allocated on the basis of a cross-community vote within the Assembly.[90] An idea of how the picture has changed over time can be gleaned from Table 9.2, which shows how departmental responsibilities have been allocated amongst the political parties after each Assembly election to date.[91]

The Executive Committee had a shaky start. The Ulster Unionist Party did not want Sinn Féin to be involved in the North-South Ministerial Council until there had been greater movement on the decommissioning of weapons; it also refused to share

---

[86] Northern Ireland Act 1998, s. 28B(1)(b) and (3). Strangely, the section does not explicitly require the Presiding Officer to rule on whether the Minister's decision may have been taken in breach of the Ministerial Code, which is another ground for the Executive Committee considering it: s. 28B(1)(a).

[87] The Executive Committee should not be confused with the Executive Office, the name given since 8 May 2016 to what was formerly the Office of the First Minister and Deputy First Minister: Departments Act (NI) 2016, s 1(1).

[88] S. 20(3), which refers to paras 19 and 20 of Strand One of the Belfast Agreement.

[89] S. 18.

[90] Northern Ireland Act 1998, s. 21A; Department of Justice Act (NI) 2010, s. 2(1).

[91] No Ministers were appointed after the 2003 and 2017 elections because the two big parties could not agree on who should be the First and Deputy First Ministers.

Table 9.2 Allocation of ministries within the Northern Ireland Executive, 1998–2017[96]

	1998	2003	2007	2011	2016[92]	2017
Ulster Unionist Party	4	n/a	2	1[93],	0	n/a
Democratic Unionist Party	2	n/a	5	5	5	n/a
Social Democratic and Labour Party	4	n/a	1	1	0	n/a
Sinn Féin	2	n/a	4	4	4	n/a
Alliance Party	0	n/a	1	2	0	n/a
Others	0	n/a	0	0	1	n/a
Total:	12[94],	n/a	13[95],	13	10	n/a

Executive papers with the DUP, whose two Ministers withdrew from the Executive because of the presence of Sinn Féin Ministers at the table. Both of these matters were brought to the High Court under judicial review proceedings and on each occasion the Ulster Unionist Party lost.[97] In *De Brun's and McGuinness's Application*[98] the Court of Appeal confirmed the High Court's view that David Trimble had acted unlawfully in refusing to nominate Sinn Féin Ministers to the North-South Ministerial Council because by doing so he was pursuing a collateral purpose (the decommissioning of weapons) rather than focusing on making the Ministerial Council work. In *Morrow's and Campbell's Application* the High Court reached the same conclusion when the First (and Deputy First) Ministers sought to 'punish' the DUP Ministers by refusing them access to Executive papers because they were refusing to sit at the Executive table.[99] The

[92] The number of ministerial departments was reduced from 12 to 9 by the Departments Act (NI) 2016, implementing part of the Stormont House Agreement of 2014, on which see pp 258–9 below.

[93] The UUP withdrew from the Executive in October 2015, whereupon the DUP took over another Ministry.

[94] The Departments (NI) Order 1999 created 11 departments but one of them has two joint heads—the Office of the First Minister and Deputy First Minister.

[95] The Department of Justice was created by the Department of Justice Act (NI) 2010; see too the Northern Ireland Act 1998, s 21(2).

[96] The Table does not include the Junior Ministers who have assisted the First and Deputy First Ministers.

[97] For more general treatment of how the Belfast Agreement has been dealt with by the courts see C. Harvey, 'On Law, Politics and Contemporary Constitutionalism' (2002) 26 *Fordham International LJ* 996, 1001–12; J. Morison and M. Lynch, 'Litigating the Agreement: Towards a New Judicial Constitutionalism for the UK from Northern Ireland?' in J. Morison, K. McEvoy and G. Anthony (eds), *Judges, Transition, Human Rights* (2007) Ch. 7; J. Morison, 'Towards a New Constitutional Doctrine for Northern Ireland? The Agreement, The Litigation and the Constitutional Future', in P. Carmichael, C. Know and R. Osborne (eds.), *Devolution and Constitutional Change in Northern Ireland* (2007) Ch. 4.

[98] [2001] NICA 43.   [99] [2002] NIQB 4.

result would no doubt have been different if DUP Ministers had challenged a decision reached by the Executive Committee at discussions from which those Ministers had deliberately absented themselves.

During the suspension of the Stormont institutions between 2002 and 2007 there was a significant power-shift in that the 2003 Assembly elections resulted in the DUP and Sinn Féin respectively outflanking the UUP and the SDLP, a trend which has continued ever since (see Table 9.1). At the talks leading up to the St Andrews Agreement in 2006 detailed discussions took place on how to make the Executive a more effective and durable institution than it had been to date. At least seven important reforms were agreed: (1) a statutory Ministerial Code would be developed which would ensure that, in the absence of any doctrine of collective responsibility, Ministers would act in accordance with provisions on ministerial accountability in the Code; (2) where a decision of the Executive could not be achieved by consensus, any three members of the Executive could require a vote to be taken on a cross-community basis; (3) new legislation would allow for important ministerial decisions to be referred from the Assembly to the Executive; (4) Ministers would be required by their pledge of office to participate fully in the Executive, the North-South Ministerial Council and the British Irish Council; (5) the largest party in the Assembly would be allowed to nominate someone for the post of First Minister; (6) the First and Deputy First Ministers would seek agreement on which, if any, functions should be transferred from their Office to other departments; and (7) an Assembly Committee would be set up on a statutory basis to hold the Office of the First and Deputy First Minister to account in the same way as other departmental scrutiny committees. All of these proposed reforms were subsequently implemented.

The two biggest challenges facing the Executive after 2007 were how to achieve and implement the devolution of policing and justice and how to respond to the austerity policies adopted by UK governments in the wake of the global financial crisis of 2008. We will look at each of these issues in turn.

POLICING AND JUSTICE

The Belfast Agreement provided for the decommissioning of paramilitary weapons, the early release of paramilitary prisoners and the establishment of a new Human Rights Commission and an Equality Commission. No consensus was reached on the reform of policing or on other aspects of the criminal justice system. Instead those issues were allocated to separate bodies for further consideration.[100]

Policing was examined by an independent Commission which was asked to report by the summer of 1999 and to include proposals for encouraging widespread community support for new policing arrangements, bearing in mind the principles that the police should be representative of the community they serve and should work in partnership with that community. The Belfast Agreement also suggested that the police should not

---

[100] Criminal justice reform is not addressed here; see McAlinden and Dwyer (eds.) under Further Reading.

be routinely armed, should be free from partisan control, should be accountable and should always operate in conformity with human rights norms. The Commission was duly appointed in June 1998 under the chairmanship of Chris Patten, a former Conservative minister, EU Commissioner for External Relations and governor of Hong Kong.[101] He was joined by five other male and two female Commissioners. During the following autumn and winter they organized 40 public meetings throughout Northern Ireland, 28 of them in December alone, and consulted widely with policing experts in the UK, Ireland, the US, Canada, Spain, South Africa, and the Netherlands. Their commendably clear and concise report was published 18 months after the Belfast Agreement, on 9 September 1999, and contained 175 recommendations.

The principal proposal was that the RUC should be disbanded and reconstituted as the Police Service of Northern Ireland (PSNI). Likewise, the body holding the police to account should no longer be the Police Authority but a new statutory body called the Northern Ireland Policing Board and in each of the 26 district council areas there should be a District Policing Partnership Board. A majority of the members of all these Boards should be elected politicians, with the remainder being 'independent' members. To ensure that the proportion of police officers coming from the Catholic community was increased from the low figure of 20 per cent in 1998, the Commission proposed that for at least ten years a system of affirmative action should be put in place to ensure that 50 per cent of all new recruits should come from that community. Perhaps most importantly of all, the first seven of Patten's recommendations stressed the need for the new PSNI to adopt a human rights based approach to policing. This was to be enshrined in the oath which all officers would have to take and also in a Code of Ethics which would integrate the European Convention on Human Rights into police practice. No major changes were suggested to the system for handling complaints against the police because that system had already been radically reformed as a result of the Hayes Report in 1997, leading to the creation of the Office of the Police Ombudsman for Northern Ireland, whose staff were completely independent of the PSNI and could investigate all complaints.[102]

These reforms to policing were duly implemented, the process being monitored by an Oversight Commissioner who had international expertise in policing. The Commissioner published three reports a year until 2007, when his role was no longer deemed necessary. His satisfaction with the process no doubt influenced Sinn Féin's decision to take their seats on the Policing Board that year. In turn this made it more likely that Sinn Féin would agree to the devolution of policing and justice to the Northern Ireland Assembly and Executive. After a series of inter-party talks on this issue consensus was finally reached in the form of the Hillsborough Castle Agreement in February 2010 and devolution took effect two months later. David Ford, the leader of the cross-community Alliance Party, was elected by the Assembly as the first Minister of Justice in the Executive. He retained the post until 2016 and during that period was

---

[101] He became Lord Patten in 2005 and has served as Chancellor of the University of Oxford since 2003.
[102] Police (NI) Act 1998, Pt VII (ss. 50–65).

able to pilot several key pieces of legislation through the Assembly. The Justice Acts (NI) 2011 and 2015 enhanced the rights of victims and witnesses, reduced expenditure on legal aid (which had allegedly risen to the highest *per capita* in the world), merged the two varieties of district council committees dealing with policing and community safety, reformed the Prison Service to make it more efficient, introduced measures to help counter domestic violence, modernized the law on jury service and improved the handling of criminal records.

Three issues have continued to bedevil policing in spite of the reforms following the Patten report. The first is the difficulty encountered in increasing the proportion of police officers from the Catholic community. In 2011 the Secretary of State (who retained responsibility for this particular issue even after the devolution of policing in 2010) brought to an end the affirmative action programme put in place in 2001 ('50-50 recruitment') even though the proportion of Catholic police officers was still only 30 per cent rather than the 43 per cent it should have been if it was to truly reflect the proportion of Catholics living in Northern Ireland. The situation today is not helped by the fact that Sinn Féin seems reluctant to openly encourage people from the Catholic community to apply to join the PSNI because doing so would allow the small 'dissident' republican community to portray Sinn Féin as somehow complicit with the British state. In addition, frequent attacks by such dissidents on serving Catholic police officers, or on members of their families, have discouraged Catholics from applying to join. In 2020 PSNI constable Peadar Heffron lost both his legs when his car was blown up by dissident republicans while he was on his way to work at a police station, and a year later Ronan Kerr, another young Catholic police officer, was killed by a car bomb in his driveway. As yet no-one has been convicted in relation to either of these attacks.

The second major challenge for policing (and for politicians) has been how to deal with the many unresolved crimes dating from the period of the troubles, in particular 3,269 unsolved murders. It was not a matter addressed in the Belfast Agreement, where the concerns of victims of violence, including those bereaved, were blandly referred to in terms of their suffering needing to be acknowledged and addressed 'as a necessary element of reconciliation'.[103] To help the bereaved, the PSNI set up a special unit, the Historical Enquiries Team (HET) in 2005 and tasked it with reviewing the unresolved killings to discover if there were any evidential leads which would merit a new investigation and possible criminal proceedings. All appeared to be going well until an academic researcher[104] and then Her Majesty's Inspectorate of Constabulary verified that the HET was using different methods to review killings committed by British soldiers than it was using for killings committed by members of paramilitary organizations such as the IRA and UVF (Ulster Volunteer Force). The Policing Board announced that it no longer had confidence in the leadership of the HET and asked for no more reviews to be completed until reforms had been introduced. At the end of 2014 it seemed as if the local political parties had reached agreement on a general set

---

[103] 'Rights, Safeguards and Equality of Opportunity', under 'Reconciliation and Victims of Violence', para. 11.
[104] Prof. Patricia Lundy of Ulster University.

of measures for dealing with the past (the Stormont House Agreement) and the Chief Constable closed down the HET. On the assumption that no further reviews were completed subsequent to the HMIC's inspection, the number of reviews the HET managed to complete before being wound up was 1,713, covering 2,209 deaths. This left at least 842 reviews, covering 1,051 deaths, either not completed or not even started.[105] In four separate cases men were successfully prosecuted on the basis of evidential leads emanating from an HET review: all four were convicted of murder or attempted murder but were required to serve only two years in prison, in line with the 'early release' provisions in the Belfast Agreement.

At the start of 2015, the HET's remaining caseload was transferred to the PSNI's Legacy Investigations Branch (LIB), the expectation being that it would soon be moved to the Historical Investigations Unit (HIU) which was one of four new bodies presaged in the Stormont House Agreement. The others were an Independent Commission for Information Retrieval, an Oral History Archive, and an Implementation and Review Group. The UK government agreed to contribute up to £150 million over five years to help fund these bodies, but at the time of writing none of them has been established and the work of the LIB is languishing. In several cases involving deaths caused by British soldiers, the PSNI have been accused of not disclosing adequate information to the coroner or judge who is looking into the case.[106] The work of the Police Ombudsman on cases where police officers are alleged to have been involved in killings, either directly or through colluding with members of unlawful paramilitary organizations in some way (e.g. by not properly investigating a killing because they did not want it known that a police informer within such an organization was implicated), has also been called into question—by families as well as by former police officers. The consensus view amongst all political parties, and of the current Chief Constable George Hamilton, is that 'policing the past' is adversely affecting the ability of the PSNI to police the present. Every time a controversy arises over the PSNI's handling of a legacy issue it damages the police's current public image, making it even harder to recruit new officers from the Catholic community, which is the one most likely to be dissatisfied with how the police have handled previous investigations.

The third challenge facing the PSNI is the threat posed by those who are still committed to using violence for political ends. These include dissident republicans, loyalist organizations such as the UVF and disgruntled former paramilitaries on both sides who still feud amongst themselves. Counter-terrorism laws and policies in Northern Ireland are still non-devolved matters and so remain the responsibility of the UK Parliament and government. As part of the St Andrews Agreement in 2006 the UK's internal security service, MI5, acquired lead responsibility for handling national security intelligence in Northern Ireland but it was affirmed that all such intelligence would be

---

[105] These figures are taken from the HMIC's Report, pp. 39 and 50, available at https://www.justiceinspectorates.gov.uk/hmicfrs/media/inspection-of-the-police-service-of-northern-ireland-historical-enquiries-team-20130703.pdf.

[106] E.g. *Flynn (John) v Chief Constable of the PSNI* [2018] NICA 3, available at www.judiciary-ni.gov.uk, under 'Judicial Decisions and Directions'.

visible to the PSNI, that the PSNI would be informed of all MI5 operations relating to Northern Ireland, that the great majority of informers in Northern Ireland would continue to be handled by PSNI officers and that there would be no reduction in the duty of the PSNI to comply with the Human Rights Act or in the power of the Policing Board to monitor that compliance. In 2015 the National Crime Agency (which does not investigate terrorist organizations but focuses instead on organized crime and child sexual exploitation) was allowed to operate in Northern Ireland, but it too is accountable to the Policing Board and must work in close liaison with the PSNI.[107]

Despite the problems connected to policing it would be inaccurate to claim that they have contributed to the current breakdown in trust between the two largest political parties, the DUP and Sinn Féin. Since the latter took up their allocation of seats on the Policing Board in 2007 they have worked reasonably harmoniously with DUP members of the Board. The Stormont House Agreement proposals on dealing with the past were not implemented after 2014 largely because there was a stand-off between the two big parties over an unrelated matter, welfare reform.[108]

AUSTERITY POLICIES AND WELFARE REFORM

When the Conservative and Liberal Democrats formed a coalition government after the UK general election in 2010 they agreed a package of austerity measures designed to eliminate within five years the nation's annual budget deficit and to reduce the national debt. As a consequence the money available for public services (except health and education) was considerably reduced and the amounts paid by way of welfare benefits were frozen. Corresponding reductions were made to the block grant to Northern Ireland under the so-called Barnett formula which, since 1979, has proportionately linked the amounts of money allocated to Scotland, Wales and Northern Ireland to that available for England. In 2013 welfare benefits were allowed to rise by 1 per cent but in the following year the UK government announced that as the budget deficit was not decreasing at the required rate the period of austerity would have to continue until 2018. In Northern Ireland there was little support for the austerity measures within political parties representing the nationalist community, who argued that as social security was a devolved issue in Northern Ireland (unlike in Scotland and Wales) the Northern Ireland Assembly did not have to follow the UK government's route.

Following a failure to secure Assembly support on a way forward regarding welfare reform a consensus on how to proceed was included in the Stormont House Agreement of 2014, the document considered above in relation to dealing with the past. The outcome was that Northern Ireland accepted the same welfare arrangements as in England but there would be 'flexibilities and top-ups from the block grant as part of a package of measures to address local need'. Northern Ireland was not exempted from

---

[107] See the Crime and Courts Act 2013 (National Crime Agency and Proceeds of Crime) (NI) Order 2015.
[108] The Northern Ireland Office eventually put out detailed legislative proposals on dealing with the past for consultation in June 2018.

the so-called 'bedroom tax', but until 2020 anyone whose housing benefit is reduced as a result of that tax can be reimbursed for their loss. Savings were to be made by selling off some government-owned assets and reducing the size of the civil service in Northern Ireland (where the public sector has for long been proportionally larger than in any other part of the UK). The UK government promised to spend almost £2 billion to assist in these processes, the plan being that this expenditure (on staff redundancy packages etc.) would in due course generate annual savings of about £500 million. The fact remains that in real terms Parliament's block grant to Northern Ireland fell by 8 per cent between 2010 and 2015. To ensure that the required changes to welfare benefits laws were put in place quickly (and to avoid nationalist parties having to formally vote for them at Stormont) they were enacted not by the Northern Ireland Assembly but by Orders in Council at Westminster.[109]

THE CURRENT IMPASSE

As already noted, the period after 2007 was marked by the growing power of the DUP and Sinn Féin within the Executive Committee. In the 2011 and 2016 Assembly elections they consolidated their dominance (see Table 9.1 above), but after the 2016 election no other party agreed to enter the Executive alongside the DUP and Sinn Féin because they did not believe that during the life of the two previous Assemblies those parties had been committed to genuine power-sharing, either between themselves or with others. They claimed that the two big parties did not so much 'share' power as 'share out' power. The Alliance Party refused to nominate one of its MLAs for the post of Minister of Justice because the DUP would not agree to curb its use of the petition of concern procedure in the Assembly. As the two big parties could not agree on an MLA from one of the unionist or nationalist parties taking up the Ministry, it was offered to an independent MLA, Claire Sugden (who nevertheless designates herself as unionist). Taking advantage of a new statutory provision allowing it to happen,[110] both the Ulster Unionist Party and the SDLP chose at this time to enter into Opposition rather than take the seats on the Executive Committee to which they were entitled under the d'Hondt system. None of the other smaller parties in the Assembly, including the Alliance Party, had enough seats to qualify for membership of the Opposition. The Opposition was to receive benefits such as research and financial assistance, extra speaking and questioning rights and the right to chair the Public Accounts Committee,[111] but no Standing Orders could be approved in time for those benefits to be activated before the Executive collapsed in January 2017.

[109] Welfare Reform (NI) Order 2015; Welfare Reform and Work (NI) Order 2016. These are the only two Northern Ireland Orders in Council made since 2009.

[110] The Assembly and Executive Reform (Assembly Opposition) Act (NI) 2016, which was an outcome of the so-called Fresh Start Agreement reached by the Northern Ireland parties and the British and Irish governments in 2015: see https://www.gov.uk/government/news/a-fresh-start-for-northern-ireland.

[111] Ibid., ss. 6–11.

The collapse occurred ostensibly because of a financial debacle linked to a Renewable Heat Incentive (RHI) scheme, but also because the two big parties differed so fundamentally over Brexit and various rights issues. In 2016 the UK government announced a prolongation of its austerity policies until 2020, though it later softened its stance on pay rises for those working in the public sector. In January 2016 Arlene Foster took over the leadership of the DUP from Peter Robinson, who retired after serving in that role since 2008. In November 2016 it came to light that the RHI scheme for which Mrs Foster had responsibility as Minister for Enterprise, Trade and Investment in the period 2012–15 did not have the same cost controls attached to it as applied to the similar scheme in England and Wales, which meant that people who took advantage of the scheme could make a profit out of it by needlessly burning subsidized wood pellets. The potential loss to the public purse was said to be close to £500 million. Mrs Foster refused to resign over the issue but on 9 January 2017 the Deputy First Minister, Martin McGuinness of Sinn Féin, resigned (he was very ill at the time), meaning that Mrs Foster had to leave office too. As his reason for resigning, Mr McGuinness cited not just the RHI scandal but the DUP's 'arrogance', giving as an example a DUP Minister's recent decision to withdraw funding from a bursary scheme for young people wanting to learn Irish in Donegal. On 17 January 2017 the Assembly voted unanimously (though Sinn Féin did not take part in the debate) to ask the Secretary of State for Northern Ireland to establish a public inquiry into the RHI scandal. The Inquiry is currently up and running and has heard considerable evidence of apparent dysfunctionality within the department of government concerned. Its report is due to be published in the Summer of 2019.

THE RELEVANCE OF BREXIT

The cleavage between the two big parties over Brexit is very significant. Prior to the referendum in June 2016 unionist parties campaigned strongly in favour of Brexit, but on the day nearly 56 per cent of all those who voted in Northern Ireland opted for the UK to remain in the EU. As in Scotland (and London) there is considerable disquiet in Northern Ireland that the area is now being required to leave the EU simply because a majority of people living in England and Wales voted for that outcome. Prior to 2016 Sinn Féin were a predominantly euro-sceptical party: in 1972 they campaigned against Ireland joining the Common Market and they subsequently objected to the Single European Act, the Maastricht Treaty, the Amsterdam Treaty, the Nice Treaty and the Lisbon Treaty. But they strongly supported the UK's continued membership of the EU in 2016, suggesting at times that a vote to leave might encourage dissident republicans to attack any border crossings that might need to be established on the island as a result of Brexit. All parties in Northern Ireland, even the DUP, as well as the British and Irish governments, have agreed that Brexit must not mean the return of any 'hard' border in Ireland. They just have not yet been able to come up with a scheme which will satisfy the EU that such a border is not required.

The DUP were also largely in favour of 'the Chequers deal', which was thrashed out by the UK cabinet in July 2018.[112] They liked the way it did not differentiate between Northern Ireland and Great Britain as regards the measures that could be taken to ensure regulatory alignment with the EU after Brexit. The EU, however, was not satisfied that the Chequers deal was compatible with fundamental EU principles. Sinn Féin and the SDLP campaigned for Northern Ireland to be given a special status whereby it would be allowed to remain in the EU's single market and even in the customs union, but that is anathema to unionists (and to the Conservative Party) because it would effectively create a border in the Irish Sea between the island of Ireland and the island of Great Britain, making Northern Ireland, in unionist eyes, less British. Nevertheless Mrs May agreed to the inclusion of a Northern Ireland Protocol in the proposed Brexit Withdrawal Agreement which tended to have that effect—the so-called 'Irish backstop'.[113] Some say that Sinn Féin are playing a long game in that by appearing to be the victims of unionist domination in the North they are positioning themselves to gain more votes in the next general election in the Republic, which has to occur before April 2021. The SDLP, for their part, have always been a pro-EU party but they are conscious of the increasingly fragile position they occupy in Northern Ireland and are considering forging a much closer relationship with Fianna Fáil, the main opposition party in the Republic: a merger or collaboration between those parties would create another all-Ireland nationalist party which could pose a bigger threat to Sinn Féin in Northern Ireland than the SDLP alone has managed to present in recent years.

As Sinn Féin refused to nominate another Deputy First Minister after Mr McGuinness's resignation, new Assembly elections had to take place in March 2017, less than a year after the previous elections. As can be seen from Table 9.1, the DUP lost 10 seats, while Sinn Féin lost just one. The DUP managed to remain the largest party, but for the first time ever the total number of unionist MLAs elected was not over 50 per cent. Despite various series of inter-party talks having occurred since then, as of April 2019 no new Executive had yet been formed. Northern Ireland has now been without its government for longer than the previous world record period of 589 days experienced by Belgium—another divided society governed on a consociational basis—in-between 2010 and 2011. In February 2018 it did seem as if an agreement to establish a new Northern Ireland Executive had been reached but at the last minute the DUP pulled out of it because they felt that their supporters on the ground would not accept the deal's provisions concerning protection of the Irish language.[114] Further talks may occur in the forthcoming months but it is hard to see where the necessary compromise will come from. While the DUP say they are ready to re-establish the Executive tomorrow, Sinn

---

[112] Sam McBride, 'Does the DUP support Theresa May's Chequers Brexit plan?', available at https://inews.co.uk/news/brexit/does-dup-support-theresa-may-chequers-brexit-plan.

[113] For the Institute for Government's useful summary of the Protocol's import see https://www.instituteforgovernment.org.uk/explainers/northern-ireland-ireland-protocol-brexit.

[114] What is alleged to be the final draft of the February 2018 agreement was subsequently leaked: see http://eamonnmallie.com/2018/02/stormont-exclusive-draft-agreement-text-eamonn-mallie-brian-rowan.

Féin insist that certain preconditions must first be met, including that same-sex marriage, abortion reform and Irish language rights be guaranteed.

THE CONFIDENCE AND SUPPLY AGREEMENT

Following the 2017 general election, the DUP struck a 'confidence and supply' agreement with the Conservatives whereby, in exchange for DUP support at Westminster
on motions of confidence, the Queen's Speech, money bills, Brexit legislation and legislation relating to national security, the UK government promised to preserve the so-
called 'triple lock' on pension rises, the universal nature of 'winter fuel payments'[115]
and the preservation until the end of the current Parliament of farm support payments.
These are matters affecting the whole of the UK, demonstrating the DUP's desire to
be considered a major political force throughout the Union.[116] In addition, the DUP
managed to wrest from the UK government a sizeable financial package for Northern
Ireland.[117] The government promised £550 million over two years for infrastructure
development, £300 million over two years to help address immediate pressures in
health and education, £100 million over five years to help the Northern Ireland Executive target pockets of severe deprivation, and £50 million over five years to provide support for improvement to mental health. This amounts to additional public expenditure
of £1 billion in Northern Ireland over five years.

   Although non-supporters of the DUP were critical of that party for agreeing to prop
up the Conservative government, they could hardly deny that the extra expenditure
secured was necessary and helpful. Unsurprisingly there was some astonishment in
Great Britain that in an age of austerity an extra £1 billion could be conjured up for
one small part of the nation quite so easily. There was even a legal challenge to the
agreement, brought by a member of the Green Party in England who alleged that it
breached the Bribery Act 2010, but the High Court ruled that that Act did not apply
to agreements reached between political parties and that ruling was not appealed.[118]
A Coordination Committee has been established to monitor implementation of the
confidence and supply agreement and brief details of its meetings are posted on the
government's website.

   The confidence and supply agreement has survived at least two political crises since
it was reached in June 2017. The first occurred in December 2017 when the Prime
Minister went to Brussels thinking she had support from the DUP in relation to an
agreement she had struck with EU negotiators over 'regulatory alignment' on the island of Ireland after Brexit (meaning, in effect, that Northern Ireland would remain
in the single market whereas the rest of the UK would not). After the DUP expressed

---

[115] I.e. this benefit will not be means-tested.

[116] The agreement, updated as of 28 June 2018, is available on the UK Government's website, www.gov.uk.

[117] The details are set out in an annex to the confidence and supply agreement, also available on the UK
Government's website under the title 'UK Government financial support for Northern Ireland'.

[118] *R. (McClean) v First Secretary of State* [2017] EWHC 3174 (Admin), 26 October 2017, available at
https://www.bailii.org/ew/cases/EWHC/Admin/2017/3174.html.

its dissatisfaction with the proposed deal, Mrs May had to return hastily to London to discuss it with that party before going back to Brussels a few days later to clinch it. The second occasion was in February 2018 when the Prime Minister (and the Taoiseach, the Prime Minister of Ireland) went to Belfast on the understanding that the DUP had struck a deal with Sinn Féin over the restoration of the Northern Ireland Executive, only to find, as mentioned above, that in fact it had not. To date, however, the DUP's MPs have tended to vote with the government in crucial House of Commons debates. On 16 July 2018, for instance, their support was crucial to the government winning a vote on its proposal that after Brexit the UK should collect tariffs on incoming goods destined for the EU provided that the EU would fully reciprocate even in the unlikely event of the UK's tariff being higher than the EU's.[119] But on 15 January 2019 the DUP's MPs joined 118 rebel Conservative MPs in voting against Mrs May's Brexit Withdrawal Agreement, helping to ensure a massive defeat for her proposals and requiring her to return to Brussels to seek further 'concessions'.

THE *BUICK* CASE

Meanwhile the difficulties involved in running Northern Ireland are increasing almost daily, partly because of an important judicial decision.

When Assembly elections took place in March 2017, existing government Ministers ceased to hold office. Since then, as no agreement has been reached on the formation of a new Executive, no replacement Ministers have been appointed. This has left civil servants in a difficult position as there are many issues on which they would like to make progress but there are no Ministers in place to take the relevant decisions. In September 2017 the Permanent Secretary of the Department for Infrastructure granted planning permission for the construction of a major incinerator and waste treatment centre in County Antrim, relying on legal advice and influenced by information that not going ahead with the project would lead to Northern Ireland failing to meet EU requirements on waste management, that the cost of disposing of waste would rise significantly, and that illegal waste activity would be encouraged. Opponents of the project judicially reviewed the civil servant's decision and Mrs Justice Keegan held that the decision was illegal because it could be taken only by a government Minister.[120]

The Court of Appeal upheld the judge's ruling, one judge doing so on the same basis as Mrs Justice Keegan and the other two on the basis that this particular decision, relating as it did to a cross-cutting issue, was one which could not be taken by a single Minister but only by the Northern Ireland Executive as a whole.[121] Under the Belfast Agreement,

---

[119] The government's Brexit proposal hammered out at Chequers a few days earlier, under which the UK promised to maintain 'a common rulebook' with the EU for all goods, was ambiguous on this point, so some MPs argued that the government was contradicting itself. It won the vote by just three votes.

[120] *Buick's (Colin) Application* [2018] NIQB 43.

[121] *Buick's (Colin) Application* [2018] NICA 26. The majority judges were Morgan LCJ and Stephens LJ; the minority judge was Treacy LJ.

as implemented by the Northern Ireland Act 1998,[122] the Executive Committee has to agree on 'issues which cut across the responsibilities of two or more Ministers'[123] and this is backed up by provisions in the Ministerial Code, also mandated by the 1998 Act.[124] In August 2018 the Attorney General for Northern Ireland referred some questions arising out of the *Buick* case to the UK Supreme Court, so that it could clarify when exactly civil servants can take decisions if no relevant Minister is in post, but in January 2019 the Supreme Court refused to rule on the matter saying that it would be better dealt with in the context of actual litigation, an example of which was pending.[125] Meanwhile the Secretary of State for Northern Ireland secured the passage of new legislation at Westminster to make it easier for senior civil servants to take decisions in the absence of Ministers.[126]

POSSIBLE FUTURES

Nationalist parties in Northern Ireland are not at all keen to see 'direct rule' in Northern Ireland, especially as Sinn Féin do not take their seats in the UK Parliament and the SDLP lost their three seats there in the 2017 general election. Those parties know that the UK government would be acting contrary to the St Andrews Agreement if it did revert to direct rule, but they are also aware that the UK government will at least keep the administration of Northern Ireland ticking over by continuing to allocate money to the area in the absence of a power-sharing government.[127] The unionist parties can also live with the halfway-house of indirect rule from London, the more so when, as at present, DUP MPs are crucial to the ability of the Conservative government to command a majority in the House of Commons.

It is conceivable that the Executive can be restored within the next few months and that the life of the current Assembly can become productive again until the next election due in 2022. As the DUP and Sinn Féin were close to reaching a deal in February 2018, they may still be able to achieve a compromise, particularly on Irish language issues. The danger is, however, that without reform to the petition of concern procedure, or without some moderation in the parties' demands, a further breakdown is likely at some future point. The outcome of the public inquiry into the RHI scandal will not be known until mid-2019 and the report may well have a destabilizing effect. This could also be a consequence of any deal struck with the EU over Brexit. Brexit without a deal would be even more dangerous as far as devolution in Northern Ireland is concerned, especially if, despite all protestations to the contrary, the EU insists

---

[122] S. 20(3).   [123] Strand One, paras. 19 and 20.
[124] S. 28(5); provision for a Ministerial Code was inserted in the Act as a result of the St Andrews Agreement 2006.
[125] Reference by the Attorney General for Northern Ireland of devolution issues to the Supreme Court pursuant to Paragraph 34 of Schedule 10 to the Northern Ireland Act 1998 (No 2) [2019] UKSC 1. The pending litigation concerns the validity of a proposed electricity interconnector between Northern Ireland and Ireland.
[126] Northern Ireland (Executive Formation and Exercise of Functions) Act 2018.
[127] See the Northern Ireland Budget Acts 2017 and 2018.

upon border controls being put in place. In short, the Assembly and Executive could limp along for the next few years but the chances of devolution operating effectively are slim. The prospects are further diminished by the fact that the DUP seems to be in denial of certain so-called British values such as equality, diversity and tolerance. Likewise Sinn Féin continues to find it hard to attract votes from non-nationalists because its leaders refuse to say that supporting the use of politically-motivated violence during the troubles was a misguided strategy which led to the needless loss of countless lives. In those important respects the 'constitutional cultures' pervading each of the two big parties are completely different and, for the foreseeable future, irreconcilable.

In theory a new effort could be made to re-design the Belfast Agreement to make it more workable. This would involve a lengthy negotiation process, with the British and Irish governments devoting a great deal of attention to the issues, but it is difficult to detect any appetite for such a process or to see any likelihood of such negotiations succeeding, especially if they occur while the current impasse persists. If they ran in parallel with a functioning Assembly and Executive they could seriously undermine the cooperative spirit that is required for such institutions to function effectively. Back in 2009 a prominent member of the Alliance Party and now its deputy leader, Stephen Farry, foresaw that the consociationalist nature of the Belfast Agreement may be its eventual undoing: 'with the exception of the use of proportionality in elections, I am generally critical of the other core aspects of consociationalism and believe that they are not in the interests of stability and the evolution to an open and modern civic society, with a sustainable economy'.[128] He advocates promoting a shared identity for those living in Northern Ireland (or 'the North' as some nationalists prefer to call it), a better strategy for improving community relations and the elimination of the 'designation' system in the Assembly so that a weighted majority would simply mean a 60 or 70 per cent approval amongst all the MLAs.[129]

It may already be too late for a re-design or even a re-tweaking of the Belfast Agreement. Brexit may well be its death-knell. One demographic reality is that the population of Northern Ireland is becoming increasingly more Catholic. In 2011 Protestants formed 48 per cent of the population (down from 53 per cent in 2001) and Catholics formed 45 per cent (up from 44 per cent in 2001). The 2011 census was the first to ask a question about national identity: 40 per cent said their identity was British only and 25 per cent said it was Irish only (the remainder said it was a mixture of both, Northern Irish or some foreign nationality). This suggests that not all Catholics would automatically vote to live in a united Ireland rather than the United Kingdom, but sooner or later it seems inevitable that there will be majority support for changing the constitutional status of Northern Ireland. The Secretary of State must arrange for a border poll 'if at any time it appears likely to him [or her] that a majority of those voting would express a wish that Northern Ireland should cease to be part of the United Kingdom and form part of a united Ireland'.[130] Depending on the kind of Brexit deal

---

[128] 'Consociationalism and the Creation of a Shared Future' in Taylor (ed.), 165 at 167, listed under Further Reading. Farry was Minister for Employment and Learning in the Northern Ireland Executive from 2011 to 2016.

[129] Ibid., 178–9. See too Robin Wilson's proposals concerning an 'intercultural' approach, ibid., 221–36.

[130] Northern Ireland Act 1998, Sched. 1, para. 2.

Table 9.3 GDP per capita in the UK and Ireland, 1957–2017[131]

	United Kingdom	Ireland
1967	2,018	1,149
1977	4,682	3,409
1987	14,328	9,405
1997	26,628	22,435
2007	50,156	60,828
2017	39,591	68,977

which is negotiated, that likelihood may become apparent to the Secretary of State within just a few years from now.

When such a vote occurs, a primary consideration for those voting will be the economic prospects of the entity they are asked to prefer. Over the last 50 years or so the comparative economic situation of the UK and Ireland has shifted remarkably. Taking Gross Domestic Product *per capita* as the prime indicator of an economy's success, the relative position of the two countries has been as shown in (Table 9.3. The figures are in US dollars. GDP *per capita* in Ireland began to exceed that in UK in 2001 and it has been in that position ever since, even in the years immediately following the collapse of Ireland's banking sector in 2008. But of course we do not know what the future holds, especially after Brexit. If the UK's economy suffers a further decline it is likely that Ireland's will as well, given the degree of dependency Ireland has on trade with the UK, but the decline in Ireland will probably be less severe given that Ireland will still benefit from the advantages of being in the EU's single market while the UK will have to strike new trade deals with both the EU and the rest of the world. Quite apart from the possible economic advantages of living in a united Ireland, the fact that the Republic is now a more liberal and diverse society than Northern Ireland may make voting for a united Ireland an attractive proposition for liberal Protestants who are not as captivated by the supposed glory of Britain's imperial past as residents of England and Wales may be. Living as people who have joint British and Irish nationality in a liberal democracy within the EU may be more appealing to such a cohort than living with that status in a marginalized part of a United Kingdom (minus Scotland perhaps) outside the EU.[132]

If a border poll were to result in a vote favouring a united Ireland it would give rise to at least three important uncertainties. First, and most worryingly, there is the potential for a

[131]   Source: https://countryeconomy.com/gdp, under 'UK' and 'Ireland'. For further comparison of the economies of the UK and Ireland see https://www.indexmundi.com/factbook/compare/united-kingdom.ireland/economy, a derivative of the CIA's 'World Factbook'. The OECD also publishes regular 'Economic Surveys' of each of its member states. For a fairly recent assessment of the economic impact of 'peace' in Northern Ireland since 1998 see Paul Teague, 'Northern Ireland: The Political Economy of Peace', available at https://www.qub.ac.uk/Research/GRI/mitchell-institute/FileStore/Filetoupload,727473,en.pdf (October 2016).

[132]   It is possible, of course, that a new federal United Kingdom might eventually emerge: see McEldowney in Chapter 14 of this book.

violent backlash on the part of disaffected loyalists. There are still many weapons within that community and loyalist paramilitary organizations which were responsible for approximately 30 per cent of the killings during the troubles could easily re-group, perhaps launching attacks in the 26 counties of the Republic as well as in Catholic areas in the six counties of the North. Second, a decision would have to be taken on whether the Assembly and Executive of Northern Ireland could continue to exist within the framework of a united Ireland. Allowing that to happen would give some comfort to unionists, who would still constitute at least a very substantial minority in that region and would be entitled, under the d'Hondt system, to be in charge of some Executive departments. Such an arrangement might be agreed on a temporary basis—say ten years—to allow the reunification of Ireland to bed down and to disincentivize any violence. The third uncertainty, not unrelated to the second, is whether the Irish government would be prepared to take over from the UK government the responsibility for subsidizing the North. In 2016–17 the UK subvention for Northern Ireland (also known as the net fiscal deficit) was £5,014 for every man, woman and child living in Northern Ireland, equating to a total of about £5.5 billion.[133] Public expenditure *per capita* in Northern Ireland was £13,954 in that year, £2,200 more than the UK average;[134] in 2016 *per capita* expenditure in the Republic was very slightly higher than the UK average but lower than in Northern Ireland, at €14,502.[135] It is unlikely that Ireland would care to carry such excessive costs, at least initially, without some subsidy either from the UK or from other international sources.

FURTHER READING

G. ANTHONY, *Judicial Review in Northern Ireland* (2nd edn., 2014)

P. CARMICHAEL, C. KNOX, and R. OSBORNE, (eds.), *Devolution and Constitutional Change in Northern Ireland* (2007)

M. COX, A. GUELKE, and F. STEPHEN, (eds.), *A Farewell to Arms? From War to Peace in Northern Ireland* (2nd edn., 2006)

B. DICKSON, *Law in Northern Ireland* (3rd edn, 2018)

J. DOYLE, (ed.), *Policing the Narrow Ground: Lessons from the Transformation of Policing in Northern Ireland* (2010)

C. HARVEY, (ed.), *Human Rights, Equality and Democratic Renewal in Northern Ireland* (2001)

A.-M. MCALINDEN, and C. DWYER, (eds.), *Criminal Justice in Transition: The Northern Ireland Context* (2015)

R. TAYLOR, (ed.), *Consociational Theory: McGarry and O'Leary and the Northern Ireland Conflict* (2009)

---

[133] *Country and Regional Public Sector Finances: Financial Year Ending 2017*, Office for National Statistics (1 August 2018) 11, Table 2.

[134] Ibid., 27, Table 6.

[135] T. A. McDonnell and P. G. Kelly, *Public Spending: How Ireland Compares and Productivity Implications*, NERI Research in Brief, No 53 (2017) 3, Table 2. The UK figure is given there as equivalent to €14,306.

10

DEVOLUTION IN SCOTLAND

Aileen McHarg

SUMMARY

Scotland's devolved Parliament and Government were established in 1999 under the Scotland Act 1998. The current devolved arrangements build upon earlier institutional arrangements for the distinctive governance of Scotland, elements of which date back to the Union of 1707. By creating both a distinct legislature and separate institutions of political representation for Scotland, the 1999 reforms were nevertheless of profound constitutional significance. This chapter traces the development of devolved government in Scotland, arguing that the history of Scottish devolution is best understood as a response to nationalist sentiment: the assertion of the right of the people of Scotland to self-governance and self-determination. The historical trajectory has been one of increasing autonomy and constitutional recognition, and this pattern has continued since 1999 (culminating in an—unsuccessful—referendum in 2014 on the question whether Scotland should become wholly independent of the United Kingdom). However, despite the extensive powers enjoyed by, and the political importance of, the Scottish Parliament and Government, the status of devolution within the United Kingdom constitution is ambiguous and contested. The chapter also explores the constitutional status of devolution across two dimensions: the juridical—i.e. how the powers of the Scottish Parliament and Government are understood and interpreted by the courts; and the political—how the devolved Scottish institutions relate to their counterparts at UK level. The chapter ends by exploring how the tensions between Scotland's powerful political claims for constitutional recognition, yet weak legal protection, have played out in relation to Brexit, and may play out in future in a Scottish political context still dominated by the independence question.

INTRODUCTION

Devolution to Scotland, in its current incarnation, is a relatively recent constitutional phenomenon. The devolved Scottish Parliament, based at Holyrood in Edinburgh, and the Scottish Government[1] were established by the Scotland Act 1998 ('the 1998 Act'), and the first elections to the Holyrood parliament, from which a government was selected, were held on 6 May 1999. It would, however, be a mistake to think that Scottish devolution only began in 1999. On the contrary, elements of a distinctive Scottish governance system have been in place ever since the Union of 1707. Although officially an 'incorporating union', in which the previously independent Scottish and English states were dissolved and merged into a new state of Great Britain, the terms of union provided certain guarantees for the smaller and weaker Scottish partner, most notably the continued existence of a separate Scottish legal system.[2] The governance of Scotland was never wholly assimilated to that of England. During the eighteenth century, 'the British state . . . was always mediated through . . . "native Scottish surrogates"'[3]—the so-called Scottish 'managers',[4] or the Lord Advocate, acting as adviser to the British Home Secretary. With the expansion of the functions of the state from the mid-nineteenth century onwards, separate administrative arrangements were frequently adopted for Scotland. In 1885, the Scottish Office was created within the UK Government, headed by a 'Secretary for Scotland', later upgraded to the status of Secretary of State, and the Scottish Office continued to accrue additional functions throughout the twentieth century.[5] Distinctive institutions of local government (albeit subject to several reorganizations) have also persisted in Scotland since the Union. Institutions of intermediate government—such as the police, the National Health Service, and nationalized industries—were often separately constituted, and sometimes substantively different from equivalent institutions elsewhere in the UK. In addition, by the late twentieth century, there were well-established arrangements in the Westminster Parliament for handling Scottish business.

By the 1990s, then, Scotland enjoyed extensive administrative devolution. The Scottish Office system was able to tailor government policies to the distinctive needs of Scotland, and sometimes to pursue different policy lines, albeit within the constraints of collective Cabinet responsibility, and subject to the political direction determined by the UK-wide majority in the Westminster Parliament. In an important sense, the new institutions established by the 1998 Act were an evolutionary development of this system of administrative devolution. The Scottish Government inherited an already-functioning government machine based in St Andrew's House in Edinburgh, and the subject areas over which the Scottish Parliament and Government were given responsibility largely mirrored the previous responsibilities of the Scottish Office, although the scope of devolved competence has since expanded, most notably via the Scotland

---

[1] The Scotland Act 1998 referred to the 'Scottish Executive'. However, this was unofficially renamed the 'Scottish Government' in 2007 by the newly-elected Scottish National Party (SNP) administration, and the name change was confirmed by the Scotland Act 2012, s. 12.

[2] Treaty of Union, Arts XVIII and XIX.

[3] L. Paterson, *The Autonomy of Modern Scotland* (1994) 34.

[4] Ibid., 32–4; J. Mitchell, *The Scottish Question* (2014) Ch. 2.

[5] See J. Mitchell, *Devolution in the UK* (2009) Ch. 2; Mitchell, *The Scottish Question* (above n. 4) Ch. 3.

Acts of 2012 and 2016, and will further increase after the UK leaves the European Union ('Brexit').[6]

Nevertheless, the 1998 Act made two fundamentally important changes to the governance of Scotland: it conferred *legislative competence* on the Scottish Parliament; and it created new institutions of *political representation* for Scotland. This has meant that the formation of law and policy in devolved areas is no longer dependent upon political forces at Westminster, but rather is determined by electoral outcomes and political choices within Scotland itself.

These twin changes have had profound implications for Scottish governance. First, they have enabled further divergence in law and policy in Scotland compared with the rest of the UK. This was muted at first, while the Labour party was in power both at Westminster and as the larger coalition partner in Edinburgh, but became more significant after 2007 when Scottish and UK electoral outcomes began to diverge. Secondly, the 1998 Act reforms have heightened political consciousness of Scotland as a distinct territorial unit within the UK, in ways which have sometimes spilled beyond the boundaries of devolved competence. This latter effect has, on the one hand, fuelled demands for greater autonomy for Scotland, culminating in the referendum of 18 September 2014 on whether Scotland should become independent. Although 55 per cent of Scottish voters opted to remain within the UK, the independence question remains a live one, and a major determinant of political behaviour within Scotland. On the other hand, heightened Scottish political self-consciousness has sometimes manifested in a demand for Scotland's distinctive political voice to be taken into account in UK-wide decision-making, most notably in relation to Brexit.

As this latter point suggests, the 1998 Act (along with the other devolution statutes) has also had broader constitutional implications beyond increasing Scottish self-government. By distributing legislative power away from the UK Parliament, and pluralizing centres of political authority, it has had an impact on the wider UK constitution. The precise nature of that impact is, however, highly contested. Should devolution be understood as a form of decentralization within a still essentially unitary constitutional order? Is it, rather, an expression of Scottish popular sovereignty and self-determination within the context of a 'union state?'[7] Or is it part of a more fundamental pluralization and federalization of the UK's territorial constitution? The answer to this question is not merely of academic importance, but may have significant practical consequences both in terms of how the courts interpret the powers enjoyed by the Scottish Parliament and Government, and in shaping the behaviour of political actors in cases of conflict between UK and Scottish institutions. But the answer given may vary depending on one's perspective. Differences in geographical position (in Scotland or elsewhere), in political objectives, both short and long term, and in broader constitutional understandings and value commitments may produce different interpretations of legal

---

[6]   European Union (Withdrawal) Act 2018, s. 12.

[7]   See S. Rokkan and D. Urwin, 'Introduction: Centres and Peripheries in Western Europe', in S. Rokkan and D. Urwin (eds.), *The Politics of Territorial Identity* (Sage Publications Ltd, London, 1992).

texts, and different readings of the significance of historical and contemporary political events. Moreover, since devolution is still an evolving process, understandings of its constitutional significance may vary over time, and it remains highly uncertain how it will develop in future. While Scotland has, in recent years, seemed to be on a path of ever-greater decentralization, Brexit has served to highlight the weak constitutional supports for devolution, and reminds us that the current level of Scottish autonomy within the UK cannot be taken for granted.

This chapter aims to do three things. First, it outlines the development of devolution in Scotland, showing how different forces and constitutional understandings have shaped contemporary arrangements. Second, it discusses the constitutional status of devolution along two—albeit inter-related—dimensions: the *juridical*—i.e., how the powers of the Scottish Parliament and Government are understood by the courts; and the *political*—i.e., the status of the devolved institutions vis-à-vis the UK Parliament and Government. Finally, it briefly considers the future of devolution in Scotland, in the light of the two key contemporary destabilizing forces, namely the ongoing pressure for independence, and the impact of Brexit.

THE DEVELOPMENT OF DEVOLVED GOVERNMENT IN SCOTLAND

The single most important explanation for the development of devolution in Scotland has been as a response to nationalism. Sometimes that has been nationalism with a capital 'N'—i.e., the electoral success of the Scottish National Party (SNP), the central aim of which is to secure Scotland's independence. At other times, it has been nationalism with a small 'n'—i.e., the perception, even amongst those committed to maintaining the Union, that Scotland is nevertheless a distinct political community with a right to self-determination and (a degree of) self-government.[8] That is not to say that there have not also been genuine constitutional weaknesses in the governance of Scotland. But the perceived urgency of responding to those problems, and the nature of the response in the form of increased autonomy for Scotland, have been a result of constitutional grievances being filtered through, and magnified by, a nationalist lens.

THE GROWTH OF ADMINISTRATIVE DEVOLUTION

The legacy of the Union of 1707 was to preserve a distinct sense of Scottish national identity, and one which was expressed in institutional as much as in cultural terms. The Union settlement preserved elements of Scots civic life which, at a time of minimal state intervention, were regarded as important markers of national identity—the legal system, the Royal Burghs and, above all, the Presbyterian church. However, Mitchell argues:

---

[8] On 'nationalist-Unionism', see C. Kidd, *Union and Unionisms: Political Thought in Scotland, 1500–2000* (2008).

The union was not simply a settlement which preserved particular Scottish institutions, but an agreement that Scottish institutions should be protected. In other words, the underlying principle was that Scottish national identity should be protected, but that might take different institutional forms at different times . . . Scotland's constitutional status was archetypically that of a component of a union state, not a unitary state.[9]

As the functions of the central state expanded, therefore, a distinct Scottish administration began to emerge—partly as a pragmatic response to distinctive local conditions, and partly for symbolic reasons. Initially, as elsewhere in the UK, this was primarily through the formation of functional boards, but these were eventually brought under the control of the Scottish Office, albeit somewhat later than the ending of the board system in England.[10] The establishment of the Scottish Office itself seems to have been motivated primarily by symbolic concerns—the need to respond to the perceived neglect of Scottish affairs.[11] Although questions of good government also played a part[12]—the desirability of ministerial and parliamentary oversight of Scottish administration—the acknowledgment of a distinct territorial dimension to the governance of Scotland was an important exception to the general principle of functional organization within central government.

The dominant constitutional question in the late nineteenth and early twentieth centuries was the question of Home Rule for Ireland. There was some interest in extending Home Rule to Scotland, as part of a programme of 'Home Rule all round', and this was official Labour Party policy until 1958. In 1949–50, 1.7 million people signed a 'National Covenant' expressing a commitment to Home Rule.[13] However, until the 1970s, there were no serious proposals for an elected Scottish assembly. Instead, the pattern was one of steady accretion of responsibilities by the Scottish Office, with opposition parties in particular willing to play 'the Scottish card' to argue for greater recognition of Scottish distinctiveness.[14] The Scottish Office became a 'state within a state,'[15] always headed by a Scottish politician, and the Secretary of State for Scotland was expected to represent Scottish interests within the Cabinet beyond the specific responsibilities of the Office.[16]

THE KILBRANDON COMMISSION AND THE SCOTLAND ACT 1978

It was only in the late 1960s that the prospect of legislative devolution for Scotland began to be taken seriously. The key impetus was rising support for the SNP (which had been at the margins of Scottish electoral politics since its formation in 1934), and in particular Winnie Ewing's unexpected victory for the party in the 1967 Hamilton by-election. The Labour Government at Westminster felt it had to react, but the scope

---

[9] Mitchell, *Devolution in the UK*, above n. 5, 10.
[10] See A. Page, *Constitutional Law of Scotland* (2015) paras. 1.26–1.29.
[11] Mitchell, *Devolution in the UK*, above n. 5, 17, 19.   [12] Ibid., 17.
[13] See Mitchell, *The Scottish Question*, above n. 4, 88–92.
[14] Mitchell, *Devolution in the UK*, above n. 5, 25, 30, 34.   [15] Page, above n. 10, para. 1.38.
[16] Mitchell, *Devolution in the UK*, above n. 5, 19.

for additional administrative devolution, and the likelihood of it paying further electoral dividends, was considered to be limited.[17] The eventual response was the establishment of the Royal Commission on the Constitution (the Kilbrandon Commission) in 1969 to consider reform of the territorial constitution. The Commission reported in 1973, recommending (with two commissioners dissenting) the creation of a legislative assembly for Scotland.[18]

In the Kilbrandon Report, we find a mixture of all three understandings of the constitutional significance of devolution, referred to above. The Report contained a diagnosis of general constitutional discontent throughout the UK, raising 'the presumption that there was a basic fault in the system of government which had nothing to do with nationalism—i.e., that government was too centralised'.[19] The sense of alienation and frustration that gave rise to a desire for greater participation in government in Scotland (and Wales) existed everywhere, and 'the basic need was for people in Britain as a whole to win back power from London'.[20] In other words, the UK constitution required fundamental reform to improve its democratic credentials.[21] However, the Commission acknowledged that it was the sense of Scottish (and Welsh) national identity that caused frustration to be felt—and expressed—more keenly in those territories, and its proposals for reform were correspondingly limited. In keeping with the understanding of the UK as a union state, diversity in governance arrangements was regarded as a source of strength, which should continue to be respected.[22] Nevertheless, devolution was understood by the Commission in essentially unitary and top-down terms, as 'the delegation of central government power without the relinquishment of sovereignty'.[23]

As far as Scotland was concerned, the constitutional problems to which legislative devolution was considered to provide the solution were threefold. First, Scotland had a separate legal system, but no dedicated legislature, giving rise to persistent complaints about the neglect of Scottish law reform by the Westminster Parliament.[24] Second, there was perceived to be an over-concentration of functions in the Scottish Office, and a corresponding lack of democratic accountability to the Scottish electorate.[25] Third, and most fundamental, was what later came to be called the 'democratic deficit', namely the divergence between voting patterns in Scotland and the rest of the UK. This was problematic because of the overwhelming dominance of England within the UK. As McCrone has put it 'so long as Scotland and England voted more or less the same way, the constitutional anomaly whereby the United Kingdom always got a government the English voted for did not matter'.[26] But the decline of the Conservative vote in Scotland from the 1950s and the rise of the SNP in the 1960s and 70s disrupted the pattern of two party politics in Scotland, increasing the risk that Scotland might get a government it had *not* voted for, and exacerbating the other democratic weaknesses in the system of administrative devolution.

---

[17] Ibid., 28–9.   [18] *Report of the Royal Commission on the Constitution 1969–73*, Cmnd 5460 (1973).
[19] Ibid., para. 6.   [20] Ibid., para. 6.   [21] Ibid., para. 269.   [22] Ibid., para. 417.
[23] Ibid., para. 543.   [24] Ibid., para 1101.   [25] Ibid., paras 363, 1101.
[26] D. McCrone, 'Scotland Out of the Union? The Rise and Rise of the Nationalist Agenda' (2012) 83 Pol Q 69 at 73.

Despite these principled arguments in favour of devolution, the response to the Kilbrandon Report was politically driven. The continued rise of the SNP, encouraged by the discovery of North Sea oil, meant that the minority Labour governments elected in February and October 1974 had little choice but to act on Kilbrandon's recommendations. However, considerable opposition remained amongst Labour MPs, and the first attempt to legislate for devolution via the Scotland and Wales Bill 1976 was abandoned in February 1977 when the government lost a timetabling motion.[27] Nevertheless, continued electoral pressure from the SNP meant that another Scotland-only Bill was introduced later the same year and, with support from the Liberal party, became the Scotland Act 1978. This was, though, a weak and grudging measure of devolution.[28] Crucially, also, in order to appease backbench critics, the government had conceded that a referendum would be held in Scotland before the Act was brought into force, and the notorious 'Cunningham amendment' required at least 40 per cent of the electorate to vote in favour of devolution.

The referendum was duly held on 1 March 1979. Although a small majority (51.6 per cent) supported the establishment of a Scottish Assembly, the threshold requirement was not satisfied. In consequence, the SNP withdrew support for the Labour Government, and on 28 March, it was defeated on a confidence vote in the House of Commons. Following the 1979 General Election, the incoming Conservative Government repealed the 1978 Act.

THE SCOTTISH CONSTITUTIONAL CONVENTION AND THE SCOTLAND ACT 1998

It was the election of four successive Conservative governments during the 1980s and 1990s that finally cemented public support in Scotland for legislative devolution. The Conservatives' ability to secure landslide majorities at Westminster, while Scots voters returned equally overwhelming majorities of Labour MPs, graphically illustrated the perceived democratic deficit in the governance of Scotland. Moreover, not only did the Conservative governments have only limited electoral support in Scotland, but (particularly under the premiership of Margaret Thatcher) they were also regarded as insensitive to Scottish distinctiveness. Unitarist rather than unionist in her instincts, Thatcher saw the Scottish Office—like local authorities—as just another layer of bureaucracy standing in the way of radical reform of the role and operation of the state.[29] The democratic deficit was epitomized by the 'Poll Tax' (or Community Charge), which was introduced in Scotland in 1989,[30] a year earlier than in England and Wales.

---

[27] Mitchell, *Devolution in the UK*, above n. 5, 120–4.   [28] Ibid., 124–6.

[29] Ibid., 30; see also C. Kidd and M. Petrie, 'The Independence Referendum in Historical and Political Context' in A. McHarg et al. (eds.), *The Scottish Independence Referendum: Constitutional and Political Implications* (2016), 38–41.

[30] Abolition of Domestic Rates etc. (Scotland) Act 1987. For an account of the opposition to the Poll Tax in Scotland and its constitutional significance, see M. Goldoni and C. McCorkindale, 'Why We (Still) Need a Revolution' (2013) 14 *German Law Journal* 2197, 2217–21.

This was a deeply unpopular, ideologically-driven reform of local government taxation which led to widespread civil disobedience in the form of a non-payment campaign. Although it was demand from within the Conservative party in Scotland that led to its early introduction north of the border, it was only the fact that the Scottish Office was controlled by a party that Scots had not voted for that enabled the policy to be adopted at all. In addition, it was not opposition in Scotland that led to the Poll Tax eventually being abandoned, but rather the fact that it proved to be equally unpopular when it was later introduced in England and Wales.

Although support for the SNP declined dramatically after 1979 (falling from 11 to just two seats), the tendency of opposition parties to 'play the Scottish card'[31] meant that opposition to Thatcherism nevertheless came to be seen in nationalist terms. The Conservative party was regarded not merely as having no mandate to govern Scotland, but in some more existential way as 'anti-Scottish'[32] and a threat to Scottish national identity.[33]

Matters came to a head after the 1987 General Election, at which the Conservatives secured a 101-seat majority, but saw their support in Scotland fall to just 10 seats out of 72 (from 22 seats out of 71 in 1979). In 1988, the Campaign for a Scottish Assembly (set up in 1980 to keep the case for devolution alive) issued a *Claim of Right for Scotland*, which asserted the 'sovereign right of the Scottish people to determine the form of Government best suited to their needs.'[34] Later signed by 58 out of Scotland's (then) 72 MPs, the Claim of Right deliberately echoed earlier *Claims* of 1689 and 1842. The Claim went on to assert the fundamental flaws in Scotland's governance arrangements—flaws which were said to undermine the spirit of the Treaty of Union—and to make the case for a Scottish assembly:

> Scotland, if it is to remain Scotland, can no longer live with such a constitution and has nothing to hope for from it. They must now show enterprise by starting the reform of their own government.[35]

In 1989, a Scottish Constitutional Convention (SCC) was established to draw up plans for devolution. This was an unofficial body that enjoyed support not only from the Labour and Liberal Democrat parties in Scotland,[36] but also from key civic institutions such as the Church of Scotland, the Scottish Trades Union Congress and the Convention of Scottish Local Authorities.[37] The SCC's final report, published in 1995,[38] recommended the establishment of a powerful devolved parliament. Unlike the weak model of devolution proposed in the Scotland Act 1978, this would be constituted on a reserved powers, rather than conferred powers basis—i.e., it would have plenary

---

[31] Mitchell, *Devolution in the UK*, 30.   [32] Ibid.

[33] See Report of the Constitutional Steering Group, *A Claim of Right for Scotland* (1988).

[34] See House of Commons Library, *Claim of Right for Scotland*, Debate Pack No 2016–0158 (2016).

[35] Constitutional Steering Group, above n. 33, epilogue.

[36] The SNP was initially represented in the Convention but withdrew when it became clear that it would not consider the option of independence.

[37] See J. McFadden, 'The Scottish Constitutional Convention' [1995] PL 215.

[38] *Scotland's Parliament, Scotland's Right*.

legislative competence subject to specific exceptions. Also in contrast to the 1978 model, it would have competence across the full range of Scottish Office responsibilities, as well as limited tax-varying powers. With only minor modifications, the SCC's blueprint for devolution was eventually enacted in the Scotland Act 1998.

Although formally a creature of the UK Parliament, its origins in the work of the SCC gave the Scottish Parliament a strongly autochthonous quality, reflecting an understanding of the UK as a union state in which Scots enjoyed a right to self-government as an expression of their distinct national identity. This was reinforced by the outcome of a pre-legislative referendum, held on 11 September 1997, in which 74.3 per cent voted in favour of establishing a Scottish Parliament, and 63.5 per cent in favour of it having tax-varying powers (on a 60.1 per cent turnout). There was some doubt about whether a referendum was either necessary or desirable, but strong popular endorsement both helped to ease the passage of the subsequent Scotland Bill through Parliament and has been regarded as giving Holyrood a degree of political entrenchment.[39]

Nevertheless, as with the Kilbrandon Report, the constitutional narrative surrounding the 1998 Act was not entirely consistent. Alongside the theme of protecting Scottish autonomy, there were strong overtones of democratic renewal. This was reflected in the design of the new Scottish institutions, which were modelled on the Westminster Parliament (i.e., with an executive chosen from and accountable to the legislature), but with some important departures. The SCC saw devolution as an opportunity to make fundamental improvements in the way Scotland was governed, increasing its openness, accountability, accessibility and responsiveness,[40] and ushering in 'a way of politics that is radically different from the rituals of Westminster: more participative, more creative, less needlessly confrontational.'[41] Thus the 1998 Act created a unicameral parliament, elected by proportional representation, and with a strong committee system in place of a second chamber. The 1999 report of the Consultative Steering Group, established to advise on the new Parliament's procedures, also emphasized principles of power-sharing, accountability, access and participation, and equal opportunities.[42]

In addition, devolution was part of a wider programme of constitutional reform pursued by the New Labour government elected in 1997, alongside enactment of the Human Rights Act, reform of the House of Lords, freedom of information legislation, regulation of political parties, and a commitment (ultimately abandoned) to reform the House of Commons' electoral system. Alongside other constraints on Westminster's legislative freedom imposed by EU law and the growth of 'common law constitutionalism', the creation of a legally-limited Scottish Parliament might be seen as part of a new model of constrained constitutionalism, rather than simply a marker of its subordinate status.[43]

---

[39] See *Report of the Independent Commission on Referendums* (2018) paras 2.13–2.17.
[40] Scottish Constitutional Convention, above n. 37, 24.   [41] Ibid., 9.
[42] Consultative Steering Group, *Shaping Scotland's Parliament* (1999). It is questionable to what extent these principles, and the desire for a 'new politics' have been achieved in practice—see Commission on Parliamentary Reform, *Your Parliament, Your Voice: Report on the Scottish Parliament* (2017).
[43] See C. McCorkindale *et al.*, 'The Courts, Devolution and Constitutional Review' (2018) 36 *University of Queensland Law Journal* 289, 291–2.

At the same time—and despite the threat that the SCC identified that it posed to Scottish autonomy[44]—the Labour government was at pains to emphasize that Parliamentary sovereignty would remain intact:

> The UK Parliament is and will remain sovereign in all matters; but as part of Parliament's resolve to modernise the British constitution Westminster will be choosing to exercise that sovereignty by devolving legislative responsibilities to a Scottish Parliament without in any way diminishing its own power.'[45]

This was underlined by the—strictly unnecessary, on an orthodox understanding of Parliamentary sovereignty—inclusion of the statement in s. 28(7) of the Scotland Act 1998 that the power of the Scottish Parliament to legislate in devolved areas 'does not affect the power of the Parliament of the United Kingdom to make laws for Scotland.' Whereas the legislative competence of the Scottish Parliament would be subject to hard, legally-enforceable limits, preventing it from straying into reserved areas, the powers of the UK Parliament would be constrained only by what was to become known as the Sewel (or Legislative Consent) Convention: the expectation that 'Westminster would not normally legislate with regard to devolved matters in Scotland without the consent of the Scottish Parliament.'[46]

Nor were there any formal changes to the organization or operation of the Westminster Parliament and Government which might have suggested a move towards a more federal understanding of the territorial constitution. Apart from a reduction in the number of Scottish MPs from 72 to 59, and the creation of a new post of Advocate-General for Scotland,[47] it was business-as-usual at Westminster. Similarly, the limited provisions in the 1998 Act for interaction between the UK and devolved governments mainly suggested a hierarchical relationship, in which the UK Government would police the boundaries of devolved decision-making through powers of judicial referral[48] or (in limited circumstances) powers of veto and direction.[49] More general machinery for intergovernmental relations was again regarded as a matter for soft rather than hard law, contained in non-statutory Concordats and Memoranda of Understanding,[50] the development of which was treated as an internal government matter and was largely based on pre-devolution administrative practice.[51]

---

[44] See Scottish Constitution Convention, *Towards Scotland's Parliament* (1989), para. 5.1.

[45] Scottish Office, *Scotland's Parliament*, Cm 3658 (1997) para. 4.2.

[46] Lord Sewel, HL Deb, Vol. 592, col. 791 (21 July 1998).

[47] Scotland Act 1998, ss. 86 and 87. The Advocate General for Scotland is the UK Government's Law Officer in relation to Scots Law. The creation of the post was necessitated by the decision that the Lord Advocate, as head of the system of criminal prosecution in Scotland, as well as Law Officer, should become a member of the Scottish Government.

[48] Scotland Act 1998, ss. 33, 98 and Sched. 6.   [49] Scotland Act 1998, ss. 35 and 58.

[50] See *Devolution Memorandum of Understanding and Supplementary Agreements between the United Kingdom Government, the Scottish Ministers, the Welsh Ministers, and the Northern Ireland Executive Committee* (2013), available at: https://assets.publishing.service.gov.uk/government/uploads/system/uploads/attachment_data/file/316157/MoU_between_the_UK_and_the_Devolved_Administrations.pdf.

[51] See R. Rawlings, 'Concordats of the Constitution' (2000) 116 LQR 257.

POST-1998 DEVELOPMENTS

Despite the relatively generous powers conferred upon the Scottish Parliament and Government by the 1998 Act, devolution was always conceived of as a dynamic rather than fixed process. Sections 30 and 63 of the Scotland Act allowed the boundary between reserved and devolved competence to be adjusted by Order in Council, and these provisions have been used on numerous occasions to transfer additional executive or (less frequently) legislative powers from London to Edinburgh. In addition, there have been two major waves of post-1998 reform to Scottish devolution, both of which have clearly been a response to the resurgence of the SNP.

For the Labour party, one of the anticipated benefits of devolution was that it would 'kill Nationalism stone dead.'[52] This was expected to occur both because devolution would satisfy Scottish demands for self-government, and because the electoral system chosen for the Scottish Parliament—the Additional Member System—would prevent any party, including the SNP, from gaining an overall majority. However, at the 2007 Holyrood election, following two terms of Labour–Liberal Democrat coalition, the SNP overtook Labour by just one seat to become the largest party and formed a minority government. Four years later, the impossible happened, and the party won an overall majority (although it returned to minority government status in 2016).

Following the 2007 election, lacking parliamentary support to take decisive steps towards its ultimate goal of independence, the SNP government launched a 'National Conversation' on Scotland's constitutional future, setting out options for independence or extensive further devolution.[53] Feeling the need to respond, the unionist parties in Scotland (Labour, the Conservatives and the Liberal Democrats), with the support of the UK Government, set up the Calman Commission to review the operation of devolution.

The Calman Commission found that devolution was popular in Scotland and had largely worked well.[54] It saw little scope for transfers of further substantive areas of policy-making competence, but it identified a major weakness of the 1998 Act in relation to the financing of devolution. The 1998 Act allowed the Scottish Parliament to vary the basic rate of income tax by three pence above or below the rate set at Westminster. This was, however, regarded as too restricted to be an effective fiscal tool and in fact it had never been used. All other fiscal powers, with the exception of local government taxation, were reserved to Westminster, and the Scottish Government also lacked borrowing powers. It was, therefore, dependent upon a block grant from the Treasury, set (as Scottish Office funding had been prior to devolution) using the so-called 'Barnett Formula' by reference to a percentage of spending in devolved policy areas for England. Although this arrangement ensured a relatively generous share of public expenditure for

---

[52] Attributed to George Robertson MP, as Shadow Secretary of State for Scotland, in 1995.

[53] Scottish Government, *Choosing Scotland's Future: A National Conversation: Independence and Responsibility in the Modern World* (2008).

[54] See Commission on Scottish Devolution, *The Future of Scottish Devolution within the Union: A First Report* (2008); Commission on Scottish Devolution, *Serving Scotland Better: Scotland and the United Kingdom in the 21st Century: Final Report* (2009).

Scotland, the Calman Commission considered it to be flawed in two main respects. First, it reduced policy flexibility by tying overall devolved expenditure to UK government choices on expenditure in England, as well as by denying Scottish governments important policy instruments. Second, Calman considered that it undermined the responsibility of devolved governments in Scotland. Since governments were responsible for spending money, but not raising it, party competition focused on expenditure rather than fiscal choices, and governments could pass the buck for policy failures by blaming Westminster for inadequate funding.

The Calman Commission's proposals for fiscal reform were partially, though not entirely, implemented by the Scotland Act 2012. This provided for a significant increase in the Scottish Parliament's tax-raising powers (and a corresponding reduction in the block grant) through an obligation (rather than merely a power) to set a 'Scottish Rate of Income Tax', to compensate for a 10 pence reduction in the basic and higher rate of income tax set by the UK Parliament for Scottish taxpayers. It also devolved power over Stamp Duty Land Tax and Landfill Tax, as well as enabling the Scottish Government to borrow (with Treasury consent) on the bond markets to finance capital expenditure.

The Calman Commission's reports are also notable for their attempt, for the first time, to articulate principled limits to devolution, via an understanding of the political, economic and cultural underpinnings of the union,[55] as well as for their emphasis on the importance of effective machinery for intergovernmental relations in order to successfully negotiate the competing demands of autonomy and integration.[56] These aspects of the reports did not, however, result in any concrete changes to devolution.

Before the 2012 Act was even enacted, the constitutional debate had moved on in Scotland. The SNP majority at the 2011 election meant it now had parliamentary support—and a popular mandate—to pursue a referendum on independence. In October 2012, via the so-called 'Edinburgh Agreement', the UK Government agreed to facilitate the holding of an independence referendum, but it refused to agree a second referendum question on a proposal for further devolution. Nevertheless, during the long independence referendum campaign it became clear that, even if there was not yet majority support for ending the union, there was substantial public appetite for additional reforms to devolution going beyond the Calman Commission's recommendations. A series of individual initiatives by the unionist parties culminated in the (in)famous 'Vow', published in the *Daily Record* on 16 September 2014, in which the three party leaders promised to deliver extensive new powers to the Scottish Parliament in the event of a No vote.

On the morning after the independence referendum, the Prime Minister, David Cameron announced the establishment of a commission, chaired by Lord Smith of Kelvin, and with representatives from all five parties with seats in the Scottish Parliament (Labour, Conservatives, Liberal Democrats, SNP and Greens), to draw up a package of measures for further devolution. By 27 November, the parties had reached

---

[55] See Commission on Scottish Devolution, *First Report*, above n. 54, Ch. 4.
[56] Commission on Scottish Devolution, *Final Report*, above n. 54, Part 4.

agreement,[57] and the Smith Commission's proposals were in due course enacted in the Scotland Act 2016, again with relatively little modification.

The 2016 Act reforms addressed three main issues. First, like the Calman Commission, Smith recommended further substantial fiscal devolution, although stopping short of the 'full fiscal autonomy' sought by the Scottish Government. Thus, the 2016 Act provided for the (almost) complete devolution of income tax, control over the Aggregates Levy and Air Passenger Duty,[58] and assignment of VAT receipts.[59] Alongside the legislation, the UK and Scottish governments negotiated a new Fiscal Framework governing the future calculation of Scotland's block grant.[60] Secondly, the 2016 Act devolved a (somewhat disparate) range of new substantive powers, although again these did not go as far as the Scottish Government sought. Of greatest significance in constitutional terms were powers over elections to and the composition of the Scottish Parliament,[61] over welfare benefits,[62] and over abortion.[63] All of these policy areas raise issues of citizenship and social citizenship, and devolution therefore paves the way for potentially significant variations in the terms of citizenship in different parts of the UK. Thirdly, and of greatest constitutional significance, were proposals to guarantee the permanence of the Scottish Parliament and Scottish Government, and to place the Sewel Convention on a statutory footing.[64] These were constitutionally significant because they appeared to address one of the key weaknesses of devolution identified by supporters of independence— its lack of constitutional entrenchment[65]—and hence to place limits on the sovereignty of the UK Parliament. In the event, the statutory language adopted by the 2016 Act was hedged around with qualifications and, as will be discussed further below, seemed designed to provide only symbolic reassurance rather than legally-enforceable guarantees.

The UK Government claimed that the 2016 Act reforms would make the Scottish Parliament 'one of the most powerful devolved parliaments in the world.'[66] Although there is some room for scepticism about this claim,[67] Holyrood clearly does enjoy extensive powers and these will increase still further following Brexit. Thanks to the reserved model of devolution, powers currently exercised at EU level in areas that are

---

[57] *Report of the Smith Commission for Devolution of Further Powers to the Scottish Parliament* (2014).

[58] Devolution of these two taxes had been recommended by the Calman Commission, but not implemented.

[59] Scotland Act 2016, Part 2.

[60] See S. Eden, 'Scotland Act 2016: Further Tax Powers Come North' (2016) 20 Edin LR 376; M. Lazarowicz and J. McFadden, *The Scottish Parliament: Law and Practice* (5th edn., 2018) Ch. 10.

[61] See P. Reid, 'Elections and Supermajorities: Simply Another Staging Post?' (2016) 20 Edin. LR 367.

[62] See T. Mullen, 'Devolution of Social Security' (2016) 20 Edin. LR 382.

[63] See M. Neal, 'Devolving Abortion Law' (2016) 20 Edin. LR 399.

[64] See Scotland Act 2016, ss. 1 and 2.

[65] See A. McHarg, 'The Constitutional Case for Independence', in A. McHarg *et al.* (eds.), above n. 29, 115–21.

[66] See, e.g., David Mundell MP, 'David Mundell Calls for End to Blame Games', BBC Website, 16 May 2016.

[67] See N McEwen, 'A Constitution in Flux: the Dynamics of Constitutional Change after the Referendum', in A. McHarg *et al.* (eds.), above n. 29, 234–40.

otherwise devolved (such as agriculture, fisheries or environmental regulation) will default to the Scottish Parliament, although this will be subject in some areas to new UK-wide common frameworks,[68] and calls by the Scottish Government for even further devolution post-Brexit (for example in relation to immigration)[69] have so far been resisted.

Clearly, however, legislative devolution has turned out to be far more than a mechanism for preserving Scotland's autonomy against the imposition of unpopular policies. Rather, it has provided a platform for the articulation of Scotland's distinctiveness, helping to embed a 'Scottish frame of reference'[70] in a way which always has the potential to generate new demands for recognition of Scotland's voice and Scottish interests spilling beyond the existing boundaries of devolved competence. But as both the Calman and Smith Commissions recognized, strong provision for Scottish 'self-rule' has not been matched by effective mechanisms for 'shared rule'—for recognition of Scotland's voice in matters of continued UK decision-making, or for mediation between competing territorial interests in areas of overlapping competence.[71] Here, the potential 'democratic deficit' remains, arguably exacerbated post-devolution by the fact that the Westminster institutions now combine roles as representatives of both the UK and England. As will be discussed further below, this has proved to be a significant source of tension, particularly in the context of Brexit.

THE CONSTITUTIONAL STATUS OF DEVOLUTION

The devolved institutions created by the Scotland Act 1998 enjoy both legislative and executive power. The Scottish Parliament has the freedom to enact new laws in areas of devolved competence, and to amend or repeal UK Parliament legislation in those areas. The executive competence of the Scottish Government mirrors the legislative competence of the Scottish Parliament, so that the Scottish Ministers are able to exercise statutory and prerogative powers in devolved areas previously exercised by UK Ministers,[72] as well as new powers or duties conferred upon them by Acts of the Scottish Parliament (ASPs). The Scottish Ministers also have a range of additional executively-devolved powers (i.e., exercised under UK legislation, where legislative power remains reserved to Westminster) conferred either by or under the Scotland Acts, or by other sectoral legislation. In addition, since competence constraints bite only on ASPs or on the exercise by Ministers of specific legal functions,[73] both the

---

[68] European Union (Withdrawal) Act 2018, s. 12.
[69] Scottish Government, *Scotland's Place in Europe* (2016) Ch. 4.
[70] McCrone, above n. 26, 75.   [71] See McEwen, above n. 67, 237–40.
[72] Scotland Act 1998, s. 53.
[73] Scotland Act 1998, ss. 29 and 54. NB: the cross-cutting constraints of EU law and Convention rights apply on a broader basis than the subject-matter constraints to executive 'acts', including failures to act—Scotland Act 1998, s. 57(2), and see further below.

Parliament and Government enjoy unrestricted power to discuss and/or advocate for policy changes even in relation to matters reserved to the UK level.

The question remains, though, how the constitutional significance of these devolved powers should be understood. As we have seen, the Scottish Parliament and Government are in legal terms creatures of statute: they were created by the Westminster Parliament and their powers remain dependent upon UK legislation. In political terms, however, self-government was clearly *demanded by* rather than granted to Scots voters. Moreover, devolution and its subsequent development has been accompanied by intimations of an alternative constitutional model of constrained, but guaranteed autonomy. How best to account for the constitutional significance of devolution is not merely an issue of academic interest. Rather it has real implications for the extent of devolved autonomy in practice, and the ways in which the Scottish Government and Parliament are able to exercise their powers. These issues play out across two, related, dimensions: first, regarding how the courts respond to legal challenges brought against the devolved institutions; and, second, concerning the relationship between Holyrood and Westminster.

DEVOLUTION AND THE COURTS

As the Scottish Parliament is not a sovereign legislature, it is uncontroversial that its Acts—as well as the decisions of the Scottish Government—can be subject to judicial challenge. As Lord Rodger stated in *Whaley v Lord Watson*,[74] Holyrood had 'joined that wider family of parliaments' which 'owe their existence and powers to statute and are in various ways subject to the law and to the courts which act to uphold the law.' It followed that, unlike Westminster, the Parliament and its members enjoyed no general legal privilege entitling them to regulate their own affairs free from judicial interference, except insofar as expressly provided for in the 1998 Act.[75]

Nevertheless, the courts have had to consider how they should approach the question of review of ASPs and, more fundamentally, how they should be categorized in legal terms. The latter question was settled by the Supreme Court in *AXA General Insurance Ltd v Lord Advocate*.[76] The case involved a challenge to the Damages (Asbestos-Related Conditions) (Scotland) Act 2009, which enabled persons exposed to asbestos and who had developed non-symptomatic pleural plaques to recover damages, reversing the decision of the House of Lords in *Rothwell v Chemical and Insulating Co Ltd*.[77] The appellants argued, *inter alia*, that ASPs should be regarded as a species of delegated legislation which were amenable to judicial review on normal common law grounds. Since the House of Lords had found in *Rothwell* that pleural plaques did not cause harm, they argued that the legislation was irrational in the *Wednesbury* sense and therefore invalid.

---

[74] 2000 SC 340, 349.   [75] See Scotland Act 1998, ss. 40–42.
[76] [2012] 1 AC 868.   [77] [2008] AC 281.

The Supreme Court rejected this argument. Although ASPs derived their authority from an Act of the UK Parliament, this did not mean that they were subject to judicial control in the same way as delegated legislation made by ministers. According to Lord Hope:

> The Scottish Parliament takes its place under our constitutional arrangements as a self-standing democratically elected legislature. Its democratic mandate to make laws for the people of Scotland is beyond question. Acts that the Scottish Parliament enacts which are within its legislative competence enjoy, in that respect, the highest legal authority.[78]

Accordingly:

> Acts of the Scottish Parliament are not subject to judicial review at common law on the grounds of irrationality, unreasonableness or arbitrariness . . . it would also be quite wrong for the judges to substitute their views on these issues for the considered judgment of a democratically elected legislature . . .[79]

For Lord Reed, the ordinary grounds of judicial review—predicated on the idea that statutory powers are conferred for a purpose which imposes limits on the lawful exercise of those powers—also had no analytical purchase in relation to ASPs. Within the limits set down by the Scotland Act, the Scottish Parliament had plenary legislative power which:

> is as ample as it could possibly be . . . The Act leaves it to the Scottish Parliament itself, as a democratically elected legislature, to determine its own policy goals. It has to decide for itself the purposes for which its legislative powers should be used, and the political and other considerations which are relevant to its exercise of those powers.[80]

However, this did not mean that ASPs were wholly immune from challenge at common law. Both Lord Hope and Lord Reed stressed that, in exceptional circumstances, the courts could strike down ASPs which breached the Rule of Law, although they arrived at this conclusion by different routes. For Lord Hope, it was a matter of first principle that there were constitutional limits that even a democratically elected legislature could not breach; given the status of the Rule of Law as 'the ultimate controlling factor on which our constitution is based . . . the judges must retain the power to insist that legislation of that extreme kind is not law which the courts will recognise.'[81] By contrast, Lord Reed relied upon the more constitutionally-orthodox route of the principle of legality. In enacting the 1998 Act:

> Parliament did not legislate in a vacuum: it legislated for a liberal democracy founded on particular constitutional principles and traditions. That being so, Parliament cannot be taken to have intended to establish a body which was free to abrogate fundamental rights or to violate the rule of law.[82]

---

[78] *AXA*, above n. 76, para. 46.   [79] Ibid., para. 52. See also Lord Reed at paras. 147–8.
[80] Ibid., para. 146.   [81] Ibid., para. 51.   [82] Ibid., para. 153.

While the decision adds an element of uncertainty to the scope of the Scottish Parliament's legislative competence which litigants will naturally attempt to exploit,[83] *AXA* nevertheless suggests that Holyrood exists within a constrained constitutional order in which the exercise of the powers of the UK Parliament, as well as its own, are to be guided by considerations of constitutional principle. This is reinforced by the decision in *H v Lord Advocate*,[84] in which the Supreme Court held that the Scotland Act 1998 is a constitutional statute which therefore cannot be impliedly repealed.

The primary grounds of challenge to ASPs, then, are those set out in section 29 of the 1998 Act.[85] The most important restrictions[86] on the Parliament's legislative competence fall into two categories. First are subject-matter restrictions, which define the division of competences between the UK and Scottish Parliaments. Holyrood may not make laws which 'relate to' the list of policy areas reserved to Westminster set out in Schedule 5.[87] In addition, it may not modify certain protected statutes listed in Schedule 4,[88] nor may it modify the 'law on reserved matters', except insofar as this is part of a reform of the general rules of Scots private or criminal law which are common to reserved and devolved matters.[89] Second are cross-cutting constraints which apply to legislation otherwise within devolved competence: ASPs must not be incompatible with rights contained in the European Convention on Human Rights nor (for the time being) with European Union (EU) law.[90]

Although there are ample opportunities for challenging legislative competence,[91] by December 2018, only 18 out of the 281 Acts enacted by the Parliament had been subject to legal challenge post-enactment,[92] plus one bill was the subject of a pre-enactment

[83] In *Moohan v Lord Advocate* [2014] UKSC 67, there was an unsuccessful attempt to argue that legislation denying prisoners the right to vote in the independence referendum was in breach of the Rule of Law. In *Re UK Withdrawal from the European Union (Legal Continuity) (Scotland) Bill* [2018] UKSC 64, it was argued that the existence of separate legislation governing the status of retained EU law after Brexit for devolved and reserved matters would breach the Rule of Law principle of legal certainty, but this was also robustly rejected by the Court (see para. 86).

[84] [2013] 1 AC 413.

[85] N.B: these limitations also apply to acts of the Scottish Ministers (Scotland Act 1998, ss. 54 and 57(2)), subject to the possibility of powers being executively devolved and therefore not subject to the subject-matter constraints.

[86] The Parliament is also prohibited from legislating extra-territorially (s. 29(2)(a)), or from removing the Lord Advocate from his position as head of the system of criminal prosecution and investigation of deaths in Scotland (s. 29(2)(e)).

[87] Scotland Act 1998, s. 29(2)(b).

[88] Scotland Act 1998, s. 29(2)(c). The Sched. 4 restrictions do not, however, occupy the policy field in the same way as the Sched. 5 restrictions. In other words, the Scottish Parliament may legislate in the same policy areas, provided that this supplements the relevant UK legislation and does not modify it, either expressly or in substance—see Continuity Bill reference, above n. 83, para. 51.

[89] Scotland Act 1998, s. 29(4) and Sched. 4, para. 2. See *Martin v Most* 2010 SC (UKSC) 40; *Henderson v HM Advocate* 2011 JC 96.

[90] Scotland Act 1998, s. 29(2)(d). When the UK leaves the EU, the latter restriction will be lifted, but UK Ministers will be able to make regulations prohibiting the Scottish Parliament from modifying retained EU law in specified areas—European Union (Withdrawal) Act 2018, s. 12(1)(2).

[91] See McCorkindale *et al.*, above n. 43, 291.

[92] Ibid., 295–8; see also Lazarowicz and McFadden, above n. 60, Ch. 9.

reference to the Supreme Court.[93] Provisions in six Acts/Bills have so far been found to be beyond competence,[94] five on grounds of breach of Convention rights, which has been by far the most common basis for challenge, and the sixth on the ground that it modified protected statutes.[95] The relative paucity of challenges has been attributed to the effectiveness of pre-legislative *vires* checks[96] and to the flexibility mechanisms built into the devolution settlement—the ability to use section 30 Orders to confer additional competences on the Parliament, or the use of the Sewel Convention to allow Holyrood to consent to UK legislation on devolved matters where doubts exist about the competence of proposed Scottish Bills.[97] Nevertheless, there is now a sufficient body of case law on the boundaries of devolved competence to allow an understanding of the nature of the interpretive challenges that arise and how the courts handle them.

Challenges brought on Convention rights or EU law grounds raise few issues peculiar to the devolved context. Although they may result in legislation being struck down, rather than simply in a declaration of incompatibility or 'disapplication' as in the case of UK statutes, it is hard to detect much difference in the way in which the courts handle such challenges against Holyrood as compared with Westminster legislation. Thus, where questions of proportionality arise, the courts show a degree of deference towards the Scottish Parliament's legislative choices (albeit varying in extent depending on the context), and there is a statutory injunction, similar to that required by section 3 of the Human Rights Act 1998 or by the *Marleasing* principle,[98] to resolve competence issues through interpretation wherever possible.[99] However, one potential difference concerns the relevance of the Scottish Parliament's limited competence to the conduct of a proportionality assessment. This was raised but not resolved in the *Scotch Whisky Association* case,[100] which involved a challenge to legislation imposing a minimum unit price for alcohol as being incompatible with Art 34 TFEU. The fact that Holyrood had no competence in relation to alcohol duty (which might have been considered a less intrusive means of achieving the policy aim of reducing alcohol-related harms) was referred to as 'the elephant in the room'.

Nevertheless, the most challenging constitutional issues arise in relation to the subject-matter constraints. Such challenges raise a number of difficult interpretive

---

[93] Under Scotland Act 1998, s. 33.

[94] See *Cameron v Cottam* 2013 JC 12; *Salvesen v Riddell* 2013 SC (UKSC) 236; *Christian Institute v Lord Advocate* 2017 SC (UKSC) 29; *P v Scottish Ministers* 2017 SLT 271; *AB v HMA* 2017 SLT 401; Continuity Bill Reference, above n. 83.

[95] Continuity Bill Reference, above n. 83. See further below at nn. 107–8.

[96] See B. Adamson, 'The Protection of Human Rights in the Legislative Process in Scotland', in Murray Hunt *et al.* (eds.), *Parliaments and Human Rights: Redressing the Democratic Deficit* (2015) and C. McCorkindale and J.L. Hiebert, 'Vetting Bills in the Scottish Parliament for Legislative Competence' (2017) 21 Edin. LR 319.

[97] McCorkindale *et al.*, above n. 43, 297.

[98] *Marleasing SA v LA Comercial International de Alimentacion SA,* Case C-106/89 (1992) 1 CMLR 305.

[99] Scotland Act 1998, s. 101. According to Lord Hope in *Salvesen v Riddell*, above n. 94, para. 46 'the obligation to construe a provision in an Act of the Scottish Parliament so far as it is possible to do so is a strong one, and the court must prefer compatibility to incompatibility.'

[100] *Scotch Whisky Association v Lord Advocate* 2018 SC (UKSC) 94.

questions, the handling of which may significantly affect the scope of Holyrood's competence, and the relative balance of policy-making power as between the Scottish and UK Parliaments.[101] These include: determining the scope of reserved policy areas; deciding what it means to 'relate to' a reserved matter or 'modify' a protected statute; determining the 'purpose' and 'effect' of an impugned ASP;[102] and—in the context of a dynamic boundary between reserved and devolved matters—determining the time at which competence is to be judged (When a Bill is passed by the Parliament? When it receives Royal Assent? When it comes into force?).

The prevailing approach, set out most clearly by Lord Hope in *Imperial Tobacco*,[103] is to treat the 1998 Act in the same way as any other statute: i.e., it is to be interpreted according to the ordinary meaning of the words used, taking account of its purpose where relevant. In the context of a reserved powers model, this tends to favour a generous understanding of devolved competence: the constraints on competence are only those explicitly set out in the 1998 Act. At the same time, though, the detail and complexity of the reservations—and exceptions to reservations—in some areas means that a literal approach to interpretation could trip up an ASP with a predominantly devolved purpose, but which nevertheless strays into reserved areas. Attitudes to this issue have differed. In *Martin v Most*, which concerned whether a modification of Scots sentencing law which affected the reserved area of road traffic offences was within competence or not, Lord Hope preferred 'a generous application . . . which favours competence':[104]

> Given that the Scottish Parliament is plainly intended to regulate the Scottish legal system I am disinclined to find a construction of Schedule 4 which would require the Scottish Parliament, when modifying that system, to invoke Westminster's help to do no more than dot the i's and cross the t's of the necessary consequences.[105]

By contrast, Lord Rodger preferred a narrower approach to construction, seeing no constitutional objection to the fact that this would leave Holyrood dependent on Westminster for the achievement of its policy purposes. However, in *Imperial Tobacco*, Lord Hope held that, where an ASP has more than one purpose, one of which 'relates to' a reserved matter, the legislation will be invalid unless the reserved purpose 'can be regarded as consequential and thus of no real significance'.[106]

There is also a risk that the approach to interpretation could vary depending on the perceived political and constitutional significance of the case. For instance, in the recent Continuity Bill reference, the UK Government appeared to be arguing for an approach to competence significantly at odds with established jurisprudence. The case involved a challenge by the UK Government—the first competence dispute between

---

[101] See further, McCorkindale *et al.*, above n. 43, 302–5.
[102] Scotland Act 1998, s. 29(4): 'the question whether a provision . . . relates to a reserved matter is to be determined . . . by reference to the purpose of the provision, having regard (among other things) to its effect in all the circumstances.'
[103] *Imperial Tobacco v Lord Advocate* [2012] UKSC 61.   [104] Above n. 89, para. 38.
[105] Ibid., para 66.   [106] *Imperial Tobacco*, above n. 103, para. 43.

the UK and Scottish Governments to reach the courts—to the UK Withdrawal from the European Union (Legal Continuity) (Scotland) Bill. This was enacted to give continuity of effect to EU law in devolved areas post-Brexit, and was passed in the context of a major dispute between the UK and Scottish Governments over the allocation of decision-making competences returning from the EU, which resulted in the Scottish Parliament refusing to grant consent under the Sewel Convention to the European Union (Withdrawal) Act 2018 (which was nevertheless extended to Scotland anyway). The UK Government challenged the Bill on multiple grounds, including that it breached EU law and the Rule of Law, as well as encroaching upon various reserved matters.[107] The latter challenges were particularly notable, not only for their very expansive approach to the scope of the relevant reservations, but also because the Government attempted to read in various restrictions on competence based on assumptions about what powers the UK Parliament would have intended the Scottish Parliament to have in the event of Brexit, and about the general constitutional principles underpinning devolution. This approach seemed inconsistent with a reserved powers model, in which power to legislate in respect of unanticipated events falls by default to the devolved level. For the most part, the UK Government's arguments were rejected, with the Supreme Court reaffirming that 'The constitutional framework underlying the devolution settlement is neither more nor less than what is contained in the Scotland Act construed on principles which are now well settled.'[108] Nevertheless, the court did accept a novel argument that section 17 of the Bill (which purported to make the exercise of UK ministerial powers under future UK legislation affecting devolved matters subject to the consent of the Scottish Ministers) amounted to an unlawful modification of section 28(7) of the 1998 Act (as a protected statute) because it sought to place conditions on the unlimited power of the UK Parliament to continue to legislate for Scotland.

HOLYROOD AND WESTMINSTER

The Continuity Bill case is a good illustration of the way in which judicial interpretation of devolved competence may affect the balance of power between Westminster and Holyrood in policy disputes in areas of intersecting devolved and reserved competence. But it also demonstrates the fact that, while Westminster's sovereignty remains intact, it will always have the upper hand in such disputes, legally at least. Although the Supreme Court regarded the Continuity Bill as having been largely *within* devolved competence at the time the reference was made, the UK Government had a trump card. The effect of its power under section 33 of the 1998 Act to refer a Bill to the Supreme Court was to delay the enactment of the Continuity Bill (because Royal Assent cannot be granted until the competence question has been resolved). In the

---

[107] See Written Submission of the Advocate General for Scotland, available at: https://www.gov.uk/government/publications/supreme-court-case-no-uksc-20180080-written-submission.

[108] Above n. 83, para. 35.

meantime, the UK Parliament enacted the EU (Withdrawal) Act, which, *inter alia*, added the Withdrawal Act itself to the list of protected statutes that the Scottish Parliament is not permitted to modify. Since the Supreme Court held that competence is to be judged at the time legislation is *enacted* rather than when it is *passed*, this rendered much of the Continuity Bill *ultra vires* to the extent that it was inconsistent with equivalent provisions in the Withdrawal Act. Moreover, even if the UK Government had lost the case, the UK Parliament could simply have repealed the Scottish legislation. In other words, while Parliamentary sovereignty remains unaffected by devolution, the UK Parliament can simply resolve disputes with the Scottish Parliament by fiat—by legislating to override Holyrood legislation and/or by removing issues from the scope of devolved competence.

As was noted above, the protections provided for the devolved institutions against Westminster encroachment in the initial devolution arrangements were political rather than legal: the legitimacy that they gained from popular endorsement, and the operation of the Sewel Convention. Since 1999, the Sewel Convention has developed into the key mechanism for managing constitutional relations between the UK and Scottish Parliaments, albeit in practice it has acted as a means of *enabling* Westminster to enact legislation on devolved matters as well as for protecting Holyrood's autonomy against unwelcome Westminster intrusion.[109] The practice has also developed of seeking consent for legislation which changes the *scope* of devolved competence, as well as to statutes in areas of existing devolved competence.[110] The importance attached to the Sewel Convention was underlined by its recognition in the Scotland Act 2016.

Until recently, Sewel appeared to be an effective way of tempering Parliamentary sovereignty. While Parliament might *as a matter of law* retain unlimited power to legislate for Scotland, the practical reality seemed different. Thus, the need for consent was respected on all but one minor occasion (and subject to some disputes about whether particular pieces of legislation engaged the Convention); the threat of consent being refused was usually sufficient to lead to negotiation and compromise over the content of UK Bills; and where, exceptionally, consent could not be obtained, this had been respected—Scotland was removed from the scope of the offending provisions, and Holyrood was permitted to introduce its own legislation.

The Convention has, however, been put under severe strain by Brexit. There have been two major disputes between the UK and Scottish Governments over its application, which risk permanently weakening the protection it provides. The first concerned the need for devolved consent to the European Union (Notification of Withdrawal) Act 2018. The Scottish Government argued that, if legislation was necessary to authorize the triggering of the EU Withdrawal process under Article 50 TEU, such legislation

---

[109] For discussion of the constitutional functions of the Sewel Convention, see A. McHarg, 'Constitutional Change and Territorial Consent: the *Miller* Case and the Sewel Convention', in M. Elliott *et al.* (eds.), *The UK Constitution After Miller: Brexit and Beyond* (2018), 159–67.

[110] See Department for Constitutional Affairs, *Post-Devolution Primary Legislation Affecting Scotland*, Devolution Guidance Note 10 (2005), available at: https://www.gov.uk/government/publications/devolution-guidance-notes.

would engage the Sewel Convention because Brexit would necessarily impact on matters within devolved competence as well as affecting the scope of devolved competences. The UK Government rejected this analysis, arguing that withdrawal from the EU was a matter of international relations, which is reserved to the UK level. In the *Miller* case,[111] the Scottish Government intervened in the proceedings seeking a declaration that consent was required. However, the Supreme Court refused to decide the question, holding that statutory recognition of the Convention had not given rise to enforceable legal obligations; according to the court, it remained purely a matter of convention, and as such disputes about its operation or scope were not justiciable. This not only handed a *de facto* victory to the UK Government, which simply insisted on its position that consent was not required for the Notification of Withdrawal Act, but also negated any suggestion that statutory recognition of the Convention and of the permanence of the Scottish Parliament and Government had effected any fundamental enhancement of the constitutional status of devolution. While an argument could be mounted that the promise in section 1 of the 2016 Act, that the devolved institutions will not be abolished unless authorized by another referendum, amounts to a 'manner and form' constraint on the exercise of Westminster's legislative sovereignty,[112] the decision in *Miller* does not give much cause to expect that such an argument would be successful.

The second dispute arose in relation to the European Union (Withdrawal) Act 2018. Here, the UK Government did accept that the Sewel Convention was engaged and, following protracted negotiations, significantly amended the Bill in response to strenuous objections by the Scottish and Welsh Governments to its original drafting. Despite these amendments, the Scottish Parliament was still unwilling to consent to the Bill. Nevertheless, for the first time ever, it was enacted anyway without further amendment. As UK Ministers pointed out, the Sewel Convention does not establish an invariable rule, but rather requires only that devolved consent is *normally* required. However, instead of explaining what it was about in the, admittedly unusual, circumstances of Brexit which made it constitutionally acceptable to ignore the refusal of devolved consent, Ministers seemed to be advancing a different understanding of the Convention, such that it requires consent to be *sought*, but does not give the devolved legislatures a veto in relation to UK legislation on devolved matters if consent cannot be *secured*.[113] According to Bogdanor, writing in 1999, 'the relationship between Westminster and Edinburgh will be quasi-federal in normal times and unitary only in crisis times.'[114] It remains to be seen whether this dramatic reassertion of Parliamentary sovereignty will

---

[111] *R. (Miller) v Secretary of State for Exiting the European Union* [2017] 2 WLR 582.

[112] For a defence of manner and form constraints, see M. Gordon, *Parliamentary Sovereignty in the UK Constitution* (2015).

[113] See, e.g., the evidence of David Lidington MP and David Mundell MP to the House of Commons Public Administration and Constitutional Reform Committee, *Devolution and Exiting the European Union: Reconciling Differences and Building Strong Relations*, 8th Report, 2017–19, HC 1485, paras. 52, 57–9.

[114] V. Bogdanor, *Devolution in the United Kingdom* (1999) 287.

turn out to be temporary, or rather a lasting confirmation of Holyrood's constitutionally subordinate status.

How the constitutional significance of devolution is understood affects not only the relationship between the UK and Scottish Parliaments, but also that between the UK and Scottish Governments. Except insofar as UK Ministers have specific statutory consent or veto powers, there is no general relationship of hierarchy between the UK and Scottish Governments, and UK Ministers may not act in devolved areas unless they are specifically empowered to do so. Indeed, it was because it considered the EU (Withdrawal) Act to breach this principle that the Scottish Government felt unable to recommend consent to it, even in its amended form.[115] Thus, the Act gives UK Ministers the power to determine via regulations, and without having to secure devolved consent, that new UK-wide frameworks are necessary in areas currently governed by EU law, and so to prohibit the Scottish Parliament from legislating in those areas.[116]

With the exception of the decision to refer the Continuity Bill to the Supreme Court, successive UK Governments have not felt the need to exercise any of their formal powers over the devolved institutions in Scotland. And they have frequently been willing to acknowledge and respect the political authority of the devolved institutions. The most vivid example of this was in relation to the independence referendum, where the UK Government acknowledged the Scottish Government's mandate to hold a referendum and was willing to facilitate it, even though it considered that it was not within devolved competence to legislate for a referendum. Nevertheless, the authority it derives from its relationship with the UK Parliament, and the informal nature of the arrangements for inter-governmental relations effectively allow the UK Government to assert its will over the devolved administration, should it choose to do so.

The UK Government dominates the inter-governmental relations process both because it is able to set the agenda for discussion—and indeed to determine whether the Joint Ministerial Councils meet at all—and because there is no independent mechanism for resolving disputes between governments. As noted above, this is particularly problematic in areas where the UK Government represents both English voters and the UK electorate as a whole. This means that where territorial conflicts arise, for instance in relation to financial allocations or because of political divergence (such as in relation to Brexit), English interests are likely to prevail. The weakness of the devolved governments in the inter-governmental relations process has been repeatedly criticized,[117] but there is no sign of any imminent change. Thus, the influence of the devolved governments in areas of intersecting competences or overlapping interests

---

[115] Scottish Government, *Supplement Legislative Consent Memorandum: European Union (Withdrawal) Bill* (2018), available at: http://www.parliament.scot/S5ChamberOffice/LCM-S5-10a.pdf.

[116] European Union (Withdrawal) Act 2018, s. 12. The Act requires a 'consent decision' by the Scottish Parliament before regulations can be made, but this requirement can be satisfied by a refusal of consent, or even by a failure to consider the matter.

[117] See, e.g, Calman Commission, *Final Report*, above n. 54, Part 4; Smith Commission, above n. 57; House of Lords Constitution Committee, *Inter-Governmental Relations in the United Kingdom*, 11th Report, 2014–15, HL Paper 146; Public Administration and Constitutional Affairs Committee, above n. 113, Ch. 8.

remains dependent upon whatever political resources they are able to muster, rather than resting upon a secure legal or constitutional foundation.

SCOTLAND'S CONSTITUTIONAL FUTURE

As we have seen in this chapter, the strongest political resource available to those seeking recognition of Scotland's political voice has historically been nationalism: the assertion of a right on the part of Scottish voters to self-government and self-determination. In the context of Brexit, the threat of Scotland exiting from the Union has been made explicit. As soon as the result of the EU referendum was known, Scotland's First Minister, Nicola Sturgeon, made clear that, unless there was some recognition and accommodation of the fact that a majority of Scots voters had chosen to remain in the EU, the option of a second independence referendum was firmly 'on the table'.[118] When, in March 2017, it became obvious that the UK Government intended to trigger the UK's withdrawal from the EU under Article 50 TEU without securing the Scottish Government's agreement to the form that Brexit should take, Sturgeon activated that threat by announcing her intention, subsequently endorsed by a vote in the Scottish Parliament,[119] to seek agreement from the UK Government for a second referendum to be held in Autumn 2019. The Prime Minister's response was to reject the request. But crucial to the credibility of that stance was the result of the snap UK general election held in May 2017, at which the SNP lost a substantial proportion of its seats and vote share (albeit from an unprecedentedly high level in 2015). Since the referendum request was a major election issue in Scotland, this undermined the Scottish Government's claim to have a mandate for another referendum.

Although Brexit is in many ways a textbook illustration of the democratic and constitutional weaknesses of Scotland's constitutional position within the UK, it has not had the dramatic impact on support for independence that might have been expected. This is perhaps explicable by a stronger attachment to a UK rather than an EU identity amongst Scottish 'Remain' voters, as well as significant uncertainty about the impact of Brexit—uncertainty having been a major factor for those voting No to independence in 2014.[120] Thus, while support for Scottish independence remains at an historically high level,[121] the immediate threat of another referendum appears to have receded (although it clearly has not gone away). This may explain the robust attitude taken by the UK Government to the recognition claims made by the Scottish Government in relation to Brexit, and its willingness to assert an essentially unitary understanding of the territorial constitution. If the only protection for the devolved institutions lies in

[118] See http://www.bbc.co.uk/news/uk-scotland-36620375.
[119] Motion S5M-04710 (Nicola Sturgeon) SPOR, 28 March 2017 (Session 5).
[120] See R. Liñeira *et al.*, 'Voters' Response to the Campaign: Evidence from the Survey', in M. Keating (ed.), *Debating Scotland: Issues of Independence and Union in the 2014 Referendum* (2017).
[121] See http://whatscotlandthinks.org/questions/how-would-you-vote-in-the-in-a-scottish-independence-referendum-if-held-now-ask#line.

convention, the only sanctions for breaching convention are political; but here the risk of a significant political backlash appears to have been neutralized.

At the same time, it must be acknowledged that the recognition claims being advanced by the Scottish Government were unusual ones.[122] This was not simply about seeking protection against Westminster interference in areas of existing Scottish autonomy, or making new claims for Scottish self-rule. Rather, it was the assertion of a right to shared rule; to influence matters of common interest which form part of the constitutional framework in which devolution is situated. Here we see the limits of the constitutional reconfiguration brought about by devolution. While high levels of Scottish autonomy may be tolerated, there is much less willingness to countenance devolved vetoes over UK-wide decision-making.

Yet, as the Scottish Parliament has become more powerful, it has become harder to maintain a watertight division between reserved and devolved matters. Both the 2012 and 2016 Scotland Acts have created significant areas of shared decision-making, particularly in relation to fiscal and welfare matters. This process is further extended by Brexit, which necessitates reconsideration of the common frameworks within which devolution operates. EU law, as a constraint on both devolved and UK decision-making, provided an important centralizing counterweight to the decentralizing effects of devolution. Thus, post-Brexit, new mechanisms are required to preserve the UK's internal market and the ability of the UK Government to enter into new trade deals. However, while the UK Government has shown an acute awareness of the dangers of the excessive decentralization and fragmentation post-Brexit,[123] there has been a failure to acknowledge that common frameworks are matters of mutual interest which need to be established and governed in a co-operative manner and not imposed unilaterally by Westminster.

It may be that, once the immediate Brexit crisis has passed, we will see a return to the gradual evolution of the territorial constitution towards a quasi-federal relationship, in which there is an acceptance of constitutionally-divided authority and the need for effective mechanisms for shared rule alongside self-rule. If not, history suggests that, given the choice between self-government and unmediated unitary decision-making at Westminster, most Scots are likely to prefer the former.

FURTHER READING

M. KEATING, *The Independence of Scotland: Self-Government and the Shifting Politics of Union* (Oxford University Press, 2009)

M. LAZAROWICZ and J. McFADDEN, *The Scottish Parliament: Law and Practice* (Edinburgh University Press, 5th edn., 2018)

---

[122] See further, McHarg, above n. 109, 159–67.

[123] On this, see A. McHarg, 'Unity and Diversity in the United Kingdom's Territorial Constitution', in M. Elliott *et. al* (eds.), *The Unity of Public Law? Doctrinal, Theoretical and Comparative Perspectives* (2018) 297–9.

C. McCorkindale, A. McHarg and P. Scott, 'The Courts, Devolution and Constitutional Review' (2018) 36 *University of Queensland Law Journal* 289

J. Mitchell, *Devolution in the UK* (Manchester University Press, 2009), Chapters 1, 2, 6, and 10

J. Mitchell, *The Scottish Question* (Oxford University Press 2018)

A. Page, *Constitutional Law of Scotland* (W. Green & Son, 2015), esp. Chapters. 1, 2, 4, 5, 7, 8, and 9

S. Tierney, 'Scotland and the Union State', in A. McHarg and T. Mullen (eds.), *Public Law in Scotland* (Avizandum Ltd, 2006)

D. Torrance, ' "The Settled Will?" Devolution in Scotland, 1998–2018', House of Commons Library Briefing Paper, No 08441, 2018

11

THE WELSH WAY/Y FFORDD GYMREIG

Richard Rawlings

SUMMARY

Welsh constitutional development in recent times is characterized by a convoluted and ongoing set of legislative transformations and by the emergence of a distinct policy approach not only for the sub-state polity itself but also under the banner of a 'new Union' for the United Kingdom as a whole. Examination of the design and dynamics of the Wales Act 2017 serves to illuminate the difficulties and rewards of the territorial constitutional journey, especially in terms of central government conservatism in the face of principled argument and of the scope afforded for home-grown democratic renewal. In terms of the extended Brexit process, where competing conceptions of the UK territorial constitution are brought to the fore, the Welsh Labour Government is seen combatting potentials for centralization under the rubric of a 'UK internal market', deal-making in the name of mutual benefit, and championing a new brand of shared governance in the UK. Today, the workings of the justice system in Wales are being examined on their own for the first time in two centuries by an independent commission established by the Welsh Government. With a new stage in the Welsh constitutional journey in prospect, a series of foundational questions is raised.

INTRODUCTION

The title of this chapter bears a dual meaning in both the official languages of Wales. First, in denoting an actual path of development, it references an extraordinary constitutional journey since the advent of democratic devolution in 1998. At the heart of which lies an ongoing series of legislative transformations, a process in which officially labelled 'devolution settlements' quickly prove otherwise by reason of basic defects and limitations and home grown innovation and expansionary pressure. Step by step the path to a reasonable and realistic form of representative government in Wales is travelled, but in arduous, even painful, fashion.

The chief milestones in this exercise in 'national devolution'[1] afford ample evidence.[2] The Government of Wales Act 1998 delivered a weak and spotty form of executive devolution on the back of a narrow majority in a devolution referendum.[3] This not only looked backwards, with powers largely cast in terms of the previous responsibilities of the UK territorial department, but also had a strange anatomy, with representative and executive functions formally combined in the new 60 strong National Assembly for Wales in Cardiff Bay. In light of an autochthonous *de facto* development, the Government of Wales Act 2006 helped to bring Wales into the comparative constitutional mainstream by formally establishing a system of parliamentary government. A step towards serious legislative status, Part III of the Act gave increased competence to make or modify legislation by 'Assembly Measures', but through a restrictive and enervating scheme of designated policy fields in a conferred powers model of devolution particular to Wales.[4] Part IV of the same Act, triggered via a larger majority in another devolution referendum, got as far as establishing a full legislative model of competence.[5] Another intricate scheme of conferred powers, this time premised on 'Acts of the Assembly' relating to listed subjects, it was however difficult to operate and quickly generated Supreme Court litigation concerned with issues of clarity and workability.[6] Following in the footsteps of Scotland, the Wales Act 2014 opened up a familiar route of constitutional development by providing for some limited tax devolution. In light however of challenging post-industrial and rural demographics, Wales would remain heavily dependent on block grant funding from London via the well-known Barnett formula.[7] Large-scale amending legislation, the Wales Act 2017 typically marks a new stage in the constitutional journey while pointing in paradoxical fashion to another stage. This is the stuff of opportunities for internal democratic renewal of, in certain respects, a more generous model of reserved powers; and, at the expense of devolved policy space, of the maintenance through that model of the unitary legal system of England and Wales.[8]

Secondly, the chapter title references the emergence of a distinct Welsh Government approach to constitutional reform, not only for the sub-state polity itself, but also, under the banner of a 'new Union', for the UK as a whole. This entails an increasingly

---

* This chapter derives from my research project 'Devolution: A Constitutional Journey in Wales', generously supported by the Leverhulme Trust. I am grateful to Sarah Nason for comments on a draft. The usual disclaimer applies.

[1] R. Rawlings, *Delineating Wales: Constitutional, Legal and Administrative Aspects of National Devolution* (2003).

[2] For a general overview, see D. Torrance, 'A Process not an Event': Devolution in Wales, 1998–2018 (2018).

[3] R. Rawlings, 'The New Model Wales' (1998) 25 *J. of Law and Society* 461.

[4] R Rawlings, 'Hastening Slowly: The Next Phase of Welsh Devolution' [2005] *Public Law* 824; D. Moon and T. Evans, 'Welsh Devolution and the Problem of Legislative Competence' (2017) 12 *British Politics* 1. See also, M. Shipton, *Poor Man's Parliament: Ten Years of the Welsh Assembly* (2011).

[5] R. Scully and R. Wyn Jones, *Wales Says Yes* (2012).

[6] Most notably, *Agricultural Sector (Wales) Bill—Attorney General Reference* [2014] UKSC 43.

[7] *Final Report of the Independent Commission on Funding and Finance for Wales* (the Holtham Commission) (2010).

[8] R. Rawlings, 'The Strange Reconstitution of Wales' (2018) *Public Law* 62.

advanced form of quasi-federalism:[9] most obviously with a view to navigating a famously uncodified constitution in a period of great unsettlement, close and creative
engagement with federal-type ideas of enabling unity while guaranteeing diversity.[10]
Cast in terms of the UK as a multi- pluri-national state,[11] and of the gradual development in the UK territorial constitution of a multi-level political system, 'new Union'
thinking naturally challenges and runs up against a central government mind-set long
conditioned by the doctrine and practice of Parliamentary Sovereignty.[12] At one and
the same time, the approach fits with a long tradition of federal-type thinking in the
UK, notably revivified in recent years;[13] the familiar difficulties of establishing a fully-
fledged federal system in the UK, more especially the sheer dominance of England;
and is all the more significant for being propounded by official actors.

Welsh constitutional policy is essentially framed by the fact of Cardiff having the
only devolved administration fully committed to the United Kingdom and, more generally, the Labour Party's continued dominance of Welsh electoral politics throughout the period of democratic devolution,[14] as indeed much of the twentieth century.[15]
Reflecting both a sense of maturation in the sub-state polity, and evolving debates in
the Party around solidarity and autonomy and/or territorial protection from a UK
Conservative Government, the approach has become more assertive and clearly defined. Set in the context of major stresses and strains in the UK territorial constitution,
and more particularly the Scottish independence referendum and the extended Brexit
process, recent Welsh Government efforts at building on the operational realities of
quasi-federalism represent a step change.

The Welsh experience further illustrates the strong role of practical concerns in
constitutional development, most obviously as regards the scope for distinctive forms
of substantive policy-making. Fitting with the early nostrum that 'devolution is a
process not an event',[16] rising policy ambition has in part driven the constitutional
case. Initially, under Assembly First Secretary, Alun Michael (1999–2000), the devolved administration appeared singularly lacking in vision.[17] In contrast, 'made in
Wales' policies would come to be much trumpeted under First Minister of Wales,
Rhodri Morgan (2000–2009), especially when in pursuit of a more egalitarian model

---

[9] For the earlier association with New Labour constitutional reform, see V. Bogdanor, *The New British Constitution* (2009).

[10] M. Burgess, *In Search of the Federal Spirit* (2012); A. Lev (ed.), *The Federal Idea* (2017).

[11] A-G. Gagnon and J. Tully (eds.), *Multinational Democracies* (2001); M. Keating, *Plurinational Democracy* (2004).

[12] See latterly, M. Loughlin and S. Tierney, 'The Shibboleth of Sovereignty' (2018) 81 *MLR* 989.

[13] Leading illustrations are D. Melding, *The Reformed Union: The UK as a Federation* (2013); D. Torrance, *Britain Rebooted: Scotland in a Federal Union* (2014); and R. Schütze and S. Tierney (eds.), *The United Kingdom and the Federal Idea* (2018).

[14] Time will tell whether Labour's resounding defeat in the 2019 European Parliament elections heralds a fundamental shift in the electoral politics of Wales.

[15] K. Morgan, *Revolution to Devolution: Reflections on Welsh Democracy* (2014). See also R. Deacon et al. (eds.), *The Government and Politics of Wales* (2018).

[16] Ron Davies (then Secretary of State for Wales), *Devolution: A Process not an Event* (1999).

[17] Alun Michael, *The Dragon on our Doorstep* (1999).

grounded in public provision than was the case with the New Labour government in London.[18] Indeed, much was heard, and under First Ministers Carwyn Jones (2009–2018) and Mark Drakeford (2018–) has continued to be heard, of a progressive consensus in Wales.[19] As regards ways of working this denotes much stress on partnership arrangements and attempts at joined-up governance. In terms of policy promotion it references official commitments to social, economic, environmental, and cultural well-being together with equalities and human rights. Designed to imbue the young constitutional construction with a particular quality, Welsh devolved legislation in the area is world-leading.[20]

Added policy potentials and problems in realizing those potentials associated with small country governance must also be factored into the equation.[21] Joint and joined-up working is further prioritized, and there are challenging issues of limited capacity, overly dependent civil society and scarce international influence to navigate.[22] At one and the same time, it does not do to gloss over continued criticism of the state of public services in Wales and the negative effects of a decade of austerity for a country ranked as one of the economically poorest UK regions.[23] So too, issues of political engagement and recognition continue to dog this young polity.[24] Though carefully grounded in the pro-devolution sentiments expressed in territorial referendums, the elite, official, character of much in the Welsh way cannot be gainsaid.

Here as elsewhere the prospect of Brexit has cast a long shadow. Together with the general wrap-around of legal rights and obligations, the place of Wales as a distinct 'region' in the EU was a foundational precept of the devolutionary project.[25] The 2016 UK referendum also left Welsh ministers awkwardly placed: a hitherto 'Remain' government in a sub-state polity (narrowly) voting 'Leave'. Subsequent documentation would speak of respecting a democratic decision while emphasizing the importance to Wales of maintaining full and unfettered access to the EU Single Market and the practical benefits of the Customs Union.[26] Attention is drawn to some local facts of economy and geography: very high proportions of international exports to the EU; Wales as a net recipient

---

[18] D. Moon, 'Rhetoric and Policy Learning: On Rhodri Morgan's "Clear Red Water" and "Made in Wales" Health Policies' (2012) 28 *Public Policy and Administration* 306.

[19] See especially, Mark Drakeford: 'Social Justice in a Devolved Wales' (2007) 15(2) *Journal of Public Finance and Public Choice* 171. For the antecedents, see R. Rawlings, '*The New Model Wales*'.

[20] For the flagship enterprise, see the Well-being of Future Generations (Wales) Act 2015.

[21] For discussion in the Welsh context, see T. Rabey, *Connection, Coherence and Capacity: Policy Making in Smaller Countries* (2015); and A. Cole and I. Stafford, *Devolution and Governance* (2015).

[22] See further, C. Saunders, 'The Challenges of Multi-Layered Constitutionalism' in L. Fisher et al. (eds.), *The Foundations and Future of Public Law* (2019).

[23] *Report of the Commission on Public Service Governance and Delivery* (the Williams Commission) (2014); Wales Governance Centre, *Government Expenditure and Revenue Wales* (2016); Office of National Statistics, *Regional Economic Activity, 1998–2017* (2018).

[24] See further, R. Scully and R. Wyn Jones, 'The Public Legitimacy of the National Assembly for Wales' (2014) 21 *J. of Legislative Studies* 515.

[25] R. Rawlings, 'Cymru yn Ewrop: Wales in Europe', in P. Craig and R. Rawlings (eds.), *Law and Administration in Europe* (2003); J. Hunt, 'Devolution' in M. Dougan (ed.), *The UK after Brexit: Legal and Policy Challenges* (2017).

[26] Welsh Government with Plaid Cymru, *Securing Wales' Future* (2017).

of EU funding; and, a particular twist among the multiple challenges for the island of Ireland associated with Brexit, heavy cargo traffic through Welsh ports. Moreover, it would have been strange if the Welsh Government had not characterized Brexit as 'an existential challenge to the UK itself', especially if it occasioned 'excessive centralisation'.[27] In due course, the National Assembly would in symbolic fashion vote to reject the November 2018 EU/UK Withdrawal Agreement and Political Declaration.[28] On closer examination, we will see local actors busily engaged in major domestic aspects of the extended Brexit process. For the proverbial 'big questions', however, Wales was fated to be on the sidelines in view of the particular histories and politics of these Atlantic Isles.

Let us put the Welsh way in comparative perspective. As England's first colony, nowhere in the common law globe has the process of legal, political and administrative assimilation been deeper or more thoroughgoing. [29] Typically seen as the junior partner in the UK's 'state of unions',[30] this small polity is also prone to being buffeted about.[31] Discrete Welsh constitutional development was thus destined to be particularly—even uniquely—challenging, an aspect now underscored by twenty years and counting of laborious polity-building. Conversely, however, from self-rule and separation of powers and on through subsidiarity and comity to shared governance, some familiar themes feature prominently in the constitutional narrative, not least because much in the Welsh way is determinedly outward-looking. We will also encounter some particularly strong pulls and interactions involving the other devolved territories, more especially Scotland in relation to the reserved powers model and the domestic dimension of the Brexit process.

Let us then consider the basic tenets of Welsh constitutional policy as recently articulated and several key aspects of 'the changing constitution' in Wales and the UK in the light of them. Examination of the design and dynamics of the Wales Act 2017 will serve to illuminate the difficulties and rewards of the constitutional journey in Wales. Not least, that is, in terms of central government conservatism in the face of principled argument and of the scope afforded for home-grown democratic renewal. The extended Brexit process has brought competing conceptions of the UK territorial constitution to the fore. The Welsh Labour Government will be seen combatting potentials for centralization under the rubric of a 'UK internal market', deal-making in the name of mutual benefit, and championing a new brand of shared governance in the UK. Today, the workings of the justice system in Wales are being examined on their own for the first time in two centuries by an independent commission established by the Welsh Government. With a new stage in the Welsh constitutional journey in prospect, a series of foundational questions is raised.

---

[27] Welsh Government, *Brexit and Devolution* (2017).

[28] On a motion supported by Labour, Plaid Cymru and Liberal Democrat Members: National Assembly for Wales, *Record of Proceedings*, 4 December 2018. See also *Record of Proceedings*, 5 March 2019.

[29] For the leading narrative, see J. Davies, *A History of Wales* (1993).

[30] J. Mitchell, *Devolution in the UK* (2009).

[31] R. Rawlings, 'Riders on the Storm: Wales, the Union, and Territorial Constitutional Crisis' (2015) 42 *JLS* 471.

WELSH CONSTITUTIONAL POLICY

In its advanced form, Welsh constitutional policy involves revisiting the concept of devolution, so challenging the easy assumption that centralization is the constitutional default position.[32] Far from some 'Greater England' form of unionism, which countenances only limited territorial difference,[33] devolution should be about how the UK as a whole is governed by several administrations which are not in a hierarchical relationship one to another. Expressions of popular sovereignty in the various territorial referendums are duly invoked to support this constitutional perspective and understanding. Different but related is the insistence on the UK as a voluntary association of nations as illustrated by both the constitutional arrangements for Northern Ireland[34] and the very fact of the Scottish independence referendum in 2014. And, in functional terms, on an economic, political, and social Union of countries which in quasi-federal fashion 'share and redistribute resources and risks between us to our mutual benefit and to advance our common interests'.[35]

As against 'the pragmatic, make do and mend' approach so familiar in the UK devolutionary context, a premium is put on longer-term, holistic perspectives; beginning, of course, with the proposition that, assuming continued territorial consent, the devolved institutions are here to stay. As regards self-rule, a strong presumption of devolution, or downwards pull of the principle of subsidiarity in the face of power-hoarding at the centre, should frame the allocation of functions across the UK territorial constitution. At the same time, recognizing the reality of interdependence in a multi-level constitutional system, a particular premium is placed in terms of shared governance on intergovernmental cooperation. This should be on the basis throughout of precepts of comity or mutual respect and parity of esteem among the several democratically legitimated centres of governmental authority which characterize a 'new Union' mind-set. A looser but interconnected United Kingdom is seen as the best hope of preserving it.

Set in terms of entrenched views of an indivisible internal sovereignty, 'new Union' thinking is optimistic. Faced with 'the old one-dimensional version of Parliamentary Sovereignty', and prompted initially by the existential threat in Scotland to the domestic Union, First Minister Carwyn Jones regularly but unsuccessfully called for a pan-UK Constitutional Convention.[36] Though forced to navigate the formal legal orthodoxy, the Welsh Government has nonetheless pursued a series of political, legal, and administrative reforms which reflect the radical spirit of 'new Union' ideas. Local actors have been able to draw here on an increasing wealth of constitutional and technical analysis

[32] Carwyn Jones, *Our Future Union—A Perspective from Wales* (2014); Mark Drakeford, *The Future of Devolution: the UK after Brexit* (2019).

[33] C. Kidd, *Union and Unionisms* (2008); L. Colley, *Acts of Union and Disunion* (2014).

[34] As discussed in the chapter by Brice Dickson.

[35] Welsh Government, written evidence to House of Lords Constitution Committee, *The Union and Devolution*, HL 151 (2015–16).

[36] Carwyn Jones, *Towards a Better Union: Past, Present and Post-Brexit prospects for the UK* (2018).

and expertise, not least among the think tanks and public interest bodies.[37] Debates in Scotland, especially in and around the Calman Commission[38] ahead of the independence referendum,[39] and, after it, the Smith Commission[40] and the Scotland Act 2016, have been a major reference point. Given however the somewhat lonely political position in the UK of the Welsh Government, gaining traction has been a major issue. Coalition-building, both internally as with the harnessing of Welsh civil society, and externally as most obviously with the nationalist Scottish Government, is a substantial part of the enterprise.

The heavy use of independent commissions is a defining feature in terms of institutional technique. Evidence-based analysis, laced with public consultation, opinion polling and latterly digital strategies, is thus made a recurring theme in the Welsh devolutionary narrative. Exemplars, the Richard Commission[41] and the Silk Commission[42] can indeed be seen as the necessary precursors to the Government of Wales Act 2006 and the Wales Acts 2014 and 2017 respectively. A further theme is highlighted, one which characterizes both the work of the independent commissions and the Welsh Government policy development more generally: high level appeals to constitutional principle and/or good governance values, not least to frame and justify demands for more devolution. Referencing no less a list than accountability, clarity, coherence, collaboration, efficiency, equity, stability, and subsidiarity,[43] the Silk Commission is itself a valuable reservoir of principles-based analysis in comparative constitutional terms. As illuminated in the work today of the independent Commission on Justice in Wales, discussed below, this approach is also part and parcel of the quest in a determinedly progressive polity for a more just, fair and prosperous Wales.

How might 'new Union' ideas be given tangible expression? In the legislative sphere, the Welsh Government has typically favoured a strong, protective convention of territorial consent to Westminster statutes. A key constitutional battleground, we observe, in the extended Brexit process. As well as the grant of autonomy to determine the size and electoral arrangements of a devolved legislature, another federal-type component would also fit: dedicated territorial representation in a reformed Upper Chamber of the UK Parliament. In the executive sphere, precepts of mutual respect and parity of esteem support exclusive political authority for each set of ministers within their legal competence, as well as targeted forms of joint working by the several administrations and robust machinery of intergovernmental relations for matters of shared interest.

---

[37] See for suitably instructive examples, Bingham Centre for the Rule of Law, *A Constitutional Crossroads* (2015); Institute for Government, *Governing in an Ever Looser Union* (2015).

[38] Commission on Scottish Devolution, *Serving Scotland Better* (2009).

[39] A. McHarg et al. (eds.), *The Scottish Independence Referendum* (2016).

[40] *Report of the Commission for Further Devolution of Powers to the Scottish Parliament* (2014); see further, A. Tomkins, *Shared Rule: What Scotland Needs to Learn from Federalism* (2016).

[41] *Report of the (Richard) Commission on the Powers and Electoral Arrangements of the National Assembly* (2004).

[42] *Report of the (Silk) Commission on Devolution in Wales: Part 1, Financial Powers to Strengthen Wales* (2012); *Part 2, Legislative Powers to Strengthen Wales* (2014).

[43] Silk Commission, Part 2 Report, paragraph 3.3.3.

Likewise, the Welsh Government has repeatedly advocated the constitutionally principled step of a transparent and jointly owned system of territorial funding based on relative need.[44] Politically very difficult, not least by reason of competing territorial interests in Scotland, this also serves, however, to point up the challenges of a 'new Union' project.

The increased constitutional ambition is well-illustrated in terms of asymmetric devolution, a chief design feature of New Labour's original approach to constitutional reform which typically saw Wales lag behind in the territorial stakes.[45] At one with the move to a reserved powers model akin to the arrangements in Scotland and Northern Ireland, 'a consistent structure across the devolved territories' is today a cardinal principle of Welsh constitutional policy.[46] Again, while there is no assumption that the reservations in respect of Wales should be identical to those operating elsewhere, in particular in tax and welfare given the challenging demographics, the policy approach increasingly tends in this subtle quasi-federal direction. As shown below, the current debate on justice functions for Wales provides multiple examples. Why centralization, the Welsh Government typically asks, when the same responsibilities are already devolved in Scotland and Northern Ireland and even to an extent within English city regions.[47]

The UK machinery of intergovernmental relations (IGR), centred on the Joint Ministerial Committee system introduced by New Labour, has been a major concern from the outset.[48] Precepts of co-operation, communication and consultation, appearing in 'soft law' terms in the agreed memorandum of understanding[49] and concordats, are all very well, but the machinery has been repeatedly criticized for being disjointed, unstable, and prone to central domination, as well as lacking in transparency and accountability.[50] At one with the emphasis on shared governance in conditions of mutual respect, the Welsh Government has been at the forefront in making proposals for reform. As discussed below, the Brexit process has given the issue a sharper edge by reason, at one level, of the very different political views about the wisdom and design of the general enterprise, and, at another level, of official efforts to elaborate common frameworks and forms of governance in terms of a 'UK internal market'.[51]

England looms large. It could hardly be otherwise given the local demographics of a porous 'border', as well as the long history of pooling of resources and shared

---

[44] So replacing the Barnett Formula; see latterly, Welsh Government, *Reforming UK funding and fiscal arrangements after Brexit* (2018).

[45] R. Rawlings, *'The New Model Wales'*.   [46] Carwyn Jones, *'Towards a Better Union'.*

[47] Commission on Justice in Wales (the Thomas Commission), WS 48.

[48] R. Rawlings, 'Concordats of the Constitution' (2000) 116 *Law Q. Rev.* 257.

[49] *Memorandum of Understanding and Supplementary Agreements* (2013 version).

[50] See for example House of Lords Constitution Committee, *Inter-Governmental Relations in the United Kingdom*, HL 146 (2014–15); House of Commons Public Administration and Constitutional Affairs Committee, *The Future of the Union: Inter-institutional relations in the UK* HC 839 (2016–17).

[51] House of Commons Public Administration and Constitutional Affairs Committee, *Devolution and Exiting the EU: Reconciling Differences and Building Strong Relationships* HC 1485 (2017–19). For the UK Government Response, see HC 1574 (2017–2019).

endeavour in many fields under the familiar administrative paradigm of 'England and Wales'. Reflecting and reinforcing the presumption of devolution, however, a recurring theme in the territorial policy analysis is the propensity in such arrangements for insufficient regard to be given to the particularities and distinct interests of the much smaller country. As illustrated below in the context of the justice system, the policy responses can take many forms, ranging through proposals for disaggregation of a previously centralized system to strengthened representation on 'cross-border' public bodies. We also touch here on the double-hatted character of Whitehall, the largescale functional fusion of UK Government with the government of England in a classically non-federal system. Essentially the flip-side of devolution to the three Celtic lands, this element has also been brought into sharp focus by the Brexit process, to the extent of conjuring up the prospect, with the removal of EU legal corsetry, of increased constitutional imbalance between the constituent nations of the UK in the light of English workings of Parliamentary Sovereignty.[52] It is hardly for the Welsh Government to pontificate on how England should be governed or indeed on the increasingly evident forces of English nationalism.[53] Rather, the question is raised of how the devolved administrations can have confidence that the UK Government will not unfairly prioritize English interests. Hence the Welsh policy line that, as part of a 'better Union based on fair rules and collaboration', there must be 'a clear and transparent demarcation' in Whitehall.[54]

REMODELLING: AUTONOMY, RESERVATION, AND UNSETTLEMENT

The making of the Wales Act 2017 was long and difficult partly because of the different motivations in Cardiff and London for providing Wales with a reserved powers model. From the standpoint of the Welsh Government, the Silk Commission had effectively paved the way by pointing up the potential benefits in terms of subsidiarity, workability, and comprehensibility.[55] Detailed proposals on such diverse matters as institutional autonomy, natural resources and economic development, and policing and youth justice, promised much by way of expanded powers. Paradoxically, however, Whitehall was envisaging greater protection of central power. The key reference point is the *Agricultural Sector* case in 2014, in which the UK Supreme Court, led by the then Lord Chief Justice of England and Wales, Lord Thomas of Cwmgiedd, ruled that Welsh legislation fairly and reasonably relating to a devolved subject was within competence even if it also related to a subject on which the conferred powers model was silent.[56] The subsequent draft Wales Bill sees ministers striking back at an unwelcome constitutional precedent.

[52] R. Rawlings, *Brexit and the Territorial Constitution: Devolution, Reregulation and Inter-governmental Relations* (2017).

[53] M. Kenny, *The Politics of English Nationhood* (2014); A. Henderson and R. Wyn Jones, *Future of England Survey* (2018).

[54] Carwyn Jones, '*Towards a Better Union*'.   [55] Silk Commission, '*Part 2 Report*', Chapter 4.

[56] *Agricultural Sector (Wales) Bill—Attorney General Reference* [2014] UKSC 43.

Indicative of some roll-back of powers, so-called 'silent subjects' would be reinvented as reserved competence under the twin flags of clarity and stability.[57]

Much in the pre-legislative processes was the very antithesis of a 'new Union' approach. First, promoted by the Secretary of State, the so-called 'St David's Day process' effectively stood for devolution by lowest common denominator. With the predictable ad hoc and limiting effects, Westminster representatives of each of the major political parties in Wales were thus allowed to veto any of the Silk Commission's recommendations in secretive fashion. Most notably, devolution of policing was taken off the agenda.[58] Secondly, Whitehall processes of trawling and reverse engineering constituted another backward-looking approach, whereby the new reserved powers model still bears the DNA of territorial department responsibilities pre-1998.[59] In-house characterizations of non-devolved matters under the conferred powers scheme were thus flipped over into draft lists of reservations in a notably closed and elite form of constitution-building. The lexicon of the Welsh constitutional journey soon contained a new phrase: 'reservation creep'.[60]

Reflecting the influence of the Scotland Act 2016, some surviving elements from the St David's Day process fit well with Welsh constitutional policy. The declaration in s. 1 of the permanency of the devolved institutions, and the formal recognition in s. 2 of the convention that Westminster will 'not normally' legislate with regard to devolved matters without the National Assembly's consent, are good examples of the continuing quest for mutual respect and parity of esteem. Other provisions, for example on control via standing orders of the composition of committees,[61] also serve to buttress the status of the Assembly as a self-governing and autonomous institution. An especially noteworthy feature is the legislative space created by the 2017 Act for further autochthonous constitutional development; namely, an Assembly reform programme intended to enhance political engagement and practical workings, but also one which may itself facilitate further devolution. Local actors are immediately seen working with a new set of competences[62] on the size of the sub-state legislature—a major issue in terms of the capacity for democratic oversight[63]—the devolved electoral system and— sitting comfortably with progressive demands for inclusivity—the (lowering of the) minimum voting age.[64] A proposed name change is intended to underwrite the very

---

[57] HM Government, *Powers for a Purpose: Towards a Lasting Devolution Settlement for Wales*, Cm. 9020, 2015; HM Government *Draft Wales Bill* Cm. 9144, 2015.

[58] HM Government, '*Powers for a Purpose*', Annex A.

[59] Theodore Huckle QC (then Counsel-General for Wales), *Fixes, Fudges and Falling Short?* (2015).

[60] Wales Governance Centre and Constitution Unit, *Challenge and Opportunity: The Draft Wales Bill 2015* (2016). The author was Rapporteur.

[61] Wales Act 2017, s. 14.

[62] Which naturally include super-majority requirements: see Wales Act 2017, s. 9.

[63] UK's Changing Union Project/Electoral Reform Society Wales, *Size Matters* (2013).

[64] Expert Panel on Assembly Electoral Reform, *A Parliament that Works for Wales* (2017); National Assembly for Wales Commission, *Creating a Parliament for Wales: Consultation Report* (2018).

different nature of the institution to the original corporate body; hence the 'Senedd' ('Welsh Parliament') .[65]

The devolved institutions naturally welcomed significant new powers in subjects like energy and transport.[66] Testimony to a growing maturation of the sub-state polity, however, local actors pushed back hard against Whitehall power-hoarding on a range of topics, typically invoking the principle of subsidiarity. A sensitive issue in many constitutional settings, not least this one, the control and management of water resources was chief among these—a joint 'cross-border' arrangement was eventually agreed.[67] Demands for less complexity and more territorial decision-making space, not least from civil society, also saw some trimming of the proposed reservations across the piece.[68] The further question of UK ministerial consents or veto powers on democratically legitimated Welsh policy preferences was particularly challenging. From a Whitehall perspective, this was a useful technique for protecting cross-border public bodies from unilateral changes of function by the devolved institutions. From the territorial standpoint, it cut hard against the constitutional nostrum of parity of esteem. Once again it required the hard slog of myriad official exchanges and dual and interacting processes of legislative scrutiny at UK and sub-state level to achieve a resolution: a lengthy schedule of shared executive powers[69] and an open list of sub-state governance infrastructure in the form of 'devolved Welsh authorities'.[70] Often arcane and from the viewpoint of Cardiff Bay significant but incomplete, the development is itself emblematic of much in the arduous Welsh constitutional journey. A Scottish-style general transfer of Minister of the Crown functions[71] to Wales was evidently a step too far for London.

Yet overarching all this is a fundamental difference of view about the relative constitutional importance of democratic devolution. Echoing earlier arguments for adopting the conferred powers model,[72] Whitehall persisted in putting the unity of the England and Wales legal system first. Operating beyond the purview of the St David's Day process, the UK Ministry of Justice (MoJ) had thus set about protecting the 'integrity' of that system in the context of a reserved powers model. Effectively this meant limiting the scale of legal divergence between the two countries by cramping the legislative capacities of one side of the representative institutional equation. With reference to the voluminous fields of civil and criminal law and procedure, the draft Wales Bill accordingly prescribed 'a general level of protection' for the unified system, whilst allowing

---

[65] National Assembly for Wales, *Record of Proceedings*, February 13, 2019; Senedd and Elections (Wales) Bill.

[66] Wales Act 2017, ss. 23–43.

[67] Wales Act 2017, ss. 48–52; *Intergovernmental Protocol on Water Resources, Water Supply and Water Quality*, HC 563 (2017–9).

[68] See Wales Governance Centre and Constitution Unit, '*Challenge and Opportunity*', Chapter 7.

[69] Wales Act 2017, s. 21 and Schedule 4 inserting new Schedule 3A to Government of Wales Act 2006.

[70] Wales Act 2017, s. 3 and Schedule 2 inserting new Schedule 7B to Government of Wales Act 2006, paragraphs. 8–12; s. 4 and Schedule 3 inserting new Schedule 9A to Government of Wales Act 2006.

[71] Scotland Act 1998, s.53.

[72] Thomas Commission, WS 142 (Counsel General); and see further below.

the Assembly 'some latitude to modify these areas'.[73] Another phrase entered the territorial constitutional lexicon: 'leeway and lock'.[74]

In operational terms, the MoJ model decreed that whether or not the National Assembly was within competence would depend in many situations on whether the relevant provision was 'necessary'. This was in addition to the general reservation of 'the single legal jurisdiction' and a cluster of specific reservations on such matters as the legal profession and legal services.[75] Further evidencing the growth of Welsh constitutional sensitivities, however, the Secretary of State 'paused' the legislation when faced with a barrage of criticism, again grounded in principle. Mutual respect and parity of esteem hardly suggested loading the burden of maintaining 'unity' on Cardiff Bay. More prosaically, in situations not covered by Convention rights (or EU law), necessity testing was clearly apt to undercut political responsibility and accountability, cause problems of workability and generate enervating legal disputes.[76] A looming block on the path to a fully rounded devolution settlement was withdrawn.

It is in this fraught context that we see the Welsh Government promoting a written constitution for the sub-state polity: the Government and Laws in Wales draft bill.[77] As such, giving tangible expression to 'new Union' thinking, the text is not only determinedly holistic and principles-based with a special emphasis on subsidiarity, but also envisions a constitutional destination as well as the transition. Indeed, in comparative constitutional terms, much in this ground-breaking documentation for Wales appears unremarkable. Why would there not be a logical progression from 'Welsh Parliament' and legislative competence and process to the Welsh Government and executive functions, and on through legal jurisdiction, finance and taxation, in such a text? Likewise, reservation of core matters such as macroeconomic policy, citizenship and foreign affairs, which itself illuminates the quasi-federal nature of the enterprise. As against the MoJ model, the Welsh draft bill stood for a 'distinct jurisdiction', formal division into the law and senior courts of England and of Wales but with a common judiciary, in a clear prioritization of responsible government over what the Welsh Government has labelled 'a relic of history'.[78] A new category of 'deferred matters' was envisaged, which would see powers over the justice system transferred at a later date, so allowing for proper preparation. There was no serious prospect of Whitehall suddenly signing up to this shadow measure. Effectively heralding another independent commission in the wake of the 2017 Act, a chief constitutional marker had however been put in place.[79]

---

[73] HM Government, *Explanatory Notes to Draft Wales Bill* (2015), paragraph 32.

[74] Wales Governance Centre and Constitution Unit, '*Challenge and Opportunity*', Chapter 5.

[75] See Wales Act 2017, s. 3 and Schedule 1 inserting new Schedule 7A Part 1 paragraph 8 and Head L to Government of Wales Act 2006.

[76] National Assembly for Wales Constitutional and Legislative Affairs Committee, *Report on the UK Government's Draft Wales Bill* (2015); House of Commons Welsh Affairs Committee, *Pre-Legislative Scrutiny of the Draft Wales Bill*, HC 449 (2015–16).

[77] See Welsh Government, *Explanatory Summary to Government and Laws in Wales Draft Bill* (2016).

[78] Thomas Commission, WS 48.

[79] The shadow draft Bill was also included in Labour's 2017 UK General Election manifesto.

The Act itself demonstrates some limited devolutionary advance in this area. With much abandonment of necessity-testing, the protection afforded the unitary legal system in the revamped model of legislative competence is softened and more targeted. Notably, Assembly legislation may modify the private law for a purpose that does not relate to a reserved matter, while, in the criminal law sphere, the National Assembly can provide for offences in relation to non-reserved matters but is prohibited from legislating on major crimes and core legal concepts.[80] The sub-state polity, in other words, is better placed to do what myriad sub-state polities around the world do, namely develop coherent statutory—regulatory—regimes encompassing rights, duties and sanctions. Not before time, there is also formal legal recognition of the facts on the ground in the guise of 'Welsh law'. Namely, primary and secondary legislation made by the devolved institutions as part of the law that applies in Wales.[81] In similar vein, the formal establishment of the office of President of the Welsh tribunals underwrites a nascent devolved model of administrative justice.[82]

Enough has been said to demonstrate the significance and more particularly the restrictive dimension of this most recent devolution legislation for Wales. At one and the same time, the making of it illuminates the role of a principles-based approach in framing and testing constitutional proposals and is a salutary reminder of the less appealing aspects of law, politics, and administration in the UK's 'changing constitution'. From the standpoint of Welsh constitutional policy, there is fresh encouragement in terms of the long march through accretion of powers and polity and institution-building. Conversely, there is much embedded restriction ranging well beyond classic fields of central power, most notably in the justice field. In comparative constitutional perspective, the new reserved powers model might even be analysed in terms of 'home rule' without 'home affairs'. The Wales Act 2017 is unfinished business—more unsettlement.

Suffice it to add that the constitutional and political significance of devolved legislative consent is well-illustrated in this context. Giving the Welsh Government some additional leverage, it was agreed that the bill would only proceed to Third Reading in the House of Lords if the National Assembly passed the relevant motion. As well as the elements of institutional autonomy and scope for democratic renewal, two key factors helped to swing the vote in Cardiff Bay in favour of accepting the reserved powers model on offer. The first one is fiscal reform in another boost for political responsibility and democratic accountability at territorial level. A more generous variant of the Barnett Formula and an increased capital borrowing limit, coupled with abolition of a referendum 'lock' on devolved income tax powers, was thus made part of a

---

[80] Wales Act 2017, s. 3 and Schedule 2 inserting new Schedule 7B paragraphs 1–4 to Government of Wales Act 2006.

[81] Wales Act 2017, s. 1.

[82] Wales Act 2017, Part 3 and Schedule 5. See further, Committee for Administrative Justice and Tribunals, Wales, *Administrative Justice: A Cornerstone of Social Justice in Wales* (2016); S. Nason (ed.), *Administrative Justice in Wales and Comparative Perspectives* (2017); S. Nason, *Administrative Justice: Wales's First Devolved Justice System* (2018).

package together with the general statutory reform.[83] Again illuminating the extraordinary reach of all things Brexit, coalition-building with Edinburgh is the second one. By aligning the Welsh constitutional model more closely to Scotland, Wales would be better placed for the looming tussles with Whitehall over the development of a UK internal market, or so the argument went.[84]

REREGULATION: CONSENT AND SHARED GOVERNANCE

Reregulation, in the general sense of regulating again or anew, is after all a key part of the extended Brexit narrative.[85] With a view to the preserving and/or substituting of EU norms in order to avoid a major legal vacuum, the European Union (Withdrawal) Act 2018 gives chapter and verse.[86] Regarding the evident pressures on the UK territorial constitution, attention is here drawn to a protracted dispute concerning the distribution to the several centres of representative government of powers expected to return from Brussels, one which has generated much political friction and also legal spill-over into the UK Supreme Court. So too, we observe a mass of intergovernmental work on the role, design and governance of common domestic frameworks in an otherwise increasingly differentiated polity; a significant element of constitutional experimentation which included as initial policy drivers a free-flowing 'UK internal market' and active international trade policy.[87] At the same time, with reference to the eventual scale, patterns and timings of release (if any) from supranational frameworks, we are reminded of the sea of uncertainty surrounding official actors in the wake of the 2016 Brexit vote, an aspect itself underscored by the later EU/UK draft documentation and seismic events at Westminster. In terms of the quasi-federal approach pursued in Wales, this most complex situation effectively mandated a careful defence of territorial interests coupled with a close and constructive engagement with the centre under the banner of shared governance. We see sterling efforts being made in this small polity to shape and influence particular aspects of the Brexit-related domestic constitutional development accordingly.

The so-called 'devolution clauses' in the Withdrawal Bill[88] went to the heart of contemporary political debate over the very nature and future of the UK, effectively exposing competing constitutional narratives.[89] Indeed, the clauses were developed in the

[83] Wales Act 2017, ss. 17–18; HM Government and Welsh Government, *Agreement on the Welsh Government's Fiscal Framework* (2016). For the obvious comparator, see HM Government and Scottish Government, *Agreement on the Scottish Government's Fiscal Framework* (2016).

[84] National Assembly for Wales, *Record of Proceedings*, 17 January 2017.

[85] R. Rawlings, *'Brexit and the Territorial Constitution'*.

[86] M. Elliott and S. Tierney, 'Political Pragmatism and Constitutional Principle: The European Union (Withdrawal) Act 2018' (2019) *Public Law* 37. For further illustration, see the (Brexit-associated) Agriculture Bill and Fisheries Bill currently before the UK Parliament.

[87] See Joint Ministerial Committee (EU Negotiations) Communiqué, 16 October 2017. For the relevant UK ministerial intervention powers in the Welsh context, see Government of Wales Act 2006, s. 82.

[88] Clauses 10–11 of the bill as originally introduced.

[89] See for example in terms of 'permissive autonomy', M. Sandford and C. Gormley-Heenan, '"Taking Back Control": The UK Constitutional Narrative and Schrodinger's Devolution' (2018) 71 *Parliamentary Affairs*.

context of some bold Prime Ministerial envisioning of a common domestic market place empowering 'a truly Global Britain' post-Brexit.[90] In this regard, the dual prospect of Whitehall gaining much by way of market regulatory and trade powers, and of the overarching requirement in the devolution legislation not to transgress EU law falling away, was an evident source of tension.[91] One-sided and provocative, especially when juxtaposed with the extraordinarily wide-ranging powers for UK ministers elsewhere in the bill, the devolution clauses in turn helped to promote a new 'devo-axis' between the Welsh Labour Government and the Scottish Nationalist one. The UK Government's initial approach of 'hold and release', whereby repatriated powers otherwise going to the three Celtic lands would be diverted to London with a view to distributing them or not in the light of the construction of common frameworks, was thus constitutional anathema not only for those advocating separation or looser confederal-type arrangements[92] but also in terms of parity of esteem from the standpoint of 'new Union' thinking.[93] In so occupying legislative and executive space at the expense of the territorial authorities in Scotland, Wales, and (if and when the power-sharing institutions were operative) Northern Ireland, Whitehall's approach stood for a reassertion of hierarchical control, and hence a strong centralizing potential, in the face of reserved powers arrangements. Conversely, as against such muscular use of formal law through the medium of Parliamentary sovereignty, the two devolved governments jointly advocated a model of 'respect and collaborate', whereby powers would be repatriated in accordance with established patterns of reserved competence and common frameworks would be constructed in consensual and collaborative fashion. Standing in practical terms for a rebalancing of negotiating strength away from the UK Government and government for England, the approach sits comfortably with the devolutionary narrative of a seriously 'changing constitution' since 1998: a multi-level political system very different from the domestic constitutional setting of the UK's entry into the then European Communities in 1973.[94] In this respect, the Welsh First Minister was commendably blunt. 'Any retreat towards a monolithic and centralised UK . . . will serve to threaten, not strengthen, our Union.'[95]

The dispute shows a basic lack of trust between the parties.[96] A revamped approach by Whitehall of 'devolve and freeze' was a step, but only a step, towards a resolution. Under this proposal, returning EU powers that intersected with devolved competence would go directly to Belfast, Cardiff and Edinburgh, but subject to a more targeted

---

[90] Prime Minister Theresa May, Lancaster House speech, 17 January 2017; Department for Exiting the European Union, *Legislating for the United Kingdom's withdrawal from the European Union*, Cm. 9446, 2017, Chapter 4.

[91] A. Page, *The Implications of EU Withdrawal for the Devolution Settlement* (2016).

[92] Scottish Government White Paper, *Scotland's Place in Europe* (2016).

[93] Welsh Government, '*Brexit and Devolution*'.

[94] See further, S. Douglas-Scott, 'Brexit, Article 50 and the Contested British Constitution' (2016) 79 *Modern Law Review* 1019; and S. Tierney, 'The Territorial Constitution after Brexit' (2019) 72 *Current Legal Problems*.

[95] Welsh Government, 'Brexit and Devolution', First Minister's preface.

[96] For a more detailed examination of the controversy, see R. Rawlings, *Brexit: Law, Constitution and Market* (2018).

regime of freezing of competence on the basis of pre-existing EU norms, again to allow space and time for the reregulatory development of more substantive pan-UK/GB arrangements.[97] Illustrating the scope with a multi-level political system for constitutional play and counter-play, the two sets of devolved authorities are found promoting their own fast-track continuity legislation aimed at occupying the disputed legislative and executive space.[98] The limits of the new-found devo-axis are also exposed, however, with Welsh ministers ultimately preferring, as part of an intergovernmental deal with the UK Government, not to pursue the conflictual routing of 'pre-empt and be challenged' in the Supreme Court.[99] Capacity problems had loomed large in this small polity in view of the extra demands for delegated legislation associated with a continuity Act. In a 'Leave' voting country with a peculiarly muddled constitutional development, the sense of a 'power grab' or centralist attack on established devolutionary principles was harder to convey. Nor of course were Welsh ministers on pro-independence manoeuvres.

The new intergovernmental agreement was itself the product of lengthy discussions between the three governments.[100] In Welsh, if not Scottish Government eyes, it was also a considerable achievement, so paving the way for the one but not the other devolved legislature to give consent to the Withdrawal Bill.[101] Though the new arrangement did not provide a veto on changes to devolved competence through UK regulations under what would become s. 12 of the 2018 Act,[102] the previous UK approach of 'devolve and freeze' was now hedged around with a mix of legal and political commitments. In this way, the UK/Welsh deal represents 'consent convention plus'. First, incorporating the familiar phraseology of 'not normally', the agreement reads the convention of devolved legislative consent across to the relevant UK order-making powers, with s. 12 then imposing further process—explanatory—requirements. Second, the deal explicitly discounts the possibility of the legislative consent convention being sidestepped in follow-up primary legislation. As well as sunset provisions for s. 12, the agreement also provides for an equivalent reregulatory 'freezing' in respect of England: a political constraint on the UK Government fitting well with Welsh constitutional policy.[103] Looking more broadly, Welsh actors—having negotiated hard and having settled on the

[97] Minister for the Cabinet Office and Chancellor of the Duchy of Lancaster David Lidington, speech on Brexit, 26 February 2018.

[98] European Union (Legal Continuity) (Scotland) Bill; Law Derived from the European Union (Wales) Act 2018.

[99] For the repeal by regulations of (what had become) the Welsh Continuity Act, see National Assembly for Wales, *Record of Proceedings*, 20 November 2018.

[100] UK Government and Welsh Government, *Intergovernmental Agreement on the European Union (Withdrawal) Bill and the Establishment of Common Frameworks and Attached Supplementary Memorandum* (2018).

[101] National Assembly for Wales, *Record of Proceedings*, 15 May 2018 (Plaid Cymru dissenting); Scottish Parliament, Official Report, 15 May 2018 (Scottish Conservatives dissenting).

[102] In contrast to the standard model of s. 109 Government of Wales Act 2006 and s. 30 Scotland Act 1998. In conferring powers on the devolved administrations to make relevant regulations within devolved competence, s. 11 and Schedule 2 of the 2018 Act also show greater generosity than the bill as published.

[103] UK Government and Welsh Government, 'Intergovernmental Agreement', paragraphs 5–9.

basis of the twin imperatives of devolutionary space and central government responsibility—could now claim a particular credibility in the ongoing negotiations on common frameworks. Moreover, from a quasi-federal viewpoint, there was clearly a case for keeping the proverbial 'nuclear option' of refusal of legislative consent in reserve. Not signing off the intergovernmental agreement effectively meant a constitutional precedent of Westminster override, as the Scottish experience promptly confirmed.

The Counsel General for Wales was naturally an interested party in the Supreme Court proceedings on the Scottish Bill.[104] Of particular concern from the Welsh perspective were the arguments by UK Law Officers for an expansive reading of the international relations reservation and of legal uncertainty in the situation of parallel UK and devolved legislation. These smacked of a firm belief in hierarchy and had evident potential across devolved competence more generally. In this regard, the more targeted nature of the Court's ruling on the content and sequencing of the Scottish Bill, whereby the challenge was partially successful, is not insensitive in 'new Union' terms. The Counsel General duly welcomed 'the clarity. . . brought to the scope of devolved powers'.[105]

Looking forwards, attempts to breathe new life into the legislative consent convention will be a significant test of Welsh constitutional positioning. At one level, we see how fostering and protection of the convention is a consistent theme in the strongly devolutionist and pro-UK sub-state policy, the basic principle being a chief form of defence for self-rule and source of leverage in an uncodified constitution. Of course as all the actors know, the UK Supreme Court robustly states in *Miller*[106] that the issue of legislative consent is for the political, not legal, sphere. At the same time, in emphasizing the important role of the convention in facilitating harmonious relationships between the different legislatures, the Court effectively echoes Welsh constitutional policy as laid out in the intervention in the case from the Counsel General.[107] At another level, we observe how the extended Brexit process has generated pressures of an unheralded scale on the convention. In this regard, neither central insistence on a free rein in self-declared abnormal conditions, nor a Scottish approach of refusal of consent to Brexit-related Bills, fits the Welsh way. First Minister Carwyn Jones is duly seen advocating a new Memorandum of Understanding on the circumstances in which refusals of consent can legitimately be overridden, and a more explicit stage of UK Parliamentary consideration of the implications of so proceeding.[108] Such proposals may just possibly have traction.[109]

---

[104] *The UK Withdrawal from the European Union (Legal Continuity) (Scotland) Bill—Reference by the Attorney General and the Advocate General for Scotland* [2018] UKSC 64; Counsel General, Written Submissions.

[105] Counsel General, Written Statement, 20 December 2018.

[106] *R (on the application of Miller and Dos Santos) v Secretary of State for Exiting the European Union* [2017] UKSC 5.

[107] Ibid., paragraph 151. See further, G. Anthony, *Devolution, Brexit and the Sewel Convention* (2018).

[108] Carwyn Jones, *Brexit and Devolution: Stresses, Strains and Solutions* (2018).

[109] See for similar recommendations, House of Commons Public Administration and Constitutional Affairs Committee, 'Devolution and Exiting the EU', paragraphs 64–8.

Issues of shared governance are naturally brought to the fore in the related work stream on common frameworks. From the standpoint of Welsh ministers, a positive approach couched in terms of subsidiarity fitted with a strong sense of interconnection between the devolved and non-devolved layers of governance. The political obligation 'to reach agreements which benefit all and harm none' in areas of devolved competence was thus readily accepted.[110] In this regard, it is important to bear in mind the multiple scope and design choices associated with reregulatory arrangements in the context of an uncertain Brexit framework. Classically a product of countervailing constitutional, political, and administrative demands for convergence and divergence in different sectors and over time, EU common frameworks themselves come in many shapes and sizes. Likewise, the important place in EU governance of composite administration, in the inclusive sense of administration by co-dependent actors, and of 'soft law' techniques such as concordats, guidance and benchmarking,[111] serves to illuminate the fact of reregulation as not simply a legislative endeavour.

Amid much by way of technical dialogue, the scale of the proposed pan-UK arrangements would be whittled down as the two devolved governments effectively pressed arguments of proportionality and subsidiarity, or more careful targeting. From a Welsh Government perspective, a principles-based agreement was of particular value in framing the continuing official dialogue and, while leaving much open in terms of practical policy tools, encouraging a more collaborative and trust-building approach. Common frameworks, it was said, would respect the devolution settlements (and adhere to the Good Friday Agreement), maintain, as a minimum, equivalent territorial flexibility for tailoring policies to that under existing EU rules, and, restating a previous UK Government policy line, lead to a significant increase in devolved decision-making powers. There were of course important limitations. Sitting comfortably with the general reservation of foreign affairs etc. in the devolution legislation,[112] outcomes were to be without prejudice to the UK's negotiations and future relationship with the EU.[113]

Drilling down, we see how the two intergovernmental deals fit with the design process at civil service level. Areas of EU law that intersect with devolved competence are identified, some 64 in the case of Wales; assessments are made of the risks associated with further divergence and the different areas classified accordingly; policy development and engagement largely focuses on some 24 core areas, such as chemicals regulation, fisheries and food labelling, where frameworks with legislative elements are considered appropriate.[114] A recurring theme is the emphasis on soft law technique,

---

[110] Welsh Government, 'Brexit and Devolution', p. 4.

[111] C. Harlow and R. Rawlings, *Process and Procedure in EU Administration* (2014); R. Rawlings, 'Soft Law Never Dies' in M. Elliott and D. Feldman (eds.) *The Cambridge Companion to Public Law* (2015).

[112] As in Wales Act 2017, s. 3 and Schedule 1 inserting new Schedule 7A Part 1 paragraph 10 to Government of Wales Act 2006.

[113] Joint Ministerial Committee (EU Negotiations) Communiqué, 16 October 2017.

[114] UK Cabinet Office, *Frameworks Analysis: Breakdown of Areas of EU Law that Intersect with Devolved Competence in Scotland, Wales and Northern Ireland* (2018).

not least with a view to intergovernmental coordination of the kind broadly favoured
by 'new Union' thinking. Predictably, the core areas themselves are subject to a hybrid
approach, whereby certain formal legal requirements of consistency are matched with
wider working arrangements through memorandums of understanding.[115] Shared
governance in action, the detailed administrative process itself involves considerable
organizational growth not unlike that in EU governance: multilateral workshops, technical working groups, a Frameworks Project Board. Notably, the early UK Government
reviews speak not only of collaborative and constructive discussions with colleagues
in the devolved governments on matters of mutual interest, but also of joint progress
sufficient to obviate the need for the exercise of order-making powers under s. 12 of
the 2018 Act.[116] Since Parliamentary sovereignty could be invoked in extremis, why,
it may be asked, all the previous Whitehall fuss exhibited in the 'devolution clauses' of
the Withdrawal Bill?

A standing commitment to review the ramshackle machinery of IGR effectively
grounds another related work stream.[117] The Welsh Government has duly envisioned
'deeper and sustained co-operation' between the several centres of executive power,
developed on the basis of agreement and fashioned in the light of EU experience.
Taking a shared governance approach to new heights, this is the stuff of negotiation
and co-decision on common frameworks through a 'UK Council of Ministers' loosely
modelled on the EU Council, and ultimately premised on a 'UK plus one devolved
administration' rule for affirmative decisions.[118] At one with another move beyond the
binary (devolved and non-devolved) approach to competence, clear and continuing
acceptance of the devolved administrations as legitimate interlocutors in UK decision-
making which bears directly on their interests is also a priority, as most obviously in
the Brexit planning with trade policy.[119] Looking forwards, it would be a remarkable
shift in position if Whitehall, and indeed the Scottish Government, signed up to comprehensive, executive-style arrangements of the 'UKCoM' type. The development or
otherwise of joint ministerial machinery under such rubrics as 'Agriculture and fisheries', 'Economic policy' and 'International trade' in turn makes for a more appropriate
test of the general Welsh policy approach in this field, subject yet again to the uncertainties of the extended Brexit process. The vexed issues with IGR-type arrangements
of transparency and accountability must also be kept in mind, however. Not least with
a view to matching shared governance with democratic oversight, National Assembly
members have taken a lead in advocating closer forms of inter-parliamentary relations
inside the UK, shaped perhaps through a 'Speakers' Conference'.[120]

[115] UK Cabinet Office, *The European Union (Withdrawal) Act and Common Frameworks, First Report*
(2018); *Second Report* (2019).

[116] Ibid.

[117] See N. McEwen et al., *Reforming Intergovernmental Relations in the United Kingdom* (2018).

[118] Welsh Government, 'Brexit and Devolution', pp. 6, 17–18.

[119] Welsh Government, *Trade Policy: The Issues for Wales* (2018). See further, Mark Drakeford, 'The Future
of Devolution'.

[120] National Assembly for Wales Constitutional and Legislative Affairs Committee, *UK governance post-
Brexit* (2018). See further, House of Commons Public Administration and Constitutional Affairs Committee,
'*Devolution and Exiting the EU*', paragraphs 138–151.

Looking across the piece, the Welsh Government is seen invoking Brexit as a 'crisis' driving constitutional change in hitherto stunted fields of development. Hence, Carwyn Jones's argument that reform of domestic intergovernmental arrangements is 'more imperative and more possible'.[121] In this regard, we see how the distinct quasi-federal positioning between London and Edinburgh has provided Cardiff with opportunities as well as challenges. Attention is here drawn to parts of the domestic constitutional narrative all too easily obscured by the bright lights of developments in Parliament Square. As for the constitutional legacy, a recognition in light of the sheer intensity of the political, administrative and legal engagement of a more central role in UK governance for the devolved governments than Whitehall had previously acknowledged would clearly fit with the Welsh way. Let us see.

JUSTICE AND JURISDICTION: FOUNDATIONAL QUESTIONS

For the reasons explained, it would have been most odd if the Welsh Government had not established the independent Commission on Justice in Wales in the wake of the Wales Act 2017. Chaired by the former Lord Chief Justice of England and Wales Lord Thomas of Cwmgiedd,[122] and expected to report in late 2019, the Commission has sufficiently wide terms of reference to suggest that its recommendations should be of much interest not only in, but also outside, Wales. As against a narrow exercise in formal constitution-building, a range of social, economic and legal concerns is included as part of the quest for a more just, fair, and prosperous country:[123]

> To review the operation of the justice system in Wales and set a long term vision for its future, with a view to:
>
> - promoting better outcomes in terms of access to justice, reducing crime and promoting rehabilitation;
> - ensuring that the jurisdictional arrangements and legal education address and reflect the role of justice in the governance and prosperity of Wales as well as distinct issues that arise in Wales;
> - promoting the strength and sustainability of the Welsh legal services sector and maximising its contribution to the prosperity of Wales.

How else to proceed than through a series of work streams, both classically subject-based (criminal justice and civil, family and administrative justice), and cross-cutting (access to justice and equalities, legal sector and the economy, knowledge, skills and innovation), and flowing into the innately constitutional discussion of governance and

---

[121] Carwyn Jones, 'Brexit and Devolution'. And see generally, V. Bogdanor, *Beyond Brexit: Towards a British Constitution* (2019).

[122] The author is a member of the Commission.

[123] First Minister Carwyn Jones, written statement, 20 November 2017. See further, Counsel General for Wales, Jeremy Miles, *Towards a Just Wales* (2018).

jurisdictional matters? Not one to lower the bar, Lord Thomas has spoken of 'a unique opportunity to set a new direction of travel', one that 'could set Wales apart as a model for excellence with a justice system and a legal system that work for all.'[124]

Let us put this in broad historical perspective. Building on the so-called 'Acts of Union' of England and Wales in Tudor times,[125] which did much to suppress an old Welsh legal history,[126] early nineteenth century Parliamentary inquiries into distinctive Welsh court structures eventually yielded the proverbial 'right answer' of assimilation.[127] Indeed, it would take until the middle of the last century for the Welsh Language to begin to be recognized inside the now unified legal system of England and Wales.[128] There are today increasing examples of Wales as a polity being recognized inside that system: from the skeleton of a Welsh tribunals structure to an element of regionalization with the Administrative Court in Wales,[129] and on through varying degrees of Welsh representation in the so-called 'justice infrastructure' of statutory agencies, executive agencies and executive and advisory non-departmental public bodies operating in the field. Patchy and often hesitant, the development illustrates not only the broadening devolutionary dynamic since 1998 but also the strong hold of the Whitehall department hitherto, while also underwriting the local demand for more principled approaches.[130] Viewed against this backdrop, the issue with the Thomas Commission is not whether, but how strong, the recommended dose of centrifugalism.[131]

Given the terms of reference, it should not be surprising to learn of a strong focus in the Thomas Commission on criminal justice and policing. Underwriting the Welsh Government's plea for an enhanced policy space in which to bring more coordinated and progressive strategies to bear in these fields, not least in view of extraordinarily high rates of imprisonment,[132] a mound of critical evidence has rapidly accumulated around a chief 'jagged edge' in the constitutional arrangements unique to Wales.[133] A classic product of an unprincipled development, this is the sometimes dizzying arrangement in which areas of self-rule such as education, housing, and social care intersect and overlap with policy fields reserved to London on the basis of the England and Wales justice paradigm, not least policing, prisons, and probation. A recipe for holistic approaches to 'reducing crime and promoting rehabilitation' this is not.

---

[124] Lord Thomas of Cwmgiedd, *A New Direction for Justice* (2018); see also, Lord Thomas of Cwmgiedd, *The Past and the Future of the Law in Wales* (2017).

[125] Laws in Wales Acts 1535/6 and 1542/3. With the Plantagenet conquest, the English common law system was introduced to Wales via the Statute of Rhuddlan in 1284.

[126] As famously expressed in the Welsh codification at the end of the first (Christian) millennium: see D. Jenkins, *The Law of Hywel Dda* (1986).

[127] Foreshadowing abolition of the Courts of Great Sessions in Wales in 1830. The Wales and Berwick Act 1746 had already included Wales in the statutory definition of England.

[128] Welsh Courts Act 1942; built on by the Welsh Language Act 1967 (which also repealed the Welsh element of the Wales and Berwick Act).

[129] D. Gardner, *Administrative Law and the Administrative Court in Wales* (2016).

[130] H. Pritchard, *Justice in Wales* (2016); H. Pritchard, 'Revisiting Legal Wales' (2019) 23 *Edinburgh Law Review* 123.

[131] See further, T. Watkin, *The Legal History of Wales* (2nd edn., 2012).

[132] Wales Governance Centre, *Sentencing and Immediate Custody in Wales* (2019).

[133] See especially, R. Jones and R. Wyn Jones, *Justice at the Jagged Edge in Wales* (2019).

Equality issues are a recurring theme. An aspect previously highlighted in terms of 'England and Wales', overrepresentation in the criminal justice system and underrepresentation in the legal profession and judiciary of ethnic minorities are particularly concerning.[134] Austerity-related problems of access to justice also show the Commission casting new light on the workings of the legal system in Wales. Contextualized in terms of legal advice 'deserts', the impact of court closures and disproportionately large cuts in legal aid in Wales feature prominently.[135] From the standpoint of the Welsh Government, such evidence is grist to the mill in formal constitution-building, so helping to ground the devolutionary argument in a very practical or 'real world' way and build (elite) consensus around it. The standard central government line that the current unified legal system works well for Wales is challenged as never before.

Despite, or perhaps partly because of, limited resources, the twin potentials of small country governance for a more joined-up approach, and for collaborative or partnership ways of working, are commonly highlighted in the engagement with the Commission.[136] A new forum has been ventured, one which in determinedly autochthonous fashion would bring together the Counsel General and senior judiciary, representatives of the legal professions and law schools, and other stakeholders in the justice system, on an all-Wales basis. Aimed at promoting knowledge and skills, best practice, and innovation, the *Law Council of Wales/Cyngor Cyfraith Cymru* would have a broad and flexible remit, including such matters as the propagation of Welsh law, access to justice, equality and diversity in the justice system, and the development of 'law tech'.[137] While not dependent on further constitutional change involving the justice system, this type of standing body could have a useful role to play in helping to deal with the implications for legal practice and generally smoothing the way.

How else to proceed on governance and jurisdictional arrangements than through a set of foundational questions? Especially when the concept of 'jurisdiction' has the chameleon-like quality of being variously associated with a defined territory, a distinct body of law, and separate institutions making and applying that law.[138] Together with accountability, key organizational values such as coherence, workability, and robustness must be factored into the constitutional equation. Recommendations for largescale legislative and executive devolution in the realm of criminal justice and policing would also help justify some general reworking in this more institutional and conceptual sphere.

First, should there be a Justice Minister in the Welsh Government? Separate that is from the classic law officer role played by the Counsel General. How otherwise, it may

---

[134] See, building on the *Lammy Review* (2017), Thomas Commission, WS 88 (Equality and Human Rights Commission). See further, EHRC, *Is Wales Fairer?* (2018).

[135] Thomas Commission, WS10 (Wales and Chester Circuit); and see generally, Wales Governance Centre, *Public Spending on the Justice System in Wales* (2019).

[136] Including by First Minister Carwyn Jones: Thomas Commission, OE1.

[137] Commission on Justice in Wales Consultation Paper, *Law Council of Wales/Cyngor Cyfraith Cymru* (2018).

[138] R. Percival, 'How to Do Things with Jurisdictions' (2017) *Public Law* 249.

be asked, can a tolerably coherent, responsive and effective justice policy for the sub-state polity be delivered? Moreover, in view of an entrenched 'vicious circle' of legal business and talent disappearing over the 'border', most obviously to (the City of) London,[139] why not some clear ministerial focus on strengthening the local legal services sector and 'maximising its contribution to the prosperity of Wales'? From the standpoint of Welsh constitutional policy, the establishment of a ministerial department would itself contribute to a consistent structure across the devolved territories. Under the disciplines of parliamentary government this would necessarily entail designated lines of scrutiny and oversight in the sub-state legislature, most obviously as in Scotland and Northern Ireland in the form of a Justice Committee.

Secondly, should there be a law of England and a law of Wales, or a continuation of the law of England and Wales? More particularly, as regards 'a long term vision' can the current framework of the law of England and Wales with different territorial applications bear the increasing weight of dual dynamics of divergence? Even with little responsibility for criminal justice, the sub-state polity had by 2019 produced over 50 Acts and Measures, and over 6,000 pieces of subordinate legislation. Meanwhile, the fact of contrasting legislative activity by the UK 'government for England' has become ever more apparent in view of so-called 'political cohabitation' and 'English votes for English laws'.[140] We also touch here on problems with the accessibility of law in Wales, associated not only with the piecemeal character of devolved powers and scarce economies of scale, but also with the customary assumption in the justice system of 'for Wales, see England'.[141] Indeed, both the Law Commission and the Counsel General have laboured long and hard on a path-breaking programme of legislative codification for the sub-state polity.[142] Contributing to a distinctive legal and constitutional milieu, this feeds into the Welsh Government's advocacy of a law of Wales.

As for the mechanics, a law of England and a law of Wales would suggest a set of choice of law rules akin to those already applying between the different territorial jurisdictions within the UK.[143] At the same time, particularly strong elements of substantive harmonization are readily envisaged in view of shared common law heritage; and, fitting with the domestic Union as a form of economic integration, the more so in key areas of commercial and private law. Market essentials such as company law, intellectual property law and insolvency law would thus be reserved.[144] Viewed in this light, a decoupling of the law of England and Wales is a less challenging constitutional change than perhaps at first appears.

---

[139] See for example, Thomas Commission, WS 10 (Wales and Chester Circuit).

[140] D. Gover and M. Kenny, 'Answering the West Lothian Question?' (2018) 71 *Parliamentary Affairs* 760.

[141] See generally, M. Ford, *For Wales, See England: Language, Nationhood and Identity* (2016).

[142] Law Commission, *Form and Accessibility of the Law Applicable in Wales*, No. 366 (2016); Welsh Government, Legislation (Wales) Bill 2018.

[143] K. Hood, *Conflict of Laws within the UK* (2007).

[144] So effectively rehearsing Schedule 5, Part II of the Scotland Act 1998: see Thomas Commission, WS 142 (Counsel General).

Thirdly, should there be a separate judiciary for Wales and if so to what level? Assuming, that is, pan-UK linkage in the Supreme Court, with of course a dedicated Welsh seat.[145] Much ink has been spilt over the years on this question, with various proposals for a High Court of Wales and (hence) a High Court of England;[146] and also, sitting comfortably with a quasi-federal project in view of the status and precedent-setting capacity, for a matching division of the Court of Appeal. Echoes of the flexible concept of a 'distinct jurisdiction', cross-border 'ticketing' of senior judiciary might in turn help to ease the transition.[147] Conversely, and helping to explain the imbroglio over the Wales Act 2017, there is a considerable history of rebuffs to Welsh constitutional development founded on the single legal jurisdiction of England and Wales.[148] Central government hostility to a reserved powers model prior to the subversive *Agricultural Sector* case was in this sense par for the course. Viewed in this light, the Thomas Commission has effectively been tasked with considering an old question afresh in the light of reversed constitutional tectonics.

Evidence to the Thomas Commission on jurisdictional arrangements reflects all this. Much is familiar from previous debates, not least around the Silk Commission.[149] As well as the ongoing legal divergence, reformists typically reference national identity and the social, cultural and linguistic condition of Wales, and also legal commercial and service opportunities in a new jurisdiction.[150] Especially given the excellent reputation of existing senior court structures, countervailing concerns are raised about local capacities and yet further leeching of legal business to England. But a new strand in the evidence suggests the inevitability of change in the jurisdictional arrangements following the introduction of the reserved powers model.[151] In this regard, future historians of Wales may well remark on how the hitherto controlling constitutional factor became decentred.

Fourthly, should there be a separate legal sector in Wales? The legal professions' own organization clearly references the constitutional status quo: the classically cross-border Wales and Chester Circuit; the Law Society of England and Wales, with a satellite office in Cardiff. Conversely, if Wales had a separate legal system, why not a new dedicated status for the local professions in the conditions of 'national devolution'? Issues are raised of education and training, and likewise of professional legal regulation, where arrangements in Scotland and Northern Ireland again provide useful comparators. In this regard, the Counsel General's support for 'dual focused expertise and dual experience' in the light of separate forms of English law and Welsh law, coupled

---

[145] So building on the individual appointment of Lord Lloyd-Jones in 2017.

[146] For a contemporary rendition, see Constitution Reform Group, *Act of Union Bill* (2018).

[147] There is already provision at tribunal level: Wales Act 2017, Part 3 and Schedule 5.

[148] T. Watkin, 'Devious Debates and Devolution' in Watkin (ed.), *The Welsh Legal Triads and Other Essays* (2012). See also, National Assembly for Wales Constitutional and Legislative Affairs Committee, *Inquiry into a Separate Welsh Jurisdiction* (2012).

[149] Silk Commission, *Legislative Powers to Strengthen Wales*, Chapter 10.

[150] Justice for Wales, *In Support of a Welsh Jurisdiction* (2015).

[151] See Thomas Commission, WS 142 (Counsel General).

perhaps with mutual recognition and/or some 'cross-border' ticketing, is suitably consistent with Welsh constitutional policy in the face of local professional concerns about cost and reputation or market perception.[152]

Fifthly, should there be separate forms of 'justice infrastructure' for Wales? Typically linked with the Home Office or Ministry of Justice on an England and Wales basis, current arrangements are sprawling and fragmented. As with legal professional regulation, parts of the infrastructure are of considerable functional significance: for example on composition, the Judicial Appointments Commission; on administration, the Courts and Tribunals Service; on criminal justice, a major cluster of bodies including the Crown Prosecution Service, the Prison and Probation Service, and the Parole Board; on access to justice, the Legal Aid Agency; and on reform, the Law Commission.[153] Issues of steering, ethos, and partnership-working, and of resources and funding, loom large here; there is also much experience in the other devolved territories to draw on. As against a general decoupling, should there be prioritization and reordering through a spectrum of approaches? Possible options include partial separation of the infrastructure into 'devolved Welsh authorities';[154] cooperative forms of joint statutory ownership by the two governments on a cross-border basis; and strengthened Welsh inputs in those remaining England and Wales (and GB and UK) justice bodies. The further possibilities of integration or amalgamation—as with criminal justice inspection in Northern Ireland—and of creation, as with the home-grown Human Rights Commission in Scotland, also need careful consideration in the conditions of small country governance.

Looking forwards, this series of questions provides benchmarks for assessing the constitutional boldness of the Thomas Commission and the responses to the recommendations in Cardiff Bay and, in light of the English doctrine of Parliamentary sovereignty, in Whitehall and Westminster. There is, after all, an evident anomaly in comparative constitutional terms. Why should Wales be odd one out in the great common law family of state and sub-state systems in not having matching legislative and executive and judicial architecture?

CONCLUSION

Wales has come a long way. At the heart of this devolutionary process is an old theme in territorial constitutional development: winning some autonomy with a view to winning more. This goes in tandem with a particularly strong role for autochthonous forms of polity-building, most obviously around the National Assembly. Along the way, a succession of so-called 'devolution settlements' has been subverted: in pointing up their basic flaws, local actors have successfully maintained a sense of constitutional unsettlement. The talisman in terms of political and administrative technique is the

---

[152] Ibid.   [153] See further, Chapter 8 by Andrew Le Sueur.
[154] Wales Act 2017, Schedule 3. As the Welsh Government would prefer with the Law Commission, for example: see Draft Government and Laws in Wales Bill, clauses 102–105 and Schedule 11.

independent commission: a repeating source in Wales of evidence-based pressures for reform. Viewed in comparative perspective, the UK's uncodified constitution has provided elements of malleability and instability for the maturing sub-state polity to exploit. Since the dawn of democratic devolution in 1998, there always has been another (Government of) Wales Act to imagine.

The very fact of a Welsh constitutional policy says much. Viewed against the backdrop of Wales as a largely unaccounted element in the UK constitution, a determinedly active approach at territorial level is a significant historical feature. Taking constitutional ideas seriously is of the essence of this, a mark of difference from the ad hoc and piecemeal approach familiarly associated with Whitehall. While quasi-federal forms of advocacy are hardly original in comparative constitutional terms, they add up to a distinct Welsh Government positioning in the contemporary UK context. As one would expect, buttressing and advancing Wales's own position is the chief aim, typically in the face of specific policy concerns, adverse institutional politics and seeming lack of trust in Whitehall. Themes of consistent structure, mutual respect, and parity of esteem have an obvious attraction for a junior partner, not least when contextualized through a critical focus on the legal scope and institutional culture of central power. At the same time, a genuine concern for the United Kingdom in conditions of territorial constitutional crisis shines through, as in the emphasis on shared governance and the mediating role of territorial consent. In light of the hitherto limited development of multilateral forms of IGR, and of the multiple reregulatory demands associated with Brexit, the Welsh way represents both a prompt and a benchmark. Not that the policy can disguise the difficulty inherent in the quasi-federal approach of dealing with Parliamentary sovereignty, or indeed a territorial lack of clout on the bigger constitutional stage, aspects highlighted in the wider Brexit process. Whether or not the United Kingdom as presently constituted survives and prospers is most unlikely to be decided in Wales.

In terms of a 'new Union' mind-set, a matching culture in London remains elusive. While 'events' in the form of the Scottish independence referendum generated favourable ripple effects for Welsh constitutional development, in the guise of the Brexit referendum vote, and hence the early processes of reregulation under the rubric of a UK internal market, they have been hard for Welsh ministers to navigate. Reworking hierarchical assumptions into equitable parameters for common frameworks is a step but only a step. Looking forwards, further devolutionary advance may readily be envisaged in the local conditions of small country governance. In view of the great constitutional as well as policy significance, issues of justice and jurisdictional arrangements rightly command attention. Wales still has far to go.

FURTHER READING

MARK DRAKEFORD, *The Future of Devolution: the UK after Brexit* (2019)

CARWYN JONES, *Our Future Union—A Perspective from Wales* (2014)

CARWYN JONES, *Towards a Better Union: Past, Present and Post-Brexit Prospects for the United Kingdom* (2018)

R. Rawlings, *Delineating Wales: Constitutional, Legal and Administrative Aspects of National Devolution* (2003)

R. Rawlings, *Brexit and the Territorial Constitution: Devolution, Reregulation and Intergovernmental Relations* (2017)

R. Rawlings, 'The Strange Reconstitution of Wales' (2018) *Public Law* 62

R. Scully, and R. Wyn Jones, *Wales Says Yes* (2012)

Lord Thomas of Cwmgiedd, *The Past and the Future of the Law in Wales* (2017)

T. Watkin, *The Legal History of Wales* 2nd edn., (2012)

T. Watkin, and D. Greenberg, *Legislating for Wales* (2018)

Welsh Government, *Brexit and Devolution* (2017)

USEFUL WEBSITES

Commission on Justice in Wales: **https://beta.gov.wales/commission-justice-wales**

PART III

NEW DIRECTIONS?

12

THE RELATIONSHIP BETWEEN PARLIAMENT, THE EXECUTIVE AND THE JUDICIARY

Alison L. Young*

SUMMARY

When examining the recent evolution of the Constitution, it is argued that the UK has become more 'legal' as opposed to 'political'. The last twenty years has seen a growth in legislation and case law, particularly that of the Supreme Court, regulating aspects of the UK constitution. This chapter investigates this claim. It argues that, whilst we can point to a growth in both legislation and case law, when we look at the case law more closely we can see that the courts balance an array of factors when determining how far to control executive actions. These factors include an analysis of the relative institutional features and constitutional role of the legislature, the executive, and the courts. This evidence, in turn, questions the traditional understanding of the separation of powers as a hidden component of the UK constitution. It is not the case that courts merely balance the rule of law and parliamentary sovereignty in order to determine how far to control executive actions. Rather, the courts determine how to make this balance through the lens of the separation of powers, evaluating institutional and constitutional features. In doing so, they are upholding necessary checks and balances in the UK constitution.

INTRODUCTION

It is impossible to talk about the relationship between Parliament, the executive, and the judiciary without thinking about the separation of powers. However, we are often told that the separation of powers plays little role, if any, in the UK constitution. Unlike

* Sir David Williams Professor of Public Law, Cambridge and Fellow of Robinson College, Cambridge.

countries with codified, entrenched constitutions, the ideology of the separation of powers has not played a key role in the creation of the UK constitution—or so we are told. Rather than being designed, the UK constitution has evolved over time. Whilst some of these evolutions may have given rise to a stronger protection of the separation of powers, it is still hard to see this principle as one which underpins the UK constitution, let alone a principle which vies for recognition as one of its key components. Moreover, rather than exemplifying a separation of powers, the UK constitution is described as having a fusion of powers between the executive and the legislature. The Government is formed from whichever political party is able to form a Government which holds the confidence of Parliament. The Prime Minister is the leader of the political party which holds either a majority of the seats in Parliament, or is the leader of the strongest party in either a coalition Government,[1] or a minority Government supported by a 'confidence and supply' agreement.[2] The Prime Minister selects her cabinet from amongst MPs from her political party. Moreover, the Government has considerable control over the initiation of legislation, the time allocated to legislative debate, and, given its majority in Parliament, over the casting of votes on legislation. It is hard to classify a constitution with such fusion between its branches in terms of personnel as one which adheres to the ideology of the separation of powers.

Despite the traditional reluctance to engage with the separation of powers, there is nevertheless growing interest in the nature of the relationship between the legislature, the executive, and the judiciary. This is particularly true of the nature of the relationship between the judiciary and either the executive or the legislature. It is easy to point to recent developments in constitutional law and to see these as evidence of a change in the nature of the UK constitution. There is an apparent move away from the UK's predominantly political controls over the executive towards greater legal controls. This move is seen as one aspect of the growing legalization or judicialization of the UK constitution.[3] It modifies the relationship between the legislature, the executive, and the judiciary by empowering the judiciary to place greater controls or limits on the powers of the executive, in addition to the controls and limits placed on the executive by the legislature.

This chapter aims to challenge both the assumption that the separation of powers has little role to play in the UK constitution and the perceived modification of the relationship between the judiciary and the executive, and the judiciary and the legislature. First, it will investigate the changing nature of the relationship between the legislature, executive, and the judiciary. It will first provide an account of evidence which supports

[1] See, for example, David Cameron during the 2010–2015 Coalition Government formed between the Conservative Party and the Liberal Democrats.

[2] See, for example, Theresa May following the snap general election called in 2017, whose minority Government is supported by the Democratic Unionist Party, which has agreed to support the Conservative Government on the budget, on votes of confidence and on Brexit.

[3] This is also described as a move towards 'juristocracy'. See, K. D. Ewing, 'The Bill of Rights Debate: Democracy or Juristocracy in Britain?' in K. D. Ewing, C. A. Gearty and B. A. Hepple, *Human Rights and Labour Law: Essays for Paul O'Higgins* (London: Mansell, 1994), 147–87 and R. Hirschl, *Towards Juristocracy: The Origins and Consequences of the New Constitutionalism* (Cambridge, Mass: Harvard University Press, 2004).

the claim of a greater judicialization of the UK constitution, with power moving from the executive and the legislature to the judiciary. However, it will then explain how there is insufficient evidence to support so broad a claim. The courts are more willing to control the executive and to interpret legislation in a manner which goes beyond merely determining the will of the legislature. However, the extent to which the court does so is determined by a range of contextual factors. Courts vary the extent to which they are willing to control acts of the executive, or creatively interpret legislation, according to the circumstances of the particular case. Moreover, whilst we can find clear examples of courts being more willing to exert their control, we can also find examples of where courts are more deferential, adopting an approach that provides fewer controls over the executive than we might otherwise have expected.

The discovery of this more contextual approach also questions the role of the separation of powers in the UK constitution. When determining the extent to which the judiciary is willing to control actions of the executive or the legislature, courts draw on factors relating to the relative institutional characteristics and the constitutional roles of all three institutions. I will argue that this contextual approach illustrates that traditional understandings of the role of the separation of powers in the UK constitution fail to fully account for the case law. We often regard the relative role of the legislature, the judiciary, and the executive as depending upon the relative weight we give to parliamentary sovereignty and the rule of law. The greater the importance of the rule of law, the greater the legitimacy of the court in developing legal controls over the executive and, to a more limited extent, over the legislature, and vice versa. However, the case law suggests that courts look more closely at the different institutional features and constitutional roles of the legislature, executive and judiciary when determining principles of judicial review.

In addition, I will argue that this illustrates that the separation of powers plays a fundamental role in the UK constitution, albeit one that remains in the background rather than being directly enforced by the courts. I will argue that it is the separation of powers that determines the relative balance between the rule of law and parliamentary sovereignty rather than it being the case that the relative importance of the rule of law and parliamentary sovereignty dictates the nature of the separation of powers between the three institutions of the UK constitution. I will argue that this provides a stronger normative justification of the UK's uncodified Constitution as well as providing a better account of the case law.

THE JUDICIALIZATION OF THE CONSTITUTION?

The UK constitution is traditionally described as uncodified, with a preference for political as opposed to legal regulation. However, following the enactment of the Constitutional Reform Act 2005[4] and the Human Rights Act 1998, there has arguably been

---

[4] For a discussion of the Act's history, see Lord Windlesham, 'The Constitutional Reform Act 2005: Ministers, Judges and Constitutional Change: Part 1' [2005] *Public Law* 806 and 'The Constitutional Reform Act: The Politics of Constitutional Reform: Part 2' [2006] *Public Law* 35.

a move away from the use of informal, or political, means of determining the relationships between the three branches of government to one which focuses more on
legally-defined, formal relationships.[5] The Act, inter alia, created the Supreme Court.
Rather than sitting as a separate committee of the House of Lords, the UK's highest
court now sits in a separate building on Parliament Square. Moreover, the Justices of
the Supreme Court are no longer also members of the second legislative Chamber of
Parliament. The Supreme Court has also made the judiciary and their role more visible,
particularly through the televising of hearings and an accessible website. This has led
to the perception that the Supreme Court is becoming more of a constitutional court,
deciding more issues of constitutional importance than were decided by the House of
Lords.[6]

The Human Rights Act 1998 has also been said to have had a huge impact on the role
of the UK's highest court.[7] It provides clear evidence of a move towards a perception of
greater legal control over actions of the legislature and the executive. Even if there are
disputes as to the extent to which the Human Rights Act provides a better control than
was, or could have been, provided by the common law alone,[8] it is hard to argue with
the conclusion that the existence of the Human Rights Act has led to a greater involvement of the Supreme Court in human rights cases. Moreover, there is a growing perception that the role of the court is to uphold the constitution, as well as the rule of law.
This perception is added to by the role of the Supreme Court when determining the
validity of Acts of the devolved legislatures, either through challenges brought after the
legislation is enacted,[9] or following the special procedure allowing for references to be
made directly to the Supreme Court when legislation has been enacted by the devolved
legislature but has not yet received royal assent.[10] However, it is not the only evidence
used by those wishing to argue that the UK constitution has become more legal, or
when illustrating the potential judicializations of the UK constitution. There is further
evidence of greater legal control over both the legislature and the executive through
developments of the common law, in addition to the role of EU law, and following exit
day, of retained EU law. The next subsection will explore these developments as regards
the relationship between the legislature and the judiciary, before going on to explore
the nature of the relationship between the executive and the judiciary.

[5] R. Hazell, 'Judicial Independence and Accountability in the UK Have Both Emerged Stronger as Result
of the Constitutional Reform Act 2005' [2015] *Public Law* 198.
[6] See, for example, the argument of K. Malleson, 'The Evolving Role of the Supreme Court' [2011] *Public
Law* 754.
[7] See S. Shah and T. Poole, 'The Impact of the Human Rights Act 1998 on the House of Lords' [2009] *Public Law* 347 and T. Poole and S. Shah, 'The Law Lords and Human Rights' (2011) 74 *Modern Law Review* 79.
[8] T.R.S. Allan, 'Parliament's Will and the Justice of the Common Law: The Human Rights Act in Constitutional Perspective' (2006) 59 *Current Legal Problems* 27.
[9] See, for example, *Martin v Most* [2010] UKSC 10, *AXA General Insurance Ltd v Lord Advocate* [2011]
UKSC 46, [2012] 1 AC 868.
[10] See Scotland Act 1998, section 33, Government of Wales Act 2006, section 112 and Northern Ireland Act
1998, sections 33 and 34. See, for example, *Re the UK Withdrawal from the European Union (Legal Continuity)
(Scotland) Bill—Reference by the Attorney General and the Advocate General for Scotland (Scotland)* [2018]
UKSC 64, [2019] 2 WLR 1.

Judicial Controls over the Legislature

It is not hard to find further evidence of what would appear to be a greater role for the court in controlling acts of the legislature. We could list: the principle of legality; the creation of constitutional statutes; examples of the disapplication of legislation that is incompatible with directly effective provisions of EU law; and judicial dicta concerning the possibility that the courts could fail to apply legislation in exceptional circumstances. Each of these examples suggests that courts no longer merely interpret legislation by looking for the clear intention of Parliament, thereby modifying the orthodox understanding of the relationship between Parliament and the courts.

The principle of legality limits the extent to which legislation can restrict or remove fundamental common law rights. General words found in legislation will be read so as to ensure that they do not remove or restrict fundamental common law rights. Fundamental common law rights can only be removed or restricted by clear and specific statutory provisions, or by necessary implication. In addition, where there are clear words enabling the restriction of fundamental common law rights, any restriction of a fundamental common law right must be to achieve a legitimate aim and must be reasonably necessary to achieve that legitimate aim. The principle finds its clearest expression in Lord Hoffmann's statement in *R. v Secretary of State for the Home Department, ex parte Simms*:

> Parliamentary sovereignty means that Parliament can, if it chooses, legislate contrary to fundamental principles of human rights. The Human Rights Act 1998 will not detract from this power. The constraints upon its exercise by Parliament are ultimately political, not legal. But the principle of legality means that Parliament must squarely confront what it is doing and accept the political cost. Fundamental rights cannot be overridden by general or ambiguous words. This is because there is too great a risk that the full implications of their unqualified meaning may have passed unnoticed in the democratic process. In the absence of express language or necessary implication to the contrary, the courts therefore presume that even the most general words were intended to be subject to the basic rights of the individual. In this way the courts of the United Kingdom, though acknowledging the sovereignty of Parliament, apply principles of constitutionality little different from those which exist in countries where the power of the legislature is expressly limited by a constitutional document.[11]

Whilst the principle of legality respects the sovereignty of Parliament in one sense, in that it is still possible for Parliament to legislate in a manner contrary to fundamental rights, it nevertheless requires the courts to interpret legislation in a manner other than through a process of discovering the actual intention of Parliament. Rather, courts presume that Parliament would not wish to legislate contrary to fundamental rights, implying an intention of Parliament that may be different from its actual intention.

One of the clearest examples of the extent to which the courts can potentially stretch parliamentary intention is found in *Evans*.[12] The case concerned the interpretation of

---

[11] [2000] 2 AC 115, 131.   [12] *R. (Evans) v Attorney General* [2015] UKSC 21, [2015] 2 WLR 813.

section 53 of the Freedom of Information Act 2000. The Freedom of Information Act, inter alia, provides a means through which individuals can obtain disclosure of information. Evans, a journalist, had used the provisions of the Act to request the disclosure of correspondence between HRH Prince Charles and various Governmental ministers. The request was originally refused by Governmental departments and the Information Commissioner. However, this refusal was overturned following a full hearing in the Upper Tribunal. Section 53 of the Act empowered, in this instance, the Attorney General to issue a certificate reversing the decision of the Upper Tribunal, when he had 'reasonable grounds' to do so. Lord Neuberger, whose judgment was agreed to by Lords Kerr and Reed, applied the principle of legality, interpreting section 53 in line with constitutional principles. Specifically, Lord Neuberger concluded that section 53 should be read in line with two aspects of the rule of law: that a court decision is binding between the parties and cannot be reversed by the executive, and that decisions of the executive should be subject to judicial review.[13] In order to maintain these elements of the rule of law, Lord Neuberger read 'reasonable grounds' narrowly, reading down this general provision such that 'reasonable grounds' would only exist when there was a 'material change of circumstances since the tribunal decision', or where 'the decision of the tribunal was demonstrably flawed in fact or in law'.[14]

Whilst Lord Neuberger did not provide the only judgment in the case, it does provide an example of how far the courts may be prepared to go when applying the principle of legality. Lord Hughes, with whom Lord Wilson agreed, provided a dissent which was highly critical of the reasoning of Lord Neuberger. For Lord Wilson, to read section 53 in this manner contradicted the clear wording of legislation which empowered the Attorney General to issue a certificate when he had reasonable grounds to do so. Moreover, the restrictive reading of Lord Neuberger essentially rendered section 53 devoid of application in practice. If the Government believed that the Upper Tribunal had made a decision that was 'demonstrably flawed in fact or in law' then there would be the possibility of reviewing the decision of the Upper Tribunal either for error of law, or for material error of relevant fact. In addition, the short time limit within which any certificate could be issued made it practically impossible for a 'material change of circumstances' to arise. As such, it was difficult for Lord Wilson to think of any circumstances under which the Attorney General would be able to exercise his powers under section 53.

In addition to the principle of legality, the courts have developed a category of constitutional statutes. The classification of statutes as 'constitutional' originates in the judgment of Laws LJ in *Thoburn v Sunderland City Council*.[15] The case concerned the 'Metric Martyrs', market traders who wished to continue selling loose fruit and vegetables in imperial measurements of pounds and ounces as opposed to adopting

---

[13] Ibid., [52].   [14] Ibid., [71].
[15] [2002] EWHC 195 (Admin), [2003] QB 151. See also *H v Lord Advocate* [2012] UKSC 24, [2013] 1 AC 413.

the metric measurements of kilograms and grams. The requirement to use metric measurements was found in delegated legislation implementing an EU Directive. The delegated legislation contradicted provisions found in the Weights and Measures Act 1985, which allowed fruit and vegetables to be sold either in metric or imperial measurements. The delegated legislation was enacted under section 2(2) of the European Communities Act 1972, which empowers the executive to enact measures to implement obligations under EU law. Section 2(4) of the Act makes it clear that any enactment passed under section 2(2) extends to any provision 'as might be made by an Act of Parliament'. In other words, the provision was a Henry VIII clause, empowering the executive to enact delegated legislation which modifies or amends primary legislation. The argument arose as to whether this power extended to include the amendment of legislation enacted after the European Communities Act 1972. In reaching his conclusion that the delegated legislation was valid, Laws LJ argued that the European Communities Act 1972 was a constitutional statute. As such, its provisions could not be impliedly repealed. Constitutional statutes can only be repealed by clear, specific, and precise words, or through express repeal. The Weights and Measures Act had not specifically or expressly repealed the provisions of the 1972 Act. This does not mean that constitutional legislation cannot be repealed at all—as is demonstrated by section 1 of the European Union (Withdrawal) Act 2018, which expressly repeals the European Communities Act 1972, by stating that '[t]he European Communities Act 1972 is repealed on exit day'.

The development of constitutional statutes modifies the relationship between the legislature and the courts in a more fundamental manner than the principle of legality. It does so by providing two challenges to the principle of parliamentary supremacy. The orthodox conception of parliamentary supremacy finds its clearest account in the work of A. V. Dicey. Dicey argued that parliamentary sovereignty requires that there are no legal limits on the substantive powers of Parliament to enact legislation and that legislation, once enacted, cannot be questioned by the courts. However, Parliament is not able to enact legislation which binds future Parliaments, either as to the content of future legislation, or as to the manner and form in which this legislation is enacted. To do so would be to restrict the substantive law-making power of future Parliaments.[16] The inability of Parliament to bind its successors as to the manner and form of future legislation provides the basis for the doctrine of implied repeal. When there is a conflict between an earlier and a later statute, the later statute prevails, impliedly repealing the provisions of the earlier legislation. Even if earlier legislation were to require that a referendum was needed to overturn its provisions, enacting legislation in the future without a referendum would impliedly repeal the requirement to hold a referendum.[17] The creation of constitutional statutes restricts the scope of the doctrine of implied repeal. It argues that it does

---

[16] A. V. Dicey, *An Introduction to the Study of the Law of the Constitution* (10th edition) Chapter 1 and J. Goldsworthy, *The Sovereignty of Parliament: History and Philosophy* (Oxford University Press, 2001).

[17] See *Ellen Street Estates v Minister of Health* [1934] 1 KB 590.

not apply to constitutional statutes. Instead, constitutional legislation can only be repealed through specific words or through express repeal.[18]

In addition, the creation of constitutional statutes creates a hierarchy between different types of legislation. Dicey argued that the orthodox theory of parliamentary sovereignty requires that all legislation be treated in the same way, each being as important as the other. However, the creation of constitutional statutes requires that some legislation be treated differently from other legislation. Constitutional statutes are more important and cannot be repealed in the same way as other legislation. In addition, Laws LJ's argument in *Thoburn* poses a more fundamental challenge to parliamentary sovereignty. Laws reaches his conclusion as he classifies parliamentary sovereignty as a principle of the common law. As such, courts have the power to modify the content of parliamentary sovereignty, including placing limits on its scope of application, or changing the nature of parliamentary sovereignty such that Parliaments are able to bind future Parliaments as to the manner and form in which they enact legislation.[19] The classification of parliamentary sovereignty as a principle of the common law suggests that it is not Parliament who is supreme, but rather the courts. Parliament only enjoys legislative supremacy to the extent that this is conferred upon it by the common law, as determined by the courts. Although it may be argued that legislation is able to override the common law, this too could also be construed as a principle of the common law. As such, it could be open to courts to modify this principle, such that there were aspects of the common law that could not be overridden by legislation, even if this was the clear and specific intention of Parliament.

This leads on to the third way in which the traditional understanding of the relationship between the legislature and the courts has changed, such that courts no longer merely interpret legislation according to the will of Parliament. Dicta can now be found in the case law suggesting that there may be exceptional circumstances in which the courts might refuse to enforce legislation. The clearest account in recent case law is found in the dicta of Lord Steyn in *Jackson v Attorney General*, which concerned the validity of the Hunting Act 2004.[20] Lord Steyn first asserted that parliamentary sovereignty was still a general principle of the UK constitution, before asserting that

> [i]n exceptional circumstances involving an attempt to abolish judicial review or the ordinary role of the courts, the Appellate Committee of the House of Lords or the new Supreme Court may have to consider whether this is a constitutional fundamental which even a sovereign Parliament acting at the behest of a complaisant House of Commons cannot abolish.[21]

---

[18] For a discussion of the impact of this conclusion on parliamentary sovereignty, see A. L. Young, 'Redefining Parliamentary Sovereignty' and J. Goldsworthy, 'Parliamentary Sovereignty and Constitutional Change in the United Kingdom', both in R. Rawlings, P. Leyland and A.L. Young (eds.) *Sovereignty and the Law: Domestic, European and International Perspectives* (Oxford, Oxford University Press, 2013).

[19] See A.L. Young, 'Hunting Sovereignty: *Jackson v Attorney General*' (2006) Public Law 187.

[20] [2005] UKHL 56, [2006] 1 AC 262.   [21] Ibid., [102].

Jackson is not the only case in which this dictum can be found. Similar statements can be found in *AXA General Insurance v Lord Advocate* which concerned the validity of the Damages (Asbestos-Related Conditions) Scotland Act 2009, an Act of the Scottish Parliament designed to reverse a court decision to provide a means of enabling those harmed by asbestos-related conditions to claim compensation.[22] One argument made before the Supreme Court was that the Scottish Act of Parliament was invalid as it breached principles of the common law. Lord Reed and Lord Hope both concluded that there were common law limits on the powers of the Scottish Parliament. Lord Reed reached this conclusion through an application of the principle of legality. The broad powers conferred on the Scottish Parliament in the Scotland Act 1998 were to be read so as not to include the power to act contrary to fundamental common law rights. Lord Hope, however, reached the same conclusion through a different route. He drew on his earlier statements in *Jackson*, where he asserted that 'the rule of law enforced by the courts is the ultimate controlling factor on which our constitution is based'.[23] He then stated that

> [i]t is not entirely unthinkable that a government which has that power may seek to use it to abolish judicial review or to diminish the role of the courts in protecting the interests of the individual . . . The rule of law requires that the judges must retain the power to insist that legislation of that extreme kind is not law which the courts will recognise.[24]

Both *Jackson* and *AXA General Insurance* concern possible exceptional circumstances that could arise were Parliament to legislate in a manner which removed judicial review from the courts, or to diminish the role of the courts to such an extent that they were no longer able to protect the rights of individuals in order to uphold the rule of law. However, these are not the only circumstances where the courts have suggested in dicta that they might refuse to enforce legislation. In *Moohan*, the courts had to determine whether preventing prisoners from voting in the referendum on Scottish Independence breached either Convention rights or fundamental common law rights.[25] Lord Hodge stated, again in dicta, that he did

> not exclude the possibility that in the very unlikely event that a parliamentary majority abusively sought to entrench its power by a curtailment of the franchise or similar device, the common law, informed by principles of democracy and the rule of law and international norms, would be able to declare such legislation unlawful.[26]

This dictum was referred to in *Shindler v Chancellor of the Duchy of Lancaster*, which concerned the exclusion of UK citizens who had lived abroad for 15 years or more from the electoral register of those entitled to vote in the European Union Referendum.[27] In *Shindler*, the Court of Appeal concluded that this exclusion of voters was not an abusive attempt to entrench power.

---

[22] [2011] UKSC 46, [2012] 1 AC 868.
[23] Ibid. [51]. His statement in *Jackson v AG* (n. 20) can be found at [107].
[24] *AXA General Insurance v Lord Advocate* (n. 22), [51].
[25] *Moohan v Lord Advocate* [2014] UKSC 67, [2015] AC 901, [35].   [26] Ibid.
[27] [2016] EWCA Civ 469, [2017] QB 226.

The only examples of where courts have disapplied legislation have occurred when the courts were dealing with conflicts between directly effective provisions of EU law and UK legislation. In *Factortame*, the courts famously granted an interim injunction to suspend the application of the Merchant Shipping Act 1988 to Spanish fishermen who were relying on their rights in EU law to fish in British waters.[28] More recently, the UK Court of Appeal and the Supreme Court have disapplied legislation which breached EU human rights under the EU's Charter of Fundamental Rights and Freedoms, where the Charter was applied to issues within the scope of EU law.[29] Although this would appear to suggest a dramatic change in the relationship between the legislature and the courts, it is important to recognize that this disapplication occurred due to the principle of the supremacy of directly effective EU law. Moreover, the courts were relying on legislation when applying the principle of the supremacy of EU law.

Following the UK's withdrawal from the European Union, it will still be possible for retained EU law to disapply legislation. However, the European Union (Withdrawal) Act 2018 (EU(W)A) makes it clear that this only applies to conflicts arising between retained EU law—i.e. provisions of EU law that have been incorporated into UK law by the Act—and legislation enacted prior to exit day,[30] or modifications of these laws enacted after exit day when this modification includes an intention to preserve the supremacy of EU law.[31] The EU(W)A expressly states that this includes the ability of retained EU law to disapply legislation.[32] However, it does so in a manner which preserves the traditional role between the legislature and the courts. Retained EU law obtains its legal validity through the provisions of the EU(W)A, with retained EU law coming into force on exit day. Although retained EU law disapplies legislation, it is disapplying legislation enacted prior to retained EU law coming into force in the UK. As such, the courts are merely giving effect to the latest will of Parliament. Moreover, there is nothing in the EU(W)A that would prevent its repeal by future legislation wishing to remove the supremacy of retained EU law. Although, if, as seems likely, the EU(W)A is classified as a constitutional statute, this repeal would either have to be express, or through words that were sufficiently precise as to express an intention to overturn the Act.[33]

All of these examples show how the relationship between Parliament and the courts has modified over time. It is not the case that courts merely interpret legislation by discerning the will of Parliament as set out in the specific wording of legislation. Instead, courts draw on background constitutional principles, either as a means of determining

---

[28] *Factortame Ltd v Secretary of State for Transport (No 2)* [1991] 1 AC 603.

[29] *Vidal-Hall v Google* [2015] EWCA Civ 311, [2016] QB 1003; *R. (Davis) v Secretary of State for the Home Department* [2015] EWCA Civ 1185, [2017] 1 All ER 62; *Benkharbouche v Secretary of State for Foreign and Commonwealth Affairs* [2017] UKSC 62, [2017] 3 WLR 957; and *Walker v Innospec Ltd* [2017] UKSC 47, [2017] 4 All ER 1004.

[30] European Union (Withdrawal) Act 2018, section 5(1).

[31] European Union (Withdrawal) Act 2018, section 5(3).

[32] European Union (Withdrawal) Act 2018, section 5(2).

[33] *Thoburn v Sunderland City Council* (n. 15) and *H v Lord Advocate* (n. 15).

Parliament's implied intention, or because these principles serve as a limitation on Parliament's law-making powers. Whilst Parliament can legislate in a manner contrary to these constitutional principles, it must do so in a manner that makes this intention clear. General words will not suffice. Nor is it the case that courts merely apply the law. Courts develop principles of the common law, creating a classification of constitutional statutes, developing the principle of legality and through modifying implied repeal and parliamentary sovereignty. Although the courts have stopped short of refusing to apply legislation or striking down legislation, save in areas of EU law where legislation can be disapplied. Given these developments, it is hard to conclude anything other than that the courts have become more important, with a perceived shift in the constitutional balance of power away from Parliament and towards the courts.

Judicial Controls over the Executive

A similar picture emerges when we examine the relationship between the judiciary and the executive. If we adopt an evaluation of the role of the judiciary derived from traditional accounts of parliamentary sovereignty and the separation of powers, then we would expect to see the courts being prepared to control acts of the executive to uphold the rule of law, but to do so in a manner that respects parliamentary sovereignty. As such, we would expect courts to look to legislation to establish the scope of power granted to an administrative body, striking down decisions beyond the scope of the administrative body's powers.[34] However, the scope of actions of judicial review has never been restricted to a mere analysis of the express wording of legislative provisions. For example, there is a long tradition of protecting principles of natural justice and procedural fairness, these principles being derived from the common law, with courts being prepared to apply these principles in the absence of legislative provisions, or in order to provide procedural protections that go above and beyond those found in legislation or in codes of procedural practice developed by administrative bodies. Courts have also developed substantive limits on discretionary powers. Public bodies must not act irrationally when exercising their discretion.[35] In addition, courts have been prepared to review the actions of non-statutory bodies,[36] in addition to controlling the way in which justiciable prerogative powers are exercised,[37] and applying common law as well as statutory limits to the scope of prerogative powers.[38]

All of these forms of control by the judiciary over the executive make it clear that courts do not merely ensure that administrative bodies act within the express wording of the legislation setting out the specific powers of an administrative authority. There is also a perception that the courts are developing more controls over the executive through the development of the common law. The principle of legality, discussed above, is a principle of statutory interpretation, but it is also used to place restrictions

---

[34] See, for example, Forsyth, 'Of Fig Leaves and Fairy Tales' (1996) 55 *Cambridge Law Journal* 122.

[35] *Associated Provincial Picture Houses Ltd v Wednesbury Corporation* [1948] 1 KB 223.

[36] *R. v Panel on Takeovers and Mergers ex parte Datafin* [1987] QB 815.

[37] *Council of Civil Service Unions v Minister for the Civil Service* [1984] 3 All ER 935.

[38] *R. (Miller) v Secretary of State for Exiting the European Union* [2017] UKSC 5, [2017] 2 WLR 583.

on executive power. In *Evans*, the court interpreted legislation to ensure that it protected fundamental common law rights. In doing so, it restricted the powers granted to the executive, here the Attorney General. Although the Attorney General had a power to issue a certificate to overturn a decision of the Upper Tribunal, the extent to which he could use this power was read down, restricting the circumstances in which he was able to issue it. Applying the principle of legality in this manner means that it is unlawful for a public authority to act in a way that would undermine fundamental common law rights, unless there were clear words in the legislation granting this power to the executive.

We can also give other examples of where the court appears to be expanding its control over executive actions. One such example is the growing use of the principle of proportionality, which has the potential to provide a more stringent standard of review than a control of rationality. To date, proportionality is not a general head of judicial review in English law.[39] Moreover, when the issue was most recently raised in the Supreme Court, the court concluded that, given the constitutional implications of a move from rationality to proportionality as a general test of review in English administrative law, it would require a court composed of more than five Justices of the Supreme Court to make such a change.[40] Nevertheless, there are clear judicial statements which appear to accept some of the arguments made in favour of the adoption of a standard of proportionality in English law. In *Kennedy v Charity Commission*, for example, Lord Mance accepted the argument of Paul Craig that both *Wednesbury* unreasonableness and proportionality involve the courts in a balancing exercise, weighing up interests in order to delineate the legal range of choices within which the administration can act when exercising its discretion.[41] In addition, Lord Mance accepted that both rationality and proportionality can be applied more or less stringently, depending on the circumstances. If there is a difference between *Wednesbury* and proportionality, it may well be one of structure and not one of content.[42] Similar statements can be found in *Pham*.[43] In *Youssef*, judicial statements illustrate broad support for the test of proportionality being used for the review of common law fundamental rights cases which fall outside of the scope of the European Convention on Human Rights.[44]

These statements suggest a general move away from a more restrictive to a more stringent standard of judicial review, with the courts being more willing to control the way in which administrative bodies exercise their discretionary powers, particularly when they concern human rights. Moreover, there is evidence of a move towards an adoption of tests of proportionality, or those akin to a proportionality analysis, in other areas of administrative law. We discussed the scope of the principle of legality in the previous section, noting how this provided courts with an opportunity to interpret

---

[39] See *R. (Association of British Civilian Internees) v Far East Region* [2003] QB 1397, [2003] 1 WLR 1813 and *Keyu v Secretary of State for Foreign and Commonwealth Affairs* [2015] UKSC 69, [2016] AC 1355.

[40] *Keyu v Secretary of State for Foreign and Commonwealth Affairs* (n. 39), [132].

[41] [2014] UKSC 20, [2015] AC 455.   [42] *Kennedy v Charity Commissioner* id., [54]-[55]

[43] *Pham v Secretary of State for the Home Department* [2015] UKSC 19, [2015] 1 WLR 1591.

[44] *Youssef v Secretary of State for Foreign and Commonwealth Affairs* [2016] UKSC 3, [2016] AC 1457.

legislation in a manner which protects fundamental common law rights. We noted that it is possible for legislation to restrict fundamental common law rights provided that it does so through clear and specific wording. However, as Lord Reed made clear in *UNISON*, 'even where primary legislation authorizes the imposition of an intrusion on the right of access to justice it is presumed to be subject to an implied limitation . . . the degree of intrusion must not be greater than is justified by the objectives which the measure is intended to serve'.[45] Lord Reed concluded that there was an analogy between this principle and the principle of proportionality: any restriction on the right of access to the court would be 'unlawful unless it can be justified as reasonably necessary to meet a legitimate objective'.[46] In addition, the test of proportionality is probably used when determining whether there are good public policy reasons for a public body to renege on a substantive legitimate expectation.[47] All provide further evidence of the court gaining greater powers to control actions of the executive.

Judicialization of the Relationship between the Executive and the Legislature

The relationship between the legislature and the executive is mostly determined through political as opposed to legal means. In particular, conventions and the internal regulations of Parliament play a prominent role. The conventions of individual and collective ministerial responsibility regulate the extent to which the legislature can hold Ministers to account for their actions. Collective ministerial responsibility applies to Cabinet Ministers. It requires those holding office in the Cabinet to stand collectively behind the Government's policies, supporting these policies even when they personally disagree with them. Where this is not possible, Cabinet Ministers should resign from their Ministerial office—as was the case with Boris Johnson and David Davis, MPs, both of whom resigned as Foreign Secretary and Secretary of State for Exiting the European Union respectively, given their inability to support the Prime Minister's Chequers plan for Britain's future relationship with the European Union.[48] The convention helps to provide for strong cabinet Government, whilst also reinforcing the accountability of the Government as a whole to Parliament for the policies it adopts. Individual ministerial responsibility is designed to ensure that Ministers are accountable to Parliament for their ministerial departments, taking responsibility for policy failures. Although it is not always the case that Ministers resign for these failures, they are often held to account and resignations occur in particular when Ministers breach internal rules of conduct. For example, Amber Rudd recently resigned following the Windrush scandal. Her resignation occurred because she misled Parliament as to whether her department had adopted targets for forced deportation.[49]

---

[45] *R. (UNISON) v Lord Chancellor* [2017] UKSC 51, [2017] 3 WLR 409, [88].   [46] Ibid., [89].

[47] *Nadarajah v Secretary of State for the Home Department* [2005] EWCA Civ 1363, *Paponette v Attorney General of Trinidad and Tobago* [2010] UKPC 32, [2012] 1 AC 1 and *R. (Bancoult) v Secretary of State for Foreign and Commonwealth Affairs* [2008] UKHL 61, [2009] AC 453.

[48] See   https://www.bbc.co.uk/news/av/uk-politics-44771278/boris-johnson-resigns-as-foreign-secretary and https://www.bbc.co.uk/news/uk-politics-44761056.

[49] See https://www.bbc.co.uk/news/uk-politics-43944988.

As was recently reinforced by *Miller*, the courts cannot enforce conventions in and of themselves.[50] Whilst their interpretation may be relevant to the meaning or application of legal doctrines, it is not unlawful in and of itself to breach a convention. As such, the relationship between the legislature and the executive is regulated by predominantly political as opposed to legal means. The Cabinet Manual both establishes and recognizes conventions, leading to a form of codification of conventions. Whilst the Cabinet Manual may clarify the scope and application of conventions, it is clear that their enforcement is through political means, dominated by whether Parliament can exert sufficient political pressure to ensure that the convention is upheld. As such, exceptions can arise. The most notable example is the war powers convention, found in paragraph 5.38 of the Cabinet Manual, which acknowledges that a 'convention had developed in Parliament that before troops were committed the House of Commons should have an opportunity to debate the matter'. However, the scope of this convention has eroded over time,[51] the most recent example being the deployment of air strikes in Syria when Parliament was not called back from recess in order to debate the matter. Instead, debate occurred after the strikes had taken place.[52]

Nevertheless, we can still point to developments which suggest there has been a legalization or juridification of the relationship between the legislature and the executive. Some conventions have been placed on a legislative basis, transforming a political obligation under a convention into a legally enforceable statutory duty. The clearest example of this is sections 20 to 25 of the Constitutional Reform and Governance Act 2010. These provisions replace the Ponsonby rule, a convention which required the Government to lay Treaties before Parliament prior to their ratification. The statutory provisions replace this convention with a legal duty, with section 20 setting out that, generally, a Treaty is not to be ratified unless it has been laid before Parliament and no resolution has been enacted within 21 sitting days to reject the ratification of the Treaty. If the Government were to ratify a Treaty in breach of these provisions, then a legal action could be brought challenging this ratification as unlawful.

However, merely placing aspects of a convention on a statutory basis may not replace a political obligation with a legal obligation. This can be seen as regards section 2 of the Scotland Act 2016 and section 2 of the Wales Act 2017, both of which referred to the Sewel Convention, stating that 'it is recognised that the Parliament of the United Kingdom would not normally legislate with regard to devolved matters without the consent' of either the Scottish Parliament or the Welsh Assembly respectively. In *Miller,* the Supreme Court concluded that this did not mean that the Sewel Convention could now be legally enforced. This was because, unlike the Constitutional Reform and Governance Act, these provisions merely recognized the existence of the convention and did not place a specific legal duty on the UK Government to obtain the consent of

---

[50] *R. (Miller) v Secretary of State for Exiting the European Union* (n. 38).

[51] V. Fikfak and H. Hooper, *Parliament's Secret War* (Hart 2018), Chapter 1 and Chapter 3.

[52] V. Fikfak and H. Hooper, 'Whither the War Powers Convention? What Next for Parliamentary Control of Armed Conflict after Syria?' U.K. Const. L. Blog (20 April 2018) (available at https://ukconstitutionallaw.org/).

the devolved legislatures before enacting legislation with regard to devolved matters. Moreover, the court concluded that the word 'normally' related to political as opposed to legal issues—politics would determine whether it was or was not 'normal' to obtain the consent of the devolved legislatures. In addition, to assess these issues would mean that courts would breach Article 9 of the Bill of Rights 1689. This provision provides for the parliamentary privilege of freedom of expression, stating that proceedings in Parliament are not to be questioned in a court.

In addition to the use of conventions as the main means through which to regulate the relationship between the legislature and the executive, parliamentary privilege prevents courts from regulating aspects of parliamentary procedures. We have already seen this when discussing the Sewel Convention and its treatment in *Miller*. Article 9 means that courts are not able to question proceedings in Parliament. This provides a strong protection of freedom of expression, ensuring that MPs are able to debate freely in Parliament with no legal recourse in the courts, even when their speech would otherwise breach human rights.[53] In addition to the privilege of freedom of expression, Parliament has the privilege to regulate its own internal affairs. There are mechanisms through which MPs who do not follow Parliament's own internal rules can be reprimanded, to the extent of being held in contempt of the House, being fined and being suspended from the House. The courts are not meant to interfere. However, as *Chaytor* makes clear, there is space for the court to regulate the behaviour of MPs, even when this does concern a proceeding in Parliament.[54] *Chaytor* concerned prosecutions for fraud over MPs' election expenses. The claim that this was part of the proceedings in Parliament, and as such within the exclusive cognizance of Parliament, was rejected by the Supreme Court. This enabled greater legal control over the regulation of the behaviour of MPs, indirectly facilitating the ability of MPs to hold the Government to account when concerned with the behaviour of MPs who are members of the Government.

In addition to conventions and internal rules, prerogative powers are used to regulate the relationship between the legislature and the executive. In particular, there are prerogative powers in the hands of the Crown, with conventions which govern how these prerogative powers should be exercised. There is also evidence of some prerogative powers relating to the relationship between the legislature and the executive being placed on a statutory basis. The clearest example is the Fixed Term Parliaments Act 2011. Prior to this Act, the Monarch possessed the prerogative power to dissolve Parliament. By convention, the Monarch would only dissolve Parliament when instructed to do so by her Ministers. The Prime Minister would ask for Parliament to be dissolved, either at a time prior to the maximum five-year term, or following the loss of a vote of no confidence in the House of Commons. The Fixed Term Parliaments Act placed this prerogative power on a statutory basis, fixing the term of Parliament at five years. It also regulates the ability of the Government to call a general election prior to the duration of the fixed five year period, requiring a vote in favour equal in number to

---

[53] *A v United Kingdom* [2002] ECHR 35373/97.   [54] *R. v Chaytor* [2010] UKSC 52, [2011] 1 AC 684.

two-thirds of all of the seats in the House of Commons.[55] Alternatively, an early general election may be called following a vote of no confidence. Following a successful vote of no confidence, there is a two-week period in which either the current Government, or a differently composed Government, can try to obtain a successful vote of confidence. If this is not achieved, then a general election is called.[56]

Although not as conclusive as our analysis of the relationship between the judiciary and the executive, and that between the judiciary and the legislature, it is possible to provide evidence of a growing legalization of the relationship between the legislature and the executive. As such, we can find support for the claim that the UK constitution is moving away from a political constitution and towards a legal constitution. Whilst this does not undermine parliamentary sovereignty, it nevertheless suggests a growing role for the judiciary and a growing importance for the rule of law. It is the judiciary and not Parliament who are beginning to take centre stage when it comes to the regulation of the executive. The next section will cast doubt on this broad conclusion, by explaining how it fails to take account of the particular circumstances when courts are more or less willing to control the executive.

A CONTEXTUAL APPROACH

The previous section has provided one view of the UK constitution, selecting examples which show that the courts play a more dominant role in the UK constitution. However, the previous section could have provided examples where this would appear not to be the case. Whilst there is evidence of the courts taking on a strong role, moving the constitution towards more legal as opposed to political forms of regulation, we can equally point to areas where the controls are more political as opposed to legal. This section will argue that the relative roles of the legislature, the executive, and the judiciary are more context-specific. It is hard to make broad generalizations as to the separation of powers without including inaccuracies. We will first re-examine the relationship between the legislature and judiciary, looking in particular at the principle of legality, before looking at the scope of proportionality in order to re-evaluate the relationship between the executive and the judiciary. Finally, we will look at legislation that has been enacted which places the relationship between the legislature and the executive on a more legal footing. The Government plays the predominant role in the initiation of legislation and when determining its content. This means that duties can often be subject to exceptions. In addition, the legislation can delegate a large degree of power to the executive. Although the courts may be able to control this executive power, the use of clear and specific wording in legislation can restrict the powers of the courts, reducing the impact of legal controls.

---

[55] Fixed Term Parliaments Act 2011, section 2(1) and (2). This was the provision used by Theresa May to hold a snap general election in 2017.

[56] Fixed Term Parliaments Act 2011, sections 2(3)–(5).

The Principle of Legality Re-Examined

The previous section argued that the principle of legality demonstrates the extent to which the courts are able to provide a strong legal control over the legislature and the executive. We focused in particular on *Evans*, arguing that this provided an example of how far courts were willing to interpret legislative provisions in order to preserve fundamental common law rights. However, it is no surprise that our example of the principle of legality concerns the preservation of access to the courts. When we examine the case law applying the principle of legality, it is clear that the courts are more willing to apply the principle of legality when faced with a legislative provision removing or undermining the rule of law—for example, through restricting the right of access to the courts,[57] or restricting the right to a fair trial.[58] In a similar manner, the courts are more willing to apply the principle of legality and read down general provisions of legislation when interpreting legislative provisions which empower the executive. For example, in *Leech*, Lord Steyn stated that

> [i]t would be a rare case in which it could be held that such a fundamental right was by necessary implication abolished or limited by statute. It will, we suggest, be an even rarer case in which it could be held that a statute authorised by necessary implication the abolition of a limitation of so fundamental a right by subordinate legislation.[59]

Both of these aspects are evident in *Evans*. The legislative provision empowered the executive to act in a manner that could undermine the rule of law. These same elements are also present in other recent cases where the courts appear to have applied the principle of legality in a way that appears to be different from the actual intention of Parliament. In *UNISON*, for example, the court read down section 42(1) of the Tribunals, Courts and Enforcement Act 2007, which empowered the Lord Chancellor to set the level of fees to be paid by those wishing to bring a legal action before a tribunal.[60] The fees set by the Lord Chancellor effectively made it impossible for those on low incomes to bring actions before Employment Tribunals. The Supreme Court reached this conclusion after analysing the level of fees required, the level of income below which it was possible to obtain remission from the payment of tribunal fees, and the average awards granted in Employment Tribunal cases. The Supreme Court read down the broad provision so as to ensure that the Lord Chancellor did not have the power to set tribunal fees that were so high that they prevented individuals from exercising their

---

[57] See, for example, *R. v Secretary of State for the Home Department ex parte Leech* [1994] QB 198, *R. v Lord Chancellor, ex parte Witham* [1998] QB 575, *R. v Secretary of State for the Home Department, ex parte Pierson* [1998] AC 539, *R. v Secretary of State for the Home Department ex parte Simms* [2002] 2 AC 115, *W (Algeria) v Secretary of State for the Home Department* [2010] EWCA Civ 898, [2010] All ER (D) 321 (Jul), *Home Office v Tariq* [2011] UKSC 35, [2012] AC 452, *R. (UNISON) v Lord Chancellor* (n. 45) and *Evans v Attorney General* (n. 12).

[58] See, for example, *Home Office v Tariq* [2011] (n. 57).

[59] *R. v Secretary of State for the Home Department, ex parte Leech* (n. 56), at 212. See also *W (Algeria) v Secretary of State for the Home Department* (n. 57) and *Ahmed v Her Majesty's Treasury* [2010] UKSC 5, [2010] 2 AC 534.

[60] *R. (UNISON) v Lord Chancellor* (n. 45).

right of access to justice. The need to protect the right of access to justice and the role of the court in protecting the rule of law is also a theme running through the dicta regarding the ability of the courts to refuse to apply or enforce legislation which contravenes fundamental common law rights. The dicta in the courts stress that courts would only refuse to recognize or enforce legislation in exceptional circumstances. These include when legislation removes the right of judicial review of executive decisions from the courts.[61]

However, it is also important to note that, when interpreting the application of the principle of legality, courts also pay close attention to the wording of the legislation in general and the specific statutory provision that the court has been asked to interpret.[62] The greater the evidence in the specific wording of an intention to restrict or abrogate fundamental rights, the more likely it is that the courts will not apply the principle of legality; there are no general words that the court can read down in order to protect fundamental common law rights.[63] The precise scope of legislative provisions also plays a role when determining whether a purported fundamental common law right exists, such that the courts should read down legislation in order to ensure that its provisions are not restricted. In *Moohan*, concerning the right to vote, the Supreme Court was willing to accept that the right to vote was a constitutional right. However, it did not have the same status as other fundamental rights in English law.[64] This was because the precise content of the right to vote had been established through a series of legislative provisions. As such, there was not, in common law, 'a right of universal and equal suffrance from which any derogation must be provided for by law and must be proportionate'.[65]

Moreover, we can point to examples where the court exercises the principle of legality in a restrained manner, even when dealing with the right of access to the courts. The clearest example of this is the recent Court of Appeal decision in *Privacy International*, concerning a clause designed to oust the jurisdiction of the court over decisions of the Investigatory Powers Tribunal (IPT).[66] Section 67(8) of the Regulation of Investigatory Powers Act 2000 states that '[e]xcept to such extent as the Secretary of State may by order otherwise provide, determinations, awards and other decisions of the Tribunal (including decisions as to whether they have jurisdiction) shall not be subject to appeal or be liable to be questioned in any court'. As such, the provision meant that decisions of the IPT could not be subject to judicial review. This ouster clause was similar to that found in *Anisminic Ltd v Foreign Compensation Commission*.[67] In *Anisminic*,

---

[61] *Jackson v AG* (n. 20) and *AXA General Insurance v Lord Advocate* (n. 22).

[62] See, for example, *R. (Gillan) v Commissioner of Police for the Metropolis* [2006] UKHL 12, *W (Algeria) v Secretary of State for the Home Department* (n. 57), *Seal v Chief Constable of South Wales* [2007] UKHL 31, [2007] 1 WLR 1910 and *R. (Privacy International) v Investigatory Powers Tribunal* [2017] EWCA Civ 1868, [2018] 1 WLR 2572, *Khaled v Secretary of State for Foreign and Commonwealth Affairs* [2017] EWHC 1422 (Admin), [2017] All ER (D) 119 (Jun).

[63] See, for example, *W (Algeria) v Secretary of State for the Home Department* (n. 57).

[64] *Moohan v Lord Advocate* [2014] UKSC 67, [2015] AC 901.

[65] Ibid., [34], (Lord Hodge).

[66] *R. (Privacy International) v Investigatory Powers Tribunal* (n. 62).   [67] [1962] 2 AC 147.

legislation appeared to prevent judicial review of determinations of the Foreign Compensation Commission. The clause which appeared to oust jurisdiction of the court was contained in section 4(4) of the Foreign Compensation Act 1950, which stated that '[t]he determination by the commission of any application made to them under this Act shall not be called in question in any court of law'. The House of Lords concluded that this provision did not fully remove judicial review from determinations of the Foreign Compensation Commission. In particular, it did not remove the jurisdiction of the court over purported determinations—that is determinations which were made by the commission, but which nevertheless were not real determinations given that they contained errors of law. Any determination which contained an error of law was not a real determination, the error of law making this determination a nullity. Whilst the courts could not question real determinations, judicial review would still remain to ascertain whether any determinations contained legal errors, such that they were not real determinations. As such, the court would only be questioning purported and not real determinations of the Commission.

The narrow interpretation of ouster clauses, exemplified in *Anisminic*, was classified by the court in *Privacy International Ltd* as an aspect of the principle of legality.[68] We argued above that the principle of legality applies with greater strength when the courts are protecting aspects of the rule of law, particularly concerning access to judicial review. As such, we would expect the Court of Appeal to have concluded that the jurisdiction of the courts to review decisions of the IPT could not be ousted by legislation. In a manner similar to the outcome in *Anisminic*, we would expect it to oust real, but not purported decisions, enabling the courts to exercise judicial review over decisions of the IPT which contained errors of law or other jurisdictional errors. However, the Court of Appeal reached the opposite conclusion. The statutory provision was capable of ousting the jurisdiction of the court.

This conclusion could be explained by the different wording of the provisions in *Privacy International* and *Anisminic*. The statutory provision in *Anisminic* stated that determinations could not be questioned by the court. The statutory provision in *Privacy International* stated that determinations, decisions and awards could not be questioned by the court, and specifically included decisions by the IPT as to whether it had the jurisdiction to act. It is clear from case law that all legal errors are classified as jurisdictional errors.[69] Therefore, there were clearer, specific words in the statutory provision expressing an intention to oust the jurisdiction of the court over errors of law that would render a decision, determination or award void. As such, Parliament had expressed its intention to oust the jurisdiction of the courts over decisions of the IPT, including purported decisions.

If the decision in *Privacy International* had been reached solely on the specific statutory wording, we might have concluded that the decision provided evidence of the

---

[68] R. *(Privacy International) v Investigatory Powers Tribunal* (n. 62).

[69] See *O'Reilly v Mackman* [1983] 2 AC 327 and R. *v Lord President of the Privy Council, ex parte Page* [1993] 2 AC 682.

courts being less willing to exercise clear legal controls over the executive. However, before reaching this conclusion, we also need to take account of the institutional nature of the IPT. The IPT is staffed by individuals with a high degree of judicial expertise and independence, such that it has equivalent standing to the High Court. Moreover, the IPT has exclusive jurisdiction to hear claims brought under section 7 of the Human Rights Act 1998 to ensure that the intelligence services are acting within the scope of Convention rights. It also has greater powers to hear proceedings in private, enabling it to reach better decisions on issues concerning aspects of national security than the High Court, which does not have a general ability to hear proceedings in private beyond that specifically granted to it under legislative provisions. These aspects of the membership and function of the IPT mean that it is more likely to uphold requisite elements of the rule of law, without the need for further control of the court over its decisions. It may have a better ability to correctly determine the scope of its jurisdiction than the Foreign Compensation Commission.

At the time of writing, the decision in the Court of Appeal in *Privacy International* is on appeal to the Supreme Court, and was heard in December 2018. It may be that the court reverses its conclusion in the Court of Appeal. Even if this were the case—with the court, for example, reading 'decision as to jurisdiction' to only exclude errors of jurisdictional fact made by the IPT as opposed to jurisdictional errors of law, or to not exclude jurisdictional errors that breached fundamental common law rights or Convention rights—this would not undermine the argument made in this section. This section is arguing that it is too simplistic to see *Evans* and *UNISON* as cases which show the courts gaining more power over the legislature, and *Privacy International* being seen as a case where the courts retreat from an earlier zenith of power. Rather, these cases are best understood as a delicate balance of specific statutory wording and context applied to background legal principles. Context plays a key role in determining the extent to which the courts are prepared to interpret legislation so as to provide stronger or weaker control over the legislature and the executive.[70]

Proportionality in Context

We argued above that there was also growing evidence of the courts developing stronger controls over the executive. This can be illustrated both by the principle of legality, and the growing use of the principle of proportionality, even if, to date, proportionality is not a general head of judicial review. The previous section explained how the

---

[70] Further evidence of this approach can be found in the decision of Lord Mance in *Lee v Ashers Baking Company* [2018] UKSC 49, [2018] All ER (D) 43 (Oct), where Lord Mance adopted a contextual approach when interpreting a statutory provision that decisions of the Northern Ireland Court of Appeal are final. Whilst this excluded judicial review over the substantive content of the decision, it did not exclude judicial review of a mistake made in the process of reaching that determination. Here, the Northern Ireland Court of Appeal had mistakenly concluded that its judicial proceedings had been determined when it had reached a decision on a case, but had not yet produced the court order confirming that decision. See J. Bell, 'The Supreme Court's Approach to the Finality Clause in *Lee v Ashers*: A Response to Anurag Deb and Conor McCormick & Looking Forward to *Privacy International*', U.K. Const. L Blog (23rd Oct. 2018) (available at https://unkconstitutionallaw.org/).

principle of legality is applied in a contextual manner. The extent to which the courts are willing to read down legislative provisions so as to protect fundamental rights from erosion by actions of the executive depends on the nature of the specific statutory wording, its context, and the nature of the fundamental right in question. A similar conclusion can be reached when we examine proportionality. Proportionality applies in a more or less stringent manner, depending upon the context of the case in which it is being applied.

When applying proportionality, courts have developed a concept of deference—although there is reluctance to use this term, given its overtones of servility.[71] The courts apply proportionality less stringently when there are good institutional, constitutional, or epistemic reasons for doing so, although there is continuing controversy both as to whether the courts should exercise deference,[72] and, if so, the grounds and the extent to which deference should be exercised.[73] Courts exercise deference on institutional grounds when the composition of the executive means that the executive has a better ability to decide the issue. This may be, for example, because the administrative body is in a better position to hear a wide variety of viewpoints, or to gather information regarding a particular decision. This is particularly the case as courts only hear the views of those coming before the court and decide issues in an adversarial as opposed to an inquisitorial manner. Courts are not able to carry out investigations in order to discover further relevant information. Deference on epistemic grounds focuses on the ability of the administrative body to reach a better conclusion given that it has greater expertise in a particular area. It is therefore more likely to evaluate information correctly than the courts. Finally, deference on constitutional grounds occurs because the decision is more legitimately made by the administration as opposed to the court. This could occur, for example, where there is a clear capacity for the executive to be held politically accountable for its actions—as, for example, would occur with regard to decisions of ministers through the application of individual ministerial responsibility. Another example of democratic deference occurs when applied to decisions of public bodies that are themselves democratically composed and democratically elected—e.g. decisions of local councils.

An example of how deference operates in practice is the decision of the House of Lords in *Belfast City Council v Miss Behavin' Ltd*, which concerned zoning and planning decisions regarding the location of sex shops in Belfast.[74] Belfast City Council had exercised statutory powers such that it would be unlawful to use premises as a sex

---

[71] See *R. (on the application of Prolife Alliance) v British Broadcasting Corporation* [2003] UKHL 23, [2004] 1 AC 185, [75], where Lord Hoffmann remarked that 'although the word "deference" is now very popular in describing the relationship between the judicial and other branches of government, I do not think that its overtones of servility, or perhaps gracious concession, are appropriate to describe what is happening.'

[72] T.R.S Allan, 'Human Rights and Judicial Review: A Critique of "Due Deference"' (2006) 63 *Cambridge Law Journal* 671.

[73] A. L. Young, 'In Defence of Due Deference' (2009) 72 *Modern Law Review* 554 and M. Elliott, 'From Bifurcation to Calibration: Twin-Track Deference and the Culture of Justification' in M. Elliott and H. Wilberg, 'The Scope and Intensity of Substantive Review: Traversing Taggart's Rainbow' (Hart, 2015).

[74] [2007] UKHL 19, [2007] 1 WLR 1420.

shop without a licence. Miss Behavin' had applied for a licence. However, Belfast City Council had decided that no licences should be granted in the locality in which Miss Behavin' had applied. Miss Behavin' argued that this was a disproportionate restriction on their right to freedom of expression under article 10 ECHR. Lord Hoffmann recognized that this was an issue of social control in which a wide area of discretion would be granted to the council. Lady Hale recognized that the Belfast City Council had greater knowledge of these issues than the court, and were in touch with the people and place involved to a greater degree. Lord Hoffmann's assessment exemplifies deference on constitutional grounds, with the local council being regarded as a more legitimate institution to decide issues of social policy than the court. Lady Hale focuses more on institutional and epistemic grounds. The local knowledge of the council, and its expertise, mean that it is more likely to reach the best conclusion on this issue.

The standard of review of proportionality can also be modified when the nature of the test is changed given the specific issue before the court. This is particularly true when courts are faced with decisions which require the balancing of complex social issues. Although courts only see the specific issue before them, the decision any court makes can have repercussions beyond that particular issue. An example of where the courts have been willing to modify the standard of proportionality is the *Bedroom Tax* case, concerning the cap on housing benefit which applied to those who lived in council premises with more bedrooms than needed.[75] It was argued that the cap on housing benefit discriminated against those with disabilities, contravening articles 8 and 14 ECHR. In determining this issue, the court applied a test examining whether the policy to introduce the cap on housing benefit was 'manifestly without reasonable foundation'. The Supreme Court confirmed that this was the correct test to be applied, relying on the test used by the European Court of Human Rights when dealing with issues of inequality in social welfare systems. Although some of the applicants in the *Bedroom Tax* case succeeded, they did so on narrow grounds. For example, previous cases had concluded that rights would be harmed when the benefits cap was applied to a husband and wife who had an extra bedroom, given that the disabilities of one of the spouses meant preventing them sharing a bedroom. In the *Bedroom Tax* case, the court concluded that, similarly, an extra room was needed to ensure that children who could normally share a bedroom had separate rooms when one of the children was disabled and these disabilities prevented the sharing of a bedroom. To conclude that the bedroom was not needed in this case would be manifestly without reasonable foundation. It is hard to distinguish this test from the standard test of rationality applied in non-Convention rights cases.

Whilst proportionality can provide a stronger form of review than rationality, it would be wrong to conclude that this provides clear and conclusive evidence of the courts obtaining greater powers to control the executive. Proportionality can be applied more or less stringently and its application in practice may be little different from

---

[75] *R. (Carmichael and Rourke) v Secretary of State for Work and Pensions* [2016] UKSC 58, [2016] 1 WLR 4550.

a rationality review. Moreover, the intensity of its application is context-specific. The courts take account of the nature of the right before the court, as well as the institutional and constitutional differences between the judiciary and the executive. Examples of cases where the courts appear to apply a less stringent form of review, or to modify the test of proportionality, are better understood as further applications of this contextual approach, rather than illustrating a potential move away from legal controls.

Legislative or Executive Dominance?

When discussing the extent to which there was a potential legalization of the relationship between the legislature and the executive, we examined how far legislation has placed conventions on a statutory basis, as well as replacing prerogative powers. We also recognized how courts, whilst respecting parliamentary privilege, both determined the confines of the application of parliamentary privilege and were able to hold parliamentarians to account for criminal behaviour, including fraud, even when this concerned proceedings in Parliament. Nevertheless, as we discovered when we re-examined the relationship between the legislature and the judiciary, and the executive and the judiciary, we can point to examples which would suggest that there are fewer legal controls over the relationship between the legislature and the executive. More worryingly, we can point to recent developments in which legislation is being used to give greater powers to the executive, challenging the justification of the fusion between the legislature and the executive as a means of facilitating the ability of the legislature to control the powers of the executive.

When discussing the extent to which the courts are beginning to regulate the behaviour of parliamentarians, we discussed the case of *Chaytor*, where the Supreme Court rejected the argument that the privilege of Parliament to regulate its own internal affairs meant that the courts were unable to apply the criminal law to regulate the behaviour of MPs with regard to claims for fraudulent expenses.[76] However, this does not mean that courts are able to regulate all aspects of the behaviour of members of either the House of Commons or the House of Lords. Nor is it the case that investigations for fraud are always able to be brought against members of either House. For example, recently, a prosecution against Lord Hanningfield was discontinued because of issues of parliamentary privilege.[77] Lord Hanningfield had been investigated by the Commissioner for Standards for the House of Lords after newspaper reports that he had claimed allowances for working in the House of Lords, despite there being evidence of him arriving, signing in as attending, and then almost immediately leaving the House. Following the investigation, the Crown Prosecution Service wished to prosecute Lord Hanningfield for false accounting. However, the prosecution could only succeed if it could be demonstrated that Lord Hanningfield had claimed a daily allowance without doing any work for the House of Lords. To determine this issue would require the courts to question proceedings in Parliament, determining what was meant by 'work'

---

[76] *R. v Chaytor* (n. 54).

[77] Sir John Saunders, 'Parliamentary Privilege and the Criminal Law' [2017] Crim L Rev 521.

in relation to working as a member of the House of Lords. Accordingly, the prosecution was dropped.

A recent case of the Supreme Court also illustrates how the Crown can be immune from legislative provisions. In *Black,* the Supreme Court had to determine whether Part 1 of the Health Act 2006, which prohibited smoking in public places, applied to the Crown, and more specifically to Her Majesty's Prisons.[78] The general presumption is that legislation does not apply to the Crown, unless there are specific words making it clear that its provisions do apply. Part 1 of the Health Act did not specifically state that its provisions applied to the Crown. The Supreme Court was invited to modify this principle of statutory presumption, recognizing instead that statutory provisions should apply to the Crown unless there was specific statutory wording making the Crown exempt from its provisions. Lady Hale, giving the main judgment for the Supreme Court, recognized both that there were good reasons for modifying the principle of statutory interpretation in general and, specifically, that there were good reasons for applying the provisions banning smoking in public places to Government-owned prisons. Nevertheless, Lady Hale did not reverse the statutory presumption.

In reaching this conclusion, Lady Hale relied on the specific wording of the legislation in question. Whilst there were no provisions in Part 1 of the Health Act which made it clear that its provisions were to apply to the Crown, other provisions of the Act did specifically and clearly apply to the Crown. Lady Hale also argued that the main aim of the legislation need not be undermined; it was possible for prisons to adopt a ban on smoking in public places, even though they were not required to do so by the legislation. More generally, to modify the legislative presumption would give rise to difficulties, given that legislation has been enacted under the current principle of statutory interpretation that its provisions would not apply to the Crown, unless specific words made it clear that it was to do so.

As with our previous examples, this may be regarded as courts being less reluctant to interpret legislation so as to limit executive power. However, a better understanding can be gleaned from focusing on the particular context. Although modifying the statutory presumption could mean that the executive is held to account by legislative provisions established by the legislature, thus upholding one element of the rule of law, in doing so it could undermine other aspects of the rule of law—legal certainty and predictability. Given the impact of a modification of this principle of statutory interpretation, it is better for this to be achieved through Parliament rather than by the courts. Moreover, there were other ways in which the policy of the legislature could be upheld through the executive choosing to adopt policies in line with the legislative provisions.

A far deeper concern arises as to whether the standards enacted in legislation provide an effective means of holding the executive to account. Replacing a convention with a legislative standard does provide a means for the court to hold the executive to account for failing to adhere to these legislative standards. However, the extent to which this is achieved depends upon the content of the duties found in legislative

---

[78] R. *(Black) v Secretary of State for Justice* [2017] UKSC 81, [2018] 2 WLR 123.

provisions. It is possible for the legislation to provide a legal duty that fails to provide a means of effectively holding the executive to account for its actions. We referred above to the provisions of the Constitutional Reform and Governance Act 2010, which replaced a convention with a statutory obligation. However, although the provisions of the Act require Treaties to be laid before Parliament, subject to the negative resolution procedure before ratification, the Act also provides a means whereby this obligation can be avoided. Even if the House of Commons, or the House of Lords, or both, resolves that a Treaty ought not to be ratified, it is nevertheless possible for the Treaty to be ratified if a Minister of the Crown lays before Parliament a statement stating that the Treaty ought nevertheless to be ratified, including an explanation of her reasons for why this should be the case. [79] There are also provisions for exceptional cases, allowing Treaties to be ratified without being laid before the House,[80] as well as a list of Treaties to which the provisions do not apply.[81] The legislation provides a series of exceptions and restrictions which effectively preserve the predominantly political means of holding the Government to account with regard to the way in which it ratifies Treaties.

A similar conclusion can be reached as regards the provisions of the Fixed Term Parliaments Act 2011. Although designed, at least in part, to restrict the ability of Prime Ministers to call a general election at a time that would suit their own political purposes, these provisions did not prevent Theresa May from calling a snap general election, predominantly because she thought doing so would strengthen her majority in the House of Commons, making it easier for her to ensure that she was able to deliver on her promise to fulfil the outcome of the Referendum and ensure a smooth and stable exit from the European Union. The 2011 Act appears to restrict Prime Ministerial powers as it requires a vote of two-thirds of the seats of the House of Commons as a whole in order to trigger an early general election. However, political pressure can be brought to bear upon opposition parties to vote in favour of an early general election, particularly as these parties can be accused of being weak and unwilling to fight a general election for fear that they would lose political seats. As such, in reality, the statutory provisions appear to do little to restrict the power of the Government.

Furthermore, the European Union (Withdrawal) Act 2018 (EU(W)A) provides an example of how legislative provisions can grant broad sweeping powers to the executive. The provision that has raised the most concerns is section 8, which empowers the executive to make regulations to deal with deficiencies in retained EU law which arise from the UK's withdrawal from the European Union. Sections 2, 3 and 4 of the EU(W)A provide the means through which to enable most provisions of EU law to continue to apply in the UK after the UK's withdrawal from the European Union. These measures are referred to as retained EU law. However, as some provisions of retained EU law are only able to operate effectively because, for example, of reciprocal arrangements with the European Union which may not continue following the UK's withdrawal, there is a

---

[79] Constitutional Reform and Governance Act 2010, sections 20(3) and (4) and sections 20(7) and (8).
[80] Constitutional Reform and Governance Act 2010, section 22.
[81] Constitutional Reform and Governance Act 2010, section 23.

need to ensure that modifications to retained EU law occur to prevent problems which may arise.

Whilst recognizing that there is a need for section 8, concerns arise since it can be triggered on very little evidence. The Minister need only consider it appropriate for a measure to be made to achieve the objective of preventing, remedying or mitigating any deficiencies in retained EU law, or failures of retained EU law to operate effectively.[82] Although section 8 provides a list of examples of possible deficiencies in retained EU law, these too are worded broadly to include where measures have no practical application, or to refer to functions that no longer need to be performed, or rely on reciprocal arrangements.[83] Moreover, the measures adopted under section 8 may contain any provision 'that could be made by an Act of Parliament'.[84] In other words, section 8 contains a Henry VIII clause, empowering the Minister to make regulations which modify, amend or repeal primary legislation. Section 8 does contain a sunset clause which limits its application to two years beginning with the day on which the UK exits the EU,[85] and also provides for specific restrictions on the measures which may be enacted.[86] Nevertheless, there are concerns that these powers place too much power in the hands of the executive, particularly given that, even with the presence of sifting committees to recommend a stricter form of scrutiny, most of these regulations can be enacted through the negative resolution procedure.[87] This means that the regulations will be enacted unless Parliament passes a resolution to refuse to enact the regulation.

Far from providing an example of increasing legal limits on the powers of the executive, these developments would suggest that legislation can serve to provide the executive with greater powers. Whilst the courts can still control delegated legislation, including using the principle of legality to place restrictions on how they interpret broad sweeping legislative powers to ensure that they do not empower the legislature to act contrary to fundamental common law rights, and to read down the general wording of Henry VIII clauses,[88] it remains to be seen whether the courts can use these powers to effectively control the executive. Moreover, it is always open to Parliament to enact legislation which provides detailed specific powers to the executive.

RE-IMAGINING THE SEPARATION OF POWERS

We have argued that a description of the relationship between the legislature, the executive, and the judiciary is more complex than an account of a gradual move towards greater legal controls, with an independent judiciary playing a greater role in checking

---

[82] European Union (Withdrawal) Act 2010, section 8(1).
[83] European Union (Withdrawal) Act 2010, section 8(2).
[84] European Union (Withdrawal) Act 2010, section 8(5).
[85] European Union (Withdrawal) Act 2010, section 8(8).
[86] European Union (Withdrawal) Act 2010, section 8(7).
[87] European Union (Withdrawal) Act 2010, Schedule 7.
[88] R. (Public Law Project) v Lord Chancellor [2016] UKSC 39, [2006] AC 1531, R. (Ingenious Media) v Commissioners for Her Majesty's Customs and Revenue [2016] UKSC 54, [2016] 1 WLR 4164.

the actions of both the legislature and the executive in order to uphold the rule of law. We can provide examples of where courts appear to play a smaller role, or provide a less intrusive form of control over the executive than we would expect. The extent to which courts are willing to control the actions of the executive and the legislature is context-dependent. Whilst providing an account of these complexities, we have spent little time examining accounts of the separation of powers. Rather, we assumed that there was no need to think about conceptions of the separation of powers, arguing that it had played little, if any, role in the UK constitution. This section will evaluate models of the separation of powers to see if understanding these models can provide a better account of the case law, as well as providing a defensible normative account of the UK constitution. It will focus on the models proposed by Roger Masterman and Se-shauna Wheatle, and will argue that the separation of powers does play a fundamental role in the UK constitution. However, it does so through establishing a balanced constitution relying on a system of checks and balances between the legislature, the executive, and the judiciary.

In their analysis of case law, Masterman and Wheatle argue that there is evidence of four possible models to explain how courts refer to the separation of powers in their judgments: the hierarchical model, a weakly normative model, a strongly normative model and a model which regards the separation of powers as a constitutional fundamental principle.[89] The hierarchical model combines the separation of powers with a strong protection of the sovereignty of Parliament. As such, it regards the role of the judiciary as being to interpret the law to ensure that it is in line with the intentions of Parliament. The role of the executive is to put the law enacted by Parliament into effect, again ensuring that it does so according to the will of Parliament. When checking the actions of the executive, the court ensures that the executive acts within the scope of powers granted to it by the legislature and implements the law according to the wishes of the legislature.

The normative models elevate the role of the separation of powers to a normative principle of the constitution, as opposed to relying on the sovereignty of Parliament as the main means through which to determine the relevant roles of the legislature, the executive, and the judiciary. Normative models focus on the role of the judiciary given its position as an institution that is independent from politics, and its role in upholding the rule of law. The weakly normative version argues that the judiciary has a role that is beyond that found in the hierarchical model, but which still respects parliamentary sovereignty. As such, courts can interpret legislation in a manner that protects fundamental rights, for example, but not in a manner that would contradict the clearly worded provisions of legislation. The weakly normative model also has aspects of comity, where the judiciary respects the relative constitutional roles of the legislature and the executive.[90] The strongly normative role gives even more importance to the

---

[89] R. Masterman and S. Wheatle, 'Unpacking Separation of Powers: Judicial Independence, Sovereignty, and Conceptual Flexibility in the UK Constitution' [2017] *Public Law* 469.

[90] P. Craig, 'Public Law, Political Theory and Legal Theory' [2000] *Public Law* 211 and P. Craig, *UK, EU and Global Administrative Law: Foundations and Challenges* (Cambridge University Press, 2015), 125–55.

independence of the judiciary, drawing on the role of the courts in protecting the rule of law, which it regards as more important than the sovereignty of Parliament. As such, it would advocate that courts could strike down legislation when this was needed to protect the rule of law.[91]

Neither of the models above regard the separation of powers as a constitutional fundamental principle. Rather, the focus is on the relative importance of the sovereignty of Parliament and the rule of law. Whilst the weakly normative model regards the sovereignty of Parliament as more important, the strongly normative model regards the rule of law as more important. This then dictates the specific role of the court and the extent to which courts apply the separation of powers, in the sense of their understanding of the checks and balances that they are to perform over the legislature and the executive. A model of the separation of powers where this principle is understood as a constitutional fundamental principle, however, would see the separation of powers as an organizing principle, playing a distinct role in organizing the relationships between the legislature, the executive, and the judiciary.

Masterman and Wheatle argue that current case-law supports either a weakly normative or a strongly normative model of the separation of powers, with less support for a hierarchical model. Our discussion above reaches a similar conclusion. The growing role of the court in holding the legislature and the executive to account for their actions would suggest that the UK constitution has moved away from a hierarchical model of the separation of powers. However, it is hard to regard the case law as demonstrating a move to a strong normative model of the separation of powers, given that references to the powers of the court often reinforce the role of the sovereignty of parliament. Although we can point to dicta suggesting that there may be exceptional circumstances in which the courts may refuse to enforce legislation, these dicta have not yet been acted upon and may never be acted upon by a future court. If our analysis has done anything in pointing out the extent to which the role of the court is dependent upon a range of factors, it may provide a means of explaining when the courts are more likely to choose to adhere to a weakly normative model, and when they may move closer to adopting a strongly normative model of the separation of powers.

I would argue that the separation of powers does operate as a fundamental principle of the UK constitution. However, it does so in a manner that is more latent than blatant— i.e. it governs relationships between the legislature, the executive, and the judiciary at a fundamental level, but not in a manner in which we would expect courts to refer to the separation of powers as a legally recognized and independent fundamental principle of the constitution, or as a distinct head of judicial review. What I mean by this is that the separation of powers may influence the balance that is made between parliamentary sovereignty and the rule of law, rather than the relative importance of the rule of law or parliamentary sovereignty determining the way in which we apply the principle of the separation of powers. However, whilst the separation of powers plays this role at a more

---

[91] T.R.S. Allan, 'The Constitutional Foundations of Judicial Review: Constitutional Conundrum or Interpretive Inquiry?' (2002) 61 *Cambridge Law Journal* 87.

fundamental level, it is not a head of judicial review, in that the courts do not strike down decisions of the executive because they breach the separation of powers, nor do they refer to the separation of powers specifically as a means of interpreting the extent to which the courts interpret legislative provisions. Rather, they refer to other principles whose content draws on the separation of powers. This explains how the separation of powers functions as a fundamental constitutional principle, despite the lack of evidence in judicial decisions of the courts referring to the separation of powers in this manner.

In earlier work, I advocated a model of the UK constitution as a whole, not just of the separation of powers, focusing on democratic dialogue. This model focuses on the nature of the relationships between the different institutions of the constitution and the way in which they interact with each other.[92] The model relies on two types of interaction between the legislature and the judiciary: constitutional counter-balancing and constitutional collaboration. Constitutional counter-balancing occurs when institutions are able to take measures to protect their role in the constitution. This can occur either pro-actively to promote their own constitutional role, or defensively to prevent the constitutional role of that institution from being eroded. Constitutional collaboration occurs when institutions work together, combining their different institutional strengths, to achieve a constitutionally valuable objective. My earlier work looked at these interactions in the field of human rights protections, looking in particular at how the legislature and the judiciary work together to provide a better protection of human rights. However, the model can also apply to the relationship between the legislature, the executive, and the judiciary more generally and can be used to further objectives other than a normatively defensible protection of human rights. This can best be explained through the use of an example.

We discussed above the dicta in *Jackson* and *AXA Insurance Ltd*, which refers to the possibility of exceptional circumstances in which the judiciary might refuse to enforce or recognize legislation. The exceptional circumstances mentioned by the Supreme Court judgments to date include the removal of judicial review from the courts,[93] in addition to an abusive measure of Parliament which would either remove or undermine the right to vote in a manner that would challenge the democratic legitimacy of Parliament.[94] These dicta are best understood as examples of constitutional counter-balancing. If legislation were to remove judicial review from the courts to such an extent as to remove their proper constitutional role, then the courts would be justified in refusing to enforce this legislation. They would do so in order to protect the separation of powers, ensuring a balanced constitution in which the legislature, the executive, and the judiciary are able to check the powers of each other. If the legislature were to act in a manner that removed its democratic legitimacy, then the courts would no longer be required to respect the acts of the legislature, the constitutional justification for its powers having been undermined to such an extent that it was no longer acting legitimately.

---

[92] A.L. Young, *Democratic Dialogue and the Constitution* (Oxford University Press, 2017).
[93] *Jackson v AG* (n. 20) and *AXA General Insurance v Lord Advocate* (n. 22).
[94] *Moohan v Lord Advocate* (n. 64) and *Shindler v Chancellor of the Duchy of Lancaster* (n. 27).

Constitutional counter-balancing measures can be contrasted with constitutional collaboration. Interactions between the legislature, the executive, and the judiciary foster constitutional collaboration when the institutions work together in a manner that respects their distinct roles in the constitution, based on their institutional and constitutional features. This can be illustrated by our discussion of proportionality and deference, where the standard of review is modified given the circumstances of the case and the relative powers of the legislature, executive and judiciary. The courts exercise deference when there are institutional reasons for doing so. For example, in *Miss Behavin' Ltd*, the court recognized that Belfast City Council had greater knowledge of Belfast, and also had more of an ability to hear a range of views concerning zoning restrictions. As such, the Council were in a better position to determine whether sex shop licences should be granted in particular areas of the city. Their knowledge, and greater expertise from determining these issues on a more regular basis, meant that the council were more likely to reach a good decision on this issue. This does not mean that the courts should not control these decisions at all. Rather, it means that when exercising their scrutiny to determine whether this is a proportionate restriction on the right to freedom of expression, courts scrutinize the decision less stringently then they would otherwise have done. Moreover, deference could be owed on democratic grounds when faced with decisions which are contestable, allowing democratically accountable institutions, like Belfast City Council, to choose from a range of reasonable policy choices, for which they are held accountable to the electorate.

In this manner, the separation of powers is influencing judicial review, but it is not being used blatantly as a head of review. Rather, concerns as to the different institutional and constitutional features of the legislature, executive and judiciary are used in the background to influence the intensity of judicial review. These factors may also be used to explain why the court reached different conclusions in *Anisminic* and *Privacy International Ltd*, perhaps in a manner that was unexpected given the strong support for the principles of access to justice in both *Evans*[95] and *UNISON*[96] and the dicta in *Jackson* and *AXA Insurance Ltd* suggesting that the removal of judicial review is one of the exceptional circumstances in which courts may refuse to enforce legislation.[97] As discussed above, the conclusion in *Privacy International Ltd* focused not just on the specific wording of legislation, but also on the institutional composition, and the powers of the Investigatory Powers Tribunal (IPT).[98] The legislation provided a clear account of Parliament's intention to empower the IPT to have the final say on issues relating to its own jurisdiction. To go against the clear wording of Parliament here would be a greater intrusion on the legislature's sphere of constitutional authority than in *Anisminic* given that the legislation specifically included jurisdictional errors in its account of the ouster clause. Moreover, although the legislature is removing an aspect of judicial review from the courts, it is not removing the constitutional ability of the

---

[95] R. (Evans) v Attorney General (n. 12).   [96] R. (UNISON) v Lord Chancellor (n. 45).
[97] Jackson v AG (n. 20) and AXA General Insurance v Lord Advocate (n. 22).
[98] R. (Privacy International) v Investigatory Powers Tribunal (n. 62).

courts to carry out judicial review over the powers of the executive more generally. As such, there is only a weak justification for the court to challenge legislation in order to preserve its own constitutional role.

In addition, the institutional features of the IPT demonstrated that it was able to uphold the rule of law, the membership of the IPT being equivalent to membership of the High Court. Moreover, the IPT had a better ability to determine good outcomes, given its ability to hear information in private so as to balance competing interests without undermining the interests of national security. It may also have gained more expertise in these issues, hearing more cases concerning the scope and application of the Regulation of Investigatory Powers Act—both the source of the powers of the IPT and the source of most of the law that the IPT was called upon to interpret. On the facts of the case, the IPT was required to determine the requisite precision of a warrant which could be used to authorize an interference with wireless telegraphy. A focus on constitutional collaboration would require a comparative evaluation of the ability of the IPT and the courts to make such a determination, including the relative ability of the courts to correct the possible mistakes of the IPT when making this determination. It may also depend on the nature of the mistake. We may be less concerned about mistakes arising from the interpretation of legislative provisions than we would be were the IPT to make a mistake when balancing fundamental human rights and national security issues.

Regarding the separation of powers as a fundamental principle of the constitution in this manner may help to provide a better account of the case law. I would also argue that this provides a better normative justification for the relative roles of the legislature, the executive and the judiciary in the UK's uncodified and un-entrenched constitution. Countries with an entrenched, codified constitution enact and modify their constitutions in a manner different from the way in which they enact ordinary legislation. As such, when a constitutional court holds either the legislature or the executive to account according to the principles set out in the constitution, it can both point to a higher form of law-making establishing these principles and, usually, though not always, to a higher form of law-making establishing the role of the court to uphold the constitution. The same is not true in the UK. Even if we are beginning to recognize a hierarchy of constitutional and ordinary norms, there is no distinct procedure for adopting constitutional norms.[99] As such, the UK does not differentiate between constituent power and legislative power. Parliamentary legislative supremacy has been interpreted as requiring that both rest in the hands of Parliament, with Parliament being able to enact constitutional measures in the same way that it enacts legislation.

We argued above that the sovereignty of Parliament is in tension with the rule of law. Those who advocate a strongly normative model of the separation of powers do so because they focus on the greater importance of the rule of law. Such theories regard the rule of law as underpinning the sovereignty of Parliament, such that legislation which does not adhere to the requirements of the rule of law is not legitimate—it is not

---

[99] A. Blick, D. Howarth and N. le Roux, *Distinguishing Constitutional Legislation: A Modest Proposal* (London: The Constitution Society, 2014).

capable of providing a good reason for those subject to the law to obey its provisions.[100] These accounts of the separation of powers effectively place constituent power in the hands of the courts. The courts determine the content of the rule of law. They also determine the content of the doctrine of parliamentary sovereignty, and the circumstances in which the courts could strike down actions of the legislature or the executive.

My theory of the separation of powers focuses on maintaining a balanced constitution, specifically aiming to ensure that constituent power does not rest fully either in the hands of the legislature or the courts. It regards the separation of powers as a fundamental normative principle of the constitution. Rather than our understanding of the relative roles of the legislature, the executive and the judiciary being dependent upon the relative importance of the separation of powers or the rule of law, it argues that their relative institutional and constitutional roles, and the need for each institution both to defend its own constitutional powers and to collaborate with other institutions, determines the extent to which the courts will maintain a balance between parliamentary sovereignty and the rule of law. Parliamentary sovereignty and the rule of law are kept in tension with each other, each playing an important role in the constitution but with neither being regarded as the foundational or the most important principle of the constitution.

To achieve this, parliamentary sovereignty, as understood by Dicey, needs to be respected. However, this is required not because Parliament should have absolute law-making power but because Parliament should not possess constituent power. It should not be able to enact legislation that binds its successors. Moreover, parliamentary sovereignty, and some principles of statutory interpretation, cannot be regarded as mere principles of the common law that can be modified through the actions of the courts alone. Rather they are best classified as customary rules, evolving over time and exemplified through the behaviour of the legislature and the courts. This ensures that constituent power cannot be exercised by the courts alone, with the court creating constitutional limits which can overturn the legislative power of Parliament. As such, it aims to ensure that, in an evolving constitution, constitutive power is shared between the legislature and the judiciary. In a similar manner, it advocates that both the legislature and the judiciary need to work together to ensure that there are sufficient checks and balances over the executive. However, these checks and balances need to respect the legitimate role of the executive, both in terms of its institutional features and its important constitutional role in administering the law in a manner which achieves the public good.

CONCLUSION

We have argued that, although we can provide evidence of growing legal controls over the executive and the legislature, we should be wary of regarding this as a conclusive and definitive move in the UK constitution towards greater legal controls and

---

[100] T.R.S. Allan, *The Sovereignty of Law: Freedom, Constitution and Common Law* (Oxford University Press, 2013).

a corresponding rise in the relative power of the judiciary. We recognized that there are also examples of more restrictive legal controls, and that the extent to which legal controls are exercised in practice is contextual. A range of factors is used to determine how far the legislature and the executive are controlled by the courts. We also argued that this was best understood as illustrating how the separation of powers operates as a fundamental principle of the UK constitution. Whilst the separation of powers was not used as an instrument of constitutional design in the UK, in the sense of providing a clear account of the relative powers of the legislature, executive and judiciary, it nevertheless performs an important role as a fundamental constitutional principle. It aims to ensure a balanced constitution, such that no one institution is capable of obtaining too much power in the UK constitution. Moreover, the institutional and constitutional features of the legislature, executive, and judiciary are used by the court to help determine the extent to which the court holds both the executive and the legislature to account.

However, this balance can only occur when there are both effective legal and political controls over the executive. Whilst the fusion of the executive and the legislature in terms of personnel may be used to facilitate checks and balances, it can also be used to provide too much power to the executive with little, if any, political oversight. We noted this in particular regarding the use of Henry VIII clauses, as well as explaining how the codification of prerogative powers and conventions may be used as a means of giving greater powers to the executive, replacing political controls with legal controls whose content is weaker than the potential political controls. If the separation of powers is to continue to perform its role as a fundamental constitutional principle in the UK's uncodified constitution, then we need to ensure that the legislature has the means and the motivation to hold the executive to account for its actions. If not, the delicate balance of power on which the UK constitution rests may be undermined; perhaps even to the extent that the courts consider that exceptional circumstances do exist in which to refuse to recognize or enforce legislation enacted by an overly dominant Government able to enact measures with little, if any, control from Parliament.

FURTHER READING

N. BARBER, 'Prelude to the Separation of Powers' (2001) 60 *Cambridge Law Journal* 59

E. BARENDT, 'Separation of Powers and Constitutional Government' [1995] *Public Law* 599

R. MASTERMAN, *The Separation of Powers in the Contemporary Constitution: Judicial Competence and Independence in the United Kingdom* (Cambridge University Press, 2011)

R. MASTERMAN and S. WHEATLE, 'Unpacking Separation of Powers: Judicial Independence, Sovereignty and Conceptual Flexibility in the UK Constitution' [2017] *Public Law* 469

D. WOODHOUSE, 'The Constitutional Reform Act 2005: Defending Judicial Independence the English Way' (2007) 5 *International Journal of Constitutional Law* 153

13

INFORMATION: PUBLIC ACCESS, PROTECTING PRIVACY AND SURVEILLANCE

Patrick Birkinshaw*

SUMMARY

The Freedom of Information Act is a statute of great constitutional significance. The Act established a right to publicly held information. Until the Act, disclosure of government held information was largely a matter of government discretion. FOIA laws have their origins in the pre-digital age and any discussion of information rights must also take on board the contemporary reality of the global digitization of communications via social media networks and the enhanced capabilities of state intelligence agencies to conduct surveillance over electronic communications. The General Data Protection Regulation seeks to give greater security to personal data. However, private information is now regularly harvested by private tech companies and used by intermediaries to influence public events, public power and elections—as illustrated by recent scandals involving the practice of 'data farming' by social media networks, and the sale of personal data to political campaign consultants seeking to affect the outcomes of national elections and referenda. Similarly, government surveillance may be age-old, but the emergence of digital power has enabled public authority to invade our private lives far more intrusively and effectively—due in part to legislation such as the Investigatory Powers Act 2016. All this poses substantial challenges for the public regulation of information access, an issue which traverses both the public and private spheres. Courts, meanwhile, have to balance demands for privacy protection, open justice and secrecy.

* Emeritus Professor of Law, University of Hull.

THE FOI JOURNEY

Lord Mance's appraisal is well known. 'Information is the key to sound decision-making, to accountability and development; it underpins democracy and assists in combatting poverty, oppression, corruption, prejudice and inefficiency.' Judges and officials depend upon it, as do the press and public interest bodies. But, he continued, 'information can be genuinely private, confidential or sensitive', and these genuine interests must be respected.[1]

The FOIA has its modern origins in the USA, whose own federal Freedom of Information Act became law in 1966. It was seen as an antidote to secret government in which citizens had no legal right to publicly held information. This problem was particularly acute in the United Kingdom where there was an overarching framework of official secrecy in which official information was protected in the widest of terms by criminal law and frequent use of the non-justiciable prerogative power in matters of governance.[2] The civil service was managed under the prerogative and anonymity, which conventionally protected the identity of civil servants. Official secrecy was buttressed by repressive legislation from 1911 (originally 1889): the notorious section 2 of which was eventually pensioned off by reforming legislation in 1989. The Official Secrets Act 1989, still in operation, removed the 'blunderbuss' protection over all official information formerly provided by the 1911 legislation. However, it pinpointed six specific areas of information for legal protection and criminalized 'damaging' unauthorized disclosures in those areas. In particular, it protects security and intelligence information—especially in the case of security and intelligence personnel—and surveillance powers in the strictest of terms.[3] There are additionally numerous other statutory provisions apart from the OSA criminally punishing unauthorized disclosures.[4] Prosecutors have also increasingly resorted to an ancient common law offence of misbehaviour in public office for unauthorized disclosures.[5]

The Law Commission in 2017 published a consultation paper on suggested reforms to the Official Secrets legislation including the 1989 Act.[6] The Commission's paper provisionally recommended significant reforms although the press was critical because of fears about tightening up secrecy controls. For example, compliance with Art 10 ECHR did not, the Commission believed, require a public interest defence against unauthorized disclosure.[7]

Against this background of secrecy and prerogative, the movement to open up government and to provide a legal right to information gathered pace from the 1970s. The

---

[1] *Kennedy v Charity Commission* [2014] UKSC 20 para 1.

[2] In the modern era, case law began to hem in the scope of the prerogative from the 1960s.

[3] S 1. 'Notified persons' under s. 1 are also similarly bound.

[4] See P. Birkinshaw and M. Varney, *Government and Information Rights* 5th ed. (2019) Annex B.

[5] *R. v Chapman* [2015] EWCA Crim 539—there has to be a specific guidance on 'damage to the public interest' for conviction.

[6] Law Commission *Protection of Official Information* Consultation Paper No. 230 (2017).

[7] *R. v Shayler* [2002] UKHL 11.

objectives of seeking to place a FOIA on the UK statute book were to achieve greater forms of accountability, greater participation by the public in government and to make government more open—in present day ubiquitous language, to make government, and the powers exercised by government, more transparent. The objective was to make the bases on which government operated open to greater scrutiny and to encourage debate on public issues on a more informed basis.

The debates, which UK advocates inherited from the USA, were nurtured before digitization—making information and data computer readable—became a mainstay of modern existence along with tech companies, social media platforms, smart phones and uses in information technology of algorithms and psychography. Digitization was well under way by 2000, the date of the UK FOIA, and the 1984 Data Protection Act was enacted in the UK to introduce safeguards for computer held personal information following a Council of Europe convention.[8] The Act of 1984 has been replaced by two successive reforming measures, both of which were enacted as a consequence of European Union requirements.[9] The 2016 General Data Protection Regulation, replacing the 1995 Directive, seeks to address the dangers posed to personal information by global resort to information technology.

The result is that general access to information is governed by one statutory framework and data and privacy protection by another. The FOIA was a domestic measure inspired by American and Commonwealth measures. Privacy and data protection and safeguards in surveillance had their provenance in European laws, especially Art. 8 of the ECHR protecting private and family life. Moreover, as the press have discovered, Art. 8 rights frequently clash with Art. 10 ECHR, which guarantees freedom of expression rights.

FOIA—THE FRAMEWORK

It is eighteen years since the Freedom of Information Act was passed and over thirteen years since it came fully into effect. Publication schemes giving pro-active disclosure of publicly held information were introduced before individual access rights took effect in 2005. Publication schemes are mandatory for public authorities (PAs) and contain classes of information on subjects, such as, who we are and what we do; how we spend money; our priorities, policies and procedures; how decisions are made and our guidance; registers; minutes; and services. Publication schemes have been facilitated by the growing sophistication of search engines and browsers as PAs put more information on-line.

The FOIA confers a right of access to information held by public authorities on anyone.[10] PAs are under a duty on request to confirm or deny whether they hold

---

[8] Convention for the Protection of Individuals with regard to the Automatic processing of Personal Data (Convention 108, 1981). A new Convention has been opened for signature.

[9] EC Directive 95/46/EC (1995); General Data Protection Regulation EU 2016/679 and Law Enforcement Directive (EU) 2016/680.

[10] *IPSA* [2015] EWCA Civ 388—FOIA allows access to *documents* not just information.

information (s. 1(1)). Requests must be made in writing. Fees may be charged although the provision of information is free up to limits.[11] Authorities are under an obligation to provide advice and assistance to requesters. Time limits apply for a response and disclosure, although these are frequently not met. Requests may be refused where they are vexatious or repetitive.[12]

PAs may refuse a request on the basis of twenty-four exemptions.[13] Virtually all exemptions contain a proviso allowing a 'neither confirm nor deny' response as set out in the exemption. Exemptions may be qualified and subject to a public interest (PI) test. This means that the Information Commissioner (IC) may decide that although the exemption applies there is a greater PI in disclosure. Where the scales are evenly balanced, the outcome favours disclosure.[14] IC decision notices and tribunal decisions have many examples of such balancing. Particularly important qualified exemptions are contained in s. 35, covering the formulation of government policy-making, and s. 36 on prejudice to the conduct of public affairs. These exemptions together with personal information (s. 40) and legal privilege (s. 42) are the most heavily invoked exemptions.

Or exemptions may be absolute. This means there is no place for a PI disclosure. Some absolute exemptions are unavoidably so. Information protected by the law of confidentiality (s. 41) or where disclosure is legally prohibited (s. 44) fall under this category. Other exemptions such as communications between a public authority and the monarch or first or second in line to the throne (s. 37)[15] or information supplied by, or relating to, the security and intelligence services (s. 23) reflect policy decisions on what must be kept secret. Opinions differ on whether an absolute exemption is needed.

In *Kennedy*, the Supreme Court ruled that an absolute exemption in s. 32, which deals with court and tribunal information, did not remove a duty upon the Charity Commission to consider using its statutory and common law powers to disclose information in its possession despite the existence of s. 32. *Kennedy* concerned a journalist's request for information about inquiries conducted by the Commission. The Commission cited the absolute exemption in s. 32 as a reason for refusing to disclose the information sought. However, the Supreme Court held that the Commission could not simply rely upon the existence of this absolute exemption as a reason for refusing disclosure. As a statutory body, it was also subject to common law duties of openness and transparency. As a result, disclosure decisions resulting in a refusal would be subject to searching judicial review—in particular because of the importance of these principles as they apply in respect of journalism on questions of real public importance.

Kennedy also featured a discussion of the influence of the jurisprudence of the European Court of Human Rights (ECHR) on whether Art. 10 ECHR on freedom of

---

[11] In the case of central government, armed forces and Parliament £600; for other public authorities £450.

[12] *Drunsfield v IC* [2015] EWCA Civ 454.

[13] Some of the sections contain more than one exemption so the number is larger than twenty-four.

[14] S. 2(2). A 'neither confirm nor deny' response to a request is also subject to a public interest override, s. 2(1).

[15] This was not originally an absolute exemption but was made so after the *Evans* litigation below.

expression contained a right of access to information. The recent CHR jurisprudence suggested it did, and the question was whether s. 32 should be interpreted under the influence of that jurisprudence.[16] The majority refused to travel along the path taken by the CHR in the absence of a judgment of the Grand Chamber of that court supporting such a conclusion. Subsequently a judgment of the Grand Chamber CHR confirmed that, in appropriate circumstances, Art. 10 can confer a right of access to information.[17]

EVANS AND THE VETO

Section 53 contains what is referred to as the veto. By this means, an 'accountable person' may form an opinion on 'reasonable grounds' that, in essence, disclosure should not be made by a PA. The decision to disclose by the IC, or tribunal which hears appeals from the IC's decision on disclosure (below), can thus be overruled by this veto power. In *Evans*, a long-running case involving communications between the Prince of Wales and government departments, the Upper Tribunal ruled that the correspondence should be disclosed.[18] The Attorney General exercised the veto. Judicial review was sought of this decision. The Supreme Court ruled by majority (5–2) that the certificate issued by the Attorney General, which basically simply stated a disagreement with the tribunal in bare terms, could not, in the absence of clear statutory language to the contrary, remove the power of the court or tribunal to determine rights between litigants and the power of review of the executive by the courts. In particular, Lord Mance concluded that the statement by the AG would require the clearest possible justification and solid reasons to disagree with the judicially determined findings of fact and rulings on the law by the Upper Tribunal. The certificate fell far short of this. The end result was that under FOIA the certificate was unlawful. None has been issued subsequently. The court also ruled by 6–1 that the certificate was in breach of EU law.[19]

BODIES COVERED

Coverage is extensive. FOIA applies to over 100,000 public authorities (PAs) with powers to designate private bodies as a PA for FOIA purposes under terms. Use of designation has been limited.[20] A long-standing and important question has concerned the designation of private sector contractors under FOIA[21] who provide public services.

---

[16]   See *Kennedy* paras. 71–99 per Lord Mance on the case law from a variety of jurisdictions. The more recent CHR decisions were from lower sections of the court, not the Grand Chamber.

[17]   *Magyar Helsinki Bizottság v Hungary* Application No 18030/11 (8 November 2016).

[18]   *Rob Evans v IC* [2012] UKUT 313 (AAC). Note *Rob Evans v IC* [2015] UKUT 303 (AAC) with the Annex of disclosed documents and the reasons for disclosure in June 2015!

[19]   *R. (Evans) v Attorney General* [2015] UKSC 21. The EU law component was by virtue of the Environmental Information Regulations (below). Including *Evans*, seven vetoes have been issued: O. Gay and E. Potton *FOI and Ministerial Vetoes* House of Commons Library (2014).

[20]   Bodies designated include the Academy Trusts, National Police Chiefs Council, the Financial Ombudsman Service, Universities Central Admissions Service and Network Rail.

Such contracts have produced highly controversial episodes.[22] Reviews of the FOIA, which are examined below, have been reluctant to recommend designation of private contractors.

There is no straightforward way of establishing the total number of FOIA requests. Only 41 central government bodies are subject to detailed central statistical analysis of FOI performance by the Cabinet Office and Ministry of Justice.[23]

Bodies not listed as PAs are effectively excluded from the Act. The most important exclusions are the Monarch and Royal Family and the security and intelligence services and GCHQ. Some, e.g. the BBC, are excluded for categories of information—journalism, art and literature.[24] Others are excluded from FOIA for specific functions.[25]

THE INFORMATION COMMISSIONER

The Act brought in a unified regulatory authority for FOI and Data Protection (DP) under the Information Commissioner's Office although the statutes have their own legislative details which differ significantly, especially under the General Data Protection Regulation (2016), which has now been implemented in UK law by the Data Protection Act 2018. The IC has considerable enforcement, information gathering and penalty powers under both statutes, and GDPR reforms have added appreciably to the DP penalties.

The standard outcome of a complaint to the IC against a refusal to disclose information under the FOIA is a decision notice after investigation. This is not available under the DPA although complaints procedures were introduced for data subjects under DPA 2018 (s. 165). The complainant may go to the tribunal if there is an inadequate response (s. 166).

To FOI and DPA have been added the Environmental Information Regulations (EIR). The regulations implement an EU Directive.[26] These are administered by the IC and although the specific provisions on what is accessible and what is exempt differ from the FOIA, the mode of enforcement is based on the FOIA. Unlike the FOIA, the EIR do not schedule public authorities that are covered by the regulations. The EIR provide broadly based definitions of a public authority and bodies acting in a public capacity. For example, these may involve private bodies which are under the control of a PA or which possess special powers. The ECJ has been more extensive on the identification of public bodies to be covered by the EU provisions than English courts.[27] The Sovereign and Royal Household are not public bodies under EIR and nor is the Prince of Wales in that capacity.[28]

---

[21] S. 5(1)(b).   [22] The collapse of Carillion in 2018.

[23] Cabinet Office, *FOI Annual Statistics 2017*.   [24] See *Sugar v BBC* [2012] UKSC 4.

[25] The Bank of England and monetary policy and financial stability operations.

[26] Directive 2003/4/EC implemented by SI 3391/2004.

[27] *Fish* [2015] UKUT 52 (AAC) applying Case C-279/12 *Fish Legal and E Shirley v IC et al.* The lead from the ECJ has been beneficial in this respect.

[28] *Cross v IC and Cabinet Office* [2016] UKUT 153 AAC; *AG v IC & M Bruton* [2016] UKUT 154 AAC.

THE INFORMATION COMMISSIONER AND TRIBUNALS

The establishment of the IC was not propitious. The Commissioner's salary was initially modest compared with senior officials and the headquarters were in Chester. Changes to improve status were soon introduced. Now there is a satellite office in London as well as offices in Belfast, Cardiff and Edinburgh. ICs have enjoyed an increasingly high profile but they have reported on shortage of resources as the ICs workload increases and austerity bites harder. The IC's 2016–17 annual report stated a 70 per cent increase in the ICO's budget for DPA work 'in the long term'. DPA work is paid for from fees received. These are expected to rise to £34.5 million by 2021. FOIA work is a grant in aid (about £3.75 million p.a.). Levies on social media companies have been suggested by the Commons Digital, Culture etc. committee to help finance and enhance the role for the IC in its recommendations for regulation of social media.[29]

The IC has described her role as upholding information rights for the UK public in the digital age.[30] She seeks to 'maintain and develop influence within the global information rights regulatory community'.[31] Her remit covers: FOIA and Environmental Information Regulations; Data Protection, the GDPR and the less publicized Law Enforcement Directive; Privacy and Electronic Communications Regulations; the Re-use of Public Sector Data Regulations; Spatial Data/INSPIRE Regulation; Electronic Identification Regulations; the Network Information Systems Regulations 2018 which seek to ensure network security in the face of cyber attacks; and the Investigatory Powers Act 2016.

Accompanying the IC is a system of tribunals to hear appeals under FOIA.[32] Originally the FOI proposals did not recommend a tribunal—the Scottish FOIA 2002 actually stuck to this blueprint and has no tribunal system. However, the FOIA as enacted saw the introduction of a tribunal as well as several other important liberalizing amendments. There are now two tribunal appellate stages after the IC's decision. The first tier is the information rights tribunal which hears appeals on law, exercise of discretion, and which possesses fact-reviewing powers. There is a further appeal on a point of law to the Upper Tribunal (AAC). A very specialized, detailed jurisprudence has developed.[33]

The annual reports of the IC contain details of complaints to the IC and appeals.[34] In 2017–18 there were 5,784 complaints, which was up by 5 per cent on the previous year. There were 284 appeals to the first-tier tribunal.[35]

---

[29] *Disinformation and Fake News Interim Report* HC 363 (2017–19). See text at note 118.

[30] ICO *Annual Report* 2017–18 p. 11.

[31] Ibid.

[32] The site for IC decision notices on complaints is https://icosearch.ico.org.uk/s/search.html?collection=ico-meta&profile=decisions&query and for tribunal case law http://informationrights.decisions.tribunals.gov.uk//Public/search.aspx and http://www.bailii.org/uk/cases/UKUT/AAC/2018/ (Upper Tribunal).

[33] Birkinshaw and Varney note 4 Chs. 1 and 3.

[34] https://ico.org.uk/media/about-the-ico/documents/2259463/annual-report-201718.pdf.

[35] Note 30.

FOIA reforms have included a specific right of access to datasets (and re-use of public sector information requirements); a qualified exemption for research and, most famously, the elevation to absolute status of the qualified exemption covering communications between PAs, the Monarch and successors (*Evans* above). The Public Records legislation has also been amended to reduce the 30-year rule before publication to 20 years.

HOW DOES THE FOI FUTURE APPEAR IN THE UK?

There have been dramatic FOIA disclosures: the scandal of MPs expenses; legal advice on invading Iraq; Michael Gove's use of personal email accounts for ministerial business was covered by FOIA; separating legal advice from national security information on drone strikes in Syria making them a qualified and not absolute exemption; the existence of a rulebook on a royal legislative 'veto'; and Prince Charles' correspondence with ministers, which has been referred to. There is constant reference to FOI releases to the BBC and media providing details for public interest reports.[36]

Disclosure has involved Cabinet discussions, where there have been vetoes as well as many unsuccessful requests, and lobbying activity at the highest levels of government. One should not forget the thousands of cases where individuals have received information that is of little public significance but of appreciable importance to them.

My belief is the FOIA has been fundamental in changing the landscape of public activity—it is 'a landmark enactment of great constitutional significance for the United Kingdom'.[37]

COMMONS JUSTICE COMMITTEE REVIEW

The first post-legislation scrutiny of FOIA took place in 2012 before the Commons Justice Committee.[38] The Committee was not impressed by the special pleading of mandarins on the alleged chilling effect of s. 35 on civil servants in official decision-making. Nor was the committee impressed by the former Prime Minister's (Blair) querulous letter to the committee about the FOIA.[39] FOIA was described as a success and 'one of the most open regimes in the world' and the 'veto was appropriate to protect policy development at the highest levels' (para. 179) which meant it would have to be exercised from time to time (para. 201). In its response, in December 2012, the government

---

[36] *Corporate Officer of the House of Commons v IC* [2008] EWHC 1084 (Admin) (MPs); *S Plowden/FCO v IC* EA/2011/0225 & 0228 (21 January 2014) (Iraq); FS5042276 (1 March 2012) (Gove); *Corderoy & Ahmed v IC, AG &CO* ([2017] UKUT 495 (AAC) (Syria)) in which the IC was criticized for not exercising the IC's full fact-finding powers; FS50425063 (26 August 2012) (rule-book).

[37] Lord Sumption *Kennedy* above para. 153.   [38] HC 96 Vols. 1–111 (2012–13).

[39] Tony Blair, *A Journey*, pp. 516–17 (2010).

addressed various points but while it did not rule out extension by designation for new bodies it felt that commercial information and government contracting should rely on voluntary arrangements. The Act had been successful in achieving some objectives but notably not in increasing confidence in government.[40]

THE INDEPENDENT COMMISSION ON FREEDOM OF INFORMATION

The Independent Commission was appointed in 2015.[41] It was to review the first ten years of the Act's existence. There was media concern that the review of the FOIA by a Cabinet Office–appointed commission would recommend significant restraints on FOIA. Its epithet was 'independent' but it had two former home secretaries in its membership—Jack Straw and Michael Howard. Neither was regarded as an apostle of openness. The terms of reference included whether there was an appropriate public interest balance between transparency, accountability and a 'safe space' for policy development. The reference to the 'burden of the Act' was not propitious.

In its foreword, the chair set out the conclusion of the Commission that the Act has helped change the culture of the public sector. It has enhanced openness and transparency. There was no evidence that FOI rights had to be restricted—in some areas they needed to be increased. Delays were a problem. There were no proposals for fee increases.

The Commission recommended that a 'safe space' should be given added weight in policy formulation to add protection for internal communications and there should be greater protection for collective Cabinet responsibility (in the era of Brexit!) and post-decision stages. The veto should be strengthened and only issued after the IC decision either for or against the PA. It would be challengeable on a judicial review. Public bodies under contract for delivery of public services where the contract was in excess of £5 million should be included within FOIA but there was no Commission agreement on this specific point. Several recommendations sought to make the Act more effective and reduce delays. Reforms in the tribunal system were also suggested, as well as an increase in IC funding. The government response came in March 2016 and, while generally supporting the 21 recommendations of the Commission, agreed that fees for requests would not be increased.[42] No reference was made to increased funding—in contrast to the situation under the new GDPR regime, which has seen additional resources allocated for data protection.[43]

---

[40] R. Hazell, B. Worthy and M. Glover, *The Impact of the Freedom of Information Act on Central Government in the UK: Does FOI Work?* (2010).

[41] *Independent Commission on Freedom of Information*, Cabinet Office (2016).

[42] https://www.opengovernment.org.uk/2016/03/01/government-responds-to-the-commission-on-freedom-of-information/ (10/10/2018).

[43] No recommendations have resulted in legislative changes but the *FOIA Code of Practice* Cabinet Office (2018) was amended to accommodate some recommendations. The code has guidance on private contractors and datasets inter alia.

PARTY MANIFESTOS

The clamour for FOI has long subsided and GDPR has been the recent focus of public attention. The Conservative Manifesto of 2017 contained a whole chapter on digitization and a digital charter and explained the need for new data protection legislation. It was the most interesting contribution on information in the manifestos. The Digital Economy Act 2017 also emerged—much of it about the digital infrastructure, on-line public services, data exchange, superfast broadband and the electronic communications code conferring special powers and rights on communications network providers. Of the four major parties, only Labour referred to FOIA in wanting to extend FOIA to private contractors running public services and, together with the Scottish National Party, in wanting to amend the Transparency of Lobbying Act 2014.[44] Media plurality, the free flow of information, and super broadband were also taken up by the 'opposition' parties.

One has to ask whether FOI has become diminished in the digital era? Transparency is now proclaimed as a beneficent feature of modern government. Many of the practices on publishing information do not take place under FOIA and many are non-statutory. More information has been made available on government expenditure, senior salaries, transparency in taxation and an Office of Tax Simplification.[45] Internet freedom of information was the *leitmotiv* of social media tech companies. One was beginning to wonder whether, with so much transparency, we need FOI. My answer is unreservedly 'yes'.

FOI, DATA PROTECTION, AND PRIVACY

The FOIA provides that requests for personal information by the subject of the information (data subject (DS)) are dealt with under the DPA 2018. For the DS, this allows access to a far greater range of 'unstructured data'[46] when held by a public authority under the UK and Scottish FOIAs than usually available under the DPA. Requests for data about others are made under the FOIA subject to DPA principles (FOIA s. 40).

We live in a digitally determined world: smartphones; wired up motor vehicles; digital assistants; CCTV; number plate recognition; automated facial recognition; satellite imagery; and psychographic classification of big data through algorithms for marketing purposes. We leave our digital foot and thumb prints in a vast, exciting and frightening range of repositories.

FOI was driven by the desire to know about 'them'. Them being those who wielded power on our behalf—our governors—to hold them to account for their stewardship

---

[44] The Act establishes a register and registrar of consultant lobbyists. *Spinwatch* suggests about 1 per cent of lobbying is regulated by the 2014 Act: see Speakers Corner's Trust http://www.speakerscornertrust.org/10529/lobbying-in-the-uk-well-regulated-or-out-of-control/ (11/10/2018).

[45] See https://www.gov.uk/government/collections/how-to-publish-central-government-transparency-data.

[46] Not digitized or part of a structured system (below).

and the trust we had to place in them. To tell us, the governed, what they did, on what basis, or what they didn't do and how they spent our money—wisely, wastefully, or corruptly. To cast light on power's all-intrusive grasp. To make power more responsive and responsible. That is a timeless unending quest. Government will always need to be scrutinized.[47]

Now the preoccupation has become 'me'. My privacy. My space. My right to be left alone or be forgotten. My information. David Cameron's government used the phrase 'personalised democracy' through use of big data.[48] The data harvesters and social media also need to be scrutinized. Is there is an emerging role for FOI here?

On the whole, the relationship between DPA and FOIA has worked pretty well in the use of Sched. 2(6) of the 1998 Act to balance a public right of access to, and protection of, personal data. The GDPR regime has similar balancing considerations and emphasizes that protection of freedom of speech/information and data protection are fundamental rights, as examined below under 'Processing for a Legitimate Interest'. But the CJEU and EU Commission have not always been so balanced and have given priority to DP over access to information. Officials and individuals acting in a public capacity have been protected against requests for information about official activity. The threshold of establishing 'necessity' to receive data under EC Regulation 45/2001 art. 8(b) has been set at a high level.[49] By contrast, the IC and tribunal have frequently drawn a more nuanced distinction under the domestic laws between individuals acting in a public or private capacity, and in the former on the status of the official. The lower the rank, usually the greater the expectation of privacy.[50]

Matching the two statutes—the DPA 1998 and the FOIA 2000—was not easy because of the perceived conflict between disclosure under the FOIA 2000 and privacy protection and regulation under the DPA 1998. The Law Lords spoke of the undoubted importance of FOIA and its liberal interpretation but emphasized that FOIA operates so as not to override privacy and data protection.[51] The jurisprudence under FOIA since 2005 has assisted the relationship between the overlapping regimes.

DPA 2018

In a context of numerous episodes revealing the dangers involved in massive retention of personal data, the Cambridge Analytica episode highlighted the abuse of data harvesting of millions of individuals' personal data. This episode involved the wrongful

---

[47] B. Worthy, *The Politics of Freedom of Information: How and Why Governments Pass Laws that Threaten their Power* (Manchester University Press, 2017).

[48] *Open Data* Cm 8353 (2012).

[49] Case C 28/08P *EU Commission v Bavarian Lager Co Ltd* Grand Chamber (29 June 2010) involving the access regulation and data protection regimes applying to EU institutions: Regulations EC 1049/2001 and EC 405/2001. See *Psara v Parliament* [2018] EUECJ T-639/15.

[50] See the early case of *Corporate Officer of House of Commons v IC* EA/2006/0074–0076 which concerned MPs' expenses.

[51] *Common Services Agency v Scottish Information Commissioner* [2008] UKHL 47 para 4.

transmission of that data from Facebook to an academic researcher who sold it to a political canvassing consultant. The latter used it to attempt to sway voters in key elections in the USA. Other examples of use of personal data include interference by governments in elections in other countries and by political campaigning groups breaching data protection. The IC has explained the methods involved in the Cambridge Analytica example.[52]

In July 2018, after a fourteen-month investigation, the IC fined Facebook £500,000 for breaches of the 1998 Data Protection Act involving Cambridge Analytica. The events in question occurred before the 2018 Data Protection Act came into effect. The fine is a trifle for Facebook and it had twenty-eight days to respond. More importantly, the investigation by the IC was aimed at the activities of EU leave campaign groups in the 2016 referendum and their use of personal data. These included Arron Banks, who had bank-rolled the leave campaign, his insurance company, Britain Stronger in Europe (Remain), Vote Leave, and UKIP. The report has serious implications for data use by universities, because of the use of personal data for research which may be wrongly transmitted as in Cambridge Analytica, and for the UK's political parties. Eleven letters were sent by the IC to the main political parties with Assessment Notices for personal data audits: 'We have concluded that there are risks in relation to the processing of personal data by many political parties'.[53] In *Democracy Disrupted?* [54] the IC reported a 'significant shortfall in transparency and provision of fair transparency information' in political campaigns. The publication has recommendations for fairer and more transparent use of data by political parties and social media in elections.

It is against this dramatic background that the Data Protection Act 2018 was enacted in order to implement the General Data Protection Regulation and the Law Enforcement Directive.[55] The DPA is tortuous and technical. The Act states 'most UK data processing' is subject to the GDPR (s. 1(2)).[56]

The 2018 DPA applies to the holding of personal data by both public and private bodies. The Act repeals and replaces the 1998 DPA, which was amended by the Freedom of Information Act 2000 (FOIA 2000). The DPA 2018 basically allows the subjects of automated (electronic/digitized) and 'structured' files to access such files (or more precisely the personal data within them) which are held on them. Requests may be written or oral. Access is free with power to charge where requests are 'manifestly unfounded or excessive' (s. 135). DCs must pay a fee to the ICO for processing unless exempt (s. 134). This varies according to the size of the organization, between £40–£2,900 p.a.

The key to effective protection would lie in privacy safeguards that establish semi-permeable membranes between the data subjects and data controllers (DC) that give

---

[52] ICO *Democracy Disrupted: Personal Information and Political Influence* (2018) https://ico.org.uk/media/action-weve-taken/2259369/democracy-disrupted-110718.pdf ICO; *Investigation Into the Use of Data Analytics in Political Campaigns* (2018) https://ico.org.uk/media/action-weve-taken/2259371/investigation-into-data-analytics-for-political-purposes-update.pdf; Demos: *The Facts of Political Campaigning* (July 2018) on the ICO website.

[53] ICO *Investigation* above p. 3.   [54] ICO *Democracy Disrupted* above p. 3.   [55] See note 9.

[56] The territorial scope is defined in Article 3 GDPR. The DPA 2018 provides that the Act applies throughout England, Northern Ireland, Scotland, and Wales.

comprehensible and effective privacy protection and set strict controls on the use of data. In the digitally determined world however, privacy, if it means a right to be left alone or to be forgotten, is impossible.[57] This has not prevented the CJEU interpreting the 1995 DP Directive in a manner to promote the right to be forgotten so that Google search engines were caught by the safeguards of the data law.[58] That court has also ruled that transfer of passenger data to the USA from EU states fell foul of DP laws.[59]

According to the *Financial Times*,[60] US companies alone who trade in Europe have reportedly spent $7.8 billion in preparing for the GDPR. The GDPR is the EU's response to privacy and data protection in an age of data harvesting—a further eprivacy regulation is proposed which will introduce further conditions for permission for collection and use of data in electronic communications. The GDPR is directly applicable although it is adapted under the DPA. In addition, the EU Law Enforcement Directive (LED) is implemented with modifications under the DPA. The GDPR came into force on 4 May 2016 and applies from 25 May 2018. Data processing under way at the time of the GDPR coming into force (4 May 2016) has two years to conform with GDPR requirements (see recital 171 GDPR).

DPA 2018 seeks to ensure a smooth legal transition in existing processing, subject to the enhanced rights provided by the GDPR. Schedule 20 deals with transitional provisions. The 1998 Act required significant updating to attempt to keep abreast of the digital age and developments in electronic communications and data processing. Furthermore, Art. 8 of the EU Charter of Fundamental Rights had promoted data rights to fundamental rights.[61] But:

> The processing of personal data should be designed to serve mankind. The right to the protection of personal data is not an absolute right; it must be considered in relation to its function in society and be balanced against other fundamental rights, in accordance with the principle of proportionality. (GDPR recital 42)

The somewhat contradictory objectives of opening up trans-border transfers of personal data and protecting personal data were to be achieved in this reform. As the EU General Data Protection Regulation expressed the point:

> Technology has transformed both the economy and social life, and should further facilitate the free flow of personal data within the Union and the transfer to third countries and

---

[57] S. D. Warren and L. D. Brandeis, 'The Right to Privacy' (1890) 4 *Harvard Law Rev* 193 is the seminal article. On subjecting artificial intelligence and digital power concentrations to the principles of constitutionalism, the rule of law, and human rights see P. Nemitz 'Constitutionalism, Democracy and Technology in the Age of Artificial Intelligence' *Philosophical Transactions of the Royal Society* 15 Oct 2018: DOI:10.1098/reta.2018.0089 https://papers.ssrn.com/sol3/papers.cfm?abstract_id=3234336 (2/11/2018).

[58] Case C-131/12 *Google Spain v AEPD; N1* and *N2 v Google LLC & IC* [2018] EWHC 799 (QB). See *Google v CNIL* Case C-507/17 (10/01/2019) on the Advocate General's Opinion limiting EU law to searches from within the EU.

[59] Case C-362/14 *Schrems* EUECJ.

[60] 19 May 2018.

[61] The EU Charter of Fundamental Rights only applies to EU institutions and Member States when they are implementing (operating within the scope of) EU law. The EU (Withdrawal) Act 2018 does not make the Charter a part of EU law that will be domesticated after Brexit.

international organisations, while ensuring a high level of the protection of personal data. (GDPR recital 6)

The UK government claimed the DPA would give more control over personal data to data subjects. There are, however, numerous qualifications and exemptions (derogations) to the Act's regulatory provisions.

The new UK statute comes at a time when the UK is set to leave the EU. While setting a new framework for data protection, the reform seeks to be compliant with EU law: a commercial necessity and, in any case, compliance would be a strict legally necessity until the UK left the Union. Furthermore, the statute seeks to prepare for the UK's future outside the EU.[62] Chapter 5 of the GDPR and Chapter V LED set out the requirements to be met in international transfers of data.

In August 2017, the UK Government published *The Exchange and Protection of Personal Data—A Future Partnership Paper*.[63] This explained why the free flow of data is essential to the UK in future trading relationships. Despite Brexit, data protection is one of many areas where our future international relationships require compatibility with EU law. The internet, commerce, law enforcement and security make this unavoidable.

While the UK remains a member of the EU, all the rights and obligations of EU membership remain in force including the directly applicable rights and duties under the GDPR. When the UK leaves the EU, the GDPR will be incorporated into the UK's domestic law as UK law under the European Union (Withdrawal) Act 2018. Decisions of the CJEU prior to Brexit Day on EU measures will still be binding on UK courts but the Supreme Court and Inner House of the Court of Session will be able to establish new precedent and not follow EU judgments. It seems that in any transitional phase EU law will apply along with the jurisdiction of the CJEU. After the transitional phase ends, on 31 December 2020, the supremacy of EU law and the jurisdiction of the CJEU will not apply. However, it is impossible to give a definitive analysis at this stage.[64]

PROCESSING COVERED BY THE DPA

There are four areas of processing provided for in the Act. These are: general data processing, which has two parts—those areas covered by EU law and those not covered but where the GDPR is applied; law enforcement data (LED) processing by competent law enforcement authorities (Sched 7); and data processing by the intelligence services.[65]

---

[62] The government has published guidance on data transfers in the event of a 'hard' Brexit: https://www.gov.uk/government/publications/data-protection-if-theres-no-brexit-deal/data-protection-if-theres-no-brexit-deal (25/09/2018); see note 119 for the IC's advice. See also Craig in Chapter 4 of this volume.

[63] And *Technical Note on Data Protection* (June 2018); *The Future Relationship Between The EU and UK* Cm 9593 Ch. 2 (July 2018), and *Draft Agreement on the Withdrawal of the United Kingdom from The European Union* (November 2018), Arts. 8, 71–4. The Political Statement outlines criminal law enforcement co-operation.

[64] On extending duration for the sovereignty of EU law see *Legislating for the Withdrawal Agreement* (Cm 9674 (2018), para. 60).

[65] The Security Service, the Intelligence Service, and GCHQ.

Part 5 concerns regulatory oversight and enforcement. The 1998 Act covered these subjects but made no separate provision for law enforcement and national security processing as the 2018 Act does.

Amendments in the Lords empowered the Secretary of State under s. 191 to prepare a document, called the Framework for Data Processing by Government, which contains guidance about the processing of personal data in connection with the exercise of the functions of—(a) the Crown, a Minister of the Crown or a United Kingdom government department, and (b) a person with functions of a public nature who is specified or described in regulations made by the Secretary of State. Section 2, which was added late in the bill's progress, provides for 'protection of personal data' under which the Information Commissioner must have regard when exercising functions under the data protection laws to the importance of securing an appropriate level of protection for personal data, taking into account the interests of Data Subjects, Data Controllers, others and matters of general public interest.

The most important part of the Act in terms of extent of coverage is Part Two. This (a) applies the GDPR to the types of processing of personal data covered by Article 2 of the GDPR and sets out some derogations from the GDPR and must be read with the GDPR and (b) extends the GDPR provisions to areas outside EU competence (the 'applied GDPR' scheme) with modifications.

The latter includes processing under the FOIA, processing for activities relating to national security and defence, but not processing by law enforcement bodies or intelligence services (Parts Three and Four DPA). The DPA does not apply to processing of personal data by an individual in the course of a purely personal or household activity.

The DPA and the GDPR apply essentially the same standards to the majority of data processing in the UK, hoping to establish a comprehensible and coherent data protection regime. There are also derogations providing exemptions from the GDPR.

As the UK Act's long title makes clear, it is not just an access statute but an Act which provides for the 'regulation of the processing of information relating to individuals', but it also makes provision in relation to functions of the Information Commissioner (IC) under information regulations.

PERSONAL DATA AND OTHER DEFINITIONS

Like the 1998 Act, the GDPR applies to 'personal data'. The GDPR's definition is more detailed and para. 12 of the Explanatory Notes explains that information 'such as an online identifier, for example a computer's IP address, can be personal data'. The wider definition provides for a wide range of personal identifiers to constitute personal data, 'reflecting changes in technology and the way organizations collect information about people. Also, personal data that has been pseudonymized, for example key-coded data, can fall within the scope of the GDPR depending on how difficult it is to attribute the pseudonym to a particular individual'.[66]

---

[66] DPA 2018 Explanatory Notes (ExN) para. 12.

The basic definitions in data protection are contained in Article 4 GDPR. They are set out in detail.

For the purposes of the GDPR and DPA, Article 4 defines:

'personal data' means any information relating to an identified or identifiable natural person ('data subject'); an identifiable natural person is one who can be identified, directly or indirectly, in particular by reference to an identifier such as a name, an identification number, location data, an online identifier or to one or more factors specific to the physical, physiological, genetic, mental, economic, cultural or social identity of that natural person. Personal data does not include corporate or 'legal' persons data (see GDPR Recital 14 and see Recital 27). S 3(2) refers to 'living individual'.

There are additionally 'special categories of personal data' (sensitive) concerning race, political opinions, health, sex life or orientation etc. which require additional safeguards.

'Data Controller' means the natural or legal person, public authority, agency or private sector body which, alone or jointly with others, determines the purposes and means of the processing of personal data. 'Processors' (DP) means those who process data.

'Processing' means any operation or set of operations which is performed on personal data or on sets of personal data, whether or not by automated means, such as collection, recording, organisation, structuring, storage, adaptation or alteration, retrieval, consultation, use, disclosure by transmission, dissemination or otherwise making available, alignment or combination, restriction, erasure or destruction.[67]

'Filing system' means any structured set of personal data which are accessible according to specific criteria, whether centralised, decentralised or dispersed on a functional or geographical basis.

'Consent' of the data subject means any freely given, specific, informed and unambiguous indication of the data subject's wishes by which he or she, by a statement or by a clear affirmative action, signifies agreement to the processing of personal data relating to him or her. The age for consent for a child in relation to information society services is thirteen.[68]

'Personal data breach' means a breach of security leading to the accidental or unlawful destruction, loss, alteration, unauthorised disclosure of, or access to, personal data transmitted, stored or otherwise processed.

'Profiling', genetic data, biometric data, data concerning health are all defined.

GENERAL DATA PROTECTION PRINCIPLES

As under the 1998 Act, processing must take place according to the 'Principles' (Data Protection Principles—DPP) unless rendered non-applicable or exempt. They (or rather some of them) may, however, be rendered non-applicable in certain processing e.g. in response to FOIA requests and unstructured data. In the 1998 Act, there were eight DPP and these are largely carried over to the GDPR as set out in the following table.[69]

---

[67] See *Johnson v MDU (No. 2)* [2007] EWCA Civ 262 for a narrow reading of processing under the 1998 DPA—'selecting' data was not processing. The dissenting judgment of Arden LJ is to be preferred. The GDPR's wording 'retrieval, consultation, use' would be broad enough to cover selecting.

[68] See s. 208 for Scotland where it is twelve years 'unless the contrary is shown' concerning understanding.

[69] Adapted from the DPA Explanatory Notes para. 14.

The 'principles' apply to the processing of personal data. The GDPR also provides a new ninth principle of accountability. The DC shall be responsible for and be able to, demonstrate compliance with the principles (Art. 5(2) GDPR). All personal data shall be processed according to the following GDPR principles. Parts 3 and 4 DPA provide their own principles largely derived from those below but modified.

Processing for the 'special purposes' is highlighted for particular protection from the controller and subject's perspective. This is processing for the purposes of journalism, academic, artistic or literary purposes. A court may stay proceedings if a special purpose is involved although the IC may certify that it is not.[70]

Lawfulness	Personal data shall be processed lawfully, fairly and in a transparent manner in relation to the data subject.
Purpose	Personal data shall be collected for specified, explicit and legitimate purposes and not further processed in a manner that is incompatible with those purposes.
Data minimization	Personal data shall be adequate, relevant and limited to what is necessary in relation to the purposes for which they are processed.
Accuracy	Personal data shall be accurate and, where necessary, kept up to date; every reasonable step must be taken to ensure that personal data that are inaccurate, having regard to the purposes for which they are processed, are erased or rectified without delay.
Storage	Personal data shall be kept in a form which permits identification of data subjects for no longer than is necessary for the purposes for which the personal data are processed; personal data may be stored for longer periods insofar as the personal data will be processed solely for archiving purposes in the public interest, scientific or historical research purposes or statistical purposes.
Access	The GDPR does not have an equivalent principle. Instead access rights are found separately in Chapter III of GDPR.
Security	Personal data shall be processed in a manner that ensures appropriate security of the personal data, including protection against unauthorized or unlawful processing and against accidental loss, destruction or damage, using appropriate technical or organizational measures.
Overseas transfer	The GDPR does not have an equivalent principle. Instead overseas transfers of personal data are addressed separately in Chapter V.
Accountability	The 1998 Act does not have an equivalent principle. The controller shall be responsible for, and be able to demonstrate, compliance with the principles.

---

[70] See *Campbell v Mirror Group Newspapers* [2002] EWCA Civ 1373 paras 108–128 and scope of protection; see now s 176 and Sched 2 Pt 5 DPA.

CONDITIONS FOR PROCESSING

There must be a condition (lawful justification) allowing processing. The concept of 'consent' is central to data processing and is also a, but not the only, condition. Paragraph 26 of the Explanatory Notes explains that 'Processing of special categories of personal data concerning e.g. race, political opinions, health, sex life or orientation (Art. 9 GDPR) is generally prohibited unless explicit consent is obtained. The GDPR allows processing to take place in certain circumstances without consent and enables domestic law to specify the conditions and safeguards around this processing.'

'The processing of special categories of data and criminal conviction and offences data must be undertaken with adequate and appropriate safeguards to ensure the absolute protection of individuals' most sensitive personal data.' This was allowed under the 1998 Act. The 2018 Act seeks to allow for 'continued processing for "substantial public interest" purposes ensuring that organisations are able to continue lawfully processing data' and also to maintain a balance between the rights of individuals (paragraph 26 of the Explanatory Notes).

To process personal data a DC/P must satisfy one of the conditions for processing. Otherwise processing is unlawful unless a condition is exempted. Exemptions for Part 2 are in Schedules 2, 3 and 4 and are extremely extensive. Although consent is the basic means to enable lawful processing (see Art 4(11)) 'it is not the only way to enable processing of data. There may also be a contractual or other legal obligation that allows data to be processed without explicit consent. Data may be processed without consent where necessary for the performance of a task carried out in the public interest or in the exercise of official authority vested in the controller' (EN para 17). Data may be processed for a vital interest, e.g. to protect life. Processing must be necessary—for special purposes data, including health, this justification cannot be used where a DS is capable of giving consent and they refuse. Conditions for processing are in Schedule 1 and for law enforcement (sensitive data only) they are in Schedule 8. Under s. 31, processing in Part 3 is for 'law enforcement purposes' which is the condition. Part 4 conditions are in Schedules 9 and 10.

PROCESSING FOR A LEGITIMATE INTEREST

Data may also be processed where there is a 'legitimate interest', although under the GDPR this can no longer be relied upon by public authorities although it is arguable that PAs may be able to invoke this reason where they act in a purely commercial (private) capacity. PAs have to rely on specific conditions. 'A legitimate interest may include processing for direct marketing purposes or preventing fraud; transmission of personal data within a group of undertakings for internal administrative purposes, including client and employee data processing for the purposes of ensuring network and information security and reporting possible criminal acts or threats to public security to a competent authority.'[71] This list is not exhaustive. The provenance of this

---

[71] Note 69 para. 18.

justification, which is likely to be widely used, is Art 6(1)(f) GDPR. It has similarities to DPA 1998 schedule 2(6) which featured widely in IC investigations under s. 40 FOIA but it is both wider and more nuanced. One should note the emphasis on protecting a child.

Art 6(1)(f) states:

> processing is necessary for the purposes of the legitimate interests pursued by the controller or by a third party except where such interests are overridden by the interests or fundamental rights and freedoms of the data subject which require protection of personal data, in particular where the data subject is a child.

The Information Commissioner has advised that 'this can be broken down into a three-part test':

> Purpose test: are you pursuing a legitimate interest?
> Necessity test: is the processing necessary for that purpose?
> Balancing test: do the DS's interests override the legitimate interest of the DC or third party (e.g. a requester under FOIA)? For instance, if the DS would not reasonably expect the processing, or if it would cause unjustified harm, a DS interests are likely to override a requester's legitimate interests.

The IC continues:[72] 'The legitimate interests can be your own interests or the interests of third parties. They can include commercial interests, individual interests or broader societal benefits. A record of the legitimate interests assessment (LIA) should be kept to help demonstrate compliance if required. Details of legitimate interests should be kept in the DC's privacy information.'

In the absence of 'explicit consent' to the processing of special categories of personal data and criminal data, there are even more restrictive conditions on when such data can be lawfully processed.

DATA SUBJECT RIGHTS

The DS rights are in Chapter III GDPR. Article 12 concerns transparency of information, communication and procedures for the exercise of the rights. The standards are strict and detailed. Specific rights include the right to be informed about details of processing, the right of DS access, rectification, erasure, restriction of processing, a right to object which is wider than the 1998 DPA, and rights in relation to automated decision-making and profiling.[73] Breaches of the GDPR or DPA may bring an entitlement to damages for material damage and/or distress.[74] Compliance orders may be issued by courts (s. 167).

---

[72] https://ico.org.uk/for-organisations/guide-to-the-general-data-protection-regulation-gdpr/lawful-basis-for-processing/legitimate-interests/ which contains the three-part test.

[73] Automated decision-making is decisions made without human involvement. Profiling is an analysis of an individual's personality, interests, behaviour or habits to make predictions or decisions about them.

[74] See *Google Inc v J Vidal Hall* [2015] EWCA Civ 311 paras. 52–95.

It is an offence to require records for employment purposes[75] and contractual terms requiring health records are rendered void. Rights of the DS under Parts 3 and 4 processing are contained in those parts along with duties imposed on DCs and security of processing. These include audits and impact assessments, reports of breaches of the DPA, appointment of DP officers (Part 3 only) and transfers to third countries. Part 3 s. 45 lists exemptions to the right to access (including a neither confirm nor deny response as under the FOIA) and Part 4 lists national security exemptions and Schedule 11 lists other Part 4 exemptions.

IC CODES AND AUDITS

The IC must produce codes on data-sharing, direct marketing, and an age-appropriate design code where children are likely to have access. There is also a duty to produce a data protection and journalism code. The specific provisions on journalism can be picked up below. The Secretary of State may direct the IC to produce other codes 'for guidance as to good practice'. Under s. 129, the IC may conduct a consensual audit of a DC's processing to establish whether there is compliance with good practice in processing.

ENFORCEMENT AND OFFENCES

Under the DPA, data subjects may go to court to enforce their individual rights under the DPA. The IC may also issue notices enforcing action, assessing data processing, or ordering production of information to the IC.

Notices can be backed up by court order and may be appealed against to the information rights tribunal. The IC is provided with entry and inspection powers on warrant including equipment-testing powers. Breaches of notices or certain provisions of the GDPR may lead to the award of a civil penalty notice by the IC of Euros 20 million or 4 per cent of annual world-wide turnover in the previous year for breaches of the DPP, breaches under Part 3, or wrongful transfers to third countries. This is the higher maximum. There is a lower standard maximum. Appeal lies to the tribunal. The Act maintains and creates criminal offences relating to wrongful obtaining, re-identification and alteration of data (ss. 170–3).

One of the greatest challenges to privacy protection comes from the global network of electronic surveillance capabilities employed by intelligence services and police. The DPA makes specific provision for these activities.

---

[75] Specific legislation provides for disclosure of certificates about criminal convictions and intelligence to prospective employers (4 million applications each year) where there will be contact with vulnerable people under the Police Act 1997, Part V and Rehabilitation of Offenders Act 1974; see *R. (AR) v Chief Constable of Greater Manchester* [2018] UKSC 47—disclosure of rape acquittal to prospective employer (college) with otherwise good character lawful. Cf. *R. (L) v Comr of Police of the Metropolis* [2009] UKSC 3; *R. (T) v Secretary of State for the Home Department & Anor* [2014] UKSC 35 and *R. (P) & Ors v Secretary of State for the Home Department* [2019] UKSC 3. On police retention and deletion of intelligence data and breach of Art 8 ECHR, see *Catt v United Kingdom* Application 43514/15 (24/01/2019) ECtHR, First section.

SURVEILLANCE

Two areas protected by the strictest of conditions under secrecy legislation are the activities of the security and intelligence services (S&IS), and interception of communications.[76] It has been explained how the S&IS have been excluded from the FOIA and how PAs are given an absolute exemption for information they hold on (i.e. communications from) S&IS. The DPA provides specifically for law enforcement and S&IS processing with the widest of exemptions (above). In the latter case the important (but not only) means of surveillance is electronic given the bulk capabilities of intercepts and bulk retention of communications data. Retention of communications data is not an 'intercept' and does not contain the content of a communication. Such data contains the identity of the communicators, their location, equipment used, and the timing of the communication.[77] UK officials widely accept that such data is crucial to protect public safety.[78]

The Regulation of Investigatory Powers Act 2000, following earlier legislation, regulated surveillance by the S&IS, police and other authorities. The main point here is that intercept material cannot be used in judicial proceedings—although there are numerous exceptions. The major reason for this is to protect intelligence material from being exposed in open court. RIPA was amended in 2014 by the Data Retention and Investigatory Powers Act (DRIPA) which had effect until December 2016. The Investigatory Powers Act 2016 (IPA) amended the provisions dealing with interceptions and data retention. This legislation has spawned litigation in EU and domestic courts which is examined below.

THE INVESTIGATORY POWERS ACT 2016

The IP Bill, which sought to find a balance between state security and individual privacy, followed a review by the Independent Reviewer of Terrorist Legislation of existing laws of investigatory powers, a review by the Intelligence and Security Committee of Parliament and by the Panel of the Independent Surveillance Review convened by the Royal United Services Institute.[79] All three agreed that current powers remained essential for the UK's security. There were also critical reactions in the media.

The Act brings together powers for the interception of communications, obtaining communications and communications data, bulk data and bulk data sets powers and it

---

[76] R. Jeffreys-Jones, *We Know All About You: The Story of Surveillance in Britain and America* (2017) and S. Zuboff, *The Age of Surveillance Capitalism* (2019).

[77] Described as the 'who', 'how', 'where' and 'when' of a communication https://www.gov.uk/government/collections/communications-datav.

[78] See notes 79 and 83 below.

[79] Independent Reviewer of Terrorism Legislation, *A Question of Trust* (2015) https://terrorismlegislation-reviewer.independent.gov.uk/wp-content/uploads/2015/06/IPR-Report-Print-Version.pdf; Intelligence and Security Committee Report: http://isc.independent.gov.uk/news-archive/12march2015 and Royal United Services Institute Report: https://rusi.org/rusi-news/rusi-responds-draft-investigatory-powers-bill.

relates to collection of data in bulk by interception, communications data acquisition and equipment interference powers—computer hacking—and collection of personal information about large numbers of individuals (most of whom will be of no interest to the S&IS) (only S&IS have the 'bulk' capabilities for national security and serious crime objectives), and internet connection records in real time. Communications and postal service providers will be under a duty to assist the S&IS and police.

This Act introduces the requirement for 'double-lock' approval by a minister and a judge (retired) for certain warrants, i.e. interception, equipment and bulk equipment interference (hacking), bulk data and bulk data sets' powers. Warrants may only be issued to nine (ten are listed) responsible intercepting bodies under three specified powers: national security, prevention of serious crime, and economic well-being in relation to national security. Warrants are not required for targeted communications data. Access to such data was originally under authorizations granted by designated senior officers in 'relevant' public authorities with stricter requirements for local authorities. In all cases, and they extend far beyond serious crime (s. 61(7)(a)–(j)), access must be 'necessary and proportionate'. Powers of the Secretary of State to require retention of communications data, which may be for up to twelve months, need the approval of a judicial commissioner.

There is to be oversight by an Investigatory Powers Commissioner (IPC), a senior judge. There are special safeguards in 'particularly sensitive material' e.g. involving lawyers, MPs, and journalists. There will be 'single point contacts' for communications data and intercept connection records within authorities. The Act retains the extra-territorial effect of the repealed 2014 Act.

Schedule 6 provides for the making of codes of practice on the operation of powers. The Act says nothing about the use of informers (child informers are being increasingly used[80]) and other forms of human, intrusive and covert surveillance which are governed by the 2000 Act.[81] The Act sets out safeguards on holding data, duration of warrants, and the role of the IC. A Technical Advisory Board has been established following the report by the Independent Reviewer and will advise on the impact of changes in technology.

The Independent Intelligence and Security Committee of Parliament issued a critical report on the Bill. Amongst other criticisms it recommended laws on universal privacy protection and that S&IS capabilities in equipment interference, bulk data sets and communications data are too broad and lack clarity.[82] The Bill was revised and introduced in Parliament to take account of some of these criticisms. The Bill was subject to further amendments in Parliament including overarching provisions on privacy protection in s. 2, safeguards in the warrant process, and enhanced protections for sensitive professions and parliamentarians, including the requirement that a Judicial Commissioner must consider that there is 'an overriding public interest' before any

---

[80] HL 168 (2017–19) *Draft Investigatory Powers etc Order* 2018.

[81] An inquiry is being conducted into use of undercover police officers since 1968: https://www.ucpi.org.uk/.

[82] HC 795 (2015–16) *Report on the Draft Investigatory Powers Bill*.

request to identify a journalist's source can be approved. The Prime Minister must also personally approve a warrant to obtain the communications of an MP or a member of another relevant legislature. The Independent Reviewer of Terrorism Legislation conducted a review of bulk powers for the government with a team of experts chosen by him. His report found that such powers are of vital importance to S&IS and alternatives were slower, more intrusive, more expensive and more dangerous.[83] One year after enactment the Home Office launched a public consultation in November 2017 on amendments to the Act to accommodate a critical judgment of the CJEU in *Watson* (below).[84]

The IP Commissioner replaces the S&IS Commissioner appointed under RIPA 2000, s. 59. The position is now governed by Part 8 IPA 2016 and the IP Commissioner has this responsibility added to his remit. The provisions concerning the Commissioner and his investigation of complaints under previous legislation were therefore repealed and taken over by RIPA 2000, and now by the 2016 Act. The IPC will deal with investigatory matters and undertake, with the assistance of the Judicial Commissioners and staff, the functions undertaken by previous S&IS, interception and surveillance Commissioners. Additional functions relating to S&IS may be added by the Secretary of State (s. 232). The Commissioner, who is, or was, a senior judge, keeps under review the exercise of the powers by the Secretary of State, inter alia, to issue warrants under ss. 5 and 7 of the ISA 1994 (which now covers the Security Service) and the powers and duties conferred or imposed upon the Secretary of State by IPA 2016 in connection with the activities of the intelligence services, as well as similar powers exercised in stated circumstances by Ministry of Defence officials and Her Majesty's forces. The Commissioner must also assist the IP Tribunal in, significantly, the investigation of complaints within the Tribunal's jurisdiction. The jurisdiction is spelt out in s. 65 and crucially covers 'proceedings against the intelligence services' or others acting on their behalf. It involves a complaint by a 'person who is aggrieved by any conduct' falling within the section. It would include a complaint by a member or former member of S&IS. Crucially, a right of appeal from the Investigatory Powers Tribunal's decisions to the Court of Appeal is introduced for the first time.

The Intelligence and Security Committee of Parliament may refer an issue to the IPC. The IPC has to inform the Committee whether the IPC has decided to carry out an audit, investigation or inspection (s. 236). Individuals may give information to the Judicial Commissioners regardless of any legal restrictions, i.e. to express concerns (s. 237).

Section 253 of the Act ensures that the Judicial Commissioners are fully informed and that access allows the IPC to conduct effective oversight. A Judicial Commissioner may require all the information and documents that are needed. Officials must also provide the Commissioner with any assistance they may need when carrying out investigations, inspections, or audits which may include access to technical systems. Officials

---

[83] *Report of the Bulk Powers Review* Cm 9326 (2016).
[84] https://www.gov.uk/government/consultations/investigatory-powers-act-2016.

include 'anyone working for a public authority, telecommunications, and postal operators who are subject to obligations under this Act and anyone who is or may be required to provide assistance under the Act' (Investigatory Powers Act ENs para 654).

Those who are under surveillance must be informed of serious relevant error in the use of investigatory powers that relates to them. 'Relevant error' is defined in s. 231. The IPC makes the judgement on what is serious and has to determine whether informing the victim is 'in the public interest'. The section's criterion of 'serious' is causing 'significant prejudice or harm to the person concerned'. In determining 'public interest' the Commissioner must balance the seriousness of the error and its impact on the victim and any prejudice to, inter alia, national security, prevention or investigation of serious crime and the effectiveness of the intelligence agencies. Where a person is informed, s/he must be informed of rights to make a claim in the IPT together 'with the details necessary to bring such a claim, to the extent that disclosing information is in the public interest' (ENs 645).

Under s. 244 the Information Commissioner must audit the security of retained data under Part 4 of the Act.

THE LITIGATION ON DRIPA AND IPA

Crucial elements of DRIPA were ruled incompatible with EU law and the EU Charter of Fundamental Rights (CFR) by the Divisional Court following the *Digital Rights* judgment of the CJEU.[85] In *Digital Rights*, the CJEU ruled the EC Data Retention Directive (2006/24/EC) disproportionate in its aim of collecting in a mass form communications data for the purposes of investigation, detection and prosecution of serious crime. Subsequently, the English court ruled that DRIPA, which replaced domestic measures implementing the Directive, did not contain clear and precise rules allowing access to retained data to be strictly restricted for the purposes of prevention/investigation or prosecution of serious crime and access to the data was not dependent on prior judicial or independent administrative authorization restricting access to what was strictly necessary for authorized purposes. The Divisional Court thus ruled s. 1 of DRIPA breached EU law, i.e. the EU CFR. The offending provisions of the Act were subject to a suspended disapplication pending amending measures or appeals and references to the CJEU.

The Court of Appeal (CA) cast doubt on the Divisional Court's ruling that the CJEU's judgment in *Digital Rights* set down mandatory requirements of EU law for national legislation in relation to access to that data by national authorities.[86] The object of the CJEU's criticism was the EC Directive, not national legislation. The CA believed that the CJEU's ruling could affect aspects of data retention and use not covered by EU law, i.e. outside EU competence, such as national security. The CA further suggested that

---

[85] Case C-293/12 [2014] ECJ. The Divisional Court ruling is *R. (Davis & Ors) v Secretary of State for the Home Department* [2015] EWHC 2093 (Admin). See also the ECtHR *Big Brother Watch v UK* [2018] ECHR 722, First section on the breach of the ECHR arts 8 and 10 by RIPA.

[86] *Secretary of State for the Home Department v D Davis MP et al* [2015] EWCA Civ 1185.

EU law according to the CJEU went further than ECHR protection. The CA accepted that Art. 8 EUCFR (a right to protection of personal data) was not limited in scope by Art. 8 ECHR on privacy. However, the CA doubted whether the CJEU intended to lay down more stringent measures for protection of data than the CHR jurisprudence established.[87] The CA referred the case to the CJEU.[88]

In December 2016, the Grand Chamber of the ECJ gave judgment in the joined case (*Watson*).[89] The court ruled that national legislation in question (DRIPA 2014 s. 1 for the UK) fell within the scope of the relevant EU law (para. 81). The right to confidentiality of communications must be strictly interpreted and derogations are limited to those set out in the Electronic Communications Directive (EC 2002/58), e.g. national security and investigation of crime. They are exhaustive. They must be interpreted in accordance with the CFR and protection of privacy and freedom of expression as well as relevant EU case law. Derogations must be interpreted as a 'necessary, appropriate and proportionate measure within a democratic society' (para. 95). The scope of the retention in the referred cases was a serious interference with privacy and freedom of expression. Only the objective of fighting serious crime could justify such a measure—the court accepted that state or national security was outside EU competence but nonetheless offered various opinions on that subject. General and indiscriminate retention of all traffic and location data would not be justified (para. 103). Even the fight against terrorism 'cannot in itself justify that national legislation providing for the general and indiscriminate retention of all traffic and location data should be considered necessary' (para. 103).

Retention must be strictly necessary for the objective of preventing or investigating serious crime and must be objectively justifiable vis-à-vis the data retained and the legitimate objective pursued. Article 15(1) of Directive 2002/58, read in the light of Articles 7, 8 and 11 and Article 52(1) of the Charter, does not prevent a Member State from adopting legislation permitting, as a preventive measure, the targeted retention of traffic and location data, for the purpose of fighting serious crime, provided that the retention of data is limited, with respect to the categories of data to be retained, the means of communication affected, the persons concerned, and the retention period adopted to what is strictly necessary (para. 108). The CJEU at this point suggested that geographical profiling based on 'objective evidence' may be permissible which raises very sensitive questions of racial and social discrimination. With regard to 'bulk' retention as the 2016 UK legislation terms it, Article 15(1) of Directive 2002/58, read in the light of Articles 7, 8 and 11 and Article 52(1) of the Charter, must be interpreted as precluding national legislation which, for the purpose of fighting crime (let alone other objectives), provides for the general and indiscriminate retention of all traffic

---

[87] Para 111. The court relied on *Kennedy v UK* [2011] 52 EHRR 4. The ECJ ruled this matter inadmissible.

[88] The questions referred to the CJEU under Art 276 TFEU are at para. 118 of the CA's judgment.

[89] EU ECJ C-203/16 [2016] *Tele2 Sverige AB v Post-och telestyrelsen* (Case C-203/15 ECJ [2016]) and *Secretary of State for the Home Department v Tom Watson* (Case C-698/15 ECJ [2016]). David Davis MP was a party in the *Watson* case but dropped out on becoming Secretary of State for Brexit. See L. Woods http://eulawanalysis.blogspot.co.uk/2016/12/data-retention-and-national-law-ecj.html [27/02/2019].

and location data of all subscribers and registered users relating to all means of electronic communication (para. 112).

The court addressed the question of security of data retained for the purposes of serious crime and access by the authorities to that data where that access is not subject to prior review by a court or independent administrative authority, and where there is no requirement that the data concerned should be retained within the EU. Only the objective of fighting serious crime is capable of justifying access to the retained data (para. 115). Safeguards, both procedural, i.e. prior review, and substantive, must be laid down in clear and legally binding rules (paras. 118–119).

> Accordingly, and since general access to all retained data, regardless of whether there is any link, at least indirect, with the intended purpose, cannot be regarded as limited to what is strictly necessary, the national legislation concerned must be based on objective criteria in order to define the circumstances and conditions under which the competent national authorities are to be granted access to the data of subscribers or registered users. In that regard, access can, as a general rule, be granted, in relation to the objective of fighting crime, only to the data of individuals suspected of planning, committing or having committed a serious crime or of being implicated in one way or another in such a crime (para. 119).[90]

In the war against terrorism, as distinguished from investigating or preventing serious crime, the court suggested:

> access to the data of other persons might also be granted where there is objective evidence from which it can be deduced that that data might, in a specific case, make an effective contribution to combating such activities. (para. 119).

As pointed out below, is this latter point a matter which is within national competence under TEU Art 4(2)?

In relation to access to retained data, the CJEU ruled that in order to ensure that those conditions are fully respected, it is essential that access of the competent national authorities to retained data should, as a general rule, except in cases of validly established urgency, be subject to a prior review carried out either by a court or by an independent administrative body, and that the decision of that court or body should be made following a reasoned request by those authorities submitted, inter alia, within the framework of procedures for the prevention, detection, or prosecution of crime.[91]

National authorities to whom access to the retained data has been granted must notify the persons affected, under the applicable national procedures, as soon as that notification is no longer liable to jeopardize the investigations being undertaken by those authorities. That notification is, in fact, necessary to enable the persons affected to exercise, inter alia, their right to a legal remedy, expressly provided for in Article 15(2) of Directive 2002/58 and relevant EU case law.

---

[90] *Zakharov v Russia*, CE:ECHR:2015:1204JUD004714306, para 260 cited.

[91] The court cited the *Digital Rights* judgment, paragraph 62; and in relation to Article 8 of the ECHR as interpreted by the European Court of Human Rights in *Szabó and Vissy v Hungary* (ECHR, 2016 paras. 77 and 80).

The CJEU's judgment presaged problems for the general and indiscriminate retention of all traffic and location data relating to all means of electronic communication
for the purpose of fighting crime which provides for such retention of all traffic (routing, duration or timing) and location data of all subscribers and registered users. Specifically, EU law precluded national legislation governing the protection and security
of such data allowing access by competent national authorities to the retained data,
where the objective pursued by that access is not restricted solely to fighting serious
crime, and where access is not subject to prior review by a court or an independent
administrative authority, and where there is no requirement that the data concerned
should be retained within the European Union.

This judgment clearly has serious implications for the legality of the newly enacted
regime of UK surveillance. The CJEU was addressing DRIPA and left little doubt that
that Act had serious incompatibilities with EU law, including the CFR. However, retention of communications data in the 2016 Act is far more extensive in subject coverage
than the CJEU would permit and the 2016 Act has provision for bulk data sets and
bulk data retention. The point has been made that EU judges take a stricter approach
to privacy protection than would British judges who acknowledge the benefits of surveillance as set out in the 2016 Act for legitimate purposes in the public interest.[92] The
judgment is also likely to prompt national judges to examine what the true significance
of Art 4(2) TEU is: 'In particular, national security remains the sole responsibility of
each Member State.' The CJEU is unclear in setting subject boundaries on this.

IPA AND NECESSARY AMENDMENTS

Amendment to the IPA was unavoidable. The future of the Act in relation to communications data and bulk data sets and bulk data would appear to have been thrown
into doubt by the CJEU judgment in *Watson*.[93] Following that judgment, the Court of
Appeal[94] declared that DRIPA s. 1, which had been enacted to place communications
on a domestic footing, was inconsistent with EU law but decided not to make a ruling in relation to blanket retention powers. References from the IPT to the CJEU have
raised wider points that the Court of Appeal did not rule upon in relation to bulk powers and the S&IS.[95] The Home Secretary also commenced a consultation on necessary
reforms to ICA to comply with the ECJ judgments.[96]

In *Liberty* the Divisional Court declared the IPA Part 4 unlawful under the CFR
because in the area of criminal justice (1) access to retained data is not limited to the

---

[92] See https://terrorismlegislationreviewer.independent.gov.uk/cjeu-judgment-in-watson/. See also House
of Lords EU Committee 7th Report HL 77 (2016–2017) *Brexit: Future UK-EU Security and Police Cooperation*
http://www.publications.parliament.uk/pa/ld201617/ldselect/ldeucom/77/7702.htm.

[93] Above note 89.

[94] *Secretary of State for the Home Department v T. Watson* [2018] EWCA Civ 70.

[95] *Privacy International v Secretary of State for Foreign Affairs* 8 September and 30 October 2017 http://www.
ipt-uk.com/judgments.asp?id=40 and https://www.ipt-uk.com/judgments.asp?id=41.

[96] https://www.gov.uk/government/consultations/investigatory-powers-act-2016. This site now contains
the government response and all updates (July 2018).

purpose of combating 'serious crime'; and (2) access to retained data is not subject to prior review by a court or an independent administrative body.[97] The government was given six months from the date of the judgment to enact the necessary changes.

To put data retention in context, from January to December 2015, 761,702 items of data were acquired by public authorities, 85.8 per cent of which was for the statutory purpose of preventing or detecting crime or of preventing disorder. And 53 per cent of the data acquired for that purpose was in relation to four types of crime: drugs offences, sexual offences, theft offences, and fraud and deception offences.[98]

The consultation did not include the S&IS and their powers because the government believed that Art 4(2) TEU made national security a domestic matter and the CFR (and CJEU) only had competence within EU law. The government believed that the CJEU judgment did not apply to 'entity data' (s. 261 IPA) but, in future, requests for such data would be authorized in the same manner as 'events data' (s. 261).[99] The CJEU case covered 'events data' i.e. trafficking and location, and views were sought. Changes to IPA would be effected by regulations and additions to the code of practice.[100] Codes will have statutory force and authorities must have regard to them in exercising powers under the legislation. The code is admissible as evidence in criminal and civil proceedings, and may be taken into account by any court, tribunal, or supervisory authority when determining a question arising in connection with those functions.[101]

In relation to the ECJ judgment's inapplicability to the retention or acquisition of data for national security purposes, the paper stated that S&IS primarily exist to manage national security threats to the UK. The government considers that their activities, including requests for communications data for the statutory purpose of crime, 'fall outside the scope of EU law and the CJEU's judgment'.[102]

The government did not consider that the existing domestic data retention regime is 'general and indiscriminate'. It currently provides that data retention is based on objective criteria.[103] However, amendments would require that the Secretary of State must specifically consider which of the operator's services the notice of retention should relate to; require consideration of whether it would be appropriate to restrict a notice by geography or exclude groups of customers; and more closely link the benefits of the notice to the statutory purpose by ensuring that the Secretary of State takes into account the statutory purpose(s) for which the notice is being given when considering the potential benefits of the notice, i.e. the Secretary of State will need to consider how the retention of data would, for instance, be beneficial in the prevention and detection of serious crime, rather than how the retention of the data would be beneficial more

---

[97] R. (Liberty) v Secretary of State HD [2018] EWHC 975 (Admin).   [98] Note 96 p. 6.

[99] See Liberty judgment note 97 para 154.

[100] https://www.gov.uk/government/uploads/system/uploads/attachment_data/file/663677/November_2017_IPA_Consultation_-_Draft_regulations_amending_the_IP_Act.pdf. See now Data Retention and Acquisition Regulations 2018 SI 1123.

[101] https://www.gov.uk/government/uploads/system/uploads/attachment_data/file/663675/November_2017_IPA_Consultation_-_Draft_Communications_Data_Code_of_Pract....pdf.

[102] Note 96 p. 11.   [103] Note 96 p. 14.

generally, i.e. a requirement of greater specificity. The government would define more carefully the 'serious crime' permitting retention and access to data and would remove three, but not all, of the current justifications: public health, taxation and financial matters. The government response is ambiguous to say the least.

The draft Regulations create a new power for the IPC to authorize access to communications data. The IPC will delegate these functions to a newly appointed body of staff, to be known as the Office for Communications Data Authorisations (OCDA). OCDA will report directly to the IPC and will be responsible for considering the vast majority of requests to access communications data made by public authorities. Senior officers as set out will be able to give authorizations in urgent cases. Because of its views on national security above, the designated senior officers will continue to authorize these requests for retention and access. S&IS will continue to authorize the 'vast majority' of their applications internally.[104] The government believed that existing safeguards removed any need to notify individuals affected as soon as notification would not jeopardize the investigation being undertaken, as the ECJ had ruled.

The IPA accompanies numerous powers of information gathering and investigation in relation to terrorist offences. The Official Reviewer of Terrorism Legislation reports on such laws to inform public and political debate.[105]

SECRET JUSTICE AND OPEN JUSTICE

National security and the threat of terrorism have promoted the movement to secret justice most strikingly under the Justice and Security Act 2013, which extended closed material procedures (CMPs) to all civil litigation after the Supreme Court ruled that such procedures needed statutory authorization and could not apply to common law actions.[106] CMPs basically involve secret litigation in the absence of the 'defendant' whose interests are represented by a security vetted special advocate. After an initial meeting there is rarely any contact between these parties after proceedings commence. The 2013 Act provided for CMPs to be under judicial control. The Act introduces absolute prohibitions via ministerial certificates on public interest grounds of disclosure of intelligence information (s. 17). But the development of secret justice is not confined to litigation involving terrorists.[107]

The 2013 Act also enhanced the status and powers of the Independent Intelligence and Security Committee of Parliament which investigates the activities of the security and intelligence services. This committee has made some very important reports of its

---

[104] Note 96 p. 19.

[105] https://terrorismlegislationreviewer.independent.gov.uk/.

[106] *Al Rawi* [2011] UKSC 34; see developments in *R. (Haralambous) v Crown Court at St Albans* [2018] UKSC 1 and *Belhaj v DPP* [2018] UKSC 33.

[107] Use of super injunctions fomented a great deal of press outrage and on secret civil proceedings, see Corruption Watch *Veil of Secrecy* July 2018. https://docs.wixstatic.com/ugd/54261c_b5a8c697963841afbb1af7cc10e27e4c.pdf.

investigations although it has clearly been hampered by refusals to disclose information and evidence.[108]

The obverse side of the coin has been a greater advance under common law principles of the benefits of open justice in a wide variety of circumstances.[109] The Investigatory Powers Tribunal has a website and it has consciously moved to greater openness in its proceedings where possible.[110]

PRIVACY AND THE COURTS

The courts have fashioned a right for the protection of a legitimate expectation of privacy. The principles have been fashioned in the face of media intrusion and attempt to strike a balance between privacy and freedom of speech. Within a period of under thirty years, courts have moved from the non-recognition of a common law right to privacy[111] to the protection of a legitimate expectation to privacy and a right to privacy and protection of personal information. This development was fomented by Art. 8 ECHR and its incorporation within UK law by the Human Rights Act. Initially the courts recognized that the domestic law of confidentiality would be coloured by Art. 8. In *Naomi Campbell v MNG*[112] the Law Lords made clear that the protection of privacy was taking a new development which fastened on protection of private personal information. In *PJS v Newsgroup*[113] the Supreme Court ruled that the new tort was not subject to the limitations of confidentiality and the courts could still prevent domestic publication of personal private information even though the information had been posted on the internet.[114] A striking case involved the singer Cliff Richard who successfully sued the BBC for a sensationalist 'scoop' broadcasting of an investigation by a police force into historical allegations of sex offences against children after the BBC had been tipped off by the police.[115]

PRESS AND MEDIA

The domestic discovery of a tort of privacy coincided with notorious abuses of privacy invasion by the press through unlawful intercepts (hacking) and disclosure of police information by corrupt officers. Sir Brian Leveson was appointed by the then Prime

---

[108] See *Detainee Mistreatment and Rendition 2001–2010* and *Current Issues* at http://isc.independent.gov. uk/.

[109] *Kennedy* note 1. *A v BBC* [2014] UKSC 25; *Khuja v Times Newspapers Ltd* [2017] UKSC 49; *R. (DSD) v Parole Board* [2018] EWHC 694 (Admin).

[110] https://www.ipt-uk.com/.

[111] *Kaye v Robertson* [1990] EWCA Civ 21; *Wainwright v Home Office* [2003] UKHL 53.

[112] [2004] UKSC 22. See Lord Nicholls at paras. 12–13 although he refers to the action as 'breach of confidence' para. 17. See *Google Inc v J Vidal Hall* [2015] EWCA Civ 311 paras. 17–51. See *In the Matter of JR 38* [2015] UKSC 42 for the threshold of engagement of Art. 8.

[113] [2016] UKSC 26.   [114] Paras. 25–35.   [115] *Sir Cliff Richard v BBC* [2018] EWHC 1837 (Ch).

Minister in 2011 to conduct an inquiry into the 'Culture, Practices and Ethics of the Press'.[116] Leveson's recommendations for press regulation were rejected and a proposed second inquiry focusing on the police and the press was aborted early in 2018. It is little wonder that Leveson was sidelined and then the second inquiry into the press and the police and government was axed. What came out of the first inquiry raised the most searching of questions about press conduct. The government adopted a form of regulation under the prerogative, not statute, with a body that would recognize a regulator which would publish an editorial standards' code. The recognized body, IMPRESS, has only a membership of a few regional outlets. A large number of newspapers formed their own self-regulatory body, IPSO.[117] This supported the government statement in March 2018 that s. 40 of the Crime and Courts Act 2013 will not be coming into effect. This provision would have made newspaper proprietors subject to awards of costs in legal proceedings, win or lose, where they had not joined a recognized regulator. It was another slap in the face for Leveson.

It will be recalled that under the DPA 2018, provision is made for the special purposes including journalism. The IC may provide assistance to an individual involved in such proceedings (s. 175). The IC must produce a code of guidance on the steps that may be taken where an individual considers that a media organization is failing, or has failed, to comply with the data protection legislation (s. 177). Under s. 178 and Schedule 17, the IC must conduct a review of the processing of personal data for the purposes of journalism in specified periods. The IC must report on the effectiveness of media alternative dispute resolution procedures.

CONCLUDING THOUGHTS

This chapter has outlined the information revolution that has dominated our public and private lives in the last two decades. The future of the FOIA seems secure although in other jurisdictions FOIA has faced limitations. One major question concerns the designation of private contractors as public bodies under FOIA where they are acting as public bodies or performing public tasks. The ICO's *Transparency in Outsourcing: A Roadmap* (ICO 2015) set out suggestions for clearer contracts between public and private bodies which in 2015 amounted to £95 billion—half of the public service costs for goods and services. The IC recommended transparency by design; agreeing who holds what information; setting out responsibilities in handling FOI requests.

The argument has force that what operates in the commercial and competitive sectors cannot be subjected to the constitutional requirements of state entities. Nevertheless, as the examination of data protection explained, there is clearly a problem with a lack of transparency in the way social media operate and in the power they possess.

---

[116] https://www.gov.uk/government/publications/leveson-inquiry-report-into-the-culture-practices-and-ethics-of-the-press (11/10/2018).

[117] https://www.ipso.co.uk/ (11/12/2018).

A Commons select committee has published an interim report on 'Fake News' and its threat to democracy when wielded through social media platforms used by governments and 'hidden persuaders'. The report recommends reforms to make regulation by Ofcom and the IC more effective. Levies on social media companies were suggested as a way of paying for more effective regulation by the IC and it hopes for 'major investment' in the IC's office in a forthcoming government white paper.[118] Electoral laws and the powers of the Electoral Commission should be increased and updated to reflect the digital context of political campaigns. There should be a greater and clearer legal liability for social media tech companies to remove and compensate for material they allow to be posted. The liability of tech companies under the Defamation Act 2013 should be assessed for effectiveness. Transparency should be ensured through more effective regulation and codes and the committee calls for an Atlantic Charter with the USA to guarantee information rights. In the era of governance by Twitter this would appear to have little to commend itself to the US executive.

There is a dramatic tone to the interim report's recommendations and the recommendations will have to be subject to clear, achievable proposals. The committee assumes that when the UK leaves the EU the benefits of the GDPR will cease. It was seen that this is by no means clear cut.[119] But the digital space has produced evidence of serious threats to the democratic process and the rule of law. Reform is obviously a long-term agenda. In *Online Harms White Paper* (CP 57, April 2019), the government launched a consultation on proposals to establish a new legal duty of care on tech companies towards users. The duty will be overseen by an independent regulator with power to issue a code of practice. Digital comapnies and senior managers may be fined by the regulator 'who will be held to account for tackling a comprehensive set of online harms, ranging from illegal activity and content to behaviour which is harmful but not necessarily illegal' (p. 10), raising the criticism of non-legally-based censorship. Platforms may be blocked. Effective complaints procedures for users will be introduced. The regulator will have power to require an annual transparency report from tech companies. The paper states that the UK is the first to establish a regulatory framework, although it acknowledges practices elsewhere. The global nature of social media and problems of jurisdiction are not really addressed beyond hoping for a 'global coalition of countries' (p. 9) and level playing fields between domestic and overseas companies (paras 6.9–6.12). Electoral manipulation is not covered by the paper.

In the field of surveillance there is much more exposure and investigation into practices of S&IS than prior to the Investigatory Powers Act 2016, although there are

---

[118] Digital, Culture Media and Sport committee *Disinformation and Fake News Interim Report* HC 363 (2017–19) and Government Response HC 1630 (2017–2019). The committee's final report calling for 'the enforcement of greater transparency in the digital sphere' is HC 1791 (2017–2019). The EU Commission has produced a Code on Disinformation, see https://ec.europa.eu/digital-single-market/en/news/code-practice-disinformation (26/09/2018). See the Lords Communications Committee's recommendations for a super digital regulatory authority in second report HL 299 (2017–19).

[119] Note 63. For the IC's advice on a no-deal withdrawal see: https://ico.org.uk/for-organisations/data-protection-and-brexit/data-protection-if-there-s-no-brexit-deal/ (23/01/2019).

limitations on available evidence on activities. One point to bear in mind is that many of the reforms in UK laws came about because of checks, not from our domestic safeguards, but from EU and ECHR institutions. The direct force of EU pressures will clearly change on Brexit. Our future in the Council of Europe and ECHR remains to be seen.[120]

FURTHER READING

M. Varney and P. Birkinshaw, *Government and Information Rights: The Law Relating to Access, Disclosure and their Regulation,* Bloomsbury Professional (5th ed. 2019).

R. Jeffreys Jones, *We Know All About You: The Story of Surveillance in Britain and America* (Oxford University Press, 2017).

B. Worthy, *The Politics of Freedom of Information: How and Why Governments Pass Laws that Threaten their Power* (Manchester University Press, 2017).

USEFUL WEBSITES

Information Commissioner's Office: **www.ico.org.uk**

The website of the Information Commissioner's Office has detailed information on Information Rights, case law, guidance, etc.

---

[120] See Cm 9593 note 63 paras. 2.5e and 2.3.19 on a first commitment by the Prime Minister to remain in the ECHR.

14

FEDERALISM

John McEldowney*

SUMMARY

Federalism, to date, has proved unattractive to the United Kingdom. The United Kingdom is commonly described as a unitary state, whereby governmental power is primarily exercised through a sovereign Parliament at Westminster. The UK may be distinguished from Federal countries, notably the United States or Germany. In federal systems, sovereign power is shared between the federal government and the states. However, the description of the United Kingdom as a unitary state is an oversimplification as there are many instances of devolved, shared and autonomous powers that do not easily fit under a centralized view of the state. These 'quasi-federal' elements of the constitution arise through the UK Parliament delegating to regional and local communities a variety of powers and responsibilities through elected local and municipal authorities as well as devolved 'deals'. Since 1989, powers have been distributed to the four nations of the United Kingdom: England, Scotland, Wales and Northern Ireland through extensive, and increasing, devolved powers (devolution) including a variety of tax-raising powers. There is also a London Assembly with devolved powers. The future of the UK after Brexit is uncertain and there are deep divisions of opinion. England and Wales voted for Brexit while London, Northern Ireland and Scotland voted to remain within the EU.

Different constitutional configurations were suggested for the four nations, during the nineteenth century, including federalism, Irish home rule, and independence as well as strengthening local government. No exact definition of federalism emerged from the different variations supported at one time or another during this period. Consequently, supporters of federalism have struggled to assert a single configuration to make their case. Overall federalism was rejected as inconsistent with the orthodoxy of a unitary state formed from an incorporating union centred around a sovereign Parliament. Has the extent of substantial devolved and delegated powers reached a tipping point that places a form of divisible federalism as a way of addressing current concerns and controversies including Brexit? Any formal adoption of federalism would alter the role of the UK Supreme Court as well as future relations with the EU after Brexit. Federalism might

---

* Professor of Law, University of Warwick.

provide a mechanism with which a changing unitary state can address twenty-first century chal-
lenges amidst a perceptible shift to a 'quasi-federal' state with devolved governments and many
shared or delegated powers.

INTRODUCTION

A useful starting point is K.C. Wheare's[1] definition of a federal constitution[2], including the implications for the institutional arrangements that accompany a federal state:

> In a federal constitution, the powers of government are divided between a government for
> the whole country and governments for parts of the country in such a way that each gov-
> ernment is legally independent in its own sphere. The government for the whole country
> has its own areas of powers and it exercises them without any control from the govern-
> ments of the constituent parts of the country, and these in their turn exercise their powers
> without being controlled by the central government. In particular, the legislatures of the
> whole country have limited powers and the legislatures of the states or provinces have
> limited powers.

Under Wheare's definition, the UK does not qualify as a federal state. In 1973, the Royal
Commission on the Constitution[3](known by the name of its Chair as 'the Kilbrandon
Commission') rejected federalism for the UK as 'not an appropriate place for federalism
and now is not an appropriate time.' Its reasoning, in a rather short and pithy chapter,
was that the UK is a unitary state and that 'undivided sovereignty was necessary for the
present-day needs of the people of the UK.'[4] Defining sovereignty as indivisible rested
on the continuity of the sovereignty of the United Kingdom Parliament. Nevertheless,
this permitted, as we shall see, substantial and significant powers to be distributed
amongst the four nations, England, Wales, Scotland and Northern Ireland.[5]

Devolution provides various powers to the nations, as a form of self-government,
but this does not create any entrenched autonomous powers because devolution maintains the sovereignty of the UK Parliament. It is important to be clear in distinguishing
devolution, where powers are transferred, but the UK Parliament does not relinquish
any of its sovereignty, from a formal federal system. Under a federal system, the UK

---

[1] K.C. Wheare, *Modern Constitutions* 2nd ed. Oxford: Oxford University Press, 1966 p. 19. Useful background material is to be found in Michael Burgess, *The British Tradition of Federalism* London: Leicester University Press, 1995 and David Marquand, 'Federalism and the British: Anatomy of a Neurosis' (2006) 77 *Political Quarterly* 175–83.

[2] D. Elazar, *Federal Systems of the World: A Handbook of Federal, Conferral and Autonomy Arrangements*
2nd ed. Harlow: Longman, 1994.

[3] *The Royal Commission on the Constitution 1969–1973 Vol. 1 Report* Cmnd., 5460 vol. 1 Chapter 13,
pp. 152–61.

[4] See: Robert Schütze and Stephen Tierney, *The United Kingdom and the Federal Idea* Oxford: Hart, 2018.

[5] See Michael Gordon, *Parliamentary Sovereignty in the UK Constitution* Oxford: Hart, 2017, Ming-Sung
Kuo, 'Administration or Federation? Constitutional Self-Image and the World Political Order in Which the EU
Finds Itself', *Perspectives on Federalism* Vol. 9 issue 2 (2017) pp. 216–39.

Parliament inevitably loses some or all of its sovereignty to the nations within the federation arrangements.

In recent years there is a more divisible form[6] of arrangement emerging, way beyond the contemplation of the Kilbrandon Commission. There is, today, an increasingly broad devolution of powers, including finance, to Scotland and Wales, and a strong movement for Scottish independence.[7] Brexit has given rise to the need for special arrangements to prevent a hard border between Northern Ireland and Ireland and divisions between 'Remainers' and those who favour Brexit (Scotland and Northern Ireland voted to remain). All are suggestive of the difficulties of accommodating within a unitary state the changing nature of the United Kingdom. Devolved powers to local government are also continuing apace. The creation of various forms of devolution in England is ongoing. The British Overseas territories and Crown dependencies possess their own spheres of autonomous power.

The House of Lords Select Committee on the Constitution[8] in 2016 criticized the current 'inattentive approach to the integrity of the Union, recommending that any proposals for further devolution in the future '. . . should be considered within an appropriate framework of constitutional principles that safeguard the integrity of the Union'. The funding arrangements for devolution need reform; the importance of English votes for English laws (EVEL) and the relationship between devolution settlements and local authorities also need to be addressed. Various principles arise such as solidarity, diversity, responsiveness, and consent for change that allow for clarity amongst members of the public as to the nature of devolved powers, their accountability, and their appropriate level of scrutiny at the different levels of power.

The prevailing constitutional arrangements are centred on the indivisible sovereignty[9] of the UK Parliament that emerged in its present form from earlier centuries through incorporating union with Scotland, Wales and Ireland. Federalism, it has to be said, has an 'uneasy relationship' with indivisible sovereignty—which is also opposed to any constitutional adaptation. Consideration of a divisible form of sovereignty may recognize that federalism, in its many forms,[10] may offer an alternative and workable constitutional architecture[11] to the current arrangements for devolved forms of government. It would offer a more accountable system of government as well as a structure to uphold the rule of law, particularly legal certainty.[12]

---

[6] C. Schmitt, *Verfassungslehre* Berlin, Duncker and Humblot, 2003 Part IV.

[7] P. Gillespie, *Scotland's Vote on Independence: The Implications for Ireland* Dublin: Institute of International and European Affairs, 2014.

[8] House of Lords Select Committee on the Constitution, *The Union and Devolution* 10th Report of Session 2015–16 HL Paper 149 (25th Many 2016) pp. 3–4.

[9] B.P. Levack, *The Formation of the British State: England, Scotland and the Union 1603–1707* Oxford: Clarendon Press, 1987.

[10] Robert Schütze and Stephen Tierney eds. *The United Kingdom and the Federal Idea* London: Hart Publishing, 2018.

[11] See the Constitution Reform Group, *Towards a New Act of Union* Discussion Paper DP01 September 2015.

[12] Richard Mayne and John Pinder, *Federal Union: The Pioneers: A History of Federal Union* London: Macmillan, 1990.

THE HISTORICAL SETTING

Early federalist influences[13] can be traced back to the seventeenth century.[14] Locke's establishment of legislative power as the supreme power of the Commonwealth, left relations within the community and its members part of a federative power dependent on an architectural institutional design. Although united, they formed separate jurisdictions.[15] A federalist vision illuminated the potential for the sharing of sovereign powers between distinct communities united in a common endeavour. An attractive feature was that a federal approach opened up possibilities of distributing power that could be tailored to particular community needs. Its flexibility allowing a widely diverse means of achieving meaningful constitutional agreements. The ebb and flow of the debates about some form of federalism continued throughout the centuries up until the present day.[16] The main obstacle to federalism came from an allegiance to sovereignty that rested on a juridical form of unitary state defined by the union.[17] Defining the Union[18] came to the fore when James VI of Scotland became James I of England on the death of Elizabeth in 1603. Unifying the Crown made good practical and economic sense as well as being a strategic alliance based on the same language with similar religion and culture. This ambition was not as easily realized as first thought and many questions over national identity and how power might be best identified were revealed. A unified Parliament required equal representation; separate Parliaments might be needed to reflect national identity; autonomy within borders might recognize national sovereignty but also distinct legal traditions and rules. Federal, however, lacked a precise meaning. It was ambiguously worded to suggest a loose covenant or compact between nations and not a legally binding constitutional structure with legal powers.[19] The vagueness of any union might also have been deliberate as pragmatic necessity dominated any theoretical influence. The Cromwellian period did not bring clarity, rather a workable military administration for England, Wales, Scotland and Ireland. The debate between a federal or incorporated union emerged rather slowly; Scotland preferring a federal structure and England an incorporated one. The precise detail of each was never clearly articulated. Pamphleteers and propagandists focused on arguments that accentuated their cause. The 1688 settlement of the sovereignty of

---

[13] M. Burgess, *Comparative Federalism: Theory and Practice* London: Routledge 2006. V. Bogdanor, *Devolution in the United Kingdom* 2nd edition Oxford: Oxford University Press. J. Kendle, *Federal Britain: A History* London: Routledge 1997.

[14] See T. Poole, *Locke on the Federative* LSE Working Papers 22/2017 https:/ssrn.com/abstract=3086173 (January 2018). See Locke's Chapter XII of the Second Treatise. John Dunn, *The Political Thought of John Locke* Cambridge: Cambridge University Press, 1969. James Tully, *Strange Multiplicity: Constitutionalism in an Age of Diversity* Cambridge: Cambridge University Press, 1995. Jeremy Waldron, *God, Locke and Equality: Christian Foundations in Locke's Political Thought* Cambridge: Cambridge University Press, 2008.

[15] John Locke (1632–1704).

[16] John E.E. Dalberg, Ist Baron Acton (1834–1902), Professor of Modern History at Cambridge and Henry Sidgwick (1838–1900) were federalists and promoted that cause.

[17] A. V. Dicey, 'Federal Government' (1885) 1 *Law Quarterly Review* 80.

[18] Peter Furtado, *Histories of Nations* London: Thames and Hudson, 2017.   [19] Ibid.

the English Parliament at Westminster threatened any ambition for Scotland to realize its own destiny through its own autonomous Parliament. The debate on the form the union would take was constrained by issues such as free trade and commerce, largely ignoring national aspirations in Scotland.

The eighteenth century further consolidated the union. English power was London based and English regionalism was highly dispersed and lacked a cohesive economic unity to forge its own identity to rival London. Wales was successfully incorporated into the English state and from the Act of Union 1707, Scotland's identity submerged into the state of the British Isles. The economic and political stability thus engendered was seen to be in preference to European instability and uncertainty of the time. At the end of the eighteenth century, coming to terms with strong and independent colonies raised the question of the extent to which a single concept of sovereignty was compatible with what many colonists saw as a divided sovereignty between colony and the sovereign power that gave the colony autonomy. What was at stake at the heart of colonialism was the sovereignty of the colony and this was not easily reconcilable with the indivisible sovereignty of the United Kingdom. Achieving close contact with the mother country and autonomy at the level of colonial government was achievable. Federalism in different forms began to be debated as an answer to a colonial world. The US constitution in the 1780s showed what was possible—the sovereignty of the people and the division of sovereignty at federal and state level. American federalism became a model for future discussions of federalism, but this was outside Britain's influence. Perhaps the adoption of a written constitution proved decisive and off putting to the English pragmatic approach to government. While many commentators such as John Locke had been influential, intellectual debate in Britain or even commentary was largely absent.

Events in Britain moved rapidly with the Act of Union in 1800 with Ireland favouring a strong centralization of the state and a London model of government that formed the basis of British rule in Ireland in Dublin Castle. Many writers in the UK, perfectly aware of the federal nature of constitution-building, were tied to the Union under a UK sovereign Parliament, and did not adopt a federal model for the way forward and considered a divided sovereignty under a federal union unattractive. Dicey and Freeman[20] were particularly resistant to any adoption of a federal model for the UK and objected to any form of divided powers and, in their minds, a weakening of unitary sovereignty. Objections to federalism came in detailed polemical treatises from Dicey who became preoccupied with, and against, Irish Home Rule. Dicey, influenced by the American version of federalism, reasoned that federalism represented a weaker form of government than a unitary state.[21] He devoted an entire chapter in *Law of the Constitution*[22]

---

[20] J. Kelly, 'The Origins of the Act of Union: An Examination of Unionist Opinion in Britain and Ireland 1650–1800' (1987) *Irish Historical Studies* 236.

[21] A.V. Dicey, 'Federal Government' (1885) *Law Quarterly Review* 1 pps. 80–99 (January 1885). See R.A. Cosgrove, *The Rule of Law: Albert Venn Dicey, Victorian Jurist* London: Macmillan, 1980 pp. 35, 103–4 and 235–6.

[22] A.V. Dicey, *Law of the Constitution* London: Macmillan, 1893 Chapter 3.

to arguing against federalism and was condemnatory of attempts in 1911 to address Irish Home Rule through a federal construction of an Imperial Parliament. In later life, however, Dicey acknowledged[23] that a form of limited federalism through some form of Home Rule[24] that maintained the Union,[25] might be possible. He raised problems such as the complexity of arrangements for the division of state powers between the regions, the problems of financial arrangements and also concerns that friction between the different parts of the federal arrangement would generally weaken the United Kingdom. Each region, however, was developing at its own pace so that it was difficult to ensure economic alignment.[26] The main response to such difficulties was to argue for a greater centralization of the state under the banner of a sovereign Parliament so that change might be accommodated but, equally, more easily controlled or at least risk from nationalistic tendencies.[27]

The long running debate over Irish Home Rule, which divided opinion, tended to distract from any mainstream debate on federalism. Vast amounts of Parliamentary time were spent on the subject of how to govern Ireland. The debates were not helped by the fact that versions of federalism were confused with devolution or local government. The absence of any uniformity in approach to federalism made the arguments in favour hard to discern. Politically federalism had no single party support and this further exacerbated the absence of clarity and coherence.

The Government of Ireland Act 1920 was an attempt to secure the union but at the same time find a way to manage nationalist expectation. It was not federalism but devolution: a fudge that enabled sovereignty to be preserved but at the same time powers granted to the Northern Ireland Parliament enabled a fully functional government. The 1920 Act was modelled on the British North American Act in respect of Canada, although little was made of this connection by the politics of the time. Constitutional reality and legal interpretation of the 1920 Act became apparent in making the governing of Northern Ireland a reality. Even if it was accepted that, in the final analysis, Northern Ireland was a subordinate legislature and fell under the sovereignty of the UK Parliament, there was little guidance on how to interpret the width and breadth of powers devolved to the Northern Ireland Parliament. The solution according to Lord Denning was to uphold the legality of government powers unless there was 'proof of abuse of power, if not of bad faith.'[28] Indeed Viscount Simonds, in 1960, went further when commenting on the way the Northern Ireland Constitution, then the Government of Ireland Act 1920, might best be interpreted: 'A flexibility of construction is

---

[23] A.V Dicey and R.S. Rait, *Thoughts on the Union between England and Scotland* London: Macmillan 1920 p. 100.

[24] Trowbridge H. Ford, 'Dicey's Conversion to Unionism' (1973) Vol 18 (72) *Irish Historical Studies* 552–82.

[25] A. V. Dicey, *A Leap in the Dark* 2nd ed. London: John Murray 1893.

[26] A. V. Dicey and R. S. Rait, *Thoughts on the Union between England and Scotland* London: Macmillan, 1920.

[27] See W. Molyneux, *The Case of Ireland Being Bound by Acts of Parliament in England*, Pamphlet Dublin, 1688.

[28] *McCann v Attorney General for N. Ireland* [1961] NI 102 at p. 133.

admissible in regard to [constitutional statutes] which might be rejected in construing ordinary statutes.'[29]

The UK and Northern Ireland courts became familiar[30] with the doctrines and interpretations of the case law of Canada and the USA, which proved helpful when considering devolution issues.[31]

Interest in Federalism emerged from South Africa and Canada. Ironically what was rejected as unsuitable for the United Kingdom, was perfectly acceptable for colonial arrangements separated from the geography of Britain. As early as the 1830s and 1840s ideas about federalism were adopted, culminating in the 1860s in the British North America Act. The result was to unite Nova Scotia, New Brunswick, Quebec and Ontario. Additional provinces were added: Manitoba (1870), British Columbia (1871) and Prince Edward Island (1873). This model of federation set the scene for the future. There was support for some form of Imperial Federalism engaging the UK, the Commonwealth of Australia 1901, and the four South African colonies in the Union of South Africa in 1910. The Round Table Movement was formed in 1910 out of interested groups throughout the dominions. The benefits of federalism remained convincing for many in wishing to maintain a link with the United Kingdom. The influential members of the group extended their debate through English statesmen.[32] The primary aim of the movement was the maintenance of the organic union of the Empire.

Federalism connected with diverse examples such as Brazil and Yugoslavia. The West German Federation was formed. Many African[33] countries found that a federal solution which was attractive for a unitary state was unsuitable to represent different ethnic groups. Its strength was the flexibility it offered of dividing powers and recognizing the power of self-government to advance good standards of living, while ensuring appropriate controls that reflected the size of small territories. The formation of a Commonwealth was achievable through the 'creation of small political entities, technically independent, but in reality, isolated and feeble' and through new principles and methods of association and integration.[34] Federalism in a colonial setting did not advance the cause of federalism within the United Kingdom. The sharing of sovereignty in the colonies helped to reinforce the authority and influence of the UK. In a domestic setting, however, it meant the opposite: fears for a diminution of British authority and a threat to the inviolable nature of legal sovereignty. Opposition to any quasi-federal arrangements was not helped by Northern Ireland. Devolution in Northern Ireland offered

---

[29] *Belfast Corporation v O.D. Cars Ltd.*, [1960] N. I. 60 at p. 86.

[30] See: Lady Hale, *Devolution and the Supreme Court—20 Years On* (Scottish Public Law Group, 2018, Edinburgh 14th June 2018) p. 16. https://www.supremecourt.uk/docs/speech-180614.pdf.

[31] See: *R. (Lynn) v Gallagher* [1937] 3 All ER 598, *O.D. Cars Ltd. v Belfast Corporation* [1959] NI 62 see Lord Sankey LC in *Edwards v Attorney General for Canada* [1930] AC 124 at p. 136. *Macleod v Attorney General for New South Wales* in *Lynn v Gallagher* above.

[32] See John Kendle, *Federal Britain* London: Routledge, 1997 Chapter 5 pp. 95–6.

[33] Trinidad, Nigeria, British Guiana, Malaya, Southern Rhodesia and East Africa, Eden and South Arabian Protectorate.

[34] Clement Atlee, Minutes of meeting 19 January 1949, Cabinet Commonwealth Affairs Committee Cab (49) 1st meeting Cab. 134/56 PRO.

some tentative first steps in the domestic sharing of powers. However, as Northern Ireland became mired in the religious and sectarian conflict that dominated its politics from the 1970s, the experience hardly offered a lesson of 'quasi-federal' power that might be emulated elsewhere. It was also inextricably tied up with competing unionist and nationalist claims over the legitimacy of the state.

FEDERALISM AND THE EUROPEAN UNION

In the run up to Britain joining the European Economic Community in 1973, federalism was debated and analysed, but rejected.[35] Serious academic writing[36] canvassed the possibilities of federalism[37] based around a 'United States of Europe' on federal lines.[38] British suspicions of closer union with the European continent came from a preoccupation with its own indivisible parliamentary sovereignty. The federalist case was not co-ordinated or coherent. Many of the arguments[39] supporting federalism were in substance a case for regionalism or devolution rather than pure federalism. As Kendle has pointed out 'federation was an anathema'.[40] In such circumstances the diminution of the ability of Britain to conduct its own affairs inhibited and restricted any future possible federal arrangement. Wheare,[41] in 1955, raised a common concern about federalism, namely that people of differing nationalities cannot form a federal union unless they are prepared to accept a government in which those that joined were 'expected to develop some common nationality in addition to their own distinct nationalities'. A common European identity is difficult to forge and its absence would remain a major obstacle to any federalist proposal. Such scepticism has endured, leaving many of the major developments in the European Union to be viewed from Britain as a major intrusion into its legal state and nationality.

The debates surrounding the EU Withdrawal Act 2018 and the referendum[42] mirrored many of the concerns about 'ever closer union', resting on long-held fears that British identity and sovereignty might be put in doubt. The Government's White Paper

---

[35] Andrea Bosco, *June 1940 and the First Attempt to Build a European Union* Newcastle Upon Tyne: Cambridge Scholars Publishing 2–16.

[36] A.J. Nicholls, 'Britain and the EC: The Historical Background' in S. Butler et al. (eds) *The United Kingdom and EC Membership Evaluated* New York: St Martin's Press, 1992. Christopher Lord, 'Sovereign or Confused? The "Great Debate" about British Entry to the European Community 20 Years on' (1992) *Journal of Common Market Studies* vol. 30(4) December 1992 pp. 419–36.

[37] John Kendle, *Federal Britain* London: Routledge 1997 pp. 150–7.

[38] John Pinder and Roy Pryce, *Europe After de Gaulle: Towards the United States of Europe* London: Penguin Books, 1969.

[39] See J.C Bank, *Federal Britain Harrap*, London, 1971. John Lambert, *Britain in a Federal Europe* London: Chatto and Windus, 1968. Philip Allott, 'Britain and Europe: A Political Analysis' (March 1975) vol. 9 no. 2 *Journal of Common Market Studies* pp. 175–83.

[40] John Kendle, *A Federal Britain* London: Routledge, 1997 p. 155. John Pinder, *The Federal Case* London: The European Movement 1991.

[41] K. Wheare, *Federalism and the Making of Nations* Oxford: Oxford University Press 1955.

[42] House of Commons Library Briefing Paper Number CP 7639, *European Union Referendum 2016* (29 June 2016).

on *The Future Relationship between the UK and the EU* envisages a 'shared future' between the UK and the EU, premised on the need for the UK and the EU to make decisions 'through a new Governing Body' established for that purpose.[43] Creating such an institutional arrangement will be challenging, and its powers and composition are not defined in the White Paper, but ironically it has the potential to create a quasi-federal relationship between a sovereign UK and a sovereign EU.[44] This form of divisible sovereignty involves the UK and the EU in working out solutions.[45] Details of any agreement, if and when reached, will have political implications that have to be fully worked out. The UK's White Paper envisages that there will be new institutions in the recently published draft Withdrawal Agreement.[46] There are two, the Joint Committee between the UK and EU and the Citizen's Rights Monitoring Authority. The former is the primary mechanism for resolving disputes as to the interpretation of the agreement and disputes over whether the EU or the UK have complied with the requirements of the agreement. The Joint Committee will make decisions that are binding on both parties and it may make non-binding recommendations.[47] The Joint Committee may also make amendments to the Withdrawal Agreement within the terms of what is agreed. Sub-committees may be established to cover sectoral areas such as the rights of citizens. The Joint Committee decisions may be given the same legal effect as the Withdrawal Agreement while recommendations may be adopted through mutual consent. Many issues need to be addressed, such as the overlapping jurisdiction of the Court of Justice of the European Union (CJEU) and the Joint Committee, as indeed is the lack of clarification of the role of the CJEU after the transition arrangement. The EU may find such a Joint Committee mechanism inadequate as an enforcement mechanism.

There are significant areas where devolved nations have powers to make their own primary and second legislation, such as the environment, and increasingly devolved nations have taken divergent legislative and policy routes.[48] Migrating retained EU law to devolved nations will require considerable dexterity and political skill. The Joint Committee offers a form of federal oversight of the devolved nations, in the sense that the devolved nations will participate in taking forward EU law. It is unclear at the time of writing how this might work.

Adopting solutions to address new constitutional governance arrangements might be facilitated by a federal arrangement that may encourage accountability, and overall

---

[43] HM Government, *The Future Relationship between the United Kingdom and the European Union* London: 2018 Cm 9593 para. 4.3.1.

[44] House of Commons Library, *Briefing Paper Brexit and Governance of the UK-EU Relationship* (14 September 2018).

[45] In addition to the White Paper, discussion has focused on the arrangements between the EU and Canada: see House of Commons Library Briefing Paper Number 7492, *CETA: The EU Canada Free Trade agreement* (20th July 2018); and, for Norway, see House of Commons Library, *Norway's Relationship with the EU* Standard Note 6522 (14th January 2013).

[46] CBP-8269, *Brexit: The Draft Withdrawal Agreement* (26 March 2018). Article 161 of the Draft Withdrawal Agreement. Also see Articles 157 and 158, 159.

[47] House of Lords EU Committee Report, *Dispute Resolution and Enforcement After Brexit* (HL 2017–19, 130) paras. 79–87.

[48] House of Commons Library Briefing Paper, *Brexit and the Environment* (8 August 2018) CBP8132.

scrutiny.[49] The short-term temporary withdrawal period has to be distinguished from the longer-term future relationship between the UK and the EU. Discussion of possible arrangements will inevitably see an emerging and divisible sovereignty. This is likely to be highly contentious within the UK. However, future relations between the UK and the EU may adopt a 'federal' form, although it is doubtful if this will qualify as federal when the UK exercises its own independent sovereignty. Murkens,[50] argues that a federal UK 'would be able to absorb EU law much more smoothly than the current centrist model' given the need for many EU competences to be exercised locally and regionally in each nation.

FEDERALISM AND DEVOLUTION

The 'quasi-federal state'[51, 52] with devolved administrations in Scotland, Wales and Northern Ireland is a remarkable shift from the theory of a unitary state with a centralized government to one with autonomy to each nation. The shift from unitary to quasi-federal is to be found in the details of how devolution is composed of a number of distinct inter-locking mechanisms.

As we have already seen, Northern Ireland was the first to experience devolution within the United Kingdom from the Government of Ireland Act 1920. This gave considerable autonomy to the Northern Ireland Parliament and government to make laws for the peace, order, and good government of Northern Ireland. The Royal Commission on the Constitution (the Kilbrandon Commission) in 1973 rejected federalism, but a form of 'quasi-federalism' is evident from some of the analysis and discussion.[53]

The Northern Ireland Act 1998[54] may be regarded[55] as a modern version of a 'Constitution for Northern Ireland'.[56] It should be noted that the original Government of Ireland Act 1920, as an exercise in devolution, gave considerable powers to the Northern Ireland government and Parliament.[57] The 1998 Act came from the Good Friday Agreement and a referendum in both parts of Ireland. It forged a different form of power than majority rule. Northern Ireland also has an important cooperation agreement through

---

[49]   House of Commons Briefing Paper 8397, *What if There's no Brexit Deal?* (10 September 2018).

[50]   Jo Eric Khushal Murkens, 'The UK's Reluctant Relationship with the EU' in Robert Schütze and Stephen Tierney, *The United Kingdom and the Federal Idea* Oxford: Hart, 2018 p. 172.

[51]   See Brice Dickson Chapter 9 for a full discussion.

[52]   V. Bogdanor, 'Asymmetric Devolution: Towards a Quasi-Federal Constitution' in P. Dunleavy et al., *Developments in British Politics* London: Palgrave Macmillan, 2003, p. 7.

[53]   *The Royal Commission on the Constitution 1969–1973 Vol. 1 Report* Cmnd, 5460.

[54]   See Brice Dickson, 'Devolution—Northern Ireland' Chapter 9.

[55]   See H. Calvert, *Constitutional Law in Northern Ireland: A Study in Regional Government* Belfast and London: Stevens 1968. *Robinson v Secretary of State for N. Ireland* [2002] UKHL 32.

[56]   The term is used for the Government of Ireland Act 1920 and subsequently. See Sir Arthur Quekett, *The Constitution of Northern Ireland* Belfast: HMSO 1928 and 1946.

[57]   H. Calvert, *Constitutional Law in Northern Ireland* Belfast, NILQ, 1968.

the North-South Ministerial Council established under the Belfast and Northern Irish Agreements. The nature of power-sharing under the Northern Ireland Act 1998 is unique and built on a power-sharing basis including a role for the Republic of Ireland's government. This has the potential to be expanded and developed. In interpreting the 1998 Act, Lord Bingham looked for an interpretation that is 'generous and purposive, bearing in mind the values which the constitutional provisions are intended to embody'.[58]

Northern Ireland is also able to increase its autonomy, for example, through the devolution of corporation tax-raising powers to the Northern Ireland Assembly under the Corporation Tax (Northern Ireland) Act 2015. This gives autonomy to the Assembly to set the main rate of corporation tax. The rate applies to the profits of large companies and in defined circumstances to medium-sized enterprises. While there are many exclusions from the scheme, such as life insurance and certain lending and investing activities, this is a substantial devolution of powers.[59] The Northern Ireland Assembly has not been sitting so it is unclear if and when such powers might be activated.

Since 1998 the UK has witnessed a gradual dispersal of powers to the devolved nations, particularly Scotland[60] and Wales. Tierney sees this as a 'federal trajectory'[61] and cites the examples of the Scotland Act 2016 and the Wales Act 2017. His analysis is well evidenced from the legislation. The Scotland Act 2016 affirms the permanence of the Scottish Parliament, and provides formal recognition of the Sewel Convention. The Sewel Convention dates from 1998 when Lord Sewel made a commitment that there should be a parliamentary convention that when the UK Parliament legislated in a devolved area it would not 'normally legislate without the consent of the Scottish Parliament'.[62] Autonomy is to be found through the Scottish Parliament having control over its own composition and electoral system. Significant tax-raising powers, also, have been acquired including the rates and bands of income tax and a share of VAT receipts. Significant powers over welfare benefits are devolved with large tracts of policy making such as employment, energy, and transport devolved. Tierney notes that Scotland 'is more heavily devolved' than many federal systems in other states.[63] If the Scotland Act 2016 is viewed as not a single moment in constitutional history but a continuous dialogue, it is path-changing in the potential for Scottish independence, if not a form of federal status.

Similarly, for Wales, there is an expectation of continuous devolution, whereby further powers will be devolved.[64] Originally conceived as a weaker form of

---

[58] *Robinson v Secretary of State for Northern Ireland* [2002] UKHL 32 at [11].

[59] House of Commons Library Briefing Papers Number 7078 Corporation Tax in Northern Ireland (16 May 2018).

[60] See Aileen McHarg, Chapter 10.

[61] Stephen Tierney, 'Drifting Towards Federalism? Appraising the Constitution in the Light of the Scotland Act 2016 and Wales Act 2017' in Robert Schütze and Stephen Tierney, *The United Kingdom and the Federal Idea* Oxford: Hart, 2018 p. 102.

[62] House of Commons Library, Briefing Paper Number 08275 *Legislative Consent and the European Union (Withdrawal) Bill (2017–19)* (23 May 2018).

[63] Ibid. Tierney p. 104.   [64] See Richard Rawlings Chapter 11.

devolution in 1998, the Wales Act 2017 shifts Welsh devolution to a fully recogniz-able reserved powers model on lines similar to Scotland.[65] Welsh ministers have been granted new executive powers over such matters as speed limits, pedestrian crossings, and onshore petroleum licences. There is overall a reduction of the re-served powers kept at Westminster and the removal of the need for a referendum on the devolution of income tax. Further devolved powers are likely to follow as the National Assembly for Wales hopes to obtain similar powers to the Scottish Parliament to control its own composition and voting arrangements. This may even extend to its own nomenclature turning the Welsh Assembly into the Welsh Parlia-ment. There is even consideration of a distinct Welsh legal jurisdiction. The Wales Act 2017 is a reflection of a growing political debate on federalism in Wales[66] and a wish to emulate Scotland. It is a reminder that while there may be constitutional significance arising out of various devolution arrangements, these are predicated on political momentum that promotes change. There is another, often overlooked aspect of devolution. namely the creation of some innovative mechanisms for in-teraction between devolved nations and Westminster. The administration of the four nations is achieved through a *Memorandum of Understanding* established in 1999. It has been reviewed twice, in 2009 and then in 2013. Joint meetings are held through the Joint Ministerial Committee (JMC), a non-statutory and broadly *ad hoc* informal system of discussion that was productive of concordats and agree-ments. The effectiveness of the JMC is open to question and its ability to initiate policy discussion in the four nations is unclear. However, its existence is significant as recognizing that inter-governmental relations exist and that the technical com-plexity of that relationship needs monitoring, if not to say accountability. In 2015, the House of Lords Constitution Committee[67] found that devolved nations were critical of the JMC, and hoped for a more systematic approach. Following the EU referendum, in June 2016, the government published its plans for Brexit on 2 Febru-ary 2017 and established the Joint Ministerial Committee for EU negotiations (JMC (EN)) as a means of taking forward future relations and Brexit with the devolved nations.[68] It remains to be seen how effective these arrangements will be in future years. Post Brexit the distinctiveness of each nation is likely to be further accentu-ated as EU-retained UK law is transferred to each nation.

A quasi-federal state is also apparent from the financial arrangements under the Barnett formula and devolved taxation as well as the development of principles for UK legislation for English laws for English votes (EVEL).

---

[65] House of Commons Library, Briefing Paper '*"A Process not an Event": Devolution in Wales, 1998–2018*' (11 July 2018) Number 08318.

[66] David Melding, *Will Britain Survive Beyond 2020?* Cardiff Institute of Welsh Affairs 2009.

[67] House of Lords Constitution Committee, Intergovernmental relations in the United Kingdom 11th re-port Session 2014–15 HL Paper 146.

[68] See House of Lords Library Briefing: *Leaving the EU: Role of the Devolved Administrations and Implica-tions for the Union* (debate 25th January 2018).

THE BARNETT FORMULA AND FINANCIAL ARRANGEMENTS BETWEEN ENGLAND AND THE DEVOLVED NATIONS

The devolved administrations receive grants[69] from the UK government to fund the majority of their spending.[70] Since the late 1970s funding arrangements between England and the devolved administrations has been undertaken on the basis of the 'non-statutory Barnett formula' which applies to the block grant, that is by far the largest item of grant provided to the devolved administrations by the UK Parliament. The Barnett formula, named after Joel Barnett, then the Chief Secretary to the Treasury, allows annual adjustments to be made to each of the devolved nations based on changes to funding for various services in England.[71] There are other grants that have to be negotiated as the amount of spending is unpredictable from year to year. The basis of the Block grant is that when there is a change in funding for comparable services in England, the same changes are introduced country wide and this includes devolved services for each nation. Changes are adjusted within each government department. There are demands for greater transparency and clarity over the Block grant that has prompted the Treasury to publish financial information on an annual basis in a revised and clearer formula.[72] Changes in the taxation basis in each of the devolved nations have not resulted in a fundamental change to the Barnett formula, rather adjustments are made in line with changed taxation.

TAXATION AND SPENDING BY THE DEVOLVED ADMINISTRATIONS

Despite substantial changes to the taxation and spending arrangements in each of the devolved administrations,[73] Scotland and Wales and Northern Ireland, there has been no corresponding adjustment to the Barnett formula to take account of how each devolved administration is able to raise its own resources. This has resulted in increasing anomalies in the Barnett system although the main political parties have refrained from any full-scale reform, even though this is clearly needed. In Scotland, the Scotland Act gave the Scottish Parliament its own tax-raising powers with the ability to deviate income tax from the standard UK rate. Similar powers covering land transactions and landfill tax were also delegated to Scotland. The Scotland Act 2016 went further and gave the Scottish Parliament control over income tax, air passenger duty and aggregates levy as well as an element of Value Added Tax receipts. Responsibilities have

---

[69] A formula for financial support to local authorities in 1888 by Georg Goschen allocated probate duties to local authorities in England and Wales (80%) Scotland (11%) and Ireland (9%).

[70] David Heald and Alastair Mcleod, 'Embeddedness of UK Devolution Finance within the Public Expenditure System' *Regional Studies* June 2005. Institute for Fiscal Studies, *Business as Usual? The Barnett Formula: Business Rates and Further Tax Devolution* November, 2014.

[71] House of Commons Library, Briefing Paper number 7386, *The Barnett Formula* (23 January 2018).

[72] HM Treasury, *The Block Grant Transparency Release,* 2017.

[73] House of Commons Library Briefing Paper, *The Barnett Formula* (23 January 2018).

also broadened to include elements of welfare. The Barnett formula[74] will need some further adjustment to take account of the changes.

In Wales, the Wales Act 2014 devolved tax-raising powers over business rates, land transaction tax, and landfill tax to the National Assembly of Wales. The Act allowed the use of a rate of income tax to be introduced from April 2019 under the Wales Act 2017 again. This will require some adjustment in the Barnett formula. In Northern Ireland more limited powers of taxation are devolved by the Northern Ireland Corporation Tax (Northern Ireland) Act 2015 which devolves corporation tax rates to Northern Ireland, subject to an agreed commencement order. There are likely to be some adjustments to the block grant for Northern Ireland once arrangements are put in place.[75]

ENGLISH VOTES FOR ENGLISH LAWS

A long-standing concern about the system of devolution is the anomaly that English MPs cannot vote on devolved laws that apply to the devolved administrations whereas, in the UK Parliament, MPs from devolved nations are able to vote on English matters.[76] This anomaly is known as the West Lothian question.[77] The introduction of devolution in the 1990s raised the issue of how to address the West Lothian question. In 1999, the House of Commons Procedure Committee made various proposals that legislation for one part of the UK might be vetted by special second reading committees. Lord Norton chaired a Commission to Strengthen Parliament in 2000 that envisaged only English MPs would effectively vote on English-only legislation through its Commons stages. The need to come up with a satisfactory solution became clear when in November 2003 MPs voted for an amendment to the Health and Social Care (Community Health and Standards) Bill to prevent the establishment of foundation hospitals in England. This was rejected by 17 votes but it would have passed if only English MPs had voted. The government's Higher Education Bill, a few months later raised a similar problem. The bill contained a controversial rise in tuition fees for English students, but it would not have passed without the votes of non-English MPs, with an embarrassing defeat for the Westminster government. English MPs alone would have defeated the Bill.

In 2013, the McKay Commission was established to provide an independent assessment of how best to proceed. The Commission accepted that the anomaly created by devolution needed to be addressed. It recommended that English MPs should be given a 'voice' at Westminster rather than a veto over English-only legislation, and this might be accomplished through procedural reforms.

---

[74] HC Deb 14 November 1977 c123. The issue was raised in the House of Commons by Tam Dalyell, then Labour MP for West Lothian.

[75] House of Commons Library, Briefing Paper, *The Barnett Formula* Number 7368 (23 January 2018). See HM Treasury, 'Funding the Scottish Parliament, National Assembly for Wales and Northern Ireland Assembly; Statement of Funding Policy' November 2015.

[76] The question was first asked by Tam Dalyell, the MP for West Lothian. See HC Deb 14 June 1977 cc 225. See Vernon Bogdanor, *Devolution in the United Kingdom* rev edition 2001 p. 19, Oxford: Oxford University Press; House of Commons Library, Standard Note: *The West Lothian Question* SN/PC/2586 (18 January 2012).

[77] House of Commons Library, Standard Note: *The West-Lothian Question* SN/PC/2586 (18 January 2012).

In October 2015, the House of Commons approved a Standing Order that gives effect to only 'English Votes for English Laws' (EVEL). A central focus is on the creation of a legislative grand committee composed of English or English and Welsh MPs with the capacity to debate and veto legislative procedures. In so doing, the EVEL arrangements admit a special category of law for English-only legislation that is addressed through a collective legislative veto for English MPs allowing an English-only voice at Westminster.

The crucial significance of the EVEL procedures is found in the details of the procedures. First, the system means that English (or English and Welsh) legislation must be approved by the whole House and by English MPs in order to become law. This is a double lock on the legislation. Second, there is a formal procedure to identify government bills that apply to England (or England and Wales). The Speaker has to ensure that each bill is checked to see if the powers in the bill are within the competence of the devolved legislatures in a different part of the UK. The Speaker has to check every clause or schedule of any proposed government bill. There is a third element, namely the setting up of legislative grand committees to ensure that the EVEL procedures operate properly. The committees are made up exclusively of English MPs (or English and Welsh MPs). The decision of the committee is mandatory and the offending clause may be deleted from the bill. Any amendments made by the House of Lords have also to be considered by such a committee, subject to a separate system of voting outside the Grand Committee.

The EVEL system at first appears convoluted and over technical. Initial research shows that from 2015–17, out of 33 government bills, over half had at least one clause, eligible to be considered under the Speaker's certificate, and almost 25 per cent of statutory instruments. This is a finding of some importance because it shows the extent of the anomaly of English-only legislation being approved by devolved MPs.

The constitutional significance of the EVEL arrangements need to be fully assessed. One analysis is that priority is being given to an English voice. Might this create different classes of MPs? Initially, this was regarded as a major objection to the EVEL procedure, but over time such objections have diminished. Another concern is that the outcome of EVEL is a form of bifurcated government. The House of Commons may be re-constituted into an English only form, inconsistent perhaps with the role of a UK government and the overarching responsibility for the Union. EVEL does not affect the need for a UK government to command the support of the House of Commons and the requirement that government enjoys the exclusive power to raise taxes and spend public money.

It is hard to know if the EVEL arrangements will survive the test of time and different formulations of a UK government, perhaps with a broader spectrum of appeal across the UK as a whole. EVEL is also susceptible to being changed in the future by any government that is minded to do so. Legislation can also be enacted in a technical manner that by-passes EVEL.

EVEL has some inherent deficiencies. It is currently constructed around a veto rather than the requirement of a positive right to do something. There are also few opportunities for the 'English' voice to be heard across the policy-making process. It is still necessary for the support of the UK-wide House to pass legislation. In such circumstances English MPs cannot force through legislation against the wishes of UK-wide MPs. There are many other areas where the opportunity to hold debates, question and conduct inquiries where there are devolved responsibilities and powers need to be addressed. There is little to suggest that the implications of EVEL has galvanized English MPs into a coherent whole. Scepticism about federalism for the UK remains entrenched and is unlikely to be considered a realistic prospect for reform at the present time.[78]

POST-BREXIT AND THE MIGRATION OF RETAINED EU LAW TO THE DEVOLVED INSTITUTIONS

Retained EU law is preserved in the European Union (Withdrawal) Act 2018.[79] A number of key competences are currently devolved within the UK but all are subject to EU law and regulation. The question of what competences will be released back to the devolved administrations is controversial.[80] Common Framework Agreements will be necessary for the United Kingdom to ensure some form of convergence and divergence between different parts of the UK. Technical skill and political judgement are necessary to ensure that the arrangements run smoothly.[81] There are 153 individual policy areas[82] with different arrangements for each of the devolved nations. Current estimates suggest that there are 82 policy areas where it will be possible to proceed without legislative intervention but there are at least 24 areas where legislation is thought to be required. Each area will require detailed discussion. Particularly difficult are areas of the Common Agricultural Policy involving standard settings for animal health and safety as well as payments to farmers and the advancement of trade.[83] It is recognized that the repatriation to devolved administrations of various retained EU law powers is likely to require considerable technical dexterity to ensure clarity and certainty in the powers each devolved nation will enjoy. The need for a common approach across the UK, so that a consistent approach to policy making is achieved for each devolved nation, is essential.[84] Particular importance is given to Northern Ireland because of the existence of the

[78] See Stephen Tierney, 'Drifting Towards Federalism? Appraising the Constitution in the Light of the Scotland Act 2016 and the Wales Act 2017' in Robert Schütze and Stephen Tierney, *The United Kingdom and the Federal Idea* Oxford: Hart, 2018 Chapter 4 and Murray Forsyth, *Unions of States: The Theory and Practice of Confederation* London: Leicester University Press, 1981.

[79] See P. Craig Chapter 4.

[80] See Richard Rawlings, *Brexit and the Territorial Constitution* London: The Constitution Society 2017.

[81] Michael Keating, *The Repatriation of Competences in Agriculture after Brexit,* Centre of Constitutional Change, January 2018.

[82] Cabinet Office, *Frameworks Analysis: Breakdown of Areas of EU Law that Intersect with Devolved Competence in Scotland, Wales and Northern Ireland* March, 2018.

[83] Michael Keating, *The Repatriation of Competences in Agriculture after Brexit* London: Centre for Constitutional Change, 2018.

[84] House of Lords, Select Committee on the Constitution 9th Report session 2017–19 EU (Withdrawal Bill) HL Paper 69 para. 260.

Anglo-Irish Agreement and the peace process. Undoubtedly, the UK will be capable of designing its own policies after Brexit but this freedom has to be considered in the context of ensuring trade with the EU and also preventing obstacles to trade within the UK. A major unknown are the various trade deals that may be negotiated after Brexit. A number of environmental policy areas are expected to be retained by the UK, in favour of achieving a UK-wide legislative approach to each area.[85]

Retained EU law and its transfer to devolved nations will also bring to the fore the complexity of financial settlements between the UK and devolved nations. Payments in support of retained EU laws will have to be annually adjusted and also considered in terms of the existing Barnett formula. There is no easy solution unless there is an appropriate adjustment to the Barnett formula and a reconsideration of the financial relations between the UK and each devolved nation.

Financial arrangements for the devolved nations provide a blueprint for increasing devolved legislative autonomy. Post-Brexit, the drawing up of complex Framework Agreements will in effect provide a constitutional settlement of the devolved competences working within a framework set by the UK Parliament. This form of administrative, legislative, and financial agreement is federal in form but remains lacking an overarching constitutional settlement that recognizes the reality of devolved powers. The setting up of a Framework agreement has proved divisive. The Scottish government refused to approve a legislative consent motion on the application of the European Union (Withdrawal) Bill and to date only the Welsh government has entered into an *Intergovernmental Agreement on the European Union (Withdrawal) Bill and the Establishment of Common Frameworks* in April 2018. Scotland wishes to maintain a high ambition for the continuation of key sectors in EU regulation such as the environment. Northern Ireland awaits the outcome of the discussion on its relations with the Irish Republic post Brexit. The special circumstances of Northern Ireland raises the question of how to maintain a frictionless border link with the Irish Republic, an EU Member State. This raises an intriguing question about the implications of any agreement negotiated with the EU on this vexed issue. Potentially, Northern Ireland may signal further asymmetry, leaving the rest of the United Kingdom in an unusual position of recognizing an exception to the UK's relations with the EU.

DEVOLUTION TO LOCAL GOVERNMENT IN ENGLAND

Traditionally few independent powers free of central control have been conferred on local government. However, in a number of areas now, such as planning, local authorities are being given more autonomy, subject in some cases to a 'call-in' by the minister,

---

[85] Chemicals and Regulation; environmental quality, ozone depletion substances and F gases, the implementation of EU Emissions Trading Systems, pesticides, Waste packaging and product regulation and GMOs. See ENDS Report 517 (April, 2018) p. 12.

or appeal to an independent inspectorate. The Localism Act 2011, however, sought significantly to enlarge the powers of local authorities by creating 'general powers of competence', which could involve them charging for their services.

One of the outcomes of the Scottish referendum in September 2014, was the decision[86] to encourage the grant of additional powers to local authorities[87] or to local areas in England.[88] This is a work in progress beginning with 'devolution'[89] deals in November 2014.[90] The arrangements are *ad hoc* in nature, negotiated in private and triggered by local needs, on the basis of bids made to central government.[91] There were 38 bids made by 4 September 2015. The model consists of strong city regions led by directly elected Mayors. This enables more powers to be granted including for housing, skills and healthcare. The Greater Manchester Combined Authority (November 2014) is one example and, by April 2018, an additional 12 area bids had been successfully agreed.[92] There are also a number of deals[93] under negotiation and it is unclear if these will be successful.[94] Enabling legislation is contained in the Cities and Local Government Devolution Act 2016 that may transfer or create powers. The deal documents are non-statutory and are initially private, but must be first published and agreed by each council involved. In some cases, councils have not agreed and the deal is then rejected. There is a striking absence of a devolution framework for this form of local government powers, although such a framework is promised by the government.[95] The range of powers that form existing devolution deals cover a number of categories. Restructuring further education in their area to encourage skills acquisition is one. There are business support schemes as well as the Work Programme. Current allocation of structural funds will be included and after Brexit there will be 'shared Prosperity' funds to be allocated. Fiscal powers are also included as are planning and land use and integrated transport schemes. There is also capacity for special areas on specific needs such as housing, health, transforming cities funds, and local industrial strategies. The arrangements proposed above have also to be considered alongside the existing devolution arrangements for London under the Greater London Authority and elected Mayor. The Greater London Authority Acts 1999 and 2007 provide a wide

---

[86] HM Treasury, Chancellor on Building a Northern Powerhouse (14 May 2015), M. Heseltine, *No Stone Unturned: In Pursuit of Growth* (2012).

[87] House of Commons Library Briefing Papers, *Devolution to Local Government in England* (4 May 2018) Number 07029.

[88] Communities and Local Government Committee, *Devolution in England: The Case for Local Government* HC-503 (2013–140 (July 2014).

[89] Ed. Hammond, *Cards on the Table: English Devolution and Governance* Centre for Public Scrutiny, March 2016.

[90] House of Commons Library, Briefing Paper: *Devolution to Local Government in England* (4 May 2018).

[91] Leader of the House of Commons, *The Implications of Devolution for England* CM 8969 December 2014.

[92] Greater Manchester, Sheffield City Region, West Yorkshire, Cornwall, North-East, North of Tyne, Tees Valley, West Midlands, Liverpool City Region, Cambridgeshire/Peterborough, Norfolk/Suffolk, West of England and Greater Lincolnshire.

[93] National Audit Office, *English Devolution Deals* HC948 2015–16 April 2016.

[94] These include the Solent, Lancashire, Devon/Somerset, and Dorset.

[95] It was expected that a framework would be forthcoming from central government.

range of powers over transport, police, economic development, fire and emergency planning. It is likely that additional devolution will be given on the basis of a further tranche of enhanced devolution powers.[96]

The policy direction in favour of increasing local government forms of devolution is favoured by many 'think-tanks'[97]keen to see local devolution reach its full potential.[98] It is also a reaction to concerns about an over-centralized state and also greater financial cuts to the traditional local government authorities.[99] It is striking that as devolution processes have been evolving, there has not been much analysis of their impact overall on the UK's social and economic development.[100]

UK CROWN DEPENDENCIES AND OVERSEAS TERRITORIES

The Crown Dependencies[101] and the 14 Overseas Territories[102] have a unique constitutional and historical relationship with the UK. They are not part of the UK or the EU and are self-governing with their own legislatures and systems of accountability.[103]

In the case of Crown Dependencies (the Channel Islands and the Isle of Man), the Kilbrandon Report in 1973 illuminated the relationship between them and the United Kingdom[104] asserting that the UK government is responsible for their defence and external relations, although their domestic affairs are largely in their own hands. Nevertheless, 'the ultimate and last resort to legislate for the Islands' rested with the UK's Parliament.[105] It was conceded, however, that the consent of the Islands was normally necessary and should always be sought.[106]

The autonomy of the Islands was considered in the UK Supreme Court decision in *R. (Application of Barclay and Another) v Secretary of State for Justice and Lord Chancellor (No. 2).*[107] It was held that the UK courts could not determine the compatibility of local legislation with the provisions of Article 6 of the ECHR as the relevant provisions of

---

[96] National Audit Office, *English Devolution Deals* HC 948 2015–16 (April 2016).

[97] Local Democracy Network, 'The County Councils Network and the Centre for Cities'.

[98] See Jack Hunter, *Rebooting Devolution: A Common Sense Approach to Taking Back Control* IPPR, 2017.

[99] Eds. Cox and Jack Hunter, Empowering Counties: Unlocking County Devolution Deals, 2015.

[100] One exception is the House of Lords Constitution Committee, *Inquiry into the Union and Devolution* 2015–16 HL Paper 55.

[101] The Crown Dependencies include the Isle of Man the Bailiwick of Jersey and the Bailiwick of Guernsey.

[102] The 14 Overseas territories include Anguilla, Ascension, Bermuda, British Virgin Islands, Cayman Islands, Falkland Islands, Gibraltar, Montserrat, Pitcairn, St Helena, the Sovereign Base areas of Akrotiri and Dhekelia, Tristan de Cunha, and Turks and Caicos Islands.

[103] See UK Overseas Joint Ministerial Council.

[104] Part XI Volume 1 of the Report of the Royal Commission on the Constitution 1969–73, *The Relationship between the United Kingdom and the Channel Islands and the Isle of Man.*

[105] Ibid. para. 513.

[106] J. Jowell, 'The Scope of Guernsey's Autonomy—A Brief Rejoinder (2001) 5 *Jersey Law Review* 271.

[107] [2014] UKSC 54.

the Human Rights Act 1998 did not apply to Channel Islands legislation. This leaves the UK courts giving due deference to the Channel Island institutions to make choices as to the national interests of their territories. Island courts can make decisions for themselves, though subject to appeal to the Judicial Committee of the Privy Council.[108] As Jowell and others have explained, the case also helps to reinforce existing conventions such as autonomy in purely domestic matters and consultation prior to the UK enacting legislation that would apply to the Dependencies.[109]

In international law, the Crown Dependencies are recognized as territories, not in their own right, but falling within the UK's responsibilities. They can make treaty arrangements when permitted to do so by 'entrustment'. Ultimately the Crown may intervene directly in the affairs of the Islands in the interest of 'peace, order and good government,' but that may, these days, apply only where there is a significant breakdown of law and order or endemic corruption.[110] Crown dependencies have a unique relationship with the European Union. Article 355(5)(c) of the TFEU provides that the Treaty will apply to the Channel Islands and the Isle of Man only to the extent necessary for the accession of new members to the EEC in 1972. Protocol 3 of the UK's Treaty of Accession allows the Crown Territories to be part of the Customs Union that includes the common customs tariff, levies, and the prohibition of quarantine restrictions. There is free movement of agricultural goods and derived products between the islands and the UK. They are not eligible for assistance from the EU structural funds and there is no free movement of persons, however they are part of the Single Market for the purposes of trade in goods but not in other respects. There are also some differences within some Crown Dependencies. The Isle of Man has a customs and excise arrangement with the UK since 1979 allowing for the sharing of VAT and other revenues. Guernsey and Jersey do not apply VAT and they have had their own customs regime since 1973. The Isle of Man is part of the UK's membership of the WTO, Guernsey and Jersey do not have this relationship, but wish to have membership of the WTO.

The Crown Dependencies offer an example of a special form of sharing close constitutional, economic and social relationships whilst maintaining their own distinctiveness. This is consistent with their autonomy but, also, maintaining a link with the Crown permits the sharing of constitutional responsibility with the UK for their protection and security, as well as some limited access to the EU.[111]

The British Overseas Territories (OTs) (a number of former British Colonies) have a similar quasi-federal relationship with the UK. However, they have their own written

[108] See J. Jowell, Iain Steele and Jason Pobjoy, 'The Barclay Cases: Beyond Kilbrandon' (2017) *The Jersey and Guernsey Law Review* 29–42.
[109] Ibid. p. 41.
[110] As suggested by the House of Commons Justice Committee, Eighth Report of Session 2009–10, *Crown Dependencies (2010), HC 56–61*.
[111] House of Lords, European Union Committee 19th Report, Brexit: The Crown Dependencies Session 2016–17 HL Paper 136 (23 March 2017).

constitutions, with bills of rights.[112] The pattern is that the governments of the OTs have full powers within the sphere of domestic affairs except those that are carved out to be exercised by the British Governor. These normally include external affairs, defence and matters of internal security, and the police. There are sometimes additional over-ride powers conferred on either the Governor or the UK Foreign Secretary. In addition, the Crown may, as with the Crown Dependencies, intervene directly in matters that offend 'peace, order and good government'.

The UK Parliament possesses sovereign power to intervene in the affairs of the Overseas Territories but by convention does not do so without their consent. However, this convention was violated in the recent Sanctions and Money-Laundering Act 2018, which authorizes an order in council to be made to require the OTs to introduce a public register of beneficial interests in companies. Although the Act was initially intended also to be applied to the Crown Dependencies, this was not carried out.

In the case of the Overseas Territories,[113] there is a Joint Ministerial Council which meets annually. The powers devolved to each of the Overseas Territories are the maximum possible to allow UK responsibility but at the same time to ensure the autonomy of the territories.[114] The UK may continue to provide infrastructure support and economic development. In a number of areas such an anti-corruption, governance, and human rights as well as environment and climate change, pensions and health, working partnerships exist between the UK and the Overseas Territories. Nine[115] of the 14 territories have the benefits of an Overseas Association Decision of 2013 (OAD) adopted by the EU.[116] This enables a relationship with the EU to develop as well as the UK. Over 80 million euros of funding has been provided, and there is free access to the EU market which has been particularly beneficial to the Falklands Islands. There is sufficient flexibility in the OAD for there to be close links between the Commission and the territories. The EU has also helped to strengthen autonomy within the territories and greater political visibility.[117] As the *Barclay's* decision is indicative of recognizing various forms of autonomy[118] in the relationship between the UK and the Crown dependencies, there are similar trends for devolution cases.

---

[112] See I. Hendry and S. Dickson, *British Overseas Territories Law*, 2nd ed. London: Hart Publishing, Bloomsbury, 2018.

[113] The UK Overseas Joint Ministerial Council 2016 Annual Communique.

[114] See Brexit in the Caribbean, *The Economist* 11 August 2018 p. 23.

[115] The nine are Anguilla, Bermuda, British Virgin Islands, Cayman Islands, Falklands, Monserrat, Pitcairn, St Helena and Turks and Caicos Islands.

[116] House of Commons Foreign Affairs Committee (2016) 'Implications of the Referendum on EU Membership for the UK's Role in the World'. Evidence EU M0029 and EUM0034.

[117] Dr. Peter Clegg, 'The United Kingdom Overseas Territories and the European Union: Benefits and Prospects', The United Kingdom Overseas Territories Association (UKOTA) June 2016.

[118] Philip Johnson, 'Sark, The Supreme Court and the Status of the Channel Islands: or Barclay Bites Back' (2016) *The Jersey and Guernsey Law Review* 126.

THE UK SUPREME COURT'S APPROACH
TO DEVOLUTION—RECOGNIZING A QUASI-
FEDERAL STATE?

Devolution, in its different forms, has provided the courts with powers[119] to potentially override statutes that are passed by the devolved legislatures.[120] The courts are nonetheless particularly sensitive to the politics of devolution as well as the autonomy of nations. The Supreme Court in *Miller*[121] on interpreting the role of the UK Parliament under TEU Article 50 in terms of exiting the EU considered the scope of devolved autonomy under the Sewel Convention and the Court acknowledged a reluctance to become engaged in devolution in terms of 'policing its scope and operation' which falls outside the remit of the courts'.[122]

This is understandable in the context of UK withdrawal from the EU but devolution as a whole has to be seen in the wider context of various constitutional developments through EU membership, the Human Rights Act 1998, and other statutory changes,[123] including devolution where the court has created a form of entrenchment[124] for 'constitutional statutes',[125] protecting them from implied repeal.[126] Such statutes may contain 'fundamental principles' that should not be amended or abolished without clear unambiguous words. The Supreme Court has accepted the approach explained by Lord Reed in *Pham*[127] in distinguishing ordinary statutory interpretation from the interpretation needed when reviewing constitutional principles. The approach in *Pham* or even *Jackson* is not novel. It is possible to find historical examples where approaches to constitutional matters were acknowledged as requiring different forms of interpretation. Lord Sankey in *British Coal Corporation v The King*[128] explained that constitutions are 'organic statutes'. Cases involving colonial constitutions attracted a 'large and liberal interpretation'[129] and judicial attitudes have had to address 'the need to provide a framework within which the state can develop'.[130]

---

[119] House of Commons Library, Briefing Paper, The Supreme Court on Devolution Number 07670 (27 July 2016).

[120] The devolved arrangements specifically retain the power of the UK Parliament to make laws for Wales, Scotland, or N. Ireland. See section 28 of the Scotland Act 1998 and section 93(5) of the Government of Wales Act 2006 and section 5(6) of the Northern Ireland Act 1998.

[121] *R. (on the application of Miller and Another) v Secretary of State for Exiting the European Union* [2017] UKSC 5 at para. 51.

[122] See C. Crumney and E. Velasco Ibarra, 'Statutory Conventions: Conception Confusion or Sound Constitutional Development', [2018] *Public Law* 613. See also Jowell, Larkin, McCrudden, Wolffe, and Gordon [2016–17] *The UK Supreme Court Yearbook*, Vol. 8 Part II.

[123] For example, the Fixed Term Parliament Act 2011.

[124] S. Dimelow, 'The Interpretation of "Constitutional Statutes"' (2013) *Law Quarterly Review* 501.

[125] See Laws LJ, in *Thoburn v Sunderland City Council* [2002] EWHC 195.

[126] See *Jackson v HM Attorney General* [2005] UKHL 56.

[127] *Pham v Secretary of State for the Home Department* [2015] UKSC 19.

[128] *British Coal Corporation v The King* [1935] AC 500 p. 518.

[129] Lord Sankey in *Edwards v Attorney General for Canada* [1930] AC 124 at p. 136.

[130] Mr Justice Holmes in *Bain Peanut Co. of Texas v Pinson* (1931) 282 US 499.

Undoubtedly, the devolution settlement created by UK legislation could be amended or reversed by the UK Parliament. Devolved legislation is a reflection of the elected opinion of the devolved nations and may receive special constitutional protection. Lord Hope observed in *H. v Lord Advocate*[131] that such statutes had a 'constitutional nature' that gave them special status in terms of protection from any implied amendment.[132] In fact, both the Human Rights Act 1998 and the devolved statutes may be the basis of legal challenge.[133]

The question that arises is whether the Supreme Court recognizes the evolving quasi-federal relationship with the devolved nations, by taking account of the large degree of autonomy granted to the devolved nation. One of the most important decisions on devolved legislatures and the courts[134] is *AXA General Insurance*.[135] The Supreme Court held that the courts had powers to strike down the statutes of devolved legislatures if the statute abrogated human rights or the rule of law. Lord Hope made clear that by their nature devolved legislatures do not have 'unconstrained' powers and are subject to oversight by the courts. Defining the grounds when the courts might decide to strike down legislation is difficult as the basis of such legislation is the result of an election mandate. Striking down such powers is rare and only exercised in 'exceptional circumstances' and the grounds are wider than *Wednesbury*[136] unreasonableness.[137]

The *Axa General Insurance* case involved a legal challenge to the Damages (Asbestos-related Conditions) (Scotland) Act 2009[138] on the grounds that it exceeded the legislative competence of the Scottish Parliament. The case was an appeal to the Supreme Court against a judgment of the Court of Session on 12 April 2011 that the 2009 Act did fall within the competence of the Scottish Parliament. The Supreme Court had to consider the law-making powers of the Scottish Parliament under section 29 of the Scotland Act 1998, which made clear that there are limitations on the legislative competence of the Scottish Parliament. The Act expressly states that Scottish legislation which is incompatible with the European Convention on Human Rights or EU law is outside the competence of the Scottish Parliament.

The insurance companies' main grounds for challenge was that the 2009 Act violated their right to peaceful enjoyment of possessions protected under the Article 1

---

[131] [2013] 1AC 413 para 30.

[132] See: *R. (On the application of HS2 Action Alliance Ltd.) v Secretary of State for Transport* [2014] UKSC 3.

[133] *Somerville v Scottish Ministers* [2007] UKHL 44 and see the Convention Rights Proceedings (Amendment) (Scotland) Act 2009.

[134] See Lewis J, *AXA General Insurance Ltd., v HM Advocate and Others* [2012]. Lewis, J., 'The Nature of Devolved Legislation and the Role of the Courts' in S. Juss and M. Sunkin, eds., *Landmark Cases in Public Law* Hart: Oxford, 2017, 271–84. See Lady Hale, 'Devolution and the Supreme Court—20 Years On (Scottish Public Law Group, 2018, Edinburgh 14 June 2018) https://www.supremecourt.uk/docs/speech-180614.pdf.

[135] *AXA General Insurance Ltd. v HM Advocate* [2012] 1 AC 688.

[136] *Associated Picture Houses Ltd., v Wednesbury Corporation* [1948] 1KB 223.

[137] P. Craig, 'The Nature of Reasonableness Review' (2013) *Current Legal Problems* pp. 1 and 31. Also see Lord Sumption in *Hayes v Willoughby* [2013] 1 WLR 935 at para. 14.

[138] The history of the 2009 Act is interesting as the Act was passed to reverse the effect of a previous Supreme Court decision that had challenged the retrospective effect of the legislation: see *Rothwell v Chemical and Insulating Co Ltd.* [2007] UKHL 39.

of Protocol 1 of the ECHR. Additional grounds included common law grounds for challenge that set limitations on the legislative powers of the Scottish Parliament and that the 2009 Act was unlawful because it was an irrational use of the Scottish Parliament's competence.

On the facts of the case, the Supreme Court rejected the grounds of incompatibility raised by EU law or the ECHR. A significant part of the analysis of the Supreme Court was directed to a mapping exercise setting out the broadest parameters of review including the rule of law. Lord Hope made clear that constraints defined by the rule of law provided considerable judicial discretion over the powers of the Scottish Parliament.[139] The assumptions that underline the Supreme Court's approach are that constitutional decisions made by the Scottish legislature have to uphold the rule of law[140] as part of the constitutional arrangements reached in the devolution settlement.

> The UK Supreme Court reserved the possibility of the common law qualifying and restricting the power of the devolved legislature in order to prevent it subverting the constitutional values that it was created to serve.[141]

The Scottish Parliament is subordinate to the common law rule of law as well as the statutory framework in which it operates. In positive terms this could be translated into a presumption of legality that surrounds devolved legislatures but one that can be rebutted in exceptional circumstances. The reason that the *Axa* case is significant in terms of the quasi-federal discussion is that the Court explicitly rejected the approach that the Scotland Act 1998 and amending legislation should be treated as akin to the exercise of any legislative power by any statutory body. It also rejected the idea that the legislative competence of the Scottish Parliament was the same as primary legislation and immune from review. Instead the courts adopted an innovative compromise in their approach according respect to the devolved legislature because of its democratic mandate but not providing complete immunity from review, preferring a form of constitutional oversight when necessary.

Devolved legislation may be invalid if it infringes Convention rights. In the *Welsh asbestos* case,[142] the Welsh Assembly proposed legislation that imposed liability for NHS treatment of victims of asbestos-related diseases on persons that are liable to pay compensation to those victims. The proposed legislation was held to infringe Article 1 of the first protocol of the European Convention (which protects property rights) because of its retrospective nature. Retrospective legislation was barred under the article unless there was special justification, which was not found in the case. This was the first case of its kind whereby a bill from a devolved legislature, that had been approved but was not enacted, fell outside the competence of the Welsh Assembly. The bill was a Private Member's bill and the mechanism to test the legality of the Bill to be considered

---

[139] Lord Hope at [2011] UKSC 46 at [51].

[140] See C. Himsworth, 'The Supreme Court Reviews the Review of Acts of the Scottish Parliament' [2012] *Public Law* 205, 210.

[141] Ibid. p. 284.

[142] *Recovery of Medical Costs for Asbestos Diseases (Wales) (Bill) (Reference by the Counsel General for Wales)* [2015] UKSC 3.

was at the initiative of the Counsel General for Wales referring the case to the Supreme Court, even though it was believed that the bill was legally within the powers of the Assembly. This allowed the Supreme Court to give guidance on the bill's legality.

In a Northern Ireland case,[143] legislation that precluded adoption of children by unmarried couples was held to have infringed Article 14 (which prohibits discrimination) of the Convention. The court concluded that adoption by an unmarried couple should be decided on a case by case basis.

In Scotland, there was a Convention challenge to Scottish legislation that required a 'named person' to be assigned to all children for child protection purposes. The sharing of private information amongst named individuals was essential. In the *Christian Institute* case,[144] the Court held that the legislation was contrary to Article 8 of the Convention because it failed to protect privacy.

Beyond convention rights, questions arise about the scope of devolved legislation in terms of reserved matters of the United Kingdom. The Scotland Act, in common with other devolved legislation, raises difficult questions as to what may 'relate to' a specific topic or area of competence, in terms of clarity as to the jurisdiction of the Scottish Parliament. Interpretation of the statute is important but the test of what is related or not is hard to define. It is possible to see the answer in terms of a loose or consequential connection or as incidental to a particular purpose. In the *Christian Institute* case the test was the ultimate aim or the central aim of the statute. Consistency of approach is important but this is very early in the case law, leaving much to be achieved in future cases. The main line of reasoning in the cases is obscure, particularly when different emphasis is given to the means of interpretation.

In *Martin v Moat* the Supreme Court considered the legality of a Scottish Act, section 45 of the Criminal Proceedings etc (Reform) (Scotland) Act 2007, which increased the maximum sentence for driving while disqualified on summary conviction to bring it into line with a conviction on indictment. Matters reserved to the UK Parliament included road traffic legislation. However, the Supreme Court narrowly (by 3–2) regarded the Scottish Act as legal as it did not relate to the reserved matters of the UK Parliament. The purpose of the Scottish Act was to contribute to reform of the justice system by reducing pressure on the higher courts.

The Scottish model of devolution that defines powers reserved to the UK Parliament is slowly being adopted in Wales. The Government of Wales Act 2006 set out specific subjects to fall within the competence of the Welsh Assembly. There have been fewer cases from Wales, significantly only three[145] and in each case the Counsel General of

[143] *In Re P and Ors (Northern Ireland)* [2008] UKHL 38.
[144] *Christian Institute* [2016] UKSC 51. Also see *Reference by the Attorney General and the Advocate General for Scotland The UK Withdrawal from the EU (Legal Continuity) (Scotland) Bill* [2018] UKSC on the powers of the Scottish Parliament to pass the European Union (Legal Continuity) Scotland Bill.
[145] Local Government Byelaws (Wales) Bill 2012—Reference by the Attorney General for England and Wales [2012] UKSC. Agricultural Sector (Wales) Bill (Attorney General for England and Wales, ref) [2014] UKSC 43 and, finally, Recovery of Medical Costs for Asbestos Diseases (Wales) Bill (reference by the Counsel General for Wales) [2015] UKSC 3.

Wales was submitting that the bill had not been passed into law. In the *Welsh Agricultural Wages* case,[146] the bill addressed the employment and wage conditions of agricultural workers. The Welsh Assembly had 'powers to make laws for agriculture, horticulture ... plant health and rural development' but no such powers for 'employment or industrial relations'. The question arises as to whether or not an Agriculture Bill could be valid. The Supreme Court held that the main substance of the bill was about agriculture and 'it does not matter that it also might be capable of being classified as relating to a subject which has not been devolved'.[147]

As the Scottish model of reserved powers is being adopted in Wales, and Northern Ireland already has such a reserved powers model, it is likely that a common jurisdiction will emerge from all devolution settlements. Constitutional focused litigation is likely to increase giving the judiciary an increased responsibility for overseeing constitutional developments. Maintaining the rule of law is essential, but it is impossible not to see as, in the *AXA* case, the development of principles and observations on how to interpret devolution arrangements.[148] There are a number of aspects to the role of the Supreme Court. The opinion of law officers in each of the devolved nations, is significant. Initially, there was a reluctance to take cases to court preferring to interpret the law in a positive way in favour of the constitutional position that each legislature will act within its legal powers. There is also an extensive range of 'custom and practice' that sets the boundaries of legality; in the case of Scotland recourse to the courts is seen as a last resort.[149] The evolving devolution arrangements are reflected in the Supreme Court acknowledging a role as a 'constitutional court' while recognizing that the quasi-federalism of the devolution form is likely to expand and deepen in the coming years. In its constitutional role, the Supreme Court will have to settle issues[150] arising from the consequences of Brexit and, going forward, the interpretation of the UK/EU withdrawal settlement including the European Union (Withdrawal) Act 2018. Acknowledging the nature of many issues before the Court as 'constitutional' makes it much clearer to the public and commentators that the court is in such cases called upon to develop a broader and more contextual analysis of legal issues. As Lady Hale has expressed recently:[151] 'a more evaluative or teleological interpretation' than would be expected in other areas of the law.[152] As Lady Hale acknowledges,[153] this turns 'the United Kingdom Supreme Court into a genuinely constitutional court'.

---

[146] Agricultural Sector (Wales) Bill (Attorney General for England and Wales, ref) [2014] UKSC 43.

[147] Ibid., para. 67.

[148] See: Lord Neuberger, 'The UK Constitutional Role of The Supreme Court in the Context of Devolution in the UK' The Lord Rodger Memorial Lecture 2016.

[149] See: R. Hazell 'Out of Court: Why Have the Courts Played No Role in Resolving Devolution Disputes in the United Kingdom' *Journal of Federalism* 2007 p. 589.

[150] *Christian Institute v Lord Advocate* [2016] UKSC 51, [2016] UKSC 29 paras 29–32.

[151] Lady Hale, *Devolution and the Supreme Court—20 Years On* (Scottish Public Law Group, 2018, Edinburgh 14 June 2018) p.16. https://www.supremecourt.uk/docs/speech-180614.pdf.

[152] *R. (HS2 Action Alliance Ltd., v Secretary of State for Transport* [2014] UKSC 3.

[153] Lady Hale Lady Hale, *Devolution and the Supreme Court—20 Years On* (Scottish Public Law Group, 2018, Edinburgh 14 June 2018) p. 16. https://www.supremecourt.uk/docs/speech-180614.pdf. p. 18.

CONCLUSIONS

Constitutional events and their significance, falling short of outright revolution, often take time to be fully realized, appreciated or easily analysed. The quasi-federal nature of the UK's arrangements that emerge from the discussion above have all come about through the politics of the day and the expression of political choices. Scotland, Wales, and Northern Ireland are examples of referendum results that in turn have stimulated constitutional change. Scotland set an example in obtaining the most devolved powers which Wales has been keen to emulate. The UK has moved on considerably from the period of the Kilbrandon Report[154] and the context of the present day calls for a re-examination of federalism in all its forms. It is easy to reflect that, if offered a binary choice between indivisible sovereignty and some form of federalism, federalism may prove to be more attractive as a means to engage with current constitutional debates in the United Kingdom. This would require political action that to date has not been forthcoming. One of the greatest ironies is that federalism may ultimately maintain the United Kingdom as a single entity, rather than allow a fracture between England, Scotland and Northern Ireland.[155] The stumbling block should not be minimized and it has to be conceded that if federalism were to be fully accepted, it has to be admitted that it is a form of divisible sovereignty. This is the essential first step towards recognizing what is already in the minds of many commentators[156]—that federalism in a variety of forms is already in existence in the UK, through devolution and EVEL. Federalism may also prove helpful for future relations with the EU. However, the prospect for the adoption of legal federalism honouring K.C. Wheare's definition remains frustratingly remote as the history of federalism has shown. At crucial moments in the UK's constitutional history, such as the nineteenth century, it appeared to offer workable solutions to political, economic, and social problems, but it failed to gain political support.[157] The current devolution settlements are changing, often in response to nationalist claims for independence and with no pre-determined end in sight for demands for further devolved powers. As matters stand, devolution does not challenge the legislative sovereignty of Parliament in the UK. However, it does change some practical constraints upon it. By convention,[158] the UK government will not usually legislate on matters where competences have been devolved without first obtaining the consent of the devolved legislatures. As the *Miller* case[159] demonstrated, the Supreme Court's rejection of the convention as offering a legally enforceable veto over the UK's decision to leave the EU, was firm, despite the fact that the convention was put on a statutory basis

---

[154] *The Royal Commission on the Constitution 1969–1973 Vol. 1 Report* Cmnd, 5460.

[155] Stephen Tierney, 'Drifting Towards Federalism: Appraising the Constitution in the Light of the Scotland Act 2016' Chapter 4 in Robert Schütze and Stephen Tierney, *The United Kingdom and the Federal Idea* Oxford: Hart, 2018]101.

[156] David Armitage, 'Conclusion: We Have Always been Federal' in Robert Schütze and Stephen Tierney, *The United Kingdom and the Federal Idea* Oxford: Hart, 2018, pp. 276–7.

[157] John Kendle, *Federal Britain* London: Routledge, 1997 p. xi.

[158] The Sewel Convention.

[159] *R. (Miller) v Secretary of State for Exiting the European Union* [2017] UKSC 5.

for Scotland[160] and Wales.[161] Placing the convention under a statutory framework simply gave the convention added political weight. In the case of Northern Ireland section 1 of the Northern Ireland Act 1998 refers to ceasing to be part of the United Kingdom without the consent of a majority of the people of Northern Ireland and giving notice to leave the EU has no bearing on section 1. The Supreme Court was unwilling to see any lessening of the rights of Northern Ireland citizens as a matter to be considered at the stage of leaving the EU under Article 50.

The quasi-federal nature of many of the UKs constitutional relationships are apparent without any tacit recognition that federalism may offer a relevant solution. Arrangements to ensure that the principle of English votes for English laws applies are over complex and lack sufficient transparency for the rules to be readily understood. As noted above, the creation of a specific recognition for the English Parliament as part of the EVEL arrangements is an illustration of how important locality has become in the UK's constitutional arrangements and how this is, in embryo, federal.

Financial relations through the existing Barnett formula recognize the diversity of regions. Migrating retained EU UK law to the devolved legislatures through complex common framework agreements further strengthens the case for clarity and accountability as well as information. Common frameworks might best be implemented and monitored through a federal structure. Ireland and the Irish border offers an intractable problem in the negotiations for the terms of any future relations between the UK and all the devolved nations. Federalism may allow greater flexibility in taking matters forward, if there is no settlement to the Northern Irish border or no deal is the outcome, recognizing the distinctiveness of each nation may offer a way forward.

However, long-standing resistance to adopting a federal UK structure remains and should not be underestimated. The strong historical legacy of the current constitutional architecture with a uniform doctrine of legal sovereignty without any major adjustments will help ensure that the unity of the UK through a traditional view of parliamentary sovereignty is preserved. This is short-sighted. In the modern world, sovereignty is ever changing. It is not static. Federalism provides a range of potentially useful arrangements and creates a greater sense of regional autonomy and self-governance that would be beneficial to the UK because it would bring clarity to the exercise of decision-making powers alongside clarity over their accountability. Finally, the importance of policy making may also tip the arguments in favour of developing some form of federal structure. Going forward, UK-retained EU law will need to be monitored across the nations and kept under review. EU law of the 27 Member States is likely to be subject to further changes. UK retained EU law may very likely have to follow. UK policy making is likely to be particularly challenged in the absence of the UK's participation in EU institutions upon leaving. Filling the policy gap will need co-ordination. Finding an effective mechanism for inspecting and enforcing all aspects of UK-retained EU law is likely to strain current constitutional arrangements,

---

[160]   Section 28(2) of the Scotland Act 1998 amended by section 2(2) of the Scotland Act 2016.
[161]   Section 2 Wales Act 2017.

particularly the courts. Federal structures may ease the burden and facilitate the transfer of ideas and debate.

The Government's White Paper envisages the creation of new institutions in the Draft EU Withdrawal Agreement,[162] including a new Joint Committee as the primary mechanism for resolving disputes over the interpretation of the agreement and whether the parties to the agreement, the EU and UK, have complied with its requirements. The Joint Committee role includes making decisions that are binding on the EU and the UK, as well as non-binding recommendations. Within the terms of the Withdrawal Agreement, it is possible to adopt amendments to the Agreement and finally it is possible for the Joint Committee to create sub-committees to supervise areas of the agreement including citizen's rights. Achieving a suitable governance structure that allows for such arrangements to work may be assisted by recognizing the federal quality of the arrangements, including the autonomy of each nation.

Similarly, maintaining a common policy framework amongst the devolved legislatures will be particularly demanding as the self-interest of each region may not be the same. In each of the devolved nations there are likely to be democratic competitors based on economic markets that will wish to compete within certain sectors, such as agricultural products, including fishing quotas and milk subsidies. Resolving such policy differences as well as maintaining a single UK market is going to be particularly challenging.

The UK Supreme Court has shown a remarkable willingness to take into account the differences in devolved powers in the case law, reflecting the particular circumstances and politics in which each nation operates. Forging a legal identity for each devolved nation will take some time as the nature and extent of devolved powers develop. The increasingly complex nature of legislation including post-Brexit agreements and the influence of future EU policy-making leave many aspects of the current constitutional arrangements lacking in clarity and accountability. Indeed there are signs that the EU may find a federalist position attractive.

It may be argued that the interpretation of legislation and constitutional doctrines will be aided by a form of federal settlement that more accurately reflects the realities of political and legal powers. Recognizing the degrees of federalism does not negate the fact that the single sovereignty of the UK Parliament may be a work in progress, but it may reward consideration. It remains, however, a matter of political choices for such recognition to take place.

FURTHER READING

M. Burgess, *The British Tradition of Federalism* London: Leicester University Press, 1995

M. Gordon, *Parliamentary Sovereignty in the UK Constitution* Oxford: Hart, 2017

[162] Draft Withdrawal Agreement Article 161 and also see Articles 157, 158 and 159.

J. Kendle, *Federal Britain: A History* London: Routledge, 1997

D. Marquand, 'Federalism and the British: Anatomy of a Neurosis' (2006) 77 *Political Quarterly* 175–83

P. Oliver, *The Constitution of Independence: The Development of Constitutional Theory in Australia, Canada, and New Zealand,* Oxford: Oxford University Press, 2005

R. Schütze, and T. Tierney, *The United Kingdom and the Federal Idea* Oxford: Hart, 2018

K.C. Wheare, *Federal Government* Oxford: Oxford University Press, 1963

15

THE DEMOCRATIC CASE FOR A WRITTEN CONSTITUTION

*Jeff King**

SUMMARY

Written constitutions have often been viewed as the bridle to unchecked political majoritarianism, as a restraint on government, and hence as a limiting device rather than form of democratic political expression. Breaking with that tradition, this chapter sets out a democratic case for a written constitution and contrasts it with the rights-based and clarity-based cases. It then proceeds to show why the case against written constitutions—which is broadly located in a conservative critique, an anti-rationalist critique, and an anti-judicialization critique—is misguided. Nevertheless, a democratic case for a written constitution necessarily raises challenging questions about how the constitution would be enacted, and how rigidly entrenched it should be. In relation to the former, the author argues for a constituent assembly consisting of party and direct citizen representation. As for the latter, he defends a model of entrenchment that permits amendment through a simple majoritarian parliamentary procedure in conjunction with a referendum, and, most controversially, a provision requiring a new constitutional convention about once in a generation. This is the type of democratic constitution, in the author's view, that accommodates the need for a UK constitutional order that takes both rights and democracy seriously.

'The English Constitution', wrote Lytton Strachey in his biography of Queen Victoria, 'that indescribable entity—is a living thing, growing with the growth of men, and assuming ever varying forms in accordance with the subtle and complex laws of human character. It is the child of wisdom and chance.'[1] My view is that the United Kingdom constitution has lately been more the issue of chance than of wisdom, and that, at any rate, neither chance nor wisdom produce legitimate constitutional children in a democratic society. Only people can do that, and they can only do it by producing a written constitution.

* Professor of Law, Faculty of Laws, University College London. Bentham House; 4–8 Endsleigh Gardens, London, WC1H 0EG. jeff.king@ucl.ac.uk. This chapter is adapted from an article by the same title published in (2019) 72 *Current Legal Problems* 1.
    [1] Lytton Strachey, *Queen Victoria* (Harcourt, Brace and Company 1921) 153.

The argument I nod to here, one steeped in principle, butts up immediately against a deep British suspicion of grand principle in politics. For instance, Edmund Burke railed against natural rights thinking which attempted to derive a 'geometrical and arithmetical constitution', from abstract principles.[2] From the opposite end of the political spectrum, John Griffith derided the work of the 'natural lawyers, the metaphysicians and the illusionists' whose work he called mere 'sleight of hand.'[3] This distrust of idealism and rationalism has deep national roots. Constitutional thinking is intimately related to national character. In this respect, it resembles philosophy, which we can consider for a moment in that light. It seems no surprise to me that idealism reached its apotheosis in Germany, existentialism in France, and that pragmatism hails from America. Britain's comparable contribution is empiricism, a theory of knowledge that tells us to base belief only on what is immediately observable, and to doubt everything else. That no-nonsense, ever-practical impulse travels well beyond philosophy. Adam Smith told us why the state should just let people get on with their own business; Edmund Burke that we should only change things with remorse; Charles Darwin that the mere passage of time leads to natural improvements; the Suffragettes that what matters is 'deeds not words'; and John Maynard Keynes that 'in the long run we're all dead.'

However much it cuts against the grain of this pragmatic thinking, the argument of this chapter is very much one of principle and one which has grand repercussions. In Part I, I will set out my idea of a democracy and then explain why I think the best case for a written constitution is the right of citizens to participate in the writing of the fundamental law. This idea revolves around authorship. A selection of arguments against a written constitution is the subject of Part II. I argue that neither conservativism, nor anti-rationalism, nor concerns over judicial supremacy defeat the case I have set out in Part I. Having dispatched these objections, I turn in Part III to clarifying what it means for the people to participate in the writing of the fundamental law—namely, the process of constitution-writing. In Part IV, I address the pressing question of how difficult it should be to amend the constitution, and more deeply, when the authorship I will speak of in Part I expires and there is a need to revisit the fundamentals.

PART I: THE DEMOCRATIC CASE

WHAT KIND OF DEMOCRACY?

I do not think Churchill was right when he said 'democracy is the worst form of government, except for all the rest.' I take the view that it is rather beautiful, and that we should prefer it over other forms of government even if those might deliver better results.

---

[2] Edmund Burke, 'Reflections on the Revolution in France' cited in Jeremy Waldron, *Nonsense Upon Stilts: Bentham, Burke and Marx on the Rights of Man* (Routledge 2015) 91.

[3] J.A.G. Griffith, 'The Political Constitution' (1979) 42 *MLR* 1, 6.

When I refer to democracy, I take the foundational value to be that of political equality: equal respect and equal status. However, this raw value can have a multitude of institutional implications, so any theory of democracy must carefully consider the role of persons, of institutions and of joint decision-making. I adhere to a tradition of liberal egalitarian democratic theory which to me reaches the high-water mark in the work of John Rawls,[4] but which shares a family resemblance with the work of Jürgen Habermas,[5] the deliberative democrats, and to a large extent the republicanism of Philip Pettit.[6] My aim is not to expound these theories. I simply want to draw attention to four features they possess which are salient to this topic. The first is that these theories seek to integrate our deep commitments to rights, distributive justice and democracy. The second salient feature is the distinction between justice and legitimacy. Justice concerns what is *right*, what is true independent of anyone's particular beliefs; legitimacy, on the other hand, is concerned with when it becomes oppressive to use coercion to impose one's view on another, even if there is good reason to think she is wrong. The importance of this distinction is founded on a recognition of what Rawls called the 'fact of reasonable pluralism' about justice; this entails an important role for political deliberation, a respect for difference opposed to both liberal elitism and populism. A third salient feature is the conception of the citizen and social cooperation that lies at the heart of such theories. The citizen is a reasonable rather than narrowly selfish person, seeking to engage in good faith social cooperation. This emphasis on social cooperation recognizes both the value of the state and of the machinery of democratic politics. The state is more a 'we' than a 'they' in this conception, and political representation and political parties play an indispensable role as conduits for collective agreement. Lastly, each of these theories affirms the value of public deliberation and of rational argument in public affairs. They place great value on deliberation, listening, education, and progress—an approach that is entirely unrecognizable in the politics of populism.

My claim is accordingly that these four features—the integration of rights, democracy, and social justice; the recognition of pluralism; the affirmation of the state and of representative politics; and the importance of deliberation—squarely reject conservatism, liberal elitism and populism. *That matters, because they are all political orientations that exert great pressure on constitutional thinking.* These liberal egalitarian theories systematize the otherwise loose collection of intuitions and tenets lying deep within the traditions of UK parliamentary democracy, the core principles of the European Union, the international human rights law framework, and the traditions of both the Christian and social democratic parties of Europe.

---

[4] John Rawls, *A Theory of Justice* (rev edn., Harvard University Press 1999); John Rawls, *Political Liberalism* (rev. edn., Columbia University Press 2005); John Rawls, *Justice as Fairness: A Restatement* (Harvard University Press 2001).

[5] Jürgen Habermas, *Between Facts and Norms* (William Rehg tr., MIT Press 1996).

[6] Philip Pettit, *On the People's Terms: a Republican Theory and Model of Democracy* (Cambridge University Press, 2012).

THE DEMOCRATIC CASE

The democratic case for a written constitution is simple: the people should participate in the writing of the fundamental laws of the community. This idea flows from the principle of equal basic liberty.[7] I want to take up the two objections that claim to expose it as simplistic.

The first objection suggests that what matters is not so much a constitution's pedigree, but what it does for us right now: its consequences. It is my view that the past very much does matter. Suppose one had two identical statutes, one which is issued from the German Bundestag and the other from the Westminster Parliament. All else being equal, should we be indifferent to which of these governs us? Of course, we are not indifferent, and indeed would normally prefer the Westminster law even if it were worse law. It is *our* law, adopted by *our* representatives, and so one in which *we* had a say. That is the force behind the idea of *self*-government.

The second objection concedes that pedigree matters, but maintains that under current political arrangements, the people *have*, as a matter of fact, accepted all of the constitution. Consider this claim by the great constitutional lawyer Sir Ivor Jennings:

> The outpourings of enthusiastic reformers must not be mistaken for the complaints of a frustrated people. If the people of this country want to overthrow capitalism, the public school system, the House of Lords or the monarchy, they have the power in their hands. If they have not done so, the explanation is that they have not wanted to do so.[8]

I think this line of argument is seriously mistaken. The mistake is one of fact: opinion polling consistently shows that people want a reformed House of Lords, a different voting system,[9] and a written constitution.[10] Nearly 90 per cent of the population are against the House of Lords remaining in its current state.[11] Inertia, rather than choice, tends to dictate the status quo. More fundamentally, this argument fails to see any significant difference between the legitimacy of acquiescence and authorship. I want to suggest that a very important distinction exists between the legitimacy of acquiescence, ratification, and authorship.

Acquiescence means passive acceptance, without overt endorsement. We sometimes have good reasons to acquiesce even where we do not consent. Until the twentieth century, most of the adult population of Britain acquiesced in constitutional arrangements

---

[7] See John Rawls, *A Theory of Justice* (n. 4) 194–200, read in conjunction with 200–6 (limitations on the principle of participation).

[8] Sir Ivor Jennings, *The British Constitution* (5th edn, Cambridge University Press, 1966), 211.

[9] Most recently, polling in 2017 by ICM on behalf of Make Votes Matter found widespread support for proportional representation: see Make Votes Matter, 'New Poll Finds Overwhelming Support for Proportional Representation' (Make Votes Matter, 5 May 2017) https://www.makevotesmatter.org.uk/news/2017/5/5/new-poll-finds-overwhelming-support-for-proportional-representation, accessed 1 June 2018.

[10] As noted in the Blackburn Report (Political and Constitutional Reform Committee, *A New Magna Carta?* (HC 2014–15, 463) para. 175), the level of support for a written constitution varies depending on the phrasing of the question.

[11] A poll conducted by BMG Research on behalf of the Electoral Reform Society in October 2017 indicated that 63% wanted a fully-elected upper house, while 27% thought it should be abolished; only 10% thought it should remain as it is.

they were unable to change democratically. Sometimes we also acquiesce if we have the democratic power to change the norm, as we do under most of the common law. Nevertheless, my view is that acquiescence is almost always a suboptimal form of legitimation. The passivity of acquiescence means that the reasons for it are rarely clear and usually diverse. And as behavioural psychologists point out,[12] inertia and paralysis can drive the failure to act more than considered choice.

Ratification is therefore a step forward. Ratification occurs where there *is* an affirmative decision in favour of the proposal or instrument through a formal procedure. In a political setting, such a procedure provides an opportunity for debate on the merits, but crucially *not* normally an opportunity to amend the details of the proposed measure; it is usually a thumbs up or down affair. A referendum is a classic example. Delegated legislation before Parliament is another. The 'take it or leave it' approach is a shoddy way of accommodating disagreement, because the choices are too stark, forcing a politics of brinksmanship rather than one of accommodation.

That is why the distinction between *ratification* and *authorship* is important. *Authorship* means participation by oneself, or one's representatives, in the writing of the laws, or in the shaping of the political decision embodied in the law. It is affirmative, constructive, and legislative in character, and hence highly proceduralized. The extent of parliamentary input into government bills in the Westminster Parliament is far more extensive than standard constitutional thinking has taught us to believe. Meg Russell and Philip Cowley explored and rejected the view that Parliament is side-lined in the law-making process. Taking 12 statutes as a core case study, these authors showed that there were 4,361 amendments proposed, 886 of which were made by the government: 117 of those government amendments embodied concessions to other parties or committees on issues of substance. On the whole, in a proper legislative process, there are manifold ways for voices to be heard on the record and, more importantly, legislatively accommodated in this process.[13]

I think there is a clear legitimacy progression from acquiescence to ratification and then to authorship. Authorship gives best expression to respect for equal basic liberty. It does so because it represents the finest procedure for the proactive accommodation of difference, and most accurate record of genuine collective approval or disapproval, accompanied by reasons.[14] Now, it is in one sense obvious that the citizens themselves do not actually write the laws in either a legislature or a constituent assembly. In either place, it would be their representatives: in most situations a committee or the government would steer or instruct the writing itself. The authorship idea is thus a metaphor, but one that finds appropriate application in this context. The normative salience of the metaphor is that it illustrates the egalitarian merits of pro-active

---

[12] Sunstein notes in Cass R. Sunstein, *Why Nudge?* (Yale University Press 2014) 151–3 that people are often unlikely to opt out of the status quo even when it is easy to do so.

[13] Meg Russell and Philip Cowley, 'The Policy Power of Westminster Parliament: The "Parliamentary State" and Empirical Evidence' (2016) 29 *Governance* 121.

[14] I address limitations to the authorship metaphor in Part I of the longer article, 'The Democratic Case for a Written Constitution' (2019) 72 *Current Legal Problems* 1.

line-by-line participation in collective law-making, and its superiority over ratification and acquiescence. And the procedural salience of the metaphor is evident because (1) participation in a legislative drafting exercise, including the power to move amendments, entitles one to claim something akin to collective co-authorship of the resulting product, and (2) participation in this fashion by genuine representatives of the people provides a legitimate attributive link between representatives and the people themselves. The representatives participate in the joint-authorship exercise, in other words, *in the name of* their constituencies.

Now, authorship of the laws in this sense is admittedly not always available as an option. We might codify the common law, but we can't realistically renew all the old law regularly. Due to scarcity of time and resources we are frequently confined to acquiescence or ratification. *But we are not required to do that for all of it.* That practical impediment does not mean we cannot or should not subject to this kind of process of authorship *the very most important laws and rules*. It is possible to democratize the constitution by subjecting its terms to this kind of comprehensive authorship process. I think equal basic liberty gives people the right, and the state the duty, to do so.

CONSEQUENTIALIST JUSTIFICATIONS FOR AUTHORSHIP

My argument thus far has been a rights-based or deontic rather than consequentialist argument for authorship of the constitution. The right to participate in writing the fundamental law flows from a more general right to self-government. I think the case for a written constitution could rest on that right alone. But other, more consequentialist, benefits also follow from the authorship exercise. One is that it forces parties to clarify their position on fundamental matters. This kind of clear, principled stance is what was attractive about the Clause IV debate in the Labour Party and about Prime Minister Thatcher's strident 'there is no such thing as society' political clarity.[15] The clarity was attractive irrespective of the content of the message, because it exposed the decision to a very clear form of political accountability.

Another merit to written constitutionalism is that a written document compels a certain respect for coherence or what Dworkin called integrity.[16] The positive and canonical statement of a constitution commends a degree of completeness and non-arbitrariness. As a social practice, it has its own internal logic and integrity, making arcane promises not impossible, but certainly more difficult. Modern constitutionalism, with its commitments to equality, rights, and self-government, does generate a certain logic and list of commitments. These ideas commend a commitment to parliamentarism, democracy, the rule of law, a clear policy on central and local relations, respect for

---

[15] For opposing views see, for instance, Nick Barber, 'Against a Written Constitution' [2008] PL 11, 15. Barber argues that some constitutional vagueness is useful, 'particularly . . . in parts of constitutional law and practice where uncertainty may mask, and allow us to avoid, a costly and unnecessary political choice'. As examples, Barber lists the jurisdiction to determine the scope of parliamentary privilege and the legal relationship between Britain and the European Union.

[16] Ronald Dworkin, *Law's Empire* (Hart Publishing 1998).

individual liberties, and multiple forms of political accountability. Even where these written commitments are ignored in practice—in other words there is a 'sham constitution'[17]—they at least serve to expose the outright hypocrisy of the government.

Perhaps the greatest consequential advantage is that the acts of writing, deciding, and legislating provide the opportunity to confront big constitutional questions and decide them. Though much of the existing British constitution would admittedly be applied in its current state without reform, a range of issues would be up for discussion: Lords reform; reconsidering the voting system; considering the constitutionalizing of social rights; putting controls on the executive and military; reforming the role of Parliament in treaty-making and so on. Most important of all, the constitution can finally provide what we do not now have—an established process for reforming and amending the constitutional framework. By any defensible metric, that would be good.

THE RIGHTS-BASED CASE

Lord Scarman made the eloquent point in 1992 that 'A written constitution embodying a Bill of Rights is needed if defenceless and grossly under-represented groups are to have their human rights and their freedoms safeguarded.'[18]

My straightforward misgiving about this argument is that the instrumentalist assumption that an entrenched charter will substantially improve real rights protection is by no means established. Of the quantitative data, to take one example, the Freedom House Report of 2018 shows that in ranking respect for civil and political liberties, seven of the top ten countries have no strong constitutional judicial review of statutes.[19] Furthermore, Australia, which has no federal charter of rights at all, ranks eighteen spots ahead of Germany and forty-six ahead of the United States. There is *no* evidence, so far as I am aware, showing that *entrenched* charters make all the difference. And we have a Human Rights Act already.

Ultimately, my view is that judicial review is an instrument of public policy that has an intimate but not necessary connection to the underlying human rights. There is no human right to the constitutional judicial review of statutes; rather it is a component of a broader account of a liberal egalitarian democratic order. Whether it is democratic depends to an important extent on whether the practice supports or detracts from a given state's capacity to secure equal participation and status for its citizens. Whether a particular polity should adopt it, ultimately, is a complex question of institutional design to be answered by the people. And above all, their answer to that question is what goes the furthest towards giving that practice its democratic legitimacy. For that very reason, the rights-based case and the democratic case come together when the former is put most persuasively.

---

[17] David S. Law and Mila Versteeg, 'Sham Constitutions' (2013) 101 *California Law Review* 863.

[18] Lord Scarman, 'Why Britain needs a Written Constitution' (The Fourth Sovereignty Lecture, London, Charter 88 Trust Publications 1992) reprinted in (1993) 19 *Commonwealth Law Bulletin* 317, 322.

[19] Freedom House, 'Freedom in the World 2018', https://freedomhouse.org/report/freedom-world-2018-table-country-scores, accessed 1 June 2018.

THE CLARITY-BASED CASE

Sydney Lowe observed in 1904 that 'British government is based upon a system of tacit understandings. But the understandings are not always understood.'[20] A number of scholars and statespersons over the years have made much of the need for clarity, and the role of a written constitution in providing it.[21] I am attracted to the argument, but its connection to the case for a written constitution can be obscure.

First, the extent to which a written constitution would provide greater clarity is often exaggerated. A huge amount of the UK constitution is written down in authoritative treatises, law reports and elsewhere. The US constitution probably generates much more uncertainty because laws on issues such as healthcare, gun control and campaign finance aren't secure until the (invariably slim) majority of the Supreme Court has spoken. Second, the argument is quiet about the costs of a written constitution. If the resulting constitution is protected by a rigid amending procedure, if it substantially increases judicial power via interpretation, if it locks in sub-optimal policy innovations, then the extra clarity will be purchased at a high price. Third, if clarity is all that is at stake, a non-binding declaratory code could be adopted. That would not be of much moment. We should aim for renewal rather than documentation.

Ultimately clarity on constitutional fundamentals should be sought by the people. The lack of clarity surrounding the status of the legislative supremacy of Parliament is the key case in point. It should be answered by a legislative process, not firmed up by judicial drift, as is now happening under the swelling common law constitution. The orthodox doctrine concerning the legislative supremacy of Parliament holds that what the Queen enacts in Parliament is law; that Parliament can make or unmake any law; that there is no hierarchy between statutes; and that there is no body that can set aside an Act of Parliament. The doctrine is not laid down in any source but derived by doctrinal writers who study the decisions of courts and attitudes of the judges.[22] It embodies what H.L.A. Hart and many judges refer to as the (ultimate) rule of recognition—the rule used by law-applying officials to identify what constitutes the highest source of valid law. (One can say that it is the ultimate rule of recognition, because judges employ a different rule of recognition to say that the common law is a valid source of law—the ultimate rule is the one that specifies which norms enjoy supremacy over any competing norm.) A rule of recognition like this is adopted as a customary behaviour. We study what law-applying officials actually do when adjudicating between competing norms.

---

[20] Sidney Lowe, *The Governance of England* (T. Fisher Unwin 1904) 12, which came to my attention in S.E. Finer, V. Bogdanor, and Bernard Rudden, *Comparing Constitutions* (Oxford University Press, 1995) 100.

[21] Vernon Bogdanor, Tarunabh Khaitan and Stevan Vogenauer, 'Should Britain Have a Written Constitution' (2007) 78 *Political Quarterly* 499; Robert Blackburn, 'Enacting a Written Constitution for the United Kingdom' (2015) 36 *Statute Law Rev* 1; Andrew Blick, 'The Merits of a Written Constitution' (2016) 21 *Judicial Review* 49.

[22] The great and classical example is A. V. Dicey, *An Introduction to the Law of the Constitution* (10th edn., Palgrave Macmillan 1959), 39ff.

Since the basis of this rule of parliamentary sovereignty is customary, there has been an enormous degree of uncertainty about its scope and certainty. Henry VIII clauses, which enable governments to amend or repeal statutes, should not be possible under the doctrine, and yet they abound. The European Communities Act 1972 empowered courts to disapply UK legislation that conflicts with EU treaties. Section 3 of the Human Rights Act 1998 is understood to empower judges to read a statute compatibly with the ECHR by reading words into or out of a statute that were plainly not intended to form part of the original law. What is interesting about these two examples of departures from the traditional doctrine is that the evident tinkering with traditional sovereignty is best explained as a knowing decision of Parliament to modify the rule of recognition.

But now we are in the situation where it is the courts that are proposing to modify or have modified the rule. In recent years, not only have three different judges of the Supreme Court suggested in obiter that they may enjoy a power to disapply a statute because it fundamentally infringes the rule of law,[23] but the entire Supreme Court has now embraced a doctrine of constitutional statutes. The idea of constitutional statutes at first looks like a good idea. It arises because of the doctrine of implied repeal: the rule in UK constitutional law that if any two statutes conflict, the later one repeals the earlier one. But what if the Dangerous Dogs Act 1991 inadvertently amended the Magna Carta 1215? The motivation for the doctrine of constitutional statutes invites us to contemplate that scenario, with the implication that it would be absurd if such an inadvertent consequence were possible. Hence in the case of *Thoburn*, Lord Justice Laws held obiter that constitutional statutes are immune from implied repeal. He gave a rather vague analytical definition of what they are and listed various examples.[24] The Supreme Court in the *Miller* case,[25] as well as in the *H2S* case,[26] essentially confirmed the existence of the doctrine. They did not confirm or reject Lord Justice Laws' analytical definition but were happy to lead from example. It is now part of the law.

While this all might seem reasonable, what has not been sufficiently appreciated is that the courts have authorized the judicial disapplication of statutes under the common law. This is the case because if an advocate can show that a later statute is incompatible with any former constitutional statute, the court will be invited to disapply that later statute. Under the doctrine as accepted by the Supreme Court thus far, this is what follows. This is a far more potent remedy than what is available under the Human Rights Act. The rulings until now have seemed pretty innocuous. In *Thoburn* Lord Justice Laws upheld the authority of regulations approved by Parliament in disapplying the Weights and Measures Act 1985 for its incompatibility with EU law.[27] In *HS2*, the Supreme Court held in obiter that they would be

---

[23] *Jackson v Attorney General* [2005] UKHL 56, [2006] 1 AC 262 (Lord Hope [107], Lord Steyn [102] and Lady Hale [159]).

[24] *Thoburn v Sunderland City Council* [2002] EWHC 195 (Admin), [2003] QB 151 [62].

[25] *R.(on the application of Miller and another) v Secretary of State for Exiting the European Union* [2017] UKSC 5, [2018] AC 61.

[26] *R.(HS2 Action Alliance Ltd) v Secretary of State for Transport* [2014] UKSC 3, [2014] 1 WLR 324.

[27] *Thoburn v Sunderland City Council* [2002] EWHC 195 (Admin), [2003] QB 151.

prepared to give priority to UK constitutional statutes over EU norms that flowed in through the mechanism of the European Communities Act. In both cases, the findings were in substance *not* hostile to the sovereign Westminster Parliament. But having come garbed in sheep's clothing, the position now is that a judge is entitled to disapply or read down a provision of an Act of Parliament if a claimant can convince the judge that it infringes on the provisions of a previous constitutional statute. That is constitutional judicial review. I agree that constitutional statutes should not be overridden accidentally, but the move being made here is very constitutionally significant; authority for the new doctrine should issue from Parliament rather than the common law or better still, from the people directly.

Another misgiving with the suggestion that authorship can remedy this kind of problem is that the whole story here is evidence of judicial usurpation, a species of judicial power, rather than a problem with the constitution itself. If the judges overreach even with this lack of mandate, the argument runs, one can only imagine what they would do with an actual mandate for constitutional judicial review. The problem with this argument is that in fact there is nothing in our constitutional order that forbids judges from making this kind of move. That is exactly the problem. When a constitution's most fundamental norm is based on custom only, it is always liable to change by some of the participants in the system simply bidding to change it, and hoping to win over other officials or members of the community. It is precisely the failure to give any authority or direction outside custom to this ultimate power of the judges that leaves us in the potentially illegitimate quandary in which we find ourselves. This is the very irony of the position that seeks to sanctify the status quo and oppose a written constitution on account of it empowering a judiciary. The status quo in fact leaves considerable power in the hands of the judiciary, at the expense of a positive political decision of what that power should be. Here again, the clarity-based case and the democratic case come together.

PART II: THE CASE AGAINST A WRITTEN CONSTITUTION

There are many arguments opposing a written constitution, but this section focuses on three.

THE CONSERVATIVE ARGUMENTS

There is a set of arguments that are conservative in the small 'c' sense, which all assume the status quo has special and presumptive weight, perhaps owing to a belief that the past arrangements have met with general acceptance. One of them is the view contained in the maxim that 'if it ain't broke, don't fix it'. Well, on one view, that the people have been excluded from writing their own fundamental law can itself be counted as 'broken'. Moreover, consider the composition of the House of Lords, the voting system, the weak state of the union, the overwhelming power of the executive, the uncertain status of rights, and the absence of an amending formula. These all count as something between embarrassments and travesties.

Turning to the argument that all written constitutions abroad are preceded by national crises like revolutions, even assuming it were true, the answer here can also be brief: prevention is better than cure. One may recall the memorable comment Lord Peter Hennessy made in the House of Lords after the Brexit vote: 'We may pride ourselves on being a back-of-the-envelope nation, but this was excessive. Never have I encountered so many people with so few ideas about what to do in the face of a first order crisis.'[28] The same is as true of the constitutional questions brought out by the Brexit process as it is of the purely political ones.

At the common core of these arguments is, in my view, an instinctive attraction to Edmund Burke's conservatism. In constitutional affairs, to say that some norm has been respected by rulers for hundreds of years is a mark of its good sense. Burke wrote that educating the masses would result in learning being 'thrown into the mud and trodden down under the hoofs of a swinish multitude.' When he wrote, recall, less than three percent of the adult population of Great Britain and Ireland could vote in parliamentary elections.[29] That was not really a problem for Burke. On the subject of creating government by consent, he was rather cynical:

> The very idea of the fabrication of a new government is enough to fill us with disgust and horror. We wished at the period of the Revolution, and do now wish, to derive all we possess as an inheritance from our forefathers . . . All the reformations we have hitherto made have proceeded upon the principle of reference to antiquity; and I hope, nay, I am persuaded, that all those which possibly may be made hereafter will be carefully formed upon analogical precedent, authority, and example.[30]

This reverence for antiquity as a form of argument is, and always has been, a serious mistake. As Bentham pointed out in his critique of Blackstone's Commentaries, 'nor is a disposition to find "everything as it should be", less at variance with itself, than with reason and utility . . . since whatever now is established, once was innovation.'[31] But Bentham's main charge was that it is at odds with reason too. As Bentham well knew, the past is a repository of enormous injustice and inequality. Disenfranchisement, villeinage, squalor, disease, illiteracy, rape, servitude, bigotry, malnutrition and short lives—some or all of that was the daily life of the vast majority of people in pre-twentieth century Britain. The past must be confronted and overcome, not revered.

---

[28]   HL Deb 5 July 2016, vol. 773, col 1963.

[29]   Neil Johnson, *The History of the Parliamentary Franchise*, House of Commons Research Paper, 13/14, 1 March 2013.

[30]   Edmund Burke, *Reflections on the Revolution in France* (J.C.D. Clark ed., Stanford University Press 2001) 181.

[31]   Jeremy Bentham, *A Comment on the Commentaries and A Fragment on Government* (H.L.A. Hart, J.H. Burns eds., Clarendon Press 2008), 400.

ANTI-RATIONALISM

Michael Oakeshott was a critic of rationalism in politics and constitutionalism, arguing that practice is where social and moral values take on their true meaning and that the enlightenment rationalists departed from these values by extracting principles from such practice and generating elaborate schemes of governance from them. Politics, Oakeshott maintained, is 'deeply veined with both the traditional, the circumstantial, and the transitory.'[32] He believed that practical knowledge was that which 'can neither be taught nor learned, but only imparted and acquired.'[33] Such knowledge was vastly superior to rationalist temperament, which would 'assimilate politics to engineering.'[34] His critique of rationalism in politics, to be brief, is that it disregards the significance of knowledge culled through extended experience in preference for schemes based on book learning or speculation. He roundly condemned the American constitution, as well as the Beveridge Report, and argued for giving preference to what is known presently rather to speculations about an uncertain future based on abstract principle.

Oakeshott underestimated the extent to which the political players in the French and American revolutions, as well as social reformers, were indeed people of action. But beyond that, the theoretical core of his argument seems to me either banal or false. It is banal if it means to take experience seriously, and it is false if it means, as he says directly, that high principle and rational planning in situations of epistemic uncertainty are most likely to be misguided. The problem with this latter claim can be illustrated by two counter-examples.

The advent of proportional representation as a voting system has greatly invigorated party plurality and coalition governments in many countries. Plurality systems, like the UK's, often return a large majority of parliamentary seats to a party with around 40 per cent of the vote (sometimes less), as with the victory of the Labour Party in 2005 (35.2 per cent of the vote). That encourages a politics of the median voter, stifling party plurality. Proportional representation has the opposite effect, encouraging a politics of compromise and increasing the likelihood of a good social policy. Proportional representation was actually the child of natural rights thinkers, barristers, philosophers and mathematicians that can be traced back to John Adams and was expounded by, among others, Thomas Wright Hill and John Stuart Mill.[35] Their rationalism was an inestimable practical boon to the politics of Europe and indeed the world.

A second example is of course the development of the post-war welfare state. When William Beveridge outlined his radical plan to eliminate the five giants of want, disease, ignorance, idleness and squalor in his report of 1942, he faced down the argument that the existing patchwork of friendly societies, national charities and diverse private

---

[32] Michael Oakeshott, *Rationalism in Politics* (Indianapolis: Liberty Fund, 1991), 7.
[33] Ibid.   [34] Ibid.
[35] The development and history of proportional representation outlined here is discussed at length in Jennifer Hart, *Proportional Representation: Critics of the British Electoral System 1820–1945* (Oxford University Press, 1992); see also Thomas Hare, *A Treatise on the Election of Representatives, Parliamentary and Municipal* (Longman 1859); and J.S. Mill, *Considerations on Representative Government* (2nd edn., Parker, Son, and Bourn 1861), Ch. 7.

insurance schemes should just be reformed. His rebuttal is now legendary: 'A revolutionary moment in the world's history is a time for revolutions, not for patching.'[36] The National Health Service was launched in 1948 and is possibly the most socialist health service in the entire world. It was driven entirely by two very simple ideas—that it meet the needs of everyone, and that it be free at the point of delivery.[37] Those simple ideals were the engine that motivated a huge exercise in rationalist bureaucracy, delivering one of the country's proudest achievements.

We might do a service to this anti-rationalist argument, however, by recasting it in the following way. One could argue as follows: we do not oppose reform, or even big reform, *but* we think that piecemeal legislative reform of the constitution is better than wholesale constitutional overhaul via the adoption of a codified but abstract scheme. Parliament can go statute by statute, crafting detailed bundles of rules rather than lonely abstract principles, while providing ample room for democratic participation along the way. And we can revise it when needed. In that form, the argument is one the political left could sign on to as much as the right. This, in my view, is one of the very best arguments from this quarter. Indeed, it almost succeeds. The major problem with it, however, is that in a first past the post electoral system, there is a structural problem with constitutional change of the piecemeal variety. Single parties dominate each Parliament, and constitutionalism, on anyone's view, ought to be a cross-party affair. In a winner takes all system of politics, a constitutional reform victory is always the Government's victory and the Opposition's concession. And neither of them, for that matter, would want to vote to substantially diminish their own powers—this is how we got here. A proper constitutional choice requires a different kind of assembly.

JUDICIALIZATION OF THE POLITICAL CONSTITUTION

Judicialization will be addressed briefly, because in my view, the whole issue of judicial power in this country is a storm in a teacup. The Judicial Power Project's list of 50 problematic cases[38] appears little more than a list of cases that are debatable on the merits and most outside the EU law cases are small fry for public policy. The constitution has a lot of problems, but that list is not one of them.[39]

Admittedly, the role for judges would likely become more prominent under a written constitution, depending on its content, than it is now. That was also true of the proposal to create a scheme of devolution in the UK, which is structured by three core legislative schemes that have been before the courts at various points. The devolution

---

[36] William Beveridge, *Social Insurance and Allied Services* (Cmd 6404, 1942) pt. 1 para. 7.

[37] In fact, the three core values outlined by Aneurin Bevan MP were that it meet the needs of everyone; that it be free at the point of delivery; and that it be based on clinical need, not ability to pay, see HC Deb 30 April 1946, vol 422, col 45. The current NHS constitution collapses the second into the third, and in fact charges are payable in limited circumstances.

[38] Judicial Power Project, '50 Problematic Cases' (Judicial Power Project, 2018) http://judicialpowerproject.org.uk/50-problematic-cases/ accessed 23 May 2018.

[39] For a critique of the Judicial Power Project and that list in particular, see Paul Craig, 'Judicial Power, the Judicial Power Project and the UK' [2018] 36(2) *University of Queensland Law Journal*.

comparison illustrates a deeper point about the judicialization critique. The devolution scheme enormously invigorated the politics of the United Kingdom, launching three legislatures, introducing proportional representation to significant parts of the UK, and as part of a broader package, bringing relative peace to Northern Ireland. Those assemblies also make a lot of law. Scotland has adopted about 270 Acts of the Scottish Parliament since its founding in 1999, in addition to some 7,500 statutory instruments. This extensive legal scheme of devolution, and the business interests it regulates, would look ripe for challenge in the courts by regulated entities, but it has not happened. The straightforwardly political benefits of the constitutional enterprise that devolution to any significant extent was, especially for Northern Ireland and Scotland, vastly dwarf the significance of any new role for judges.

We should similarly recall that we already have a bill of rights in the form of the Human Rights Act 1998, so we largely know what judges will do with a constitutional bill of rights. I have gone through all the section 4 declarations of incompatibility, which is the equivalent of Britain's 'strike down power', and examined all the parliamentary debates and committee reports in response to them.[40] Three short take-away points are pertinent here. First, one must look with a magnifying glass for serious disagreement in Parliament about what the courts are doing. Second, nearly all cases were brought by politically marginalized groups. And third, nearly all cases concerned a very tiny proportion of the public or involved remedies that constrained Parliament to a minor extent. Anti-democratic the scheme is not.

Now, if we take for granted that we already have a quasi-federal scheme in which there is little evidence of legal opportunism, and a human rights charter that has largely functioned as predicted, then the question is—just how much of an expanded role for judges would there be under a written constitution? I suspect not much. And that is why I see this objection as much ado about not much. It lies, moreover, right in the way of a potentially huge contribution to democratic renewal.

PART III: THE PROCESS OF ENACTMENT

Clearly, if the case for a written constitution is largely democratic, the participation by the people in the end product is essential. Looking abroad, the usual method is popular approval through a referendum. But that is ratification; I made a case for authorship. Authorship requires representation, because drafting requires discussion and a procedure for agreement. This is where the question gets very interesting—what kind of representation?

---

[40] Jeff King, 'Parliament's Role following Declarations of Incompatibility under the Human Rights Act' in Hunt and others (eds.), *Parliaments and Human Rights: Redressing the Democratic Deficit* (Hart Publishing 2015). See similarly Alison Young, 'Is Dialogue Working Under the Human Rights Act?' [2011] PL 773; Aruna Sathanapally, *Beyond Disagreement: Open Remedies in Human Rights Adjudication* (Oxford University Press 2012).

The first obvious place to consider is Parliament. It is the supreme assembly of the state, with the legitimacy, pedigree, and a complex set of customs, practices and conventions that have shaped it into the nation's best conduit for political dialogue, decision and scrutiny. But it is the wrong place to draft a written constitution. It is the very nature of the UK Parliament that the leadership of one—normally divided—party dominates every major vote in the Commons, at least outside the select committees, and can prevail over any resistance by the House of Lords. And all that with as little as a third of the popular vote behind it.

Neither should the process be executive led by the government for precisely the same reasons. Esteemed commentators have thus suggested other options broadly within executive powers but at some distance from government itself. For example, Robert Blackburn's preferred body for drafting a written constitution as a bill to Parliament is a 'Commission for Democracy'.[41] He suggests this be formed through ministerial prerogative following cross-party negotiations and agreement of its general aims and composition. Although lacking direct participation from the public, an advisory unit could be established to facilitate the process by informing and engaging the public. It would also be possible to establish executive bodies such as a Royal Commission or some other form of Commission that is independent, staffed by representatives and experts, and properly resourced.[42] Such a body could run appropriate public consultation and give the appearance of independence from Government and Parliament. However, the main problem here is that if this body is too remote from Parliament, it will lack the legitimacy for bold recommendations. And if on the other hand it is too close, it will exhibit the politics of tribalism. At any rate, the almost insurmountable problem for any executive-run process is that the final product must be passed by Parliament. It would lack the legitimacy to bypass Parliament. That downstream sluice will send powerful upstream currents, forcing the appointed commission to be more judicious than just in its findings.

Perhaps for such reasons, the idea of a constitutional convention seems particularly apt. Such conventions could take many forms. Alan Renwick and Robert Hazell, for example, envisage representation through a citizens' convention which allows ordinary members of the public to take evidence, deliberate, and make recommendations.[43] The members of the convention are to be selected through stratified random sampling, and politicians should be engaged without being full members, so that the convention is not overly detached from Parliament or the Government. Proposals by the convention would ultimately be left to the Government to respond to through parliamentary debate or legislation. In my view, while this proposal takes us quite far to the correct position, it falls at the same hurdle identified above. If Parliament controls the final product, it can act as a conservative veto point that will block the convention's work,

---

[41] Robert Blackburn, 'Enacting a Written Constitution for the United Kingdom' [2015] 36(1) *Statute Law Review* 21–25.

[42] Robert Blackburn, 'Enacting a Written Constitution for the United Kingdom' [2015] 36(1) *Statute Law Review* 15–17.

[43] Alan Renwick and Robert Hazell, 'Blueprint for a UK Constitutional Convention' (The Constitution Unit, UCL, June 2017).

and all the more so if the deliberations of citizens are considered too remote from the realities of the workings of everyday government.

This is why I believe a constituent assembly is the best option if we are to respect the democratic case I have laid out. A constituent assembly is a body—a type of constitutional convention—convened for the particular purpose of drafting or revising a constitution, and which, crucially, *has its own legislative authority*. Constituent assemblies are there to constitute, not only to deliberate and report. My case for the constituent assembly does not rest on the metaphysical idea of constituent power, ranking it as superior to parliamentary authority.[44] To be clear on this deeper point, my references to 'the people' don't seek to essentialize the idea; I simply mean the citizenry and electors. At any rate, my case for the constituent assembly is altogether more practical—it is about the right design of a representative process for enacting a constitution. It does not deny that Parliament is also representative. It makes the case for a different form of representativeness for an altogether different kind of task.

In my contention, to be suitable for the task of writing a constitution, the assembly must do three core things: represent the people; debate the right questions in an informed and complete manner; and have the real authority that will lead to its conclusions being accepted by those holding political power. In other words, it must produce a constitution that is *representative*, *informed*, and *effective*. I have shown already why Parliament and Government will fail to be representative in the required way, so it might at first seem contradictory to argue that it is essential that political parties are given a prominent role in the constituent assembly. Let me focus here on their epistemic role and their role in generating effectiveness. As to the former, it is a very real fact that when it comes to constitutional reform, the issues are complex and there is a need to have people involved who understand the art of the possible as well as the art of the probable. In this scenario, the whole constitution is on the table; only grizzled party hacks are likely to fully understand the mosaic.

The astute observer might object here that if the role is epistemic, why not just call in the party members for hearings, alongside other experts, rather than give them a vote? However, this would overlook the importance of effectiveness. Recall that in the proposed scheme the constituent assembly has *original* legislative authority. It does not send its product to Parliament for approval—though it would consult it regularly. That original legislative authority only starts to look feasible if the parties are involved intimately at the decision-making stage about content. The approval or disapproval of the parties is likely to be important to the referendum outcome, and to daily functioning in politics thereafter. Of course, neither can it be forgotten that the parties have a key representative role too. Parties have constituencies and can bargain on their behalf. They have a *mandate* to seek accommodation. Tribes do not disappear at the (re)founding.

But at the end of the day, the parties *are* tribes, and that can raise conflicts of interest, produce myopia, and result in a reluctance to change minds through deliberation.

---

[44] Daniel Lee, *Popular Sovereignty in Modern Constitutional Thought* (Oxford University Press 2016); Bruce Ackerman, *We the People, Vol 1: Foundations* (Harvard University Press 1991).

To compensate for these problems, therefore, I would propose the appointment of a substantial body of non-party citizens. So the assembly would have mixed composition in this sense: an elected component along party lines and an appointed element for reasons just given. For the election, a closed list proportional representation system would be best. In that way, parties can put forward the candidates they think are best suited to the task of writing a constitution. And of course any group can form a party for the purposes of participation in such an election. As to the appointees, the question is a touch more complicated. Either we can appoint persons who are experts, that is, persons of eminence and ability such as those appointed as cross-bench peers in the House of Lords. Or we can appeal to a representative body of citizens—by which I mean descriptively representative (i.e. there is a correspondence between the characteristics of the population and the characteristics of the persons in the assembly). For the latter, we can appeal to sortition, a technique used for jury trials which has been done for a variety of citizens' assemblies and citizens' juries around the world. Proper sortition is a demographic science, and it would, if applied, constitute a body that is truly representative in the descriptive sense along gender, race, income, employment, age, region and other lines—informed, one hopes, by the feminist insight about the importance of critical mass in voices being heard. Since what I propose would be a long-term daily gathering, most likely stretching a few years, the participants would need adequate compensation and job security. I favour this option, over the appointed persons model, because I think it is the most legitimate. I imagine a constitution drafted by a panel of constitutional law experts and eminent persons would be just my kind of process. But that is exactly why we should not go with it. Such persons should and would be heard, but not decide.

PART IV: THE STATUS AND AMENDMENT OF THE CONSTITUTION

A landmark report prepared by Robert Blackburn and Andrew Blick for a parliamentary inquiry on a written constitution canvasses three options for its status:[45]

1. A non-binding declaratory code.

2. A statute.

3. An entrenched constitution with a super-majority amendment formula.

My view is that the constitution should be entrenched, but flexible. Entrenched because without that, it could be overwritten by a simple Act of Parliament, inadvertently even. But *how deeply* entrenched? A constitution protected by a strict amending procedure effectively allows the people at one point in time—1787 in the US or 1949

---

[45] Political and Constitutional Reform Committee, *A New Magna Carta?* (HC 2014–15, 463), 29.

in Germany—to prevail over often vastly larger and often much more representative majorities at a later point in time.

The argument has a lot to be said for it. But it is hard to give a universal answer to the question of how rigid a constitutional amendment formula should be. In post-war Germany, there was good reason—to put it mildly—to make the constitution's defence of fundamental rights, the federal structure, the political parties and the unions quite firmly entrenched. In post-revolutionary America, the strains of holding a huge federation together suggested that stability would depend on a measure of security. In other highly divided societies like Northern Ireland, and sometimes new democracies like post-apartheid South Africa, there are often good reasons why a deeper entrenchment would be attractive. Eternity clauses offer a way to protect the 'sacrosanct principles'[46] of a constitution by limiting amendment power over provisions which preserve the contemporary polity or which are especially vulnerable because they run counter to the pre-constitutional political arrangement.

But in many other countries, there is no clear political demand for anything like this kind of strict entrenchment. All of the Scandinavian countries, France, Ireland and many other nations have amending formulas that require either one or more Acts of the legislature, or a referendum, or both.

At one end of the spectrum, amending the Finnish Constitution is regarded as the function of the legislature alone. An amending bill must pass with a simple majority upon its second reading, followed by an abeyance until after the next general parliamentary election. After this first stage the amendment succeeds with a two-thirds majority in Parliament.[47]

Sweden, too, provides that the amendment competence belongs to the legislature, but with the possibility that a referendum may be invoked. The Swedish Constitution requires two simple majorities either side of a parliamentary election with the possibility that a motion for a referendum be brought by one-tenth of members of parliament, to be approved by one third.[48] Under the French Constitution referenda provide an alternative to approval by Congress as a route to amendment, following the passage of the bill through Parliament.[49]

Other constitutions, at the opposite end of the spectrum, unconditionally integrate referenda into the amendment procedure. Under the Danish Constitution, a referendum follows majorities in two consecutive parliamentary terms in favour of an amendment.[50] The Norwegian Constitution is similar, with the additional requirement that the proposal be circulated in print ahead of the intervening election.[51] The Irish Constitution requires simple majorities of both houses for an amendment then to be put to a referendum.[52]

---

[46] Arnold Brecht, *Federalism and Regionalism in Germany—The Division of Prussia* (Oxford University Press 1945), 138.

[47] Suomen perustuslaki, 6 luku, 73§.   [48] *Regeringsformen* 8 kap 18 §.

[49] Const., Art. 18.   [50] Grl § 88, Lov nr. 169 af 5.6.1953.   [51] Grl § 121.

[52] Art. 46, Constitution of Ireland, 1937.

In my view, an amendment procedure should *always* be designed to ensure that the political decision is extremely careful. But subject to that, in principle I think the baseline or starting position should be that it is respectful of ongoing equal political status—i.e. not fiercely counter-majoritarian. One can depart from that presumption when the case is made out, as in the examples of rigidity as set out in some of the stricter formulas examined above. However, the political case for that type of rigidity I think will more often be the exception than the norm in a mature democracy.

It is also evident that in none of the countries mentioned above is the amendment process anywhere near as flexible—as easy—as it is in the United Kingdom. Indeed, there are not even agreed criteria for what would constitute a constitutional amendment in the UK, and hence nothing to prevent 'amendments' being effected *even without an Act of Parliament*.[53] So there is, in other words, some gulf between the quite rigid formulas of anywhere from a two-thirds majority upwards and the current position in the UK.

For these reasons, I think the democratic case for a written constitution for a country like the UK commends an amending formula of the following sort: a bill passed by both Houses of Parliament under a special procedure (Speaker's conference, committees of the whole house), and ratified by public referendum, before it takes effect as an amendment of the constitution. This means that referenda must be *preceded* by a carefully debated and concrete initiative passed by Parliament; a popular ratification is an antidote to some of the problems in the legislative process. This approach ensures that Parliament will play a key role in the amendment process, but also that there is a national conversation and popular ratification of amendments. The legislative form of the proposal will ensure that the conversation is focused and the outcome relatively concrete.

This flexibility might be enough, one could think, to answer definitively the objection that the constitution is lacking in the democratic credentials I set out in Part I. However, I do not think that is true. Existing arrangements take on inertia. People get attached. Nick Barber has argued against a written constitution precisely because it would force some awkward conversations unnecessarily, because, to put it another way, a constitutional rewrite would be gauche.[54] I take a different view. The constitution is something that should belong to each generation in the important sense of authorship that I have outlined in Part I. We cannot renew it every Parliament. Yet we *can* sit down and explore it front to back once in a generation. And that is why I would suggest that a constituent assembly be convened along the lines I have identified above, about once in a generation.[55] That means putting a sunset clause into the constitution, to prevent

---

[53] The institution of English Votes for English Laws would be such an example, which was effected by way of the amendment of the standing orders of the House of Commons rather than by legislation: Richard Kelly, *English Votes for English Laws*, House of Commons Library Research Paper, 17/7339, 20 June 2017. The proposed plan to promptly increase the number of peers in the House of Lords, mooted in the People's Budget crisis in 1909, is another example: see Chris Ballinger, *The House of Lords 1911–2011: A Century of Non-Reform* (Hart Publishing 2012) Ch.1.

[54] See for example Nicholas Barber, 'Against a Written Constitution' [2008] PL 11; Nicholas Barber, 'Why Entrench?' (2016) 14 ICON 325.

[55] This might range anywhere between 20–40 years.

political opportunism in fixing the date.[56] The proposal is hence different from the situation that exists with respect to a number of state constitutions in the United States. In New York, for example, the constitution provides that a referendum take place every 20 years on whether to hold a new constitutional convention.[57] Voters normally decline. The proposal I put down here is that the convention take place automatically, precisely to engage the spirit of authorship outlined above. The people and even the parties will not know, until they engage in the process, whether the status quo really is fine as it is. They cannot know, because it requires an extensive national conversation and a large investment of time and attention.

A number of persons would fear doing this, particularly when populist sentiments are all the rage. They might rather argue to let sleeping dogs lie.[58] However, it would be well to recall on the one hand that the constituent assembly I have suggested is still composed by a two-thirds elected component along party lines, and on the other that there is empirical evidence that mini-publics are conducted in a respectful, balanced and public-oriented way even in a country with a significant politics of populism.[59] I side with the deliberative democrats in seeing deliberative constitutionalism, which the proposed constituent assembly would embody, as a solution to rather than aggravation of populist politics. As Simone Chambers has observed, '[d]eliberation, whether in the jury, a mini-public, between judges, in a parliament or even in the chaotic unstructured public sphere, implies a multiplicity of voices, opinions and claims being voiced. [. . .] Arguments, not votes, pose the more serious threat to populism.'[60]

CONCLUSION

The journey to this conclusion has been a long one, so it will help to summarize the key arguments. First, a democratic case requires participation by the people's representatives in the authorship of the fundamental rules of the polity. Rights-based and clarity-based arguments support this view above, but both are conditioned by the democratic argument in important ways. Second, the case against the written constitution often

---

[56] See Thomas Jefferson, Letter to James Madison, 6 Sept. 1789, in *Thomas Jefferson: Writings*, ed. Merrill D. Peterson (New York: Library of America 1984), 959–64; Antonios Kouroutakis, *The Constitutional Value of Sunset Clauses: An Historical and Normative Analysis* (Routledge 2017); Sofia Ranchordás, *Constitutional Sunsets and Experimental Legislation: A Comparative Perspective* (Edward Elgar Publishing 2014).

[57] N.Y. CONST. art. XIX, § 2–3.

[58] For a general discussion see Eleonora Bottini, 'Who is Afraid of the Constitutional Convention? The Rejection of Constitutional Change in the State of New York' (I·CONnect: the blog of the International Journal of Constitutional Law, 22 November 2017), http://www.iconnectblog.com/2017/11/who-is-afraid-of-the-constitutional-convention-the-rejection-of-constitutional-change-in-the-state-of-new-york/ accessed 1 June 2018.

[59] See Stephen Elstub and Gianfranco Pomatto, 'Mini-Publics and Deliberative Constitutionalism' in Ron Levy, Hoi Kong, Graeme Orr and Jeff King (eds), *The Cambridge Handbook of Deliberative Constitutionalism* (Cambridge University Press, 2018) ch.22 (exploring two Italian citizens' juries on federal reform of the state of Italy).

[60] Simone Chambers, 'Afterword: Populist Constitutionalism v. Deliberative Constitutionalism' in Levy, Kong, Orr and King (eds), ibid., at 370-71.

fetishizes the past without justification, it opposes rationalist reform when it has delivered some of our most lasting achievements, and it overemphasizes the role of courts, which is both less than supposed and dwarfed by the positive potential for democratic renewal. Third, the best way past the stranglehold the Westminster Parliament holds over the reform process is a constituent assembly featuring a combination of party members and members of the general public. And fourth and finally, the status of the constitution should be that it is entrenched but amendable by Act of Parliament and referendum; and that it come up for renewal about once a generation. That is, in my view, the democratic case for a written constitution.

There is an important question about how that democratic case relates to a truly seismic event in United Kingdom constitutional politics: the planned departure of the UK from the European Union (or, colloquially, Brexit). There is a common tendency at the time of writing to refer to all the shifting fault-lines made evident in the Brexit crisis as grounds for comprehensive constitutional reform. These include the constitutional tensions between the Westminster and devolved governments; the lack of clarity about fundamental constitutional norms, such as whether the Queen could withhold Royal Assent to a bill that passed both Houses if the Prime Minister advised her to do so; the secrecy and unreliability of constitutional conventions; and the extraordinary enhancement of executive power to make important policy decisions using delegated legislation and Henry VIII powers under the European Union (Withdrawal) Act 2018. My view is that while these issues expose genuine problems and may well provoke a full-blown constitutional crisis akin to those that precede most foreign experiences of constitutional overhaul, they provide a political occasion rather than clear justification for a constitutional reform process. Whether the problems created by Brexit are solved by a comprehensive constitutional reform process is a deep and difficult question. The prior question is, Brexit aside, what precisely is the case for a written constitution and what kind of process and degree of entrenchment would such a case support? The democratic case does not make the case for the substance of a *particular* constitution. Therefore, the argument here does not enable one to hold up a particular constitution as the answer to the problems that the crisis has arguably exposed. At best, it can point to a process in which the relevant conversation can be held, and prescriptions for the enactment and status of a written constitution which will answer the more powerful objections to having one in the first place. But that conversation should be held for good democratic reasons entirely independent of the reasons attributable to Brexit. On the other hand, Brexit may lead to a serious crisis—perhaps even a 'good crisis' that the advocates of a written constitution should 'never let go to waste.'[61] Whether true or not, the democratic case for a written constitution stands on its own feet.

---

[61] The expression 'Never let a good crisis go to waste' is often attributed to Winston Churchill, but it is unclear whether the claim is more than apocryphal.

FURTHER READING

SIR JOHN BAKER, 'Our Unwritten Constitution' (Maccabaean Lecture in Jurisprudence, British Academy London, November 2009)

NICK W. BARBER, 'Against a Written Constitution' [2008] *Public Law* 11

ROBERT BLACKBURN, 'Enacting a Written Constitution for the United Kingdom' [2015] 36(1) *Statute Law Review* 2.

ANDREW BLICK, *Beyond Magna Carta: A Constitution for the United Kingdom* (Hart Publishing 2015)

VERNON BOGDANOR, TARUNABH KHAITAN and STEFAN VOGENAUER, 'Should the UK Have a Written Constitution?' (2007) 78 *The Political Quarterly* 499

LORD HAILSHAM, 'Elective Dictatorship' (Richard Dimbleby Lecture, London, October 1976)

IAN MCLEAN, *What's Wrong with the British Constitution?* (Oxford University Press 2009)

DAWN OLIVER, 'Written constitutions: principles and problems' (1992) 45 *Parliamentary Affairs* 135

GEOFFREY PALMER and ANDREW BUTLER, *Toward Democratic Renewal: Ideas for Constitutional Change in New Zealand* (Victoria University Press, 2018)

POLITICAL and CONSTITUTIONAL REFORM COMMITTEE, *A New Magna Carta?* (HC 2014–15, 463).

LORD SCARMAN, 'Why Britain needs a Written Constitution' (The Fourth Sovereignty Lecture, Charter 88 Trust London, 1992).

INDEX